An Introduction to
Econometrics

To Annemarie, Isabel and Robert
and in memory of Akos and Eddie

# An Introduction to Econometrics

Michael Pokorny

Basil Blackwell

First published 1987

Basil Blackwell Ltd
108 Cowley Road, Oxford, OX4 1JF, UK

Basil Blackwell Inc.
432 Park Avenue South, Suite 1503
New York, NY 10016, USA

*British Library Cataloguing in Publication Data*

Pokorny, Michael
    Introduction to econometrics.
    1. Econometrics
    I. Title
    330'.028    HB139

    ISBN 0-631-15002-1
    ISBN 0-631-15003-X Pbk

*Library of Congress Cataloging in Publication Data*

Pokorny, Michael
    An introduction to econometrics.
    Includes bibliographies and index.
    1. Econometrics.    I. Title.
HB139.P635    1987    330'.028    86-32707
ISBN 0-631-15002-1
ISBN 0-631-15003-X (pbk.)
Typeset by Advanced Filmsetters (Glasgow) Ltd
Printed by Page Bros (Norwich), Ltd

# ntents

# Preface

The primary objective of this text is to provide a relatively non-technical exposition of the more commonly used techniques of applied econometrics. It is not to be interpreted as an attempt to present a comprehensive exposition of all the varied techniques which fall within the subject area of econometrics. Such a text would be considerably lengthier than this one, and would contain material well beyond that which could be reasonably covered in an introductory course.

This text is intended for use on a one-year introductory econometrics course, where, typically, the student would not be majoring in econometrics. Such courses are now common at both undergraduate and postgraduate levels, and on degree programmes whose main subject area may not necessarily be economics. Indeed, the techniques which are covered in this text could be interpreted within a wider context of being illustrative of the role of statistical inference in the social sciences in general. However all the illustrations which are used are drawn from economics. It is assumed that the reader has a basic understanding of the techniques of calculus and statistical inference, although it is also assumed that the reader's background in these areas is limited. Given the central role which the theory of statistical inference plays in econometrics, an introductory chapter is provided which reviews this theory, and which the reader may find useful. A further feature of this text is that no use is made of matrix algebra. This is firstly because I doubt its value as an expository device at an introductory level, and secondly, because only a limited emphasis is placed on the rigorous derivation of many of the results presented, thus obviating the need for the notational efficiency afforded by a matrix representation.

The attempt throughout has been to develop a central core as directly and efficiently as possible, keeping to a minimum the need to deviate from this core. Consequently, many results are presented without proof, with reliance placed on intuitive justifications, and the more mathematically-inclined reader being directed to other references. However, some of the more fundamental results are discussed in further detail in appendices.

Chapters 2 and 3 are concerned with developing the essentials of the single equation regression model, the model which forms the basis of much applied econometrics. Care is taken to provide detailed explanations and illustrations of the assumptions of this model, as it is via a detailed understanding of these assumptions that the important extensions of the model can be better understood. Some of these extensions are then discussed in Chapters 4 and 5. In Chapter 6 an introductory discussion of simultaneous equation modelling is presented, and the issues associated with econometric forecasting and policy evaluation are outlined. Finally, Chapter 7 covers material which is perhaps not normally associated with an introductory econometrics course, but which is useful for providing an introduction to some of the issues and controversies which have recently been associated with econometric modelling.

Central to the approach taken in this text is use of detailed numerical examples to illustrate most of the theoretical results which are presented. Often these examples are discussed at considerable length, and their objective is not only to convey the manner in which econometric theory can be applied, but also to illustrate the difficulties and ambiguities which are associated with this application. Limited discussion of published econometric work is presented, as most published work represents the end product of what is generally a lengthy and detailed experimentation process. The attempt here is to convey some of the flavour of this experimentation process, albeit at a relatively simplified level. Where appropriate, all the data which are used in these examples are presented, and the reader is encouraged to experiment with these data in order to obtain a more detailed appreciation of the techniques involved. Given the wide availability of relatively inexpensive microcomputers and relevant software, such an objective is considerably more realistic than it would have been only a few years ago.

The process of writing a text such as this is certainly not the independent activity that is implied by the single name appearing on the cover. Thanks must first go to Peter Jeffreys and the Polytechnic of North London Computing Service. The numerical examples which appear throughout the text represent but a fraction of the empirical work which was actually carried out, and the frustrations involved in this process were greatly eased by the efficiency and flexibility of PNLCS. Particular thanks must go to Lindsay Dean who always dealt cheerfully (well, almost always) and efficiently with what must have seemed like my incessant demands on the computing facilities. Thanks are also owed to Warwick Dean and Alison Mackinlay who patiently tolerated the extra work I generated for them. I would also like to thank John Curran for reading through a number of the earlier chapters and for making numerous suggestions which improved the exposition. Richard

Baillie kindly read various drafts of the book and a number of areas have benefitted from his thoughtful and rigorous criticisms.

However, undoubtedly my greatest debt is owed to Ken Holden. He patiently read each draft of the book, providing detailed comments and countless suggestions for improvement. Just as importantly, he often provided encouragement for a project that on many occasions seemed never-ending. There is no doubt that this book would have been very much the poorer but for his contributions.

I would also like to thank the Biometrika Trustees for kindly allowing me to reproduce the statistical tables in Appendices I to V. Appendices I, II, III and V were adapted and abridged from Pearson, E. S. and Hartley, H. O. (eds) *Biometrika Tables for Statisticians* Vol I 3rd Edition (London, Charles Griffin and Company, 1976). Appendix IV was reprinted from Durbin, J. S. and Watson, G. S. 'Testing for Serial Correlation in Least Squares Regression' *Biometrika* Vol 38, 1951, pp. 159–77.

Thanks for the typing of the earlier drafts of the manuscript go to Vi Warburton, Ruth Denison and Margaret Frankling. Finally, I would like to thank my wife, Isabel. She uncomplainingly took on the tedious task of proof reading, and greatly eased the pressure at this hectic stage of the production process. But more importantly she provided much needed support during those times when this project threatened to get the better of me.

# 1 A Review of the Theory of Statistical Inference

## 1.1 Introduction

In this chapter we will provide a brief review of the methodology involved in using sample information to draw inferences about the population from which the sample was drawn. We will outline the procedures involved in estimating the population parameters (typically, the population mean and variance), and the manner in which hypotheses concerning the population parameters can be tested. We will also discuss the concept of correlation, before completing this chapter with a discussion of the role of statistical inference in economics, and hence the nature of econometrics.

## 1.2 The Role of Sampling

The primary objective in selecting and analysing a sample of data is to derive information concerning the population from which the sample was drawn. The term 'population' is used in the widest sense to indicate any collection of objects (animate or inanimate) which is in some sense self-contained. Statistical theory, therefore, is concerned with deriving methods of analysing sample data in order to draw the most precise inferences possible about the population under investigation.

We can distinguish between two forms of data – **cross-section** and **time-series** data. Cross-section data are data which have been collected at a point in time. Thus we could select a sample of firms at a point in time, or a sample of households, or a sample of individuals, and so on. Time-series data are data which are collected over time. Examples would be a series of, say, monthly observations on a firm's or industry's output, or annual observations on

1

**Table 1.1**   Pre-tax profits per employee in a sample of 30 mechanical engineering establishments 1982 (£'000)

| Establishment number | Pre-tax profits/ employee | Establishment number | Pre-tax profits/ employee | Establishment number | Pre-tax profits/ employee |
|---|---|---|---|---|---|
| 1 | 4.94 | 11 | 0.00 | 21 | 0.70 |
| 2 | 0.51 | 12 | −0.24 | 22 | −0.17 |
| 3 | −0.83 | 13 | −3.83 | 23 | −0.58 |
| 4 | 2.83 | 14 | −1.93 | 24 | −1.09 |
| 5 | 0.08 | 15 | 1.01 | 25 | 1.18 |
| 6 | 0.00 | 16 | 3.46 | 26 | 0.06 |
| 7 | 1.17 | 17 | 2.98 | 27 | −1.00 |
| 8 | −0.76 | 18 | 0.71 | 28 | −2.86 |
| 9 | 2.88 | 19 | −0.17 | 29 | 0.65 |
| 10 | −8.91 | 20 | 2.26 | 30 | 0.18 |

*Source*: A sample survey of British mechanical engineering establishments carried out by the author, V. Lintner, M. Woods and M. Blinkhorn.

**Table 1.2** Index of industrial production UK manufacturing industries 1948 to 1983 (1975 = 100)

| Year | Index | Year | Index | Year | Index | Year | Index |
|---|---|---|---|---|---|---|---|
| 1948 | 46.9 | 1957 | 64.9 | 1966 | 87.4 | 1975 | 100.0 |
| 1949 | 50.3 | 1958 | 64.3 | 1967 | 87.9 | 1976 | 101.4 |
| 1950 | 54.1 | 1959 | 68.0 | 1968 | 94.1 | 1977 | 103.0 |
| 1951 | 55.7 | 1960 | 73.5 | 1969 | 97.6 | 1978 | 104.0 |
| 1952 | 53.0 | 1961 | 73.7 | 1970 | 98.0 | 1979 | 104.3 |
| 1953 | 56.7 | 1962 | 73.8 | 1971 | 97.5 | 1980 | 95.4 |
| 1954 | 59.8 | 1963 | 76.5 | 1972 | 100.0 | 1981 | 89.4 |
| 1955 | 63.6 | 1964 | 83.4 | 1973 | 108.4 | 1982 | 89.5 |
| 1956 | 63.4 | 1965 | 85.8 | 1974 | 106.6 | 1983 | 91.2 |

*Source*: *Economic Trends*, Annual Supplement, HMSO, 1984.

various performance measures at the macroeconomic level, such as the unemployment rate, output, or consumption expenditure. For illustrative purposes we present a sample of cross-section data in Table 1.1, and a sample of time-series data in Table 1.2.

Data may also be available in a form which is a combination of cross-section and time-series data. An example would be the collection of data on the incomes of a sample of individuals, where these data are collected at regular time intervals. Thus we would be interested in assessing how the features of this sample of incomes change through time. Such data are referred to as **panel** data. However, in the remainder of this text we will be concerned with data which are either strictly time-series or strictly cross-sectional.

If the population which is being analysed is sufficiently small (or resources sufficiently unconstrained) to allow a total enumeration of the population (a census) then the problem of sampling and inference does not arise. However, even if resources are unlimited, there are a number of situations in which a total enumeration is not possible. For example, if we wished to determine the breaking strength of some industrial component then a census would require that the population be destroyed. Or if the component is produced by some production-line process then the population can be considered as effectively infinite – the census can only be completed when all production ceases, at which time the census information will presumably no longer be of any use.

A sample of time-series data could also be interpreted as having been selected from an 'infinite population', in the sense that a time-series extends into the unbounded (infinite) future and past. We often wish to analyse a time-series in order to draw inferences about the future (the process of forecasting), and it is of course not possible to select a sample from the future.

So there are situations in which sampling is the only way of obtaining information about the population. Indeed, if a population is so large that a census would involve a substantial amount of (human) error, a sample may even provide more accurate information than a census.

As we have already indicated, the central objective of sampling is to obtain an accurate description of the population. In general, this is achieved by deriving estimates of a number of population **parameters** (typically, the population mean and variance). These estimates will be based on the sample information or, in particular, on sample statistics (the sample mean and variance).

Thus we can begin by defining the population mean and variance, and their sample counterparts, the sample mean and variance.

Let $X$ denote the variable of interest. For example, in terms of the data in Table 1.1, $X$ would denote 'pre-tax profits per employee', and in terms of the data in Table 1.2, $X$ would represent the 'index of industrial production'. Let $X_i$ denote the value of the variable $X$ at the $i$th sample point. In terms of Table 1.1, $i$ can take any integer value between 1 and 30. Therefore pre-tax profits of establishment number 14, say, would be denoted by $X_{14}$, and from Table 1.1 we have $X_{14} = -1.93$ (that is, establishment number 14 made a pre-tax loss of £1930 per employee). In terms of the data in Table 1.2 the subscript $i$ would refer to year $i$, and for notational convenience we could refer to 1948 as year 1, 1949 as year 2, and so on to 1983 and year 36. (In order to distinguish cross-section from time-series data the commonly used convention is to use a subscript of $t$ rather than $i$ when analysing time-series data. Thus we would denote the value of the Index of Industrial Production in year $t$ by $X_t$.)

The population mean (or population average) is defined as the average value of the variable $X$ in the population. Denote the population mean by the

Greek letter $\mu$ (mu), and thus we can write:

$$\mu = \frac{\sum\limits_{i=1}^{N} X_i}{N}$$

Equation 1.1

where $N$ is the size of the population (the number of elements in the population), and the notation $\Sigma_{i=1}^{N}$ reads as 'the sum over $i$, where $i$ runs in increments of 1 from 1 to $N$' (see Appendix 1.1 for a fuller discussion of summation notation). If $X$ referred to time-series data then the subscript $i$ in Equation 1.1 could be replaced by $t$.

The population variance is a measure of the extent of **dispersion** or **variation** of the variable, $X$, in the population. Thus consider the deviation of each value of $X$ from the population mean, $\mu$. These deviations would be denoted by $X_i - \mu$, for $i = 1, 2, \ldots, N$. If we then square these deviations (in order to eliminate the signs of the deviations, as we are interested in the absolute level of dispersion in the population), then the variance is defined as the average value of these squared deviations. That is, denoting the population variance by $\sigma^2$ (where $\sigma$ is the Greek letter sigma), then we can write:

$$\sigma^2 = \frac{\sum\limits_{i=1}^{N} (X_i - \mu)^2}{N}$$

Equation 1.2

In order to return to the original units of measurement we could take the square root of this expression, which would be denoted by $\sigma$, and is referred to as the population **standard deviation**.

The terms $\mu$ and $\sigma^2$ (or $\sigma$) are referred to as **population parameters**. Typically, they will be unknown (unless a census has been performed), and a sample would be selected from the population in order to estimate these parameters. The obvious estimators[1] of these parameters are the sample mean and variance, which we will denote by $\bar{X}$ and $V^2$, respectively. That is, we have:

$$\bar{X} = \frac{\sum\limits_{i=1}^{n} X_i}{n}$$

Equation 1.3

and

$$V^2 = \frac{\sum\limits_{i=1}^{n} (X_i - \bar{X})^2}{n}$$

Equation 1.4

where $n$ is the size of the sample.

The numerator of Equation 1.4 can be re-expressed so as to produce a computationally more convenient expression for $V^2$. Squaring out this numerator we can write[2]:

$$\sum_i (X_i - \bar{X})^2 = \sum (X_i^2 - 2X_i\bar{X} + \bar{X}^2)$$
$$= \sum X_i^2 - 2\bar{X}\sum X_i + \sum \bar{X}^2$$
$$= \sum X_i^2 - 2\bar{X}\sum X_i + n\bar{X}^2$$

Now, consider the term $2\bar{X}\sum X_i$. If we multiply this term by $n/n$, which will leave its value unchanged, we have:

$$2\bar{X}\sum X_i = (n/n)2\bar{X}\sum X_i = 2n\bar{X}(\sum X_i/n) = 2n\bar{X}^2$$

Thus we can now write:

$$\sum (X_i - \bar{X})^2 = \sum X_i^2 - 2n\bar{X}^2 + n\bar{X}^2$$

or

$$\sum (X_i - \bar{X})^2 = \sum X_i^2 - n\bar{X}^2 \qquad \text{Equation 1.5}$$

Therefore:

$$V^2 = \frac{\sum X_i^2 - n\bar{X}^2}{n} \qquad \text{Equation 1.6}$$

In order to illustrate the use of Equations 1.3 and 1.6, we can consider the sample data in Tables 1.1 and 1.2. From Table 1.1 we have $\sum X_i = 3.23$ and $\sum X_i^2 = 182.035$, and therefore:

$$\bar{X} = \frac{3.23}{30} = 0.108$$

$$V^2 = \frac{182.035 - (30)(0.108)^2}{30} = 6.056$$

or

$$V = \sqrt{6.056} = 2.461$$

From Table 1.2 we have $\sum X_t = 2923.1$ and $\sum X_t^2 = 29{,}820.55$, and therefore:

$$\bar{X} = 81.197$$
$$V^2 = 346.507$$

or

$$V = 18.615$$

However, in the case of time-series data, summary measures such as the mean and variance are often not particularly illuminating in capturing the important features of the data. Thus, while the mean and variance of the data in Table 1.2 capture some of the features of the data, they also ignore or conceal some of the more interesting and important aspects of the data. In particular, the one distinguishing characteristic of time-series as compared to cross-section data is that time-series data occur in a natural ordering – they are ordered by time. Consequently, a natural graphical representation of

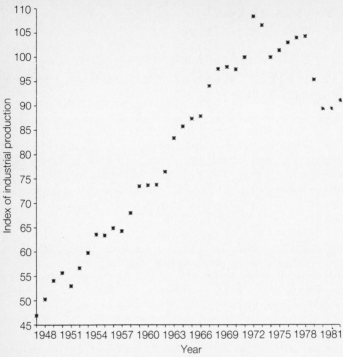

**Figure 1.1** Index of industrial production against time.

time-series data is available, and that is to plot the data against time, and therefore to observe how the data vary over time. Figure 1.1 shows the data in Table 1.2 graphed against time.

From Figure 1.1 it can now be seen that the most interesting feature of the data is the steady increase in the level of the observations for most of the sample period, and then the quite abrupt decline in the observations towards the end of the sample period. To observe that the mean of the data is 81.197 conveys none of this information, and indeed a mean of 81.197 could be consistent with the data increasing over time or decreasing over time, or any combination of these movements. This will also be the case with the standard deviation of the data.

Consequently, time-series data are not generally summarised and analysed in terms of their mean and standard deviation. Of more interest will be the movement of the data over time, and thus a starting point for analysis will be a graphical representation of the form shown in Figure 1.1. We can then proceed to analyse the data in terms of their trend through time, the movements around this trend, and the growth rate of the data. Many of the examples which we will discuss in this text will concern time-series data, and the various methods of analysing such data will be discussed as we proceed.

So far we have briefly discussed the way in which sample data might be analysed so as to begin the process of drawing inferences about the population. However, we have not as yet indicated how large a sample should be selected, nor have we discussed methods of sample selection.

As a generalisation, the larger the sample used then the more precise (or reliable) will be the parameter estimators, although resource constraints will often be the major determinant of sample size rather than strict theoretical considerations. However, while it is generally true that precision increases with sample size, beyond some point the increase in precision may be so small that further increases in sample size are not justified. An extreme example would be if each element of the population was identical – the population has no variance. In such a case a sample size of one would be sufficient to describe the population fully – a larger sample would be superfluous (as of course would be a census). More realistically, the smaller the variance of a population then the smaller is the sample required to achieve a given level of precision. Conversely, when sampling from a population with a large variance the decision as to sample size is very much a trade-off between resource expenditure and the precision required.

Together with the choice of sample size, the method of sample selection must also be determined. Sampling theory is a major branch of statistics, and we do not propose to present any detailed discussion here.[3] The simplest method (at least conceptually) is **simple random sampling**, whereby a sample is selected in such a way as to ensure that each element in the population has an equal chance of selection. Thus if there are $N$ elements in the population, then the sample is chosen in such a way as to ensure that each element has the same chance, $1/N$, of being selected.

In the absence of any further information (for example, that some elements of the population are in some sense more important than other elements, thus requiring a greater probability of selection) simple random sampling would appear to be the most sensible method of sampling and, in addition, has certain theoretical advantages. In particular, the elements of a simple random sample can be considered as independent – the probability of any element being selected does not depend on the selection (or omission) of any other element. The advantages of independence will be seen when we discuss estimation methods in more detail in Section 1.4.

## 1.3  Probability Distributions

A complete description of any population is contained in its **probability distribution**, and the process of sampling and estimation could be characterised as the attempt to derive an approximation to this probability distribution.

In order to illustrate the nature of a probability distribution, consider the data in Table 1.3. These data refer to the size distribution of households in Great Britain in 1981[4] (note that these data derive from a census of the population). Let the variable $X$ denote the number of individuals residing in each private household in Great Britain in 1981, and thus $X_i$ would denote the number of individuals residing in household number $i$, where, from Table 1.3, it can be seen that $i$ runs from 1 to 19,492,000, and $X$ can take on any integer value between 1 and 9. Note that $X$ is a **discrete** variable, in the sense that it can only take on integer values. This contrasts with the variables in Tables 1.1 and 1.2, which are **continuous**, and can therefore take on any value, integer or fractional. However, discrete variables are somewhat more convenient for developing the concepts associated with probability distributions, and hence, for illustrative purposes, we will develop these concepts in the context of Table 1.3.

**Table 1.3** Size distribution of households in Great Britain 1981

| Number of individuals residing in a household | Number of households (thousands) |
|---|---|
| 1 | 4242 |
| 2 | 6222 |
| 3 | 3327 |
| 4 | 3532 |
| 5 | 1436 |
| 6 | 455 |
| 7 | 179 |
| 8 | 79 |
| 9 | 20 |
| Total | 19,492 |

*Source*: Adapted from *Social Trends*, HMSO, 1982.

Consider a particular value of $X$, $X_i$ – that is, the observation of $X_i$ individuals per household. Let $f_i$ be the number of households out of the total of $N$ households that contain $X_i$ individuals. That is, $f_i$ is the **frequency** with which $X_i$ occurs. For example, from Table 1.3 if we consider the value of 4 for $X$, then the corresponding frequency is 3532 (thousand), where the total number of households, $N$, is 19,492 (thousand).

Consider the **relative frequency** of $X_i$ – that is, the number of times $X_i$ occurs relative to the total size of the population. This relative frequency is given by $f_i/N$. Thus in the case of $X = 4$, the corresponding relative frequency is 3532/19,492, or 0.181. As we are here considering the total population then $f_i/N$ can be defined as the **probability** of $X_i$ occurring. That is, if we were to select a household at random then the probability that this household contained $X_i$ individuals would be $f_i/N$. Thus the probability that in 1981 a randomly selected household in Great Britain contained four individuals is 0.181 (or the chance of such a household being selected is 18.1 per cent).

Thus, notationally, the probability that $X$ takes on the value $X_i$ can be written as:

$$P(X = X_i) = \frac{f_i}{N}$$   Equation 1.7

A common convention is to shorten the expression $P(X = X_i)$ to just $P(X_i)$, a convention which we will adopt.

Thus given knowledge of the total population, the relative frequency or probability of each value of $X$ could be evaluated, and this would constitute the **probability distribution** of $X$. Thus in the case of Table 1.3 we present in Table 1.4 the associated probability distribution. Note that, by definition, the

**Table 1.4** Probability distribution of the number of individuals residing in households in Great Britain 1981

| Number of individuals residing in a household $X$ | Probability $P(X)$ |
|---|---|
| 1 | 0.218 |
| 2 | 0.319 |
| 3 | 0.171 |
| 4 | 0.181 |
| 5 | 0.074 |
| 6 | 0.023 |
| 7 | 0.009 |
| 8 | 0.004 |
| 9 | 0.001 |
| Total | 1.000 |

*Source*: As for Table 1.3.

probabilities of each of the possible outcomes must sum to one. Note also that this probability distribution is a complete statement of the characteristics or nature of the population – it is a detailed statement of precisely how the population is distributed. Graphically, this probability distribution could be presented as in Figure 1.2, which provides an alternative means of highlighting the characteristics of the population. Note that the width of each bar of the histogram in Figure 1.2 is one unit, and the height of each bar is equal to the probability of the corresponding value of $X$. That is, the area enclosed by each bar is equal to the probability of the corresponding value of

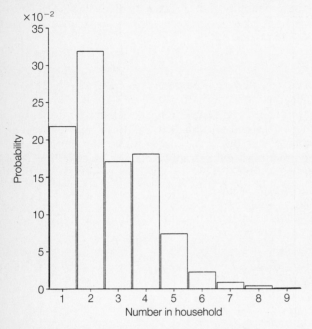

**Figure 1.2**  Probability distribution of $X$ in Table 1.4.

$X$ occurring, and hence the area enclosed by the entire histogram must be one (square unit). This will be a property of the graphical representations of all probability distributions.

It is straightforward to derive the population mean and variance directly from the probability distribution in Table 1.4. Thus recall the definition of the population mean in Equation 1.1. That is:

$$\mu = \frac{\sum\limits_{i=1}^{N} X_i}{N} \hspace{4cm} \text{Equation 1.8}$$

Now if $X_i$ occurs $f_i$ times in the population, and if $X$ can take on a total of $k$ different or distinct values (in our example $k = 9$) then we could re-express the population mean as follows:

$$\mu = \frac{\sum\limits_{i=1}^{k} f_i X_i}{N}$$

Equation 1.9

and note that by definition

$$\sum_{i=1}^{k} f_i = N$$

Equation 1.10

Re-expressing Equation 1.9, we have:

$$\mu = \sum_{i=1}^{k} X_i \frac{f_i}{N}$$

Equation 1.11

or

$$\mu = \sum_{i=1}^{k} X_i P(X_i)$$

Equation 1.12

where, as previously, $P(X_i)$ is the probability that $X$ takes on the value $X_i$.

Thus the population mean can be interpreted as the sum of each value of $X$ weighted by its corresponding probability or relative frequency, and therefore can be derived directly from the probability distribution of $X$.

Similarly, the population variance in Equation 1.2 can be re-expressed as follows:

$$\sigma^2 = \frac{\sum\limits_{i=1}^{k} f_i (X_i - \mu)^2}{N}$$

Equation 1.13

or

$$\sigma^2 = \sum_{i=1}^{k} (X_i - \mu)^2 \frac{f_i}{N}$$

Equation 1.14

or

$$\sigma^2 = \sum_{i=1}^{k} (X_i - \mu)^2 P(X_i)$$

Equation 1.15

That is, the population variance can be interpreted as a weighted average of the squared deviations of each $X_i$ from $\mu$, where again the weights are the probabilities of each $X_i$ occurring.

However, just as in the case of deriving a computationally more convenient expression for $V^2$ in Equation 1.6, Equation 1.15 can also be re-expressed. Thus squaring out the right-hand side of Equation 1.15 we can write:

$$\sigma^2 = \sum (X_i^2 - 2X_i\mu + \mu^2) P(X_i)$$
$$= \sum X_i^2 P(X_i) - 2\mu \sum X_i P(X_i) + \mu^2 \sum P(X_i)$$

noting that $\mu$ is a constant (as is $\sigma^2$). Recall from Equation 1.12 that $\sum X_i P(X_i) = \mu$ and that by definition $\sum P(X_i) = 1$, and therefore $\sigma^2$ can be expressed as:

$$\sigma^2 = \sum X_i^2 P(X_i) - \mu^2 \qquad\qquad \text{Equation 1.16}$$

We can demonstrate the use of Equations 1.12 and 1.16 via the probability distribution in Table 1.4. Thus from Table 1.4 we have:

$$\mu = (1)(0.218) + (2)(0.319) + \ldots + (9)(0.001)$$
$$= 2.705$$

That is, there was an average of 2.705 individuals per household in Great Britain in 1981. (Note that we could not of course observe a household with '2.705' individuals. The value 2.705 is a measure of central tendency of the probability distribution of $X$, rather than some measure of the size of the 'typical' or representative household.)

Similarly, the value of $\sigma^2$ can be derived as follows:

$$\sum X_i^2 P(X_i) = (1)(0.218) + (4)(0.319) + \ldots + (81)(0.001)$$
$$= 9.385$$

and therefore:

$$\sigma^2 = 9.385 - (2.705)^2$$
$$= 2.068$$

or

$$\sigma = 1.438$$

While we have developed the concepts associated with a probability distribution in the context of a discrete variable, these ideas all extend directly to the case of a continuous variable. Graphically, a probability distribution of a continuous variable would be in the form of a smooth curve, rather than the histogram of Figure 1.2.

A common form of a continuous probability distribution is the **normal distribution**. Thus consider a continuous variable, $X$, which is known to have a normal distribution (or is normally distributed), with a mean of $\mu$ and a variance of $\sigma^2$. Then, graphically, this distribution would appear as in Figure 1.3. As in the case of the probability distribution in Figure 1.2, the area enclosed by the curve in Figure 1.3 must equal one (square unit). Let this curve be denoted by $f(X)$. That is, this curve is a **function** of $X$ which, notationally, is generally shortened to $f(X)$. Thus in Figure 1.3 the values of $X$ are graphed on the horizontal axis and the corresponding values of $f(X)$ are graphed on the vertical axis (it is common to omit the vertical axis from the graphical representations of continuous probability distributions, a convention which we will adopt).

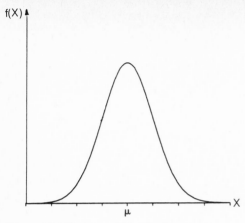

**Figure 1.3** The normal distribution.

The term $f(X)$ is referred to as the **probability density function** (p.d.f.) of $X$. It describes a curve which encloses an area of one, and is such that the various component areas equal the probabilities of the corresponding ranges of $X$ occurring. In the case of the normal distribution $f(X)$ has a well behaved mathematical form, which is given by the following expression:

$$f(X) = \frac{1}{\sqrt{2\pi\sigma^2}} \, e^{-(X-\mu)^2/2\sigma^2}$$

Equation 1.17

where both $\pi$ and $e$ are constants (approximately equal to 3.14159 and 2.71828, respectively), and $\mu$ and $\sigma^2$ are the mean and variance of $X$. That is, the formula for $f(X)$ in Equation 1.17 (given values of $\mu$ and $\sigma^2$) will trace out a smooth curve enclosing an area of one square unit. The general properties of the normal distribution are that it is a continuous, bell-shaped, symmetrical distribution, with approximately 68 per cent of the distribution contained within one standard deviation of the mean, approximately 95 per cent of the distribution contained within two standard deviations of the mean, and 99.7 per cent of the distribution contained within three standard deviations of the mean. Thus given any variable which is known to have a normal distribution then once the mean and variance of this variable are known these can be substituted into Equation 1.17, hence fully specifying the probability distribution of $X$. Given the full specification of the p.d.f. of $X$ then various probabilities concerning $X$ can be directly evaluated.

However, first note that as $X$ is a continuous variable, then summation notation is no longer appropriate and we must use the notation of **integration**. Thus in all the previous formulae which we have derived for the case of discrete variables, we simply replace the summation notation with integration notation.

Therefore, if $X$ is continuous then the mean of $X$ can be written as:

$$\mu = \int_a^z Xf(X)\mathrm{d}X \qquad\qquad \text{Equation 1.18}$$

where $a$ is the minimum value of $X$ in the population, and $z$ is its maximum value. This can be compared to Equation 1.12 above. In the case of the normal distribution $a = -\infty$ and $z = +\infty$, and therefore $f(X)$ in Figure 1.3 is asymptotic to the $X$ axis.

Similarly, the variance of $X$ can be written as:

$$\sigma^2 = \int_a^z (X-\mu)^2 f(X)\mathrm{d}X \qquad\qquad \text{Equation 1.19}$$

which can be compared to Equation 1.15.

As in the case of the expression for the variance of a discrete variable in Equation 1.15, Equation 1.19 can also be simplified. Thus squaring out Equation 1.19 we have:

$$\sigma^2 = \int_a^z (X^2 - 2\mu X + \mu^2) f(X)\mathrm{d}X$$

Now, as the area enclosed by $f(X)$ is 1 then we must have:

$$\int_a^z f(X)\mathrm{d}X = 1$$

and also recall from Equation 1.18 that $\int_a^z X f(X)\mathrm{d}X = \mu$ and therefore we can write:

$$\sigma^2 = \int_a^z X^2 f(X)\mathrm{d}X - 2\mu^2 + \mu^2$$

or

$$\sigma^2 = \int_a^z X^2 f(X)\mathrm{d}X - \mu^2 \qquad\qquad \text{Equation 1.20}$$

which can be compared to Equation 1.16 above.

Note further the way in which probabilities concerning $X$ can be expressed in terms of $f(X)$. For example, the probability of $X$ falling between the values $c$ and $d$, say, would be written as:

$$P(c < X < d) = \int_c^d f(X)\mathrm{d}X \qquad\qquad \text{Equation 1.21}$$

The probability of $X$ exceeding the value $g$ would be written as:

$$P(X > g) = \int_g^z f(X)\mathrm{d}X \qquad\qquad \text{Equation 1.22}$$

The probability of $X$ being less than $k$ is:

$$P(X < k) = \int_a^k f(X)\mathrm{d}X \qquad \text{Equation 1.23}$$

In Table 1.5 we present a summary of the various expressions for the mean and variance, for the variable $X$, at the levels of both the population and the sample. In the case of discrete data we assume that $X$ can take on $k$ distinct values, and in the case of continuous data $X$ can take on a minimum value of

**Table 1.5** Formulae for the mean and variance

|  | POPULATION | SAMPLE |
|---|---|---|
| MEAN | Discrete data:<br>$$\mu = \sum_{i=1}^{k} X_i P(X_i)$$<br>Continuous data:<br>$$\mu = \int_a^z X f(X)\mathrm{d}X$$ | $$\bar{X} = \frac{\sum\limits_{i=1}^{n} X_i}{n}$$ |
| VARIANCE | Discrete data:<br>$$\sigma^2 = \sum_{i=1}^{k} (X_i - \mu)^2 P(X_i)$$<br>Continuous data:<br>$$\sigma^2 = \int_a^z (X - \mu)^2 f(X)\mathrm{d}X$$ | $$V^2 = \frac{\sum\limits_{i=1}^{n} (X_i - \bar{X})^2}{n}$$ |

$a$ and a maximum of $z$. In both cases the population contains $N$ elements and the sample is of size $n$.

The normal distribution has been found to describe adequately many natural phenomena (in the biological and physical sciences) and also occurs commonly in many industrial applications. That is, while the normal distribution is a theoretical probability distribution there are many applications in which it provides an adequate approximation to the population distribution under investigation, and hence can be used to provide a detailed description of this population. Thus the role of sampling in such situations is to derive sample data in order to estimate the population mean and variance, so that these estimates can be substituted into Equation 1.17, hence providing an approximation to the population p.d.f.

Given the population p.d.f. there are then a range of detailed characteristics of the population which can be examined. Returning to the discrete probability distribution in Table 1.4, note that not only can we derive the population mean and variance from this information, but we can determine, for instance, the proportion of the population that resides in households of six or more individuals $(P(6)+P(7)+P(8)+P(9))$, or the proportion of the population residing in households with fewer than three individuals $(P(1)+P(2))$, and so on. Similarly, in the case of $X$ having a normal distribution, with some known (or estimated) mean and variance, analogous probabilities can be evaluated. For example, the proportion of the population exceeding, say, 5.5 would be expressed as:

$$\int_{5.5}^{+\infty} f(X)dX$$

or the proportion of the population lying between 6 and 9, say, would be:

$$\int_{6}^{9} f(X)dX$$

where $f(X)$ is given by Equation 1.17.

However, in the case of the normal distribution, evaluating these integrals to derive the required probabilities is exceedingly tedious, and different integrations would have to be performed for normal variables with differing means and/or variances.

Fortunately, a solution to this problem is available which greatly facilitates the calculation of normal probabilities. In particular, it can be shown that any normal variable, $X$, with a mean, $\mu$, and variance, $\sigma^2$, can be transformed to another normal variable which has a mean of 0 and variance of 1. Therefore all normal probabilities can be expressed in terms of this transformed distribution, and thus derived from this distribution. This distribution is referred to as the **standard normal distribution**. It is derived by subtracting from the original variable, $X$, its mean, $\mu$, and then dividing by its standard deviation, $\sigma$ (note, standard deviation and not variance). This transformed variable is denoted by $Z$ and can be written as:

$$Z = \frac{X-\mu}{\sigma} \qquad\qquad \text{Equation 1.24}$$

Note that all we have done to the original variable, $X$, is to subtract a constant ($\mu$) and then divide by another constant ($\sigma$). Therefore the distributional properties of $X$ have been left unchanged (if $X$ is normally distributed then so must be $Z$), the origin of $X$ having just been shifted to 0 and its variance standardised to 1 (we will demonstrate this more explicitly below).

Thus probabilities involving any normal variable, $X$, can all be expressed in terms of $Z$. In addition, rather than explicitly evaluating integrals to obtain any given probability, statistical tables are available in which these integrals are tabulated for various values of $Z$. A table of probabilities for the standard normal distribution is given in Appendix I.

Before proceeding, we will briefly introduce some notational conventions.

Consider a variable, $X$, which has a normal distribution with a mean of $\mu$ and a variance of $\sigma^2$. This statement is generally shortened to:

$$X \sim N(\mu, \sigma^2)$$

which reads as '$X$ follows a normal distribution with a mean $\mu$ and a variance $\sigma^2$'. Therefore the transformed variable, $Z$, where

$$Z = \frac{X - \mu}{\sigma}$$

also has a normal distribution, but with a mean of 0 and a variance of one, which can be expressed as:

$$Z \sim N(0, 1)$$

In order to demonstrate the use of the standard normal tables in Appendix I, consider a variable, $X$, which is known to have a normal distribution with a mean of ten and a variance of four. That is,

$$X \sim N(10, 4)$$

Consider evaluating the probability that $X$ is greater than, say, 11.3. That is, notationally, we require $P(X > 11.3)$. Transforming to the standard normal distribution we can write:

$$P(X > 11.3) = P\left(\frac{X - \mu}{\sigma} > \frac{11.3 - \mu}{\sigma}\right)$$
$$= P\left(Z > \frac{11.3 - 10}{2}\right)$$
$$= P(Z > 0.65)$$

That is, the probability that a normally distributed variable, $X$, with a mean of ten and a variance of four exceeds 11.3 is equivalent to the standard normal variable, $Z$, exceeding 0.65. From Appendix I the entry corresponding to 0.65 is 0.258 (the probabilities tabulated in Appendix I indicate the probability of $Z$ exceeding the tabulated value). Thus we can deduce that $P(X > 11.3)$ is 0.258, or that about 26 per cent of this population exceeds 11.3.

Similarly, consider the probability that $X$ lies between nine and twelve – that is, $P(9 < X < 12)$. Again, transforming to the standard normal distribution, we can write:

$$P(9 < X < 12) = P\left(\frac{9-10}{2} < Z < \frac{12-10}{2}\right)$$

$$= P(-0.5 < Z < 1)$$

$$= 1 - [P(Z < -0.5) + P(Z > 1)]$$

Noting that the normal distribution is symmetrical, then we must have:

$$P(Z < -0.5) = P(Z > 0.5)$$

and therefore from Appendix I we have:

$$P(Z > 0.5) = 0.309 \quad \text{and} \quad P(Z > 1) = 0.1587$$

Thus we can deduce that:

$$P(-0.5 < Z < 1) = 1 - (0.309 + 0.159)$$

$$= 0.532$$

That is, approximately 53 per cent of a distribution which is $N(10, 4)$ falls between nine and twelve, or equivalently, there is a 53 per cent chance that a randomly selected observation from this population will lie between nine and twelve.

As we shall see in the following section when we discuss the process of estimation in more detail, the normal distribution has further applications that are of considerable practical relevance.


## 1.4   Estimation

While we have implied that the process of sampling and estimation could be characterised as an attempt to derive an approximation to the population probability distribution, a sample of data is rarely used for such an ambitious task. In practice, there will be no way of actually knowing that the population is, say, normally distributed (or has any other form of well-behaved distribution), and thus that all that is required is an estimate of the population mean and variance in order to specify this distribution fully. Typically, the population distribution will be unknown, and all we can realistically hope to achieve is an approximation to some of the broader characteristics of this population – estimates of the mean and variance, say.

Thus the basic sampling and estimation problem can be expressed as follows:

We are interested in a population which has an unknown probability distribution, with an unknown mean ($\mu$) and an unknown variance ($\sigma^2$). A sample is randomly selected from this population, and we wish to derive a method of estimating these unknown parameters from the sample data.

Additionally, we also require some indication as to the accuracy of the estimation method we have used, and hence the confidence which can be placed in the derived estimates.

Although we have indicated that estimates of both $\mu$ and $\sigma^2$ are required, we will here only concentrate on the problem of estimating $\mu$, and we will only briefly indicate how $\sigma^2$ can be estimated.

We can distinguish between two types of estimates:

1  *Point estimates.*   That is, the sample is used to produce a single number which can be interpreted, in some sense, as the most likely value of the population parameter.
2  *Interval estimates.*   That is, the sample is used to produce a range or interval of values which is considered likely to contain the true value of the population parameter.

Which of these two methods is used in practice will depend very much on the objectives of the estimation exercise. A point estimate provides a definitive statement and provides an unambiguous basis for taking decisions about the population. However, it can say nothing of how accurately the parameter is being estimated and hence the risks involved in any decisions which are taken.

An interval estimate, on the other hand, provides information about the accuracy of the estimation method. However, it implies a range of decisions which can be taken, and hence the qualifications which must be made about any conclusions which are drawn. Interval estimates contain a more useful summary of the sample information, but decisions generally have to be taken on the basis of point estimates. The distinction between point and interval estimates will become clearer as these concepts are developed in more detail below.

Before proceeding, we will discuss the concept of **mathematical expectation** which is useful for providing a straightforward basis for comparing various estimation methods.

*Digression 1.1:   Mathematical Expectation*

As discrete variables allow a more direct probability interpretation, we will develop concepts using a discrete variable, $X$.

Consider the population of $X$ values. From Equation 1.12 above the mean of this population can be written as:

$$\mu = \sum_{i=1}^{k} X_i P(X_i)$$

where there are $k$ distinct values of $X$ in the population.

This expression for the population mean of $X$ is also referred to as the **expected value of** $X$ – it is the sum of all the values of $X$ weighted by their respective probabilities, and in this sense can be interpreted as the value of $X$ which we would expect to occur, or it is the most 'likely' value of $X$.

The expected value of $X$ is generally shortened to $E(X)$, and thus we can write:

$$E(X) = \sum_{i=1}^{k} X_i P(X_i) \qquad \text{Equation 1.25}$$

We can evaluate the expected value of any *function* of $X$ in a directly analogous manner. That is, for some function of $X$, $f(X)$, the expected value of $f(X)$ is simply the weighted sum of $f(X)$, where the weights are the probabilities of each $X_i$ occurring, and summation is over all values of $X$. Thus we can write:

$$E[f(X)] = \sum_{i=1}^{k} f(X_i) P(X_i) \qquad \text{Equation 1.26}$$

For example, the expected value of $X^2$ can be written as:

$$E(X^2) = \sum_{i=1}^{k} X_i^2 P(X_i) \qquad \text{Equation 1.27}$$

Further, recall from Equation 1.15 that the population variance can be written as:

$$\sigma^2 = \sum_{i=1}^{k} (X_i - \mu)^2 P(X_i)$$

Therefore, $\sigma^2$ can be interpreted as the expected value of $(X - \mu)^2$ – the weighted sum of the squared mean deviations, where the weights are the probabilities of the $X_i$s. That is, we can write:

$$\sigma^2 = E(X - \mu)^2 \qquad \text{Equation 1.28}$$

If $X$ is now assumed to be a continuous variable then the above still applies but with summations replaced by integrals. Thus for continuous $X$ we have:

$$\mu = E(X) = \int_{-\infty}^{+\infty} X f(X) \mathrm{d}X$$

and

$$\sigma^2 = E(X - \mu)^2 = \int_{-\infty}^{+\infty} (X - \mu)^2 f(X) \mathrm{d}X$$

where $f(X)$ is the p.d.f. of $X$.

The advantage of expressing population values (parameters) in terms of expectations is that the expectations operator, $E$, can be manipulated just like any other mathematical operator. Thus, consider two variables, $X$ and $Y$, and two constants, *a* and *b*. Then the basic rules for manipulating the expectations operator are as follows:

$$E(bX) = bE(X)$$ 

Equation 1.29

$$E(a+bX) = a+bE(X)$$ 

Equation 1.30

$$E(X+Y) = E(X)+E(Y)$$ 

Equation 1.31

*but*

$$E(XY) \neq E(X)E(Y)$$ 

Equation 1.32

unless $X$ and $Y$ are statistically independent – that is, the expected value of the multiple of $X$ and $Y$ will only equal the multiple of the expected values if the occurrence (or non-occurrence) of $X$ in no way influences the probability of $Y$ occurring (and vice versa).

Equations 1.29 to 1.31 are intuitively obvious, but Equation 1.32 is perhaps not so clear-cut.

In order to provide a justification for Equation 1.32 consider the case of two discrete variables, $X$ and $Y$. Now consider the concept of the **joint probability distribution** of $X$ and $Y$, which we could denote by $P(XY)$. That is, for specific values of $X$ and $Y$, $X_i$ and $Y_j$ say, $P(X_iY_j)$ would be the probability that $X_i$ and $Y_j$ occur simultaneously. For example, consider the experiment of throwing two dice. Let $X$ denote the number of spots which occur on the first die, and $Y$ the number of spots which occur on the second die. Thus both $X$ and $Y$ can take on any integer value from one to six, and there will be 36 possible combinations of $X$ and $Y$ values (when $X$ takes on the value one, $Y$ can take on any value from one to six; when $X$ takes on the value two, $Y$ can take on any value from one to six, and so on). Thus the joint probability distribution of $X$ and $Y$ will consist of the probabilities of each of these 36 outcomes. Further, we would expect $X$ and $Y$ to be independent – the number of spots which occur on the first die can in no way influence the number of spots which occur on the second die, and vice versa. Therefore each of the 36 possible $X$ and $Y$ combinations would be equiprobable (each with a probability of $\frac{1}{36}$), and thus we can write:

$$P(XY) = P(X)P(Y)$$ 

Equation 1.33

That is, the probability of, say, a four occurring on the first die and a five on the second die would be equal to the multiple of the individual probabilities $((\frac{1}{6})(\frac{1}{6}) = \frac{1}{36})$, as would be the case with all the possible $X$ and $Y$ combinations. Indeed, Equation 1.33 is the precise definition of statistical independence – as no relationship exists between $X$ and $Y$ the joint probability distribution of $X$ and $Y$ can be deduced directly from the individual probability distributions.

Thus again consider Equation 1.32, but consider the case of $X$ and $Y$ being independent. As a direct extension of the definition of the expectations operator in Equation 1.26 we can deduce that:

$$E(XY) = \sum_{i=1}^{k} \sum_{j=1}^{m} X_i Y_j P(X_i Y_j) \qquad \text{Equation 1.34}$$

where $X$ can take on $k$ distinct values and $Y$ can take on $m$ distinct values. Now, if $X$ and $Y$ are independent then we can write from Equation 1.33:

$$P(X_i Y_i) = P(X_i) P(Y_i) \qquad \text{Equation 1.35}$$

and therefore Equation 1.34 can be rewritten as:

$$E(XY) = \sum_i \sum_j X_i Y_j P(X_i) P(Y_i)$$

or

$$E(XY) = \sum_i X_i P(X_i) \sum_j Y_j P(Y_j) \qquad \text{Equation 1.36}$$

That is, if $X$ and $Y$ are independent then from Equation 1.36 we have:

$$E(XY) = E(X) E(Y) \qquad \text{Equation 1.37}$$

However, if there is any form of dependence between $X$ and $Y$ then Equation 1.35 will not hold, and Equation 1.37 will not follow. Therefore in the case of any form of relationship between $X$ and $Y$, $E(XY)$, by definition, cannot equal the product of the individual expected values.

As an example of the use of the expectations operator, we can derive the mean and variance of the standard normal variable, $Z$. Thus from Equation 1.24 we have:

$$Z = \frac{X - \mu}{\sigma}$$

$$= \frac{X}{\sigma} - \frac{\mu}{\sigma}$$

Now, both $\mu$ and $\sigma$ are constants (they will generally be unknown, but they are none the less constants). Thus we can write:

$$E(Z) = E\left(\frac{X}{\sigma}\right) - \frac{\mu}{\sigma}$$

as $\mu/\sigma$ is a constant. Therefore

$$E(Z) = \frac{1}{\sigma} E(X) - \frac{\mu}{\sigma}$$

$$= \frac{1}{\sigma} \mu - \frac{\mu}{\sigma} \quad \text{as} \quad E(X) = \mu$$

$$= 0$$

Writing the variance of $Z$ as Var$(Z)$, we also have:

$$\text{Var}(Z) = E[Z - E(Z)]^2$$
$$= E(Z^2)$$

as we have confirmed above that $E(Z) = 0$. Therefore we can write:

$$\text{Var}(Z) = E\left(\frac{X - \mu}{\sigma}\right)^2$$

$$= \frac{1}{\sigma^2} E(X - \mu)^2$$

$$= \frac{\sigma^2}{\sigma^2} \quad (\text{as } E(X - \mu)^2 = \sigma^2)$$

$$= 1$$

That is, we have confirmed our earlier informal justification of the mean and variance of $Z$ being 0 and one, respectively.

We will now go on to discuss in more detail the process of using a sample to estimate the population mean, $\mu$. In order to be concrete, we will consider an application.

Consider the problem of estimating average household income in the United Kingdom. A random sample of $n$ households is selected, and the income of each of these households is recorded. Assume that 144 households are randomly selected, and that monthly income is the variable of interest. Assume further that the true population variance is known and is equal to 10,000 (in units of £²). That is, assume that $\sigma^2 = 10,000$. (Note that this is an unrealistic assumption as it is highly unlikely that the population variance would be known and not the population mean – in order to calculate the population variance knowledge of the population mean is required. However, there may be rare cases where knowledge of the population variance is available from other sources. In any event, this assumption is introduced here simply for ease of exposition, and will be relaxed below.)

We require an estimate of the true population average monthly income, $\mu$. In the absence of any other information, the obvious point estimate is simply the mean of the sample of 144 households. Let $\bar{X}$ denote the sample mean, and assume here that the mean of the sample is £415. That is:

$$\bar{X} = 415$$

For purposes of developing estimation theory, it is very important to recognise that $\bar{X}$ is a variable. If we were to randomly select a second sample of 144 households then it is likely that the mean of this second sample would be different from 415. Thus, in general, the value of $\bar{X}$ will vary from sample to sample (although in practice only one sample would be selected). That is, $\mu$ is a constant (but unknown), whereas $\bar{X}$ is a variable.

Although, intuitively, $\bar{X}$ appears to be the most sensible estimator of $\mu$, we require more formal criteria for judging how satisfactory an estimator $\bar{X}$ is. This is particularly the case if decisions have to be taken on the basis of the sample, decisions which may involve costs and benefits.

Given that $\bar{X}$ is a variable, it will itself have a probability distribution, with some mean and variance. Conceptually, at least, the distribution of $\bar{X}$ could be built up by drawing all the possible samples of size 144 from the population of households in the United Kingdom, obtaining the means of these samples, and thereby deriving the population of $\bar{X}$ values (clearly we would never actually undertake such an exercise – it would be considerably more tedious and costly than simply taking a census of the population, which would of course obviate the need for sampling).

Now, the mean of all the possible $\bar{X}$ values – the expected value of $\bar{X}$ – can be derived as follows:

$$E(\bar{X}) = E \left( \frac{\sum\limits_{i=1}^{n} X_i}{n} \right)$$

$$= \frac{1}{n} E[\sum X_i]$$

$$= \frac{1}{n} [E(X_1) + E(X_2) + \ldots + E(X_n)]$$

$$= \frac{1}{n}(n\mu)$$

$$= \mu$$

That is, if we draw all the possible samples of size $n$ from the population and calculate the means of each of these samples, then the average of all these sample means will be equal to the true population mean, $\mu$. This result may seem intuitively obvious, and is not a particularly startling result – drawing all possible samples of size $n$ from the population effectively involves enumerating the population a number of times. However, it is comforting to know that the estimator, $\bar{X}$, will on average produce an estimate which equals $\mu$.

$\bar{X}$, then, is referred to as an **unbiased** estimator of $\mu$. In general, any estimator which has an expected value equal to the population parameter it is estimating is referred to as unbiased.

Unbiasedness is generally the minimum we would require of any estimator. However, of equal (if not greater) importance, is the extent of dispersion of the estimator around the population parameter – in the present context, the dispersion of $\bar{X}$ around $\mu$, or the variance of $\bar{X}$. The larger the variance of $\bar{X}$ the more imprecise will $\bar{X}$ be as an estimator of $\mu$ – the larger the variance of $\bar{X}$ the more likely it is that a given sample will produce a value for $\bar{X}$ which is considerably different from the value of $\mu$. As there will usually be just one sample available for analysis – particularly in a social science context – then a means of controlling the variance of an estimator is essential in order to ensure that the sample produces useful information. Before explicitly deriving the variance of $\bar{X}$, we will state three results, without proof, which are useful when deriving variances.

Consider some variable, $X$, which has a variance of $\sigma^2$, and let $a$ and $b$ be two constants. As previously, we will write the variance of $X$ as $\mathrm{Var}(X)$. Thus it can be shown that:

(a) $\mathrm{Var}(bX) = b^2\,\mathrm{Var}(X)$

or

$$\mathrm{Var}(bX) = b^2\sigma^2 \qquad\qquad \text{Equation 1.38}$$

(b) $\mathrm{Var}(a+bX) = \mathrm{Var}(bX)$

or

$$\mathrm{Var}(a+bX) = b^2\sigma^2 \qquad\qquad \text{Equation 1.39}$$

(c) For a random sample of size $n$, $X_1, X_2, \ldots, X_n$:

$$\mathrm{Var}\left(\sum_{i=1}^{n} X_i\right) = \mathrm{Var}(X_1 + X_2 + \ldots + X_n)$$

$$= \mathrm{Var}(X_1) + \mathrm{Var}(X_2) + \ldots + \mathrm{Var}(X_n)$$

$$= \sigma^2 + \sigma^2 + \ldots + \sigma^2$$

or

$$\mathrm{Var}\left(\sum_{i=1}^{n} X_i\right) = n\sigma^2 \qquad\qquad \text{Equation 1.40}$$

This last result holds only if the sample is randomly selected, thus implying that each element of the sample is independent of all the others.

In order to demonstrate why Equation 1.40 holds, consider deriving the expression for the sum of just two variables. Denote these variables by $R$ and $S$, say, and thus we require the expression for $\mathrm{Var}(R+S)$. For notational ease, let $Y = R+S$, and thus we can write:

$$\mathrm{Var}(R+S) = \mathrm{Var}(Y) = E(Y^2) - [E(Y)]^2 \qquad\qquad \text{Equation 1.41}$$

Now,

$$E(Y^2) = E(R+S)^2$$

which upon expansion can be written as:

$$E(Y^2) = E(R^2) + E(S^2) + 2E(RS)$$

Equation 1.42

Similarly, we can write:

$$[E(Y)]^2 = [E(R) + E(S)]^2$$

or

$$[E(Y)]^2 = [E(R)]^2 + [E(S)]^2 + 2E(R)E(S)$$

Equation 1.43

Thus substituting Equations 1.42 and 1.43 into Equation 1.41 and simplifying produces:

$$\text{Var}(R+S) = \{E(R^2) - [E(R)]^2\} + \{E(S^2) - [E(S)]^2\}$$
$$+ 2[E(RS) - E(R)E(S)]$$

or

$$\text{Var}(R+S) = \text{Var}(R) + \text{Var}(S)$$
$$+ 2[E(RS) - E(R)E(S)]$$

Equation 1.44

Now, recall from Equation 1.37 that the last term in Equation 1.40 will be zero only if $R$ and $S$ are independent. Therefore if $R$ and $S$ are independent then we can write:

$$\text{Var}(R+S) = \text{Var}(R) + \text{Var}(S)$$

Equation 1.45

Therefore Equation 1.40 can be interpreted as a generalisation of Equation 1.45, thus implying that the variance of the sum of $n$ variables will simply be equal to the sum of the variances of these variables, provided that these variables are all independent. In the case of a randomly selected sample each sample element, by definition, is independent of all other sample elements, therefore providing the justification for the use of Equation 1.40.

(We would emphasise here that the expression for $\text{Var}(\Sigma X_i)$ only has an interpretation before the sample is actually drawn, when $X_1, X_2, \ldots, X_n$ are variables, each of which can take on any value in the population. Once the sample is drawn $\Sigma X_i$ will be some number, which cannot of course have a variance.)

With these results we can now derive the expression for the variance of the sample mean, $\bar{X}$. That is:

$$\text{Var}(\bar{X}) = \text{Var}\left(\frac{\Sigma X_i}{n}\right)$$

$$= \frac{1}{n^2}\text{Var}(\Sigma X_i) \qquad\qquad \text{using Equation 1.38}$$

$$= \frac{1}{n^2} n\sigma^2 \qquad\qquad\qquad \text{using Equation 1.40}$$

Therefore

$$\mathrm{Var}\,(\bar{X}) = \frac{\sigma^2}{n}$$                     Equation 1.46

and recall that for any given population, $\sigma^2$ is a *constant*.

The implication of this expression for $\mathrm{Var}\,(\bar{X})$ is that the larger the sample (the larger is $n$) the smaller will be the variance of $\bar{X}$. This is just a formal statement of what is intuitively obvious – namely, the larger the sample, the more confident we can be in the sample mean as a reflection of the population mean. That is, the larger the sample size the more precise will the sample mean be as an estimator of the population mean. Assuming that we have no control over the size of the population variance, $\sigma^2$, then the precision of $\bar{X}$ as an estimator of $\mu$ can only be controlled via the sample size (subject of course to resource constraints).

Thus in summary we can now write:

$$\bar{X} \sim D(\mu, \sigma^2/n)$$

where ' $\sim D$' reads as 'follows some distribution'.

Now, if the form of the distribution of $\bar{X}$ were known, then we could make probability statements concerning $\bar{X}$, and therefore make definitive statements concerning the precision of $\bar{X}$ as an estimator of $\mu$. We now go on to indicate how the form of the distribution of $\bar{X}$ can be deduced.

First, consider the case of sampling from a population which is known to have a normal distribution. Then it can be shown that $\bar{X}$ will also have normal distribution ($\bar{X}$ is just a linear transformation of a set of variables – $X_1, X_2, \ldots, X_n$ – which are themselves normally distributed, and thus it is to be expected that $\bar{X}$ will also be normally distributed). That is, if:

$$X \sim N(\mu, \sigma^2)$$

then

$$\bar{X} \sim N(\mu, \sigma^2/n)$$

However, in practice, it will be rare for the form of the population distribution to be known, although in many cases an assumption of normality may seem reasonable (in the absence of any other information). The more interesting and realistic cases are those in which the form of the population distribution is either unknown, or where it is known that an assumption of normality is inappropriate. In our example concerning the estimation of average household income, it is highly unlikely that the population distribution is normal, or even symmetrical – income distributions are typically skewed.

Thus for practical purposes we will generally be concerned with determining the distribution of $\bar{X}$ when sampling from a population with an unknown distribution, or with a distribution which is known to be non-normal. In such cases appeal can be made to one of the most important and basic results of statistical theory – the **Central Limit Theorem**. Broadly, the theorem can be stated as follows:

> Assuming random sampling, the distribution of $\bar{X}$ will approach the normal distribution as sample size increases, irrespective of the form of the population distribution of $X$.

This is a quite remarkable result, and leads to the great generality and power of the techniques of statistical inference.[5] There are a number of exceptions to the theorem (in particular, it does not apply if the population has an infinite variance), but these are of a very theoretical nature and have virtually no practical consequences.

As stated, the theorem implies that $\bar{X}$ only becomes normal as sample size approaches infinity. In practice, however, the distribution of $\bar{X}$ will be virtually normal for sample sizes in excess of about 25 or 30, and indeed reasonable approximations can occur for sample sizes as small as 15 or so. Therefore, for practical purposes, we can state that:

> Irrespective of how $X$ is distributed, $\bar{X}$ will be approximately normally distributed for sample sizes in excess of about 25.

The Central Limit Theorem (CLT), then, allows for the full specification of the probability distribution of $\bar{X}$, for reasonably large samples. Thus when sampling from (virtually) any population we can write:

$$\bar{X} \sim N(\mu, \sigma^2/n)$$

provided $n$ is larger than about 25, and the sample is selected randomly.

We are now in a position to make probability statements about $\bar{X}$, and in particular, we can derive **interval estimators** for $\mu$.

Returning to our example of estimating average household income, note that we can first deduce from Equation 1.46 that:

$$\mathrm{Var}(\bar{X}) = \frac{10,000}{144} = 69.44$$

and therefore we can write that for sample sizes of 144:

$$\bar{X} \sim N(\mu, 69.44)$$

We can transform $\bar{X}$ to the standard normal variable, $Z$, by subtracting its mean and dividing by its standard deviation. That is:

$$Z = \frac{\bar{X} - \mu}{\sqrt{69.44}} \sim N(0, 1)$$

Now, approximately 95 per cent of the distribution of $Z$ lies within $\pm 1.96$ of its mean (or zero). This can be confirmed from the standard normal tables in Appendix I, and thus we can write:

$$P[-1.96 < Z < 1.96] = 0.95$$

or

$$P\left[-1.96 < \frac{\bar{X} - \mu}{\sqrt{69.44}} < 1.96\right] = 0.95$$

This statement can be re-expressed as a statement concerning $\mu$, the parameter of interest, as follows:

$$P[(-1.96)(\sqrt{69.44}) < \bar{X} - \mu < (1.96)(\sqrt{69.44})] = 0.95$$

or

$$P[\bar{X} - (1.96)(\sqrt{69.44}) < \mu < \bar{X} + (1.96)(\sqrt{69.44})] = 0.95$$

or

$$P[\bar{X} - 16.33 < \mu < \bar{X} + 16.33] = 0.95$$

In words, if we were to randomly select a sample of size 144 from a population which has a variance of 10,000, then there will be a 95 per cent chance that the true population mean, $\mu$, will be within 16.33 of the mean of that sample.

The CLT, then, has allowed for a very precise statement of how accurately $\mu$ is being estimated. However, probability statements such as the above must be interpreted with great care. A level of probability can only be attached to statements which involve variables, and so statements such as the above are only valid before the sample is actually drawn, when $\bar{X}$ is capable of taking on any value in the population. Once a sample is drawn, a direct probability interpretation is no longer possible.

In the context of our household income example, the actual sample drawn produced a mean of £415. We can now state that the interval estimate (or **confidence interval**) for $\mu$ is:

$$[415 - 16.33 \quad \text{to} \quad 415 + 16.33]$$

or

$$[£398.67 \quad \text{to} \quad £431.33]$$

Thus note that we cannot state that there is a 95 per cent chance of $\mu$ lying between £398.67 and £431.33; $\mu$ is a constant (although unknown) and will either lie between £398.67 and £431.33 with certainty, or outside this range, with certainty. In order to make this point explicit, assume that $\mu = £410$ (although this is of course unknown to the investigator). Then to state that there is a 95 per cent chance of £410 lying between £398.67 and £431.35 is clearly nonsensical. Describing £398.67 to £431.33 as a 95 per cent interval estimate for $\mu$ refers not to the actual interval itself, but rather to the method by which it was derived. We can state that the **random** interval:

$$\bar{X} - 16.33 \quad \text{to} \quad \bar{X} + 16.33$$

will produce a **fixed** interval that 95 per cent of the time will contain the true population mean, $\mu$. That is, 95 per cent of all the possible samples of size 144 which can be drawn from the population will produce fixed intervals containing $\mu$. In general, only one sample is drawn, and so we hope that this is one of the 95 out of 100 samples which produce intervals containing $\mu$. Or, equivalently, we hope we have not been so unlucky as to have selected a sample which produces an interval not containing $\mu$, the chance of this occurring being only 5 per cent.

Thus, in summary, the general statement of the interval estimator of $\mu$ is:

$$P[\bar{X} - z_{\gamma/2}\sigma/\sqrt{n} < \mu < \bar{X} + z_{\gamma/2}\sigma/\sqrt{n}] = 1 - \gamma \qquad \text{Equation 1.47}$$

where $\sigma/\sqrt{n}$ is the standard deviation of $\bar{X}$ (see Equation 1.46), and $z_{\gamma/2}$ is the appropriate value from the standard normal distribution which ensures that a probability level of $1 - \gamma$ is achieved. For example, for a 95 per cent interval estimate (the most commonly used in practice) $\gamma = 0.05$ and $z_{0.025} = 1.96$. For a 99 per cent interval estimate we would have $\gamma = 0.01$ and $z_{0.005} = 2.57$ (see Appendix I).

An equivalent expression for a $[(1 - \gamma) \times 100]$ per cent interval estimate is simply:

$$\bar{X} \pm z_{\gamma/2}\sigma/\sqrt{n}$$

Now, clearly, the shorter the interval estimate the more useful will this interval estimate be as a basis for reaching decisions concerning $\mu$. Thus note the control that the investigator has over the length of the interval:

$$\bar{X} - z_{\gamma/2}\sigma/\sqrt{n} \quad \text{to} \quad \bar{X} + z_{\gamma/2}\sigma/\sqrt{n}$$

The standard deviation of $\bar{X}$, $\sigma/\sqrt{n}$, can be reduced (and hence the interval estimate shortened) by increasing the sample size, $n$ (the population standard deviation, $\sigma$, will generally be beyond the control of the investigator). However, resource limitations will probably constrain the extent to which $n$ can be increased.

The interval estimate can also be shortened by selecting a smaller value of $z_{\gamma/2}$. But the smaller is the value of $z_{\gamma/2}$ the greater is the chance of selecting a sample which produces an interval not containing $\mu$.

Thus, in obtaining a more precise interval estimate for $\mu$ the trade-off involves the costs incurred in increasing the sample size, $n$, and/or increasing the value of $\gamma$ thereby incurring a greater risk of deriving an interval not containing $\mu$.

So far we have made the unrealistic assumption that $\sigma^2$ is known. This will rarely be the case in practice, and so $\sigma^2$ must also be estimated.

Recall from Equation 1.4 that the sample variance, $V^2$, was defined as follows:

$$V^2 = \frac{\sum_{i=1}^{n} (X_i - \bar{X})^2}{n}$$

and this would seem to be an obvious estimator of $\sigma^2$. However, we show in Appendix 1.2 that $V^2$ is in fact a *biased* estimator of $\sigma^2$, and that the unbiased estimator involves a denominator of $n-1$ and not $n$. That is, denoting this unbiased estimator of $\sigma^2$ by $S^2$, then we have[6]:

$$S^2 = \frac{\sum_{i=1}^{n} (X_i - \bar{X})^2}{n-1} \qquad\qquad \text{Equation 1.48}$$

Now, using the CLT to conclude that $\bar{X}$ is normally distributed requires that $\sigma^2$ be known. Consequently if $\sigma^2$ is unknown and estimated by $S^2$ then, strictly, $\bar{X}$ can no longer be assumed to have a normal distribution. However, it can be shown that a different probability distribution – the 'Student's $t$' distribution[7] – is appropriate when $S^2$ is used in place of $\sigma^2$. Otherwise the methodology is virtually the same as in the case of known $\sigma^2$. That is, instead of using the standard normal variable, $Z$, where:

$$Z = \frac{\bar{X} - \mu}{\sigma/\sqrt{n}}$$

we now use the variable, $T$, where:

$$T = \frac{\bar{X} - \mu}{S/\sqrt{n}}$$

and

$$S = \sqrt{\frac{\sum (X_i - \bar{X})^2}{n-1}}$$

The only difference in using $T$ is that there exists a family of $t$-distributions, rather than a single distribution as in the case of $Z$. The particular distribution used in a given sampling application will depend on the sample size, $n$. Thus $T$ is said to have a $t$-distribution with $n-1$ 'degrees of freedom', or:

$$T = \frac{\bar{X} - \mu}{S/\sqrt{n}} \sim t_{n-1}$$

The reason that there are $n-1$ degrees of freedom is that in calculating $S^2$ we must use the squared deviations from the sample mean, $\bar{X}$, rather than from the unknown population mean, $\mu$. In using $\bar{X}$ rather than $\mu$ in the expression for $S^2$ a 'degree of freedom' has been lost. That is, given the value of $\bar{X}$ used in the expression for $S^2$ then only $n-1$ of the sample values are 'freely determined' – if we have some value for $\bar{X}$ and for any $n-1$ of the sample observations then there will be only one possible value for the final sample observation which will be consistent with the given value of $\bar{X}$. In this sense, one sample observation is not freely determined (given a value for $\bar{X}$), and one degree of freedom is therefore lost (in effect, this is also the reason why $S^2$, rather than $V^2$, is an unbiased estimator for $\sigma^2$ – as the numerator of $V^2$ contains $\bar{X}$ and not $\mu$, a denominator of $n-1$ rather than $n$ must be used in order to reflect this lost degree of freedom).

The $t$-distribution, like the normal distribution, is symmetrical and bell-shaped but has a larger variance than the normal, resulting from the increased uncertainty which is produced by having to estimate $\sigma^2$. The smaller is the sample size (or the fewer degrees of freedom) the larger is the variance of the corresponding $t$-distribution, reflecting the greater unreliability of $S^2$ as an estimator of $\sigma^2$. As the sample size increases then the $t$-distribution will approach the normal distribution (that is, in the limit, if the sample size equals the size of the population, then $S^2$ will equal $\sigma^2$, and hence $T$ will be equivalent to $Z$).

We present tables of probabilities derived from the $t$-distribution in Appendix II. Note that the probabilities are tabulated according to the appropriate degrees of freedom (the left-hand column of the table), and commonly employed probabilities (the top row of the table).

Strictly, the $t$-distribution can only be used if the population from which the sample is drawn is normally distributed. If normality cannot be assumed then the interval estimates derived from the application of the $t$-distribution are only approximate, this approximation becoming more satisfactory as sample size increases.

In order to illustrate the use of the $t$-distribution we will consider an example.

Example 1.1

Consider again the data shown in Table 1.1 relating to pre-tax profits per employee in a sample of 30 mechanical engineering establishments.

Consider estimating average pre-tax profits per employee in the population of mechanical engineering establishments – that is, the average of all mechanical engineering establishments in the UK. As a point estimate, we would use the sample average. Thus recall that the average of the observations in Table 1.1 was 0.108.

Recall that the value of $V^2$ for the data in Table 1.1 was 6.056. $V^2$, however, is a biased estimator of $\sigma^2$ (it has a denominator of $n$ rather than $n-1$). Thus multiplying both sides of Equation 1.4 by $n/(n-1)$ produces:

$$\frac{nV^2}{n-1} = \frac{n}{n-1}\frac{\sum(X_i - \bar{X})^2}{n}$$

$$= \frac{\sum(X_i - \bar{X})^2}{n-1}$$

$$= S^2$$

As we here have $V^2 = 6.056$ and $n = 30$, then we can write:

$$S^2 = (6.056)(30/29)$$

$$= 6.265$$

As $n = 30$ we require the $t$-distribution for 29 degrees of freedom, and from Appendix II we can write, for the case of a 95 per cent interval estimate:

$$P(T > 2.05) = 0.025$$

(recall that the corresponding value from the standard normal distribution is 1.96).

Thus the interval estimate for $\mu$, average profitability in the UK mechanical engineering industry, can be written as:

$$0.108 - (2.05)(\sqrt{(6.265)}/30) \quad \text{to} \quad 0.108 + (2.05)(\sqrt{(6.265)}/30)$$

or

$$-0.829 \quad \text{to} \quad 1.045$$

As the units of measurement are £'000, then the 95 per cent interval estimate of average profitability is:

$$-£829 \quad \text{to} \quad £1,045$$

Also recall that in order to derive this interval estimate we must strictly assume that profitability in the population is normally distributed, as $\sigma^2$ is unknown. Of course we have no way of knowing here whether the population is normally distributed, and all that can be done is to argue that there is no evidence to suggest that such an assumption should not be made. In practice, this is the approach which would generally have to be taken.

The discussion of this section can be summarised as follows:

*Sampling from a Population when $\sigma^2$ is Known*

a   If the population is normally distributed, then $\bar{X}$ will also be normally distributed, irrespective of sample size, and we can state that:

$$\bar{X} \sim N(\mu, \sigma^2/n)$$

and hence we can write:

$$P\left[-z_{\gamma/2} < \frac{\bar{X}-\mu}{\sigma/\sqrt{n}} < z_{\gamma/2}\right] = 1-\gamma$$

or

$$P[\bar{X}-(z_{\gamma/2})(\sigma/\sqrt{n}) < \mu < \bar{X}+(z_{\gamma/2})(\sigma/\sqrt{n})] = 1-\gamma \qquad \text{Equation 1.49}$$

b    If the population is not normally distributed then the distribution of $\bar{X}$ will be approximately normal, provided $n$ is large.

*Sampling from a Population when $\sigma^2$ is Unknown*

$S^2$ is used as an estimator of $\sigma^2$

a    If the population is normally distributed, then the variable:

$$T = \frac{\bar{X}-\mu}{S/\sqrt{n}}$$

will have a $t$-distribution with $n-1$ degrees of freedom, and we can write:

$$P[\bar{X}-t_{\gamma/2,n-1}(S/\sqrt{n}) < \mu < \bar{X}+t_{\gamma/2,n-1}(S/\sqrt{n}) = 1-\gamma$$
$$\text{Equation 1.50}$$

b    If the population is not normally distributed, then provided that $n$ is large Equation 1.50 will be approximately true, this approximation becoming more satisfactory as $n$ increases.

Finally, we are left with situations of drawing small samples from non-normal populations, where $\sigma^2$ is either known or unknown. In these situations we come to a dead end, in a sense – not enough information is available to make useful statements about $\mu$. If we are to use the above methodology in such situations, then the only alternatives are to obtain larger samples, or to obtain specific information concerning the form of the population distribution.

## 1.5   Hypothesis Testing

The results which we have introduced above in our discussion of estimation can also be used for a somewhat different application – the testing of statistical hypotheses. We use exactly the same theoretical results, but a different emphasis is taken in the questions which are asked of the population from which we are sampling. Again, the concepts involved can be more easily introduced and discussed via an application.

Consider a pharmaceutical company which markets pills that have the effect of inhibiting the desire for food, and hence are considered useful as an aid in the process of weight reduction. The company is currently deciding whether to introduce the product into a new geographical market. In order to determine whether there will be sufficient demand in this market the company must first decide whether there is an adequate incidence of overweight individuals in the population. Assume further that on the basis of past experience the company believes that the demand for this product will come primarily from adult females.

The obvious population parameter to investigate, in the first instance, is the population mean – the average weight of adult females in the potential market. Assume that on the basis of the company's past experience of marketing the product elsewhere it believes that there will only be sufficient demand for the product if average female weight exceeds 130 pounds. The company therefore wishes to determine whether this is the case in the new market.

Formally, this can be set up as a test of the hypothesis that the population mean, $\mu$, equals 130 pounds. If the company were to accept this hypothesis then this would imply that there is insufficient potential demand in the market – only if average weight exceeds 130 pounds would the company consider it worthwhile entering the market.

An hypothesis of this form is referred to as the **null** hypothesis, and is denoted by $H_0$. Thus the company wishes to test:

$$H_0: \mu = 130$$

The only alternative to this hypothesis that is of real interest to the company is that of average weight being more than 130 pounds. The other possibility, of average weight being less than 130 pounds, would still result in the company not entering the market, and in this sense is subsumed in the null hypothesis. So the full hypothesis test can be written explicitly as follows:

$$H_0: \mu = 130$$
$$H_1: \mu > 130$$

where $H_1$ is referred to as the **alternative** hypothesis.

The company now wishes to determine which of these two hypotheses to accept. In order to assist in this decision it randomly selects a sample of 50 adult females. Assume that this sample produces a mean of 135 pounds, and for ease of exposition, assume that the population variance, $\sigma^2$, is known and is equal to 225 (pounds squared) (we will relax this assumption below).

The way we would then proceed to test the above null hypothesis is as follows:

We begin by assuming that $H_0$ is true and that the sample was actually selected from a population with a mean of 130 and a variance of 225. Given this assumption we can therefore deduce from the CLT that:

$$\bar{X} \sim N(130, 225/50)$$

Thus we can now evaluate the probability of observing a value of $\bar{X}$ as extreme as 135, if the sample was in fact selected from the $H_0$ population. That is:

$$P(\bar{X} > 135) = P\left(\frac{\bar{X} - \mu}{\sigma/\sqrt{n}} > \frac{135 - 130}{15/\sqrt{50}}\right)$$

$$= P(z > 2.36)$$

$$\cong 0.01$$

Thus only about 1 per cent of samples of size 50, randomly drawn from a population with a mean of 130 and a variance of 225, will have means greater than 135. Therefore, any sample (of size 50) which produces a mean of 135 or more can be explained in only one of two ways:

a   $H_0$ is true ($\mu$ does equal 130), but unfortunately an extreme sample was selected (the probability of this occurring being only about 0.01).
b   The sample was not in fact selected from a population with a mean of 130, and hence $H_0$ is false.

Clearly, it is more reasonable to accept the second of these two explanations, and it is on this basis that $H_0$ would be rejected in favour of the alternative hypothesis, $H_1$.

Note that there are two types of errors which can be made in testing a null hypothesis in this way. First, as implied above, there is still the possibility that $H_0$ is actually true, but we were unfortunate in selecting an extreme sample. This is referred to as a **Type I error** – rejecting $H_0$ when it is true. The other possible error is to accept $H_0$ when it is in fact false – this is referred to as a **Type II error**. For example, assume that the sample of 50 produced a mean of 130 rather than 135. Then assuming $H_0$ to be true, we have:

$$P(\bar{X} > 130) = P\left(Z > \frac{130 - 130}{15/\sqrt{50}}\right)$$

$$= P(Z > 0)$$

$$= 0.50$$

That is, there is a 50 per cent chance of observing a sample mean of 130 or more from a population with a mean of 130, and this would be considered as too high a probability to allow the confident rejection of $H_0$ – indeed, if the sample produced a mean of 130 this could be interpreted as being perfectly consistent with the hypothesised mean of 130, and thus we could argue that there are no grounds for rejecting $H_0$. However, note that even though $H_0$ would be accepted in such a situation, there is still the possibility that it is false, and that the actual value of the population mean exceeds 130.

While we would wish to limit the probability of making both of these types of error, in practice this will not generally be possible. For if we require a very small Type I error (and therefore would only reject $H_0$ if a relatively large sample mean were observed) then this must necessarily increase the probability of making a Type II error – if we are going to be very conservative about rejecting $H_0$ then it follows that there will be a higher chance of accepting $H_0$ when it is false.

Thus, in practice, emphasis is generally placed on the control of the Type I error, and the hypothesis test is then constructed so as to ensure that the consequences of making a Type II error are less serious than those of making a Type I error. In the example we have been discussing, the Type I error would be to conclude that average weight exceeds 130 pounds, when in fact it equals (or is even less than) 130 pounds. The consequence of making this error is that the company would incur the costs of launching a product in a non-existent market. Conversely, the Type II error would be for the company to conclude that average weight is 130 pounds, when it is in fact higher. This would then lead to the decision not to market the product. While the company may forgo potential profits as a consequence of this error, it at least would not incur any costs.

So, in general, an hypothesis test is constructed in such a way as to ensure that $H_0$ is the conservative hypothesis – it is the hypothesis which represents the *status quo*, and its acceptance would typically result in the continuance of current behaviour. Ensuring that a decision rule is selected with a small Type I error means that the investigator would require convincing sample evidence in order to reject $H_0$, and therefore to alter behaviour to that implied by $H_1$. In most applications a probability of a Type I error (or a **significance level**) of 5 per cent is considered adequate, although there may be situations in which the consequences of making a Type I error are so serious or costly that the investigator may want to limit its size even further. However, the smaller the significance level of the hypothesis test the more likely it is that $H_0$ will be accepted in those cases where $H_1$ is true – that is, the more likely it is that a Type II error will be made. The investigator must decide on the balance between these two types of errors.

The method of carrying out an hypothesis test which we have so far described is somewhat tedious, and a simple short-cut can be used.

We first determine an acceptable significance level (the probability of making a Type I error), and then the associated decision rule is derived directly in terms of the standard normal distribution. The significance level which would generally be used is 5 per cent, and thus in our above example, $H_0$ would be rejected if the observed sample mean, when standardised to the standard normal distribution, exceeds 1.645 (assuming $H_0$ to be true). That is, from Appendix I we can deduce (by simple interpolation) that:

$P(Z > 1.645) = 0.05$

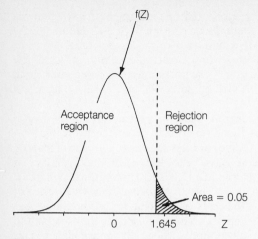

**Figure 1.4** Distribution of $Z$ assuming $H_0$ is true.

and for a sample mean of 135, the observed value of $Z$, $z_0$, is:

$$z_0 = \frac{\bar{X} - \mu}{\sigma/\sqrt{n}} = \frac{135 - 130}{15/\sqrt{50}} = 2.36$$

As this value exceeds 1.645 then $H_0$ would be rejected – there is less than a 5 per cent chance of observing a value as extreme as 135 in a normal population with a mean of 130 and a variance of 225/50. Diagrammatically, this is illustrated in Figure 1.4. Thus all standardised sample means which fall in the shaded area of Figure 1.4 would lead to the rejection of $H_0$. For this reason this area is often referred to as the **rejection region** or the **critical region**. All other values of $Z$ would lead to the acceptance of $H_0$ (they would fall into the **acceptance region**). That is, these values of $Z$ (or corresponding values of $\bar{X}$) would not provide sufficiently convincing evidence to allow the rejection of $H_0$ – such values would be consistent with a relatively high probability of $H_0$ being true.

If the investigator were more conservative, and required a significance level of, say, just 1 per cent, then a value for $z_0$ in excess of 2.33 would be required for the rejection of $H_0$. Note that in our example a sample mean of 135 would still lead to the rejection of $H_0$ at a significance level of 1 per cent.

So far we have discussed hypothesis tests in which the alternative hypothesis is **one-sided** only. That is, we have developed a method for testing a null hypothesis against an alternative of the form:

$$H_1: \mu > b$$

where $b$ is some constant.

In the case of one-sided alternatives which are of the form:

$$H_1: \mu < b$$

the methodology is exactly the same, except that the critical region will fall in the left-hand tail of Figure 1.4, rather than the right-hand tail (that is, relatively large and negative values of $z_0$ will result in the rejection of $H_0$).

A one-sided alternative is appropriate in those cases where it is known *a priori* that the possible change in the parameter under investigation can only be in one direction.

For example, consider a firm which is deciding whether to use a new production process, and assume that this process incorporates certain technical innovations in comparison with the process which the firm is currently using. So, if anything, the new process may be an improvement over the old one, although it may also be the case that the technical innovations which have been made are not sufficient to render the new process significantly better than the old one. So the company would test the null hypothesis that the new process is no better than the old one, against the alternative that the new process is in fact an improvement (for example, a sample of output could be taken from the new process and the mean compared with the known mean for the old process).

The important point here is that information may be available to the investigator, generally of a theoretical nature, which allows the specification of a one-sided alternative prior to the analysis of any sample data.

The nature of $H_1$ may also be conditioned by the objectives of the hypothesis testing exercise. Thus in our above example concerning the pharmaceutical company, the company was only interested in investigating the possibility of the population mean exceeding the hypothesised value, and therefore $H_1$ was constructed to reflect this emphasis.

A **two-sided** alternative, by contrast, would be of the following form:

$$H_1: \mu \neq b$$

A two-sided alternative would be appropriate in those cases in which no *a priori* information is available as to the possible direction of change of the parameter under investigation. Interest therefore centres on whether the parameter is simply different from (either greater or less than) the value specified in $H_0$.

For example, in our example concerning the pharmaceutical company, if the company was now interested in whether average weight was simply different from 130 pounds, then the appropriate test would be:

$$H_0: \mu = 130$$

$$H_1: \mu \neq 130$$

The decision rule for this test must now explicitly allow for the possibility of average weight being less than 130 pounds, in addition to the possibility that it may exceed 130 pounds. In terms of the standardised normal variable, $Z$, this means that we must now test for the significance of negative values of $z_0$ as well as positive values. If we still require a significance level of 5 per cent then the rejection (or critical) region for this test would be the shaded areas in Figure 1.5. That is, if the significance level is 5 per cent then we must have $2\frac{1}{2}$

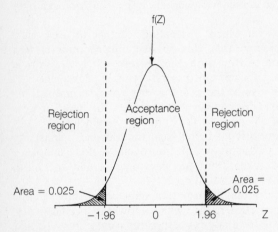

**Figure 1.5** The distribution of $Z$ under $H_0$.

per cent in each tail, and therefore we require an observed value of $Z$ which is either greater than 1.96 or less than $-1.96$ in order to reject $H_0$.

Note, then, that in comparison to a one-sided test, a two-sided test requires a higher absolute value of $z_0$ in order to reject $H_0$, for a given significance level. This simply reflects the greater amount of *a priori* information which is available for a one-sided test thus, in a sense, implying a more 'efficient' test of $H_0$ – that is, a greater possibility of rejecting $H_0$ when it is false.

To this point we have assumed that the population variance, $\sigma^2$, is known. We have therefore been able to apply the normal distribution directly. In general, however, $\sigma^2$ will be unknown, and will have to be estimated by $S^2$.

If $S^2$ is used then the $t$-distribution must be applied in place of the standard normal distribution, in exactly the same way as the $t$-distribution was used in deriving interval estimates in Section 1.4 above.

For example, assume that in the case of the pharmaceutical company, $\sigma^2$ is now unknown, and that the value of $S^2$ from the sample of 50 is 230. So instead of calculating an observed value of $Z$, an observed value of $T$ is calculated.

Assume that a sample mean of 135 was obtained. Then we have:

$$t_0 = \frac{135 - 130}{15.16/\sqrt{50}} = 2.33$$

In order to test the null hypothesis that $\mu = 130$, this value must be compared to the appropriate value from the tables for the $t$-distribution. With a sample size of 50 the $t$-distribution with 49 degrees of freedom must be used. For a significance level of 5 per cent, the appropriate value for a one-sided test can be seen from Appendix II to be (approximately) 1.68, and for a two-sided test the appropriate $t$-value from Appendix II is approximately 2.01.

Finally, it is useful to appreciate the connection between hypothesis testing and interval estimation.

Consider a two-sided hypothesis test concerning a population mean. This test can be formally expressed as:

$$H_0: \mu = b$$

$$H_1: \mu \neq b$$

where $b$ is some constant.

A sample is then selected to test $H_0$. This sample, of course, can also be used to derive an interval estimate for $\mu$. Assume that the $[(1-\gamma) \times 100]$ per cent interval estimate for $\mu$ is:

$$a < \mu < c$$

Now, this range of values, $a$ to $c$, comprises the set of null hypotheses which would all be accepted at a significance level of $100\gamma$ per cent. That is, if $H_0$ specified as a value for $\mu$ any value in the range $a$ to $c$, then $H_0$ would be accepted at a significance level of $\gamma$ (in the case of a two-sided alternative).

This observation highlights an important point to be recognised in the interpretation of a test of some given null hypothesis. Accepting a null hypothesis of the form $\mu = b$, on the basis of sample information, means only that there appears to be no marked inconsistency between $H_0$ and the sample information – $H_0$ is not contradicted by the sample. Acceptance of $H_0$ is not to be interpreted literally as meaning that the true value of $\mu$ can now be assumed to be exactly $b$ – the corresponding interval estimate for $\mu$ contains a set of values for $\mu$ which are all as acceptable as $b$ (at a fixed significance level of $\gamma$).

## 1.6   The Concept of Correlation

So far we have been concerned with how a single sample of data can be analysed so as to draw inferences concerning the population. However, the analysis of a single sample will generally only be the first step in the process of deriving a complete description of the characteristics of the population. In this section we will introduce a number of concepts which extend the single sample approach of analysing a population, and which will form the basis of much of what follows in this book.

Thus consider again the data on profitability in the sample of 30 establishments shown in Table 1.1. There are a number of questions which can be asked of these data. First, what does this sample tell us of the average profitability of all mechanical engineering establishments in the UK (the population)? That is, how confident can we be in the sample mean as an accurate reflection of the true (and unknown) population mean? The confidence interval which we derived in Example 1.1 could be used to throw some light on this question.

However, a second, and more interesting, question concerns the reasons for the variation in the sample data. That is, why are some establishments making large profits and others making large losses? Thus we seek to explain why profitability should vary from establishment to establishment, and therefore to identify those factors, and their relative importance, which account for this variation. In turn, on the basis of such an analysis of the sample data, we then wish to draw inferences concerning the role of these factors in the population.

Similarly, consider the data on the Index of Industrial Production in Table 1.2 and Figure 1.1. Thus, in addition to seeking a simple summary description of these data, we seek to explain why the data behave as they do. That is, what are the reasons for the growth in industrial production for most of the sample

**Table 1.6** Index of industrial production, UK manufacturing industries and an index of the Gross Domestic Product at factor cost in 1975 prices. 1948 to 1983 (1975 = 100)

| Year | Industrial production | Gross Domestic Product | Year | Industrial production | Gross Domestic Product | Year | Industrial production | Gross Domestic Product |
|------|------------|------------|------|------------|------------|------|------------|------------|
| 1948 | 46.9 | 52.2 | 1960 | 73.5 | 71.8 | 1972 | 100.0 | 97.9 |
| 1949 | 50.3 | 54.1 | 1961 | 73.7 | 73.1 | 1973 | 108.4 | 103.6 |
| 1950 | 54.1 | 56.0 | 1962 | 73.8 | 74.2 | 1974 | 106.6 | 102.0 |
| 1951 | 55.7 | 57.1 | 1963 | 76.5 | 76.6 | 1975 | 100.0 | 100.0 |
| 1952 | 53.0 | 56.7 | 1964 | 83.4 | 81.3 | 1976 | 101.4 | 101.8 |
| 1953 | 56.7 | 59.0 | 1965 | 85.8 | 83.5 | 1977 | 103.0 | 104.6 |
| 1954 | 59.8 | 61.5 | 1966 | 87.4 | 85.0 | 1978 | 104.0 | 108.1 |
| 1955 | 63.6 | 63.5 | 1967 | 87.9 | 86.5 | 1979 | 104.3 | 110.3 |
| 1956 | 63.4 | 64.2 | 1968 | 94.1 | 90.2 | 1980 | 95.4 | 107.1 |
| 1957 | 64.9 | 65.3 | 1969 | 97.6 | 92.0 | 1981 | 89.4 | 104.5 |
| 1958 | 64.3 | 65.2 | 1970 | 98.0 | 93.6 | 1982 | 89.5 | 105.8 |
| 1959 | 68.0 | 68.2 | 1971 | 97.5 | 94.9 | 1983 | 91.2 | 107.9 |

*Source*: As for Table 1.2.

period, and then the abrupt decline towards the end of the period? Note, that in the case of time-series data, the population could be defined as relating to all time periods, and in particular, to all time periods in the future. Thus an explanation for the variation in the data in Table 1.2 would provide a basis for deducing how they might vary in the future, and therefore provides a basis for forecasting.

It is this approach of seeking explanations for the variation in a given (economic) data set which can be characterised as the essence of econometrics.

In order to be concrete, consider once again the data on the Index of Industrial Production in Table 1.2. One issue we may wish to consider is the extent to which these data are related to movements in the overall level of economic activity. If we measure the overall level of economic activity by an index of the Gross Domestic Product then a starting point in explaining the variation of the data in Table 1.2 is to determine how closely related these data are to the Gross Domestic Product, or how highly **correlated** the two variables are. Note that this is only a starting point, as a full explanation for the data in Table 1.2, in turn, requires an explanation for the variation in the overall level of economic activity, which is a considerably more complex task.

In Table 1.6 we reproduce the Industrial Production data of Table 1.2, together with the corresponding annual data on the Index of Gross Domestic Product.

We will denote the Index of Industrial Production in year $t$ by $Y_t$ and the Index of Gross Domestic Product by $X_t$. The simplest method of examining the relationship between $Y$ and $X$ is to graph $Y$ against $X$. Thus plotting $Y$ on the vertical axis and $X$ on the horizontal axis produces Figure 1.6. From Figure 1.6 we can deduce that there does indeed appear to be a strong and positive relationship between $Y$ and $X$ – high levels of $Y$ tend to be associated with high levels of $X$, and similarly for low levels of $Y$ and $X$, although the relationship does not appear quite so strong for the higher values. Note further that the relationship appears to be approximately linear – the observations could be interpreted as being distributed around a straight line. The relationship is certainly not a perfect one, however, as the observations do not produce an exact straight line.

While graphs such as Figure 1.6 are useful for informally examining the strength of a relationship between two variables, such an examination is essentially subjective. Thus we require a more rigorous and objective method of summarising the information in Figure 1.6. In particular, we require a measure of the strength of the relationship between the variables. This measure can then be compared to the corresponding measure derived from other bivariate data sets, thereby enabling conclusions to be drawn concerning the relative strength or weakness of a relationship.

First consider the relationship between $Y$ and $X$ in the population (which is of course unobservable). Now, recall from Equation 1.28 that the population variance of $X$ can be expressed as $E(X-\mu)^2$, or $E[X-E(X)]^2$. Similarly, the

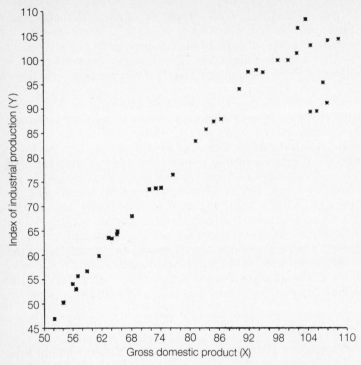

**Figure 1.6**  Index of industrial production against Gross Domestic Product.

population variance of $Y$ can be expressed as $E[Y - E(Y)]^2$. Define a third expression which is the expected value of products of the mean deviations of $Y$ and $X$. This expression is referred to as the population **covariance** between $Y$ and $X$ and is denoted by $\mathrm{Cov}(Y, X)$. That is, we can write:

$$\mathrm{Cov}(Y, X) = E[Y - E(Y)][X - E(X)] \qquad \text{Equation 1.51}$$

Thus $\mathrm{Cov}(Y, X)$ could be interpreted as reflecting the extent to which $Y$ and $X$ vary together, or co-vary. In particular, if the relationship between $Y$ and $X$ is positive (high values of $Y$ tend to be associated with high values of $X$, and low values of $Y$ tend to be associated with low values of $X$ – as is the implication of the sample data in Figure 1.6), then the products of the mean deviations will also tend to be positive. That is, for large values of $Y$ we have:

$$Y > E(Y)$$

and hence

$$[Y - E(Y)] > 0$$

Similarly, for large values of $X$ we have:

$$[X - E(X)] > 0$$

Thus the products of these mean deviations will be positive.
Conversely, for small values of $Y$ and $X$ we have:

$$[Y - E(Y)] < 0$$

and

$$[X - E(X)] < 0$$

and, again, the products of these mean deviations will be positive.

In the case of a negative relationship between $Y$ and $X$, the products of the mean deviations will tend to be negative. If the association between $Y$ and $X$ were linear and negative then this would be reflected in a scatter of sample observations on $Y$ and $X$ being distributed around a straight line extending from the top left-hand corner of the graph to the bottom right-hand corner. As high values of $Y$ will be associated with low values of $X$ then positive $[Y - E(Y)]$ terms will be associated with negative $[X - E(X)]$ terms thus producing negative $[Y - E(Y)][X - E(X)]$ terms. Similarly, low values of $Y$ will be associated with high values of $X$ and hence negative $[Y - E(Y)]$ terms will occur with positive $[X - E(X)]$, again producing negative $[Y - E(Y)][X - E(X)]$ terms.

Thus we can deduce that $\text{Cov}(Y, X)$ will be positive in the case of a positive relationship between $Y$ and $X$, and negative in the case of a negative relationship. Further, consider re-expressing $\text{Cov}(Y, X)$ by multiplying out the right-hand side of Equation 1.51. That is:

$$\text{Cov}(Y, X) = E[YX - YE(X) - XE(Y) + E(X)E(Y)]$$
$$= E(YX) - E(Y)E(X) - E(X)E(Y) + E(X)E(Y)$$

or

$$\text{Cov}(Y, X) = E(YX) - E(Y)E(X) \qquad \text{Equation 1.52}$$

Now, recall from Equation 1.37 that if $Y$ and $X$ are independent, and hence there is no relationship between $Y$ and $X$, then $E(YX) = E(Y)(X)$. That is, in the absence of a relationship between $Y$ and $X$ we must have:

$$\text{Cov}(YX) = 0$$

(note also from Equation 1.44, where we derived the expression for the variance of the sum of the two variables, $R$ and $S$, that Equation 1.52 now allows us to write:

$$\text{Var}(R + S) = \text{Var}(R) + \text{Var}(S) + 2\,\text{Cov}(R, S) \qquad \text{Equation 1.53}$$

Thus the value of $\text{Cov}(Y, X)$ can be used to deduce the nature of the relationship between $Y$ and $X$. If $\text{Cov}(Y, X)$ is positive, then $Y$ and $X$ are positively related; if negative, $Y$ and $X$ are negatively related; and if zero this would imply the absence of a relationship (however, as we shall emphasise below, a zero value for $\text{Cov}(Y, X)$ only implies the absence of a **linear** relationship between $Y$ and $X$, and not necessarily the absence of any form of a relationship – that is, independence between $Y$ and $X$ must result in a zero covariance, but a zero covariance does not necessarily imply independence).

However, the magnitude of $\text{Cov}(Y, X)$ cannot be used to measure the strength of the relationship between $Y$ and $X$. The simplest illustration of this is to consider multiplying all the observations on $Y$ and $X$ by, say, ten (perhaps as a result of changing the units in which $Y$ and $X$ are measured). Clearly this would in no way alter the strength of the association between $Y$ and $X$, but it would produce a hundred-fold increase in $\text{Cov}(Y, X)$ (this can be easily deduced from Equation 1.51). Thus we require an adjustment for the variation in both $Y$ and $X$ in order to derive a measure which is independent of the units in which $Y$ and $X$ are measured. This can be achieved by dividing $\text{Cov}(Y, X)$ by the product of the standard deviations of $Y$ and $X$, and therefore any change in the units in which $Y$ and $X$ are measured would be equally reflected in the numerator and denominator of such an expression, leaving its value unchanged. This expression is referred to as the **population correlation coefficient** between $Y$ and $X$, and is generally denoted by $\rho$ (the Greek letter rho). That is, we can write:

$$\rho = \frac{E[Y - E(Y)][X - E(X)]}{\sqrt{E[Y - E(Y)]^2 E[X - E(X)]^2}} \qquad \text{Equation 1.54}$$

Using Equations 1.16 and 1.52, $\rho$ can be re-expressed as follows:

$$\rho = \frac{E(YX) - E(Y)E(X)}{\sqrt{\{E(Y^2) - [E(Y)]^2\}\{E(X^2) - [E(X)]^2\}}} \qquad \text{Equation 1.55}$$

It can be shown that $\rho$ can take on a maximum value of one (when there is a perfect and positive linear relationship between $Y$ and $X$) and a minimum value of minus one (in the case of a perfect negative linear relationship). Note that in absence of a linear relationship the numerator of Equation 1.54 (or Equation 1.55) will be zero, and thus so must be $\rho$. Thus we can write:

$$-1 \leqslant \rho \leqslant 1$$

It is straightforward to establish that Equation 1.54 will produce an absolute value of one if there is a perfect linear relationship between $Y$ and $X$. Thus assume that the relationship between $Y$ and $X$ is:

$$Y = a + bX \qquad \text{Equation 1.56}$$

where $a$ and $b$ are constants. From Equation 1.56 we can deduce that:

$$E(Y) = a + bE(X) \qquad \text{Equation 1.57}$$

Thus substituting Equations 1.56 and 1.57 into the numerator of Equation 1.54 we have:

$$\text{Cov}(Y, X) = E[a + bX - (a + bE(X))][X - E(X)]$$
$$= bE[X - E(X)]^2$$

Substituting Equations 1.56 and 1.57 into the denominator of Equation 1.54 we have:

$$\sqrt{E[a + bX - (a + bE(X))]^2 E[X - E(X)]^2} = \sqrt{b^2 E[X - E(X)]^2}$$
$$\times E[X - E(X)]^2$$
$$= bE[X - E(X)]^2$$

Therefore in the case of the relationship between $Y$ and $X$ being perfect and linear we have deduced that the numerator and the denominator of the expression for $\rho$ must be identical, and therefore that the absolute value of $\rho$ must be one. Note also that if the relationship between $Y$ and $X$ is positive then the value of $b$ in Equation 1.56 will be positive and hence $\rho$ will equal $+1$. If the relationship is negative then $b$ will be negative and therefore $\rho$ will equal $-1$.

We have developed the concept of a correlation coefficient in the context of the population relationship between $Y$ and $X$. As this relationship is never observable, we must consider how $\rho$ could be estimated from a sample of data on $Y$ and $X$. The obvious estimator would be the sample counterpart of the expression in Equation 1.54 or Equation 1.55. Thus expressing Equation 1.55 in terms of sample equivalents produces the **sample correlation coefficient**, which we will denote by $r$. That is:

$$r = \frac{\frac{1}{n}\sum Y_t X_t - \bar{Y}\bar{X}}{\sqrt{\left[\frac{1}{n}\sum Y_t^2 - \bar{Y}^2\right]\left[\frac{1}{n}\sum X_t^2 - \bar{X}^2\right]}} \qquad \text{Equation 1.58}$$

Multiplying the numerator and denominator of Equation 1.58 by $n^2$ produces the following computationally more convenient expression for $r$:

$$r = \frac{n\sum Y_t X_t - \sum Y_t \sum X_t}{\sqrt{[n\sum Y_t^2 - (\sum Y_t)^2][n\sum X_t^2 - (\sum X_t)^2]}} \qquad \text{Equation 1.59}$$

Note from Equations 1.51 and 1.58 that the sample covariance between $Y$ and $X$, which we will denote by $\widehat{\text{Cov}}(Y, X)$, can be written as:

$$\widehat{\text{Cov}}(Y, X) = \frac{1}{n}\sum (Y_t - \bar{Y})(X_t - \bar{X}) \qquad \text{Equation 1.60}$$

or

$$\widehat{\mathrm{Cov}}\,(Y, X) = \frac{1}{n}\sum Y_t X_t - \bar{Y}\bar{X}$$

Equation 1.61

Thus given a sample of data on $Y$ and $X$ Equation 1.59 can be used to estimate the strength of the relationship between $Y$ and $X$, and hence to draw inferences concerning the strength of the relationship between $Y$ and $X$ in the population.

As an illustration of the use of Equation 1.59 consider again the data in Table 1.6. From these data we obtain:

$$\sum Y_t = 2923.1 \quad \sum X_t = 2979.3 \quad \sum Y_t X_t = 254{,}060.33$$
$$\sum Y_t^2 = 249{,}820.55, \quad \sum X_t^2 = 259{,}478.89$$

and substituting into Equation 1.59 produces:

$$r = 0.957$$

Thus given that this value for $r$ is close to one we would conclude on the basis of the data in Table 1.6 that output in the manufacturing industries appears to be highly correlated with Gross Domestic Product. We might then argue that manufacturing output appears to be largely dependent on the overall level of economic activity. However, note that such an argument does not follow directly from the simple observation that there is a high correlation between manufacturing output and Gross Domestic Product. It could just as plausibly be argued that the level of the Gross Domestic Product depends on the

**Table 1.7** Hypothetical sample data on $Y$ and $X$

| Y | X |
|------|------|
| 1.25 | 1.50 |
| 1.50 | 1.00 |
| 1.50 | 3.00 |
| 1.75 | 1.75 |
| 1.75 | 2.25 |
| 1.75 | 2.50 |
| 2.25 | 2.50 |
| 2.25 | 1.25 |
| 2.25 | 2.75 |
| 2.50 | 1.00 |
| 2.50 | 3.00 |
| 2.75 | 1.50 |

**Table 1.8** Hypothetical sample data on $Y$ and $X$

| Y | X |
|----|----|
| 45 | 0 |
| 33 | 1 |
| 23 | 2 |
| 15 | 3 |
| 9 | 4 |
| 5 | 5 |
| 3 | 6 |
| 3 | 7 |
| 5 | 8 |
| 9 | 9 |
| 15 | 10 |
| 23 | 11 |
| 33 | 12 |
| 45 | 13 |

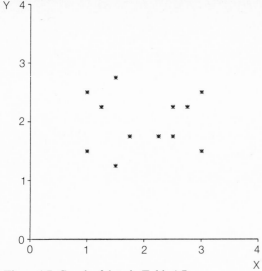

**Figure 1.7** Graph of data in Table 1.7.

success of the manufacturing industries, and that the direction of causality is not therefore from Gross Domestic Product to output, but rather vice versa. Indeed, it might even be argued that the observed correlation between the two variables is spurious.

Therefore it is important to emphasise that a correlation coefficient provides no information concerning the direction of causality between two variables. We must appeal to theoretical argument to postulate the direction of causality, with a correlation coefficient being used only to support (or perhaps counter) such an argument.

As an illustration of a zero correlation coefficient between two variables, consider the two sets of data in Tables 1.7 and 1.8, and the graphs of these data in Figures 1.7 and 1.8.

From Table 1.7 we have:

$$\bar{Y} = \bar{X} = 2, \quad \sum Y_t X_t = 48$$

Thus from Equation 1.61 the sample covariance between $Y$ and $X$ is:

$$\widehat{\text{Cov}}(Y, X) = (1/12)(48) - (2)(2) = 0$$

As the sample covariance is the numerator of the expression for $r$ (see Equation 1.58), then $r$ here must also be zero, irrespective of the values of $\sum Y_t^2$ and $\sum X_t^2$. Thus we can conclude that the data in Table 1.7 exhibit zero correlation, and therefore no evidence of a linear association between $Y$ and $X$ is provided.

For the data in Table 1.8, we have:

$$\bar{Y} = 19, \quad \bar{X} = 6.5, \quad \sum Y_t X_t = 1729$$

Therefore the sample covariance between $Y$ and $X$ is:

$$\widehat{\text{Cov}}\,(Y, X) = (1/14)(1729) - (19)(6.5) = 0$$

again producing a zero sample correlation coefficient, and hence providing no evidence of any linear association between $Y$ and $X$.

However, note from Figure 1.8 that the data in Table 1.8 exhibit a very strong (indeed, perfect) non-linear association between $Y$ and $X$. We could

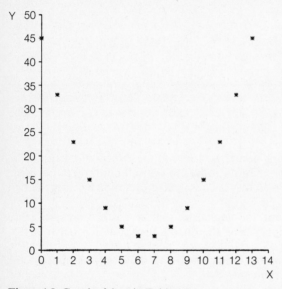

**Figure 1.8** Graph of data in Table 1.8.

interpret the data in Figure 1.8 as tending towards a negative relationship for values of $X$ below 6.5, and a positive relationship for values of $X$ above 6.5. The net result is therefore of no overall linear association.

Thus care must be taken in interpreting the value of a correlation coefficient. In particular, before concluding from a low (absolute) correlation coefficient that only a weak (or no) relationship exists between two variables, we must be sure first to examine the data for the possibility of a non-linear relationship.

Finally, it is important to recognise that the central issue of correlation analysis is the way in which the sample correlation coefficient, $r$, can be used to draw inferences concerning the strength of the population relationship between the two variables of interest. We will take up this issue of testing for the significance of the population relationship in Chapter 2.

## 1.7  Statistical Inference and Econometrics

Having introduced the concepts of estimation, hypothesis testing and correlation we can now go on to make some comments concerning the nature of econometrics.

Econometrics, in its broadest sense, can be defined as the application of statistical theory to estimation and inference in economics. The 'population parameters' with which econometrics is concerned are derived directly from economic theory.

For example, a parameter which is of central interest to macroeconomic policy makers is the **marginal propensity to consume** – the proportion of an extra unit of income that, in aggregate, the economy devotes to consumption. Economic theory would predict that this parameter lies between zero and one, but is able to say little further as to its precise magnitude. The role of econometrics, then, is to develop techniques which allow an estimate of this parameter to be derived, an estimate which can then be used by policy makers as an input into the process of policy formulation. Closely associated with the process of policy formulation is the role of forecasting. Econometrics also provides the means of producing forecasts of variables which may be of interest to the policy maker or economic analyst.

It is important to emphasise the connection between econometrics and economic theory. Econometrics is a valuable and important tool for the economic theorist (although it is a tool that the theorist may not necessarily employ). The role of the theorist is to provide explanations for the behaviour of the economy (or sectors of the economy), and of agents within the economy. It may be that theoretical analysis alone will be sufficient to provide satisfactory explanations, in which case the role of econometrics is to provide an empirical base for this theory – parameters of the theoretical 'models' must be estimated, or hypotheses concerning these parameters tested, so that the models can be of direct use to the policy maker and forecaster. By a 'model' we mean the detailed specification of the various factors which are hypothesised to explain or determine the variation in the variable (or set of variables) which is the focus of the theoretical investigation. That is, econometrics can be characterised as the process of estimating the relationships which are posited to exist between economic variables, and is therefore very much concerned with notions of cause and effect.

However, in practice, this process is generally not so straightforward. Typically, empirical analysis of an accepted theoretical model will highlight weaknesses, omissions or even inconsistencies in the model, thus indicating the need for some form of theoretical modification. So this process of model building and estimation can be very much an iterative one.

There will also be cases in which economic theory produces a number of conflicting models and theoretical analysis alone will not be able to provide a basis for discrimination. In such cases econometric (or empirical) analysis should be able to determine which of the competing models is the most satisfactory – that is, which of the competing models is most consistent with the available data.

However, for a number of reasons, empirical analysis will not always be able to resolve theoretical conflicts. Sufficiently sophisticated or sensitive statistical techniques may not be readily available to test the competing theories rigorously. The theories or models may be expressed in terms of variables for which no sample data are available, or indeed in terms of variables which are unmeasurable. But perhaps the greatest difficulty the econometrician faces is the very nature of economics as a social science. In common with all the social sciences, the scope for experimentation in economics is extremely limited. The economy cannot be made to repeat its behaviour over, say, the last ten years, in order to observe how a number of key variables would have behaved under different sets of conditions. The econometrician does not have the advantages of the natural scientist who works under laboratory conditions, enabling him to perform experiments as many times as desired and under as many sets of conditions as required. In economics 'experiments' can generally be performed only once, and the influence of factors which are indirectly related to the variable of interest (the *ceteris paribus* assumption) can be controlled for only imperfectly. It is from the outcomes of these single, imperfect experiments that generalisations have to be made.

Even to the casual observer it is quite clear that the behaviour of the economy, and the agents within the economy, is highly complex. Economic theory, with the aid of econometrics, has made significant advances in explaining this behaviour. However, much still remains unexplained. In addition, economic theories which were once acceptable, even five or ten years ago, no longer appear to be satisfactory. Indeed, the very process of explanation, in terms of the extra information which is generated, may contribute to the alteration in the behaviour of important economic agents or institutions. So the concept of universal and all-embracing economic theories is probably a misleading one – it may be that in economics, theories, at least to some extent, have only temporary explanatory power.

The role of the econometrician, then, can be seen very much as a monitoring one. The behaviour of the economy can change for a number of reasons – as a result of political changes, for example, or as a result of upheavals in the foreign sector – and it is clearly important that the consequences of these changes are evaluated as efficiently as possible. Many econometric techniques have been developed which are of great assistance to the policy maker and forecaster. But econometrics is still very much in a state of evolution, and many problems remain to be solved.

## 1.8   Summary

In this chapter we have provided a brief review of the methodology involved in using sample data to draw inferences concerning the population from which the sample was drawn.

We outlined the procedures involved in estimating the population parameters, and illustrated these procedures in the context of estimating the population mean. We also discussed the closely associated application of hypothesis testing. We described how a sample of data could be used to examine specific propositions concerning the value of the unknown population mean. Using probability theory and the results of the CLT, we developed criteria for judging whether a sample of data was consistent (or otherwise) with some hypothesised value for the population mean – that is, we developed criteria for accepting or rejecting some given null hypothesis. We also emphasised the close connection between interval estimation and hypothesis testing – a given interval estimate contains the set of acceptable null hypotheses.

We then introduced the concept of correlation as a means of extending the analysis of a given data set. In particular, correlation analysis provides a starting point in the process of seeking to explain the variation or behaviour of the data.

Finally, we completed this chapter with a discussion of the nature of statistical inference in economics – and hence the nature of econometrics – and thereby provided an introduction to the subject matter of the remainder of this book.

## Notes

[1] We will draw a distinction between an **estimator** and an **estimate**. An estimator is a statement of how individual estimates are produced – in general, it is the formula, which upon substitution of the sample observations, produces an estimate.

[2] In using summation notation it is common to shorten this notation and thus, for example, to write:

$$\sum_{i=1}^{n} X_i = \sum_i X_i$$

or even:

$$\sum_{i=1}^{n} X_i = \sum X_i$$

provided there is no ambiguity concerning the reference of the summation. We will adopt this convention throughout this book.

[3] The interested reader is referred to C. A. Moser and G. Kalton, *Survey Methods in Social Investigation*, 2nd edn (London, Heinemann Educational Books, 1971) or W. G. Cochran, *Sampling Techniques*, 3rd edn (New York, Wiley, 1977).

[4] In fact, we have slightly amended the published table by approximating values for households of sizes six, seven, eight and nine. The published table only has a category for 'six or more'. In addition to assuming frequencies for six, seven, eight and nine, we have also assumed, for simplicity, that there are no households in excess of nine individuals.

[5] A proof of the Central Limit Theorem can be found in most advanced texts on mathematical statistics. For example, see R. V. Hogg and A. T. Craig, *Introduction to Mathematical Statistics*, 4th edn (New York, Macmillan, 1978), pp. 192–4.

[6] In exactly the same way as we have discussed estimating $\mu$ via distributional statements which can be made about $\bar{X}$, we can also deal with the problem of estimating $\sigma^2$ via distributional statements about $S^2$. However, in the case of $S^2$ the appropriate distribution is not the normal but another distribution, referred to as the **chi-square** ($\chi^2$) distribution. We will not, however, concern ourselves with this problem here.

[7] 'Student' was the pen name of the statistician who first derived the $t$-distribution.

## References and Further Reading

For a discussion of summary measures of sample information see, for example: T. H. and R. J. Wonnacott, *Introductory Statistics for Business and Economics*, 3rd edn (New York, Wiley, 1984), Ch. 2, or P. G. Hoel and R. J. Jessen, *Basic Statistics for Business and Economics*, 3rd edn (New York, Wiley, 1982), Ch. 2.

A discussion of sampling techniques can be found in C. A. Moser and G. Kalton, *Survey Methods in Social Investigation*, 2nd edn (London, Heinemann Educational Books, 1971), or W. G. Cochran, *Sampling Techniques*, 3rd edn (New York, Wiley, 1977).

A more detailed discussion of probability and probability distributions, still at an introductory level, can be found in Wonnacott and Wonnacott, *Introductory Statistics*, Chs 3 and 4, or Hoel and Jessen, *Basic Statistics*, Chs 3 and 4.

For a discussion at an intermediate level see: J. Kmenta, *Elements of Econometrics*, 2nd edn (New York, Macmillan, 1986), Ch. 3.

For an advanced discussion, for the mathematically inclined reader, see: R. V. Hogg and A. T. Craig, *Introduction to Mathematical Statistics*, 4th edn (New York, Macmillan, 1978), Chs 1 to 3.

For an introductory discussion of estimation and hypothesis testing, see: Wonnacott and Wonnacott, *Introductory Statistics*, Chs 6 to 9, or Hoel and Jessen, *Basic Statistics*, Chs 6 to 8. An intermediate discussion can be found in Kmenta, *Elements of Econometrics*, Chs 4 to 6, and an advanced discussion can be found in Hogg and Craig, *Introduction to Mathematical Statistics*, Chs 4 to 7.

An introductory discussion of correlation can be found in Hoel and Jessen, *Basic Statistics*, Ch. 9, or Wonnacott and Wonnacott, *Introductory Statistics*, Ch. 5, pp. 132–5, and Ch. 15.

For those readers wishing to brush up on their mathematics, the following texts might be useful:

Allen, R. G. D., *Mathematical Analysis for Economists* (London, Macmillan, 1938).
Casson, M., *Introduction to Mathematical Economics* (London, Nelson, 1973).
Timbrell, M., *Mathematics for Economists* (Oxford, Basil Blackwell, 1985).

**Exercises**

*Section 1.2    The Role of Sampling*

Exercise 1

The following data refer to total new car registrations in Great Britain, in each of the years 1956 to 1980. The data are measured in thousands, and in terms of monthly averages.

| Year | Regis-trations | Year | Regis-trations | Year | Regis-trations | Year | Regis-trations |
|------|------|------|------|------|------|------|------|
| 1956 | 33.3 | 1963 | 84.1 | 1970 | 91.4 | 1977 | 107.1 |
| 1957 | 35.4 | 1964 | 99.2 | 1971 | 108.5 | 1978 | 130.1 |
| 1958 | 46.3 | 1965 | 93.5 | 1972 | 138.6 | 1979 | 139.7 |
| 1959 | 53.8 | 1966 | 88.8 | 1973 | 137.1 | 1980 | 124.1 |
| 1960 | 67.1 | 1967 | 93.1 | 1974 | 102.8 | | |
| 1961 | 61.9 | 1968 | 93.1 | 1975 | 97.2 | | |
| 1962 | 65.4 | 1969 | 82.3 | 1976 | 104.7 | | |

*Source: Economic Trends,* Annual Supplement, HMSO, 1982.

(a)  Draw a graph of new car registrations against time, and comment on the main features of this graph. Can you provide any possible explanations for some of the major movements in the data?

(b)  Calculate the mean and variance of the data. How useful do you consider these to be as summary measures of the data?

Exercise 2

The following table shows the unemployment rates in a sample of 35 towns and cities throughout Great Britain, in 1971 and 1982.

Calculate the mean and the variance of the data in 1971 and 1982, and comment on your results.

| Town | Unemployment rate (%) March 1982 | March 1971 | Town | Unemployment rate (%) March 1982 | March 1971 |
|------|------|------|------|------|------|
| Brighton | 11.4 | 3.6 | Leicester | 10.5 | 1.7 |
| Canterbury | 11.7 | 4.8 | Nottingham | 11.1 | 3.1 |
| Luton | 12.0 | 1.9 | Barnsley | 13.9 | 5.7 |
| Maidstone | 7.0 | 1.8 | Bradford | 14.1 | 4.2 |
| Oxford | 8.1 | 2.7 | Hull | 14.4 | 4.7 |
| Portsmouth | 11.5 | 3.6 | Leeds | 11.4 | 3.2 |

| Town | Unemployment rate (%) | | Town | Unemployment rate (%) | |
|------|-------------------|----------------|------|-------------------|----------------|
|  | March 1982 | March 1971 |  | March 1982 | March 1971 |
| Reading | 7.4 | 1.5 | Rotherham | 20.2 | 3.8 |
| Southampton | 8.8 | 4.1 | Lancaster | 13.1 | 5.4 |
| Cambridge | 5.3 | 1.1 | Liverpool | 18.6 | 5.6 |
| Ipswich | 8.3 | 3.2 | Manchester | 12.8 | 2.8 |
| Bristol | 10.3 | 2.9 | Durham | 13.3 | 4.2 |
| Exeter | 8.6 | 4.0 | Teesside | 18.1 | 4.4 |
| Plymouth | 15.3 | 4.4 | Cardiff | 13.7 | 3.5 |
| Birmingham | 16.2 | 3.3 | Swansea | 15.8 | 3.5 |
| Rugby | 12.0 | 2.2 | Edinburgh | 11.1 | 4.4 |
| Stoke-on-Trent | 13.5 | 3.2 | Glasgow | 16.2 | 6.3 |
| Worcester | 11.4 | 2.6 | Perth | 10.0 | 3.2 |
| Derby | 8.9 | 2.8 | | | |

*Source: Employment Gazette*, April 1982, HMSO. *Department of Employment Gazette*, April 1971, HMSO.

Exercise 3
The following data give the sterling exchange rate in terms of the US dollar, from 1956 to 1983.

| Year | Exchange rate | Year | Exchange rate | Year | Exchange rate | Year | Exchange rate |
|------|------|------|------|------|------|------|------|
| 1956 | 2.796 | 1963 | 2.800 | 1970 | 2.396 | 1977 | 1.746 |
| 1957 | 2.794 | 1964 | 2.793 | 1971 | 2.444 | 1978 | 1.920 |
| 1958 | 2.810 | 1965 | 2.796 | 1972 | 2.502 | 1979 | 2.122 |
| 1959 | 2.809 | 1966 | 2.793 | 1973 | 2.453 | 1980 | 2.328 |
| 1960 | 2.808 | 1967 | 2.828 | 1974 | 2.340 | 1981 | 2.025 |
| 1961 | 2.802 | 1968 | 2.394 | 1975 | 2.220 | 1982 | 1.749 |
| 1962 | 2.808 | 1969 | 2.390 | 1976 | 1.805 | 1983 | 1.516 |

*Source: Economic Trends*, Annual Supplement, 1984, HMSO.

(a)    Graph the data and comment on the main features of the data.
(b)    What explanations can you provide for some of the more obvious movements in the data?

*Section 1.3    Probability Distributions*

Exercise 4
Consider a variable, $X$, which can only take on the values 1, 2, 3, 4, and 5. Let

the probability distribution of $X$ be given by:

$$P(X) = \frac{X}{15}$$

(a) Confirm that $P(X)$ satisfies the definition of a probability distribution.
(b) Find the mean and variance of $X$.
(c) Derive the following probabilities:
   (i) $P(X > 3)$
   (ii) $P(0 \leqslant X \leqslant 4)$
   (iii) $P(X \leqslant 2)$

## Exercise 5

(Requires knowledge of the technique of integration.) Let the p.d.f. of a variable, $X$, be given by:

$$f(X) = \frac{X+2}{18}$$

where $X$ can take on any value in the range $-2 < X < 4$.

(a) Confirm that $f(X)$ satisfies the definition of a p.d.f.
(b) Find the mean and variance of $X$.
(c) Find the following probabilities:
   (i) $P(X \geqslant 0)$
   (ii) $P(1 < X < 3)$
   (iii) $P(X \leqslant -1)$

## Exercise 6

Consider a variable, $X$, which has a normal distribution with a mean of 6 and a variance of 16. Find the following probabilities:

(a) $P(X > 8)$
(b) $P(X \leqslant 3)$
(c) $P(6 \leqslant X \leqslant 10)$
(d) $P(-2 \leqslant X \leqslant 2)$

## Exercise 7

Assume that the distribution of the weights of adult males in Great Britain can be reasonably approximated by a normal distribution with a mean of 176 pounds and a variance of 784 (pounds squared). If a male is selected at random, calculate the following probabilities:

(a) The probability that this male weighs more than 224 pounds.
(b) The probability that this male weighs less than 140 pounds.
(c) The probability that this male weighs between 154 and 196 pounds.

*Section 1.4    Estimation*

Exercise 8

Recall from Equations 1.38 and 1.39 that:

$$\mathrm{Var}\,(bX) = b^2\,\mathrm{Var}\,(X)$$

and

$$\mathrm{Var}\,(a+bX) = b^2\,\mathrm{Var}\,(X)$$

Prove these two statements.
(Hint: Define two new variables:

$$Y = bX$$

and

$$Z = a+bX$$

and then use Equation 1.28 to simplify $\mathrm{Var}\,(Y)$ and $\mathrm{Var}\,(Z)$ to Equations 1.38 and 1.39.)

Exercise 9

Assume that a sample of 25 households is randomly selected, at some point in time, and data collected on expenditure on food in the immediately preceding week. Let the variable $X$ denote food expenditure, and assume that the sample statistics are as follows:

$$\bar{X} = \pounds 26.35$$
$$S = \pounds 10.89$$

Derive the 95 per cent interval estimate of the mean level of weekly household food expenditure in the population.

Exercise 10

Consider the data in Exercise 2. Assume further that the sample is randomly selected from all the towns and cities throughout Great Britain.

Derive 95 per cent interval estimates of the average unemployment rate in both 1971 and 1982.

*Section 1.5    Hypothesis Testing*

Exercise 11

Under British criminal law, the accused is considered to be innocent until proven guilty. How might a null and an alternative hypothesis be expressed within the context of a criminal trial? What are the Type I and Type II errors within this context, and how might the relative costs of making these two types of error be interpreted?

Exercise 12

A motor vehicle manufacturer claims that his vehicles consume fuel at the rate of at least 45 miles per gallon, on average. To test this claim a consumer organisation took a random sample of 12 of these vehicles and recorded fuel consumption during a period of three weeks, under a variety of driving conditions. The average fuel consumption (in miles per gallon) of these 12 vehicles was as follows:

39  43  48  39  40  40  50  45  46  41  43  48

(a)  Test the manufacturer's claim, and state any necessary assumptions.
(b)  Define the Type I and Type II errors in the context of this example.

Exercise 13

Consider again the data in Exercise 2. Derive a new variable which is the difference, for each town, between the unemployment rates in 1982 and 1971. Denote this variable by $Y$.

Test the hypothesis that the average level of $Y$ is zero, against the alternative that it exceeds zero.

*Section 1.6    The Concept of Correlation*

Exercise 14

The following table shows personal disposable income and consumers' expenditure in Great Britain, both in 1975 prices, from 1956 to 1980, in £'000m.

| Year | Income | Consumer expenditure | Year | Income | Consumer expenditure |
|------|--------|-----------|------|--------|-----------|
| 1956 | 42.48 | 40.29 | 1969 | 61.24 | 56.31 |
| 1957 | 43.16 | 41.12 | 1970 | 63.74 | 57.81 |
| 1958 | 43.87 | 42.10 | 1971 | 64.70 | 59.72 |
| 1959 | 46.13 | 43.91 | 1972 | 70.35 | 63.27 |
| 1960 | 49.14 | 45.62 | 1973 | 75.25 | 66.33 |
| 1961 | 51.13 | 46.68 | 1974 | 74.24 | 65.11 |
| 1962 | 51.50 | 47.65 | 1975 | 73.88 | 64.75 |
| 1963 | 53.77 | 49.72 | 1976 | 73.36 | 64.82 |
| 1964 | 55.78 | 51.27 | 1977 | 72.36 | 64.58 |
| 1965 | 57.20 | 52.13 | 1978 | 78.44 | 68.22 |
| 1966 | 58.50 | 53.18 | 1979 | 83.73 | 71.41 |
| 1967 | 59.38 | 54.38 | 1980 | 84.87 | 71.45 |
| 1968 | 60.61 | 56.03 | | | |

*Source: Economic Trends,* Annual Supplement, 1981, HMSO.

Denote personal disposable income in year $t$ by $D_t$, and consumers' expenditure in year $t$ by $C_t$. Given that the above data produce the following sums and sums of squares, calculate the correlation coefficient between $D$ and $C$, and comment on the strength of the relationship between these two variables:

$$\sum D_t = 1548.81, \quad \sum C_t = 1397.86, \quad \sum D_t^2 = 99{,}862.2789$$
$$\sum C_t^2 = 80{,}432.8466, \quad \sum D_t C_t = 89{,}571.9504$$

Exercise 15

(a) The following diagram is a graph of the new car registration data in Exercise 1, against personal disposable income from Exercise 14. On the basis of this graph comment on the relationship between registrations and income.

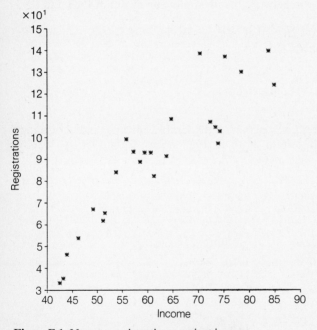

**Figure E.1** New car registrations against income.

(b) Given the following sums and sums of squares (together with the relevant ones given in Exercise 14) calculate the correlation coefficient between $D$ and $R$, where $R$ denotes registrations. Comment.

$$\sum R_t = 2278.6, \quad \sum R_t^2 = 230{,}084.68, \quad \sum D_t R_t = 149{,}686.437$$

Exercise 16

The following graph is a graph of the unemployment data from Exercise 2 (the unemployment rates in 1982 are plotted on the vertical axis and the corresponding rates in 1971 are plotted on the horizontal axis).

The correlation coefficient between these two sets of data is 0.610. Comment on this correlation in the light of the graph.

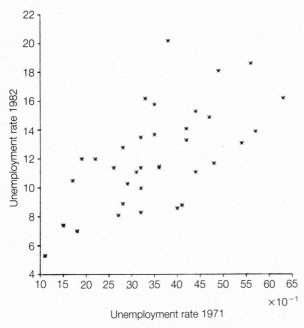

**Figure E.2** Unemployment in 1982 against unemployment in 1971.

Exercise 17

The following table shows the unemployment rates in the United States and the United Kingdom from 1956 to 1983.

(a)  Plot the sterling exchange rate data of Exercise 3 above against:
   (i)   The UK unemployment rate.
   (ii)  The US unemployment rate.
   (iii) The UK unemployment rate relative to the US rate (that is, derive a new variable which is the ratio of the UK rate to the US rate).

(b)  The correlation coefficient between the sterling exchange rate and the UK unemployment rate is −0.882, the correlation between the exchange rate and the US unemployment rate is −0.663, and the correlation between the exchange rate and the relative unemployment rate is −0.882. How might both the signs and magnitudes of these correlation coefficients be explained?

| Unemployment (%) | | | Unemployment (%) | | | Unemployment (%) | | |
|---|---|---|---|---|---|---|---|---|
| Year | US | UK | Year | US | UK | Year | US | UK |
| 1956 | 4.2 | 1.0 | 1966 | 3.8 | 1.4 | 1976 | 7.5 | 6.0 |
| 1957 | 4.3 | 1.3 | 1967 | 3.8 | 2.2 | 1977 | 6.9 | 6.4 |
| 1958 | 6.8 | 1.9 | 1968 | 3.6 | 2.4 | 1978 | 5.9 | 6.3 |
| 1959 | 5.5 | 2.0 | 1969 | 3.4 | 3.1 | 1979 | 5.7 | 5.6 |
| 1960 | 5.6 | 1.5 | 1970 | 4.8 | 3.1 | 1980 | 7.0 | 6.9 |
| 1961 | 6.7 | 1.4 | 1971 | 5.7 | 3.8 | 1981 | 7.5 | 10.6 |
| 1962 | 5.6 | 1.8 | 1972 | 5.4 | 4.1 | 1982 | 9.5 | 12.3 |
| 1963 | 5.7 | 2.2 | 1973 | 4.7 | 2.8 | 1983 | 9.5 | 13.1 |
| 1964 | 5.2 | 1.6 | 1974 | 5.5 | 2.9 | | | |
| 1965 | 4.5 | 1.3 | 1975 | 8.3 | 4.6 | | | |

*Source: National Institute Economic Review, 1967, 1976, 1985.*

**Appendix 1.1**    *Summation Notation*

Consider the expression:

$$\sum_{i=1}^{n} X_i$$

which reads as 'the sum of $X_i$ where $i$ runs from 1 to $n$ in increments of 1'.
    Thus we can write:

$$\sum_{i=1}^{n} X_i = X_1 + X_2 + \ldots + X_n \qquad \text{Equation A1.1.1}$$

For example, for $n = 4$ we have:

$$\sum_{i=1}^{4} X_i = X_1 + X_2 + X_3 + X_4$$

Similarly, we can also write:

$$\sum_{i=1}^{n} X_i^2 = X_1^2 + X_2^2 + \ldots + X_n^2 \qquad \text{Equation A1.1.2}$$

Thus irrespective of the function of $X$ involved in the summation expression, the appropriate sum is derived by substituting the successive values of the index of the summation (here denoted by $i$) into the expression.
    Let $c$ be a constant. Thus consider the following expression:

$$\sum_{i=1}^{n} cX_i$$

This can be expanded as:

$$\sum_{i=1}^{n} cX_i = cX_1 + cX_2 + \ldots + cX_n$$

$$= c(X_1 + X_2 + \ldots + X_n)$$

That is:

$$\sum_{i=1}^{n} cX_i = c \sum_{i=1}^{n} X_i \qquad \text{Equation A1.1.3}$$

Further:

$$\sum_{i=1}^{n} c = c + c + \ldots + c$$

or

$$\sum_{i=1}^{n} c = nc \qquad \text{Equation A1.1.4}$$

Note also that we need not necessarily use the index $i$. Thus we could write:

$$\sum_{j=1}^{n} X_j = X_1 + X_2 + \ldots + X_n \qquad \text{Equation A1.1.5}$$

or

$$\sum_{k=1}^{n} X_k = X_1 + X_2 + \ldots + X_n \qquad \text{Equation A1.1.6}$$

However we must ensure that there is a correspondence between the index in the summation and the function of $X$ referred to. Thus, for example:

$$\sum_{j=1}^{n} X_i = X_i + X_i + \ldots + X_i$$

or

$$\sum_{j=1}^{n} X_i = nX_i \qquad \text{Equation A1.1.7}$$

as $X_i$ is constant with respect to the index $j$.

Further, we can write:

$$\sum_{i=1}^{n} (X_i + Y_i) = (X_1 + Y_1) + (X_2 + Y_2) + \ldots + (X_n + Y_n)$$

$$= (X_1 + X_2 + \ldots + X_n) + (Y_1 + Y_2 + \ldots + Y_n)$$

or

$$\sum_{i=1}^{n} (X_i + Y_i) = \sum_{i=1}^{n} X_i + \sum_{i=1}^{n} Y_i \qquad \text{Equation A1.1.8}$$

Next consider:

$$\sum_{i=1}^{n} (X_i + Y_i)^2$$

This expression can be expanded as follows:

$$\sum_{i=1}^{n} (X_i + Y_i)^2 = (X_1 + Y_1)^2 + (X_2 + Y_2)^2 + \ldots + (X_n + Y_n)^2$$

$$= (X_1^2 + 2X_1Y_1 + Y_1^2) + (X_2^2 + 2X_2Y_2 + Y_2^2) + \ldots$$
$$+ (X_n^2 + 2X_nY_n + Y_n^2)$$

$$= (X_1^2 + X_2^2 + \ldots + X_n^2) + 2(X_1Y_1 + X_2Y_2 + \ldots + X_nY_n)$$
$$+ (Y_1^2 + Y_2^2 + \ldots + Y_n^2)$$

or

$$\sum_{i=1}^{n} (X_i + Y_i)^2 = \sum_{i=1}^{n} X_i^2 + 2\sum_{i=1}^{n} X_iY_i + \sum_{i=1}^{n} Y_i^2 \qquad \text{Equation A1.1.9}$$

Alternatively, we can write:

$$\sum_{i=1}^{n} (X_i + Y_i)^2 = \sum_{i=1}^{n} (X_i^2 + 2X_iY_i + Y_i^2)$$

$$= \sum_{i=1}^{n} X_i^2 + 2\sum_{i=1}^{n} X_iY_i + \sum_{i=1}^{n} Y_i^2$$

We can also define **double summation**. For example:

$$\sum_{j=1}^{m} \sum_{i=1}^{n} X_{ij} = \sum_{j=1}^{m} (X_{1j} + X_{2j} + \ldots + X_{nj})$$

$$= \sum_{j=1}^{m} X_{1j} + \sum_{j=1}^{m} X_{2j} + \ldots + \sum_{j=1}^{m} X_{nj}$$

or

$$\sum_{j=1}^{m} \sum_{i=1}^{n} X_{ij} = (X_{11} + X_{12} + \ldots + X_{1m}) + (X_{21} + X_{22} + \ldots + X_{2m})$$
$$+ \ldots + (X_{n1} + X_{n2} + \ldots + X_{nm}) \qquad \text{Equation A1.1.10}$$

Further:

$$\sum_{j=1}^{m} \sum_{i=1}^{n} X_iY_j = \sum_{j=1}^{m} (X_1Y_j + X_2Y_j + \ldots + X_nY_j)$$

$$= X_1 \sum_{j=1}^{m} Y_j + X_2 \sum_{j=1}^{m} Y_j + \ldots + X_n \sum_{j=1}^{m} Y_j$$

$$= \sum_{j=1}^{m} Y_j[X_1 + X_2 + \ldots + X_n]$$

That is:

$$\sum_{j=1}^{m} \sum_{i=1}^{n} X_i Y_j = \sum_{j=1}^{m} Y_j \sum_{i=1}^{n} X_i \qquad \text{Equation A1.1.11}$$

**Appendix 1.2**  *The Biasedness of the Sample Variance, $V^2$, as an Estimator of the Population Variance*

Recall from Equation 1.4 that we defined $V^2$ as:

$$V^2 = \frac{\sum_{i=1}^{n} (X_i - \bar{X})^2}{n} \qquad \text{Equation A1.2.1}$$

Consider the numerator of Equation A1.2.1. This can be re-expressed as follows:

$$\begin{aligned}
\sum (X_i - \bar{X})^2 &= \sum (X_i - \mu + \mu - \bar{X})^2 \\
&= \sum [(X_i - \mu) - (\bar{X} - \mu)]^2 \\
&= \sum [(X_i - \mu)^2 + (\bar{X} - \mu)^2 - 2(X_i - \mu)(\bar{X} - \mu)] \\
&= \sum (X_i - \mu)^2 + n(\bar{X} - \mu)^2 - 2(\bar{X} - \mu)\sum (X_i - \mu)
\end{aligned}$$

Now,

$$\begin{aligned}
2(\bar{X} - \mu)\sum (X_i - \mu) &= 2n(\bar{X} - \mu)\frac{1}{n}(\sum X_i - n\mu) \\
&= 2n(\bar{X} - \mu)(\bar{X} - \mu) \\
&= 2n(\bar{X} - \mu)^2
\end{aligned}$$

Therefore:

$$\begin{aligned}
\sum (X_i - \bar{X})^2 &= \sum (X_i - \mu)^2 + n(\bar{X} - \mu)^2 - 2n(\bar{X} - \mu)^2 \\
&= \sum (X_i - \mu)^2 - n(\bar{X} - \mu)^2
\end{aligned}$$

We can now evaluate the expected value of the numerator of Equation A1.2.1 as follows:

$$E[\sum(X_i - \bar{X})^2] = E[\sum(X_i - \mu)^2] - nE(\bar{X} - \mu)^2$$
$$= \sum E(X_i - \mu)^2 - nE(\bar{X} - \mu)^2$$
$$= n\sigma^2 - n(\sigma^2/n)$$
$$= n\sigma^2 - \sigma^2$$

noting that $E(\bar{X} - \mu)^2$ is just the variance of $\bar{X}$, which we derived in Equation 1.46.

Therefore we now have:

$$E(V^2) = \frac{1}{n}E[\sum(X_i - \bar{X})^2]$$

$$= \frac{1}{n}(n\sigma^2 - \sigma^2)$$

$$= \frac{\sigma^2(n-1)}{n}$$

which we note is not equal to $\sigma^2$, and therefore we can conclude that $V^2$ is a biased estimator of $\sigma^2$. However, we can deduce the expression for an unbiased estimator. For we have:

$$\sigma^2 = \frac{n}{n-1}E(V^2)$$

Therefore an unbiased estimator of $\sigma^2$ is:

$$S^2 = \frac{n}{n-1}V^2 = \frac{\sum(X_i - \bar{X})^2}{n-1}$$

and note that it must be the case that $E(S^2) = \sigma^2$.

# 2 The Simple Regression Model

## 2.1 Introduction

In this chapter we begin the discussion of the subject matter of econometrics proper. We will extend our discussion of the correlation coefficient in Chapter 1 by describing the model which provides a formal context for evaluating the extent to which some given variable can be considered to be determined or explained by some other variable. In particular, we will outline the role of estimation and hypothesis testing in developing causal models in economics.

We will also emphasise that the simple regression model – where only one variable is considered to determine the variable of interest – will generally be unrealistic or inappropriate in the context of economics. Typically, a given variable will be influenced by a number of different factors. Thus we require a more generalised model in order to account for these separate influences, and we will go on to develop this model in Chapter 3. The simple regression model, therefore, can be most usefully interpreted as the first step in developing generalised causal models.

## 2.2 Model Specification

The simplest form that any economic theory can take is to postulate that a variable, $X$, in some way influences another variable, $Y$. This can be expressed notationally as:

$$Y = f(X) \qquad \text{Equation 2.1}$$

That is, $Y$ is a function of $X$, or the level of $Y$ is determined by the level of $X$.

For example, an application which we will discuss at various points in this book concerns the **consumption function**. The aggregate level of consumption expenditure in the economy is one of the major influences on the overall level of economic activity, and therefore isolating the determinants of consumption expenditure is central to understanding the behaviour of the economy.

The simplest theory relating to the determination of consumption expenditure is that the level of consumption is determined only by the level of income, or in particular, by the level of disposable income – income net of taxation payments. Thus if we let $C$ denote consumption expenditure and $D$ denote disposable income, then we could write:

$$C = f(D) \qquad\qquad \text{Equation 2.2}$$

The direction of causality implied by Equation 2.1 or Equation 2.2 – from $X$ to $Y$, or from $D$ to $C$ – is the minimum requirement of a theory that purports to have any explanatory power. Empirical observation may establish that $X$ and $Y$ (or $C$ and $D$) move together (for example, on the basis of a high correlation coefficient), but it is only on the basis of some theory that it can be argued whether the direction of causality is from $X$ to $Y$ or from $Y$ to $X$.

The theory may be more specific than just stating that $Y$ depends on $X$ in some way. The sign of the relationship between $Y$ and $X$ – whether $X$ influences $Y$ positively or negatively – may be postulated *a priori*, or the theory may be able to specify the form of the relationship between $Y$ and $X$ – that is, whether the relationship is linear or non-linear, and perhaps the form that any non-linearity may take.

Thus in the case of the consumption function, we would expect consumption expenditure to be positively related to income – the higher is disposable income then the higher will be consumption expenditure. However the question as to whether the relationship is linear or non-linear is perhaps not so clear-cut, and theory may have little to offer on this aspect of the relationship.

As a starting point, and in the absence of any other information, we can begin by assuming that the relationship between $Y$ and $X$ is linear. Thus we would postulate:

$$Y = \alpha + \beta X \qquad\qquad \text{Equation 2.3}$$

$\alpha$ (alpha) and $\beta$ (beta) are the unknown **parameters** for which we require estimates in order to fully specify the relationship between $Y$ and $X$. $\beta$ (the **slope** coefficient) measures the response of $Y$ to a one unit change in the level of $X$, and $\alpha$ (the **intercept** term) is the level of $Y$ when $X$ equals zero. $Y$ is generally referred to as the **dependent** variable and $X$ as the **independent** variable.

Thus assuming a linear consumption function, we can write:

$$C = \alpha + \beta D \qquad\qquad \text{Equation 2.4}$$

Note that Equation 2.4 can have both a cross-section and a time-series interpretation. In the cross-section, Equation 2.4 could represent the relationship between consumption and income within a population of households or individuals, at some point in time. Higher income households would be expected to consume more than lower income households, and the precise relationship between the level of household consumption and household income is postulated to be reflected in Equation 2.4.

Equation 2.4 could also be interpreted as a time-series relationship. At the macroeconomic level, aggregate consumption in the economy will be determined by aggregate income, and the form of this relationship may be constant over time. Thus at time points when aggregate disposable income is high, high levels of consumption would be observed, and low levels of consumption would occur at periods of low levels of disposable income.

The term $\beta$ in Equation 2.4 measures the response of consumption expenditure to a one-unit change in income – it is a measure of the marginal propensity to consume. Economic theory would predict that $\beta$ is positive (and less than one – consumers can only spend a fraction of an extra unit of income). Therefore, *a priori*, we would expect a positive relationship between $C$ and $D$.

As they stand, Equations 2.3 and 2.4 both imply that the relationship between the dependent and independent variable is an exact one – that is, that the independent variable explains or accounts for all of the variation in the dependent variable. In reality, and especially in the social sciences, it is highly unlikely that exact relationships will be observed between variables – there will always be some element of imprecision, although if the theory underlying the relationship is a satisfactory one, then this imprecision will be relatively unimportant.

Thus we could complete the specification of the relationship between $Y$ and $X$ by adding a **disturbance term** which represents the variation in $Y$ which is not accounted for by the variation in $X$. We will denote this disturbance term by $\varepsilon$ (epsilon) and therefore the equation which purports to provide a complete explanation for the variation in $Y$ can be written as:

$$Y = \alpha + \beta X + \varepsilon \qquad \text{Equation 2.5}$$

The addition of $\varepsilon$ can be justified in three ways:

a   $Y$ is in fact determined by a number of variables, but $X$ is postulated as being the most important determinant. These other variables may be unobservable or unmeasurable but are considered to be relatively unimportant and, for completeness, $\varepsilon$ is included to account for these.

b   To a large extent social science data reflect human responses and $\varepsilon$ is included to account for the random or unpredictable elements in these responses.

c   The true relationship between $Y$ and $X$ is in fact the exact relationship in Equation 2.3. However there may be errors in measuring $Y$, and $\varepsilon$ is included to account for these measurement errors.

Our objective here is to develop a method for estimating $\alpha$ and $\beta$ so that the relationship between $Y$ and $X$ can be fully specified. However before proceeding it is important to emphasise how Equation 2.5 should be interpreted.

The theory underlying Equation 2.5 is an attempt to explain the variation in the level of $Y$ – the variable $Y$ is the focus of the theoretical investigation. The theory postulates that the variation in $Y$ can be largely explained by the variation in another variable $X$, and the variation in $Y$ not explained by $X$ can be accounted for by a third variable, $\varepsilon$. The level of $\varepsilon$ is often referred to as the *residual*, and if the theory is a satisfactory one, then this residual (or unexplained) component of $Y$ should be small.

Such an interpretation implies that $\varepsilon$ can be considered to be a random variable. By definition, $X$ captures all the systematic variation in $Y$, the remaining variation being represented by $\varepsilon$. The value of $\varepsilon$, then, cannot be predicted or explained, and in this sense can be considered as random. Sometimes the value of $\varepsilon$ will represent an addition to the level of the systematic component of $Y$ (the $\alpha + \beta X$ term) and sometimes it will represent a subtraction. On average, the value of $\varepsilon$ would be expected to be zero. Thus, by assumption, we have:

$$E(\varepsilon) = 0 \hspace{4cm} \text{Equation 2.6}$$

As $Y$ contains a random component ($\varepsilon$), $Y$ is referred to as a **stochastic** variable. $X$, on the other hand, we will initially assume to be **non-stochastic**. This implies that we do not require an explanation for the variation in $X$, and that $X$ can therefore be interpreted as given or fixed. In effect, we assume that the level of $X$ is determined entirely independently of $Y$; $X$ determines the level of $Y$, but $Y$ in no way influences the level of $X$. In turn, as $\varepsilon$ is random or unpredictable, and as $X$ is determined in a completely unrelated context to $Y$, then $X$ and $\varepsilon$ can be assumed to be independent. If $X$ and $\varepsilon$ are independent then we have:

$$E(X\varepsilon) = E(X)E(\varepsilon)$$
$$= 0 \quad \text{as} \quad E(\varepsilon) = 0$$

That is, in addition to assuming that $\varepsilon$ must have a zero mean, we can also assume that:

$$E(X\varepsilon) = 0 \hspace{4cm} \text{Equation 2.7}$$

In order to be concrete, we will consider a simple application.

Consider the case of attempting to formulate a model which explains the variation in the consumption of natural gas over time. Such a model might be useful for the gas-supplying industry, for example, in order to forecast gas consumption, and hence to make appropriate supply decisions. As one of the major uses of gas is for heating purposes then an important determinant will presumably be weather conditions and, in particular, atmospheric temperature. Thus in terms of the general notation of the simple regression model in Equation 2.5, $Y$, the dependent variable, would here denote the level of gas consumption, and $X$ would denote atmospheric temperature. Note that we would expect low temperatures to result in high levels of gas consumption, and high temperatures to result in low consumption levels. Thus $X$ will negatively influence $Y$, and consequently we would expect the value of $\beta$ in Equation 2.5 to be negative.

Now, the model is required to explain gas consumption over time, and given forecasts of temperature, the model can then be used to forecast consumption (given values of $\alpha$ and $\beta$). Thus the model is a time-series model and, in particular, will be identical at each point in time. That is, for any time period, the observed level of gas consumption can be explained by the temperature which occurred during that time period, and any random fluctuation which may have occurred. Therefore if we let $Y_t$ denote observed gas consumption during time period $t$ and $X_t$ denote atmospheric temperature in time period $t$ then the model can be written as:

$$Y_t = \alpha + \beta X_t + \varepsilon_t \qquad \qquad \text{Equation 2.8}$$

where $\varepsilon_t$ is the random component of $Y_t$ in period $t$ and $\alpha$ and $\beta$ are constants (they do not vary over time). It is in this sense that the model is assumed to be the same at all points in time.

In order to examine the empirical support for the model in Equation 2.8, we could begin by obtaining a sample of data. We first note that the model is not specific as to the appropriate time period – that is, as to whether $t$ refers to days, weeks, months, or whatever. The model as specified is a general one, and presumably should be equally appropriate irrespective of the time period.

Quite arbitrarily, we will let $t$ refer to months. Thus the model can now be interpreted as postulating that the monthly level of gas consumption is determined by some measure of monthly temperature (say, average daily temperature during a given month). In Table 2.1 we present a sample of monthly data for Great Britain over the two years 1980 and 1981. Mean daily air temperature is defined in terms of a regional average over Great Britain.

Note that the model in Equation 2.8 implies that the only influence on gas consumption is temperature. In effect, the model is a short-term model, as we have ignored various other factors which might be expected to influence the level of gas consumption in the medium to longer term. Thus, for example, we might expect that the price of gas (relative to alternative forms of energy – electricity, coal, etc.) might influence the demand for gas. However, in the short term, the ability of consumers to switch between gas and other forms of energy will be limited, and therefore we would expect price to play a role only in the medium to longer term. Consequently, the data we have selected here extend only over the relatively short period of two years.

In Figure 2.1 we present a graph of the gas consumption observations in

**Table 2.1** Monthly gas consumption and air temperature, Great Britain 1980 to 1981

| Year and month | Gas sent out (weekly averages) million therms $Y$ | Mean daily air temperature (centigrade) $X$ | Year and month | Gas sent out (weekly averages) million therms $Y$ | Mean daily air temperature (centigrade) $X$ |
|---|---|---|---|---|---|
| 1980 Jan | 508.4 | 3.1 | 1981 Jan | 461.7 | 5.2 |
| Feb | 446.4 | 6.3 | Feb | 466.3 | 3.7 |
| Mar | 452.9 | 5.4 | Mar | 428.6 | 8.3 |
| Apr | 331.4 | 9.0 | Apr | 340.8 | 8.2 |
| May | 281.1 | 11.3 | May | 296.3 | 11.6 |
| Jun | 215.1 | 14.3 | Jun | 212.6 | 13.8 |
| Jul | 199.1 | 15.0 | Jul | 185.7 | 16.0 |
| Aug | 162.6 | 16.3 | Aug | 159.3 | 16.6 |
| Sep | 188.0 | 15.2 | Sep | 182.3 | 15.1 |
| Oct | 313.4 | 9.6 | Oct | 327.0 | 8.9 |
| Nov | 401.0 | 7.0 | Nov | 391.7 | 8.1 |
| Dec | 450.3 | 6.0 | Dec | 499.5 | 1.4 |

*Source: Monthly Digest of Statistics, HMSO; Annual Abstract of Statistics, HMSO.*

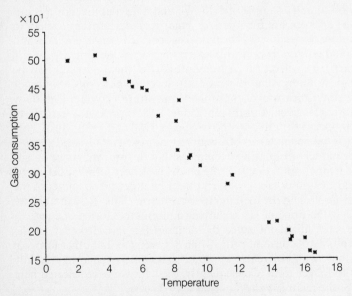

**Figure 2.1** Gas consumption against temperature.

Table 2.1 against temperature. We note from Figure 2.1 that the data would appear to support the hypothesis of an approximately linear and negative relationship between gas consumption and temperature. It would therefore seem sensible to proceed to estimate this relationship (that is, to estimate the values of $\alpha$ and $\beta$ in Equation 2.8).

Before proceeding to the estimation of $\alpha$ and $\beta$, it is instructive to consider the precise interpretation of the independent variable, $X$, and the disturbance term, $\varepsilon$, in the context of the gas consumption model in Equation 2.8.

$X$ is of course a variable in the sense that its value varies over time. However for any given time-period – period $t$, say – the value of $X$, $X_t$ – is fixed or given in the sense that its value is determined outside the model. In particular, $X_t$ is determined entirely independently of $Y_t$ ($X$ is thus an independent variable); the level of gas consumption in month $t$ can in no way influence average temperature during month $t$, the only possible direction of causality being from $X$ to $Y$.

The term $\varepsilon_t$ represents the random or unpredictable component in $Y_t$. Thus there will be instances of the same average temperature occurring in different months, and yet of differing levels of $Y$ being observed. The implication, therefore, is that given the value of $X_t$, $Y_t$ can take on any one of a range of possible values. This range of values for $Y_t$ is accounted for by the influence of $\varepsilon_t$. If the model is a satisfactory one then the range of possible values for $Y_t$ will be small – the level of $Y_t$ is primarily determined by $X_t$, but none the less a (small) range of values for $Y_t$ is consistent with the fixed value of $X_t$.

The manner in which the model is expressed in Equation 2.8 implies that we cannot explain why $Y_t$ varies, for a given value of $X_t$, and we must attribute this variation to random or unpredictable factors. However if there does appear to be some systematic component in the variation in $Y_t$, over and above that accounted for by $X_t$, then this will indicate the need to identify further systematic influences on $Y$. That is, modelling the variation in $Y$ can be characterised as the process of identifying all the systematic influences on $Y$, until only a random or unpredictable component remains.

This example is useful for allowing an interpretation to be made of how a set of sample observations is generated. In month $t$ some (given) average temperature, $X_t$, will occur. An associated value of gas consumption, $Y_t$, will be observed. However, as we have already noted, $Y_t$ is a random variable – a range or distribution of values of $Y_t$ will be associated with $X_t$ – and thus the actual value of $Y_t$ which is observed can be characterised as having been randomly 'selected' from this distribution of values of $Y_t$.

Given this interpretation, we can derive a graphical representation of the simple regression model, in the context of our gas consumption model. This is shown in Figure 2.2 where an attempt is made to represent the three dimensions of the regression model – the levels of $Y$ and $X$ and the distribution associated with a given value of $X$, $X_t$.

At each point in time a distribution of values for $Y$ occurs, the

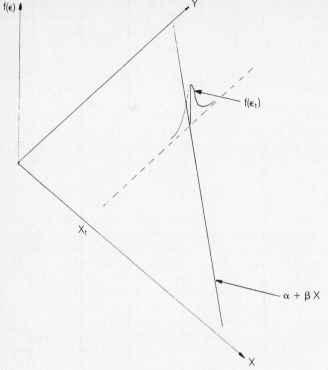

**Figure 2.2** Graphical interpretation of the simple regression model.

characteristics of this distribution being determined by the nature of the disturbance term, $\varepsilon$. In Figure 2.2 this distribution is shown for a given value of $X$, $X_t$. We therefore require a number of further assumptions concerning the properties of this distribution.

We have already concluded that given the definition of $\varepsilon$ then $\varepsilon$ would be expected to have a mean of zero, and, in particular, this will be the case at any given time-period, $t$. That is,

$$E(\varepsilon_t) = 0 \qquad\qquad\qquad \text{Equation 2.9}$$

and Equation 2.9 would hold for all values of $t$. We also require an assumption concerning the variance of $\varepsilon_t$. The simplest assumption which could be made is that the variance of $\varepsilon_t$ is constant at each point in time – that is, for time-period $s$, where $s \neq t$, the variance of the distribution of $\varepsilon_s$ would be the same as that for $\varepsilon_t$ shown in Figure 2.2. If we denote this constant variance by $\sigma_\varepsilon^2$ then this assumption can be written as:

$$\text{Var}(\varepsilon_t) = \sigma_\varepsilon^2 \quad \text{for all } t \qquad\qquad \text{Equation 2.10}$$

As drawn in Figure 2.2 the distribution of $\varepsilon_t$ is symmetrical and bell-shaped implying that $\varepsilon_t$ has a normal distribution. Thus in the absence of any other information concerning the distribution of $\varepsilon_t$ an assumption of normality is generally made.

In the simplest form of the model, we also assume that the $\varepsilon_t$s are independent or unrelated. That is, for all $s \neq t$, $\varepsilon_t$ and $\varepsilon_s$ are independent. This means, for example, that if in month $t$ an abnormally high (or low) level of gas consumption was observed (that is, abnormal relative to the temperature in month $t$ – a high (or low) value of $\varepsilon_t$ occurred) then this would have no effect on the disturbance terms in subsequent time-periods.

If $\varepsilon_t$ and $\varepsilon_s$ are independent then their covariance will be zero. Thus we can write:

$$\text{Cov}(\varepsilon_t \varepsilon_s) = E\{[\varepsilon_t - E(\varepsilon_t)][\varepsilon_s - E(\varepsilon_s)]\} \qquad\qquad \text{Equation 2.11}$$

and as we have:

$$E(\varepsilon_t) = E(\varepsilon_s) = 0$$

then

$$\text{Cov}(\varepsilon_t \varepsilon_s) = E(\varepsilon_t \varepsilon_s)$$

and we therefore assume that:

$$E(\varepsilon_t \varepsilon_s) = 0 \quad \text{for all } t \neq s \qquad\qquad \text{Equation 2.12}$$

Note that when $t = s$ we have:

$$E(\varepsilon_t \varepsilon_s) = E(\varepsilon_t^2)$$

and $E(\varepsilon_t^2)$ is just the variance of $\varepsilon_t$ as $E(\varepsilon_t) = 0$.

Finally, following the above discussion of Equation 2.7, we also assume that, for a given time-period, the disturbance term is independent of $X$. That is, the level of temperature is independent of the random component in $Y$. Therefore, we can write:

$$E(X_t \varepsilon_t) = 0 \quad \text{for all } t$$

Thus in terms of Figure 2.2 the systematic component of the true population relationship between $Y$ and $X$ $(\alpha + \beta X)$ can be interpreted as the line which passes through the means of the distributions associated with the temperature at each time period.

Thus, in summary, the full specification of the simple regression model can be presented as follows:

The model can be expressed as:

$$Y_t = \alpha + \beta X_t + \varepsilon_t \qquad\qquad \text{Equation 2.13}$$

In order to be consistent with our above discussion, and as many of the examples we will discuss in this book will involve time-series data, we will retain time-series notation here. However, we would emphasise that Equation 2.13 is a perfectly general statement, and in particular, is equally applicable for cross-section and time-series models. That is, the $t$ subscripts in Equation 2.13 (and the assumptions which follow) could be replaced by $i$ (and $s$ by $j$ in Assumption (c) below).

The following assumptions are made:

a   $E(\varepsilon_t) = 0$   for all $t$
b   $\mathrm{Var}(\varepsilon_t) = E(\varepsilon_t^2) = \sigma_\varepsilon^2$   for all $t$
c   $E(\varepsilon_t \varepsilon_s) = 0$   for all $t \neq s$
d   $\varepsilon_t$ is normally distributed, and thus we can write:

$$\varepsilon_t \sim N(0, \sigma_\varepsilon^2)$$

e   The independent variable and the disturbance term are independent. That is,

$$E(X_t \varepsilon_t) = 0$$

The assumption of $\varepsilon_t$ being normally distributed (Assumption d) is required for hypothesis testing and estimation purposes when estimating the parameters of the model in Equation 2.13 ($\alpha$ and $\beta$). However for the same reasons as were outlined in Chapter 1, this assumption becomes less important if a relatively large sample is available.

Note also that this full specification of the simple linear regression model has introduced a further parameter in addition to $\alpha$ and $\beta$ – that is, $\sigma_\varepsilon^2$, the variance of the disturbance term. In general we will also require an estimate of this parameter.

It must be emphasised that the specification of the model in Equation 2.13, and the associated assumptions, is the simplest form that this specification can take. Much of the remainder of this book will be concerned with examining the consequences of relaxing some of these assumptions, and developing methods of estimation and inference for the more complex models which result.

We will now go on to discuss methods of estimating $\alpha$, $\beta$ and $\sigma_\varepsilon^2$.

## 2.3   Estimation Methods

We have postulated that the true relationship between $Y$ and $X$ is given by:

$$Y_t = \alpha + \beta X_t + \varepsilon_t \qquad\qquad \text{Equation 2.14}$$

where $\alpha$ and $\beta$ (and $\sigma_\varepsilon^2$) are unknown. Given a set of sample observations on $Y$ and $X$ our problem is to derive a method of estimating $\alpha$, $\beta$ and $\sigma_\varepsilon^2$. Thus we can return to our gas consumption model, and the sample data in Table 2.1 and Figure 2.1, and we can interpret Equation 2.14 as the model which explains the variation in monthly gas consumption $(Y)$ in terms of average monthly temperature $(X)$.

Our objective here is to derive an estimate of the true population relationship which produced the observations in Figure 2.1 – that is, we require an estimate of Equation 2.14. However, as the disturbance term is unpredictable or random, we can only attempt to derive an estimate of the systematic component of this relationship – that is, to derive estimates of $\alpha$ and $\beta$.

Given the sample observations in Figure 2.1, we could interpret the estimate of the true population relationship as the equation which in some sense 'best' fits these data. Let this equation be denoted by:

$$\hat{Y} = \hat{\alpha} + \hat{\beta}X \qquad \text{Equation 2.15}$$

Note that $\hat{Y}$ represents the estimated systematic component of $Y$, and, in general, $\hat{Y}$ will not equal the observed value of $Y$ due to the influence of $\varepsilon$. $\hat{\alpha}$ and $\hat{\beta}$ denote the estimated values of $\alpha$ and $\beta$, respectively.

One method of deriving Equation 2.15 is simply to draw that line in Figure 2.1 which appears to be the line of 'best fit'. We can then geometrically determine $\hat{\alpha}$ and $\hat{\beta}$ and thus obtain Equation 2.15. However the disadvantage of such a method is that it is subjective, and different investigators will tend to have (slightly) different interpretations of what appears to be the line of best fit. Thus we require an objective method of deriving Equation 2.15. The most commonly employed method of obtaining values for $\hat{\alpha}$ and $\hat{\beta}$ is the **method of least squares**.

Consider Figure 2.3 where we have reproduced the data in Figure 2.1 and we have drawn through the data the (as yet to be determined) line of best fit. The equation of this line is denoted by $\hat{Y} = \hat{\alpha} + \hat{\beta}X$.

Now, at any given sample point (time period, $t$, say), an observed (actual) value of $Y_t$ will occur and from the line of best fit an estimated value – $\hat{Y}_t$ – can be derived (given the value of $X_t$). That is:

$$\hat{Y}_t = \hat{\alpha} + \hat{\beta}X_t \qquad \text{Equation 2.16}$$

The difference between $\hat{Y}_t$ and $Y_t$ we will denote by $e_t$, and this can be interpreted as an estimate of $\varepsilon_t$ ($e_t$ will be an estimate as $\hat{\alpha}$ and $\hat{\beta}$ are only estimates of $\alpha$ and $\beta$). Thus we can write:

$$e_t = Y_t - \hat{Y}_t \qquad \text{Equation 2.17}$$

Therefore the actual or observed value of $Y_t$ can be expressed as:

$$Y_t = \hat{\alpha} + \hat{\beta}X_t + e_t \qquad \text{Equation 2.18}$$

In Figure 2.3 we also provide a diagrammatic interpretation of $Y_t$, $\hat{Y}_t$ and $e_t$, for a given value of $X_t$.

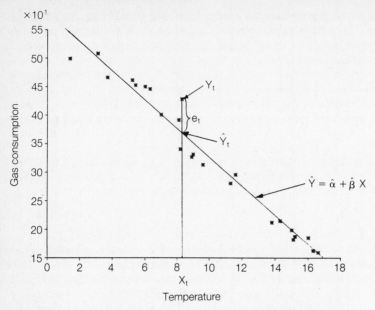

**Figure 2.3** Line of best fit to gas consumption and temperature data.

Define the line of best fit as that line which minimises the dispersion of the observations around the line. A sensible criterion, then, for determining the line of best fit is to derive those values of $\hat{\alpha}$ and $\hat{\beta}$ which ensure that the $e_t$ terms (for all values of $t$) are as small as possible – we require that the $e_t$ terms are minimised in some sense.

First note, however, that the value of $e_t$ can be either positive or negative, depending on whether $Y_t$ is greater than or less than $\hat{Y}_t$. Thus it would not be sensible to minimise the sum of the $e_t$ terms as the positive values will off-set the negative values, given that we must have $\Sigma\, e_t = 0$. Ensuring that $\Sigma\, e_t = 0$ will not, however, define a unique straight line. For example, a straight line which is perpendicular to the observations in Figure 2.3 and passing through the means of $Y$ and $X$ will have the property that $\Sigma\, e_t = 0$. Indeed any line with an even distribution of the $e_t$ terms above and below the line will ensure that $\Sigma\, e_t = 0$, but will not necessarily be the line of best fit.

In order to overcome this problem we could consider the square of each of the $e_t$ terms, thus eliminating the signs of the $e_t$s, and therefore consider the sum of the squared residuals. That is,

$$\Sigma\, e_t^2$$

Thus the least squares estimators of $\alpha$ and $\beta$ – denoted by $\hat{\alpha}$ and $\hat{\beta}$ – are defined as those estimators which minimise the sum of the squared residuals around the fitted line (or the **regression** line). Note that as $\Sigma e_t^2$ is just the numerator in the expression for the variance of the $e_t$ terms (the average of the $e_t$s must be zero, consistent with the assumption that $E(\varepsilon_t) = 0$), then the least squares estimators can be interpreted as those estimators which minimise the variance of the residuals.

Now, we have from Equation 2.18:

$$e_t = Y_t - \hat{\alpha} - \hat{\beta}X_t$$

Therefore

$$e_t^2 = (Y_t - \hat{\alpha} - \hat{\beta}X_t)^2$$

and thus

$$\Sigma e_t^2 = \Sigma (Y_t - \hat{\alpha} - \hat{\beta}X_t)^2 \qquad \text{Equation 2.19}$$

$\Sigma e_t^2$ is generally referred to as the sum of squares (denoted by SS) and thus we require those expressions for $\hat{\alpha}$ and $\hat{\beta}$ which minimise SS. This is a straightforward problem in differential calculus and in Appendix 2.1 we explicitly derive the formulae for $\hat{\alpha}$ and $\hat{\beta}$.

Thus from Appendix 2.1, Equations A2.1.10 and A2.1.6, the least squares estimators of $\alpha$ and $\beta$ can be written as:

$$\hat{\beta} = \frac{\sum_{t=1}^{n}(X_t - \bar{X})(Y_t - \bar{Y})}{\sum_{t=1}^{n}(X_t - \bar{X})^2} \qquad \text{Equation 2.20}$$

and

$$\hat{\alpha} = \bar{Y} - \hat{\beta}\bar{X} \qquad \text{Equation 2.21}$$

Therefore, in order to obtain values for $\hat{\alpha}$ and $\hat{\beta}$ we simply substitute the sample observations into Equations 2.20 and 2.21.

However Equation 2.20 is inconvenient for computational purposes, and in Appendix 2.1 we derive a computationally more convenient expression for $\hat{\beta}$. Thus from Appendix 2.1, Equation A2.1.9, an equivalent expression for $\hat{\beta}$ can be written as:

$$\hat{\beta} = \frac{n\sum Y_t X_t - \sum Y_t \sum X_t}{n\sum X_t^2 - (\sum X_t)^2} \qquad \text{Equation 2.22}$$

Using the sample data in Table 2.1 we can now derive values for $\hat{\alpha}$ and $\hat{\beta}$. From Table 2.1, we have:

$$\sum Y_t = 7901.5, \quad \sum X_t = 235.4$$
$$\sum X_t^2 = 2798.74, \quad \sum Y_t X_t = 65,080.63, \quad n = 24$$

Therefore:

$$\hat{\beta} = \frac{(24)(65,080.63)-(7901.5)(235.4)}{(24)(2798.74)-(235.4)^2}$$

$$= -25.354$$

and from Equation 2.21 we have:

$$\hat{\alpha} = \frac{7901.5}{24} - \frac{(-25.354)(235.4)}{24}$$

$$= 577.910$$

Therefore the estimated relationship between gas consumption and temperature, derived from the data in Table 2.1, can be written as:

$$\hat{Y} = 577.910 - 25.354X \qquad\qquad \text{Equation 2.23}$$

Note the interpretation which can be placed on the estimates of $\alpha$ and $\beta$. The estimate of $\alpha$ (577.910) implies that when average monthly temperature is zero we would predict monthly gas consumption to be 577.91 (million therms, in terms of weekly averages). The estimate of $\beta$ ($-25.354$) implies that when temperature increases by one degree centigrade we would expect gas consumption to fall by an average of 25.354 (million therms, in terms of weekly averages).

Note further how Equation 2.23 can be used for prediction purposes. For example, for a temperature of nine degrees, say, predicted gas consumption would be:

$$\hat{Y} = 577.910 - (25.354)(9)$$

$$= 349.724$$

From Table 2.1 a temperature of nine degrees actually occurred in April 1980, and the associated gas consumption was 331.4. Thus the estimated disturbance term for April 1980 (the fourth observation) is (from Equation 2.17):

$$e_4 = 331.4 - 349.724$$

$$= -18.324$$

For a temperature of 16 degrees, predicted gas consumption would be:

$$\hat{Y} = 577.910 - (25.354)(16)$$

$$= 172.246$$

A temperature of 16 degrees occurred in July 1981, and thus the estimated disturbance term for July 1981 (the nineteenth observation) is:

$$e_{19} = 185.7 - 172.246$$

$$= 13.454$$

Equation 2.23 could of course be used for any given temperature, not only for those which actually occurred during the sample period. However care should be taken in using Equation 2.23 for temperatures which fall outside the range of the sample. Thus for extreme values (very low or very high temperatures) it may be that Equation 2.23 will not produce reliable predictions – the form of the relationship between $Y$ and $X$ for extreme temperatures may differ considerably from the relationship implied by Figure 2.1 and reflected in Equation 2.23.

Note also that by definition the sum of the estimated residuals (the sum of the $e_i$s) will be zero if $\alpha$ and $\beta$ are estimated by Equations 2.20 and 2.21. This is demonstrated in Appendix 2.1. The reader can also confirm this by calculating the residuals for each sample point in Table 2.1 using Equation 2.23, and then summing these residuals.

Although the method of least squares is the most common method of estimation – at least for the simple regression model – it is not the only method. Another method which has certain theoretical advantages over least squares, particularly in more complex models, is the **maximum likelihood method**. We provide a discussion of the principle of maximum likelihood estimation, and the derivation of the maximum likelihood estimators for the simple regression model, in Appendix 2.2. We also show in Appendix 2.2 that for the simplest form of the regression model (the form which we have outlined here), the maximum likelihood estimators of $\alpha$ and $\beta$ are in fact equivalent to the least squares estimators.

At various points in the remainder of this book we will make reference to maximum likelihood estimation but we will not present any rigorous exposition of the methodology involved. The reason for introducing maximum likelihood estimation here is to emphasise that the method of least squares is not the only estimation method available. However for a wide range of applications least squares and maximum likelihood estimation will be equivalent and so detailed discussion of the maximum likelihood approach will not be required. None the less there will be cases where the maximum likelihood approach is superior to that of least squares and we will emphasise these when they arise.

We will now go on to discuss a further application of least squares estimation.

Example 2.1

We have already made brief reference to the theory of the consumption function when introducing the simple regression model above (see Equations 2.2 and 2.4). We will here consider the estimation of a consumption function.

Consider Equation 2.4 again. By adding a disturbance term we derive the full specification of the simple consumption function. That is:

$$C = \alpha + \beta D + \varepsilon$$

Equation 2.24

Now, in Exercise 14 of Chapter 1 we presented a sample of time-series data on personal disposable income and consumers' expenditure in Great Britain from 1956 to 1980. We will use these data to estimate Equation 2.24. Thus we will estimate a time-series consumption function. The explicit form of this relationship is shown in Equation 2.25.

$$C_t = \alpha + \beta D_t + \varepsilon_t$$

Equation 2.25

where the subscript $t$ refers to year $t$.

In Figure 2.4 we present a graph of consumers' expenditure against

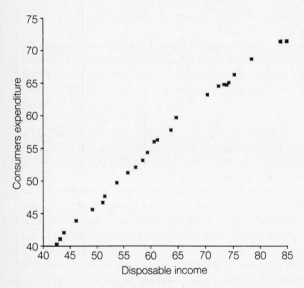

**Figure 2.4** Consumers' expenditure against disposable income.

disposable income, where it can be seen that a very strong and positive linear relationship exists between $C$ and $D$. Thus it would seem sensible to go on to estimate this relationship.

Using Equation 2.22, with $C$ substituted for $Y$ and $D$ substituted for $X$, the least squares estimator of $\beta$ in Equation 2.25 can be written as:

$$\hat{\beta} = \frac{n \sum C_t D_t - \sum C_t \sum D_t}{n \sum D_t^2 - (\sum D_t)^2}$$

Equation 2.26

From the sample data in Exercise 14, Chapter 1, we have:

$$\sum C_t = 1397.86, \quad \sum D_t = 1548.81, \quad \sum D_t^2 = 99{,}862.2789$$
$$\sum C_t D_t = 89{,}571.9504, \quad n = 25$$

Thus substituting in Equation 2.26 we have:

$$\hat{\beta} = \frac{(25)(89{,}571.9504) - (1397.86)(1548.81)}{(25)(99{,}862.2789) - (1548.81)^2}$$

$$= 0.76$$

and from Equation 2.21:

$$\hat{\alpha} = \bar{C} - \hat{\beta}\bar{D}$$

$$= \frac{1397.86}{25} - \frac{(0.76)(1548.81)}{25}$$

$$= 8.83$$

Therefore we can write the least squares estimate of Equation 2.25 as:

$$\hat{C}_t = 8.83 + 0.76 D_t \qquad\qquad \text{Equation 2.27}$$

Note the theoretical interpretation which can be placed on $\alpha$ and $\beta$ in Equation 2.25. $\beta$ is the marginal propensity to consume. From the least squares estimate of the model in Equation 2.27 the resulting estimate of $\beta$ is 0.76, which, as theory would predict, is positive and less than one. The interpretation of this value is that, in aggregate, the economy devotes 76 per cent of any additional income to consumption, the remainder presumably going into savings. Note that it is from $\beta$ that the simple Keynesian multiplier is derived – that is, $1/(1-\beta)$, which from Equation 2.27 would be estimated as 4.17.

The interpretation of $\alpha$ in Equation 2.25 is perhaps not as useful or meaningful as that of $\beta$, since $\alpha$ reflects the level of consumption in the economy when disposable income is zero. Of course no such observation occurs during the sample period used to estimate Equation 2.25, nor an observation anywhere near zero. Thus we should be careful in interpreting the estimate of 8.83 for $\alpha$ in Equation 2.27. It may well be the case that the nature of consumption behaviour in the economy, and hence the features of the consumption function, will be very different at much lower levels of income. Therefore it may not be sensible to conclude that consumption would be 8.83 (£'000m) if income were zero – in the long run if income is zero then consumption expenditure must be zero, although over the short run we might observe a higher level of consumption (via borrowing) than is consistent with the given level of income.

## 2.4   Evaluation of the Estimated Model

So far, in deciding whether a given model might be a reasonable description of reality we have only resorted to an informal inspection of the scatter diagram of the dependent variable against the independent variable, using the sample of data which is available on these variables (Figures 2.1 and 2.4, for example). That is, we have informally concluded whether or not a relationship might be held to exist between the two variables, and whether an assumption of linearity might be reasonable.

However, in general, we will require more formal and precise criteria for assessing the adequacy of a given model, in the same way as in Chapter 1 we assessed in detail the properties of the sample mean, $\bar{X}$, as an estimator of the population mean, $\mu$. In terms of the simple regression model, we wish to assess the estimators, $\hat{\alpha}$ and $\hat{\beta}$, in relation to the conclusions which can be drawn about the unknown population parameters, $\alpha$ and $\beta$.

For example, in terms of our consumption function application in Example 2.1 above, we require a means of assessing how confident we can be in the estimated marginal propensity to consume of 0.76. The value of $\beta$ will have important implications for the effectiveness of certain forms of government policy, and thus it is important to deduce the 'margin of error' which is associated with this estimate.

### 2.4.1   *Hypothesis Testing in the Regression Model*

Simple estimation of some postulated model provides very little information as to how sensible or realistic the model is, or how well the theory underlying the model is reflected in the sample data. Obtaining values for $\hat{\alpha}$ and $\hat{\beta}$ is a purely mechanical process in the sense that any set of sample data can be substituted into the formulae for $\hat{\alpha}$ and $\hat{\beta}$, and values for $\hat{\alpha}$ and $\hat{\beta}$ produced, irrespective of whether or not the variables in the model are theoretically related.

Recall from Section 1.6 that the calculation of a correlation coefficient between two variables provides a measure of the strength of association between the variables. Thus for our gas consumption model the expression for the correlation coefficient between gas consumption and temperature is (see Equation 1.59):

$$r = \frac{n \sum Y_t X_t - \sum Y_t \sum X_t}{\sqrt{[n \sum Y_t^2 - (\sum Y_t)^2][n \sum X_t^2 - (\sum X_t)^2]}} \qquad \text{Equation 2.28}$$

From the sample data in Table 2.1, we have:

$$\sum Y_t = 7901.5, \quad \sum X_t = 235.4, \quad \sum Y_t^2 = 2{,}927{,}577.37,$$
$$\sum X_t^2 = 2798.74, \quad \sum Y_t X_t = 65{,}080.63, \quad n = 24$$

and substitution of these data into Equation 2.28 produces a value for $r$ of $-0.982$. Thus a large and negative correlation coefficient is produced, confirming our informal conclusion of a strong and negative linear relationship between $Y$ and $X$.

However, a correlation coefficient, while certainly an objective measure of the strength of a relationship, must none the less still be interpreted with care. In particular, the size of the sample used to calculate $r$ should be considered before concluding that a strong relationship exists between two variables. For consider the extreme case of only two sample observations being available. Then a correlation coefficient of either one or minus one must necessarily result. Graphically, two sample observations will define a unique straight line, thus implying a 'perfect' linear relationship. However, a sample of two can hardly be used to infer that a perfect linear relationship exists in the population.

Thus, in general, the smaller the sample used to calculate $r$ then the less reliable will $r$ be as a measure of the strength of the overall relationship between the two variables – the smaller the sample the less reliable will $r$ be as a basis for drawing conclusions concerning the strength of the population relationship. Therefore, in the terminology of Chapter 1, we require a statistical test, based on $r$, that will allow inferences to be drawn concerning the significance of the population relationship. However, while such a test can be derived explicitly in terms of $r^1$, the test would be equivalent to determining whether the sample data provide evidence of the slope coefficient, $\beta$, being different from zero. For consider our gas consumption model in Equation 2.8. That is:

$$Y_t = \alpha + \beta X_t + \varepsilon_t \qquad \text{Equation 2.29}$$

Now, if there is no relationship between $Y$ and $X$ then $\beta$ must be zero. If $\beta$ were zero then this would mean that differing levels of $X$ would produce no response in $Y$ and hence that no relationship between $Y$ and $X$ exists.

Thus we wish to establish from the sample data whether there is sufficient evidence to conclude that the actual value of $\beta$ is different from zero.

A formal test of the significance of the relationship between $Y$ and $X$ can therefore be expressed as:

$$H_0: \beta = 0$$

$$H_1: \beta \neq 0$$

A sample of data could then be obtained, and the above null hypothesis tested. The approach here is precisely the same as in Section 1.5, where null hypotheses concerning the value of some unknown population mean, $\mu$, were tested on the basis of a sample of data.

First, then, we require a test statistic (such as the test statistics $Z$ and $T$ in Chapter 1). Now, we have already derived an estimator for $\beta$. Thus we must determine the properties of $\hat{\beta}$ as an estimator of $\beta$, just as $\bar{X}$ was assessed as an estimator of $\mu$ in Chapter 1. As in the case of $\bar{X}$, it is important to recognise that $\hat{\beta}$ is a variable – different samples of data will tend to produce different values for $\hat{\beta}$. In the case of our gas consumption model, were we to use a different sample of 24 monthly observations (say, the 24 observations in 1978 and 1979, rather than the observations in 1980 and 1981), then it is highly probable that the resulting estimate of $\beta$ would differ from the value of $-25.354$ presented in Equation 2.23 (although if the relationship is a stable one then this difference should be small). Therefore $\hat{\beta}$ will have some mean and variance, and if a probability distribution for $\hat{\beta}$ can be deduced then a statistical test can be derived.

Recall that given the regression model

$$Y_t = \alpha + \beta X_t + \varepsilon_t \qquad \text{Equation 2.30}$$

the least squares estimator of $\beta$ can be written as (see Equation 2.20)

$$\hat{\beta} = \frac{\sum (X_t - \bar{X})(Y_t - \bar{Y})}{\sum (X_t - \bar{X})^2} \qquad \text{Equation 2.31}$$

Equation 2.31 can be re-expressed as follows:

$$\hat{\beta} = \frac{\sum [(X_t - \bar{X}) Y_t - \bar{Y}(X_t - \bar{X})]}{\sum (X_t - \bar{X})^2}$$

$$= \frac{\sum (X_t - \bar{X}) Y_t - \bar{Y} \sum (X_t - \bar{X})}{\sum (X_t - \bar{X})^2}$$

By definition we must have $\sum (X_t - \bar{X}) = 0$. That is:

$$\sum (X_t - \bar{X}) = \sum X_t - n\bar{X} = \sum X_t - \sum X_t = 0$$

and therefore $\hat{\beta}$ can be expressed as:

$$\hat{\beta} = \frac{\sum (X_t - \bar{X}) Y_t}{\sum (X_t - \bar{X})^2}$$

or

$$\hat{\beta} = \sum \frac{(X_t - \bar{X})}{\sum (X_t - \bar{X})^2} Y_t \qquad \text{Equation 2.32}$$

If we let

$$W_t = \frac{(X_t - \bar{X})}{\sum (X_t - \bar{X})^2} \qquad \text{Equation 2.33}$$

then $\hat{\beta}$ can be written as:

$$\hat{\beta} = \sum W_t Y_t \qquad \text{Equation 2.34}$$

From Equation 2.34, $\hat{\beta}$ can now be interpreted as a weighted sum of the $Y_t$s, where the weights – the $W_t$ terms – are functions only of the non-stochastic $X_t$s. Thus $W_t$ will also be non-stochastic or fixed, and therefore $\hat{\beta}$ can be seen to be a linear combination of the $Y_t$s – $\hat{\beta}$ is a linear estimator of $\beta$, in the same way that $\bar{X}$ in Chapter 1 is a linear estimator of $\mu$, where in the case of $\bar{X}$ the weights are all equal to $1/n$. That is, $\bar{X}$ can be written as:

$$\bar{X} = \sum \left(\frac{1}{n}\right) X_t$$

As we shall see, the expression for $\hat{\beta}$ in Equation 2.34 allows for a more direct and convenient derivation of the properties of $\hat{\beta}$.

First, consider the $W_t$ terms. The $W_t$s have the two following properties:

$$\sum W_t = 0 \qquad\qquad\qquad \text{Equation 2.35}$$
$$\sum W_t X_t = 1 \qquad\qquad\qquad \text{Equation 2.36}$$

This can be seen as follows:

$$\sum W_t = \sum \frac{(X_t - \bar{X})}{\sum (X_t - \bar{X})^2}$$

$$= \frac{1}{\sum (X_t - \bar{X})^2} \sum (X_t - \bar{X})$$

$$= 0$$

as $\sum (X_t - \bar{X}) = 0$, and

$$\sum W_t X_t = \sum \frac{(X_t - \bar{X})}{\sum (X_t - \bar{X})^2} X_t$$

$$= \frac{1}{\sum (X_t - \bar{X})^2} \sum (X_t - \bar{X}) X_t$$

Consider the term $\sum (X_t - \bar{X}) X_t$. As $\sum (X_t - \bar{X}) = 0$, then we have:

$$\bar{X} \sum (X_t - \bar{X}) = 0$$

thus we can write:

$$\sum (X_t - \bar{X}) X_t = \sum (X_t - \bar{X}) X_t - \bar{X} \sum (X_t - \bar{X})$$
$$= \sum [(X_t - \bar{X}) X_t - \bar{X}(X_t - \bar{X})]$$
$$= \sum [(X_t - \bar{X})(X_t - \bar{X})]$$
$$= \sum (X_t - \bar{X})^2$$

Therefore, we now have:

$$\sum W_t X_t = \frac{1}{\sum (X_t - \bar{X})^2} \sum (X_t - \bar{X})^2$$
$$= 1$$

thus confirming Equation 2.36.

Now, consider again the expression for $\hat{\beta}$ in Equation 2.34. First we have to determine the mean of the distribution of $\hat{\beta}$, and thus establish whether $\hat{\beta}$ is an unbiased estimator of $\beta$. Thus we have:

$$E(\hat{\beta}) = E[\sum W_t Y_t]$$
$$= \sum W_t E(Y_t)$$

as $W_t$ is non-stochastic. However, note that:

$$E(Y_t) = E(\alpha + \beta X_t + \varepsilon_t)$$
$$= \alpha + \beta X_t + E(\varepsilon_t)$$

as we are treating $X_t$ as a constant. By assumption, $E(\varepsilon_t) = 0$, and therefore we can write:

$$E(Y_t) = \alpha + \beta X_t \qquad \text{Equation 2.37}$$

Therefore:

$$E(\hat{\beta}) = \sum W_t(\alpha + \beta X_t)$$

or

$$E(\hat{\beta}) = \alpha \sum W_t + \beta \sum W_t X_t \qquad \text{Equation 2.38}$$

As $\sum W_t = 0$ and $\sum W_t X_t = 1$, then we have:

$$E(\hat{\beta}) = \beta \qquad \text{Equation 2.39}$$

We have therefore established that $\hat{\beta}$ is an unbiased estimator of $\beta$.

Although we are here concentrating on assessing the properties of $\hat{\beta}$, we can also derive the mean of $\hat{\alpha}$. That is, from Appendix 2.1, Equation A2.1.6, the expression for the least squares estimator of $\hat{\alpha}$ is:

$$\hat{\alpha} = \bar{Y} - \hat{\beta}\bar{X} \qquad \text{Equation 2.40}$$

$$\therefore \quad E(\hat{\alpha}) = E(\bar{Y}) - \bar{X}E(\hat{\beta}) \qquad \text{Equation 2.41}$$

Now,

$$E(\bar{Y}) = E\left(\frac{\sum Y_t}{n}\right)$$
$$= \left(\frac{1}{n}\right)E(\sum Y_t)$$

$$= \left(\frac{1}{n}\right) \sum E(Y_t)$$

$$= \left(\frac{1}{n}\right) \sum (\alpha + \beta X_t)$$

$$= \left(\frac{1}{n}\right) \left(\sum \alpha + \beta \sum X_t\right)$$

That is,

$$E(\bar{Y}) = \alpha + \beta \bar{X} \qquad \qquad \text{Equation 2.42}$$

From Equation 2.39 we have $E(\hat{\beta}) = \beta$, and thus Equation 2.41 can be written as:

$$E(\hat{\alpha}) = \alpha + \beta \bar{X} - \beta \bar{X}$$

or

$$E(\hat{\alpha}) = \alpha \qquad \qquad \text{Equation 2.43}$$

Therefore we have established that the least squares estimators of $\alpha$ and $\beta$ – $\hat{\alpha}$ and $\hat{\beta}$ – are both unbiased.

Now consider the derivation of the variance of $\hat{\beta}$.

$$\text{Var}(\hat{\beta}) = \text{Var}\left(\sum W_t Y_t\right)$$

Given that we interpret the sample of observations on $Y$ as having been selected randomly, then we can treat the $Y_t$s as independent and thus we can write:

$$\text{Var}(\hat{\beta}) = \sum \text{Var}(W_t Y_t)$$
$$= \sum W_t^2 \text{Var}(Y_t)$$

(recall the simplifying expressions for variances in Equations 1.38 to 1.40 of Chapter 1).

Also note that we have:

$$\text{Var}(Y_t) = \text{Var}(\alpha + \beta X_t + \varepsilon_t)$$
$$= \text{Var}(\varepsilon_t) \qquad \qquad \text{(see Equation 1.39)}$$

and therefore:

$$\text{Var}(Y_t) = \sigma_\varepsilon^2 \qquad \qquad \text{Equation 2.44}$$

(from Assumption b of the regression model in Equation 2.13). That is, for any given time period, $t$, the only source of variation in $Y_t$ derives from $\varepsilon_t$, and hence the variance of $Y_t$ must equal that of $\varepsilon_t$.

Therefore, we can now write:

$$\text{Var}(\hat{\beta}) = \sum W_t^2 \sigma_\varepsilon^2$$

or

$$\text{Var}(\hat{\beta}) = \sigma_\varepsilon^2 \sum W_t^2 \qquad\qquad \text{Equation 2.45}$$

Consider the term $\sum W_t^2$.

$$\sum W_t^2 = \sum \left( \frac{(X_t - \bar{X})}{\sum (X_t - \bar{X})^2} \right)^2$$

$$= \sum \frac{(X_t - \bar{X})^2}{[\sum (X_t - \bar{X})^2]^2}$$

$$= \frac{1}{[\sum (X_t - \bar{X})^2]^2} \sum (X_t - \bar{X})^2$$

That is,

$$\sum W_t^2 = \frac{1}{\sum (X_t - \bar{X})^2} \qquad\qquad \text{Equation 2.46}$$

Therefore we can write:

$$\text{Var}(\hat{\beta}) = \frac{\sigma_\varepsilon^2}{\sum (X_t - \bar{X})^2} \qquad\qquad \text{Equation 2.47}$$

Similarly it can be shown that:

$$\text{Var}(\hat{\alpha}) = \frac{\sigma_\varepsilon^2 \sum X_t^2}{n \sum (X_t - \bar{X})^2} \qquad\qquad \text{Equation 2.48}$$

(the derivation of $\text{Var}(\hat{\alpha})$ is left as an exercise for the reader).

Thus, in summary, we have established that $\hat{\beta}$ has some distribution with a mean equal to $\beta$ and a variance given by Equation 2.47. Similarly, $\hat{\alpha}$ has a mean of $\alpha$ and a variance given by Equation 2.48. That is,

$$\hat{\beta} \sim D\left( \beta, \frac{\sigma_\varepsilon^2}{\sum (X_t - \bar{X})^2} \right)$$

and

$$\hat{\alpha} \sim D\left( \alpha, \frac{\sigma_\varepsilon^2 \sum X_t^2}{n \sum (X_t - \bar{X})^2} \right)$$

Now, we have established that $\hat{\beta}$ is an unbiased estimator of $\beta$, and unbiasedness is certainly a desirable property for any estimator to possess. However $\hat{\beta}$ is not the only unbiased estimator of $\beta$ that could be derived.

Recall from Equation 2.34 that $\hat{\beta}$ is just a weighted sum of the sample observations on $Y$, where the weights are given by Equation 2.33. In turn, the unbiasedness of $\hat{\beta}$ resulted from the $W_t$s having the properties given by Equations 2.35 and 2.36 (see Equation 2.38). Thus we could derive a different set of weights – different expressions for the $W_t$ terms – and provided that these weights satisfied Equations 2.35 and 2.36 then the resulting estimator of $\beta$ (obtained by substituting these weights into Equation 2.34) would still be unbiased. So why should the least squares estimator ($\hat{\beta}$) – derived from the weights in Equation 2.33 – be preferred to any other unbiased estimators of $\beta$?

The answer is that the least squares estimator can be shown to have the smallest variance amongst the class of all linear and unbiased estimators. That is, $\hat{\beta}$ will be the most precise of all the possible linear and unbiased estimators (the reason that we only consider linear estimators is the purely pragmatic one that linear estimators are much easier to analyse than non-linear estimators, which can take on a wide range of complicated and relatively intractable forms). Thus $\hat{\beta}$ is referred to as the **Best Linear Unbiased Estimator** of $\beta$. That is, $\hat{\beta}$ is that estimator with the smallest variance – it is the Best estimator – of all Linear and Unbiased Estimators. This is generally shortened to defining $\hat{\beta}$ as the **BLUE** of $\beta$.

A proof of this result can be derived by first noting that the general expression for a linear estimator of $\beta$ is given by:

$$\hat{\beta} = \sum W_t Y_t \qquad \text{Equation 2.49}$$

where the $W_t$s can take on any values (in the case of the least squares estimator, the $W_t$s would be given by Equation 2.33). If we require that this linear estimator be unbiased, then the $W_t$s must be selected such that they satisfy Equations 2.35 and 2.36.

The general expression for the variance of a linear estimator of $\beta$ is given by:

$$\text{Var}(\hat{\beta}) = \sigma_\varepsilon^2 \sum W_t^2 \qquad \text{Equation 2.50}$$

which can be deduced from Equation 2.45, and the $W_t$s correspond to the values selected in Equation 2.49. Thus $\text{Var}(\hat{\beta})$ will be minimised when $\sum W_t^2$ is minimised ($\sigma_\varepsilon^2$ is a constant). Thus the problem of deriving the BLUE of $\beta$ can be expressed as follows:

We require the expressions for $W_t$, for $t = 1, 2, \ldots, n$, such that $\sum W_t^2$ is at a minimum, and the constraints $\sum W_t = 0$ and $\sum W_t X_t = 1$ are satisfied.

This is a relatively straightforward problem in differential calculus, although we will not present the details of the derivation here.[2]

The solution to this problem, then, is that the expressions for $W_t$, for $t = 1, 2, \ldots, n$, are simply those given in Equation 2.33, and therefore we can deduce that the least squares estimator of $\beta$ is in fact the BLUE of $\beta$.

We can consider a simple numerical example at least to illustrate this result.

Consider a sample of just four observations, and assume that the observations on $Y$ and $X$ are those given in Table 2.2 below. Four observations are of course far too small a sample to carry out a sensible regression analysis and thus we would emphasise that these data are used here for illustrative purposes only.

**Table 2.2** Hypothetical observations on $Y$ and $X$

| $t$ | $Y$ | $X$ |
|---|---|---|
| 1 | 1 | 1 |
| 2 | 2 | 2 |
| 3 | 3 | 3 |
| 4 | 5 | 3 |

The model relating $Y$ to $X$ can be written as:

$$Y_t = \alpha + \beta X_t + \varepsilon_t \qquad \qquad \text{Equation 2.51}$$

The least squares estimate of $\beta$ can be derived by obtaining the values of the weights as defined in Equation 2.33, and then substituting these into Equation 2.34. That is, from Table 2.2 we have:

$$\sum (X_t - \bar{X})^2 = \sum X_t^2 - n\bar{X}^2$$
$$= 23 - 4(2.25)^2$$
$$= 2.75$$

Thus for $W_1$ we have:

$$W_1 = \frac{1 - 2.25}{2.75} = -0.4545$$

The values for $W_2$, $W_3$ and $W_4$ can be similarly derived, and the reader should confirm that these are equal to $-0.0909$, $0.2727$ and $0.2727$, respectively. Therefore, the value of $\beta$ can now be derived from Equation 2.33. That is:

$$\hat{\beta} = \sum_{t=1}^{4} W_t Y_t$$
$$= (-0.4545)(1) + (-0.0909)(2) + (0.2727)(3) + (0.2727)(5)$$
$$= 1.545$$

(The reader should confirm that the same value is produced by the direct application of Equation 2.22.)

Note also that these values of $W_t$ satisfy Equations 2.35 and 2.36. That is:

$$\sum_{t=1}^{4} W_t = (-0.4545) + (-0.0909) + (0.2727) + (0.2727)$$
$$= 0$$

and

$$\sum_{t=1}^{4} W_t X_t = (-0.4545)(1) + (-0.0909)(2) + (0.2727)(3) + (0.2727)(3)$$
$$= 1 \quad \text{(rounded to three decimal places)}$$

Now consider a second set of (arbitrarily) selected weights which also satisfy Equations 2.35 and 2.36. In particular, let:

$$W'_1 = -0.6, \quad W'_2 = 0.2, \quad W'_3 = 0.2, \quad W'_4 = 0.2$$

These weights clearly sum to zero, and the reader should confirm that the sum of the products of these weights and the $X$ values in Table 2.2 is one. That is, we can define a second unbiased estimator of $\beta$ as:

$$\ddot{\beta} = \sum_{t=1}^{4} W'_t Y_t$$

and substituting the observations on $Y$ from Table 2.2 into this expression produces a value for $\ddot{\beta}$ of 1.4.

Thus we have two possible estimates for $\beta$ (1.545 and 1.4) both of which have been derived from unbiased estimators. However, as $\hat{\beta}$ is the BLUE of $\beta$ we would expect that $\hat{\beta}$ will have the smaller variance of these two estimators. This is straightforward to establish. Thus from Equation 2.50 we have:

$$\text{Var}(\hat{\beta}) = \sigma_\varepsilon^2 \sum W_t^2$$

and for the above derived weights we have:

$$\sum W_t^2 = (-0.4545)^2 + (-0.0909)^2 + (0.2727)^2 + (0.2727)^2$$
$$= 0.364$$

and therefore

$$\text{Var}(\hat{\beta}) = 0.364\sigma_\varepsilon^2$$

In the case of $\ddot{\beta}$ we have:

$$\sum W_t^2 = (-0.6)^2 + (0.2)^2 + (0.2)^2 + (0.2)^2$$
$$= 0.480$$

and therefore:

$$\text{Var}(\ddot{\beta}) = 0.480\sigma_\varepsilon^2$$

That is, we have deduced that $\hat{\beta}$ has a smaller variance than $\ddot{\beta}$, and therefore is to be preferred as an estimator of $\beta$. Thus in the case of the data in Table 2.2 we would select the estimate of 1.545, on the basis that this estimate has been produced by an estimator with a smaller variance. We provide a diagrammatic interpretation of the distributions of $\hat{\beta}$ and $\ddot{\beta}$ in Figure 2.5. The figure emphasises the smaller variance of $\hat{\beta}$ as compared to $\ddot{\beta}$ although both estimators are unbiased. In other words, for any given sample, $\hat{\beta}$ is likely to produce an estimate closer to $\beta$ than is the case with $\ddot{\beta}$ and consequently is to be preferred to $\ddot{\beta}$.

As we indicated above, this result generalises to the conclusion that $\hat{\beta}$ has the smallest variance amongst the class of all linear and unbiased estimators (in

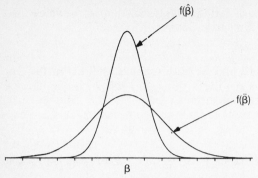

**Figure 2.5** Hypothetical sampling distributions of $\hat{\beta}$ and $\ddot{\beta}$.

terms of the data in Table 2.2, the reader can arbitrarily select other sets of weights which satisfy Equations 2.35 and 2.36 and confirm that in all cases the variance of the resulting estimator will be at least as great as $0.364\sigma_\varepsilon^2$).

Finally, therefore, we wish to establish whether the distribution of $\hat{\beta}$ has some specific form, thereby allowing hypotheses concerning $\beta$ to be tested and interval estimates for $\beta$ to be derived.

Now, our general statement of the simple regression model is:

$$Y_t = \alpha + \beta X_t + \varepsilon_t$$

We have assumed $X_t$ to be a constant, and of course $\alpha$ and $\beta$ are constants (although unknown). Thus the nature of the distribution of $Y_t$ will be entirely determined by the nature of the distribution of $\varepsilon_t$ – by assumption, the only reason that $Y_t$ has a distribution is because of the influence of $\varepsilon_t$.

Recall that Assumption d of the full specification of the regression model in Equation 2.13 is that $\varepsilon_t$ is normally distributed. Therefore if $\varepsilon_t$ is normally distributed, and as the distribution of $Y_t$ is entirely determined by $\varepsilon_t$, then we can (informally) conclude that $Y_t$ must also be normally distributed.[3]

Finally, as we can express $\hat{\beta}$ as a linear function of the $Y_t$s (see Equation 2.34), then $\hat{\beta}$ can be interpreted as just a weighted sum of $n$ normally distributed variables (the $n$ $Y_t$s), and therefore must itself be normally distributed.

Thus we can now fully specify the distribution of $\hat{\beta}$, and we can write:

$$\hat{\beta} \sim N\left(\beta, \frac{\sigma_\varepsilon^2}{\sum (X_t - \bar{X})^2}\right)$$

By the same reasoning, a similar statement can be made for $\hat{\alpha}$ (that is, $\hat{\alpha}$ can also be expressed as a linear function of the $Y_t$s). That is we can write:

$$\hat{\alpha} \sim N\left(\alpha, \frac{\sigma_\varepsilon^2 \sum X_t^2}{n \sum (X_t - \bar{X})^2}\right)$$

However, note that the Central Limit Theorem is also applicable here. That is, we do not have to assume that $\varepsilon_t$ is necessarily normally distributed in order to conclude that $\hat{\alpha}$ and $\hat{\beta}$ are normally distributed. Provided that a reasonably large sample is available then the assumption of normally distributed $\hat{\alpha}$ and $\hat{\beta}$ will be approximately true, irrespective of the distribution of $\varepsilon_t$.

Thus we can now return to our gas consumption model in Equation 2.29, and the problem of deducing from the sample data whether a significant relationship exists between gas consumption and temperature. Recall that this problem could be interpreted as one of deriving a statistical test to determine whether there is any evidence that the slope coefficient, $\beta$, is different from zero – if the sample data do provide evidence that $\beta$ is different from zero then different levels of $X$ will result in different levels of $Y$ and we can therefore conclude that $X$ has a significant influence on $Y$.

However, note here that our gas consumption model would only be theoretically sensible if $\beta$ were negative – that is, if low temperatures lead to high gas consumption, and high temperatures lead to low consumption. Thus *a priori* theoretical analysis would imply only a one-sided alternative hypothesis, and thus our test becomes:

$$H_0: \beta = 0$$

$$H_1: \beta < 0$$

Following the logic of hypothesis testing outlined in Chapter 1, we test the above hypothesis as follows:

We begin by assuming that $H_0$ is true – that is, we assume that $\beta = 0$ (and hence that $X$ does not have a significant influence on $Y$). Thus under $H_0$ $\hat{\beta}$ is normally distributed with a mean of zero. We then calculate the value of $\hat{\beta}$ from the sample data and decide whether this observed value of $\hat{\beta}$ is consistent with the null hypothesis – that is, we decide whether it is likely that the observed value of $\hat{\beta}$ was in fact selected from a distribution with a mean of zero. Figure 2.6 shows the distribution of $\hat{\beta}$ assuming $H_0$ to be true. Assuming

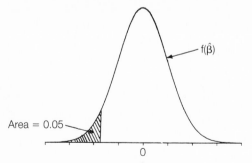

**Figure 2.6**  Distribution of $\hat{\beta}$ under $H_0$.

a significance level of 5 per cent, we also indicate in Figure 2.6 the critical region of the test.

Recall that substituting the data in Table 2.1 into Equation 2.22 produced an estimate for $\beta$ of $-25.354$ (see Equation 2.23). We therefore wish to establish whether this value is significantly different from zero, thereby implying the rejection of the above null hypothesis – that is, does $-25.354$ fall in the critical region of Figure 2.6?

Rather than carry out this test explicitly in terms of the distribution of $\hat{\beta}$ in Figure 2.6, we can adopt the same methodology as in Section 1.5, and carry out the test in terms of the standard normal distribution. Therefore, from the standard normal tables in Appendix I the critical $Z$ value which cuts off an area of 5 per cent in the left-hand tail is $-1.645$. Thus $H_0$ would be rejected here if the standardised value of $\hat{\beta}$ is less than $-1.645$. If we denote the variance of $\hat{\beta}$ by $\mathrm{Var}(\hat{\beta})$, then we can standardise $\hat{\beta}$ as follows (see Equation 1.24 of Chapter 1):

$$Z = \frac{\hat{\beta}-0}{\sqrt{\mathrm{Var}(\hat{\beta})}} = \frac{\hat{\beta}}{\sqrt{\mathrm{Var}(\hat{\beta})}} \sim N(0,1)$$

Thus in order to calculate the observed value of $Z$, and therefore to test $H_0$, we require the value of $\mathrm{Var}(\hat{\beta})$. We derived the expression for $\mathrm{Var}(\hat{\beta})$ in Equation 2.47 above, and thus we have:

$$\mathrm{Var}(\hat{\beta}) = \frac{\sigma_\varepsilon^2}{\sum(X_t - \bar{X})^2}$$

The value of the denominator of this expression can be derived directly from the sample data. However, we do not have a value for $\sigma_\varepsilon^2$, the population variance of the disturbance terms. Therefore this variance will have to be estimated.

In the absence of any other information, the obvious estimator for $\sigma_\varepsilon^2$ is the variance of the estimated disturbance terms – the $e_t$s. Thus, given values of $\hat{\alpha}$ and $\hat{\beta}$, then the corresponding sample of observations on the $e_t$s can be generated by the equation:

$$e_t = Y_t - \hat{\alpha} - \hat{\beta}X_t \qquad\qquad \text{Equation 2.52}$$

(see Equation 2.18). Thus an estimator of $\sigma_\varepsilon^2$ can be written as:

$$\tilde{\sigma}_\varepsilon^2 = \frac{\displaystyle\sum_{t=1}^{n} e_t^2}{n} \qquad\qquad \text{Equation 2.53}$$

(we demonstrate in Appendix 2.1 that if $\hat{\alpha}$ and $\hat{\beta}$ are the least squares estimators then, by definition, the mean of the $e_t$ terms will be zero, and hence that $\sum(e_t - \bar{e})^2 = \sum e_t^2$).

However, it can be shown that $\tilde{\sigma}_\varepsilon^2$ is a biased estimator of $\sigma_\varepsilon^2$, and that the unbiased estimator requires a denominator of $n-2$ in Equation 2.53, rather than $n$ (the reason is exactly analogous to the reason that the expression for $S^2$ in Equation 1.48 requires a denominator of $n-1$ – that is, in deriving the estimated disturbances we require two estimates, $\hat{\alpha}$ and $\hat{\beta}$, and consequently two degrees of freedom are lost).

Therefore an unbiased estimator of $\sigma_\varepsilon^2$ can be written as:

$$\hat{\sigma}_\varepsilon^2 = \frac{\sum\limits_{t=1}^{n} e_t^2}{n-2}$$

or

$$\hat{\sigma}_\varepsilon^2 = \frac{\sum (Y_t - \hat{\alpha} - \hat{\beta} X_t)^2}{n-2} \qquad \text{Equation 2.54}$$

The numerator of Equation 2.54 can be expressed in a computationally more convenient form, and thus it can be shown that:

$$\sum e_t^2 = \sum Y_t^2 - \hat{\alpha} \sum Y_t - \hat{\beta} \sum Y_t X_t \qquad \text{Equation 2.55}$$

and therefore an equivalent expression for $\hat{\sigma}_\varepsilon^2$ is:

$$\hat{\sigma}_\varepsilon^2 = \frac{\sum Y_t^2 - \hat{\alpha} \sum Y_t - \hat{\beta} \sum Y_t X_t}{n-2} \qquad \text{Equation 2.56}$$

We can now finally derive an expression for the estimator of $\text{Var}(\hat{\beta})$. We will denote this estimated variance by $S_{\hat{\beta}}^2$, and therefore we can write:

$$S_{\hat{\beta}}^2 = \frac{\hat{\sigma}_\varepsilon^2}{\sum (X_t - \bar{X})^2} \qquad \text{Equation 2.57}$$

where $\hat{\sigma}_\varepsilon^2$ is given by Equation 2.56.

Thus from the data in Table 2.1 we have:

$$\sum Y_t = 7901.5, \quad \sum X_t = 235.4, \quad \sum Y_t^2 = 2,927,577.37$$

$$\sum X_t^2 = 2798.74, \quad \sum Y_t X_t = 65,080.63, \quad n = 24$$

and recall that $\hat{\alpha} = 577.910$ and $\hat{\beta} = -25.354$.

From Equation 2.56, we have:

$$\hat{\sigma}_\varepsilon^2 = \frac{2,927,577.37 - (577.910)(7901.5) + (25.354)(65,080.63)}{22}$$

$$= 512.536$$

and

$$\sum (X_t - \bar{X})^2 = \sum X_t^2 - n\bar{X}^2$$

$$= 2798.74 - (24)(235.4/24)^2$$

$$= 489.858$$

Therefore we have:

$$S_{\hat{\beta}}^2 = \frac{512.536}{489.858} = 1.046$$

However, note that, just as in Chapter 1, as we have had to estimate $\text{Var}(\hat{\beta})$, then the standard normal distribution is no longer strictly appropriate, and we must use the $t$-distribution. Thus, provided $\varepsilon_t$ is normally distributed, we can deduce that:

$$T = \frac{\hat{\beta} - \beta}{S_{\beta}} \sim t_{n-2}$$

where $S_{\beta}$ is the estimated standard deviation of $\hat{\beta}$ (that is, the square root of the expression in Equation 2.57).

For our gas consumption model $n = 24$, and thus we require the $t$-distribution with 22 degrees of freedom. From Appendix II the critical value for a significance level of 5 per cent is $-1.72$ (rather than the value of $-1.645$ from the standard normal). Therefore, we can now finally test the null hypothesis that the value of $\beta$ is zero. The observed $t$ value is:

$$t_0 = \frac{\hat{\beta} - 0}{S_{\beta}} = \frac{-25.354}{\sqrt{1.046}} = -24.79$$

As this $t_0$ value falls well into the critical region we would conclude that the value of $\hat{\beta}$ is highly significant – the sample data provide very convincing evidence that $\beta$ is different from zero, and that temperature exerts a significant influence on gas consumption.

It is important to emphasise here that the method we have outlined for hypothesis testing in the regression model is derived directly from the methodology in Chapter 1. When encountering hypothesis testing in the context of the regression model for the first time it is very easy to lose sight of the basic methodology involved. The reason is the length and tediousness of some of the calculations which have to be performed. However, in practice, these will be performed by a computer, and for our purposes it is much more important to understand the underlying logic.

Thus, to summarise, recall from Section 1.5 that to test hypotheses concerning the unknown mean, $\mu$, of some population, we derived a test based on the sample mean, $\bar{X}$. Assuming the population to be normally distributed, or by invoking the Central Limit Theorem, we could deduce that $\bar{X}$ is itself normally distributed, with a mean of $\mu$ and a variance of $\sigma^2/n$. Thus given an hypothesised value for $\mu$ we could calculate the corresponding observed $Z$ value ($\bar{X}$ minus $\mu$ divided by the standard deviation of $\bar{X}$, $\sigma/\sqrt{n}$). This value is then compared to the tabulated value from the standard normal distribution, and conclusions drawn concerning the likelihood of $H_0$ being true.

In practice, $\sigma^2$, the population variance will be unknown, and will have to be estimated by $S^2$. In this case the $t$-distribution will have to be used, but in all other respects the approach is identical to the case of $\sigma^2$ being known (although, strictly, we would have to assume that the population is normally distributed).

In the case of the regression model we wish to test hypotheses concerning the value of the unknown slope coefficient, $\beta$. We base the test on the least squares estimator of $\beta$, $\hat{\beta}$. Assuming that $\varepsilon_t$ is normally distributed (or invoking the CLT) we can deduce that $\hat{\beta}$ is normally distributed with a mean of $\beta$ and a variance given by Equation 2.47. Thus given an hypothesised value for $\beta$ we can calculate the corresponding $Z$ value ($\hat{\beta}$ minus $\beta$ divided by the standard deviation of $\hat{\beta}$). In the case of the regression model, however, the specific null hypothesis that $\beta$ equals zero can be interpreted as a test of the significance of the relationship between the dependent and independent variable. This is the hypothesis which, initially at least, is generally tested, although the methodology is perfectly general and can be applied to any hypothesised value of $\beta$.

In practice, Var $(\hat{\beta})$ will be unknown (as the variance of $\varepsilon_t$ will be unknown). Thus an estimate of Var $(\hat{\beta})$ will be required, and the corresponding test is then expressed in terms of the $t$-distribution rather than the standard normal (strictly requiring the assumption that $\varepsilon_t$ is normally distributed). In Equation 2.57 we presented the commonly employed estimator of Var $(\hat{\beta})$, $S_{\hat{\beta}}^2$, and thus the sample data can be used to derive a value for $S_{\hat{\beta}}^2$ (and hence $S_{\hat{\beta}}$) and a value for $t_0$ thereby obtained.

So far we have emphasised the role of hypothesis testing only in the context of the slope parameter, $\beta$. However we can also test hypotheses concerning the intercept term, $\alpha$, in exactly the same way.

We stated previously that $\hat{\alpha}$ can be shown to be an unbiased estimator of $\alpha$, with a variance given by Equation 2.48. Further, we also indicated that $\hat{\alpha}$ can be assumed to be normally distributed, for the same reasons that $\hat{\beta}$ can be assumed to be normally distributed. That is, we can write:

$$\hat{\alpha} \sim N\left(\alpha, \frac{\sigma_\varepsilon^2 \sum X_t^2}{n \sum (X_t - \bar{X})^2}\right)$$

Finally, using $\hat{\sigma}_\varepsilon^2$ as an estimator of $\sigma_\varepsilon^2$, and substituting $\hat{\sigma}_\varepsilon^2$ into Equation 2.48, we derive an estimator of Var $(\hat{\alpha})$, which we can denote by $S_{\hat{\alpha}}^2$. Thus we can deduce that:

$$T = \frac{\hat{\alpha} - \alpha}{S_{\hat{\alpha}}} \sim t_{n-2}$$

Therefore we can carry out hypothesis tests concerning $\alpha$ in the same way as we test hypotheses concerning $\beta$.

For example, for our gas consumption model, we could consider the hypothesis that $\alpha$ is equal to zero. That is:

$$H_0: \alpha = 0$$

Thus the value of $S_{\hat{\alpha}}^2$ can be derived as follows (given the data in Table 2.1):

$$S_{\hat{\alpha}}^2 = \frac{\hat{\sigma}_{\varepsilon}^2 \sum X_t^2}{n \sum (X_t - \bar{X})^2} = \frac{(512.536)(2798.74)}{(24)(489.858)}$$

$$= 122.013$$

From Equation 2.23 we have:

$$\hat{\alpha} = 577.910$$

Thus the observed value of $t$ is:

$$t_0 = \frac{577.910}{\sqrt{122.013}}$$

$$= 52.32$$

Given such a large observed $t$-value we would conclude that there is very strong evidence that $\alpha$ is different from zero. However, in general, hypothesis tests concerning the intercept term will be of only limited interest, and much greater emphasis will be placed on tests concerning $\beta$.

In the context of the gas consumption model the intercept term measures the amount of gas which will be consumed when the temperature is zero. We have concluded that the level of this consumption will be significantly different from zero (and *a priori* we would expect it to be positive). However this is not a particularly interesting result, and there is no reason why a temperature of zero degrees should be singled out for special attention – a temperature of zero degrees is of no more inherent interest than a temperature of five degrees or a temperature of 20 degrees, or any other temperature. So, in general, in the estimation of regression models, tests concerning the intercept term will be of only secondary, if of any, interest, although in some specialised applications the intercept term may have some economic or theoretical interpretation.

Thus we could summarise our estimated gas consumption model as follows:

$$\hat{Y}_t = 577.910 - 25.354X_t \qquad \text{Equation 2.58}$$
$$(11.046) \quad (1.023)$$

where the numbers in brackets are the estimated standard deviations of the corresponding estimators – that is, the square roots of the values of $S_{\hat{\alpha}}^2$ and $S_{\hat{\beta}}^2$ which we derived above (these estimated standard deviations are generally referred to as the **standard errors**). Note that the $t$-statistic associated with each coefficient, for the null hypothesis that the corresponding parameter is zero, is simply obtained by dividing the parameter estimate by its corresponding standard error.

It is also common to present such summary equations with the absolute value of the corresponding *t*-statistics in brackets (the sign of the *t*-statistic must be the same as the sign of the associated parameter estimate). Thus an equivalent version of the summary in Equation 2.58 is:

$$\hat{Y}_t = 577.910 - 25.354X_t \hspace{3cm} \text{Equation 2.59}$$
$$(52.32) \hspace{0.5cm} (24.78)$$

Clearly, Equations 2.58 and 2.59 are equivalent, in the sense that either equation can be derived directly from the other. However, Equation 2.58 provides a more general summary of the regression results, in the sense that the standard errors of the estimators provide for a more direct evaluation of the precision of these estimators, and hence allow for the direct testing of other hypothesised values for the parameters, rather than the zero values which are tested for directly in Equation 2.59. However we will tend to present regression results in the form of Equation 2.59, rather than Equation 2.58, as we will generally be concerned with testing for zero values of the slope coefficients.

### 2.4.2 Interval Estimation in the Regression Model

We have deduced that $\hat{\alpha}$ and $\hat{\beta}$ are normally distributed, and in the previous section we used these results for purposes of hypothesis testing. However, these distributional statements concerning $\hat{\alpha}$ and $\hat{\beta}$ can also be used to derive interval estimates for $\alpha$ and $\beta$.

Thus for the general regression model:

$$Y_t = \alpha + \beta X_t + \varepsilon_t$$

we can write as a direct extension of Equation 1.50 of Chapter 1:

$$P[\hat{\alpha} - t_{\gamma/2, n-2}S_{\hat{\alpha}} < \alpha < \hat{\alpha} + t_{\gamma/2, n-2}S_{\hat{\alpha}}] = 1 - \gamma \hspace{2cm} \text{Equation 2.60}$$

and

$$P[\hat{\beta} - t_{\gamma/2, n-2}S_{\hat{\beta}} < \beta < \hat{\beta} + t_{\gamma/2, n-2}S_{\hat{\beta}}] = 1 - \gamma \hspace{2cm} \text{Equation 2.61}$$

where

$$S_{\hat{\alpha}} = \sqrt{\frac{\hat{\sigma}_\varepsilon^2 \sum X_t^2}{n \sum (X_t - \bar{X})^2}} \hspace{3cm} \text{Equation 2.62}$$

and

$$S_{\hat{\beta}} = \sqrt{\frac{\hat{\sigma}_\varepsilon^2}{\sum (X_t - \bar{X})^2}} \hspace{3cm} \text{Equation 2.63}$$

and $t_{\gamma/2, n-2}$ is the appropriate value from the *t*-distribution with $n-2$ degrees of freedom which ensures that a probability level of $1 - \gamma$ is achieved.

Returning to our gas consumption model, we can now derive interval estimates for $\alpha$ and $\beta$. First consider the slope coefficient, $\beta$. We have already obtained an estimate of the standard error of $\hat{\beta}$. That is:

$$S_{\hat{\beta}} = \sqrt{1.046} = 1.023$$

and for $\gamma = 0.05$ the appropriate value from the $t$-distribution in Appendix II is:

$$t_{22,0.025} = 2.07$$

Therefore given

$$\hat{\beta} = -25.354$$

the 95 per cent interval estimate for $\beta$ can be written as:

$$[-25.354-(2.07)(1.023) \quad \text{to} \quad -25.354+(2.07)(1.023)]$$

or

$$[-27.472 \quad \text{to} \quad -23.236]$$

In other words, a relatively narrow range of possible values for $\beta$ is produced, and we can conclude that we have estimated $\beta$ with a high degree of precision.

Similarly, consider the intercept term, $\alpha$. From the calculations in the previous section, we have:

$$S_{\hat{\alpha}} = \sqrt{122.013} = 11.046$$

and as $\hat{\alpha} = 577.910$ then the 95 per cent interval estimate for $\alpha$ is:

$$[577.910-(2.07)(11.046) \quad \text{to} \quad 577.910+(2.07)(11.046)]$$

or

$$[555.045 \quad \text{to} \quad 600.775]$$

However, for reasons outlined above, the interval estimate for $\alpha$ is only of limited (if any) interest in this application, and we have derived it here purely for illustrative purposes.

### 2.4.3    The Role of Correlation in the Regression Model

We began our discussion of the evaluation of an estimated regression model by briefly discussing the role of the correlation coefficient. Thus we suggested that the correlation coefficient provides an indication of whether a relationship might be held to exist between two variables, and therefore whether it was worthwhile proceeding to estimate this relationship (thereby, in effect, testing the significance of the observed correlation coefficient). We will here present a more detailed discussion of the role of the correlation coefficient, and indicate how it should be interpreted in the overall context of an estimated regression model.

Consider again our gas consumption model. Recall that from Equation

2.28 we derived a value for the correlation coefficient between gas consumption and temperature of $-0.982$. When presenting a correlation coefficient in the context of the associated regression model the normal convention is to present the square of this correlation coefficient. One reason for this is that squaring the correlation coefficient removes the sign of the coefficient (or, specifically, eliminates negative signs), and hence the resulting value can be interpreted as an absolute measure of the strength of the association between two variables (the sign of the relationship will of course be indicated by the sign of the estimated slope coefficient, $\hat{\beta}$). However, as we shall see, considering the square of the correlation coefficient also produces a number of additional interpretations.

The square of the correlation coefficient is referred to as the **coefficient of determination**, and is denoted by $R^2$. Thus for the gas consumption model we have:

$$R^2 = (-0.982)^2 = 0.964$$

When presenting regression results, it is common also to quote the value of $R^2$, in addition to the summary of the estimation results as presented in Equations 2.58 or 2.59. Thus a summary of the estimated gas consumption model could be presented as follows (using Equation 2.59):

$$\hat{Y}_t = 577.910 - 25.354X_t, \quad R^2 = 0.964 \qquad \qquad \text{Equation 2.64}$$
$$(52.32) \quad (24.78)$$

Therefore, we can conclude from Equation 2.64 that temperature exerts a very significant influence on gas consumption, which is indicated by the high $t$-statistic associated with temperature (or, equivalently, from Equation 2.58, the low standard error of $\hat{\beta}$ relative to its observed value). This significant association between gas consumption and temperature is also reflected in the high value of $R^2$. However, we will now consider a somewhat different interpretation of $R^2$.

Our objective in estimating the gas consumption model has been to explain why the level of gas consumption should vary from month to month. We began by postulating that the monthly variation in atmospheric temperature might be expected to be an important determinant of gas consumption.

Now, the variation in gas consumption is reflected in the variance of $Y$, and we could describe the process of model building and estimation as one of explaining this variance. In a sense, the larger is the variance in $Y$, or any dependent variable, then the more interesting and useful is any model which explains this variance – a variable which varies very little is almost by definition uninteresting, and in general, not worth further investigation.

The variance of $Y$ in the sample is:

$$\frac{\sum (Y_t - \bar{Y})^2}{n}$$

and hence for a fixed sample size, $n$, the variance of $Y$ will be directly proportional to $\Sigma (Y_t - \bar{Y})^2$. This expression is referred to as the **total sum of squares** (SST), or

$$SST = \sum (Y_t - \bar{Y})^2 \qquad \text{Equation 2.65}$$

It is this variation – the total variation in $Y$ – that the model seeks to explain.

Now, the estimated model can be written as:

$$Y_t = \hat{\alpha} + \hat{\beta} X_t + e_t \qquad \text{Equation 2.66}$$

where $e_t$ is that component of $Y_t$ which is not explained by the model, or specifically, that component of gas consumption which is not explained by temperature. Clearly, we require that the $e_t$ terms be relatively small if the model is to be a satisfactory one.

The variance of the $e_t$ terms will be directly proportional to

$$\sum (e_t - \bar{e})^2$$

and as $\bar{e} = 0$, by definition, then the variation in the $e_t$ terms will be reflected by:

$$\sum e_t^2$$

This expression is referred to as the **error sum of squares** (SSE) or the **unexplained** sum of squares, and thus we can write:

$$SSE = \sum e_t^2 = \sum (Y_t - \hat{Y}_t)^2 \qquad \text{Equation 2.67}$$

Thus the proportion of the variation in the dependent variable (gas consumption) which is not explained by the model (that is, not explained by the variation in temperature) can be written as:

$$\frac{SSE}{SST} = \frac{\sum (Y_t - \hat{Y}_t)^2}{\sum (Y_t - \bar{Y})^2} \qquad \text{Equation 2.68}$$

Therefore, we can deduce that the proportion of the variation in $Y$ which is explained by $X$ is:

$$1 - \frac{SSE}{SST} = 1 - \frac{\sum (Y_t - \hat{Y}_t)^2}{\sum (Y_t - \bar{Y})^2} \qquad \text{Equation 2.69}$$

Now, it can be shown that the expression in Equation 2.69 is in fact equivalent to $R^2$. That is, $R^2$ can be interpreted as the proportion of the variation in the dependent variable which is explained by the model (or which is explained by the variation in the independent variable).[4] It can also be shown that we can write:

$$\sum (Y_t - \bar{Y})^2 = \sum (\hat{Y}_t - \bar{Y})^2 + \sum (Y_t - \hat{Y}_t)^2 \qquad \text{Equation 2.70}$$

Now, consider the term $\Sigma (\hat{Y}_t - \bar{Y})^2$. $\hat{Y}_t$ is the value of $Y_t$ which is predicted by the model – it is the component of $Y_t$ that can be predicted directly from the corresponding value of $X_t$. Note also that the average value of the $\hat{Y}_t$s is just $\bar{Y}$. That is:

$$\bar{Y} = \frac{\sum Y_t}{n} = \frac{\sum(\hat{\alpha} + \hat{\beta}X_t + e_t)}{n}$$

$$= \frac{n\hat{\alpha} + \hat{\beta}\sum X_t + \sum e_t}{n}$$

or

$$\bar{Y} = \hat{\alpha} + \hat{\beta}\bar{X} \quad \text{as} \quad \sum e_t = 0$$

and

$$\frac{\sum \hat{Y}_t}{n} = \bar{\hat{Y}} = \frac{\sum(\hat{\alpha} + \hat{\beta}X_t)}{n}$$

$$= \frac{n\hat{\alpha} + \hat{\beta}\sum X_t}{n}$$

or

$$\bar{\hat{Y}} = \hat{\alpha} + \hat{\beta}\bar{X} \qquad \text{Equation 2.71}$$

That is

$$\frac{\sum \hat{Y}_t}{n} = \bar{\hat{Y}} = \bar{Y} \qquad \text{Equation 2.72}$$

Thus the term, $\sum(\hat{Y}_t - \bar{Y})^2$, is the variation in the predicted or explained component of $Y_t$, and therefore can be interpreted as that component of the total sum of squares which is explained by the regression, or the **regression sum of squares** (SSR). That is, Equation 2.70 can be written as:

$$\text{SST} = \text{SSR} + \text{SSE} \qquad \text{Equation 2.73}$$

and therefore $R^2$ can be written as:

$$R^2 = 1 - \frac{\text{SSE}}{\text{SST}} = \frac{\text{SST} - \text{SSE}}{\text{SST}} = \frac{\text{SSR}}{\text{SST}} \qquad \text{Equation 2.74}$$

or

$$R^2 = \frac{\sum(\hat{Y}_t - \bar{Y})^2}{\sum(Y_t - \bar{Y})^2} \qquad \text{Equation 2.75}$$

Thus we can see directly from Equation 2.75 that $R^2$ is the proportion of the total variation in the dependent variable which is accounted for by the predicted or explained variation.

(Note also from Equation 2.74 that we can write:

$$R^2 = 1 - \frac{\sum e_t^2}{\sum (Y_t - \bar{Y})^2}$$                    Equation 2.76

which is sometimes a more convenient form for computational purposes.)

Therefore, in terms of the summary of the gas consumption model in Equation 2.64, we can now interpret the value of $R^2$ of 0.964 as indicating that temperature accounts for 96.4 per cent of the variation in gas consumption – that is, not only does temperature exert a significant influence on gas consumption, but it also accounts for most of the variation in gas consumption.

The point here is that there are two broad features of any estimated model which must be examined. First, we need to establish whether the independent variable can be considered to be significant as a determinant of the dependent variable. This is achieved by means of a $t$-test on the slope coefficient. The second issue is the relative importance of the independent variable as a determinant of the dependent variable. This will be reflected in the value of $R^2$. Thus, in practice, when specifying and estimating a model, it can often be the case that a particular independent variable will produce a significant $t$-statistic, but may only exhibit a relatively low correlation with the dependent variable. The conclusion that would be drawn in such cases is that while the given independent variable appears to be a significant determinant, it is perhaps not a particularly important determinant, and further variables should be identified to account for the remaining variation in the dependent variable. We will examine these issues in more detail in Chapter 3, but we can illustrate this point with an example.

Consider the data in Exercise 2 of Chapter 1. Recall that these data related to unemployment rates·across a sample of British towns and cities in both 1971 and 1982. The simplest model which we could postulate is that the 1982 rates are determined by the 1971 rates. That is, while the overall level of unemployment may increase or decrease over time, the regional distribution of unemployment rates is more or less constant. Thus, if we let $UN82_i$ denote the unemployment rate of town/city $i$ in 1982, and $UN71_i$ denote the corresponding rate in 1971, then the postulated model could be written as:

$$UN82 = f(UN71)$$                    Equation 2.77

Assuming a linear model, then we have:

$$UN82_i = \alpha + \beta UN71_i + \varepsilon_i$$                    Equation 2.78

Using the method of least squares to estimate Equation 2.78 produces the following summary of the estimated model (the detailed calculations are left as an exercise for the reader):

$$UN82_i = 6.226 + 1.686UN71_i, \quad R^2 = 0.372$$                    Equation 2.79
$$\quad\quad\quad (4.37) \quad (4.42)$$

The numbers in brackets are the $t$-statistics associated with the respective coefficients.

Note from Equation 2.79 that an $R^2$ of only 0.372 is produced – the 1971 unemployment rates explain only about 37 per cent of the variation in the 1982 rates. However also notice that the $t$-statistic associated with the coefficient on $UN71_i$ is significant (from Appendix II, for $35 - 2 = 33$ degrees of freedom, and for a significance level of 0.025, the tabulated value for $t$ is approximately 2.04). Therefore we would conclude here that UN71 does appear to exert a significant influence on UN82, but much of the variation in UN82 remains unexplained (a similar conclusion could be informally drawn from the graph of these data which was presented in Exercise 16 of Chapter 1). The next step, then, would be to identify additional variables which might be held to influence UN82. This extension of the simple regression model will be the focus of Chapter 3.

We will complete this chapter with two further examples.

Example 2.2

We will continue with our example of estimating a consumption function which we introduced in Example 2.1.

Recall that we estimated a time-series consumption function of the form:

$$C_t = \alpha + \beta D_t + \varepsilon_t \qquad \text{Equation 2.80}$$

and using the data of Exercise 14 of Chapter 1, the resulting estimated equation was given in Equation 2.27 as:

$$\hat{C}_t = 8.83 + 0.76 D_t \qquad \text{Equation 2.81}$$

We can now go on to derive estimates of the variances of $\hat{\alpha}$ and $\hat{\beta}$, and consequently to test the significance of $\alpha$ and $\beta$ in Equation 2.80. Thus we can write:

$$S_{\hat{\alpha}}^2 = \frac{\hat{\sigma}_\varepsilon^2 \sum D_t^2}{n \sum (D_t - \bar{D})^2} \qquad \text{Equation 2.82}$$

and

$$S_{\hat{\beta}}^2 = \frac{\hat{\sigma}_\varepsilon^2}{\sum (D_t - \bar{D})^2} \qquad \text{Equation 2.83}$$

where

$$\hat{\sigma}_\varepsilon^2 = \frac{\sum C_t^2 - \hat{\alpha} \sum C_t - \hat{\beta} \sum C_t D_t}{n - 2} \qquad \text{Equation 2.84}$$

From the sample data (see Example 2.1 and Exercise 14, Chapter 1) we have:

$$\sum C_t = 1397.86, \quad \sum C_t^2 = 80{,}432.8466, \quad \sum D_t = 1548.81$$
$$\sum D_t^2 = 99{,}862.2789, \quad \sum C_t D_t = 89{,}571.9504, \quad n = 25$$

Thus substituting into Equation 2.84 we have:

$$\hat{\sigma}_\varepsilon^2 = \frac{80,432.8466 - (8.83)(1397.86) - (0.76)(89,571.9504)}{23}$$

$$= 0.6548$$

Therefore upon substitution into Equations 2.82 and 2.83 we can write:

$$S_{\hat{\alpha}}^2 = \frac{(0.6548)(99,862.2789)}{(25)(3909.7822)}$$

$$= 0.669$$

and

$$S_{\hat{\beta}}^2 = \frac{0.6548}{3909.7822}$$

$$= 0.000167$$

noting that:

$$\sum (D_t - \bar{D})^2 = \sum D_t^2 - \frac{(\sum D_t)^2}{n}$$

$$= 3909.7822$$

First consider the slope coefficient, $\beta$. The observed value of $t$ corresponding to the null hypothesis that $\beta = 0$ is:

$$t_0 = \frac{0.76}{\sqrt{0.000167}}$$

$$= 58.81$$

Therefore, given such a high $t_0$ value we can very confidently reject $H_0$, and conclude that there appears to be a very significant relationship between $C$ and $D$.

Similarly, for the null hypothesis that $\alpha = 0$, we have:

$$t_0 = \frac{8.83}{\sqrt{0.669}}$$

$$= 10.80$$

Again, given this high value for $t_0$, $H_0$ would be rejected, and we can conclude that the intercept term is different from zero.

Finally, we can calculate the coefficient of determination, $R^2$. Now, we can derive the value of $R^2$ here as we have done previously. That is, we substitute the data into Equation 2.28 to obtain the correlation coefficient and then square the resulting value to obtain $R^2$. However, given the calculations which we made above to test for the significance of $\alpha$ and $\beta$, the value of $R^2$ can be obtained more conveniently.

Recall from Equation 2.76 that $R^2$ can be expressed as (substituting $C$ for $Y$):

$$R^2 = 1 - \frac{\sum e_t^2}{\sum (C_t - \bar{C})^2} \qquad \text{Equation 2.85}$$

Now, $\sum e_t^2$ is simply the numerator of Equation 2.84, and therefore we have:

$$\sum e_t^2 = (n-2)\hat{\sigma}_\varepsilon^2 \qquad \text{Equation 2.86}$$

As $\hat{\sigma}_\varepsilon^2 = 0.6548$ then:

$$\sum e_t^2 = (23)(0.6548) = 15.0604$$

and

$$\sum (C_t - \bar{C})^2 = \sum C_t^2 - \frac{(\sum C_t)^2}{n}$$

$$= 80{,}432.8466 - \frac{(1397.86)^2}{25}$$

$$= 2272.3434$$

Therefore, from Equation 2.85 we can write:

$$R^2 = 1 - \frac{15.0604}{2272.3434}$$

$$= 0.993$$

(The reader can confirm that this is the same value as is produced by the direct application of Equation 2.28, allowing for slight rounding errors.) Therefore we can conclude that $D$ appears to be highly significant as a determinant of $C$, and that $D$ accounts for virtually all of the variation in $C$. The results of the regression analysis can be summarised as follows ($t$-statistics in brackets):

$$\hat{C}_t = 8.83 + 0.76 D_t, \quad R^2 = 0.993 \qquad \text{Equation 2.87}$$
$$(10.80)(58.81)$$

Equation 2.87 would be described as a **well determined** equation – that is, all $t$-statistics are highly significant and the $R^2$ value is very close to one. In other words, it would appear that the parameters of the model – $\alpha$ and $\beta$ – have been very precisely estimated.

While the estimated consumption function in Equation 2.87 certainly appears to be highly satisfactory, at least in pure statistical terms, estimated consumption functions of this form have been found to perform poorly in practice, particularly in terms of forecasting. This can be demonstrated here by using Equation 2.87 to forecast consumption expenditure.

Using this equation to forecast consumption is straightforward. Assume we require a forecast of consumption $k$ periods into the future. If we let $t$ denote the current time period, then we require a forecast of $C_{t+k}$. Given the value of income at period $t+k$, $D_{t+k}$, then the forecast of $C_{t+k}$ is derived by direct substitution into Equation 2.87. That is:

$$\hat{C}_{t+k} = 8.83 + 0.76 D_{t+k} \qquad \text{Equation 2.88}$$

Thus the error made in forecasting consumption at $t+k$ is simply the difference between the actual value of consumption, $C_{t+k}$, and the forecast value, $\hat{C}_{t+k}$. That is, the forecast error can be written as:

$$\text{Forecast Error} = C_{t+k} - \hat{C}_{t+k} \qquad \text{Equation 2.89}$$

Of course, in deriving $\hat{C}_{t+k}$ we first require a value for $D_{t+k}$. In practice, a forecast for income will have to be derived from some source before a forecast for consumption can be obtained from Equation 2.87. However, our purpose here is simply to examine Equation 2.87 with respect to its forecasting performance. Thus to overcome the difficulty of obtaining corresponding forecasts for income we will forecast within the sample period, where the actual values of income are known. Specifically, we will divide the sample period into two sub-periods – an estimation period and a forecast period. We will re-estimate the model over the period 1956 to 1975 (the new estimation period) and then we will treat the remaining five years, 1976 to 1980, as the 'unknown' forecast period. The actual values of income are of course known over this period and thus forecasts of consumption can be derived directly from the re-estimated consumption function. Further, the actual values of consumption are also known over the forecast period and thus we can calculate the forecast errors and hence directly evaluate the forecasting performance of the model.

The re-estimated model, over the 20 years 1956 to 1975, is as follows ($t$-statistics in brackets):

$$C_t = 7.03 + 0.79 D_t, \quad R^2 = 0.995 \qquad \text{Equation 2.90}$$
$$(8.94)(59.20)$$

Thus the broad features of Equation 2.87 are reproduced.

We can now derive the forecasts for the five years 1976 to 1980. Denote these by $\hat{C}_{76}$, $\hat{C}_{77}$, $\hat{C}_{78}$, $\hat{C}_{79}$, $\hat{C}_{80}$. Substituting the levels of income into Equation 2.90, for each of the five years, produces the following forecasts:

$$\hat{C}_{76} = 7.03 + (0.79)(73.36) = 64.98$$

$$\hat{C}_{77} = 7.03 + (0.79)(72.36) = 64.19$$

$$\hat{C}_{78} = 7.03 + (0.79)(78.44) = 69.00$$

$$\hat{C}_{79} = 7.03 + (0.79)(83.73) = 73.18$$

$$\hat{C}_{80} = 7.03 + (0.79)(84.87) = 74.08$$

We can now calculate the forecast errors over the forecast period. However it is more useful to express these errors in relative terms – that is, relative to the actual level of consumption in each year. Thus the forecast error as a percentage of actual consumption can be written as:

$$\frac{C_{t+k} - \hat{C}_{t+k}}{C_{t+k}} \times 100$$

These percentage errors are as follows:

1976: $-0.25$

1977: $\quad 0.60$

1978: $-1.14$

1979: $-2.48$

1980: $-3.68$

Thus we note that, except for 1977, consumption has been over-predicted in all cases, and the forecast errors show a disturbing tendency to increase over time. A graph of the actual and forecast values of consumption, from 1976 to 1980, highlights these features, and is shown in Figure 2.7 (actual consumption is shown as the unbroken line, and asterisks denote the forecasts). We conclude, therefore, that this simple formulation of the consumption function is unsatisfactory, even though it appears to provide an adequate description of a given set of sample data. Once we move outside this given data period, the estimated equation appears to break down.

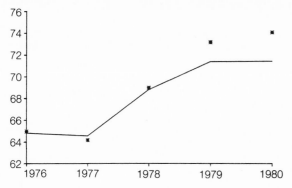

**Figure 2.7** Forecasts of consumption expenditure derived from Equation 2.90, and actual consumption expenditure, 1976 to 1980.

There are a number of reasons why this form of the consumption function is unsatisfactory, and consequently a number of ways in which it can be improved, and we will discuss these at various points in the remainder of this book. However, at this stage we can note that the theory underlying the formulation we have used here is far too simplistic.

The above consumption function implies that in reaching decisions concerning their current consumption expenditure consumers make reference only to current income. However, it would be more realistic to assume that there will be other factors which will be of relevance, such as the role of habit, wealth, expectations about the future and so on. Thus it could be argued that the above consumption function is theoretically inadequate, and this may explain its poor forecasting performance.

## Example 2.3

Consider again the data on profitability in Table 1.1. A very naive hypothesis explaining the variation in these data would be that larger establishments tend to be more profitable, and hence larger establishments will tend to be associated with larger profits per employee. Thus we could postulate that size of establishment influences or determines establishment profitability. Denoting profits by $X$ and turnover by $Z$, the following model could be postulated:

$$X = f(Z)$$

and assuming a linear relationship:

$$X_i = \alpha + \beta Z_i + \varepsilon_i \qquad \text{Equation 2.91}$$

where $i$ denotes the establishment number.

Using annual turnover as a measure of size, we reproduce in Table 2.3 the profits data of Table 1.1, together with the corresponding turnover of each establishment. From the sample data in Table 2.3, we have:

$$\sum X_i = 3.23, \quad \sum Z_i = 212.98, \quad \sum X_i Z_i = 131.955,$$
$$\sum X_i^2 = 182.035, \quad \sum Z_i^2 = 3500.462, \quad n = 30$$

The reader should confirm that using these sample data, the following estimates are produced:

$$\hat{\beta} = 0.055, \quad \hat{\alpha} = -0.282, \quad \hat{\sigma}_\varepsilon^2 = 6.275,$$
$$S_{\hat{\alpha}}^2 = 0.368, \quad S_{\hat{\beta}}^2 = 0.00316, \quad R^2 = 0.033$$

Therefore a summary of the regression equation can be presented as follows (absolute values of $t$-statistics in parentheses):

$$\hat{X}_i = -0.282 + 0.055 Z_i, \quad R^2 = 0.033 \qquad \text{Equation 2.92}$$
$$\phantom{\hat{X}_i = } (0.46) \quad (0.98)$$

**Table 2.3** Pre-tax profits per employee (£'000) and annual turnover (£m) in a sample of 30 UK mechanical engineering establishments 1982

| Establishment number | Profitability | Turnover | Establishment number | Profitability | Turnover |
|---|---|---|---|---|---|
| 1 | 4.94 | 5.00 | 16 | 3.46 | 24.00 |
| 2 | 0.51 | 2.00 | 17 | 2.98 | 14.98 |
| 3 | −0.83 | 0.08 | 18 | 0.71 | 3.59 |
| 4 | 2.83 | 0.85 | 19 | −0.17 | 28.21 |
| 5 | 0.08 | 2.30 | 20 | 2.26 | 34.00 |
| 6 | 0.00 | 3.00 | 21 | 0.70 | 5.61 |
| 7 | 1.17 | 0.08 | 22 | −0.17 | 5.20 |
| 8 | −0.76 | 0.65 | 23 | −0.58 | 6.60 |
| 9 | 2.88 | 8.50 | 24 | −1.09 | 1.67 |
| 10 | −8.91 | 8.00 | 25 | 1.18 | 8.41 |
| 11 | 0.00 | 2.00 | 26 | 0.06 | 4.00 |
| 12 | −0.24 | 4.00 | 27 | −1.00 | 5.50 |
| 13 | −3.83 | 1.86 | 28 | −2.86 | 14.36 |
| 14 | −1.93 | 6.00 | 29 | 0.65 | 7.23 |
| 15 | 1.01 | 2.00 | 30 | 0.18 | 3.30 |

*Source*: As for Table 1.1.

From an inspection of this summary equation (and particularly the very low $t$-statistic associated with $\hat{\beta}$) there is no evidence of a significant linear association between $X$ and $Z$.

In order to examine the possibility of a non-linear relationship between $X$ and $Z$ we present in Figure 2.8 the graph of $X$ against $Z$. From Figure 2.8 it can be seen that no evidence of any non-linear relationship between $X$ and $Z$ is provided. We would therefore conclude that there is no statistical evidence to support the hypothesis of profitability being primarily determined by size.

However, care must be taken in drawing conclusions from such a simple regression analysis. As was the case in the previous example concerning the consumption function, the central issue here is the correct theoretical specification of the relationship between profits and turnover. The model in Equation 2.91 postulates that the only influence on profits is turnover (or size). However, there will be many factors which influence profitability, and therefore Equation 2.91 could be argued to be far too simplistic a representation of reality.

Thus some of the factors which might be expected to influence profits are the nature and age structure of the establishment's capital equipment, the level of investment expenditure undertaken in the past, the establishment's cost structures, the demand conditions faced by the establishment and so on. Therefore such theoretical considerations would lead to a much more detailed and complex relationship than is reflected in Equation 2.91. Indeed,

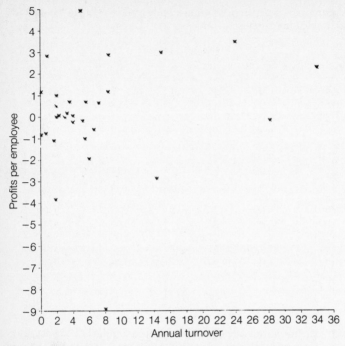

**Figure 2.8** Profitability against turnover from Table 2.3.

once account is taken of all these factors, and any others which might be relevant, it might well be found that establishment size (as reflected in turnover) does in fact exert a significant influence on profitability. These issues will be discussed in more detail in the following chapter, but the point to emphasise here is that a regression analysis is only sensible or meaningful within an appropriate theoretical context. In this respect the above regression analysis is virtually meaningless as there is no theory underlying the model, except at the most naive level. The only conclusion we can draw from this analysis is that size or turnover is not an important or major determinant of profits. However the estimated model cannot be used to conclude that size has no influence – only when all the possible influences on profits have been isolated and accounted for can we then examine the question of the statistical significance of each of these factors.

## 2.5 Summary

In this chapter we have discussed the specification, estimation and evaluation of the simple regression model. In particular, we have outlined the model that is applicable in cases where a given dependent variable can be considered to be influenced by just one independent variable. Further, we have only considered cases in which the relationship between these two variables can be assumed to be linear. The method we described for estimating this model was based on the principle of least squares. The method was derived from the intuitively appealing criterion of minimising the sum of the squared residual terms around the estimated regression line. This method produced estimators for the model parameters, $\alpha$ and $\beta$, namely, $\hat{\alpha}$ and $\hat{\beta}$.

We next considered the properties of the least squares estimators. In particular, we deduced that $\hat{\alpha}$ and $\hat{\beta}$ are the BLUEs of $\alpha$ and $\beta$. Further, we deduced that $\hat{\alpha}$ and $\hat{\beta}$ are normally distributed if the disturbance term, $\varepsilon_t$, is normally distributed, or alternatively, if a sufficiently large sample was available so that the Central Limit Theorem could be invoked. However, as the variance of $\varepsilon_t$, $\sigma_\varepsilon^2$, will generally be unknown and the sample variance, $\hat{\sigma}_\varepsilon^2$, used as an estimator, then the $t$-distribution rather than the normal must be used. The reason is exactly the same as that in Chapter 1, where the use of $S^2$ for $\sigma^2$ implied the application of the $t$-distribution rather than the normal.

Given the distributional statements that could be made about $\hat{\alpha}$ and $\hat{\beta}$, we could then go on to derive interval estimates for $\alpha$ and $\beta$, and to test hypotheses concerning the values of $\alpha$ and $\beta$. However, we noted that a test of the specific hypothesis that $\beta = 0$ was equivalent to testing whether there was a significant relationship between the dependent and independent variable. Therefore the test of this hypothesis is generally the first to be performed once a regression model has been estimated.

We also discussed the role of the correlation coefficient – or, specifically, its square, the coefficient of determination – and interpreted its role as reflecting the proportion of the variation in the dependent variable which is explained by the independent variable. Thus we were able to distinguish between independent variables with high explanatory power and those which possessed only low, but still significant, explanatory power.

Finally, we emphasised the role that economic theory plays, both in the specification and evaluation of a given model. Models which appear satisfactory according to pure statistical criteria can often be found wanting when subjected to theoretical scrutiny. The broad objective of econometric model building is to produce models which satisfy both statistical and theoretical criteria. But, as we shall see as we build on the simple regression model in the remainder of this book, such an objective will often be difficult to achieve in practice.

We will now go on to discuss the obvious extension of the simple regression model – the consideration of the more realistic case of a given dependent variable being influenced by more than one independent variable.

116   *The Simple Regression Model*

## Notes

[1] See, for example, T. H. and R. J. Wonnacott, *Introductory Statistics for Business and Economics*, 3rd edn (New York, Wiley, 1984), pp. 430–2, or P. G. Hoel and R. J. Jessen, *Basic Statistics for Business and Economics*, 3rd edn (New York, Wiley, 1982), pp. 277–8.

[2] See, for example, J. Kmenta, *Elements of Econometrics*, 2nd edn (New York, Macmillan, 1986), pp. 216–20.

[3] It must be emphasised that this derivation of the distribution of $Y_t$ here is very much an informal and intuitive one. Strictly, consideration of the *Jacobian* of the transformation from $\varepsilon_t$ to $Y_t$ is required. In this case the Jacobian is 1, leading to the (deceptively) straightforward transformation from $\varepsilon_t$ to $Y_t$.

[4] See, for example, Kmenta, *Elements of Econometrics*, pp. 237–43.

## References and Further Reading

There are now a wide variety of econometrics texts available, offering treatments of the subject at varying levels of sophistication. Most of these texts will contain a chapter or chapters on the simple regression model (or the two-variable regression model). However, we will not present a comprehensive survey of these texts here, but rather will simply indicate a selected number of texts that we think the reader might find useful.

A very useful introductory text, which uses a minimum of mathematical exposition, is J. Stewart, *Understanding Econometrics*, 2nd edn (London, Hutchinson, 1984). Further texts which offer introductory treatments of the simple regression model are:

Gujarati, D., *Basic Econometrics* (New York, McGraw-Hill, 1978).
Johnston, J., *Econometric Methods*, 3rd edn (New York, McGraw-Hill, 1984).
Kelejian, H. H. and Oates, W. E., *Introduction to Econometrics – Principles and Applications* (New York, Harper and Row, 1981).
Kmenta, J., *Elements of Econometrics*, 2nd edn (New York, Macmillan, 1986).
Koutsoyiannis, A., *Theory of Econometrics*, 2nd edn (London, Macmillan, 1977).
Maddala, G. S., *Econometrics* (New York, McGraw-Hill, 1977).
Pindyck, R. J. and Rubinfeld, D. L., *Econometric Models and Economic Forecasts*, 2nd edn (New York, McGraw-Hill, 1981).
Stewart, M. B. and Wallis, K. F., *Introductory Econometrics* (Oxford, Basil Blackwell, 1981).
Wonnacott, R. J. and Wonnacott, T. H., *Econometrics*, 2nd edn (New York, Wiley, 1979).

## Exercises

### Exercise 1

In Equation 2.4 we specified a linear form of a simple consumption function (and subsequently completed this specification with the addition of a disturbance term). Do you consider the assumption that disposable income (*D*) is a strictly independent variable a reasonable one? Why?

## Exercise 2

Consider the full specification of the simple regression model in Equation 2.13, and the associated Assumptions a to e. In particular, consider Assumption b – that the variance of the disturbance term at all sample points is equal to some constant ($\sigma_\varepsilon^2$). Can you conceive of applications of the simple regression model where such an assumption might not be reasonable? (Hint: This assumption is more likely to be violated in cross-section models than time-series models. Thus you should attempt to think of applications where, for example, it is likely that the variance of the disturbance term increases (or perhaps decreases) as the level of the independent variable increases.)

## Exercise 3

Consider again the full specification of the model in Equation 2.13. Now consider Assumption c – that the disturbance terms are unrelated across sample points. Can you think of any applications where this assumption might be unreasonable? (Hint: In contrast to the previous question, this assumption is more likely to be violated in time-series models. Thus you should consider applications where it is likely that the level of the disturbance term in some given time period – the 'shock' which occurs during that time period – might influence the level of the disturbance term (or the non-systematic component in the dependent variable) in subsequent time periods.)

## Exercise 4

Consider Exercise 15 of Chapter 1, where a graph of the new car registration data of Exercise 1 against the personal disposable income data of Exercise 14 was presented. Denote new car registrations in year *t* by $R_t$ and personal disposable income in year *t* by $D_t$. Specify the linear model which explains *R* in terms of *D*. How reasonable, theoretically, do you consider this model to be?

## Exercise 5

Consider the sterling exchange rate data of Exercise 3 of Chapter 1, and the unemployment data of Exercise 17. Denote the exchange rate in year *t* by $E_t$, the UK unemployment rate in year *t* by $UK_t$, the US unemployment rate by $US_t$, and the UK unemployment rate relative to the US unemployment rate by $RU_t$.

(a) Specify the linear model which explains *E* in terms of UK.
(b) Specify the linear model which explains *E* in terms of US.
(c) Specify the linear model which explains *E* in terms of RU.
(d) Theoretically evaluate these models.

Exercise 6

Derive Equation 2.48. (Hint: We have:

$$\hat{\alpha} = \bar{Y} - \hat{\beta}\bar{X}$$

Substituting Equation 2.34 we can write:

$$\hat{\alpha} = \bar{Y} - \bar{X}\sum W_t Y_t$$

or

$$\hat{\alpha} = (1/n)\sum Y_t - \bar{X}\sum W_t Y_t$$
$$= \sum (1/n - \bar{X}W_t) Y_t$$

Now use Equation 1.38, recalling the properties of $W_t$ in Equations 2.35 and 2.36, and simplify to the expression in Equation 2.48.)

Exercise 7

Use the data in Exercise 2 of Chapter 1 to derive the least squares estimate of Equation 2.78, as shown in Equation 2.79. Use the following summary data:

$$\sum \text{UN82}_i = 426.0, \quad \sum \text{UN71}_i = 123.4,$$
$$\sum \text{UN82}_i^2 = 5578.62, \quad \sum \text{UN71}_i^2 = 486.50,$$
$$\sum (\text{UN71}_i)(\text{UN82}_i) = 1588.67, \quad n = 35$$

Exercise 8

Estimate and evaluate the car registration model which you specified in Exercise 4 above. Use the following summary data:

$$\sum R_t = 2278.6, \quad \sum D_t = 1548.81, \quad \sum R_t^2 = 230{,}084.68,$$
$$\sum D_t^2 = 99{,}862.2789, \quad \sum R_t D_t = 149{,}686.437, \quad n = 25$$

In the light of your estimated model, discuss your original specification of the model. How satisfactory do you consider this model to be?

Exercise 9

The following estimated equations refer to the three versions of the exchange rate model specified in Exercise 5 above ($t$-statistics in brackets):

(a)  $\hat{E}_t = 2.865 - 0.108\text{UK}_t, \quad R^2 = 0.779$
     (48.91)  (9.56)

(b)  $\hat{E}_t = 3.382 - 0.164\text{US}_t, \quad R^2 = 0.439$
     (15.43)  (4.51)

(c)  $\hat{E}_t = 3.069 - 0.991\text{RU}_t, \quad R^2 = 0.777$
     (40.02)  (9.52)

Comment on these estimated models.

**Appendix 2.1** *The Derivation of the Least Squares Estimators of α and β in the Simple Regression Model*

Consider the model:

$$Y_t = \alpha + \beta X_t + \varepsilon_t \qquad\qquad \text{Equation A2.1.1}$$

Let $\hat{\alpha}$ and $\hat{\beta}$ denote the least squares estimators of $\alpha$ and $\beta$ in Equation A2.1.1. Thus we can write:

$$Y_t = \hat{\alpha} + \hat{\beta} X_t + e_t \qquad\qquad \text{Equation A2.1.2}$$

and therefore:

$$SS = \sum e_t^2 = \sum (Y_t - \hat{\alpha} - \hat{\beta} X_t)^2 \qquad\qquad \text{Equation A2.1.3}$$

In order to derive the expressions for $\hat{\alpha}$ and $\hat{\beta}$ which minimise SS in Equation A2.1.3, we partially differentiate SS with respect to each of $\hat{\alpha}$ and $\hat{\beta}$, and set the resulting equations to zero. The following equations are therefore produced (upon simplification):

$$\frac{\partial SS}{\partial \hat{\alpha}} = \sum Y_t - n\hat{\alpha} - \hat{\beta} \sum X_t = 0 \qquad\qquad \text{Equation A2.1.4}$$

and

$$\frac{\partial SS}{\partial \hat{\beta}} = \sum Y_t X_t - \hat{\alpha} \sum X_t - \hat{\beta} \sum X_t^2 = 0 \qquad\qquad \text{Equation A2.1.5}$$

Equations A2.1.4 and A2.1.5 are referred to as the **normal** equations. Solving for $\hat{\alpha}$ in Equation A2.1.4 we can write:

$$\hat{\alpha} = \frac{\sum Y_t}{n} - \hat{\beta} \frac{\sum X_t}{n} = \bar{Y} - \hat{\beta}\bar{X} \qquad\qquad \text{Equation A2.1.6}$$

Substituting Equation A2.1.6 into Equation A2.1.5 we have:

$$\sum Y_t X_t - (\bar{Y} - \hat{\beta}\bar{X}) \sum X_t - \hat{\beta} \sum X_t^2 = 0 \qquad\qquad \text{Equation A2.1.7}$$

and solving Equation A2.1.7 for $\hat{\beta}$ we have:

$$\hat{\beta} = \frac{\bar{Y} \sum X_t - \sum Y_t X_t}{\bar{X} \sum X_t - \sum X_t^2} \qquad\qquad \text{Equation A2.1.8}$$

Equation A2.1.8 can be expressed in a number of forms. Multiplying the numerator and the denominator by $-n$ produces the following expression, which is particularly useful for computational purposes:

$$\hat{\beta} = \frac{n \sum Y_t X_t - \sum Y_t \sum X_t}{n \sum X_t^2 - (\sum X_t)^2} \qquad\qquad \text{Equation A2.1.9}$$

Dividing the numerator and the denominator of Equation A2.1.9 by $n$ we have:

$$\hat{\beta} = \frac{\sum Y_t X_t - \frac{1}{n} \sum Y_t \sum X_t}{\sum X_t^2 - \frac{1}{n}(\sum X_t)^2}$$

$$= \frac{\sum Y_t X_t - n\bar{Y}\bar{X}}{\sum X_t^2 - n\bar{X}^2}$$

$$= \frac{\sum (Y_t - \bar{Y})(X_t - \bar{X})}{\sum (X_t - \bar{X})^2} \qquad \text{Equation A2.1.10}$$

noting that:

$$\sum (Y_t - \bar{Y})(X_t - \bar{X}) = \sum Y_t X_t - \bar{X} \sum Y_t - \bar{Y} \sum X_t + n\bar{Y}\bar{X}$$

$$= \sum Y_t X_t - n\bar{Y}\bar{X} - n\bar{Y}\bar{X} + n\bar{Y}\bar{X}$$

$$= \sum Y_t X_t - n\bar{Y}\bar{X}$$

and from Equation 1.5 of Chapter 1:

$$\sum (X_t - \bar{X})^2 = \sum X_t^2 - n\bar{X}^2$$

Equation A2.1.10 is in a convenient form for establishing the properties of the least squares estimators.

It is straightforward to establish that $\hat{\alpha}$ and $\hat{\beta}$ minimise rather than maximise SS (this can be established via the consideration of the appropriate second order conditions). Note, also, that given the expressions for $\hat{\alpha}$ and $\hat{\beta}$ we must have $\sum e_t = 0$, by definition. That is:

$$\sum e_t = \sum (Y_t - \hat{\alpha} - \hat{\beta}X_t)$$

$$= \sum Y_t - n\hat{\alpha} - \hat{\beta} \sum X_t$$

$$= \sum Y_t - n(\bar{Y} - \hat{\beta}\bar{X}) - \hat{\beta} \sum X_t$$

$$= \sum Y_t - n\bar{Y} + \hat{\beta}n\bar{X} - \hat{\beta} \sum X_t$$

$$= \sum Y_t - \sum Y_t + \hat{\beta} \sum X_t - \hat{\beta} \sum X_t$$

$$= 0$$

**Appendix 2.2**   *The Derivation of the Maximum Likelihood Estimators of the Parameters of the Simple Regression Model*

In order to use the maximum likelihood principle we require the assumption that $\varepsilon_t$ is normally distributed (note that this assumption was not required for the derivation of the least squares estimators). Consider the simple regression model:

$$Y_t = \alpha + \beta X_t + \varepsilon_t \qquad \qquad \text{Equation A2.2.1}$$

Now, as $\alpha$ and $\beta$ are constants, and $X_t$ is assumed to be non-stochastic (and thus is also a constant) the nature of the distribution of $Y_t$ will be entirely determined by the nature of the distribution of $\varepsilon_t$. Thus if $\varepsilon_t$ is normally distributed, then so must $Y_t$ be (although see Note 3).

The mean and variance of $Y_t$ can be derived as follows:

$$\begin{aligned} E(Y_t) &= E(\alpha + \beta X_t + \varepsilon_t) \\ &= \alpha + \beta X_t + E(\varepsilon_t) \\ &= \alpha + \beta X_t \end{aligned}$$

and

$$\text{Var}(Y_t) = \sigma_\varepsilon^2$$

from Equation 2.44. Therefore we can conclude that $Y_t$ has a normal distribution with a mean of $\alpha + \beta X_t$ and a variance of $\sigma_\varepsilon^2$. That is, we can write:

$$Y_t \sim N(\alpha + \beta X_t, \sigma_\varepsilon^2)$$

Using Equation 1.17 of Chapter 1, the full mathematical representation of the p.d.f. of $Y_t$ can be written as:

$$f(Y_t) = (\sqrt{2\pi\sigma_\varepsilon^2})^{-1} e^{-(Y_t - \alpha - \beta X_t)^2 / 2\sigma_\varepsilon^2} \qquad \qquad \text{Equation A2.2.2}$$

Now consider the random sample of the $n$ $Y_t$s. That is:

$$Y_1, Y_2, \ldots, Y_n$$

The **likelihood function** of the $Y_t$s (or the likelihood function of the sample) is defined as:

$$l = f(Y_1, Y_2, \ldots, Y_n)$$

An informal interpretation of this expression is that it represents the probability of selecting a sample consisting of the $n$ $Y_t$s – that is, the probability of selecting a sample consisting of $Y_1$ and $Y_2$ and ... and $Y_n$. As the sample is selected randomly then the $Y_t$s are independent and the likelihood function can be written as:

$$l = f(Y_1)f(Y_2)\ldots f(Y_n)$$

(see Equation 1.33 of Chapter 1 for an interpretation in terms of discrete variables). That is, using Equation A2.2.2 we can write:

$$l = (\sqrt{2\pi\sigma_\varepsilon^2})^{-1} e^{-(Y_1 - \alpha - \beta X_1)^2 / 2\sigma_\varepsilon^2} \ldots (\sqrt{2\pi\sigma_\varepsilon^2})^{-1} e^{-(Y_n - \alpha - \beta X_n)^2 / 2\sigma_\varepsilon^2}$$

or

$$l = (\sqrt{2\pi\sigma_\varepsilon^2})^{-n} e^{-(1/2\sigma_\varepsilon^2)\sum(Y_t - \alpha - \beta X_t)^2} \qquad \text{Equation A2.2.3}$$

The maximum likelihood approach to estimating $\alpha$ and $\beta$ (and $\sigma_\varepsilon^2$) is to derive expressions for these parameters which maximise the likelihood function of the $Y_t$s in Equation A2.2.3. An informal and intuitive justification for this approach is that the resulting estimates of $\alpha$, $\beta$ and $\sigma_\varepsilon^2$ can be interpreted as the most likely values of these parameters which generated the given sample of $Y_t$s. That is, Equation A2.2.3 could be considered to represent the joint probability of the $n$ $Y_t$s having been selected – the probability of selecting the entire sample – and the values of $\alpha$, $\beta$ and $\sigma_\varepsilon^2$ which maximise this probability are therefore the most likely values of these parameters in the population from which the sample was selected.

In order to obtain the maximum likelihood estimators of $\alpha$, $\beta$ and $\sigma_\varepsilon^2$ we maximise Equation A2.2.3 with respect to $\alpha$, $\beta$ and $\sigma_\varepsilon^2$. This is a straightforward problem in differential calculus.

Now, it can be shown that the values of $\alpha$, $\beta$ (and $\sigma_\varepsilon^2$) which maximise the expression in Equation A2.2.3 are the same as those which maximise the logarithm of this expression – the logarithm of Equation A2.2.3 being a more convenient expression to manipulate. Thus we can write the logarithm of Equation A2.2.3 as:

$$L = -n/2 \ln(2\pi\sigma_\varepsilon^2) - 1/(2\sigma_\varepsilon^2)\sum(Y_t - \alpha - \beta X_t)^2 \qquad \text{Equation A2.2.4}$$

Let the maximum likelihood estimators be denoted by $\tilde{\alpha}$, $\tilde{\beta}$ and $\tilde{\sigma}_\varepsilon^2$. Then, we have:

$$\frac{\partial L}{\partial \tilde{\alpha}} = -1/(\tilde{\sigma}_\varepsilon^2)\sum(Y_t - \tilde{\alpha} - \tilde{\beta} X_t)(-1) = 0 \qquad \text{Equation A2.2.5}$$

$$\frac{\partial L}{\partial \tilde{\beta}} = -1/(\tilde{\sigma}_\varepsilon^2)\sum(Y_t - \tilde{\alpha} - \tilde{\beta} X_t)(-X_t) = 0 \qquad \text{Equation A2.2.6}$$

$$\frac{\partial L}{\partial \tilde{\sigma}_\varepsilon^2} = -n/(2\tilde{\sigma}_\varepsilon^2) + 1/2(\tilde{\sigma}_\varepsilon^2)^2 \sum(Y_t - \tilde{\alpha} - \tilde{\beta} X_t)^2 = 0 \qquad \text{Equation A2.2.7}$$

Multiplying Equations A2.2.5 and A2.2.6 by $\tilde{\sigma}_\varepsilon^2$ produces the same equations as in the derivation of the least squares estimators and thus we must have:

$$\tilde{\alpha} = \hat{\alpha}$$

and

$$\tilde{\beta} = \hat{\beta}$$

Solving Equation A2.2.7 for $\tilde{\sigma}_\varepsilon^2$ gives:

$$\tilde{\sigma}_\varepsilon^2 = \frac{\sum (Y_t - \tilde{\alpha} - \tilde{\beta} X_t)^2}{n}$$

$$= \frac{\sum (Y_t - \hat{\alpha} - \hat{\beta} X_t)^2}{n}$$

$$= \frac{\sum e_t^2}{n}$$

However, $\tilde{\sigma}_\varepsilon^2$ is a biased estimator of $\sigma_\varepsilon^2$, and the expression for the unbiased estimator is given in Equation 2.54 (and Equation 2.56).

The reader requiring a more rigorous exposition of maximum likelihood estimation is referred to any mathematical statistics text. For example, see A. M. Mood, F. A. Graybill and D. C. Boes, *Introduction to the Theory of Statistics*, 3rd edn (New York, McGraw-Hill, 1974), pp. 276–86.

# 3 The Multiple Regression Model

## 3.1 Introduction

In this chapter we will relax the assumption of just a single independent variable, and discuss the more general model which allows for the joint influence of a number of independent variables. It is this model – the multiple regression model – which provides a more realistic context for model building and hypothesis testing in economics. However, we will still retain the assumption of linear relationships between the dependent and independent variables, and leave to the following chapter the consideration of non-linearities.

As we shall see, in theory, the multiple regression model is a straightforward extension of the simple regression model, with the methods of estimation and hypothesis testing being identical in both cases. However, in practice, the interpretation of estimated multiple regression models can cause difficulties, due to what is referred to as the problem of **multicollinearity**. That is, it will often be difficult to separate out and quantify the individual influences of each of the independent variables.

We will complete this chapter with a discussion of the use of computer packages for estimating regression models. These are now widely available and, in general, easy to use, and free the investigator from having to perform the tedious and laborious calculations involved in estimation. Therefore, they allow the investigator to concentrate on the more difficult and important tasks of model specification and interpretation.

## 3.2 Model Specification

The multiple regression model can be specified in an analogous manner to the specification of the simple regression model in Equation 2.13. Thus instead of one independent variable, we assume that $K$ independent variables influence the dependent variable, $Y$. Formally, the model can be written as follows:

$$Y_t = \beta_0 + \beta_1 X_{1t} + \beta_2 X_{2t} + \ldots + \beta_K X_{Kt} + \varepsilon_t \qquad \text{Equation 3.1}$$

Thus there are $K+1$ parameters to be estimated, $\beta_0, \beta_1, \ldots, \beta_K$.

Econometrics texts vary in the notation used for the number of independent variables in the multiple regression model. The model is often specified as containing $K$ coefficients, and therefore, notationally, two forms of the model could be presented. That is, either:

$$Y_t = \beta_0 + \beta_1 X_{1t} + \beta_2 X_{2t} + \ldots + \beta_{K-1} X_{(K-1)t} + \varepsilon_t$$

or

$$Y_t = \beta_1 + \beta_2 X_{2t} + \beta_3 X_{3t} + \ldots + \beta_K X_{Kt} + \varepsilon_t$$

However, we prefer to describe the general form of the model as containing $K$ independent variables, therefore requiring the estimating of $K+1$ coefficients (including the constant term).

The assumptions concerning the disturbance term, $\varepsilon$, in Equation 3.1, are the same as in the case of the simple regression model. That is:

a  $E(\varepsilon_t) = 0$  for all $t$.
b  $\text{Var}(\varepsilon_t) = E(\varepsilon_t^2) = \sigma_\varepsilon^2$  for all $t$.
c  $E(\varepsilon_t \varepsilon_s) = 0$  for all $t \neq s$.
d  $\varepsilon_t$ is normally distributed.
e  Each of the independent variables and the disturbance term is independent. That is,

$$E(X_{kt} \varepsilon_t) = 0 \quad \text{for } k = 1, 2, \ldots, K$$

In the simplest form of the multiple regression model the independent variables are generally assumed to be non-stochastic, thus ensuring that this assumption is satisfied.

Finally, there are two further assumptions which are required in order to ensure that Equation 3.1 can be estimated. That is:

f  The number of observations used to estimate the model ($n$) exceeds the number of parameters (the $\beta$s).
g  No exact linear relationship exists between any of the independent variables.

Assumption f ensures that the regression actually 'explains' some of the variation in $Y$. The analogous assumption in the case of the simple regression model of Chapter 2 is that more than two observations are available on $X$ and $Y$. Clearly, if just two observations are used to estimate a simple regression model then the regression line would 'fit' the data exactly – an $R^2$ value of 1 must necessarily result. However, using just two observations on $X$ and $Y$

would hardly be a firm basis for inferring that $X$ explains all of the variation in $Y$.

Thus in the case of the multiple regression model a perfect 'fit' can always be achieved if exactly $K+1$ observations are used to estimate Equation 3.1. Thus, for some given value of $R^2$, the larger the number of observations relative to the number of parameters in the model, the greater explanatory power the model can be interpreted as having.

Assumption g ensures that a regression line can actually be calculated. In pure statistical terms, if an exact linear relationship exists between any two (or more) of the independent variables then only one of these need be included in order to take account of their joint variation. In practice, it will rarely be the case that any of the independent variables are perfectly correlated. Typically, the problem is one of a high degree of correlation amongst the independent variables which may cause difficulties in interpreting the estimated model, even though a regression line can still be calculated. This problem, as noted earlier, is that of multicollinearity, and will be discussed in more detail in Section 3.5 below.

Thus apart from the inclusion of extra explanatory variables, the interpretation of the multiple regression model is exactly the same as that of the simple regression model outlined in Chapter 2.

Before proceeding to discuss how the parameters in Equation 3.1 might be estimated, it is useful to draw a distinction between the interpretation of the multiple regression model in the social sciences and its interpretation in the natural or laboratory-based sciences. In order to be concrete, we will place the discussion in the context of our gas consumption model of Chapter 2. However, we will extend this model to allow for the influence of an additional explanatory variable, namely the price of gas relative to the price of electricity. Thus, it could be argued, a decrease in the price of gas relative to that of electricity will induce a substitution of gas for electricity, and therefore increase the consumption of gas (and vice versa).

If we let $X_{1t}$ denote temperature in time period $t$, and $X_{2t}$ denote the price of gas relative to that of electricity in period $t$, then our simple model in Equation 2.8 can now be written as:

$$Y_t = \beta_0 + \beta_1 X_{1t} + \beta_2 X_{2t} + \varepsilon_t \qquad \text{Equation 3.2}$$

Note that Equation 3.2 can be interpreted as a model which purports to explain the longer term variation in gas consumption, given that the substitution of one form of energy for another can presumably only occur over a longer time period.

Now, the objective of the multiple regression model is to measure the separate influence of each of a number of independent variables which are held to influence the dependent variable simultaneously. Thus in terms of the model in Equation 3.2, $\beta_1$ measures the influence of temperature on gas consumption, over and above the influence exerted by price. Similarly, $\beta_2$

measures the influence of price on consumption, having taken account of the influence of temperature. Ideally, if laboratory conditions were available, an estimate of $\beta_1$ would be derived by first holding price constant, and then observing the response of gas consumption to variations in the level of temperature – that is, assuming Equation 3.2 to be the correct model, if price is held constant then any variation in gas consumption which occurs must be a result only of variations in temperature (and a disturbance term). Similarly, an estimate of $\beta_2$ would be obtained by holding temperature constant, and then observing the response of gas consumption to variations in price.

In other words, under laboratory conditions there would be no need to estimate a multiple regression model. The separate influence of each of the independent variables would be measured by performing a series of simple regressions, of the dependent variable on each of the independent variables, ensuring that in each case the levels of the remaining independent variables were held constant.

In the social sciences, however, laboratory conditions are rarely available and thus the multiple regression model can be interpreted in this sense as a 'second-best' solution – the objective is still to measure the separate influence of each of the independent variables, but given that these variables will vary simultaneously (and hence will tend to be correlated) it will often be difficult to disentangle their separate influences.

In terms of estimating $\beta_1$ and $\beta_2$ in Equation 3.2, it is perhaps possible to conceive of methods for holding each of the independent variables constant, and thus being able to perform two separate simple regressions. Indeed this is precisely what was attempted in Chapter 2 when estimating the gas consumption model – the length of the sample period was sufficiently short so as to ensure that relative prices were unlikely to have shown much variation (and/or, given that time lags are involved in switching between alternative forms of energy, little switching behaviour would have taken place in any event).

Next, in order to examine the influence of price on consumption, we require a set of observations over which temperature is constant. Thus we could select months in which the same average temperature obtained, and then observe the response of consumption to the price variations which occurred over these months. Clearly, in order to build up an acceptable sample size, observations would have to be selected from a period extending over considerably longer than two years. Alternatively, we could use annual observations (arguing that temperature variations cancel out during the year and thus we would not expect a temperature effect to be present in annual data). If annual data were used then we would require a period of 20 or 30 years in order to generate sufficient observations. However, irrespective of the length of the sample period, we must still assume that the observed variation in gas consumption results solely from price variation (and the effect of a disturbance term). But it may be difficult to justify such a *ceteris paribus* assumption given a sample period as long as 20 or 30 years (whether the data be monthly observations with some fixed temperature, or annual observations). That is, there are a range of additional factors which might be expected to influence gas consumption, over and above price variation, over such an extended sample period.

For example, we must consider the supply-side and determine the extent to which gas was as widely available at the beginning as at the end of the period. Related to this factor is the extent to which it can be assumed that gas was at all times a readily available substitute for electricity (and vice versa). There are population changes to consider. There is also technological change to allow for, in terms of technical developments which may have occurred in the efficiency of gas-using appliances relative to electricity-using appliances. In short, it would be unrealistic to assume that the only influence on annual gas consumption over, say, a 30-year period, is its price relative to that of electricity. Thus a regression of consumption on price over such a period is unlikely to reflect pure price effects. To isolate the price effect all the factors described above must be held constant.

Clearly, however, such an experimental approach becomes less and less practicable the larger is the number of factors that must be controlled for. In the social sciences the ability to control directly for the influence of additional factors is extremely limited, and the approach of the laboratory-based scientist is, in effect, unavailable. This point will become clearer in our discussion of multicollinearity in Section 3.5, where we will see that including all the relevant influences on the dependent variable in our multiple regression model does not necessarily ensure that each of these influences can be isolated.

However, note that the role of theory is just as important whether experimentation can be carried out under laboratory conditions or not. In a laboratory experiment the role of theory is to identify all the factors that influence the dependent variable and then to ensure that these are controlled for when the experiment is performed – failure to control for an important influence will result in the conclusions of the experiment being misleading or even meaningless. Similarly, in constructing a multiple regression model all relevant variables must be included in the model so that, firstly, as much of the variation in the dependent variable as possible is accounted for, and secondly, that theoretically sensible inferences are drawn concerning the influences of each of the independent variables.

We will now go on to outline methods of estimating the multiple regression model.

## 3.3   Estimation Methods

Consider the estimation of our postulated gas consumption model in Equation 3.2 above. That is, we require estimates of $\beta_0$, $\beta_1$, and $\beta_2$ in the equation:

$$Y_t = \beta_0 + \beta_1 X_{1t} + \beta_2 X_{2t} + \varepsilon_t \qquad \text{Equation 3.3}$$

The approach here is identical to that of the simple regression model. Thus the estimated model can be written as:

$$Y_t = \hat{\beta}_0 + \hat{\beta}_1 X_{1t} + \hat{\beta}_2 X_{2t} + e_t \qquad \text{Equation 3.4}$$

Using the method of least squares, we require expressions for $\hat{\beta}_0$, $\hat{\beta}_1$ and $\hat{\beta}_2$ such that the sum of the squared residuals – $\Sigma\, e_t^2$ – is minimised (as there are two independent variables here we can geometrically interpret the least squares principle as minimising the sum of the squared residuals around the regression **plane**, rather than the regression line; however, models which contain more than two independent variables can no longer have a geometrical interpretation).

The sum of squares can be written as:

$$\text{SS} = \sum e_t^2 = \sum (Y_t - \hat{\beta}_0 - \hat{\beta}_1 X_{1t} - \hat{\beta}_2 X_{2t})^2 \qquad \text{Equation 3.5}$$

Thus we minimise Equation 3.5 with respect to $\hat{\beta}_0$, $\hat{\beta}_1$ and $\hat{\beta}_2$, and the resulting expressions for $\hat{\beta}_0$, $\hat{\beta}_1$ and $\hat{\beta}_2$ will be the least squares estimators of $\beta_0$, $\beta_1$ and $\beta_2$ in Equation 3.3. This is a straightforward (although tedious) problem in differential calculus and we will not explicitly derive these estimators here – for our purposes it is only important to understand the principle by which they are derived. However, for illustrative purposes we can present the expression for the least squares estimator of $\beta_1$ in Equation 3.3. That is, it can be shown that for the case of two independent variables:

$$\hat{\beta}_1 = \frac{\left[\sum (Y_t - \bar{Y})(X_{1t} - \bar{X}_1)\right]\left[\sum (X_{2t} - \bar{X}_2)^2\right] - \left[\sum (Y_t - \bar{Y})(X_{2t} - \bar{X}_2)\right]\left[\sum (X_{1t} - \bar{X}_1)(X_{2t} - \bar{X}_2)\right]}{\left[\sum (X_{1t} - \bar{X}_1)^2\right]\left[\sum (X_{2t} - \bar{X}_2)^2\right] - \left[\sum (X_{1t} - \bar{X}_1)(X_{2t} - \bar{X}_2)\right]^2}$$

$$\text{Equation 3.6}$$

Clearly, Equation 3.6 is a relatively complex expression and a tedious one to manipulate for purposes of obtaining a value for $\hat{\beta}_1$, given a set of sample observations. Indeed as the number of independent variables increases, the expressions for the corresponding least squares estimators rapidly become even more complex, although their derivation is formally straightforward. Thus it is not practicable to obtain estimated multiple regression equations other than by means of a computer. Fortunately, computer programs which calculate the least squares estimates are now widely available, and we will discuss the use of some of these in Section 3.6 below. The estimated regression equations which we will subsequently present and discuss will all be generated via a computer package. Emphasis will therefore be placed on the specification and interpretation of these equations, rather than on the mechanics of their estimation.

The maximum likelihood estimators of the parameters in the multiple regression model can also be derived, and are direct extensions of the corresponding simple regression estimators (which we discussed in Appendix 2.2). As in the case of the simple regression model, it can be shown that the maximum likelihood estimators are equivalent to the least squares estimators, given the simplest form of the model in Equation 3.1.

For illustrative purposes, let us now consider deriving the least squares estimate of our gas consumption model in Equation 3.3. First, we require a sample of data. As Equation 3.3 can be interpreted as a longer-term model of gas consumption, we can use data extending over a longer time period than just the two years we have so far used. We will use data for the 12-year period 1971 to 1982. In order to limit the sample size we will use quarterly data

**Table 3.1** Gas consumption, temperature, and relative prices Great Britain 1971 to 1982 quarterly

| Year and quarter | | Gas consumption | Temperature | Relative prices | Year and quarter | | Gas consumption | Temperature | Relative prices |
|---|---|---|---|---|---|---|---|---|---|
| 1971 | 1 | 8.0 | 5.4 | 90.8 | 1977 | 1 | 20.0 | 5.6 | 57.6 |
| | 2 | 6.2 | 11.0 | 83.1 | | 2 | 14.1 | 10.4 | 57.8 |
| | 3 | 5.2 | 16.0 | 83.7 | | 3 | 10.5 | 15.2 | 57.2 |
| | 4 | 9.4 | 8.7 | 83.7 | | 4 | 18.2 | 8.6 | 57.2 |
| 1972 | 1 | 11.6 | 5.5 | 88.7 | 1978 | 1 | 21.7 | 4.7 | 56.0 |
| | 2 | 9.5 | 10.8 | 83.9 | | 2 | 14.4 | 10.8 | 52.8 |
| | 3 | 7.4 | 14.6 | 83.9 | | 3 | 10.4 | 15.0 | 52.2 |
| | 4 | 12.4 | 8.2 | 83.9 | | 4 | 18.6 | 8.7 | 53.0 |
| 1973 | 1 | 12.9 | 5.7 | 83.9 | 1979 | 1 | 24.9 | 2.7 | 52.2 |
| | 2 | 9.5 | 11.6 | 83.9 | | 2 | 15.4 | 10.9 | 51.8 |
| | 3 | 7.4 | 15.9 | 83.9 | | 3 | 10.8 | 15.3 | 51.4 |
| | 4 | 14.4 | 7.4 | 78.5 | | 4 | 20.2 | 8.5 | 48.1 |
| 1974 | 1 | 16.0 | 6.3 | 82.7 | 1980 | 1 | 24.7 | 4.9 | 48.1 |
| | 2 | 11.5 | 11.2 | 73.2 | | 2 | 14.6 | 11.5 | 47.7 |
| | 3 | 9.3 | 14.6 | 65.7 | | 3 | 10.3 | 15.5 | 45.5 |
| | 4 | 16.1 | 7.9 | 63.6 | | 4 | 20.8 | 7.5 | 46.8 |
| 1975 | 1 | 17.0 | 5.9 | 67.4 | 1981 | 1 | 24.3 | 5.7 | 47.4 |
| | 2 | 12.1 | 11.2 | 53.5 | | 2 | 15.2 | 11.2 | 48.5 |
| | 3 | 9.1 | 16.7 | 51.2 | | 3 | 10.1 | 15.9 | 48.8 |
| | 4 | 17.2 | 7.6 | 59.0 | | 4 | 22.5 | 6.1 | 56.3 |
| 1976 | 1 | 19.3 | 5.5 | 60.9 | 1982 | 1 | 25.3 | 5.2 | 54.5 |
| | 2 | 12.2 | 12.5 | 54.2 | | 2 | 13.8 | 12.2 | 55.3 |
| | 3 | 9.0 | 16.6 | 52.7 | | 3 | 10.5 | 16.0 | 55.5 |
| | 4 | 18.3 | 6.9 | 57.6 | | 4 | 22.1 | 8.0 | 60.2 |

*Source: Department of Employment Gazette, HMSO*
*Annual Abstract of Statistics, HMSO*

rather than monthly data, thus producing a sample size of 48 observations. Of course, the implicit assumption here is that a period of 12 years is not long enough for any additional factors (such as those discussed above) to exert a significant influence on gas consumption. We will proceed on the basis that this assumption is reasonable.

The sample data are shown in Table 3.1. The temperature data refer to the average daily temperature over the corresponding quarter, and price is measured by the ratio of an index of gas prices to an index of electricity prices – that is, it measures the price of gas relative to that of electricity. Gas consumption is here measured on a different basis to that of our previous measure (it is measured in terms of million tonnes of coal equivalent), but it is still a physical (or real) measure of consumption.

From Table 3.1 we note that considerable variation occurs in the price series, particularly as between the beginning and the end of the sample period, and thus we would expect that this variation would have some effect on gas consumption.

The (computer-generated) least squares estimate of Equation 3.3, using the data in Table 3.1, is as follows:

$$\hat{Y}_t = 39.145 - 1.085 X_{1t} - 0.220 X_{2t} \qquad \text{Equation 3.7}$$

We note from Equation 3.7 that the estimated coefficients on $X_{1t}$ and $X_{2t}$ are both negative, as expected. That is, high temperatures lead to low levels of consumption, and high relative gas prices also result in lower consumption. However, we are not yet in a position to discuss the adequacy of the estimated model – that is, whether $X_1$ and $X_2$ are significant as determinants of $Y$, and whether the model has accounted for most of the variation in $Y$. We will now go on to discuss these issues.

## 3.4    Evaluation of the Estimated Model

Model evaluation in the case of the multiple regression model is a direct extension of the results for the simple regression model. Thus it can be shown that the least squares estimators of the $\beta$s in Equation 3.1 are in fact the Best Linear Unbiased Estimators – that is, $\hat{\beta}_0, \hat{\beta}_1, \ldots, \hat{\beta}_K$ can be shown to be the BLUEs of $\beta_0, \beta_1, \ldots, \beta_K$ respectively. Similarly, assuming the disturbance terms are normally distributed (or that a sufficiently large sample is available) the least squares estimators can each be shown to be normally distributed. That is, we can write:

$$\hat{\beta}_k \sim N[\beta_k, \text{Var}(\hat{\beta}_k)] \quad \text{for } k = 0, 1, \ldots, K \qquad \text{Expression 3.8}$$

The expression for $\text{Var}(\hat{\beta}_k)$ is a relatively complex one, just as in the case of the expression for $\hat{\beta}_k$ (see Equation 3.6 for the case of two independent variables). Again, we will not explicitly derive the expression for $\text{Var}(\hat{\beta}_k)$, and we will rely on computer programs for purposes of deriving estimates of $\text{Var}(\hat{\beta}_k)$.[1]

However, for illustrative purposes, we present in Equations 3.9 and 3.10 the expressions for $\text{Var}(\hat{\beta}_1)$ and $\text{Var}(\hat{\beta}_2)$, for the case of the simplest form of the multiple regression model – the model with just two independent variables. That is, it can be shown that:

$$\text{Var}(\hat{\beta}_1) = \frac{\sigma_\varepsilon^2 \sum (X_{2t} - \bar{X}_2)^2}{\sum (X_{1t} - \bar{X}_1)^2 \sum (X_{2t} - \bar{X}_2)^2 - [\sum (X_{1t} - \bar{X}_1)(X_{2t} - \bar{X}_2)]^2}$$

Equation 3.9

and

$$\text{Var}(\hat{\beta}_2) = \frac{\sigma_\varepsilon^2 \sum (X_{1t} - \bar{X}_1)^2}{\sum (X_{1t} - \bar{X}_1)^2 \sum (X_{2t} - \bar{X}_2)^2 - [\sum (X_{1t} - \bar{X}_1)(X_{2t} - \bar{X}_2)]^2}$$

Equation 3.10

(a similar expression can also be derived for $\text{Var}(\hat{\beta}_0)$, the variance of the constant term).

Note from Equations 3.9 and 3.10 that just as in the case of the simple regression model, $\text{Var}(\hat{\beta}_k)$ will depend on $\sigma_\varepsilon^2$, and thus Expression 3.8 is strictly correct only if $\sigma_\varepsilon^2$ is known. In general, $\sigma_\varepsilon^2$ will not be known, and will have to be estimated. An unbiased estimator for $\sigma_\varepsilon^2$ can be shown to be:

$$\hat{\sigma}_\varepsilon^2 = \frac{\sum e_t^2}{n - (K+1)}$$

Equation 3.11

$K+1$ is the number of coefficients which have to be estimated (the number of $\beta$s in Equation 3.1), and thus Equation 3.11 is directly analogous to the expression for $\hat{\sigma}_\varepsilon^2$ in the simple regression model, where the denominator was $n-2$ (see Equation 2.54) – that is, in the simple regression model there are just two coefficients to be estimated and thus $K+1 = 2$.

The use of $\hat{\sigma}_\varepsilon^2$ in place of $\sigma_\varepsilon^2$ requires that the $t$-distribution be used rather than the normal, and thus we can now write:

$$\frac{\hat{\beta}_k - \beta_k}{S_\beta} \sim t_{n-(K+1)}$$

Expression 3.12

where $S_\beta$ is the square root of the estimated variance of $\hat{\beta}_k$ (obtained by substituting $\hat{\sigma}_\varepsilon^2$ for $\sigma_\varepsilon^2$ in the expression for $\text{Var}(\hat{\beta}_k)$). It is now necessary to assume that $\varepsilon_t$ is normally distributed, irrespective of sample size, but this assumption becomes less important as the sample size increases. Note also that Expression 3.12 implies the use of a $t$-distribution with $n-(K+1)$ degrees of freedom – $K+1$ degrees of freedom have been 'lost' as estimates of the $K+1$ $\beta$s have to be used rather than their (unknown) actual values.

In addition to testing for the significance of each of the independent (or explanatory) variables, we also require a measure of the extent to which the independent variables have jointly explained the variation in the dependent variable – that is, we require the multiple regression equivalent of the coefficient of determination which we discussed in Chapter 2.

The approach here is directly analogous to the case of the simple regression model where we interpreted the coefficient of determination – $R^2$ – as measuring the proportion of the variation in $Y$ which is explained by the model. Thus recall from Equations 2.73 and 2.74 that $R^2$ could be written as:

$$R^2 = \frac{\text{SSR}}{\text{SST}}$$  Equation 3.13

where SSR is the sum of squares explained by the regression (or the model) and SST is the total sum of squares, and measures the total variation in the dependent variable, $Y$. That is, as a direct extension of Equation 2.70 it can be shown that for the multiple regression model we can also write:

$$\sum (Y_t - \bar{Y})^2 = \sum (\hat{Y}_t - \bar{Y})^2 + \sum e_t^2$$
$$\text{(SST)} \qquad\quad \text{(SSR)} \qquad \text{(SSE)}$$  Equation 3.14

where we now have:

$$\hat{Y}_t = \hat{\beta}_0 + \hat{\beta}_1 X_{1t} + \ldots + \hat{\beta}_K X_{Kt}$$  Equation 3.15

Thus the coefficient of determination in the multiple regression model can be interpreted as:

$$R^2 = \frac{\sum (\hat{Y}_t - \bar{Y})^2}{\sum (Y_t - \bar{Y})^2}$$  Equation 3.16

or, equivalently:

$$R^2 = 1 - \frac{\sum e_t^2}{\sum (Y_t - \bar{Y})^2}$$  Equation 3.17

and measures the proportion of the variation in the dependent variable which is jointly explained (or accounted for) by the $K$ independent variables.

However, we should note that $R^2$ must necessarily increase as extra explanatory variables are added to the model, irrespective of the theoretical justification for including these variables. Indeed, as we have already indicated, in the limit, when there are as many explanatory variables (plus the constant term) as there are sample observations (that is, $n = K + 1$) then the estimated model will, in a sense, 'explain' nothing, although an $R^2$ of one must necessarily result (see Assumption g of Equation 3.1).

So we require a goodness-of-fit measure which takes some account of the number of explanatory variables included in the regression relative to the number of observations. Such a measure would be useful when it is necessary to discriminate between a number of regression equations, each explaining the same dependent variable, but containing different numbers of independent variables.

We define a statistic called the **corrected** $R^2$ (or $R^2$ adjusted for the degrees of freedom), which is denoted by $\bar{R}^2$ (R-bar-squared), and is given by:

$$\bar{R}^2 = R^2 - \frac{K}{n-(K+1)}(1-R^2) \qquad \text{Equation 3.18}$$

Thus given two equations explaining the same dependent variable and both having the same $R^2$ and $n$, then that equation with the larger number of explanatory variables will have the smaller $\bar{R}^2$ (and hence in this sense will have lower 'explanatory power'). That is, the larger is $K$, *ceteris paribus*, the smaller will be $\bar{R}^2$.

Also note that $\bar{R}^2 \leqslant R^2$ and can even be negative if $R^2$ is small and $K$ is large relative to $n$. If a model produces a negative $\bar{R}^2$ there can be no question but that the model has no explanatory power, or formally, that the independent variables are insignificant in explaining the dependent variable. But note that a positive $\bar{R}^2$ does not necessarily imply significance – this can only be assessed via a formal test of significance.

It must be stressed that the derivation of the expression for $\bar{R}^2$ in Equation 3.18, and its interpretation, is essentially informal – it has an intuitive justification rather than a rigorous mathematical one. That is, the consideration of the value of $\bar{R}^2$ is only one element in the overall evaluation of a given estimated equation. In particular, $\bar{R}^2$ is a purely statistical measure and of itself provides no information concerning the theoretical properties of the model – it must be interpreted within the context of a full statistical evaluation of the model.

We can now return to our estimated gas consumption model in Equation 3.7 and consider the evaluation of this model.

First, we will derive the $t$-statistics associated with $X_1$ and $X_2$ and hence test for their significance as determinants of $Y$. From Equation 3.7 we can write:

$$e_t = Y_t - 39.145 + 1.085X_{1t} + 0.220X_{2t} \qquad \text{Equation 3.19}$$

Thus an estimate of $\sigma_\varepsilon^2$ could be obtained by deriving the $e_t$s from Equation 3.19 and substituting these values into Equation 3.11. That is, for $n = 48$ and $K = 2$ we have:

$$\hat{\sigma}_\varepsilon^2 = \frac{\sum e_t^2}{48-3} = \frac{\sum e_t^2}{45} \qquad \text{Equation 3.20}$$

Substituting the data in Table 3.1 in Equations 3.19 and 3.20 produces:

$$\hat{\sigma}_\varepsilon^2 = 3.537$$

In order to derive estimates of $\text{Var}(\hat{\beta}_1)$ and $\text{Var}(\hat{\beta}_2)$, we substitute this value of $\hat{\sigma}_\varepsilon^2$ for $\sigma_\varepsilon^2$ in the expressions for $\text{Var}(\hat{\beta}_1)$ and $\text{Var}(\hat{\beta}_2)$ (Equations 3.9 and 3.10, above). Thus the estimated variances can be shown to be:

$$\text{Var}(\hat{\beta}_1) = S_{\hat{\beta}_1}^2 = 0.0047693$$

and

$$\text{Var}(\hat{\beta}_2) = S_{\hat{\beta}_1}^2 = 0.0003736$$

Therefore the *t*-statistic associated with $X_1$ in Equation 3.7 is:

$$t = \frac{-1.085}{\sqrt{0.0047693}} = -15.71$$

and the *t*-statistic for $X_2$ is:

$$t = \frac{-0.220}{\sqrt{0.0003736}} = -11.38$$

Thus given such large (negative) *t*-statistics, we can conclude that both $X_1$ and $X_2$ are highly significant as determinants of $Y$ (from Appendix II we require a *t*-distribution with $48 - 3 = 45$ degrees of freedom, and assuming a one-sided alternative hypothesis (theory would imply that both $X_1$ and $X_2$ can only negatively influence $Y$) then for a significance level of 5 per cent the critical value of the *t*-statistic is approximately $-1.68$).

Next we require the value of $R^2$ associated with Equation 3.7. Consider the definition of $R^2$ in Equation 3.17. Thus we require the values of $\Sigma e_t^2$ and $\Sigma (Y_t - \bar{Y})^2$. For $\Sigma e_t^2$, we have from Equation 3.20:

$$\sum e_t^2 = (45)(\hat{\sigma}_\varepsilon^2)$$

and given the value for $\hat{\sigma}_\varepsilon^2$ of 3.537 we have:

$$\sum e_t^2 = 159.165$$

From the data in Table 3.1 we obtain:

$$\sum (Y_t - \bar{Y})^2 = 1385.007$$

Therefore, we can finally deduce from Equation 3.17 that:

$$R^2 = 1 - \frac{159.165}{1385.007}$$

$$= 0.885$$

We can also obtain the value of $\bar{R}^2$, and thus from Equation 3.18 we have:

$$\bar{R}^2 = 0.885 - \frac{2}{45}(1 - 0.885)$$

$$= 0.880$$

Therefore we can now present a full summary of our estimated gas consumption model as follows (absolute values of *t*-statistics in brackets, with the *t*-statistic for the constant term obtained directly from the computer package used to estimate the model):

$$\hat{Y}_t = 39.145 - 1.085 X_{1t} - 0.220 X_{2t}$$
$$\quad\;\; (26.52)\;\; (15.71) \qquad (11.38)$$

$$R^2 = 0.885, \quad \bar{R}^2 = 0.880$$

Equation 3.21

While estimation and hypothesis testing in the multiple regression model is a direct and straightforward extension of the procedures in the simple regression model, a number of further issues arise in the multiple regression model, particularly in relation to hypothesis testing. Three additional types of hypothesis tests can be identified:

(a) As may have been implied in our discussion of the use of $\bar{R}^2$, situations may arise when we need to test for the significance of $R^2$ – that is, we may wish to deduce whether the set of independent variables as a whole can be considered to explain a significant proportion of the variation in the dependent variable. Recall that such a test was not required in the case of the simple regression model as testing for the significance of $R^2$ was equivalent to simply testing for the significance of the single independent variable. However, in the case of the multiple regression model situations can occur in which none of the independent variables is found to be significant according to simple *t*-tests, and yet, as a whole, the independent variables do in fact explain a significant proportion of the variation in the dependent variable. The problem which has occurred in such situations is that the independent variables are so highly intercorrelated that it is not possible to separate out their individual influences (the problem of multicollinearity).

Thus, formally, the appropriate hypothesis test can be written as follows:

$H_0: \beta_1 = \beta_2 = \ldots = \beta_K = 0$   (that is, none of the independent variables
is significant)

$H_1:$ At least one of the $\beta_k$s is different from zero.

In order to test $H_0$ we need to deduce how $R^2$ is distributed when $H_0$ is true.

Now, it can be shown that a simple transformation of $R^2$ does in fact have a well-behaved distribution. Therefore we can define a variable, $F$, where:

$$F = \frac{n - (K+1)}{K} \frac{R^2}{1 - R^2}$$

Equation 3.22

Note that using Equations 3.13 and 3.14, $F$ can also be expressed as:

$$F = \frac{\text{SSR}/K}{\text{SSE}/[n - (K+1)]}$$

Equation 3.23

Now, it can be shown that when $H_0$ is true then $F$ will have an **F-distribution**

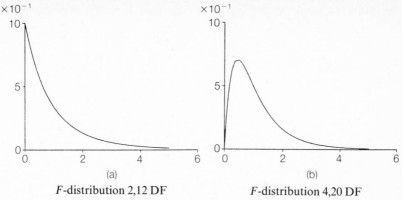

(a)

*F*-distribution 2,12 DF

(b)

*F*-distribution 4,20 DF

**Figure 3.1**

with $K$ and $n-(K+1)$ degrees of freedom. That is, under $H_0$ we can write:

$$F \sim F_{K,n-(K+1)}$$

The $F$-distribution, unlike the normal and $t$-distributions, is an asymmetrical distribution, and its specific shape will depend on the values of its degrees of freedom. For example, in Figures 3.1(a) and (b) we present graphs of the $F$-distribution for 2,12 degrees of freedom and 4,20 degrees of freedom, respectively.

Therefore, in order to test the above null hypothesis, for some given estimated regression equation, we calculate the value of $F$, using either Equation 3.22 or 3.23, and then using tables of the $F$-distribution, decide whether the observed value of $F$ is sufficiently large to allow the rejection of $H_0$.

Note from Equation 3.22 that the smaller is $R^2$ (for given values of $n$ and $K$) then the smaller will be $F$, and in the limit, when $R^2 = 0$ then $F = 0$. Thus in order to reject $H_0$ we require a 'large' value for $F$, the definition of 'large' being derived by reference to the appropriate entry in the tables of the $F$-distribution. In Appendix III we present tables of the $F$-distribution. Note that these are tabulated according to the degrees of freedom of the numerator and the denominator of Equation 3.23 ($K$ and $n-(K+1)$, respectively).

As an example of the use of the $F$-test, we can consider the estimated model in Equation 3.21 above. However note here that as both of the variables in this equation are significant then an $F$-test is superfluous – just one significant variable in any estimated regression equation is sufficient to conclude that the corresponding $R^2$ must also be significant. Thus we will perform an $F$-test here for illustrative purposes only.

First we require the observed value of $F$ associated with Equation 3.21. Using Equation 3.22, with $R^2 = 0.885$ and $n = 48$, $K = 2$, we have:

$$F = 173.15$$

(the reader should confirm that the same value for $F$ is produced by Equation 3.23 (allowing for rounding errors).)

The next step is to determine whether this value of $F$ is sufficiently large to lead to the rejection of $H_0$. We require the tables for the $F$-distribution with 2,45 degrees of freedom. Using a significance level of 5 per cent, the critical value for $F$ from Appendix III lies between 3.23 and 3.15 (that is, the entries in the table for 40 and 60 degrees of freedom for the denominator, given two degrees of freedom for the numerator, as there is no specific entry for 45 degrees of freedom for the denominator). Thus given such a large observed value of $F$ relative to the tabulated value we can confidently reject $H_0$. (This conclusion was of course to be expected given the significant $t$-statistics in Equation 3.21.)

(b) A second type of hypothesis test which may be appropriate in a multiple regression framework concerns the expected (or theoretical) relationships which may exist among some of the parameters (coefficients). The simplest forms that such hypotheses can take are the following:

$$H_0: \beta_j = \beta_k, \quad j \neq k$$

or

$$H_0: \beta_j + \beta_k = w, \quad j \neq k$$

where $w$ is some constant.

That is, theoretically, two of the parameters may be expected to be equal (typically, equal but opposite in sign), or the sum of two parameters is equal to some known constant.

A common example in which such tests arise (especially tests of the second type) is in the estimation of **production functions**. A production function can be defined as a function which describes the way in which the output (of a firm, industry or economy) is related to the inputs which are used. At the most general level, the inputs are divided into just two broad components – labour inputs and capital inputs.

A common form of production function which has been used in empirical work is the Cobb–Douglas function which has the following form:

$$Q = AK^\alpha L^\beta \qquad\qquad \text{Equation 3.24}$$

where $Q$ is output, $K$ is a measure of capital inputs, $L$ is a measure of labour inputs, and $A$, $\alpha$ and $\beta$ are the parameters to be estimated. The terms $\alpha$ and $\beta$ are often referred to as the **scale** parameters. If $\alpha + \beta = 1$ then the production function, and hence the production process which it describes, is said to exhibit constant returns to scale – that is, a given percentage increase in the capital and labour inputs will result in the same percentage increase in output. If $\alpha + \beta < 1$, then decreasing returns to scale occur (a given percentage increase in $K$ and $L$ results in a lower percentage increase in output). If

$\alpha + \beta > 1$, increasing returns are present. Therefore, having estimated a production function (the above function can be 'linearised' by taking logarithms – a fuller discussion of non-linearities will be presented in Chapter 4), the question then arises as to what the estimates of $\alpha$ and $\beta$ indicate about the true parameter values – that is, for example, whether it is reasonable to assume that constant returns to scale are implied.

Assume we wish to test:

$$H_0: \alpha + \beta = 1$$

against

$$H_1: \alpha + \beta > 1,$$
$$\alpha + \beta < 1, \text{ or}$$
$$\alpha + \beta \neq 1$$

whichever is appropriate.

Given the least squares estimators, $\hat{\alpha}$ and $\hat{\beta}$, we have:

$$E(\hat{\alpha} + \hat{\beta}) = E(\hat{\alpha}) + E(\hat{\beta}) = \alpha + \beta \qquad \text{Equation 3.25}$$

Therefore $\hat{\alpha} + \hat{\beta}$ is an unbiased estimator of $\alpha + \beta$.

Now, recall from Equation 1.53 that given two variables, $R$ and $S$, we showed that:

$$\text{Var}(R + S) = \text{Var}(R) + \text{Var}(S) + 2\,\text{Cov}(R, S) \qquad \text{Equation 3.26}$$

Here we have two variables – $\hat{\alpha}$ and $\hat{\beta}$ – and thus we can write from Equation 3.26:

$$\text{Var}(\hat{\alpha} + \hat{\beta}) = \text{Var}(\hat{\alpha}) + \text{Var}(\hat{\beta}) + 2\,\text{Cov}(\hat{\alpha}, \hat{\beta}) \qquad \text{Equation 3.27}$$

where $\text{Cov}(\hat{\alpha}, \hat{\beta})$ is the covariance between $\hat{\alpha}$ and $\hat{\beta}$. Thus we have derived the mean and variance of the estimator of the returns to scale parameter, $\hat{\alpha} + \hat{\beta}$, and given the distribution of this estimator we can then test hypotheses concerning the actual value of the parameter.

As the returns to scale estimator is just the sum of $\hat{\alpha}$ and $\hat{\beta}$, then its distribution will be the same as that of $\hat{\alpha}$ and $\hat{\beta}$. Thus assuming a normal distribution, we can write:

$$\hat{\alpha} + \hat{\beta} \sim N[\alpha + \beta, \text{Var}(\hat{\alpha} + \hat{\beta})] \qquad \text{Expression 3.28}$$

and the approach to hypothesis testing is exactly the same as previously. The only superficial difference here is that the expression for the variance in Equation 3.27 is somewhat more complex than we are used to because of the inclusion of the covariance term. But otherwise the methodology is unchanged.[2]

In general, of course, $\text{Var}(\hat{\alpha} + \hat{\beta})$ will be unknown and will have to be estimated, thus requiring use of the $t$-distribution rather than the normal.

That is, we can write:

$$\frac{\hat{\alpha}+\hat{\beta}-(\alpha+\beta)}{S_{\hat{\alpha}+\beta}} \sim t_{n-(K+1)}$$    Expression 3.29

where

$$S_{\hat{\alpha}+\beta} = \sqrt{S_{\hat{\alpha}}^2+S_{\hat{\beta}}^2+2\,\widehat{\text{Cov}}\,(\hat{\alpha},\hat{\beta})}$$

and $\widehat{\text{Cov}}\,(\hat{\alpha},\hat{\beta})$ is the estimated covariance between $\alpha$ and $\beta$. Again, we will not here derive or even present the expression for the estimator of the covariance between $\hat{\alpha}$ and $\hat{\beta}$ and we will rely on appropriate computer packages to generate the required estimates.

In terms of the specific hypothesis relating to the existence of constant returns to scale for some estimated production function, the observed value of $t$ is calculated as follows (that is, assuming $H_0$ to be true):

$$t = \frac{\hat{\alpha}+\hat{\beta}-1}{S_{\hat{\alpha}+\beta}}$$    Equation 3.30

Thus we substitute the respective estimates into Equation 3.30 and compare the resulting $t$-value to the corresponding tabulated value.

So, in summary, hypothesis tests concerning relationships among a number of parameters can generally be reduced to straightforward $t$-tests, the only change being that covariance terms are introduced – in all other respects these tests are based on exactly the same principles as in the case of testing for individual parameter values.

(c) A final type of hypothesis test which may be appropriate in certain cases is to determine whether the introduction of an additional set of explanatory variables adds to the significance of the regression – that is, whether the resulting increase in $R^2$ is a significant one. Formally, the test could be expressed as follows (assuming that $p$ additional variables are added to the regression):

$H_0$: $\beta_{K+1} = \beta_{K+2} = \ldots = \beta_{K+p} = 0$

$H_1$: The $p$ additional independent variables add significantly to the explanatory power of the regression.

This test is based on the $F$-distribution. If $H_0$ is true then it can be shown that the variable:

$$F = \frac{(\text{SSR}_T - \text{SSR}_K)/(T-K)}{\text{SSE}_T/(n-T)}$$    Equation 3.31

has an $F$-distribution with $T-K$ and $n-T$ degrees of freedom. $\text{SSR}_T$ is the sum of squares due to the regression when all $T$ explanatory variables are included (that is, the $K$ original variables plus the additional variables –

$T = K + p$), SSR$_K$ is the sum of squares due to the regression containing just the original $K$ variables, and SSE$_T$ is the error (or unexplained) sum of squares from the regression containing all $T$ variables. Note, that the value of $F$ in Equation 3.30 will be larger the greater the difference between SSR$_T$ and SSR$_K$–that is, the greater is the difference between the explanatory power of the regression with all $T$ variables and the regression containing just the original $K$ variables. The $F$-test here is, in effect, a test of the significance of this difference.

We will now go on to discuss another numerical example in order to further illustrate the estimation and interpretation of a multiple regression model.

Example 3.1

In this example we will specify and estimate a model which explains the annual variation in the consumption of beer in the United Kingdom.

The simplest model which we could postulate is that the level of beer consumption is determined by the price of beer and the level of income. Thus, if we let $B_t$ denote beer consumption in year $t$, $P_t$ denote price and $D_t$ denote income, then the model could be expressed as follows:

$$B_t = f(D_t, P_t) \qquad\qquad \text{Equation 3.32}$$

If we assume a linear relationship, then we can write:

$$B_t = \beta_0 + \beta_1 D_t + \beta_1 P_t + \varepsilon_t \qquad\qquad \text{Equation 3.33}$$

In effect, we are here formulating a demand function for beer, a function which incorporates both an income effect (that is, the influence of income on beer consumption, assuming price unchanged) and a price effect (the influence of price on beer consumption, assuming income unchanged).[3] *A priori*, income would be expected to exert a positive influence on beer consumption, and price would be expected to exert a negative influence.

We next require a sample of data in order to estimate Equation 3.32.

In Table 3.2 we present a sample of annual data, from 1963 to 1979, on total beer consumption in the UK, real personal disposable income, and the price of beer relative to the prices of all other consumer goods. Note, that as the variable measuring beer consumption is measured in quantity or 'real' terms, then so must be the variables which explain it. Therefore, real (or constant price) income is the appropriate income variable. In terms of the appropriate price variable, it would seem reasonable to assume that consumers of beer will respond to the real price of beer rather than its money (or nominal) price. The real price of beer could be defined as its money price relative to the money prices of all consumer goods – that is, the money price of beer deflated by the index of retail prices, and this is the series which is presented in Table 3.2.

**Table 3.2** Beer consumption, personal disposable income and relative price of beer, United Kingdom 1963 to 1979

| Year | Beer consumption (million bulk barrels) | Personal disposable income (1975 prices) (&'000 m) | Relative price of beer |
|------|------|------|------|
| 1963 | 28.7 | 53.77 | 91.67 |
| 1964 | 30.0 | 55.78 | 94.09 |
| 1965 | 30.3 | 57.20 | 96.06 |
| 1966 | 30.8 | 58.50 | 96.21 |
| 1967 | 31.5 | 59.38 | 94.69 |
| 1968 | 32.0 | 60.61 | 93.25 |
| 1969 | 33.4 | 61.24 | 94.76 |
| 1970 | 34.4 | 63.71 | 90.56 |
| 1971 | 35.8 | 64.64 | 85.25 |
| 1972 | 36.7 | 70.08 | 81.80 |
| 1973 | 38.3 | 75.09 | 78.93 |
| 1974 | 39.1 | 75.02 | 73.92 |
| 1975 | 40.1 | 73.77 | 74.33 |
| 1976 | 40.7 | 73.30 | 71.48 |
| 1977 | 40.3 | 71.76 | 68.41 |
| 1978 | 41.4 | 77.70 | 66.41 |
| 1979 | 41.7 | 82.13 | 65.91 |

*Source: Annual Abstract of Statistics,* HMSO

The least squares estimate of Equation 3.32 is as follows (absolute values of $t$-statistics in brackets):

$$\hat{\beta}_t = 26.004 + 0.327D_t - 0.146P_t, \quad R^2 = 0.962$$
$$\quad\;\; (2.70) \quad (4.34) \qquad (2.55)$$

Thus both variables (and the constant term) are significant at the 5 per cent level ($t_{0.05,14} = 1.76$). Note also that the signs on the independent variables are as expected and that a highly satisfactory $R^2$ is produced. There is little point in performing an $F$-test here as both independent variables are significant and thus $R^2$ must also be significant. Therefore, given the various criteria for assessing a regression equation which we have so far discussed, this estimated equation can be considered as highly acceptable. However, there are a number of further tests which can be performed on this equation, particularly with respect to the estimated disturbance terms (the $e_t$s), which are required before the equation can be considered as entirely satisfactory. These will be discussed in Chapter 4.

## 3.5 The Problem of Multicollinearity

On a number of occasions we have made brief reference to the problem of multicollinearity, and we will now present a more detailed discussion of the problem. A useful starting point is to examine the two extremes of multi-collinearity – that is, the case of perfect correlation amongst the explanatory variables, and the case of zero correlation amongst the variables.

Consider the following three-variable regression model:

$$Y_t = \beta_0 + \beta_1 X_{1t} + \beta_2 X_{2t} + \varepsilon_t \qquad \text{Equation 3.34}$$

Given a sample of data on $Y$, $X_1$, and $X_2$, perfect multicollinearity occurs if $X_1$ and $X_2$ are perfectly correlated – that is, if the absolute value of the correlation coefficient between $X_1$ and $X_2$ is one. The result in such situations is that the estimation procedures which we have discussed break down, and estimates for $\beta_0$, $\beta_1$ and $\beta_2$ cannot be obtained (recall that this is the reason for Assumption g in the specification of the model in Equation 3.1). This can be seen by considering the expression for the least squares estimator of $\beta_1$ in the three-variable regression model, which we presented in Equation 3.6. From Equation 3.6 we have:

$$\hat{\beta}_1 = \frac{\left[\sum (Y_t - \bar{Y})(X_{1t} - \bar{X}_1)\right]\left[\sum (X_{2t} - \bar{X}_2)^2\right] - \left[\sum (Y_t - \bar{Y})(X_{2t} - \bar{X}_2)\right]\left[\sum (X_{1t} - \bar{X}_1)(X_{2t} - \bar{X}_2)\right]}{\left[\sum (X_{1t} - \bar{X}_1)^2\right]\left[\sum (X_{2t} - \bar{X}_2)^2\right] - \left[\sum (X_{1t} - \bar{X}_1)(X_{2t} - \bar{X}_2)\right]^2}$$

$$\text{Equation 3.35}$$

If we divide the numerator and denominator of this equation by:

$$\sum (X_{1t} - \bar{X}_1)^2 \sum (X_{2t} - \bar{X}_2)^2$$

then the denominator of Equation 3.35 becomes:

$$1 - r_{12}^2$$

where $r_{12}^2$ is the square of the correlation coefficient between $X_1$ and $X_2$. That is, we can write $r_{12}^2$ as follows:

$$r_{12}^2 = \frac{\left[\sum (X_{1t} - \bar{X}_1)(X_{2t} - \bar{X}_2)\right]^2}{\sum (X_{1t} - \bar{X}_1)^2 \sum (X_{2t} - \bar{X}_2)^2}$$

Therefore, if $X_1$ and $X_2$ are perfectly correlated (that is, $r_{12}^2 = 1$) then the denominator of Equation 3.35 must be zero, and $\hat{\beta}_1$ will be undefined. This can also be shown to be the case for $\hat{\beta}_2$ and $\hat{\beta}_0$. In statistical terms, the model need include only one of $X_1$ or $X_2$ in order to fully reflect the variation in these variables.

At the other extreme, of zero correlation between $X_1$ and $X_2$ (and hence no multicollinearity in the data), no difficulties arise in the derivation of the least squares estimates. Further, it can be shown that the estimates of $\beta_1$ and $\beta_2$ obtained from the direct estimation of Equation 3.34 are the same as those obtained from the two simple regressions of $Y$ on $X_1$ and $Y$ on $X_2$. This can be seen by considering the expression for $\hat{\beta}_1$ in Equation 3.35 above.

Now, if the correlation between $X_1$ and $X_2$ is zero, then the covariance between $X_1$ and $X_2$ will be zero, and thus we have:

$$\sum (X_{1t} - \bar{X}_1)(X_{2t} - \bar{X}_2) = 0 \qquad \text{Equation 3.36}$$

Substituting Equation 3.36 into Equation 3.35, the least squares estimator of $\beta_1$ collapses to:

$$
\begin{aligned}
\hat{\beta}_1 &= \frac{[\sum (Y_t - \bar{Y})(X_{1t} - \bar{X}_1)][\sum (X_{2t} - \bar{X}_2)^2]}{[\sum (X_{1t} - \bar{X}_1)^2][\sum (X_{2t} - \bar{X}_2)^2]} \\
&= \frac{\sum (Y_t - \bar{Y})(X_{1t} - \bar{X}_1)}{\sum (X_{1t} - \bar{X}_1)^2}
\end{aligned}
$$

which is just the expression for the least squares estimator of $\beta_1$ in the simple regression model:

$$Y_t = \beta_0 + \beta_1 X_{1t} + \varepsilon_t$$

(see Equation 2.20). This same result can also be shown to apply in the case of the least squares estimator of $\beta_2$.

Therefore, the implication is that if the data which are used to estimate some multiple regression model exhibit no multicollinearity – the independent variables are uncorrelated – then the least squares estimates can be generated either by directly estimating the multiple regression, or by estimating each of the separate simple regressions.

However, while it is the case that the values of the least squares estimates will be the same whether the multiple or the simple regressions are performed, the variances of the respective estimators will differ. In particular, the variances of $\hat{\beta}_1$ and $\hat{\beta}_2$ will be larger in the case of the two separate simple regressions than in the case of the single multiple regression. In turn, this means that the multiple regression will produce more precise estimators than the simple regressions. This result can be established quite easily.

Recall that in the case of the simple regression:

$$Y_t = \beta_0 + \beta_1 X_{1t} + \varepsilon_t$$

the variance of the least squares estimator of $\beta_1$ can be written as:

$$\text{Var}(\hat{\beta}_1) = \frac{\sigma_\varepsilon^2}{\sum (X_{1t} - \bar{X}_1)^2} \qquad \text{Equation 3.37}$$

(see Equation 2.47).

Now, recall that in Equation 3.9 we presented the expression for $\text{Var}(\hat{\beta}_1)$

for the case of the three-variable regression model. That is:

$$\text{Var}(\hat{\beta}_1) = \frac{\sigma_\varepsilon^2 \sum (X_{2t} - \bar{X}_2)^2}{\sum (X_{1t} - \bar{X}_1)^2 \sum (X_{2t} - \bar{X}_2)^2 - [\sum (X_{1t} - \bar{X}_1)(X_{2t} - \bar{X}_2)]^2}$$

Equation 3.38

If there is zero correlation between $X_1$ and $X_2$ (and therefore $\widehat{\text{Cov}}(X_1, X_2) = 0$) then Equation 3.38 collapses to:

$$\text{Var}(\hat{\beta}_1) = \frac{\sigma_\varepsilon^2}{\sum (X_{1t} - \bar{X}_1)^2}$$

Equation 3.39

Although Equations 3.37 and 3.39 appear to be the same, superficially, they differ in one very important respect – the value of $\sigma_\varepsilon^2$ in the two equations is different. In the case of the multiple regression, $\sigma_\varepsilon^2$ will be smaller as account is being taken of the variation in both $X_1$ and $X_2$. The multiple regression must necessarily explain a larger proportion of the variation in $Y$ than either of the simple regressions. Consequently there will be less variation in the resulting disturbance terms, and the value for $\sigma_\varepsilon^2$ will be lower than in the case of either simple regression. Therefore, in the absence of multicollinearity, the value of $\text{Var}(\hat{\beta}_1)$ in Equation 3.39 will be smaller than that in Equation 3.37, with the result that the multiple regression produces a more precise estimator for $\beta_1$, which can similarly be shown to be the case for $\beta_2$.

An alternative way of expressing this is that as the multiple regression is the correctly specified equation (both $X_1$ and $X_2$ are theoretically held to influence $Y$) then it is to be expected that it will be more accurate in measuring the influences of $X_1$ and $X_2$ than will either of the simple regressions.[4]

We can illustrate some of these issues by returning to the estimate of our gas consumption model in Equation 3.21. As we shall emphasise below, the problem of multicollinearity is not one of determining whether it is simply present or absent, but rather the issue is the extent to which it exists within the sample of observations on the independent variables. Thus in the case of Equation 3.21, the extent of multicollinearity can be measured by the correlation coefficient between temperature and price. From the data in Table 3.1 it can be shown that the correlation coefficient between $X_1$ and $X_2$ is $-0.092$, and we can therefore conclude that a very low level of multicollinearity is present in the data. Thus we would expect that broadly similar least squares estimates of the coefficients on $X_1$ and $X_2$ will be produced, whether the multiple regression is estimated or the two separate simple regressions. This can be seen by explicitly estimating the two simple regressions, of $Y$ on $X_1$, and $Y$ on $X_2$. These are shown in Equations 3.40 and 3.41 ($t$-statistics in brackets):

$$\hat{Y}_t = 24.586 - 1.012 X_{1t}, \quad R^2 = 0.554$$
$$\phantom{\hat{Y}_t = } (17.06) \quad (7.55)$$

Equation 3.40

$$\hat{Y}_t = 26.550 - 0.192X_{2t}, \quad R^2 = 0.255 \qquad\qquad \text{Equation 3.41}$$
$$\phantom{\hat{Y}_t = 26.550}(8.51)\quad(3.97)$$

Note that the coefficient on $X_{1t}$ in Equation 3.40 is similar to that in Equation 3.21 (which was $-1.085$), and likewise for the coefficient on $X_{2t}$ ($-0.220$). The $R^2$s in Equations 3.40 and 3.41 must of course be lower, as in each case account is being taken of only one of the two variables which influence $Y$.

However, note also that the $t$-statistics in Equations 3.40 and 3.41 are much lower than the corresponding statistics in Equation 3.21. As was implied by the above discussion, this results from the larger estimates of the residual variance which are associated with the simple regressions as compared to the multiple regression. This can be seen by deriving the estimated coefficient variances. First, recall that the $t$-statistic associated with an estimated coefficient is derived by dividing the coefficient by its estimated standard deviation (the square root of its variance). Therefore, from Equation 3.21, the estimated standard deviation associated with $X_1$ is:

$$S_{\beta_1} = \frac{1.085}{15.71}$$

$$= 0.069$$

The estimated standard deviation associated with $X_2$ is:

$$S_{\beta_2} = \frac{0.220}{11.34}$$

$$= 0.019$$

Now, in the cases of the simple regressions in Equations 3.40 and 3.41, the corresponding estimated standard deviations are as follows:

For $X_1$:
$$S_{\beta_1} = \frac{1.012}{7.55}$$
$$= 0.134$$

For $X_2$:
$$S_{\beta_2} = \frac{0.192}{3.97}$$
$$= 0.048$$

Thus, it can be seen that in moving from the multiple to the separate simple regressions, the estimated standard deviations increase by a factor of about two, even though the coefficient estimates are little affected. Therefore, we have confirmed that the multiple regression produces more precise estimates of the coefficients (for the case of zero or very low levels of multicollinearity), which in turn results from the smaller disturbance term variation associated with the multiple regression.

Note that it is also possible for the simple regressions to produce insignificant *t*-statistics, given that the effect of estimating the simple regressions is to increase the variances of the coefficient estimators. That is, we might draw the quite erroneous conclusion from the simple regressions that none of the explanatory variables is significant – they may only appear as significant once the multiple regression model has been estimated. But it is the multiple regression which is the correctly specified model – it takes account of all the influences on the dependent variable – and thus it is the appropriate context for assessing the significance of the explanatory variables.

Although the consideration of these two extremes is useful for introducing the concept of multicollinearity, they will rarely occur in practice. As indicated above, the problem is not so much of determining whether multicollinearity is absent or present, but rather of determining the degree to which it exists, and the consequences that this has for the estimated model. It is highly unlikely that any set of sample data will exhibit perfect multicollinearity and so least squares estimates can generally be obtained. Similarly, it is highly unlikely that multicollinearity will be entirely absent from the sample data. The question, then, is how the least squares estimation procedure is affected by the level of multicollinearity, and whether there are any methods of overcoming or minimising the resulting problems.

For illustrative purposes, we will continue to consider a multiple regression model with just two explanatory variables. In Equation 3.9 (and Equation 3.38) we presented the expression for the variance of the least squares estimator of $\beta_1$. If we divide the numerator and denominator of this expression by $\Sigma (X_{1t} - \bar{X}_1)^2 \Sigma (X_{2t} - \bar{X}_2)^2$ then we can write:

$$\text{Var}(\hat{\beta}_1) = \frac{\sigma_\varepsilon^2}{(1 - r_{12}^2)\sum (X_{1t} - \bar{X}_1)^2} \qquad \text{Equation 3.42}$$

From Equation 3.42 it can be seen that the higher the correlation between $X_1$ and $X_2$, then the larger will be $\text{Var}(\hat{\beta}_1)$ (for given values of $\sigma_\varepsilon^2$ and $\Sigma (X_{1t} - \bar{X}_1)^2$). That is, $\hat{\beta}_1$ will be more imprecise the greater the extent of multicollinearity. This will have the effect of reducing the *t*-statistic associated with $X_1$, with the possibility that $X_1$ may even appear as insignificant as a determinant of $Y$. This same result can be shown to apply in the case of the interpretation of $\hat{\beta}_2$. That is, dividing the numerator and denominator of the expression for $\text{Var}(\hat{\beta}_2)$ (which we presented in Equation 3.10) by $\Sigma (X_{1t} - \bar{X}_1)^2 \Sigma (X_{2t} - \bar{X}_2)^2$ produces:

$$\text{Var}(\hat{\beta}_2) = \frac{\sigma_\varepsilon^2}{(1 - r_{12}^2)\sum (X_{2t} - \bar{X}_2)^2} \qquad \text{Equation 3.43}$$

For models with more than two explanatory variables, this general conclusion still holds – the higher the multicollinearity within the sample data on the explanatory variables, the larger will be the associated estimated variances, and consequently the more difficult it becomes to quantify precisely the separate influence of each of these variables.

However, multicollinearity can take on a variety of forms when there are more than two explanatory variables. For example, consider a model with three explanatory variables. That is:

$$Y_t = \beta_0 + \beta_1 X_{1t} + \beta_2 X_{2t} + \beta_3 X_{3t} + \varepsilon_t \qquad \text{Equation 3.44}$$

In addition to multicollinearity being exhibited in the pair-wise correlations between each of these variables (that is, the correlation between $X_1$ and $X_2$, $X_1$ and $X_3$, and $X_2$ and $X_3$, denoted by $r_{12}, r_{13},$ and $r_{23}$, respectively), a high degree of multicollinearity would also be present if any of the explanatory variables was an approximate linear combination of the other two variables. Indeed, in the extreme, perfect multicollinearity would be present if one explanatory variable was an exact linear combination of the other two variables, and this may well occur even if each of the pair-wise correlations was less than one. For example, if it were the case that:

$$X_{1t} = aX_{2t} + bX_{3t} \qquad \text{Equation 3.45}$$

where $a$ and $b$ are constants, then the estimation procedure would still break down, and least squares estimates could not be obtained.

In summary, then, the general conclusion which can be drawn is that the effect of multicollinearity is to increase the variances of the parameter estimators, hence reducing the precision of these estimators. In turn, this will lower the $t$-statistics associated with the parameter estimates, thereby reducing their statistical significance.

However, irrespective of the degree of multicollinearity which is present, it can be shown that the least squares estimators are still the BLUEs – they are still the best available linear estimators. As we shall emphasise below, multicollinearity is not a problem associated with the specification of the model, but rather it is a property of the sample data which is used to estimate the model. Thus, in practice, the problem is one of how to interpret an insignificant $t$-statistic, given that virtually all sample data will exhibit some degree of multicollinearity. That is, given an estimated multiple regression model, a variable which produces an insignificant $t$-statistic can be interpreted in one of two ways:

a   The variable is in fact theoretically irrelevant as a determinant of the dependent variable, and should therefore be dropped from the model.

b   The variable is relevant as an explanatory factor (it may even be an important factor), but unfortunately the available sample data possess such a high degree of multicollinearity that it is not possible to quantify accurately the influence of this variable. However, irrespective of the statistical properties of the sample data, the variable should still be retained in the model in order to ensure that the model remains correctly specified.

An obvious first step, then, when faced with insignificant $t$-statistics, is to quantify the extent of multicollinearity.

For an equation with just two independent variables this is straight-forward – the extent of multicollinearity is reflected in the correlation coefficient between $X_1$ and $X_2$. In the case of more than two explanatory variables the degree of multicollinearity will be reflected not only in the pair-wise correlation coefficients between the independent variables, but also in the $R^2$s which result from 'regressing' each independent variable, in turn, on all the other independent variables. High values of these multiple correlation coefficients would indicate that some of the independent variables are approximate linear combinations of the other variables, and hence that a high degree of multicollinearity is present.

If there is a high degree of intercorrelation amongst the independent variables, then all that can be concluded is that any insignificant $t$-statistics which occur may result from multicollinearity. Certainly if all the $t$-statistics are insignificant (apart from that associated with the constant term), but a significant $F$-statistic is produced by the regression, then it can be concluded that multicollinearity is a problem. However, it does not follow that if multicollinearity were absent then all the independent variables would have significant $t$-statistics – all that can be concluded is that at least one of the variables would appear as significant. Conversely, a high degree of multi-collinearity will not necessarily result in insignificant $t$-statistics. In practice, it is quite common to obtain quite well determined equations (in the sense of a large proportion of significant $t$-statistics) in the presence of high levels of multicollinearity – the only general conclusion which can be drawn is that such equations would be even better determined if there were a lower degree of multicollinearity.

It is therefore not possible to define in any absolute sense what constitutes an unacceptable level of multicollinearity. Nor is it possible to determine whether an insignificant $t$-statistic results from multicollinearity or whether it reflects the theoretical irrelevance of the variable. So it is poor econometric methodology to discard a variable simply because its $t$-statistic is insigni-ficant – only if it can also be argued that there are weak theoretical grounds for retaining the variable would such an approach be justified. If this were the case then this would mean that the theoretical reasons for including the variable in the first place must have been dubious. However, this can typically occur in cases where very little theory relating to the phenomenon under investigation has been developed, and so the regression analysis is very much experimental in nature. The question then arises as to how the problem can be overcome.

As we indicated above, it is important to recognise that multicollinearity, by definition, is a problem of the sample data, and not of the population. This point can be made explicit by considering our gas consumption model in Equation 3.2, and the data used to estimate the model in Table 3.1.

Now, in theory, we would not expect there to be any relationship between the two independent variables in this model – atmospheric temperature is presumably entirely independent of the price of gas. The extent of multi-collinearity in the data used to estimate the model is here measured by the correlation coefficient between the temperature and price observations in Table 3.1. As theory would predict, a low correlation coefficient of $-0.092$ was produced, and multicollinearity was not therefore a problem in the estimation of the model. However, note that even though temperature and price are independent in the population (and thus will have a zero population correlation coefficient), this does not necessarily mean that this property will be exactly reflected in a sample of data on these variables. Although the sample of data used here exhibits a very low correlation coefficient, this coefficient is not zero. And the smaller the sample which is used, the greater will be the tendency for non-zero (and possibly high) sample correlation coefficients to be observed, even though the variables are independent in the population.

For example, if we consider only the first 24 observations in Table 3.1 (the observations from 1971 to 1976), then the correlation between price and temperature is now $-0.226$, and a higher level of multicollinearity would therefore be present if these data were used to estimate the model, rather than if all the data in Table 3.1 were used. That is, if two variables are independent then the sample correlation between these variables will tend to become smaller as sample size increases (although it is not necessarily the case that the correlation coefficient must fall for any given increase in sample size). It is in this sense that multicollinearity is a sample problem, and that increasing the sample size will tend to reduce the problem – multicollinearity cannot occur in the population, as the explanatory variables are independent of each other, by assumption.[5]

So while increasing sample size is in many respects the optimum method of overcoming or reducing the multicollinearity problem, this option will not be available in most applications – presumably the investigator will already be using all available data.

In some specialised cases alternative methods for at least limiting the problem can be taken. For example, some or all of the variables may have strong time trends thus resulting in some level of correlation between the explanatory variables. If the time trends are of a linear form then taking first differences[6] of the data will eliminate the trends, and then analysis can proceed using the differenced data. However, such an approach may introduce estimation problems of a more complex nature, and so create more problems than it solves (these problems will be discussed in Chapter 5). In any event, the investigator may also require explanations for the time trends, and so eliminating them from the data may not even be an acceptable approach in principle.

Another approach which has been used in certain applications is to obtain estimates of some of the parameters from other sources, and then to impose these on the equation being estimated. For example, in estimating a time-series consumption function the investigator may be able to draw upon other studies of consumption behaviour (cross-section studies, say) in which satisfactory estimates of some of the relevant parameters may have been obtained (for instance, it may be the case that there is a general consensus concerning the value of the marginal propensity to consume). Imposing these parameter estimates on the equation reduces the number of parameters to be estimated, thereby reducing the multicollinearity problem. However, it will only be in very specialised applications that such an approach will be possible, and it is therefore by no means a general method of overcoming the problem.

In practice, therefore, the problem of multicollinearity just has to be tolerated, with the result that in certain applications it may not be possible to draw definitive and unambiguous conclusions from the regression analysis.

There is one final point that should be made. So far we have discussed multicollinearity within the context of a given set of independent variables, and concluded that the higher the intercorrelation amongst these variables then the less precise will the resulting least squares estimators be. In practice, it will often be the case that the investigator may wish to add one or more variables to an estimated equation (presumably because a relatively large proportion of the variation in the dependent variable still remains unexplained). However, while the addition of extra variables must increase the intercorrelation amongst the expanded set of variables, it does not follow that the precision of the resulting estimators must necessarily fall – that is, it does not follow that smaller $t$-statistics will be produced.

Recall that the expressions for the variances of the estimators will each contain the term $\sigma_\varepsilon^2$ (or in the cases of the estimators of these variances, $\hat{\sigma}_\varepsilon^2$). So if the addition of one or more variables to the regression reduces $\hat{\sigma}_\varepsilon^2$ sufficiently to overcome the increased multicollinearity, then it may well be the case that some of the $t$-statistics are increased rather than reduced. The general condition under which this will be the case is if the added variables are important in explaining the dependent variable, and therefore the original equation was mis-specified – the imprecision of the original estimators derived not so much from multicollinearity, but from the relatively small proportion of the variation which was explained in the dependent variable.

We can illustrate some of these issues by reconsidering and extending Example 3.1, which concerned the estimation of a model explaining the variation in beer consumption.

Example 3.2

Recall that using the data in Table 3.2, the regression of beer consumption on income and price produced the following estimated equation ($t$-statistics in brackets):

$$\hat{\beta}_t = 26.004 + 0.327D_t - 0.146P_t, \quad R^2 = 0.962$$
$$\quad\;\; (2.70) \quad (4.34) \qquad (2.55)$$

Although the equation is well determined (all $t$-statistics are significant and the $R^2$ is high), it is instructive to quantify the extent of multicollinearity in the data. Thus we require the correlation coefficient between $D$ and $P$, which can be expressed as follows:

$$r_{12} = \frac{\sum (D_t - \bar{D})(P_t - \bar{P})}{\sqrt{\sum (D_t - \bar{D})^2 \sum (P_t - \bar{P})^2}}$$

From the data in Table 3.3, we have:

$$\sum (D_t - \bar{D})(P_t - \bar{P}) = \sum D_t P_t - n\bar{D}\bar{P} = -1476.1234$$
$$\sum (D_t - \bar{D})^2 = \sum D_t^2 - n\bar{D}^2 = 1206.8566$$
$$\sum (P_t - \bar{P})^2 = \sum P_t^2 - n\bar{P}^2 = 2071.2876$$

and therefore:

$$r_{12} = -0.934$$

Thus the data, in fact, exhibit a very high degree of multicollinearity, and yet a well-determined equation is none the less produced. That is, although the independent variables are highly correlated, they each appear to explain a significant proportion of the variation in beer consumption which is not explained by the other variable.

Note also the possible reasons for this high degree of multicollinearity here. Thus, as we are using time-series data, it may be that both $D$ and $P$ have strong time trends, resulting in a high correlation between them (although in no way implying any causal relationship between $D$ and $P$). We are also using a relatively small sample of only 17 observations, producing a high sample correlation coefficient, even though we would expect zero correlation in the population.

Now consider adding a further variable to the regression. For example, it is sometimes argued that at times of high unemployment beer consumption increases (holding income and price constant). Such an argument generally has some sociological justification, but we will here only examine the statistical, rather than the theoretical, support for such an argument.

Table 3.3 presents the unemployment rate in the UK, from 1963 to 1979. If we denote the unemployment rate in year $t$ by $U_t$, then the regression of $B_t$ on $D_t$, $P_t$ and $U_t$ produces the following equation ($t$-statistics in brackets):

$$B_t = 12.161 + 0.378D_t - 0.043P_t + 0.530U_t, \quad R^2 = 0.969$$
$$\quad\;\; (0.97) \quad (4.84) \qquad (0.51) \qquad (1.60)$$

The most noticeable effect of introducing $U_t$ is that the coefficient on $P_t$ is now insignificant. However the coefficient on $D_t$ remains stable (changing

**Table 3.3** Percentage unemployed in the UK 1963 to 1979

| Year | Percentage unemployed |
| --- | --- |
| 1963 | 2.6 |
| 1964 | 1.7 |
| 1965 | 1.5 |
| 1966 | 1.6 |
| 1967 | 2.5 |
| 1968 | 2.5 |
| 1969 | 2.4 |
| 1970 | 2.6 |
| 1971 | 3.5 |
| 1972 | 3.8 |
| 1973 | 2.7 |
| 1974 | 2.6 |
| 1975 | 4.1 |
| 1976 | 5.7 |
| 1977 | 6.2 |
| 1978 | 6.1 |
| 1979 | 5.8 |

*Source: Annual Abstract of Statistics*, HMSO

only from 0.327 to 0.378) and the *t*-statistic even marginally improves (increasing from 4.34 to 4.84).

As an extra variable has been added to the regression $R^2$ must necessarily increase, and therefore a more useful comparison of goodness of fit is via the corrected $R^2$s. For the regression of $B_t$ on $D_t$ and $P_t$ we have from Equation 3.18:

$$\bar{R}^2 = 0.957$$

and for the regression of $B_t$ on $D_t$, $P_t$ and $U_t$ we have:

$$\bar{R}^2 = 0.961$$

and thus a (marginal) improvement in $\bar{R}^2$ is achieved.

Note also that the coefficient on $U_t$ is of the expected sign (the higher the unemployment rate then the higher is beer consumption). However $U_t$ is significant only at the 10 per cent level, assuming a one-sided alternative ($t_{0.10,13} = 1.35$, but $t_{0.05,13} = 1.77$).

The introduction of $U_t$ has increased what even before was a high degree of multicollinearity and, it can be argued, this has resulted in the insignificance of $P_t$. In fact, the correlation coefficient between $D_t$ and $U_t$ is 0.764 and the correlation between $P_t$ and $U_t$ is $-0.890$, and thus in addition to the correlation of $-0.934$ between $D_t$ and $P_t$ we can conclude that a very high degree of multicollinearity is present, without having to go on to regress each of $D_t$, $P_t$ and $U_t$ on the remaining two variables.

As it appears that the insignificance of $P_t$ results from the interaction between $P_t$ and $U_t$ (the coefficient on $D_t$ remains relatively unaffected) then there are statistical grounds for excluding $P_t$. A regression of $B_t$ on just $D_t$ and $U_t$ produces the following equation:

$$B_t = 5.890 + 0.412D_t + 0.658U_t, \quad R^2 = 0.968, \quad \bar{R}^2 = 0.963$$
$$\quad\;\; (2.82) \quad (10.68) \qquad (3.17)$$

In pure statistical terms this is the best of all three equations (it has the highest $\bar{R}^2$, the $t$-statistic on $D_t$ is the highest of all three equations, and the coefficient on $U_t$ is now highly significant). However, unless it can be argued that there are poor theoretical grounds for retaining $P_t$ (for example, it might be argued that the demand for beer is little influenced by price – habit is a much stronger determinant), then $P_t$ should be kept in the equation. That is, it would be a brave assumption which argued that price has absolutely no influence on the level of beer consumption – the implication being that retailers of beer need not be concerned with the prices they charge.

The conclusion of the regression analysis, then, is that income, price and the unemployment rate appear to explain most of the variation in beer consumption, but because of the high degree of multicollinearity which is present in the data it is not possible to measure accurately the influence of price and, to a lesser extent, the influence of the unemployment rate. However, it must be emphasised that we have not here presented a particularly convincing theoretical justification for the role that unemployment might play in this model, and thus it may be argued that it is unemployment which should in fact be omitted, and hence we return to the model as originally specified and estimated.

### 3.6   The Use of Computer Packages

We will complete this chapter with a brief outline of the use of computer packages for estimating regression models.

There are now a wide variety of commercially available regression packages, many of which can be run on either mainframe or micro computers. We will make no attempt to provide a survey of these packages here,[7] but our objective will rather be simply to demonstrate how a particular package can be used, and how the output from this package can be interpreted. We will discuss the use of two specific packages, and we will show how these packages can be used to estimate the gas consumption model in Equation 3.2, using the data in Table 3.1. The two packages which we will use are 'MINITAB' and 'TSP'.

The first step in using a regression package is to enter the data which are to be used into the computer so that they can be read by the package. The mode of data input will depend on the nature of computer hardware which is available and we will not discuss this aspect here. Thus we will assume that the data have been satisfactorily entered and read into the package. Once the data have been read by the package there will generally be a number of procedures available to the investigator before the actual estimation of the model is performed. Thus the investigator may wish to print the data out in order to check that they have been correctly entered. Plots of the data may also be useful so that their broad properties can be examined.

Outputs 1 and 2 are the outputs of the two regression packages.

First consider Output 1, which was produced by MINITAB. The data in Table 3.1 have been read into the package as the three variables, C1, C2 and C3, where C1 denotes gas consumption, C2 denotes temperature and C3 denotes relative price. These data have been printed out, following the instruction 'PRINT C1 C2 C3'. Plots of the data are also produced, in response to the instructions 'PLOT C1 C2' and 'PLOT C1 C3'. That is, the output produces a plot of gas consumption against temperature, and gas consumption against price. In both cases, broadly negative relationships are implied, as expected, although in neither case is the relationship particularly strong – we cannot satisfactorily explain gas consumption in terms of either one of these variables, and thus the need for a multiple regression model is implied.

In fact, this form of graphical analysis can often be quite misleading in the context of a multiple regression model and in general will not be particularly useful. Recall that what the multiple regression model attempts to capture is the influence of each independent variable on the dependent variable, having taken account of the influence of the remaining independent variables. The plots in Output 1 do not of course account for the influence of the other independent variable, and therefore they offer only limited insights into the expected form of the estimated multiple regression. A more useful plot might be a graph of the residuals from each simple regression against the variable omitted from the regression – a plot of what is not explained by one variable against the other variable. It is not difficult to produce such plots using this package, but we will not do so here. However, as we shall see, it is very simple to produce estimated equations, and examination of the form of the relationship between the dependent and independent variables is therefore more effectively carried out by directly estimating the relationship, rather than by experimenting with graphical analyses.

The least squares estimate of the relationship between gas consumption, temperature and price is presented in Output 1, following the plots, in response to the instruction 'REGRESS C1 2 C2 C3' – that is, regress C1 on two independent variables, these being C2 and C3.

First, the simple estimate of the equation is presented, with the dependent variable denoted by $Y$, and the independent variables denoted by $X1$ and $X2$.

OUTPUT 1

```
-- PRINT C1 C2 C3
COLUMN        C1            C2            C3
COUNT         48            48            48
ROW
  1        8.0000        5.4000       90.8000
  2        6.2000       11.0000       83.1000
  3        5.2000       16.0000       83.7000
  4        9.4000        8.7000       83.7000
  5       11.6000        5.5000       88.7000
  6        9.5000       10.8000       83.9000
  7        7.4000       14.6000       83.9000
  8       12.4000        8.2000       83.9000
  9       12.9000        5.7000       83.9000
 10        9.5000       11.6000       83.9000
 11        7.4000       15.9000       83.9000
 12       14.4000        7.4000       78.5000
 13       16.0000        6.3000       82.7000
 14       11.5000       11.2000       73.2000
 15        9.3000       14.6000       65.7000
 16       16.1000        7.9000       63.6000
 17       17.0000        5.9000       67.4000
 18       12.1000       11.2000       53.5000
 19        9.1000       16.7000       51.2000
 20       17.2000        7.6000       59.0000
 21       19.3000        5.5000       60.9000
 22       12.2000       12.5000       54.2000
 23        9.0000       16.6000       52.7000
 24       18.3000        6.9000       57.6000
 25       20.0000        5.6000       57.6000
 26       14.1000       10.4000       57.8000
 27       10.5000       15.2000       57.2000
 28       18.2000        8.6000       57.2000
 29       21.7000        4.7000       56.0000
 30       14.4000       10.8000       52.8000
 31       10.4000       15.0000       52.2000
 32       18.6000        8.7000       53.0000
 33       24.9000        2.7000       52.2000
 34       15.4000       10.9000       51.8000
 35       10.8000       15.3000       51.4000
 36       20.2000        8.5000       48.1000
 37       24.7000        4.9000       48.1000
 38       14.6000       11.5000       47.7000
 39       10.3000       15.5000       45.5000
 40       20.8000        7.5000       46.8000
 41       24.3000        5.7000       47.4000
 42       15.2000       11.2000       48.5000
 43       10.1000       15.9000       48.8000
 44       22.5000        6.1000       56.3000
 45       25.3000        5.2000       54.5000
 46       13.8000       12.2000       55.3000
 47       10.5000       16.0000       55.5000
 48       22.1000        8.0000       60.2000
```

-- PLOT C1 C2

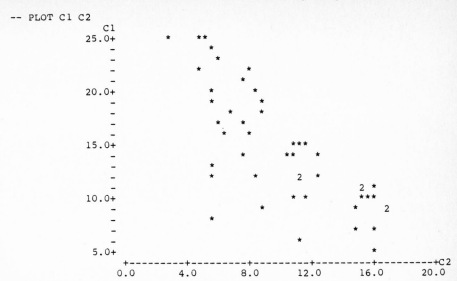

-- PLOT C1 C3

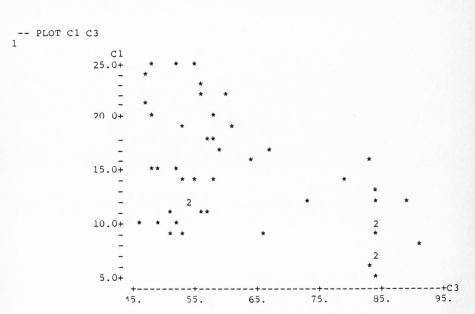

```
-- REGRESS C1 2 C2 C3

THE REGRESSION EQUATION IS
Y =    39.1 -  1.08 X1 - 0.220 X2

                                         ST. DEV.    T-RATIO =
            COLUMN      COEFFICIENT      OF COEF.    COEF/S.D.
            --            39.145           1.476        26.52
X1   C2               -1.08466          0.06906       -15.71
X2   C3               -0.22024          0.01933       -11.39

THE ST. DEV. OF Y ABOUT REGRESSION LINE IS
S = 1.881
WITH (   48- 3) =   45 DEGREES OF FREEDOM

R-SQUARED = 88.5 PERCENT
R-SQUARED = 88.0 PERCENT, ADJUSTED FOR D.F.

ANALYSIS OF VARIANCE

   DUE TO     DF            SS        MS=SS/DF
REGRESSION    2      1225.823        612.912
RESIDUAL     45       159.184          3.537
TOTAL        47      1385.007
```
1
```
FURTHER ANALYSIS OF VARIANCE
SS EXPLAINED BY EACH VARIABLE WHEN ENTERED IN THE ORDER GIVEN

   DUE TO     DF            SS
REGRESSION    2      1225.823
C2            1       766.609
C3            1       459.215

            X1          Y      PRED. Y    ST.DEV.
ROW         C2          C1       VALUE    PRED. Y    RESIDUAL     ST.RES.
  1        5.4       8.000      13.290      0.660      -5.290      -3.00R
 11       15.9       7.400       3.421      0.661       3.979       2.26R
 45        5.2      25.300      21.502      0.468       3.798       2.09R
 48        8.0      22.100      17.209      0.311       4.891       2.64R

R DENOTES AN OBS. WITH A LARGE ST. RES.

DURBIN-WATSON STATISTIC = 1.16

-- CORREL C1 C2 C3

            C1         C2
C2        -0.744
C3        -0.505     -0.092


-- STOP
```

A more detailed summary of the regression then follows, indicating the standard deviations and the *t*-statistics associated with each independent variable, thus enabling significance tests to be performed, or interval estimates to be derived. Much of the remainder of the printout is self-explanatory, although some of the information is presented in a form somewhat different from that which we have so far discussed. Thus, 'THE ST. DEV. OF Y ABOUT THE REGRESSION LINE' is simply the standard deviation of the estimated residuals, or the square root of $\hat{\sigma}_\varepsilon^2$ as given by Equation 3.11. That is, we can deduce that:

$$\hat{\sigma}_\varepsilon^2 = \frac{\sum e_t^2}{45} = (1.881)^2$$

and therefore:

$$\sum e_t^2 = (45)(1.881)^2 = 159.22$$

Following the values of $R^2$, the 'ANALYSIS OF VARIANCE' is presented. This is simply a summary of the decomposition of the total sum of squares (SST) into its explained (SSR) and unexplained components (SSE). Notice that SSE is just the value of $\sum e_t^2$ which we have derived above (allowing for rounding errors). From this analysis of variance data we can confirm the value of $R^2$ (the ratio of SSR to SST), and we can also calculate the *F*-statistic (the ratio of the **mean squares** – 'MS' – 612.912/3.537 = 173.28).

Following the analysis of variance, the printout indicates those observations on gas consumption which the model does not appear to explain particularly well – that is, those observations for which there is a relatively large difference between the predicted and actual value of the dependent variable ($\hat{Y}$ and $Y$). The investigator may then wish to go on to seek explanations for the model's poor performance with respect to these observations, which may then imply that extra variables should be added to the model. However, in this case only four of the total of 48 observations are relatively poorly predicted, and this level of imprecision might be considered as acceptable.

The final statistic on the regression printout is the 'DURBIN–WATSON STATISTIC', with a value here of 1.16. We will discuss the role of this statistic in Chapter 4. However we can note that the value of 1.16 does in fact indicate that a problem still remains with the estimated regression equation, and that the equation is not therefore in a fully acceptable form.

Finally, Output 1 presents **the correlation matrix** of the data, in response to 'CORREL C1 C2 C3'. That is, correlation coefficients are produced between all the variables indicated on the CORREL statement. Thus note the correlation between C2 and C3 of $-0.092$, indicating a low level of multicollinearity. The other two correlation coefficients are just the simple correlations between the dependent variable and each of the independent variables (note that these are just the square roots of the $R^2$ values in Equations 3.40 and 3.41 above).

In Output 2 we present the same information, but using TSP (we have omitted a printout of the data and the plots, although TSP can generate these if required).

OUTPUT 2

```
 1
    LOAD $
 2
    SMPL 1 48$
 3
    CORREL GAS PR TMP$
 4
    OLSQ GAS C TMP PR$
 5
    STOP$
 6
    END$

    LINE   2
                    SMPL
 0                      SMPL VECTOR
                          1  48
 0                      LINE   3
                    CORREL
                    GAS
                    PR
                    TMP




    LINE      3




 0                      CORRELATION OUTPUT
                        ******************
```

|  | MEAN | STANDARD DEVIATION |
|---|---|---|
| GAS | 14.4667 | 5.4285 |
| PR | 62.8229 | 14.2531 |
| TMP | 9.9958 | 3.9893 |

CORRELATION MATRIX

```
      GAS      PR       TMP
OCOL   1       2        3
  ROW
   1   1.0000 -0.5050 -0.7440
   2  -0.5050  1.0000 -0.0919
   3  -0.7440 -0.0919  1.0000
```

OLSQ    LINE    4

EQUATION 1
***********
SMPL VECTOR
  1  48
ORDINARY LEAST SQUARES

VARIABLES....

GAS
C
TMP
PR

MEAN OF DEPENDENT VARIABLE IS    14.4667

| INDEPENDENT VARIABLE | ESTIMATED COEFFICIENT | STANDARD ERROR | T-STATISTIC | MEAN OF VARIABLE |
|---|---|---|---|---|
| C | 3.91447380E+01 | 1.47612440E+00 | 2.65185890E+01 | 1.00000000E+00 |
| TMP | -1.08466040E+00 | 6.90610710E-02 | -1.57058150E+01 | 9.99583350E+00 |
| PR | -2.20237880E-01 | 1.93297880E-02 | -1.13937040E+01 | 6.28229160E+01 |

RSQ STATISTICS AND F STAT ARE AUTOMATICALLY ADJUSTED WHEN THE CONSTANT TERM IS ABSENT

RSQ= 0.8851    RSQ ADJUSTED FOR D.F= 0.8800
F-STATISTIC( 2, 45) =    173.265
DURBIN-WATSON STATISTIC (ADJ. FOR 0 GAPS) =   1.1650
NOTE: D-W STAT HAS NOT BEEN ADJUSTED FOR GAPS IN ZT3SLS WHERE IT IS RELEVANT ONLY FOR SINGLE EQUATION OLS WITH RESTRICTIONS.
NUMBER OF OBSERVATIONS =    48
SUM OF SQUARED RESIDUALS =    159.184
STANDARD ERROR OF THE REGRESSION =    1.88080
ESTIMATE OF VARIANCE-COVARIANCE MATRIX OF ESTIMATED COEFFICIENTS

  2.1789E+00 -5.5380E-02 -2.4699E-02
 -5.5380E-02  4.7694E-03  1.2265E-04
 -2.4699E-02  1.2265E-04  3.7364E-04

***********************************************************************************

The output begins with the statements that are required to produce the correlation and regression information. Thus we must first indicate the number of observations which are to be used ('SMPL 1 48'). We then request the correlation matrix (the variables on consumption, price and temperature are now denoted by GAS, PR and TMP, respectively). Finally, we run the regression ('OLSQ' stands for 'Ordinary Least SQuares', and 'C' indicates that we require a constant (or intercept) term in the estimated equation).

The correlation output is similar to that of Output 1, and requires no further comment. In terms of the regression output, there are differences in the way in which the information is presented, but the information is essentially the same (note that Output 2 uses scientific notation in dealing with decimal places; $E+0k$ indicates that the decimal place is to be moved $k$ places to the right, $E-0k$ indicates that it is to be moved $k$ places to the left). Output 2 does not present an explicit analysis of variance, but this information can easily be derived if required. Thus the $F$-statistic is presented, and the 'SUM OF THE SQUARED RESIDUALS' ($\Sigma e_t^2$), from which we could deduce SST and SSR (the value of $R^2$ could also be used).

The only additional feature of Output 2 is that it presents the 'ESTIMATE OF THE VARIANCE–COVARIANCE MATRIX OF ESTIMATED CO-EFFICIENTS'. The terms on the diagonal of this matrix are simply the estimated variances of the coefficient estimators (the square roots of which are shown as the 'STANDARD ERROR' in the estimated equation). The off-diagonal terms indicate the estimated covariances between the coefficient estimators, and allow hypotheses to be tested concerning possible relationships between the coefficients (that is, see Equation 3.27 and the associated discussion). The variances and covariances in this matrix appear in the same order as the variables that appear in the equation. Thus, the covariance between the estimators of the coefficients on TMP and PR is '1.2265E-04' or 0.00012265. The other off-diagonal terms in the matrix are the covariances between the constant term estimator and the estimators on TMP and PR.

## 3.7   Summary

In this chapter we have discussed the model that forms the basis of estimation and hypothesis testing in economics. In principle, it is a straightforward generalisation of the simple regression model and allows for the consideration of the range of factors which influence the dependent variable of interest.

However, we have emphasised that the multiple regression model only provides a second-best means for evaluating some given economic theory, given the inability of the investigator to have full control over the relevant *ceteris paribus* conditions. This results in the problem of multicollinearity and leads to a degree of imprecision in the estimation process. In general, there is little that can be done about this problem (save for using large samples), with the result that it will often be difficult to separate out the specific influence of each of the hypothesised set of explanatory variables.

Our discussion in this chapter has been concerned with the simplest form of the multiple regression model. In the remainder of this book we will extend this model to allow for a much greater degree of generality in the process of testing and evaluating economic theory. However, as we have already seen, and will continue to see, the testing of economic theory will often cause ambiguity. Partly, this may result from the theory itself being specified at too general a level. But difficulties also arise because the methods of estimation and hypothesis testing that are available to us, or the available data, are not sufficiently sensitive to discriminate adequately between competing hypotheses. In turn, this results from the very nature of economics as a social science, and the inherent difficulties of deriving specific, well-defined and directly testable hypotheses.

In the final section of this chapter we briefly discussed the use of computer packages for estimating regression models. The reader is strongly urged to become familiar with the use of such a package, as it is only via first hand experience of estimating regression models that a real insight can be gained into the application of econometric methodology.

## Notes

[1] The interested reader is referred to any intermediate or advanced econometrics text for the derivation of the variances of the least squares estimators (although, in general, texts resort to the use of matrix algebra for deriving both the least squares estimators and their variances.) For example, see J. Kmenta, *Elements of Econometrics*, 2nd edn (New York, Macmillan, 1986), pp. 403–8.

[2] Note that should the relevant hypothesis test concern the difference between the values of two parameters, then we can write:

$$\text{Var}(\hat{\alpha} - \hat{\beta}) = \text{Var}(\hat{\alpha}) + \text{Var}(\hat{\beta}) - 2\,\text{Cov}(\hat{\alpha}, \hat{\beta})$$

[3] We are here raising the issue of the identification problem, an issue which is of fundamental importance. In essence, if beer consumption and beer production are equal in each year (that is, producers do not stock-pile) then a function relating beer consumption (or production) to price, while being the classic textbook example of a demand function, could equally well represent a supply function – that is, if price changes in the market place, producers as well as consumers will respond. The inclusion of income in our function, then, allows us to describe the resulting function as a demand function, as it may be argued that producers respond to cost factors rather than to the incomes of consumers – that is, we would not expect a supply function to contain an income term. But even so, some may disagree with such an analysis, arguing that producers will take some account of 'what the market will bear'. However, we now raise issues of market imperfections and the characteristics of the competitive environment which we will not dwell on here. Suffice it to say that these issues can become theoretically complex and are beyond the scope of this book.

Specific questions concerning the identification problem will be taken up in greater detail in Chapter 6.

[4] We are here assuming of course that $X_1$ and $X_2$ are theoretically related to $Y$. A reduction in the variances of the estimators in any regression model can always be achieved by adding a further explanatory variable which is uncorrelated with any of the other explanatory variables. However, if this additional variable has no theoretical relationship to the dependent variable then the resulting equation is, by definition, incorrectly specified, and hence theoretically unacceptable.

[5] It may well be the case, of course, that correlation amongst the independent variables results from a (population) relationship between some of the variables. If this is the case then the model has been incorrectly specified and such a relationship should be explicitly incorporated into the model. This leads to the consideration of multiple equation models, rather than the single equation models which we have so far considered. These will be discussed in Chapter 6.

[6] Consider a variable, $X_t$, where the subscript $t$ refers to the time period, and the variable is measured over $n$ periods, that is, $t = 1, \ldots, n$. Then the first difference of this variable is defined as:

$$D_t = X_t - X_{t-1}$$

and so a new variable, $D_t$, is produced which measures the differences between successive observations on $X$.

[7] For a more comprehensive survey of available regression/econometrics packages see, for example, D. G. Mayes, *Applications of Econometrics* (London, Prentice-Hall, 1981), Ch. 10.

### References and Further Reading

The same references as those in Chapter 2 are also relevant in the case of the multiple regression model. An additional useful reference is: R. L. Thomas, *Introductory Econometrics – Theory and Applications* (London, Longman, 1985).

### Exercises

### Exercise 1

In the light of your estimated car registration model from Exercise 8 of Chapter 2, discuss how this model might be expanded to include the influence of additional explanatory factors. That is, identify any additional independent variables which you consider to be relevant, provide a theoretical justification for their inclusion, and briefly outline how you might obtain data to measure the influence of these variables.

### Exercise 2

Taking the same approach as in Exercise 1 above, reconsider your estimated exchange rate models from Exercise 9 of Chapter 2.

## Exercise 3

Assume that in a certain small country the demand function for coffee has been estimated and is given by:

$$\hat{D}_t = 42.22 - 3.07P_t^C + 2.63P_t^T + 0.80Y_t + 0.06t$$

where:

$D_t$ = annual demand for coffee in year $t$ (in hundreds of thousands of lbs)

$P_t^C$ = real price of coffee (in £ per lb)

$P_t^T$ = real price of tea (in £ per lb)

$Y_t$ = total real disposable income (in £ billion)

$t$ = time trend (that is, the value of $t$)

Currently (1987) the values of each of these variables are:

$D_t = 50$

$P_t^C = 1.63$

$P_t^T = 0.95$

$Y_t = 5$

$t = 87$

Assume further that all marketing of coffee in this country is controlled by one organisation – that is, this organisation can be assumed to be a monopolist.

(a)  If the price of coffee were increased by 10 per cent, what would be the approximate response of demand?
(b)  If the price of tea were reduced by 15 per cent, by how much would the price of coffee have to be reduced in order to maintain the current level of demand?
(c)  Forecast the demand for coffee in 1988, assuming:
   (i)   the price of coffee will be unchanged,
   (ii)  a 10 per cent increase in real income, and
   (iii) an 8 per cent fall in the price of tea.
(d)  You are now given the various statistics associated with this estimated demand function. That is,

$$\hat{D}_t = 42.22 - 3.07P_t^C + 2.63P_t^T + 0.80Y_t + 0.06t, \quad R^2 = 0.834, \quad n = 20$$
$$\phantom{\hat{D}_t = 42.22 -}(6.53)\ (4.21)\quad\ (0.82)\quad\ (1.13)\ \ (2.45)$$

(The values in brackets are the absolute values of the $t$-statistics associated with each estimate.)

Given this information, comment on your calculations in (a) to (c) above. Would you now amend any of these calculations?

Exercise 4

An econometrician is attempting to explain the variation in a certain variable, $Y_t$. He collects just ten observations on $Y$, and ten observations on each of five possible explanatory variables, $X_1$ to $X_5$. He runs three regressions, the results of which are as follows (*t*-statistics in brackets):

(i)  $\hat{Y}_t = 51.5 + 3.21X_{1t}, \quad R^2 = 0.63$
     $\quad\;\;(3.45)(5.21)$

(ii)  $\hat{Y}_t = 33.43 + 3.67X_{1t} + 4.62X_{2t} + 1.21X_{3t}, \quad R^2 = 0.75$
      $\quad\;\;(3.61) \;\;(2.56) \qquad (0.81) \qquad (0.22)$

(iii)  $\hat{Y}_t = 23.21 + 3.82X_{1t} + 2.32X_{2t} + 0.82X_{3t} + 4.10X_{4t} + 1.21X_{5t},$
       $\quad\;\;(2.21) \;(2.33) \qquad (0.62) \qquad (0.12) \qquad (2.10) \qquad (1.11)$

$$R^2 = 0.80$$

Which do you consider to be the most satisfactory regression and why?

What further information would you require to carry out a fuller assessment of these regressions?

Exercise 5

If you have access to a computer and an appropriate regression package, estimate the model in Equation 3.2, but using the monthly gas consumption and temperature data in Table 2.1, and the corresponding monthly price data which we present below. Discuss your estimation results. (If you have not used a regression package before, but you have access to such a package, you might familiarise yourself with using this package by attempting to reproduce the estimated equations of this chapter – for example, the estimated gas consumption model in Equation 3.21, or the estimated beer consumption model in Example 3.1.)

Price of gas relative to electricity, Great Britain 1980 to 1981 monthly

| | Month | | | | | | | | | | | |
|---|---|---|---|---|---|---|---|---|---|---|---|---|
| Year | Jan | Feb | Mar | Apr | May | Jun | Jul | Aug | Sep | Oct | Nov | Dec |
| 1980 | 60.6 | 60.6 | 60.6 | 60.5 | 60.2 | 60.0 | 60.1 | 59.6 | 57.2 | 56.3 | 57.2 | 58.8 |
| 1981 | 59.6 | 59.6 | 59.6 | 59.9 | 60.5 | 61.6 | 61.4 | 61.4 | 61.4 | 62.4 | 67.4 | 70.7 |

*Source: Monthly Digest of Statistics*, HMSO.

Exercise 6

Construct your own multiple regression model, using as a dependent variable any variable which you consider to be of interest. Limit the number of explanatory variables to just two or three, and provide a theoretical justification for the inclusion of these variables in your model.

Next, collect a sample of data on the variables in your model. You might find it useful to consult a number of Government statistical publications in order to give yourself some idea of the scope of available data, and perhaps to identify an interesting variable (in the UK, publications such as the *Monthly Digest of Statistics, Annual Abstract of Statistics,* or *Economic Trends* (Annual Supplements), all published by HMSO, are useful starting points).

Finally, if you have access to a regression package, estimate your model using the data which you have collected (for convenience, collect no more than 15–20 observations on each of your variables). Discuss your estimated model. Indicate how you think your model could be improved.

# 4 Extensions of the Regression Model – I

<hr/>

## 4.1 Introduction

In this chapter we will relax a number of the assumptions which we have so far made in the specification of both the simple and multiple regression models. We will begin by relaxing the assumption of there only being a linear relationship between the dependent and independent variables. Thus, we will discuss how non-linear relationships might arise in economics, and how these relationships can then be modelled and estimated.

We will then relax the assumptions we have made concerning the disturbance term, $\varepsilon_t$. First, we will consider situations in which it might be unrealistic to assume that the disturbance terms have the same variance at each sample point (the assumption of homoskedasticity – Assumption b in the model specifications in Equations 2.13 and 3.1). That is, we will consider the problem of **heteroskedasticity**. We will then consider cases in which the disturbance terms are correlated across sample points, and therefore consider the problem of **autocorrelation** (that is, we will relax Assumption c of the model specifications in Equations 2.13 and 3.1). We will also outline the adjustments which are required in our estimation procedures in the presence of heteroskedastic and autocorrelated disturbance terms.

## 4.2 Non-linearities

In the models which we have so far specified and estimated, we have assumed that the dependent variable and the independent variables are linearly related. However, in practice, many relationships will be non-linear, whether this be the case theoretically or empirically.

There are many relationships in economics that, *a priori*, we would expect to be non-linear. Thus, at the microeconomic level, a firm's total cost function would be expected to be 'S' shaped, such as in Figure 4.1, reflecting increasing

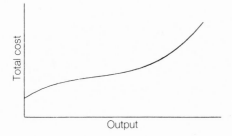

**Figure 4.1** A firm's theoretical total cost function.

returns to scale at low levels of output, and decreasing returns at high output levels.

Production function theory would also imply a range of non-linearities. Thus in the case of just two factors of production (capital and labour, say), we would expect an **isoquant** to be convex to the origin, such as in Figure 4.2. This convexity simply reflects the fact that, in general, capital and labour will not be perfect substitutes – the larger the amount of capital which is used to produce some given level of output, the more difficult it becomes to substitute further units of capital for labour (the marginal rate of substitution of capital for labour will decrease as the level of capital increases).

These examples are cases of non-linearities which can be predicted theoretically. However, in many applications theory will not be sufficiently detailed or specific to enable the *a priori* prediction of non-linear relationships.

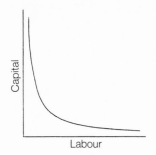

**Figure 4.2** A typical isoquant.

In such cases any non-linearities will have to be determined empirically – that is, essentially by trial and error. Graphical analysis may aid in this process, but in the case of multiple regression models it becomes very difficult to interpret the separate graphs of the dependent variable against each of the independent variables. Thus the approach which is generally taken is one of experimenting with a range of different functional forms, and selecting that form which produces the most satisfactory regression results.

The regression model can be quite easily extended to accommodate a wide range of non-linear forms. In Figure 4.3, Panels (a), (b), (c) and (d) we present

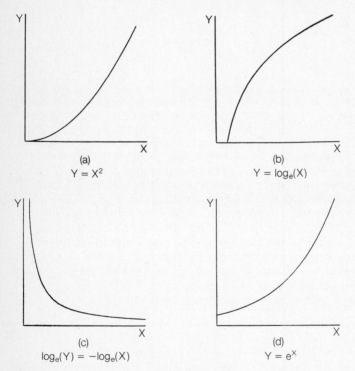

(a)
$Y = X^2$

(b)
$Y = \log_e(X)$

(c)
$\log_e(Y) = -\log_e(X)$

(d)
$Y = e^X$

**Figure 4.3**   Common non-linear relationships.

graphs of a number of common non-linear relationships (although these certainly do not represent an exhaustive range of possibilities).

Assume, for example, that in a simple regression context a plot of the sample observations on some dependent variable ($Y$) against the observations on the independent variable ($X$) produces a graph similar to that of Figure 4.3 (a). Therefore we would conclude that $Y$ is non-linearly related to $X$, and specifically, that $Y$ appears to be directly related to the square of $X$. That is, if each value of $Y$ was graphed against the square of each corresponding value of $X$ (rather than the level of $X$, as in Figure 4.3(a)) then a linear relationship would be produced – $Y$ can be interpreted as being linearly related to $X^2$.

Assuming that a sample of data produces a plot such as that in Figure 4.3 (a), we would then proceed to estimate the relationship by regressing $Y$ on $X^2$, rather than on $X$. In order to be explicit, we could define a third variable, $Z$, where:

$$Z = X^2 \qquad \text{Equation 4.1}$$

and then proceed to estimate the linear relationship:

$$Y_t = \alpha + \beta Z_t + \varepsilon_t \qquad \text{Equation 4.2}$$

Note, that in the case of Figure 4.3(a) such a regression would produce an estimate for $\alpha$ of approximately zero (the relationship passes through the origin) and an estimate for $\beta$ of approximately one (there is a one-to-one relationship between $Y$ and $X^2$). However, $\alpha$ and $\beta$ could take on any values, thus producing a wide range of variations on the basic shape in Figure 4.3(a), while still retaining the basic property of a linear relationship between $Y$ and $X^2$.

Similarly, the relationships in the remaining panels of Figure 4.3 can all be 'linearised' in the same way as in the case of (a), and variations on each of these basic shapes can be produced by varying the values of $\alpha$ and $\beta$ of the implied linear relationships.

A numerical example will help to illustrate some of these issues.

Example 4.1

In Table 4.1 we present a sample of 20 hypothetical observations on some

**Table 4.1** A hypothetical sample of data on a dependent variable $Y$ and an independent variable $X$

| Observation number | $Y$ | $X$ | Observation number | $Y$ | $X$ |
|---|---|---|---|---|---|
| 1 | 2692.50 | 42 | 11 | 2751.51 | 37 |
| 2 | 2839.79 | 32 | 12 | 2779.17 | 34 |
| 3 | 2814.48 | 51 | 13 | 2708.88 | 46 |
| 4 | 2814.18 | 33 | 14 | 2691.85 | 40 |
| 5 | 2718.43 | 45 | 15 | 2758.82 | 49 |
| 6 | 2750.05 | 47 | 16 | 2718.54 | 39 |
| 7 | 2768.31 | 35 | 17 | 2738.79 | 38 |
| 8 | 2750.69 | 36 | 18 | 2702.16 | 41 |
| 9 | 2744.47 | 48 | 19 | 2698.57 | 43 |
| 10 | 2807.75 | 50 | 20 | 2719.70 | 44 |

dependent variable, $Y$, and an independent variable, $X$. A graph of these data is shown in Figure 4.4, where it can be seen that the relationship between $Y$ and $X$ is clearly non-linear, and specifically, the relationship appears to be 'U-shaped' (or parabolic). In addition, a disturbance term appears to be present which results in the relationship between $Y$ and $X$ being an approximate rather than an exact one.

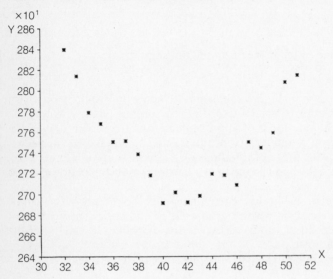

**Figure 4.4**    Graph of data in Table 4.1.

Now, the general form of a parabolic relationship between $Y$ and $X$ is as follows:

$$Y_t = \beta_0 + \beta_1 X_t + \beta_2 X_t^2 \qquad \text{Equation 4.3}$$

where $\beta_0$, $\beta_1$ and $\beta_2$ are parameters which determine the precise shape and positioning of the parabola (note that the relationship in Figure 4.3(a) is a special case of Equation 4.3, where $\beta_0 = \beta_1 = 0$ and $\beta_2 = 1$). Thus in terms of the data in Table 4.1 and Figure 4.4, we require estimates of $\beta_0$, $\beta_1$ and $\beta_2$ in Equation 4.3. The full specification of the relationship between $Y$ and $X$ can be written as:

$$Y_i = \beta_0 + \beta_1 X_i + \beta_2 Z_i + \varepsilon_i \qquad \text{Equation 4.4}$$

where

$$Z_i = X_i^2$$

and $i$ denotes 'Observation Number'.

Thus we can obtain the least squares estimates of $\beta_0$, $\beta_1$ and $\beta_2$ by simply regressing $Y$ on $X$ and a third variable, $Z$, which is just the square of $X$.

In Equation 4.5 below we present the least squares estimate of Equation 4.4, using the data in Table 4.1 (absolute values of $t$-statistics in brackets):

$$\hat{Y}_i = 5158.197 - 117.074\,X_i + 1.395\,Z_i \qquad \text{Equation 4.5}$$
$$\quad\;\;(37.11)\quad\;(17.25)\quad\;\;(17.09)$$

$$R^2 = 0.947$$

Thus the estimated equation can be seen to be very well determined, with a high $R^2$ and highly significant $t$-statistics. Equation 4.5 can therefore be interpreted as the equation of the parabola which 'best' fits the data in Figure 4.4.

It is instructive also to estimate the 'naive' *a priori* model – that is, the model which implies a simple linear relationship between $Y$ and $X$, which might be postulated before carrying out any graphical analysis of the data in Table 4.1. Thus the simple regression of $Y$ on $X$ produces the following equation:

$$\hat{Y}_i = 2802.173 - 1.295\,X_i \qquad \text{Equation 4.6}$$
$$\quad\;\;(38.48)\quad\;(0.74)$$

$$R^2 = 0.030$$

As expected, Equation 4.6 provides no evidence of a significant linear relationship between $Y$ and $X$ – the line of best fit to the data is a line approximately parallel to the $X$ axis in Figure 4.4, producing an even distribution of estimated residuals around the line.

It is also worth noting that if the investigator were to examine the estimated residuals from Equation 4.6 (by graphing them against $X$, for example) then the non-linearity which Equation 4.6 fails to capture would still be reflected in these residuals – they would retain the basic parabolic shape of the original data. As we shall see in Sections 4.3 and 4.4 (and in Chapter 7), the examination of the estimated residuals from a regression equation provides an important means of examining for the correct specification of the model.

In this example we have highlighted how we might proceed to determine empirically the form of a non-linearity which exists between a dependent and an independent variable. That is, a simple graphical analysis of the data highlighted both the existence and the nature of the underlying non-linearity. Thus we have illustrated how we might proceed in those cases in which the theory is not specific as to the form of the relationship between the dependent and independent variable(s).

Theory may simply imply that there should be, say, a positive relationship between $Y$ and $X$. But this would be consistent with $Y$ being linearly related to the level of $X$, or the square of $X$, of the cube of $X$, or the logarithm of $X$, and so on. The investigator would then, in effect, have to employ trial and error methods, and perhaps graphical methods, to determine the appropriate variable transformation.

Thus, $Y$ could be regressed, in turn, on a range of transformations of $X$ and that regression with the most satisfactory statistical properties (highest $R^2$, highest $t$-statistics) would be selected as containing the appropriate transformation. However, in the case of a multiple regression the graphical identification of any non-linearities can become difficult given that each independent variable will only partially explain the dependent variable, and there will not necessarily be a close association between the dependent variable and each of the independent variables.

However, economic theory can often be quite specific as to the expected form of non-linearity between two variables. Thus we have already mentioned that the theory of the firm and production function theory would imply a range of non-linear relationships (indeed, the form of the relationship between the variables in Figure 4.4 would be expected of a firm's average cost function). A common variable transformation which is used in much empirical work is the logarithmic transformation. This is particularly so in the case of the estimation of demand functions.

Consider the simplest specification of a demand function where the demand for some good in period $t$ $(D_t)$ depends on the price of that good in period $t$ $(P_t)$ and consumer income in period $t$ $(Y_t)$. That is:

$$D_t = f(P_t, Y_t). \hspace{3cm} \text{Equation 4.7}$$

Now, if Equation 4.7 is specified in logarithmic form then the coefficients on the independent variables can be interpreted directly as **elasticities**. That is, if the following equation is estimated:

$$\log_e(D_t) = \beta_0 + \beta_1 \log_e(P_t) + \beta_2 \log_e(Y_t) + \varepsilon_t \hspace{2cm} \text{Equation 4.8}$$

then the estimates of $\beta_1$ and $\beta_2$ will be estimates of the price and income elasticities of demand, respectively (see any mathematical economics text for an illustration of this result, such as those indicated in the references to Chapter 1).

While estimating demand functions in logarithmic form has the convenient property of the coefficients being elasticities, such a transformation should strictly only be used if there is also some theoretical justification for doing so. In the case of a demand function such a justification can perhaps be made. That is, a strictly linear demand function would imply that there is some finite price level at which the demand for the given good would be reduced to zero. However, it might be argued that even at very high prices there will be some demand for the good, and thus, in a two-dimensional context, we would expect a demand curve to be asymptotic to the price axis – that is, demand will approach zero but never actually reach zero as price increases. A log-linear demand function possesses this property and this represents the theoretical justification for this type of formulation.

The non-linear models which we have so far discussed could all be estimated by transforming the variables in some way and then applying the usual estimation methods – these models could be linearised via an appropriate variable transformation. Such models are described as being non-linear in the variables but linear in the parameters, and as such do not cause any estimation problems. However, there is another class of non-linear models which cannot be estimated in such a straightforward manner. These models are non-linear in the parameters and more complex estimation procedures have to be employed. The complexities involved can be illustrated by considering a number of relatively simple models.

First, recall from Appendix 2.1 the method by which we derived the least squares estimators for the simple regression model. Thus, if we consider a simple linear relationship between a dependent variable, $Y$, and an independent variable, $X$, and if for ease of exposition we assume there is no constant term, then the model can be written as:

$$Y_t = \beta X_t + \varepsilon_t \qquad \text{Equation 4.9}$$

The estimated model can be written as:

$$Y_t = \hat{\beta} X_t + e_t \qquad \text{Equation 4.10}$$

and the least squares estimator of $\beta$ is that expression for $\hat{\beta}$ which minimises $\Sigma e_t^2$. That is:

$$SS = \sum e_t^2 = \sum (Y_t - \hat{\beta} X_t)^2 \qquad \text{Equation 4.11}$$

Differentiating SS with respect to $\hat{\beta}$ and setting this expression equal to zero we have:

$$2\sum (Y_t - \hat{\beta} X_t)(-X_t) = 0 \qquad \text{Equation 4.12}$$

or

$$\hat{\beta} = \frac{\sum Y_t X_t}{\sum X_t^2} \qquad \text{Equation 4.13}$$

The essential point here is that this least squares procedure produces an equation (Equation 4.12) which is linear in $\hat{\beta}$, and thus solving for $\hat{\beta}$ to produce Equation 4.13 is straightforward.

Now consider a non-linear relationship between $Y$ and $X$, such as the following:

$$Y_t = \beta X_t^2 + \varepsilon_t \qquad \text{Equation 4.14}$$

Using the least squares procedure as above, we write the estimated model as:

$$Y_t = \hat{\beta} X_t^2 + e_t \qquad \text{Equation 4.15}$$

and

$$SS = \sum e_t^2 = \sum (Y_t - \hat{\beta} X_t^2)$$    Equation 4.16

Differentiating SS with respect to $\hat{\beta}$ and setting to zero we have:

$$2 \sum (Y_t - \hat{\beta} X_t^2)(- X_t^2) = 0$$    Equation 4.17

or

$$\hat{\beta} = \frac{\sum Y_t X_t^2}{\sum X_t^4}$$    Equation 4.18

Note that this least squares procedure has still resulted in an equation which is linear in $\hat{\beta}$ (Equation 4.17), and thus solving for $\hat{\beta}$ again presents no difficulties – the model in Equation 4.14 still remains linear in terms of the unknown parameter, $\beta$. (Note that explicitly substituting $Z$ for $X^2$ in Equations 4.14 to 4.18 would result in the equivalent analysis as implied by Equations 4.1 and 4.2 (minus the constant term).)

Now consider a different form of non-linear association between $Y$ and $X$, and in particular the following relationship:

$$Y_t = \beta^{X_t} + \varepsilon_t$$    Equation 4.19

The estimated model can be written as:

$$Y_t = \hat{\beta}^{X_t} + e_t$$    Equation 4.20

and thus

$$SS = \sum e_t^2 = \sum (Y_t - \hat{\beta}^{X_t})^2$$    Equation 4.21

Now, the difficulty here is that differentiating Equation 4.21 with respect to $\hat{\beta}$, and setting the resulting expression equal to zero, produces an equation which is non-linear in $\hat{\beta}$ (in contrast to Equations 4.12 and 4.17). Therefore a unique estimator for $\beta$ cannot be derived.

There are methods available for overcoming this problem – in general, these methods are referred to as **non-linear least squares** – but we will not describe these here (we will briefly discuss them in Chapter 7). In essence, they involve trial and error or iterative procedures in order to determine that value of $\hat{\beta}$ which minimises the appropriate sum of squares, such as the expression in Equation 4.21. The calculations involved are typically lengthy and tedious, but are easily performed on a computer.

There are a variety of non-linear models that result in similar estimation problems to those of the model in Equation 4.19. Common examples are **multiplicative** models which contain **additive** disturbance terms.

For example, consider the log-linear demand function in Equation 4.8. If we ignore the disturbance term then an equivalent form of this equation is the following:

$$D_t = e^{\beta_0} P_t^{\beta_1} Y_t^{\beta_2} \qquad\qquad \text{Equation 4.22}$$

Taking logarithms to the base $e$ of both sides of Equation 4.22 and adding $\varepsilon_t$ produces Equation 4.8.[1] However, such a procedure implicitly assumes that $\varepsilon_t$ enters Equation 4.22 multiplicatively. That is, the strict specification of the model in Equation 4.22 is:

$$D_t = e^{\beta_0} P_t^{\beta_1} Y_t^{\beta_2} e^{\varepsilon_t} \qquad\qquad \text{Equation 4.23}$$

If, instead, $\varepsilon_t$ entered Equation 4.22 additively, then we would have:

$$D_t = e^{\beta_0} P_t^{\beta_1} Y_t^{\beta_2} + \varepsilon_t \qquad\qquad \text{Equation 4.24}$$

and it is now not possible to take logarithms of both sides of Equation 4.24 and thereby produce a linear model – the expression:

$$\log_e(e^{\beta_0} P_t^{\beta_1} Y_t^{\beta_2} + \varepsilon_t) \qquad\qquad \text{Equation 4.25}$$

cannot be simplified any further and some non-linear estimation procedure would have to be used.

Now, while Equation 4.23 is certainly in a more convenient form for estimation purposes, it is often difficult to justify theoretically the way in which the disturbance term enters this equation. Formulations such as Equation 4.24 generally have a stronger theoretical justification, and therefore models such as Equation 4.8 can be best interpreted as representing a compromise between theoretical purity and empirical expediency.

## 4.3   Heteroskedastic Disturbance Terms

One of the assumptions of the model specifications in Chapters 2 and 3 was that the disturbance terms are identically distributed at each sample point, and in particular, that these distributions have the same variance. That is, we assumed that $\text{Var}(\varepsilon_t) = \sigma_\varepsilon^2$, for all $t$ (Assumption b of Equations 2.13 and 3.1). We will now consider cases in which it will be necessary to relax this assumption, and we will also describe the implications that this will have for our estimation procedures.

If the variances of the disturbance terms are constant across sample points then the disturbance terms are referred to as being **homoskedastic**. If these variances are not all equal, then the disturbance terms are described as being **heteroskedastic**, and we are therefore concerned with the problem of **heteroskedasticity**.

### 4.3.1   The Nature of the Problem

In general, heteroskedasticity is a problem which is more likely to occur in cross-section data than in time-series data.

As an example, consider the estimation of a consumption function, which we considered briefly in Examples 2.1 and 2.2. However, consider the case of estimating a consumption function using cross-section data rather than time-series data.

A cross-section consumption function could be estimated by selecting a sample of households at some point in time, collecting data on household consumption expenditure and household income, and then regressing the observations on consumption expenditure on the observations on income. However, it is very likely that higher income households will exhibit greater variation in their consumption expenditures than lower income households – higher income households will have greater flexibility or choice with respect to their consumption patterns, and we would expect this to be reflected in greater variation in observed consumption expenditure. Diagrammatically, we might expect to observe an association between household consumption and income such as that shown in Figure 4.5.

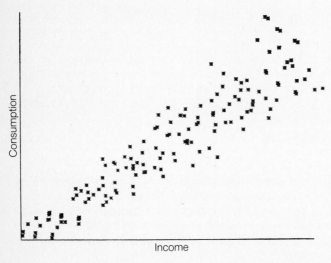

**Figure 4.5**  A hypothetical cross-section relationship between consumption and income data.

Note from Figure 4.5 that the level of household consumption expenditure increases with the level of income, as would be expected, but as income increases the variation in consumption expenditure also appears to increase. Consequently, it would be more realistic to assume that the variance of the disturbance terms is a variable rather than a constant, and we could write:

$$\text{Var}(\varepsilon_i) = \sigma_i^2 \qquad\qquad \text{Equation 4.26}$$

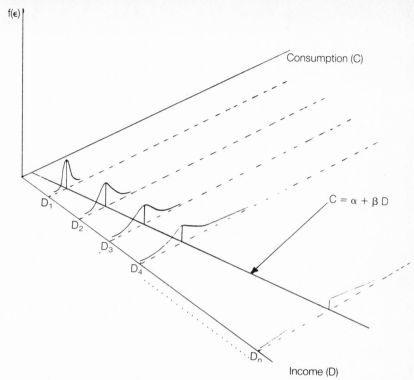

**Figure 4.6** A regression model with heteroskedastic disturbance terms.

where the subscript $i$ refers to the $i$th household and, as we have argued here, $\sigma_i^2$, in turn, depends on the income of the $i$th household.

In an analogous manner to Figure 2.2, where a diagrammatic interpretation of the simple regression model was presented, a model of the consumption function in which the variance of the disturbance terms increases with the level of income could be interpreted as in Figure 4.6. Note that as income increases the variance of the distribution of the disturbance term at each income level also increases. Thus a sample of observations could be interpreted as being generated by randomly selecting an observation on consumption at each income level, with the variation in consumption expenditure increasing as income increases.

Another application in which we might expect heteroskedastic disturbances would be a cross-section study involving a sample of firms – larger firms would probably exhibit greater variability with reference to some performance indicator, for example. Cross-section studies of geographical regions or countries are likely to require an assumption of heteroskedasticity – again, we might expect larger regions (countries) to be more variable in terms of their output, say.

So far we have emphasised that heteroskedasticity will tend to be a problem with cross-section data, and we have illustrated the nature of the problem using cross-section examples. However, time-series data can also exhibit heteroskedasticity. This will typically be the case with long runs of data where the variation in the data will often appear to increase over time. As an example, we present in Figure 4.7 a graph of quarterly consumers'

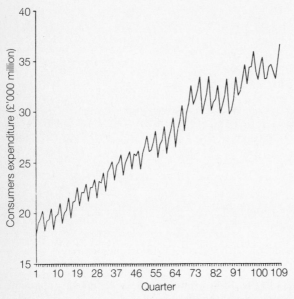

**Figure 4.7**   Quarterly consumers' expenditure in the UK, 1980 prices 1955 to 1982. *Source: Economic Trends*, Annual Supplement, 1984, HMSO.

expenditure in the UK, in 1980 prices, over the period 1955 to 1982. It can be seen from this graph that the data appear to 'fan out' over time, and thus can be interpreted as exhibiting heteroskedasticity.

### 4.3.2   The Consequences of Heteroskedasticity

Assuming that the model under investigation possesses heteroskedastic disturbance terms, we need to determine the consequences of estimating the parameters of this model using our simple least squares procedures. However, before examining these issues in detail we will first introduce a number of additional criteria which are useful for assessing the properties of a given estimator.

*Digression 4.1:   Consistency and Asymptotic Efficiency*

In Chapter 2 we described two desirable properties which we would expect of any estimator – that is, we would expect the estimator to be unbiased (on average, it will produce a value equal to the true parameter value), and we would expect the estimator to be efficient (its variance is the smallest of all available unbiased estimators, and hence it is the most precise estimator available). In practice, however, when dealing with more complex model specifications, two problems can arise.

A given estimator, or the commonly used estimator, may be biased, under the now more complex assumptions of the model. However, there may be no obvious alternative estimator available and thus we wish to determine whether, as a 'second-best' alternative, it might still be reasonable to use this biased estimator.

A second problem which can arise is that although a given model specification does allow for the derivation of what appears to be a sensible estimator, this estimator may have such a complex and intractable form that it is not possible to determine the properties of the estimator – that is, it is not possible to determine analytically whether the estimator is unbiased and, in particular, efficient.

In such cases appeal is made to the **large sample** or **asymptotic** properties of the estimator – that is, an examination of the properties of the estimator as sample size increases and, in the limit, approaches infinity. In general, these asymptotic properties are much easier to establish than the corresponding small (or finite) sample properties.

There are two asymptotic properties which can be interpreted as the large sample counterparts of unbiasedness and efficiency.

The first is **consistency**. Thus an estimator is defined as consistent if, as sample size increases, any bias which the estimator may possess approaches zero, and in addition, the variance of the estimator also approaches zero. That is, the distribution of a consistent estimator will collapse on the true value of the unknown parameter as sample size approaches infinity.

The second property concerns **asymptotic efficiency**. Thus, an estimator is asymptotically efficient if, in addition to being consistent, the **asymptotic variance** of the estimator is at least as small as the asymptotic variances of all other competing consistent estimators. The asymptotic variance of an estimator is the variance of the estimator's distribution just prior to this distribution collapsing on the population parameter – that is, just prior to this distribution becoming **degenerate**.

Now, as already indicated, the essential point about asymptotic properties for our purposes is that they are generally much easier to establish than the finite sample properties of unbiasedness and efficiency, which require generalising for all sample sizes. Therefore if, for example, a given estimator is so complex that it is not possible to establish whether the estimator is, say, efficient, but it can be established that the estimator is asymptotically efficient, then we may consider this to be an adequate justification for proceeding to use the estimator. Alternatively, a given estimator may be found to be biased but none the less consistent and asymptotically efficient. Thus if there is no alternative unbiased estimator available, then we may consider the use of this estimator to be acceptable, and particularly so if a large sample could be obtained. Finally, an unbiased and efficient estimator may be available, but it may be so complex and hence its use so costly, that it may be more convenient to use a simpler estimator with desirable asymptotic properties, even though this estimator has undesirable finite sample properties.

A more detailed discussion of consistency and asymptotic efficiency is provided in Appendix 4.1.

We now return to the consideration of using our ordinary least squares procedures for estimating the parameters of a model with heteroskedastic disturbance terms.

If we proceed to estimate such a model without taking any account of the heteroskedasticity the least squares estimators can still be shown to be unbiased, but they will no longer be BLUE – that is, an alternative unbiased and linear estimator can be derived which will have a smaller variance. Further, it can be shown that the simple least squares estimators will not even be asymptotically efficient[2] – irrespective of how large is the available sample, an estimator can still be derived that is more efficient than the ordinary least squares estimator.

We will not explicitly derive the BLUEs for the regression model with heteroskedastic disturbance terms. Rather, we will simply indicate why the expressions for these estimators must differ from the simple least squares estimators which we have so far used. Thus consider the simple regression model:

$$Y_i = \alpha + \beta X_i + \varepsilon_i \qquad \text{Equation 4.27}$$

(As heteroskedasticity tends to occur more commonly in a cross-section context, we will use a subscript of $i$, rather than time-series notation of $t$.)

Consider the estimation of $\beta$. Now, in Chapter 2 we interpreted the least squares estimator of $\beta$ as just a weighted sum of the $Y_i$s, and in general any estimator of $\beta$ could be interpreted as a weighted sum of the $Y_i$s. That is, we could write:

$$\tilde{\beta} = \sum W_i Y_i \qquad \text{Equation 4.28}$$

where $\tilde{\beta}$ is some estimator and the $W_i$s are the weights attached to the $Y_i$s. Recall also from Chapter 2 that if $\tilde{\beta}$ is to be an unbiased estimator of $\beta$ then the weights in Equation 4.28 must possess the two following properties:

$$\sum W_i = 0 \qquad \text{Equation 4.29}$$

and

$$\sum W_i X_i = 1 \qquad \text{Equation 4.30}$$

(see Equation 2.38). Now, from Equation 4.28 we can directly deduce the variance of $\tilde{\beta}$. That is:

$$\text{Var}(\tilde{\beta}) = \text{Var}\left(\sum W_i Y_i\right) \qquad \text{Equation 4.31}$$

or

$$\text{Var}(\tilde{\beta}) = \sum W_i^2 \text{Var}(Y_i) \qquad \text{Equation 4.32}$$

Recall from Chapter 2 that we indicated that the BLUE of $\beta$ can be obtained by deriving the expressions for $W_i$ (for $i = 1, \ldots, n$) that minimise Equation 4.32 subject to satisfying Equations 4.29 and 4.30. Recall further that in the simplest specification of the regression model in Chapter 2. Equation 4.32 could be simplified to:

$$\text{Var}(\tilde{\beta}) = \sigma_\varepsilon^2 \sum W_i^2 \qquad \text{Equation 4.33}$$

as the $\varepsilon_i$s were all assumed to have the same variance. Thus minimising $\text{Var}(\tilde{\beta})$ was equivalent to simply minimising $\sum W_i^2$.

However, if the $\varepsilon_i$s are heteroskedastic, then Equation 4.32 cannot be simplified to Equation 4.33. In particular, Equation 4.32 can be written as:

$$\text{Var}(\tilde{\beta}) = \sum W_i^2 \sigma_i^2 \qquad \text{Equation 4.34}$$

where $\sigma_i^2$ is the variance of the disturbance term at the $i$th sample point.

Thus in minimising Equation 4.34, again subject to Equations 4.29 and 4.30, we need simply note that the resulting expression for the BLUE of $\beta$ must involve the term $\sigma_i^2$. Therefore we can conclude that the expression for the BLUE of $\beta$ for a model containing heteroskedastic disturbances will differ from that for a model containing homoskedastic disturbances. It can be shown that the expression for the BLUE of $\beta$ is as follows:

$$\tilde{\beta} = \frac{\sum (1/\sigma_i^2) \sum [(X_i Y_i)/\sigma_i^2] - \sum (X_i/\sigma_i^2) \sum (Y_i/\sigma_i^2)}{\sum (1/\sigma_i^2) \sum (X_i^2/\sigma_i^2) - [\sum (X_i/\sigma_i^2)]^2} \qquad \text{Equation 4.35}$$

(the explicit derivation of this expression is left as an exercise for the reader).

The obvious procedure, then, is to employ this estimator whenever an assumption of heteroskedasticity is warranted. However, first note that the $\sigma_i^2$s, for $i = 1, \ldots, n$, are parameters, and generally will be unknown. Therefore in order to employ the BLUE we require estimates of the $\sigma_i^2$s. But in practice it will rarely be the case that the $\sigma_i^2$s can even be estimated. Estimation of the $\sigma_i^2$s would require a sample of observations at each level of the dependent variable. In terms of our example of a cross-section consumption function, this would require that a number of observations on household consumption be available at each observed level of household income. The form of the sample required is shown diagrammatically in Figure 4.8. However, given a sample of data, most households will probably have different incomes (perhaps only marginally different in some cases), and so estimation of $\sigma_i^2$ at each income level will not be possible. That is, the sample of data would appear as in Figure 4.5 rather than as in Figure 4.8.

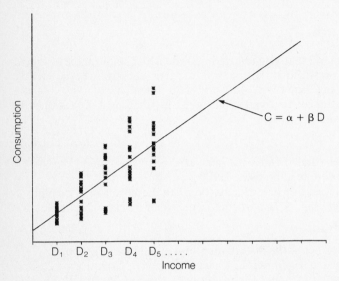

**Figure 4.8**   Data requirements for the BLU estimation of a model with heteroskedastic disturbances.

Therefore given that, in general, estimates of the $\sigma_i^2$s cannot be obtained, we will not be able to employ the BLUE of $\beta$ (nor of $\alpha$). However, as we shall see below, efficient estimation of a regression model with heteroskedastic disturbances is still possible if additional assumptions can be made about the way in which the $\sigma_i^2$s are generated.

First we will briefly reconsider the 'second-best' alternative of using the ordinary least squares estimators. Recall that these estimators are still unbiased but inefficient. The question then arises as to whether we can still use these estimators while recognising that they will not be as 'accurate' or 'precise' as the theoretically superior estimators. That is, to what extent is it worthwhile attempting to derive the appropriate BLU estimators rather than using the much simpler and straightforward least squares estimators?

Consider a simple two-variable regression model which is identical to the model specified in Equation 2.13, except that we now relax Assumption b of this specification to allow for heteroskedastic disturbances. That is:

$$Y_i = \alpha + \beta X_i + \varepsilon_i \qquad \text{Equation 4.36}$$

and

$$\text{Var}(\varepsilon_i) = \sigma_i^2 \quad i = 1,\ldots,n \qquad \text{Equation 4.37}$$

Recall from Equation 2.20 that the least squares estimator of $\beta$ can be written as:

$$\hat{\beta} = \frac{\sum (X_i - \bar{X})(Y_i - \bar{Y})}{\sum (X_i - \bar{X})^2} \qquad \text{Equation 4.38}$$

or

$$\hat{\beta} = \sum W_i Y_i \qquad \text{Equation 4.39}$$

where

$$W_i = \frac{(X_i - \bar{X})}{\sum (X_i - \bar{X})^2} \qquad \text{Equation 4.40}$$

Now, as previously:

$$\begin{aligned} E(\hat{\beta}) &= \sum W_i E(Y_i) \\ &= \sum W_i(\alpha + \beta X_i) \\ &= \alpha \sum W_i + \beta \sum W_i X_i \\ &= \beta \end{aligned}$$

as $\sum W_i = 0$ and $\sum W_i X_i = 1$.

Thus $\hat{\beta}$, the simple least squares estimator, is still unbiased, irrespective of whether or not the disturbance terms are heteroskedastic. This can also be shown to be the case for $\hat{\alpha}$.

Now consider the derivation of the expression for the variance of $\hat{\beta}$, under an assumption of heteroskedastic disturbance terms. Thus:

$$\begin{aligned} \text{Var}(\hat{\beta}) &= \text{Var}\left(\sum W_i Y_i\right) \\ &= \sum W_i^2 \text{Var}(Y_i) \end{aligned}$$

But

$$\text{Var}(Y_i) = \text{Var}(\varepsilon_i) = \sigma_i^2$$

Therefore

$$\text{Var}(\hat{\beta}) = \sum W_i^2 \sigma_i^2 \qquad \text{Equation 4.41}$$

or

$$\text{Var}(\hat{\beta}) = \frac{\sum (X_i - \bar{X})^2 \sigma_i^2}{[\sum (X_i - \bar{X})^2]^2} \qquad \text{Equation 4.42}$$

Now, the expression for $\text{Var}(\hat{\beta})$ in Equation 4.42 is the correct expression for the variance of the least squares estimator of $\beta$ if the disturbance terms are heteroskedastic. Note that it differs from the expression for $\text{Var}(\hat{\beta})$ which we derived in Chapter 2. That is, recall from Equation 2.47 we had:

$$\text{Var}(\hat{\beta}) = \frac{\sigma_\varepsilon^2}{\sum(X_i - \bar{X})^2} \qquad \text{Equation 4.43}$$

Thus, as $\text{Var}(\varepsilon_i)$ is now not a constant Equation 4.42 cannot be simplified to Equation 4.43.

In practice $\text{Var}(\hat{\beta})$ will itself have to be estimated. From Chapter 2, the conventional estimator for $\text{Var}(\hat{\beta})$ is:

$$S_{\hat{\beta}}^2 = \frac{\hat{\sigma}_\varepsilon^2}{\sum(X_i - \bar{X})^2} \qquad \text{Equation 4.44}$$

where

$$\hat{\sigma}_\varepsilon^2 = (1/n - 2)\sum(Y_i - \hat{\alpha} - \hat{\beta}X_i)^2 \qquad \text{Equation 4.45}$$

The question, then, is how reasonable is it to proceed to estimate $\text{Var}(\hat{\beta})$ using Equation 4.44, if the disturbance terms are in fact heteroskedastic?

Now, the use of Equation 4.44 implies that $\text{Var}(\varepsilon_i)$ is a constant (and can be estimated by $\hat{\sigma}_\varepsilon^2$). Therefore such an approach is clearly inappropriate. It can be shown, not surprisingly, that the expression for $S_{\hat{\beta}}^2$ in Equation 4.44 is a biased estimator of $\text{Var}(\hat{\beta})$ if the disturbance terms are heteroskedastic – that is, $E(S_{\hat{\beta}}^2)$ does not equal the expression for $\text{Var}(\hat{\beta})$ in Equation 4.42.[3]

The important point to recognise is that if we decide to ignore the fact that the disturbances are heteroskedastic, and proceed to employ the ordinary least squares estimation procedure outlined in Chapters 2 and 3, then while we may justify using this approach by arguing that the parameter estimators are still unbiased, the estimators of their variances will be biased. The consequence will be that all the resulting confidence intervals and hypothesis tests involving the regression parameters will be invalid. Thus although we can obtain a theoretically acceptable 'point' estimate of our model, we can carry out virtually no statistical evaluation of this estimated model. Such an estimation procedure, therefore, would be of very limited (if any) use.

We can still use our ordinary least squares procedure but add the refinement of using Equation 4.42 as the expression for $\text{Var}(\hat{\beta})$ (and a corresponding expression for $\text{Var}(\hat{\alpha})$). This approach will then allow a valid statistical evaluation to be performed on the estimated model. However, note that this will then require that $\sigma_i^2$ be estimated at each sample point. But if we are in a position to actually obtain estimates of the $\sigma_i^2$s then the model can be more efficiently estimated by direct use of the appropriate BLU estimators (Equation 4.35 for the case of $\beta$).

Therefore we return to our original problem of how to proceed given that the $\sigma_i^2$s are unknown and cannot even be estimated.

### 4.3.3 *Alternative Estimation Methods*

A straightforward solution to this problem can be derived if an assumption can be made of a relationship between $\sigma_i^2$ and the level of the independent variable (in a multiple regression context a relationship between $\sigma_i^2$ and one of the independent variables could be assumed). If such an assumption can be made then an appropriate variable transformation will produce a model satisfying the assumptions of the simple regression model, and this model can then be estimated by ordinary least squares. We will discuss a simple example to illustrate this approach.

Consider the problem discussed above of estimating a cross-section consumption function. We can postulate the following model:

$$C_i = \alpha + \beta D_i + \varepsilon_i \qquad\qquad \text{Equation 4.46}$$

where

$C_i$ = Consumption expenditure of the $i$th household

$D_i$ = Disposable income of the $i$th household

and we also assume:

$$\text{Var}(\varepsilon_i) = \sigma_i^2 \qquad\qquad \text{Equation 4.47}$$

We argued previously that we would expect the dispersion of household consumption expenditure to increase with household income. Thus $\sigma_i^2$ could be assumed to be positively related to $D_i$. For illustrative purposes consider the (arbitrary) assumption that $\sigma_i^2$ is linearly related to the square of household income. That is,

$$\sigma_i^2 = bD_i^2 \qquad\qquad \text{Equation 4.48}$$

where $b$ is some constant.

Now, if we divide Equation 4.46 throughout by $D_i$ we will obtain an equation which is suitable for the direct application of ordinary least squares. That is, our transformed model becomes:

$$\frac{C_i}{D_i} = \alpha\frac{1}{D_i} + \beta + \frac{\varepsilon_i}{D_i} \qquad\qquad \text{Equation 4.49}$$

Thus the disturbance term of Equation 4.46 has become $\varepsilon_i/D_i$, and note that the variance of this transformed disturbance term is now a constant. That is:

$$\text{Var}\left(\frac{\varepsilon_i}{D_i}\right) = \frac{1}{D_i^2}\text{Var}(\varepsilon_i)$$

$$= \frac{1}{D_i^2}bD_i^2 \quad \text{from Equation 4.48}$$

$$= b$$

Therefore Equation 4.49 now satisfies all the assumptions of the simple regression model, and in particular, the disturbance terms in this equation are homoskedastic (with a variance equal to the constant $b$). Thus $\alpha$ and $\beta$ can be estimated by regressing $C_i/D_i$ on $1/D_i$. The coefficient on $1/D_i$ in this regression will be the least squares estimate of $\alpha$ and the constant term of the regression will be the estimate of $\beta$.

Note also that these estimators of $\alpha$ and $\beta$ must be the BLUEs – we indicated in Chapter 2 that provided all the assumptions of the simple regression model were satisfied then the least squares estimators, by definition, are the BLUEs.

We can make alternative assumptions concerning the relationship between $\sigma_i^2$ and $D_i$, rather than the assumption given in Equation 4.48. For example, if we assumed that:

$$\sigma_i^2 = bD_i \qquad\qquad \text{Equation 4.50}$$

then the appropriate variable transformation would be to divide Equation 4.47 throughout by the square root of $D_i$. The disturbance term of this transformed equation would then become:

$$\frac{\varepsilon_i}{\sqrt{D_i}}$$

and therefore

$$\begin{aligned}
\text{Var}\,(\varepsilon_i/\sqrt{D_i}) &= 1/D_i\,\text{Var}\,(\varepsilon_i)\\
&= 1/D_i bD_i\\
&= b \quad \text{as previously.}
\end{aligned}$$

Thus each assumption concerning the specific relationship between $\sigma_i^2$ and $D_i$ will imply a different variable transformation. The determination of the appropriate relationship, however, may not be a straightforward matter and may involve some experimentation and perhaps the collection of additional information.

Note also that we need not necessarily assume that $\sigma_i^2$ is related to one of the independent variables in the model. In certain applications it may be appropriate to assume that $\sigma_i^2$ is related to some variable outside the model, and then the appropriate transformation will be based on this additional variable.

Finally, in the case of time-series data exhibiting heteroskedasticity (such as in Figure 4.7), some non-linear transformation of the data often provides a simple and effective means of 'removing' the heteroskedasticity. The logarithmic transformation is commonly employed in such situations.

For example, in the case of Figure 4.7, if the logarithm of consumers' expenditure were used, this would have the effect of reducing the rate of increase in the variance over time. That is, the logarithmic transformation would reduce the larger observations proportionately more than the smaller observations (if the data range from 1 to 1000, say, then the natural logarithm of the data would range from 0 to 6.91). We will discuss heteroskedasticity in time-series data in more detail in Section 7.2.5.

A numerical example will help to fix ideas.

Example 4.2

We will carry out a simple experiment in order to compare the various methods of estimating a model with heteroskedastic disturbance terms.

We will continue to consider the estimation of a cross-section consumption function. However, instead of collecting data on consumption and income in order to estimate the parameters of some postulated model we will, in a sense, reverse this process.

We begin by assuming that the true model is the following:

$$C_i = 500 + 0.75D_i + \varepsilon_i \qquad \qquad \text{Equation 4.51}$$

That is, we assume that $\alpha$ and $\beta$ are known and are equal to 500 and 0.75 respectively. We then proceed by (arbitrarily) selecting a sample of values for $D_i$, which are treated as our given sample of observations on the independent variable.

Next, we make certain assumptions about the way in which the $\varepsilon_i$s are generated – in particular, we will assume that the $\varepsilon_i$s are heteroskedastic – and then substitute the resulting values of $D_i$ and $\varepsilon_i$ into Equation 4.51, and so generate a sample of observations on $C_i$. This sample of observations on $C_i$ can then be interpreted as being determined by the model in Equation 4.51.

Given this sample of observations on $C$ and $D$ we can then apply various estimation methods to these data in order to estimate the parameters of the model which generated the $C_i$s. But of course we know the true values of these parameters, and therefore we can directly evaluate the relative performance of the competing estimation methods.[4]

We will use a sample size of 50. The arbitrarily selected values of $D_i$ are shown in Table 4.2 (these could be interpreted as the annual income of each household in some hypothetical sample, where in this particular sample the range of income runs from £1000 to £11,000).

The sample of values for $\varepsilon_i$ was obtained by assuming that the heteroskedasticity was of the following form:

$$\text{Var}(\varepsilon_i) = bD_i^2 \qquad \qquad \text{Equation 4.52}$$

The value of $b$ was set at 0.009.

The 50 observations on $\varepsilon_i$ were then generated by first randomly selecting 50 values from a standard normal distribution (these can either be generated by a computer or extracted from a table of random normal numbers). These are shown as $u_i$ in Table 4.2. Given these values for $u_i$, the observations on $\varepsilon_i$ were generated by the expression:

$$\varepsilon_i = u_i\sqrt{0.009\ D_i^2} \qquad\qquad\qquad \text{Equation 4.53}$$

Note that the use of Equation 4.53 implies that:

$$\begin{aligned}
\text{Var}\,(\varepsilon_i) &= \text{Var}\,[u_i\sqrt{0.009\ D_i^2}] \\
&= 0.009\ D_i^2\ \text{Var}\,(u_i) \\
&= 0.009\ D_i^2 \text{ as Var}\,(u_i) = 1
\end{aligned}$$

which is the assumption made in Equation 4.52. That is, the use of Equation 4.53 to generate observations on $\varepsilon_i$ must necessarily produce a set of heteroskedastic disturbances. The values for $\varepsilon_i$ are also shown in Table 4.2, and note how the absolute value of $\varepsilon_i$ tends to increase as $D_i$ increases, as required.

Finally, the observations on $C_i$ were derived by substituting the values of $D_i$ and $\varepsilon_i$ into Equation 4.51.

**Table 4.2**  Data on consumption, income and a disturbance term in a hypothetical sample of 50 households

| $i$ | $D_i$ | $u_i$ | $\varepsilon_i$ | $C_i$ | $i$ | $D_i$ | $u_i$ | $\varepsilon_i$ | $C_i$ |
|---|---|---|---|---|---|---|---|---|---|
| 1 | 1000 | −1.787 | −169.5 | 1080.5 | 26 | 6051 | 1.297 | 744.3 | 5782.6 |
| 2 | 1020 | −0.261 | −25.2 | 1239.8 | 27 | 6200 | −1.613 | −948.6 | 4201.4 |
| 3 | 1200 | 1.237 | 140.7 | 1540.7 | 28 | 6406 | 1.241 | 754.2 | 6058.7 |
| 4 | 1500 | 1.046 | 148.8 | 1773.8 | 29 | 6802 | −1.016 | −655.5 | 4946.0 |
| 5 | 1990 | −0.508 | −96.0 | 1896.5 | 30 | 7000 | −0.090 | −59.7 | 5690.3 |
| 6 | 2000 | −1.630 | −309.0 | 1691.0 | 31 | 7043 | 0.261 | 174.3 | 5956.6 |
| 7 | 2010 | −0.146 | −27.9 | 1979.6 | 32 | 7100 | −1.883 | −1268.4 | 4556.6 |
| 8 | 2020 | −0.392 | −75.0 | 1940.0 | 33 | 7600 | −0.181 | −130.5 | 6069.5 |
| 9 | 2900 | −0.627 | −172.5 | 2502.5 | 34 | 7992 | 1.675 | 1269.9 | 7763.9 |
| 10 | 3000 | 0.561 | 159.6 | 2909.6 | 35 | 8000 | −0.324 | −246.0 | 6254.0 |
| 11 | 3032 | −0.420 | −129.3 | 2644.7 | 36 | 8056 | −1.029 | −786.3 | 5755.7 |
| 12 | 3200 | −0.286 | −87.0 | 2813.0 | 37 | 8201 | −0.185 | −144.0 | 6506.8 |
| 13 | 3400 | −0.050 | −16.2 | 3033.8 | 38 | 8407 | 0.004 | 3.3 | 6808.6 |
| 14 | 3990 | −0.481 | −182.1 | 3310.4 | 39 | 8900 | −0.101 | −85.2 | 7089.8 |
| 15 | 4000 | 1.521 | 577.2 | 4077.2 | 40 | 9000 | −1.187 | −1013.4 | 6236.6 |
| 16 | 4010 | −1.367 | −519.9 | 2987.6 | 41 | 9072 | −0.791 | −680.7 | 6623.3 |
| 17 | 4100 | 0.609 | 237.0 | 3812.0 | 42 | 9300 | −0.528 | −465.9 | 7009.1 |
| 18 | 4400 | 0.292 | 121.8 | 3921.8 | 43 | 9700 | 0.946 | 870.6 | 8645.6 |
| 19 | 4800 | 0.048 | 22.2 | 4122.2 | 44 | 9990 | 1.673 | 1585.5 | 9578.0 |
| 20 | 5000 | 0.592 | 280.8 | 4530.8 | 45 | 10,000 | −0.680 | −645.0 | 7355.0 |
| 21 | 5025 | −0.475 | −226.5 | 4042.2 | 46 | 10,030 | −0.784 | −746.1 | 7276.4 |
| 22 | 5103 | −1.210 | −585.6 | 3741.6 | 47 | 10,100 | 1.494 | 1431.6 | 9506.6 |
| 23 | 5500 | 0.183 | 95.4 | 4720.4 | 48 | 10,506 | −0.086 | −85.8 | 8293.7 |
| 24 | 5920 | 0.526 | 295.5 | 5235.5 | 49 | 10,709 | −1.071 | −1088.1 | 7443.6 |
| 25 | 6000 | 0.495 | 281.7 | 5281.7 | 50 | 11,000 | −1.196 | −1248.0 | 7502.0 |

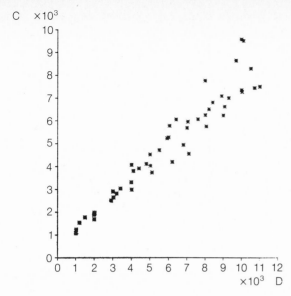

**Figure 4.9**   $C_i$ against $D_i$ from Table 4.2.

In Figure 4.9 we present a graph of $C_i$ against $D_i$, from which the disturbance terms can be seen to be heteroskedastic.

Ignoring the heteroskedasticity, and simply regressing $C_i$ on $D_i$, produces the following estimated model (standard errors in brackets):

$$\hat{C}_i = 539.422 + 0.731\, D_i \qquad\qquad \text{Equation 4.54}$$
$$(197.910)\ (0.030)$$

$$R^2 = 0.927$$

The $t$-statistics associated with the constant term and $D_i$ are therefore 2.73 and 24.37, respectively, and thus both $\alpha$ and $\beta$ are significantly different from zero. However, as $\alpha$ and $\beta$ are known in this particular example then the corresponding interval estimates provide a more convenient means of assessing the estimated model. That is, do these intervals contain the true values of $\alpha$ and $\beta$, and how accurately are $\alpha$ and $\beta$ estimated (how narrow are these intervals)?

Recall from Equations 2.60 and 2.61 that the 95 per cent interval estimators of $\alpha$ and $\beta$ can be written as:

$$\hat{\alpha} - S_{\hat{\alpha}}\, t_{0.025,48} < \alpha < \hat{\alpha} + S_{\hat{\alpha}} t_{0.025,48}$$

and

$$\hat{\beta} - S_{\hat{\beta}} t_{0.025,48} < \beta < \hat{\beta} + S_{\hat{\beta}} t_{0.025,48}$$

and thus the resulting 95 per cent interval estimates are:

For $\alpha$: 141.623 to 937.221

For $\beta$: 0.671 to 0.791

Therefore both intervals contain the true values of $\alpha$ and $\beta$.

However, recall from our discussion of the simple least squares estimation of a model with heteroskedastic disturbances that the usual expressions for the variances of the estimators of $\alpha$ and $\beta$ are incorrect. Consequently the above interval estimates and $t$-tests are invalid, and the conclusions drawn from them could be quite misleading.

From Equation 4.42 the correct expression for the variance of the least squares estimator of $\beta$ is given by:

$$\text{Var}(\hat{\beta}) = \frac{\sum (D_i - \bar{D})^2 \sigma_i^2}{[\sum (D_i - \bar{D})^2]^2} \qquad \text{Equation 4.55}$$

The expression for $\text{Var}(\hat{\alpha})$ can be similarly derived and is given by:

$$\text{Var}(\hat{\alpha}) = \sum \left[ 1/n - \frac{\bar{D}(D_i - \bar{D})^2}{\sum (D_i - \bar{D})^2} \right]^2 \sigma_i^2 \qquad \text{Equation 4.56}$$

(the derivation of Equation 4.56 is left as an exercise for the reader).

Now, we are in the unusual position here of actually knowing the values of the $\sigma_i^2$s. That is,

$$\sigma_i^2 = 0.009\, D_i^2$$

and so we can calculate the true variances of the least squares estimators of $\alpha$ and $\beta$ and hence obtain the correct interval estimates for $\alpha$ and $\beta$.

Substituting for $\sigma_i^2$ in Equations 4.55 and 4.56 we obtain:

$$\text{Var}(\hat{\beta}) = \frac{\sum (D_i - \bar{D})^2 0.009\, D_i^2}{[\sum (D_i - \bar{D})^2]^2} \qquad \text{Equation 4.57}$$

and

$$\text{Var}(\hat{\alpha}) = \sum \left[ 1/n - \frac{\bar{D}(D_i - \bar{D})^2}{\sum (D_i - \bar{D})^2} \right]^2 0.009\, D_i^2 \qquad \text{Equation 4.58}$$

Upon substitution of the observations on $D_i$ into Equations 4.57 and 4.58, we have:

$$\text{Var}(\hat{\beta}) = 0.0010448$$

and

$$\text{Var}(\hat{\alpha}) = 19{,}858.005$$

Therefore the resulting interval estimates for $\alpha$ and $\beta$ become:

For $\alpha$:  $539.422 \pm (2.01)\sqrt{19{,}858.005}$,   or
256.176 to 822.668

For $\beta$:  $0.731 \pm (2.01)\sqrt{0.0010448}$,   or
0.666 to 0.796

Comparing these interval estimates with the incorrect estimates calculated previously it can be seen that the interval estimate for $\beta$ is little affected, but that the correct interval estimate for $\alpha$ is somewhat narrower than the incorrect estimate – ignoring the heteroskedasticity implies (in this example) a greater level of imprecision than is in fact the case.

It is not possible to generalise about the effect that heteroskedasticity has on the precision of the ordinary least squares estimators. Depending on the form of heteroskedasticity (that is, the form of the relationship between $\sigma_i^2$ and the independent variable) ordinary least squares estimation (ignoring heteroskedasticity) will either give an impression of greater or less precision than is warranted. The essential point is that ignoring heteroskedasticity and applying ordinary least squares will simply result in incorrect inferences concerning the population parameters, and it is not even possible to generalise about the direction of the bias involved. Unlike our present example, the true variances of the least squares estimators will generally be unknown, and so we cannot even use ordinary least squares estimation with the variances of the estimators appropriately adjusted.

In the context of our (artificial) example it is instructive finally to derive the BLUEs of $\alpha$ and $\beta$. Recall that we have:

$$\sigma_i^2 = 0.009\, D_i^2$$

and therefore estimating the model:

$$C_i/D_i = \alpha 1/D_i + \beta + \varepsilon_i/D_i \qquad\qquad \text{Equation 4.59}$$

by ordinary least squares will produce the BLUEs of $\alpha$ and $\beta$. The least squares estimate of Equation 4.59 is (standard errors in brackets):

$$C_i/D_i = 476.377\ 1/D_i + 0.743 \qquad\qquad \text{Equation 4.60}$$
$$(58.545) \qquad\ (0.019)$$

$$R^2 = 0.580$$

Therefore the resulting interval estimates for $\alpha$ and $\beta$ are:

For $\alpha$:  358.702 to 594.052

For $\beta$:  0.705 to 0.781

Comparing these interval estimates with the correct simple least squares estimates derived from Equations 4.57 and 4.58 it can be seen that a considerable gain in efficiency has been achieved.

### 4.3.4   *Testing for Heteroskedasticity*

Having illustrated a method for overcoming the problem of heteroskedasticity we must now discuss the more fundamental and practical problem of how to determine whether or not the disturbance terms are heteroskedastic in the first place, and if so, the form that this heteroskedasticity takes. Unfortunately there are no straightforward or generalised procedures available for testing for the presence of heteroskedasticity. The tests which can be used will depend on the data that are available.

For example, if data are available in the form illustrated in Figure 4.8 then standard statistical tests could be used to infer whether or not the variance of the disturbance term varies with the level of the independent variable. That is, the variance of the disturbance term could be estimated at each level of the independent variable and inferences drawn concerning the variation in the true disturbance term variances. However, data will rarely be available in this form.

In certain cases it may be possible to group the data and compare the variances of the disturbance terms within these groups. For example, in the case of the consumption and income data in Table 4.3, the income data could be grouped into low, medium and high income groups and the variances of each of these groups compared. Of course the implicit assumption is that the variance of the disturbance terms within each of these groups is constant, or more or less constant, and hence the income groups must be selected with a view to satisfying this assumption.

Simple graphical analysis, such as Figure 4.9, may at least indicate whether an assumption of heteroskedasticity warrants further consideration. Having estimated a model by simple least squares, the estimated residuals from the model could be graphed against any variable which might be considered to be related to the disturbance term variances, and thus an informal examination for the possibility of heteroskedasticity carried out.

A simple test for heteroskedasticity which is often employed is the **Goldfeld–Quandt** test. Although the test is quite straightforward to perform, it is not a particularly detailed or powerful test, in the sense that it only tests for the presence of heteroskedasticity in relatively general terms. Thus, given a sample of data on a dependent and a set of independent variables, the data would first be ordered according to the nature of the suspected heteroskedasticity. For example, if it is thought that $\sigma_i^2$ increases with the level of one of the independent variables then the data would be ordered according to this independent variable. Note that the data in Table 4.2 are already in such an order, and thus in a form suitable for the application of the Goldfeld–Quandt test.

Now, if the disturbance terms are heteroskedastic then the variances of the disturbance terms in the latter segment of the data would on average exceed those in the first segment of the data. The test proceeds by estimating two separate models over the partitioned data set, and then comparing the estimated disturbance term variances from these regressions.

Let $\hat{\sigma}_1^2$ denote the estimated variance of the disturbance term over the first segment of the data, and $\hat{\sigma}_2^2$ the estimated variance over the second segment of the data. Then a formal test of significance can be derived by noting that, under the null hypothesis of no heteroskedasticity, the ratio of $\hat{\sigma}_2^2$ to $\hat{\sigma}_1^2$ can be shown to have an $F$ distribution with degrees of freedom equal to those of the two separate regressions. That is, it can be shown that:

$$\frac{\hat{\sigma}_2^2}{\hat{\sigma}_1^2} \sim F_{n_1-(K+1),\, n_2-(K+1)} \qquad\qquad \text{Equation 4.61}$$

where $n_1$ and $n_2$ are the numbers of observations in the first and second segments of the data, respectively, and $K$ is the number of independent variables in the model. In practice, it is common to drop some of the middle observations from the data set, as the disturbance terms at the end of the first half of the data might be expected to have similar variances to those at the beginning of the second half of the data, thus having the effect of reducing the power of the test to discriminate between the variances of the two data sets. The common rule of thumb is to omit the middle sixth of the observations.

We can illustrate the use of the Goldfeld–Quandt test by using the data in Table 4.2. We will omit the eight middle observations, and thus re-estimate the model over the first 21 observations, and over the last 21 observations. These two regressions produce the following estimates of the disturbance term variances:

$$\hat{\sigma}_1^2 = 56{,}493.053$$
$$\hat{\sigma}_2^2 = 746{,}778.000$$

and, as expected, $\hat{\sigma}_2^2$ exceeds $\hat{\sigma}_1^2$.

In order to determine whether this difference is significant we calculate the observed value of $F$ (the ratio of these two estimates), which is 13.22 (note that because of the way in which $F$ is defined in Equation 4.63, 'large' values of $F$ will lead to the rejection of $H_0$). The corresponding tabulated $F$ value from Appendix III, for 19 degrees of freedom for both the numerator and the denominator and a significance level of 5 per cent, is approximately 2.16. Thus we would conclude that the observed value of $F$ is sufficiently large to allow the rejection of the null hypothesis of homoskedastic disturbances.[5]

Once it has been established that heteroskedasticity is present, we then require information concerning the form of this heteroskedasticity so that an appropriate estimation procedure can be used.

In the unlikely event that data are available in the form illustrated in Figure 4.8 the approach is straightforward. Estimates of $\sigma_i^2$ for $i = 1, \ldots, n$ can be obtained and the BLUEs can then be directly employed (the expression for the BLUE of $\beta$ was given in Equation 4.35). Otherwise a relationship between an independent variable and $\sigma_i^2$ will have to be determined so that an appropriate data transformation can be used and the BLUEs thereby obtained.

Typically, insufficient data will be available to allow a rigorous determination of such a relationship and informal methods will have to be used. For example, observations could be grouped, as described above, the variance of the disturbances within these groups estimated, and then a relationship determined between these estimated variances and the midpoint of each of the data groupings. This relationship could then be interpreted as an approximation of the relationship between $\sigma_i^2$ and the level of the independent variable. Or theory may suggest the form of the appropriate relationship. In our consumption function example theory implied that the dispersion of consumption expenditure increases with the level of income, and the theory may even be so specific as to imply that $\sigma_i^2$ would be expected to be linearly related to the square of income, rather than just the level of income or the square root of income, or whatever.

## 4.4    Autocorrelated Disturbance Terms

We will now consider the consequences of relaxing the assumption that the disturbance terms are independently distributed. That is, we will consider the implications for our estimation procedures of relaxing the assumption that:

$$E(\varepsilon_t \varepsilon_s) = 0 \quad \text{for all} \quad t \neq s \qquad \text{Equation 4.62}$$

(Assumption c of the model specifications in Equations 2.13 and 3.1). If this assumption is violated then the disturbance terms are said to be **autocorrelated**, and we are therefore concerned with the problem of **autocorrelation**.

### 4.4.1    *The Nature of the Problem*

Given some model specification, autocorrelation occurs if any form of relationship exists between the disturbance terms at different sample points. That is, if the disturbance terms are autocorrelated (correlated 'amongst themselves') then there will be some predictability in the levels of the disturbance terms from sample point to sample point. As the objective of constructing any model is to describe all the systematic or predictable variation in the dependent variable then any form of autocorrelation which might exist should be explicitly included in the model specification. That is, the only unexplained variation which remains in the dependent variable should be strictly random or unpredictable.

Autocorrelation is a problem which more commonly occurs in time-series data. For example, consider estimating a model which seeks to explain the variation in the level of some manufacturer's quarterly output over, say, a ten-year period. Presumably, output will be determined by the level of inputs into the production process (capital, labour), the extent of technological progress which may have occurred over the period, and any other factors that may be specific to the manufacturer's operations.

Now consider the interpretation of a disturbance term within such a context. The disturbance term captures the unpredictable or non-systematic factors which affect the level of output. For example, an item of machinery may unexpectedly break down during a given quarter thus unavoidably reducing output during that quarter. Over the following quarter the manufacturer will presumably compensate for this loss of output by increasing production (again through some non-systematic mode of operation – by increasing the effort of the workforce or increased overtime working, rather than by increasing the number of employees or units of capital). Consequently, the disturbance term in one quarter (or time period) can be interpreted as influencing the disturbance term in the following quarter (or time period).

The essential feature of time-series data which makes the occurrence of autocorrelation likely is that the data occur in a natural ordering. Therefore, autocorrelation in time-series data is generally defined as a relationship between disturbance terms over successive time periods.

However, it is also possible that cross-section data may occur in an ordering in which autocorrelation might be observed. For example, consider a sample of firms which are selected over a range of industries. Further assume that the sample is then ordered by industry groupings, in such a way as to reflect some interconnection between the industries – for example, the output of each industry might be used as an input by the next ranked industry. Thus any 'random shock' which affects the operations of a given industry or firm is likely to have an influence on the activities of related industries or firms. Hence in such a case disturbance terms could be characterised as being related across sample observations. Another example would be a sample of farms in some given region which would all be affected by severe (unpredictable) weather conditions. However, as a generalisation, autocorrelation can be characterised as a feature of time-series data, whereas heteroskedasticity can be interpreted as a property of cross-section data.

We will now proceed to a more detailed discussion of the nature and consequences of autocorrelation, and we will concern ourselves only with the more common case of autocorrelation in time-series data.

Let $\varepsilon_t$ denote the disturbance term in time-period $t$. The simplest assumption which can be made about the nature of autocorrelation is that the disturbance terms are directly related between successive time periods. That is:

$$\varepsilon_t = f(\varepsilon_{t-1}) \qquad\qquad\qquad \text{Equation 4.63}$$

Assuming this relationship to be linear we can write:

$$\varepsilon_t = \rho\varepsilon_{t-1} + u_t \qquad\qquad\qquad \text{Equation 4.64}$$

where $\rho$ (the Greek letter 'rho') is a parameter (which is generally unknown and therefore will also require estimation), and $u_t$ is a further disturbance term but with all the desirable properties originally ascribed to $\varepsilon_t$ in the simple regression model – that is, independence and homoskedasticity. We will also assume that the $\varepsilon_t$s are homoskedastic.

Equation 4.64 does not contain a constant term as it would still seem sensible to retain our assumption of $\varepsilon_t$ having a zero mean, for all $t$. If $\rho$ is positive then the disturbance terms are referred to as being positively autocorrelated, and if $\rho$ is negative then the disturbances are negatively autocorrelated. In Equation 4.64 $\rho$ can be directly interpreted as the correlation coefficient between $\varepsilon_t$ and $\varepsilon_{t-1}$. Thus from Equation 1.55, we can write (noting that $E(\varepsilon_t) = E(\varepsilon_{t-1}) = 0$):

$$\mathrm{Corr}\,(\varepsilon_t, \varepsilon_{t-1}) = \frac{E(\varepsilon_t \varepsilon_{t-1})}{\sqrt{E(\varepsilon_t^2)E(\varepsilon_{t-1}^2)}} \qquad \text{Equation 4.65}$$

Now,

$$E(\varepsilon_t \varepsilon_{t-1}) = E[(\rho\varepsilon_{t-1} + u_t)(\varepsilon_{t-1})]$$
$$= \rho E(\varepsilon_{t-1}^2) + E(u_t \varepsilon_{t-1})$$

As, by assumption, $u_t$ is independent of $\varepsilon_{t-1}$ ($u_t$ is independently distributed across time periods) then $E(u_t \varepsilon_{t-1}) = 0$. Further, as the $\varepsilon_t$s are homoskedastic, then $E(\varepsilon_t^2) = E(\varepsilon_{t-1}^2)$, and therefore Equation 4.65 becomes:

$$\mathrm{Corr}\,(\varepsilon_t, \varepsilon_{t-1}) = \frac{\rho E(\varepsilon_t^2)}{E(\varepsilon_t^2)}$$

or

$$\mathrm{Corr}\,(\varepsilon_t, \varepsilon_{t-1}) = \rho \qquad \text{Equation 4.66}$$

By definition, then, we must have $|\rho| < 1$. Thus, the closer is the absolute value of $\rho$ to one, then the higher is the correlation between $\varepsilon_t$ and $\varepsilon_{t-1}$, and the more strongly autocorrelated is $\varepsilon_t$.

We can also derive the variance of $\varepsilon_t$. That is:

$$\mathrm{Var}\,(\varepsilon_t) = \mathrm{Var}\,(\rho\varepsilon_{t-1} + u_t)$$
$$= \rho^2\, \mathrm{Var}\,(\varepsilon_{t-1}) + \mathrm{Var}\,(u_t)$$

As the $\varepsilon_t$s are homoskedastic, and denoting $\mathrm{Var}\,(u_t)$ by $\sigma_u^2$, then we can deduce that:

$$\sigma_\varepsilon^2 = \frac{\sigma_u^2}{1 - \rho^2} \qquad \text{Equation 4.67}$$

Note that Equation 4.64 is a quite general statement in that it implies that $\varepsilon_t$ is indirectly related to all past values of the disturbance term. Thus, lagging

Equation 4.64 by one period (that is, substituting $t-1$ for $t$), we can write:

$$\varepsilon_{t-1} = \rho\varepsilon_{t-2} + u_{t-1} \qquad \text{Equation 4.68}$$

and substituting Equation 4.68 into Equation 4.64, we can see that $\varepsilon_t$ is indirectly related to $\varepsilon_{t-2}$. Thus, repeatedly substituting in this way $\varepsilon_t$ can be seen to be indirectly related to all past values of $\varepsilon$.

The relationship in Equation 4.64 is generally referred to as a **first order autoregressive scheme** (which is often abbreviated to $AR(1)$). However, more complex assumptions can be made about the form of autocorrelation. For example, a second-order autoregressive scheme – an $AR(2)$ – would be written as:

$$\varepsilon_t = \rho\varepsilon_{t-1} + \delta\varepsilon_{t-2} + u_t \qquad \text{Equation 4.69}$$

Higher order and hence more complex schemes can be similarly derived. However, for our present purposes we will only consider the case of first-order autocorrelation (in Chapter 7 we will consider a range of alternative structures for the disturbance term and examine this issue in more general terms).

Before going on to discuss the consequences of autocorrelation for our ordinary least squares estimation procedures, we will first illustrate the nature of autocorrelation via a numerical example.

We will artificially generate two series of autocorrelated disturbances, in much the same way as we generated a series of observations on a hetero-skedastic disturbance term in Example 4.2. Thus we will generate a series of positively autocorrelated disturbance terms, and a series of negatively auto-correlated disturbance terms. The absolute value of $\rho$ which we will use is 0.85. That is, the two following autoregressive schemes will be used:

$$\varepsilon_t = 0.85\varepsilon_{t-1} + u_t \qquad \text{Equation 4.70}$$

and

$$\varepsilon_t = -0.85\varepsilon_{t-1} + u_t \qquad \text{Equation 4.71}$$

As previously, the new disturbance term, $u_t$, will be assumed to be homo-skedastic and independently distributed. In addition, we will also assume that $u_t$ is normally distributed, with a mean of zero and a variance of $\sigma_u^2$. That is, we can write:

$$u_t \sim \text{NID}(0, \sigma_u^2)$$

where 'NID' denotes 'normally and independently distributed'.

In order to generate two series of autocorrelated residuals from Equations 4.70 and 4.71, we first require a sample of observations on $u_t$. These can be either generated by a computer or taken from a table of random normal numbers. We will here set the value of $\sigma_u^2$ to 10,000, and we will use the same sample of 50 observations on $u_t$ for generating both the positively and negatively autocorrelated residuals.

In order to begin the process of building up a series of autocorrelated residuals we first need a starting value for the $\varepsilon_t$ series. Denote this value by $\varepsilon_0$. Thus to start the process of building up a set of autocorrelated disturbances we will randomly select a value for $\varepsilon_0$. In the case of the positively autocorrelated series a value of $-14.224$ was selected, and in the case of the negatively autocorrelated series a value of $-167.940$ was chosen.

Consider first the positively autocorrelated series. For the first observation, $\varepsilon_1$, we can write:

$$\varepsilon_1 = 0.85\varepsilon_0 + u_1$$

Using the randomly selected value of $\varepsilon_0$ and the first value of the $u_t$ series (which was 26.667), we have:

$$\varepsilon_1 = (0.85)(-14.224) + 26.667$$
$$= 14.576$$

Similarly, for $\varepsilon_2$ we have (where $u_2 = -40.441$):

$$\varepsilon_2 = (0.85)(14.576) + (-40.441)$$
$$= -28.051$$

and this process is continued until 50 observations have been generated. We will denote this series of positively autocorrelated disturbances by $P\varepsilon_t$. The series on the negatively autocorrelated disturbances is generated in exactly the same way, but with a starting value of $-167.940$ and of course $\rho = -0.85$. We will denote this series by $N\varepsilon_t$.

First, it is instructive to examine graphs of these two autocorrelated disturbance term series against time. A graph of $P\varepsilon_t$ against time is shown in Figure 4.10(a) and $N\varepsilon_t$ against time is shown in Figure 4.10(b). For comparative purposes we also present a graph of the random series, $u_t$, in Figure 4.10(c). In all cases the observations have been joined by straight lines so that the disturbance term patterns can be seen more clearly. In the case of the positively autocorrelated series in Figure 4.10(a) we note that the main feature of the series is the tendency for its level to change only slowly through time. That is, as successive values of the series are highly and positively correlated then each value of the series will tend to be preceded by a value of the same sign and similar magnitude.

By contrast, the negatively autocorrelated series in Figure 4.10(b) could be interpreted as exhibiting the opposite pattern. The level of the series changes markedly through time as a result of the negative correlation between successive values – large and negative values of the series tend to be preceded by large and positive values.

In either case, however, we can see that the relatively high level of

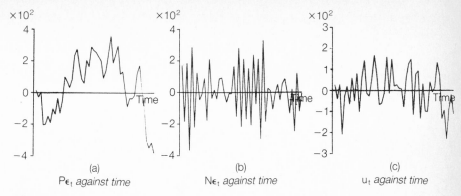

(a)
$P\varepsilon_t$ *against time*

(b)
$N\varepsilon_t$ *against time*

(c)
$u_t$ *against time*

**Figure 4.10**

autocorrelation introduces a degree of predictability into the series (from one value to the next), and hence the series are clearly not random. In terms of the actual observations, the $P\varepsilon_t$ series will be characterised by long runs of negative observations followed by long runs of positive observations, and in the case of $N\varepsilon_t$, the series would tend to regularly alternate between positive and negative values.

By comparison, the randomly generated series in Figure 4.10(c) can be seen to be not as 'well-behaved' as the series in Figures 4.10(a) and (b) in the sense of there being no clearly discernible (or predictable) pattern between successive values.

An alternative way of examining the extent of 'predictability' or 'structure' in each of the three disturbance term series is simply to run the three regressions of $P\varepsilon_t$ on $P\varepsilon_{t-1}$, $N\varepsilon_t$ on $N\varepsilon_{t-1}$, and $u_t$ on $u_{t-1}$. In the cases of the regressions of $P\varepsilon_t$ on $P\varepsilon_{t-1}$ and $N\varepsilon_t$ on $N\varepsilon_{t-1}$, we would expect significant relationships to be produced (with estimated slope coefficients of approximately 0.85 and $-0.85$ respectively). In the case of the regression of $u_t$ on $u_{t-1}$ we would expect an insignificant relationship to result. In all cases we would expect constant terms which are insignificantly different from zero.

Thus, first we lag each of the disturbance series. That is, in each case the lagged series is generated by simply moving the original series forward one period, such that for any given time-period, $t$, the observation on the lagged series is the observation at period $t-1$ of the original series. Note that by generating these lagged series one observation is lost as we do not have an observation at $t = 0$; when $t = 1$ there is no corresponding value at $t-1 = 0$, and therefore the lagged series will contain only 49 observations (strictly, we do have observations for $P\varepsilon_0$ and $N\varepsilon_0$ as these were used to initiate the process of generating the two autocorrelated series – but we will proceed here, as we would have to in practice, by assuming that no observations exist at $t = 0$).

Thus the simple regressions of $P\varepsilon_t$ on $P\varepsilon_{t-1}$, $N\varepsilon_t$ on $N\varepsilon_{t-1}$, and $u_t$ on $u_{t-1}$ are as follows, over the 49 observations which are available (*t*-statistics in brackets):

$$P\varepsilon_t = -3.506 + 0.909 P\varepsilon_{t-1}, \quad R^2 = 0.736 \qquad \text{Equation 4.72}$$
$$\phantom{P\varepsilon_t = -}(0.25)\ \ (11.45)$$

$$N\varepsilon_t = -0.648 - 0.801 N\varepsilon_{t-1}, \quad R^2 = 0.656 \qquad \text{Equation 4.73}$$
$$\phantom{N\varepsilon_t = -}(0.05)\ \ \ (9.47)$$

$$u_t = -0.797 + 0.102 u_{t-1}, \quad R^2 = 0.010 \qquad \text{Equation 4.74}$$
$$\phantom{u_t = -}(0.06)\ \ \ (0.70)$$

Thus the regression results in Equations 4.72 to 4.74 are as expected. That is, the interval estimates derived from these regressions would all contain the true values of the population parameters used to generate the data, and in the cases of Equations 4.72 and 4.73, significant regressions are produced.

### 4.4.2    The Consequences of Autocorrelation

Of central importance, then, is to determine the consequences of auto-correlated disturbance terms for our ordinary least squares estimation procedures and if, therefore, any adjustments to these procedures are required.

The consequences of autocorrelation are in fact very similar to those of heteroskedasticity. That is, it can be shown that if the disturbance terms are autocorrelated then the simple least squares estimators are still unbiased and consistent, but they are no longer efficient nor even asymptotically efficient – superior estimators of the parameters of the model can be derived. In turn, the specific form of these efficient estimators will depend on the specific nature of the autocorrelation – that is, whether the autocorrelation is of the form in Equation 4.64 (AR(1)) or Equation 4.69 (AR(2)), or any other generalisation of these structures.

But more seriously, and again as in the case of heteroskedasticity, the conventional expressions for the variances of the simple least squares estimators will be biased, and consequently all confidence intervals and hypothesis tests derived from least squares estimation will be invalid. Further (also as in the case of heteroskedasticity), it is not even possible to generalise about the direction of the bias involved – depending on the nature of the autocorrelation, an impression will be given either of greater or less precision than is justified.

In order to illustrate why the use of the conventional expressions for the estimator variances is invalid, consider the case of $\hat{\beta}$. As previously, expressing $\hat{\beta}$ as a weighted sum of the $Y_t$s, we have:

$$\mathrm{Var}(\hat{\beta}) = \mathrm{Var}\left(\sum W_t Y_t\right)$$
$$= \mathrm{Var}\left[\sum W_t(\alpha + \beta X_t + \varepsilon_t)\right]$$

$$= \text{Var}\,[\alpha \sum W_t + \beta \sum W_t X_t + \sum W_t \varepsilon_t]$$
$$= \text{Var}\,[\beta + \sum W_t \varepsilon_t]$$

and thus:

$$\text{Var}\,(\hat{\beta}) = \text{Var}\,[\sum W_t \varepsilon_t] \qquad\qquad \text{Equation 4.75}$$

Now, if the $\varepsilon_t$s were independent then we would proceed as in Chapter 2 and the variance of $\hat{\beta}$ could be written as:

$$\text{Var}\,(\hat{\beta}) = \sum \text{Var}\,(W_t \varepsilon_t) \qquad\qquad \text{Equation 4.76}$$

or

$$\text{Var}\,(\hat{\beta}) = \sigma_\varepsilon^2 \sum W_t^2 \qquad\qquad \text{Equation 4.77}$$

However, if the $\varepsilon_t$s are not independent (but are autocorrelated), then $\text{Var}\,(\hat{\beta})$ cannot be simplified to Equation 4.77 – the variance of the sum of the $W_t \varepsilon_t$ terms will not be equivalent to the sum of the variances of each of the $W_t \varepsilon_t$ terms (see the discussion associated with Equation 1.40). This is the reason, then, why the use of the conventional estimator for $\text{Var}\,(\hat{\beta})$ (Equation 4.77, with $\hat{\sigma}_\varepsilon^2$ substituted for $\sigma_\varepsilon^2$) is invalid in the case of autocorrelated disturbance terms.

Given the interpretation of autocorrelation which we provided in Figure 4.10 (and in Equations 4.72 and 4.73) we can provide an intuitive explanation of why ignoring autocorrelation leads to inefficient estimation.

Autocorrelation implies that the disturbance terms possess some structure. If we ignore this systematic component in the disturbance terms (and hence in the dependent variable) then, in effect, we are ignoring a component of the variation in the dependent variable which can be accounted for. Therefore an estimated model which ignores autocorrelation (should it be present) will possess a greater level of unexplained variation than is necessary, thus resulting in larger estimator variances, and hence greater inefficiency in estimation. Note also that as the level of an autocorrelated disturbance term can be predicted, at least in part, from time period to time period then ignoring autocorrelation will also result in less accurate forecasts of the dependent variable.

### 4.4.3 Alternative Estimation Methods

Given that the simple least squares estimation of a model with autocorrelated disturbances is inefficient we must consider the derivation of an efficient estimation method.

The derivation of such a method is relatively straightforward. In what follows we will only consider the case of a regression model with a single independent variable. However the estimation method which we will outline is perfectly general and can easily be extended to the case of a multiple regression model. We will also only consider the case of first order auto-correlation, although again the method can be adjusted to accommodate higher order structures.

Thus the generalised model can be specified as follows:

$$Y_t = \alpha + \beta X_t + \varepsilon_t \qquad \text{Equation 4.78}$$

where

$$\varepsilon_t = \rho \varepsilon_{t-1} + u_t \qquad \text{Equation 4.79}$$

and

$$u_t \sim \text{NID}(0, \sigma_u^2)$$

with all the other assumptions of the simple regression model unchanged.

First consider multiplying Equation 4.78 throughout by $\rho$ and then lagging the resulting equation by one period, thus producing the following equation:

$$\rho Y_{t-1} = \rho \alpha + \rho \beta X_{t-1} + \rho \varepsilon_{t-1} \qquad \text{Equation 4.80}$$

Subtracting Equation 4.80 from Equation 4.78 produces:

$$Y_t - \rho Y_{t-1} = \alpha(1-\rho) + \beta(X_t - \rho X_{t-1}) + \varepsilon_t - \rho \varepsilon_{t-1} \qquad \text{Equation 4.81}$$

But note from Equation 4.79 that we can write:

$$u_t = \varepsilon_t - \rho \varepsilon_{t-1} \qquad \text{Equation 4.82}$$

and therefore Equation 4.81 can be rewritten as:

$$Y_t - \rho Y_{t-1} = \alpha(1-\rho) + \beta(X_t - \rho X_{t-1}) + u_t \qquad \text{Equation 4.83}$$

Thus Equation 4.83 now has a disturbance term ($u_t$) possessing all the properties which were assumed in the simplest specification of the regression model, thereby allowing for the efficient estimation of the parameters of this equation by the direct application of ordinary least squares. That is, given the value of $\rho$, we simply create the two new variables:

$$W_t = Y_t - \rho Y_{t-1} \qquad \text{Equation 4.84}$$

and

$$V_t = X_t - \rho X_{t-1} \qquad \text{Equation 4.85}$$

and then use ordinary least squares to estimate the equation:

$$W_t = \alpha(1-\rho) + \beta V_t + u_t \qquad \text{Equation 4.86}$$

This approach will produce the BLUEs of the constant term ($\alpha(1-\rho)$) and $\beta$. To obtain an estimate of $\alpha$ we simply divide the constant term of Equation 4.86 by $1-\rho$.

However, the use of this approach requires that $\rho$ be known. In practice, $\rho$ will be unknown (in contrast to our artificial numerical example above). Thus we require a method for estimating $\rho$ in order to employ the above estimation method.

There are a number of methods which are available for estimating $\rho$ but the most widely used is derived from the **Cochrane–Orcutt procedure**.[6] The procedure is an iterative one and consists of the following steps:

1   The original equation is first estimated by ordinary least squares. That is, least squares is applied to:

$$Y_t = \alpha + \beta X_t + \varepsilon_t$$

where

$$\varepsilon_t = \rho \varepsilon_{t-1} + u_t$$

2   The estimated residuals from this regression are then obtained. That is:

$$e_t = Y_t - \hat{\alpha} - \hat{\beta} X_t \quad \text{for } t = 1, \ldots, n$$

3   The $e_t$s are treated as a set of estimated observations on the true disturbances, $\varepsilon_t$. An initial estimate of $\rho$ is then obtained by regressing $e_t$ on $e_{t-1}$ (in the same way in which the actual residuals in our numerical example were used to produce the regressions in Equations 4.72 to 4.74).

4   With this estimate of $\rho$ ($\hat{\rho}$) two new variables are generated, namely:

$$\hat{W}_t = Y_t - \hat{\rho} Y_{t-1}$$

and

$$\hat{V}_t = X_t - \hat{\rho} X_{t-1}$$

5   $\hat{W}_t$ is then regressed on $\hat{V}_t$ and a second set of estimates of $\alpha$ and $\beta$ is obtained – that is, ordinary least squares is applied to Equation 4.86 above where $\hat{W}_t$ and $\hat{V}_t$ are substituted for $W_t$ and $V_t$.

6   With these second-round estimates of $\alpha$ and $\beta$ ($\hat{\hat{\alpha}}$ and $\hat{\hat{\beta}}$, say) a new set of estimated residuals can be derived. That is:

$$e_t = Y_t - \hat{\hat{\alpha}} - \hat{\hat{\beta}} X_t \quad \text{for } t = 1, \ldots, n$$

7   We then return to Step 3 above and continue re-estimating $\rho$, $\alpha$ and $\beta$ in this manner until the difference between successive estimates of $\rho$ is negligible – that is, until the estimates of $\rho$ converge. This final estimate of $\rho$ is then used to generate a final set of estimated observations on $W_t$ and $V_t$ and the final estimates of $\alpha$ and $\beta$ are thereby obtained.

While it may appear from the above description that the practical application of the Cochrane–Orcutt method is tedious, it is ideally suited to a computerised routine. Given a regression program which possesses the facility for Cochrane–Orcutt estimation (as will be the case with most available programs) it is not necessary for the investigator to perform each of the above described iterations – they will be automatically carried out by the computer and only the final estimate of the equation presented. Thus, in practice, the use of the Cochrane–Orcutt procedure is quite straightforward.

Finally, note that the Cochrane–Orcutt procedure must produce a higher $R^2$ than in the case of ordinary least squares (given that autocorrelation is present). This simply reflects the fact that the Cochrane–Orcutt procedure takes account of the systematic variation in the disturbance term which is ignored by ordinary least squares and therefore must result in less disturbance term variation.

Although the Cochrane–Orcutt procedure is the most commonly used method for estimating a model with autocorrelated residuals, it is not the only method. Another method is that proposed by Hildreth and Lu,[7] which involves the consideration of a range of values for $\rho$, and finally selecting that value which produces an estimated equation with the minimum sum of squared residuals.

A further method is that proposed by Durbin.[8] This, conceptually, is perhaps the simplest of the available methods. It simply involves applying ordinary least squares to Equation 4.83 above, but with the equation slightly rewritten. That is, Equation 4.83 can be rewritten as:

$$Y_t = \alpha(1-\rho) + \rho Y_{t-1} + \beta X_t - \beta \rho X_{t-1} + u_t \qquad \text{Equation 4.87}$$

Equation 4.87 can now be efficiently estimated by ordinary least squares ($u_t$ possesses all the desirable properties). An estimate of $\rho$ will be given by the coefficient on $Y_{t-1}$, $\beta$ is estimated by the coefficient on $X_t$, and an estimate of $\alpha$ can be derived by dividing the estimated constant term of Equation 4.87 by the estimated coefficient on $Y_{t-1}$.

### 4.4.4    Testing for Autocorrelation

Our discussion to this point has assumed that autocorrelation is known to be present, and therefore we have been concerned with the consequences of the problem and how it might be overcome. In practice, of course, given some postulated model, we will not know *a priori* whether or not the disturbance terms in the model are autocorrelated. Therefore we first require a method of inferring from the sample data whether an assumption of autocorrelated disturbance terms should be made, and hence whether an adjustment in our estimation procedures is required.

An obvious starting point would be to begin by ignoring the possibility of autocorrelation, and thus simply to estimate the postulated model by the direct application of ordinary least squares. The residuals from the estimated model could then be derived, and examined in terms of the likelihood that they were produced by autocorrelated disturbance terms.

Thus we could graphically examine the estimated residuals, by plotting them against time, as we did with the artificially generated residuals in Figure 4.10. We would therefore be looking for some form of non-randomness in the residuals – that is, a divergence from the random graphical pattern of the residuals in Figure 4.10(c). However, such an approach would involve an element of subjectivity, and graphically detecting non-randomness would become the more difficult the weaker the autocorrelation – that is, the smaller the absolute value of $\rho$ in Equation 4.64.

A more formal approach would be to perform regressions such as those in Equations 4.72 to 4.74, and thus to regress $e_t$ on past values of itself to determine whether any significant association exists between successive values of the $e_t$s, but, strictly, we require a formal statistical test for autocorrelation. Again, we will concern ourselves only with the possibility of the disturbance terms being generated by a first-order autoregressive scheme, and thus the null and alternative hypotheses of such a test could be expressed as follows:

$H_0$: The disturbance terms are independently and randomly distributed.

$H_1$: The disturbance terms are generated by a first-order autoregressive scheme.

The most commonly employed test of the above null hypothesis is the **Durbin–Watson test**.[9] This test is based on the following test statistic:

$$d = \frac{\sum_{t=2}^{n}(e_t - e_{t-1})^2}{\sum_{t=1}^{n} e_t^2} \qquad \text{Equation 4.88}$$

where $e_t$, for $t = 1, 2, \ldots, n$, is the series of estimated residuals resulting from the initial application of ordinary least squares to the hypothesised model (ignoring the possibility of autocorrelation).

First, consider the population value of $d$ – that is, the expression that results from substituting $\varepsilon_t$ for $e_t$ in Equation 4.88 and summing over the population rather than the sample. Thus, using the expectations operator, $E$, and denoting this (unobservable) population value by $\delta$ (the Greek letter 'delta') we can write:

$$\delta = \frac{E(\varepsilon_t - \varepsilon_{t-1})^2}{E(\varepsilon_t^2)} \qquad \text{Equation 4.89}$$

Expanding the numerator of Equation 4.89 we have:

$$\delta = \frac{E(\varepsilon_t^2) + E(\varepsilon_{t-1}^2) - 2E(\varepsilon_t \varepsilon_{t-1})}{E(\varepsilon_t^2)} \qquad \text{Equation 4.90}$$

Now as $\varepsilon_t$ is assumed to be homoskedastic then we must have $E(\varepsilon_t^2) = E(\varepsilon_{t-1}^2)$, and therefore Equation 4.90 can be simplified to:

$$\delta = 2 - \frac{2E(\varepsilon_t \varepsilon_{t-1})}{E(\varepsilon_t^2)} \qquad \text{Equation 4.91}$$

Note that the final term in Equation 4.91 is just twice the (population) correlation coefficient between $\varepsilon_t$ and $\varepsilon_{t-1}$ (see Equation 4.65 above), and thus Equation 4.91 can be written as:

$$\delta = 2(1-\rho) \qquad\qquad \text{Equation 4.92}$$

Note from Equation 4.92 that we can deduce directly the effect that autocorrelation will have on the magnitude of $\delta$. Thus if no autocorrelation is present (that is, $\rho = 0$) then $\delta$ will equal two. If the disturbance terms are perfectly and positively autocorrelated ($\rho = 1$) then $\delta$ will equal zero. If the disturbance terms are perfectly and negatively autocorrelated ($\rho = -1$) then $\delta$ will equal four.

Therefore, in general, positive (but not 'perfect') autocorrelation will produce a value for $\delta$ between zero and two, and negative autocorrelation will result in $\delta$ lying between two and four.

In practice $\delta$ is unobservable (we only have a sample of observations and not the population), but we would expect the sample statistic, $d$ to reflect approximately the properties of $\delta$. That is, $d$ can be used to draw inferences concerning the value of $\delta$. Thus the closer is $d$ to zero, the stronger is the evidence of positive autocorrelation, the closer is $d$ to four the stronger is the evidence of negative autocorrelation, and a value close to two implies the absence of autocorrelation. Therefore in order to carry out a formal statistical test of the null hypothesis of no autocorrelation, we first require the distribution of $d$, under the null hypothesis. The form of this distribution is relatively complex (in contrast to our previous applications of hypothesis testing where the normal and $t$-distributions could be used) and we will make no attempt to derive it here. (Note, however, that we have already informally concluded that the expected value of $d$ (under $H_0$) is two.)

In order to test the null hypothesis of no autocorrelation we make reference to the tables of the Durbin–Watson statistic, which are derived from the sampling distribution of $d$. These are shown in Appendix IV, at various levels of significance. To carry out the Durbin–Watson test we first estimate the hypothesised model by ordinary least squares, and then from the resulting estimated residuals we calculate the value of the statistic, $d$, as given by Equation 4.88. In order to determine whether this observed value of $d$ is significant (that is, sufficiently different from two so as to lead to the rejection of $H_0$) we refer to the tables of the Durbin–Watson statistic.

Now, from Appendix IV it can be seen that these statistics are tabulated according to sample size and the number of independent variables, given the predetermined level of significance. Thus, we select the entry in this table which corresponds to the number of independent variables in the model and the size of the sample used to estimate this model. Note, that there are two tabulated values corresponding to each entry – $d_L$ and $d_U$. These entries are referred to as the **lower bound** and **upper bound**, respectively, and the values contained between these bounds are referred to as the **inconclusive region**.

Thus, if the value of $d$ falls between $d_L$ and $d_U$ ($d$ falls in the inconclusive region) then no conclusions can be drawn concerning the presence or absence of autocorrelation. From Appendix IV it can be seen that this inconclusive region will be the larger the smaller is the sample size and the greater the number of independent variables – that is, the smaller is the number of degrees of freedom available to estimate the model. That is, few degrees of freedom result in greater imprecision in the estimation of the parameters of the model, and therefore it is to be expected that this greater level of uncertainty produces relatively large inconclusive regions.

This feature of inconclusiveness is the major disadvantage of the Durbin–Watson test. It must also be emphasised that the valid application of the Durbin–Watson test assumes that the model contains a constant term and that the explanatory variables are independent of the disturbance term.

In Figure 4.11 we present a diagrammatic interpretation of the acceptance,

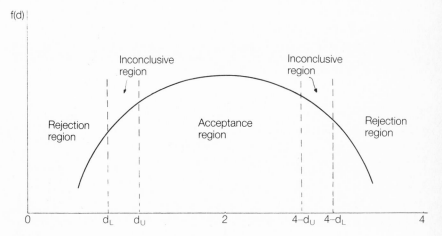

**Figure 4.11** The distribution of $d$ under $H_0$.

rejection and inconclusive regions of the Durbin–Watson test. However, the direct use of the tables in Appendix IV is only appropriate if the observed value of $d$ is less than two. That is, the method of testing $H_0$ described above should be prefaced by: 'provided the observed value of $d$ is less than two'.

If the observed value of $d$ exceeds two (thus implying the possibility of negative autocorrelation) then a simple adjustment to the entries in the Durbin–Watson tables is first required before testing $H_0$. Specifically, if the observed value of $d$ is greater than two then we obtain the appropriate entries for $d_L$ and $d_U$ from Appendix IV as previously, but we then subtract these entries from four. $H_0$ is then rejected if $d$ exceeds the larger of these two values – that is, the larger the observed value of $d$ ('large' relative to two) then the stronger is the possibility of negative autocorrelation (recall our discussion of Equation 4.92). If $d$ is less than the smaller of these two derived 'tabulated' values then $H_0$ must be accepted. A value between these two values falls in the inconclusive region, thus implying 'no decision'.

The Durbin–Watson test is not the only test for autocorrelation that could be used. However, it is a very straightforward test to apply and hence it is the most widely employed. As we have already indicated, its main disadvantage is its associated inconclusive region. In those cases where the observed value of $d$ falls in this region alternative (and more complex) test procedures are available. We will not however discuss these here.[10] An informal and pragmatic approach in those cases where $d$ falls in the inconclusive region, which is often employed in practice, is to assume the 'worst' and thus to proceed on the basis that $\varepsilon_t$ is autocorrelated. Note that such an approach, in effect, simply implies an increase in the significance level of the test (an increase in the probability of incorrectly rejecting $H_0$) – that is, a value of $d$ which falls in the inconclusive region at the 5 per cent level, say, must fall in the critical region at some higher (and generally only marginally higher) level of significance.

We will now illustrate the use of the Durbin–Watson test and the Cochrane–Orcutt procedure via an example.

Example 4.3

In Table 4.3 below we present quarterly, seasonally adjusted consumption and income data for the United Kingdom for the period 1963 to 1979, in 1975 prices. We will use these data to estimate the simple consumption function:

$$C_t = \alpha + \beta D_t + \varepsilon_t \qquad \qquad \text{Equation 4.93}$$

The least squares estimate of Equation 4.93 is as follows ($t$-statistics in brackets):

$$\hat{C}_t = 2729.246 + 0.734 D_t, \quad R^2 = 0.975, \quad d = 1.21, \quad n = 68$$
$$\phantom{\hat{C}_t = }(11.30)\ (51.07) \qquad\qquad\qquad\qquad \text{Equation 4.94}$$

Superficially, then, Equation 4.94 appears satisfactory – both parameter estimates are highly significant and a very high $R^2$ is produced. However, we have yet to consider the Durbin–Watson statistic.

As indicated, the value of $d$ associated with Equation 4.94 is 1.21. The tabulated values for $d$ from Appendix IV are (for a significance level of 2.5 per cent, and interpolating between $n = 65$ and $n = 70$):

$$d_L = 1.51 \quad \text{and} \quad d_U = 1.57$$

As the observed value of $d$ here falls below $d_L$ then we must reject $H_0$, and we would conclude that $\varepsilon_t$ is autocorrelated. Therefore we could now proceed to re-estimate Equation 4.93, using the Cochrane–Orcutt procedure, and hence incorporate an estimate of the implied AR(1) structure into the model.

**Table 4.3** Consumers' expenditure and personal disposable income quarterly – seasonally adjusted United Kingdom 1963–1979 1975 prices (£ million)

| Year | Qtr | Cons. Expend. | Income | Year | Qtr | Cons. Expend. | Income | Year | Qtr | Cons. Expend. | Income |
|---|---|---|---|---|---|---|---|---|---|---|---|
| 1963 | 1 | 12,086 | 13,100 | 1969 | 1 | 13,960 | 15,270 | 1975 | 1 | 16,285 | 19,096 |
|  | 2 | 12,446 | 13,237 |  | 2 | 13,988 | 15,243 |  | 2 | 16,301 | 18,379 |
|  | 3 | 12,575 | 13,670 |  | 3 | 14,089 | 15,254 |  | 3 | 15,970 | 18,266 |
|  | 4 | 12,618 | 13,760 |  | 4 | 14,276 | 15,477 |  | 4 | 15,868 | 18,027 |
| 1964 | 1 | 12,691 | 13,799 | 1970 | 1 | 14,217 | 15,579 | 1976 | 1 | 16,083 | 18,359 |
|  | 2 | 12,787 | 13,844 |  | 2 | 14,359 | 16,027 |  | 2 | 16,122 | 18,176 |
|  | 3 | 12,847 | 14,069 |  | 3 | 14,597 | 16,119 |  | 3 | 16,153 | 18,674 |
|  | 4 | 12,949 | 14,069 |  | 4 | 14,641 | 15,984 |  | 4 | 16,284 | 18,095 |
| 1965 | 1 | 12,959 | 14,149 | 1971 | 1 | 14,603 | 15,721 | 1977 | 1 | 15,898 | 17,788 |
|  | 2 | 12,960 | 14,165 |  | 2 | 14,867 | 16,173 |  | 2 | 15,901 | 17,530 |
|  | 3 | 13,095 | 14,418 |  | 3 | 15,071 | 16,268 |  | 3 | 16,102 | 17,973 |
|  | 4 | 13,117 | 14,473 |  | 4 | 15,183 | 16,481 |  | 4 | 16,339 | 18,472 |
| 1966 | 1 | 13,304 | 15,089 | 1972 | 1 | 15,503 | 16,885 | 1978 | 1 | 16,748 | 18,437 |
|  | 2 | 13,458 | 14,481 |  | 2 | 15,766 | 17,842 |  | 2 | 16,844 | 19,280 |
|  | 3 | 13,258 | 14,442 |  | 3 | 15,930 | 17,554 |  | 3 | 17,210 | 19,888 |
|  | 4 | 13,164 | 14,486 |  | 4 | 16,071 | 17,797 |  | 4 | 17,272 | 20,091 |
| 1967 | 1 | 13,311 | 14,486 | 1973 | 1 | 16,731 | 18,312 | 1979 | 1 | 17,406 | 20,124 |
|  | 2 | 13,527 | 14,781 |  | 2 | 16,528 | 19,082 |  | 2 | 18,242 | 20,417 |
|  | 3 | 13,726 | 15,127 |  | 3 | 16,568 | 18,912 |  | 3 | 17,417 | 20,399 |
|  | 4 | 13,821 | 14,991 |  | 4 | 16,505 | 18,780 |  | 4 | 17,751 | 21,194 |
| 1968 | 1 | 14,290 | 15,337 | 1974 | 1 | 16,144 | 18,405 |  |  |  |  |
|  | 2 | 13,691 | 15,249 |  | 2 | 16,163 | 18,537 |  |  |  |  |
|  | 3 | 13,962 | 14,921 |  | 3 | 16,262 | 18,981 |  |  |  |  |
|  | 4 | 14,083 | 15,106 |  | 4 | 16,312 | 19,100 |  |  |  |  |

*Source: Economic Trends, Annual Supplement, 1981, HMSO*

The final estimate of Equation 4.93, using the Cochrane–Orcutt procedure, is as follows:

$$\hat{C}_t = 3148.742 + 0.709D_t, \quad R^2 = 0.978, \quad d = 2.15, \quad \hat{\rho} = 0.4226, \quad n = 67$$
$$\quad (8.16) \ (31.11)$$

Equation 4.95

where $\hat{\rho}$ is the estimate of $\rho$ in the assumed AR(1) structure – that is, $\rho$ in Equation 4.64.

In order to confirm that the Cochrane–Orcutt procedure has adjusted for the autocorrelation, we can test for the significance of the value of $d$ associated with Equation 4.95. From the Durbin–Watson tables (but with $n = 67$) the approximate values of $d_L$ and $d_U$ are 1.50 and 1.56. However, as $d$ exceeds two, we must subtract these tabulated values from four before carrying out the test. That is:

$$4 - d_U = 2.44 \quad \text{and} \quad 4 - d_L = 2.50$$

As the observed value of $d$ of 2.15 is less than $4 - d_U$, we would accept $H_0$ and conclude that there is no evidence of any remaining autocorrelation.

Our discussion to this point has assumed that a significant value for the Durbin–Watson statistic necessarily implies that the disturbance terms are autocorrelated. However, while it is certainly the case that an autocorrelated disturbance term must produce a significant value for $d$ (at least in large samples), it does not follow that the converse is necessarily true. That is, a significant value for $d$ can be produced by factors other than autocorrelation. In particular, if the postulated model is **misspecified** (the model fails to take account of any appropriate non-linearities or omits relevant explanatory variables) this can often result in a significant value for $d$.

We have interpreted autocorrelation in terms of the disturbance term possessing a degree of structure or predictability. Thus, given that the objective of any regression model is to account for all of the systematic variation in the dependent variable, an estimate of this structure must be explicitly incorporated into the estimation process. This is the precise approach of the Cochrane–Orcutt procedure. Note that the underlying assumption of such an approach is that the estimated disturbances accurately reflect the properties of the actual disturbance terms. However, if the estimated model has failed to account for some systematic influence on the dependent variable, then the estimated disturbances must reflect, in part, the effect of this omitted influence. Thus even if the true disturbance terms are random and independent, the estimated disturbances will possess some structure if the model is misspecified.

In order to illustrate this point consider again the data in Table 4.1 above. However we will reorder these data in ascending order of the independent variable, $X$. Thus in Table 4.4 below we present these reordered data. Note that in simply reordering these data we have not changed the relationship

**Table 4.4** A hypothetical sample of observations on a dependent variable, *Y*, and an independent variable, *X*

| Observation number | Y | X | Observation number | Y | X |
|---|---|---|---|---|---|
| 1 | 2839.79 | 32 | 11 | 2692.50 | 42 |
| 2 | 2814.18 | 33 | 12 | 2698.57 | 43 |
| 3 | 2779.17 | 34 | 13 | 2719.70 | 44 |
| 4 | 2768.31 | 35 | 14 | 2718.43 | 45 |
| 5 | 2750.69 | 36 | 15 | 2708.88 | 46 |
| 6 | 2751.51 | 37 | 16 | 2750.05 | 47 |
| 7 | 2738.79 | 38 | 17 | 2744.47 | 48 |
| 8 | 2718.54 | 39 | 18 | 2758.82 | 49 |
| 9 | 2691.85 | 40 | 19 | 2807.75 | 50 |
| 10 | 2702.16 | 41 | 20 | 2814.48 | 51 |

between *Y* and *X* in any way. Thus a plot of *Y* against *X* must produce exactly the same graph as in Figure 4.4, the relationship between *Y* and *X* remaining a non-linear one.

Regressing *Y* on *X* (the naive model) must produce exactly the same regression equation as presented in Equation 4.6. That is (*t*-statistics in brackets):

$$\hat{Y}_i = 2802.173 - 1.295X_i, \quad R^2 = 0.030 \qquad \text{Equation 4.96}$$
$$(38.48) \quad (0.74)$$

Thus we would conclude from Equation 4.96 (as previously) that there does not appear to be a (linear) relationship between *Y* and *X*.

However, we now have a further statistic to interpret – the Durbin–Watson statistic. The estimated residuals from Equation 4.96 produce a value for *d* of 0.24 (that is, this value of *d* is calculated from the data as ordered in Table 4.4), and reference to the tables in Appendix IV will confirm that this value is highly significant. That is, it would appear that the disturbance terms associated with Equation 4.96 are strongly autocorrelated.

It is instructive to examine a graph of the estimated residuals from Equation 4.96 against the independent variable, *X*. This graph is presented in Figure 4.12. Note that the residuals in Figure 4.12, in effect, still contain the non-linearity between *Y* and *X* which the naive model has failed to capture. That is, the estimated residuals are clearly not randomly distributed in relation to the ordering of the independent variable, and thus a significant value for *d* is produced. However, this significant *d* value does not result from autocorrelation in the actual disturbance terms, but rather from the non-linearity which the model has ignored. The implication, therefore, is that if the correctly specified model is estimated an insignificant value for *d* should be produced.

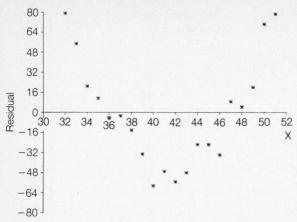

**Figure 4.12**    Graph of the residuals from Equation 4.96 against $X$.

Recall that we presented the estimate of this model in Equation 4.5. That is ($t$-statistics in brackets):

$$\hat{Y}_i = 5158.197 - 117.074X_i + 1.395Z_i, \quad R^2 = 0.947 \qquad \text{Equation 4.97}$$
$$\quad\;(37.11)\quad\;(17.25)\quad\;(17.09)$$

where

$$Z_i = X_i^2$$

The estimated residuals derived from Equation 4.97 now produce an insignificant value for $d$ of 2.19. That is, in this particular example, what initially appeared to be a problem of autocorrelation, on closer investigation, was shown to be one of misspecification.

This example is somewhat artificial in the sense that an inspection of the graph of the estimated residuals from the initial model quite clearly indicated a misspecification problem. In practice we will not often be able to draw such clear-cut and unambiguous conclusions. The more complex the theory that underlies any given model then, in general, the more difficult it will be to attribute a significant Durbin–Watson statistic unambiguously to either autocorrelation or misspecification. Often, a combination of both factors will be at work.

Note also that in the above example the Durbin–Watson statistic was significant only because the data were reordered according to the magnitude of $X$. Therefore the non-linearity was not only reflected in the graph of the residuals against $X$, but would also be reflected in a graph of the residuals against 'Observation Number' in Table 4.4 (or 'time-period' if the data were a time-series). That is, the Durbin–Watson statistic only examines structure in the disturbance terms in the order in which the data are presented. From the definition of $d$ in Equation 4.88 the Durbin–Watson test can only detect autocorrelation if the residuals are sequentially related. This is why the Durbin–Watson test is normally associated with time-series data, where the data occur in a natural ordering. But in our introductory remarks to this section we noted that autocorrelation, in general, refers to any relationship amongst the disturbance terms, a time-series relationship simply being the most common form of such a relationship.

Thus, for example, again consider the data as ordered in Table 4.1. The naive model will still produce the same statistical results except that the associated Durbin–Watson statistic is now the insignificant value of 1.42 and not 0.24 as produced by the ordering of the data in Table 4.4. Of course, the model is still misspecified (the relationship between $Y$ and $X$ remains unchanged irrespective of how the data are ordered) but this misspecification is now not reflected in the value of the Durbin–Watson statistic. That is, a graph of the residuals against Observation Number in Table 4.1 would not highlight the misspecification (athough the misspecification would still be apparent in the graph of the residuals against $X$).

The general conclusion we can draw is that any model misspecification must necessarily be reflected in the estimated residuals. However, only if this misspecification is related to the order in which the data appear will it also be reflected in the Durbin–Watson statistic.

Other forms of model misspecification, therefore, can be perfectly consistent with an insignificant Durbin–Watson statistic, and thus alternative methods of detecting such misspecifications are required (for example, in a cross-section context the data might be reordered according to the magnitude of one of the independent variables). As we shall see in much of the remainder of this book, developing methods for detecting model misspecifications is central to the effective application of econometric methodology.

Note also that our assumption of an autocorrelated disturbance term in the consumption function in Example 4.3 should now be re-examined in relation to the possibility of a model misspecification. In Example 2.2 we made reference to the possibility that consumption function formulations such as those in Equation 4.93 are too simplistic. Hence the significant Durbin–Watson statistic in Equation 4.94 may be a reflection of model misspecification rather than the actual disturbance terms being auto-correlated.

We shall return to the consideration of specifying and estimating the consumption function, and we shall see that the specification in Equation 4.93 can indeed be argued to be misspecified. However, as we shall also see, the detection of such misspecifications, in practice, is far from straightforward.

## 4.5 Summary

In this chapter we have discussed a number of refinements which could be made to the regression model. We began by considering cases in which it might be appropriate to relax the assumption of linearity. Thus we examined ways in which non-linear relationships between the dependent and independent variables could be specified and estimated. We showed that, in general, the incorporation of non-linear relationships into the modelling process was relatively straightforward.

We then examined in some detail the assumptions that could be made concerning the properties of the disturbance terms. In particular, we relaxed our initial assumptions of homoskedasticity and independence. We indicated that if the disturbance terms were heteroskedastic then ignoring this heteroskedasticity in the estimation process would produce inefficient estimators, although they would still be unbiased. But, more importantly, if the heteroskedasticity were ignored then the ordinary least squares estimation procedures would produce biased estimators of the estimator variances thus precluding a valid statistical evaluation of the estimated model.

We showed that a regression model with heteroskedastic disturbances could be efficiently estimated provided that the variance of the disturbance terms could be related to the level of some other variable – typically, one of the independent variables in the model. If such an assumption can be made then a simple variable transformation will produce a model which can be efficiently and validly estimated by ordinary least squares. However, first establishing whether or not the disturbance terms are heteroskedastic and then, if necessary, identifying an appropriate variable transformation may not be so straightforward in practice.

We then discussed the problem of autocorrelation amongst the disturbance terms and focused our discussion on the case of time series data. Autocorrelation was seen to have exactly the same consequences as heteroskedasticity – ignoring autocorrelation produces inefficient, although unbiased, estimators but produces biased estimator variances. We outlined a method for testing for autocorrelation (the Durbin–Watson test) and described an efficient estimation method (the Cochrane–Orcutt procedure). However, our discussion only concerned the simplest form of autocorrelation – first-order autocorrelation.

### Notes

[1] Let $X$ and $Y$ be variables and $a$, $b$, and $c$ be constants. Then some basic properties of logarithms are as follows:

a   $\log(XY) = \log(X) + \log(Y)$
b   $\log(X/Y) = \log(X) - \log(Y)$
c   $\log(X^b) = b\log(X)$, and therefore
d   $\log(aX^bY^c) = \log(a) + b\log(X) + c\log(Y)$
e   $\log_e e = 1$

Note also that the general non-linear relationship:

$$Y = aX^b$$

can be 'linearised' by taking logarithms of both sides. That is:

$$\log(Y) = \log(a) + b\log(X)$$

Thus the logarithmic relationship illustrated in Figure 4.3(c) can be interpreted as the log-linear form of:

$$Y = X^{-1}$$

[2] See J. Kmenta, *Elements of Econometrics*, 2nd edn (New York, Macmillan, 1986), pp. 270–6.

[3] Ibid., pp. 276–9.

[4] This type of 'experiment' is generally referred to as a Monte Carlo experiment. This approach is particularly useful in evaluating estimation methods in small samples. It is often not possible to determine analytically the properties of various estimators in small samples and this type of approach can at least be used to draw some conclusions concerning the performance of such estimators.

[5] For a fuller discussion of the tests which are available for heteroskedasticity, see Kmenta, *Elements of Econometrics*, pp. 292–8 or J. Johnston, *Econometric Methods*, 3rd edn (New York, McGraw-Hill, 1984).

[6] See D. Cochrane and G. Orcutt, 'Application of least squares regressions to relationships containing autocorrelated error terms', *Journal of the American Statistical Association*, 44 (1949), pp. 32–61.

[7] See G. Hildreth and J. Y. Lu, 'Demand relations with autocorrelated disturbances', Michigan State University Agricultural Experimental Station, *Technical Bulletin 276*, November, 1960. See also R. J. Pindyck and D. L. Rubenfeld, *Econometric Models and Economic Forecasts*, 2nd edn (New York, McGraw-Hill, 1981), pp. 157–8 for a brief summary of this method.

[8] See J. Durbin, 'Estimation of parameters in time-series regression models', *Journal of the Royal Statistical Society*. Ser. B. 22 (1960), pp. 139–53, or Pindyck and Rubenfeld, *Econometric Models*, p. 158, for a brief summary.

[9] The test was derived by J. Durbin and G. S. Watson. See J. Durbin and G. S. Watson, 'Testing for serial correlation in least squares regression', *Biometrika*, 38 (1951), pp. 159–77.

[10] The interested reader is referred to J. Johnston, *Econometric Methods*, 3rd edn (New York, McGraw-Hill, 1984), pp. 314–21, or any other intermediate or advanced econometrics text.

## References and Further Reading

All of the references in Chapters 2 and 3 are also relevant for non-linearities, heteroskedasticity and autocorrelation. The reader should note, however, that in the case of autocorrelation, terminology does vary somewhat. Thus the terms 'auto-correlation', 'autoregressive errors' (or 'disturbance terms') and 'serially correlated errors' (or 'serial correlation') are all interchangeable.

**Exercises**

*Section 4.2    Non-linearities*

Exercise 1

Show that $\beta_1$ and $\beta_2$ in the log-linear demand function in Equation 4.8 are the price and income elasticities of demand, respectively.

Exercise 2

Consider the following deterministic models:

(i)   $Y_t = X_t^\beta$

(ii)  $Y_t = \beta^{X_t}$

(iii) $Y_t = \dfrac{1}{e^{\alpha + \beta X_t}}$

(a)   Re-express each of these relationships so that they are in a form suitable for ordinary least squares estimation.

(b)   Now consider the role of a disturbance term in each of these models. How must a disturbance term enter these models so as to justify your transformations in part (a)? How reasonable do you consider these assumptions to be?

*Section 4.3    Heteroskedasticity*

Exercise 3

Divide Equation 4.36 throughout by $\sigma_i$, and explain why the least squares estimator of $\beta$ in this transformed equation must be the BLUE of $\beta$.

Derive the expression for the least squares estimator of $\beta$ from this transformed equation and show that it is equivalent to the expression in Equation 4.35. (Hint: consider Equation 3.6.)

Finally, show that if the disturbance terms are homoskedastic then Equation 4.35 collapses to the expression for the ordinary least squares estimator of $\beta$ in Equation 2.22.

Exercise 4

Derive Equation 4.56.

Exercise 5

Consider the car registration and income data in Exercise 15 of Chapter 1, and particularly the graph of registrations against income. If you have access to a regression package, perform a Goldfeld–Quandt test on these data to examine the possibility of heteroskedastic disturbances in the simple model which relates registrations to income. Making any assumptions which you consider appropriate concerning the nature of heteroskedasticity in this model, estimate the model, adjusting for heteroskedasticity. Compare this estimated model with your estimated model in Exercise 8 of Chapter 2.

*Section 4.4 Autocorrelation*

Exercise 6

The Durbin–Watson statistics associated with the various models we estimated in Chapters 2 and 3 are as follows:
a   2.51, for the gas consumption model in Equation 2.64.
b   0.55, for the consumption function in Equation 2.87.
c   1.16, for the gas consumption model in Equation 3.21.
d   0.87 and 0.90, for the beer consumption models which were estimated in Examples 3.1 and 3.2, respectively.

Test for the significance of these statistics. In those cases in which a significant Durbin–Watson statistic is produced discuss the possibility of these having resulted from model misspecification, and outline the various respecifications that you would experiment with. If you have access to a regression package, re-estimate these models using the Cochrane–Orcutt procedure. Also re-estimate these models trying some of your proposed respecifications.

**Appendix 4.1** *Consistency and Asymptotic Efficiency*

Consider the generalised problem of estimating some parameter $\theta$ (the Greek letter 'theta'). Let $\hat{\theta}$ denote an estimator of $\theta$.

$\hat{\theta}$ is said to be a **consistent** estimator of $\theta$ if the distribution of $\hat{\theta}$ collapses on $\theta$ as sample size increases. That is, as the size of the sample approaches infinity the variance of $\hat{\theta}$ approaches zero and $E(\hat{\theta})$ approaches $\theta$ – as the sample size increases without limit our estimator produces the correct value of the parameter. Thus a consistent estimator is asymptotically unbiased and its variance is a decreasing function of sample size.

More formally, $\hat{\theta}$ will be a consistent estimator of $\theta$ if, for any small positive number $\delta$, the following holds:

$$\lim_{n\to\infty} \Pr\left[\theta - \delta < \hat{\theta} < \theta + \delta\right] = 1 \qquad \text{Equation A4.1.1}$$

where $\lim_{n\to\infty}$ reads as 'the limit as $n$ (sample size) approaches infinity'. In words, Equation A4.1.1 states that as $n$ approaches infinity then $\hat{\theta}$ will lie within $\pm\delta$ of $\theta$ with certainty, where $\delta$ is any arbitrarily selected small number. This is generally abbreviated to stating that the 'probability limit' of $\hat{\theta}$ is equal to $\theta$, or:

$$\text{plim}\,(\hat{\theta}) = \theta \qquad \text{Equation A4.1.2}$$

A simple example will help to illustrate these concepts.

Consider the problem of estimating the mean, $\mu$, of some population. Recall from Chapter 1 that the 'best' estimate of $\mu$ is the mean of a randomly selected sample from this population, $\bar{X}$. That is, $\bar{X}$ is unbiased ($E(\bar{X}) = \mu$) and from Equation 1.46 its variance is given by:

$$\text{Var}(\bar{X}) = \frac{\sigma^2}{n} \qquad\qquad \text{Equation A4.1.3}$$

Thus as we have established that $\bar{X}$ is unbiased for any sample size then it is certainly asymptotically unbiased. Note from Equation A4.1.3 that $\text{Var}(\bar{X})$ is inversely related to $n$ and therefore we can conclude that $\bar{X}$ is consistent – $\text{Var}(\bar{X})$ approaches zero as $n$ approaches infinity.

Now consider two further estimators of $\mu$, which we will denote by $\hat{\mu}$ and $\ddot{\mu}$. In particular, let these estimators be:

$$\hat{\mu} = \frac{\displaystyle\sum_{i=1}^{n} X_i}{n-1} \qquad\qquad \text{Equation A4.1.4}$$

and

$$\ddot{\mu} = \frac{1}{2} \left( \frac{\displaystyle\sum_{i=1}^{n-1} X_i}{n} + X_n \right) \qquad\qquad \text{Equation A4.1.5}$$

That is, $\hat{\mu}$ is simply the sum of the sample values divided by the sample size minus one, and $\ddot{\mu}$ is the simple average of the first $n-1$ sample observations divided by the sample size and the last sample observation.

First, we must establish whether or not $\hat{\mu}$ and $\ddot{\mu}$ are unbiased. Thus, for $\hat{\mu}$ we have:

$$E(\hat{\mu}) = E(\sum X_i / n - 1)$$
$$= \sum E(X_i)/(n-1)$$
$$= n\mu/(n-1)$$

Therefore as $E(\hat{\mu}) \neq \mu$ then we can conclude that $\hat{\mu}$ is biased. The extent of the bias in $\hat{\mu}$ is simply given by the difference between $E(\hat{\mu})$ and $\mu$. That is,

$$\text{Bias}(\hat{\mu}) = E(\hat{\mu}) - \mu$$
$$= n\mu/(n-1) - \mu$$
$$= \mu[n/(n-1)-1]$$
$$= \mu[1/(n-1)]$$

However, note that as sample size increases this bias becomes smaller and, in the limit, approaches zero as $n$ approaches infinity. Thus we can conclude that $\hat{\mu}$ is asymptotically unbiased.

Next, consider the variance of $\hat{\mu}$. That is,

$$
\begin{aligned}
\text{Var}(\hat{\mu}) &= \text{Var}\left(\sum X_i/n-1\right) \\
&= [1/(n-1)^2][\sum \text{Var}(X_i)] \\
&= [n/(n-1)^2]\sigma^2
\end{aligned}
$$

Note that as $n$ increases $\text{Var}(\hat{\mu})$ will become smaller, and in the limit, $\text{Var}(\hat{\mu})$ will approach zero as $n$ approaches infinity. Thus as $\hat{\mu}$ is asymptotically unbiased and as $\text{Var}(\hat{\mu})$ is inversely related to sample size then we can conclude that $\hat{\mu}$ is a consistent estimator of $\mu$. However, note that $\bar{X}$ is still a superior estimator of $\mu$ as it is unbiased, and it has a smaller variance (for all $n > 1$).

Next consider $\ddot{\mu}$. In order to establish whether there is any bias in $\ddot{\mu}$ we have:

$$
\begin{aligned}
E(\ddot{\mu}) &= E\left[\sum_{}^{n-1} X_i/2n + X_n/2\right] \\
&= (n-1)\mu/2n + \mu/2 \\
&= (2n-1)\mu/2n
\end{aligned}
$$

Thus $\ddot{\mu}$ is biased, and the extent of this bias is:

$$
\begin{aligned}
\text{Bias}(\ddot{\mu}) &= E(\ddot{\mu}) - \mu \\
&= [(2n-1)\mu/2n] - \mu \\
&= -\mu/2n
\end{aligned}
$$

However, again note that this bias will approach zero as sample size increases and thus we can conclude that $\ddot{\mu}$ is at least asymptotically unbiased.

Finally, we require the variance of $\ddot{\mu}$ in order to determine whether $\ddot{\mu}$ is a consistent estimator. That is,

$$
\begin{aligned}
\text{Var}(\ddot{\mu}) &= \text{Var}\left[\sum_{}^{n-1} X_i/2n + X_n/2\right] \\
&= 1/4n^2 \sum_{}^{n-1} \text{Var}(X_i) + 1/4\,\text{Var}(X_n) \\
&= (n-1)\sigma^2/4n^2 + \sigma^2/4
\end{aligned}
$$

Now, note that the first term in this expression for $\text{Var}(\ddot{\mu})$ will approach zero as $n$ increases, but the last term is independent of $n$ and thus will remain irrespective of sample size. Therefore $\text{Var}(\ddot{\mu})$ will tend to the value $\sigma^2/4$ as sample size increases and therefore $\ddot{\mu}$ is not a consistent estimator of $\mu$.

As indicated in the body of the text, in evaluating estimators with particularly complex forms it will generally be easier to establish whether or not these estimators are consistent rather than examining these estimators with respect to the finite sample property of unbiasedness. The reason is that the manipulation of the 'plim' operator is much easier than the manipulation of the expectations operator, $E$. Thus, for example, given any two random variables $X$ and $Y$, say, then we can write:

$$\text{plim}(X\,Y) = \text{plim}(X)\,\text{plim}(Y)$$

and

$$\text{plim}\left(\frac{X}{Y}\right) = \frac{\text{plim}(X)}{\text{plim}(Y)}$$

However the corresponding 'finite sample' statements do not hold. That is:

$$E(X\,Y) \neq E(X)E(Y)$$

(unless $X$ and $Y$ are independent)

and

$$E\left(\frac{X}{Y}\right) \neq \frac{E(X)}{E(Y)}$$

While the estimators which we have examined here have been relatively straightforward in the sense that we have been able to examine them with respect to both their unbiasedness and consistency, this will not always be the case in practice. That is, we will not be able to deduce analytically the small sample properties of certain classes of complex estimators. However, we will not consider any examples here.

Finally, we must consider the property of **asymptotic efficiency**. We will not provide a detailed discussion here, as the mathematics can become quite complex. We simply define the asymptotic variance of an estimator as the variance of the distribution of the estimator just prior to the distribution of the estimator collapsing on the true value of the population parameter. That is, we would only examine consistent estimators with respect to their asymptotic efficiency, and as all consistent estimators will, by definition, collapse on the true value of the population parameter we need a criterion for discriminating between competing consistent estimators. Thus we would select that consistent estimator with the smallest asymptotic variance – or that estimator whose variance approaches zero most rapidly as sample size increases.

It must be emphasized, however, that while it is generally easier to establish the asymptotic properties of estimators, particularly consistency, it is the small sample properties of estimators that will be of far greater relevance – after all, in practice, only relatively small samples will be available. Thus, in a sense, the performance of estimators in large samples is quite irrelevant if only small samples are available. It is the lack of knowledge of small sample properties of estimators that represents the greatest single gap in the current state of estimation theory.

# 5 Extensions of the Regression Model – II

## 5.1 Introduction

In this chapter we will discuss a number of further refinements which can be made to the regression model. We will begin by describing the use of a particular type of independent variable – a **dummy** or **binary** variable – which is a variable that can only take on the values zero or one. These variables are used in situations in which the influence of some explanatory factor could be interpreted as being discrete rather than continuous in nature.

We will then go on to discuss the way in which any available theoretical information concerning the values, or relative values, of the parameters in a model can be incorporated into the estimation process.

Finally, we will discuss the estimation of time-series models in more general terms. In particular, we will examine the specification and estimation of models in which the past values of some independent variable influence the current value of the dependent variable – that is, we will discuss the estimation of **distributed lag models**. We will then generalise this discussion to describe some of the issues involved in the specification and estimation of **dynamic** models in economics.

## 5.2 The Use of Dummy Variables

There are a number of applications in which it will be appropriate to use dummy (or binary) variables as additional explanatory variables. Such variables can only take on the values of zero or one at each sample point, and their purpose is simply to indicate the presence or absence of some explanatory factor or characteristic (typically, a dummy variable would take on the value one if the explanatory factor were present at a given sample point, and the value zero if the factor were absent). Dummy variables can also be useful in situations in which the influence of an explanatory factor is not quantifiable, *a priori*.

As an example of the use of a dummy variable, consider a simple model which seeks to explain the variation in the level of expenditure on alcoholic beverages across some given population of individuals. Such a model could be estimated by first randomly selecting a sample of individuals from this population and collecting data on alcohol expenditure (over the previous week or month, say), and the corresponding values of appropriate explanatory variables. For simplicity, we will assume that income is considered to be the major influence on the level of alcohol expenditure. Thus our simple model could be specified as follows:

$$A_i = \alpha + \beta Y_i + \varepsilon_i \qquad\qquad \text{Equation 5.1}$$

where

$A_i$ = expenditure on alcohol by individual $i$

$Y_i$ = income of individual $i$.

Assume that, given a sample of data, the estimation of Equation 5.1 certainly results in $Y$ being significant as a determinant of $A$, but that considerable unexplained variation still remains in $A$ (that is, a significant $t$-statistic on $Y$ is produced, but with a relatively low $R^2$). Thus the investigator would seek to add further explanatory variables to Equation 5.1 in order to reduce the unexplained variation.

One possible reason for the low explanatory power of Equation 5.1 is that the level of expenditure on alcohol may differ as between males and females. That is, at any given level of income, males may tend to spend more on alcohol than females. This may result from actual consumption levels differing between males and females, or perhaps from social conventions, whereby males tend to bear a greater proportion of expenditure on alcohol even though consumption levels are similar – or indeed both of these factors may be at work. However, whatever the precise reason for expenditure levels differing between males and females, a scatter graph of the expenditure data against income might produce something like Figure 5.1.

Note from Figure 5.1 that there certainly appears to be a positive relationship between $A$ and $Y$ (as expected), but there seem to be separate relationships for males and females. It is therefore clear from Figure 5.1 why fitting a single regression line to the data results in a relatively low $R^2$ – the line of best fit would lie somewhere between the male and female observations, resulting in a large dispersion of observations around this line. Note also that ignoring this male–female differential could even lead to the

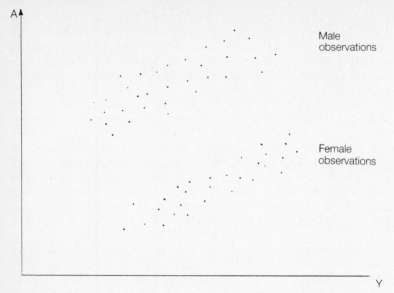

**Figure 5.1** Scatter of hypothetical observations on alcohol expenditure and income in a random sample of individuals.

conclusion that $Y$ is insignificant. That is, the vertical distance between the male and female observations may be so large that the relatively high value for $\hat{\sigma}_\varepsilon^2$ which is produced by a single regression line fitted to the data will result in an insignificant $t$-statistic on $Y$. We might therefore draw the quite erroneous conclusion that income does not exert a significant influence on alcohol expenditure.

Clearly, then, the model in Equation 5.1 is misspecified as it fails to account for this male–female differential. We therefore require a means of incorporating this differential into the model.

An obvious solution would be to fit separate regression lines to the male and female observations. Thus we could postulate that, for males:

$$A_i = \alpha_1 + \beta_1 Y_i + \varepsilon_i \qquad\qquad \text{Equation 5.2}$$

and, for females:

$$A_i = \alpha_2 + \beta_2 Y_i + \varepsilon_i \qquad\qquad \text{Equation 5.3}$$

and the two sets of observations would then be used to estimate these two models. However, note that the data in Figure 5.1 appear to imply that the two regression lines have the same slope, and differ only in terms of their intercepts. That is, while it certainly seems to be the case that the level of expenditure differs between males and females, the expenditure of both males and females appears to respond similarly to changes in the level of income. Thus in estimating Equations 5.2 and 5.3 we would wish to impose the condition that:

$$\beta_1 = \beta_2 = \beta \qquad \text{Equation 5.4}$$

Now, separately estimating Equations 5.2 and 5.3 will not guarantee that Equation 5.4 is satisfied – the probable outcome is that marginally different estimates of $\beta_1$ and $\beta_2$ would be obtained. But more importantly, such an approach would be an inefficient use of the available data. If we consider the assumption in Equation 5.4 to be an acceptable one then it would be much more sensible to use the entire data set to obtain a single estimate of the common slope coefficient, $\beta$ – formally, this would result in a more efficient estimator for the slope coefficient as a larger sample would be used and a degree of freedom saved.

This can be quite easily achieved through the appropriate use of a dummy variable. Thus we define a dummy variable, $X_1$, as follows:

$$X_1 = \begin{cases} 1 & \text{for male observations} \\ 0 & \text{for female observations} \end{cases}$$

The model can now be respecified as:

$$A_i = \alpha_3 + \alpha_4 X_{1i} + \beta Y_i + \varepsilon_i \qquad \text{Equation 5.5}$$

Thus note that for male observations $X_{1i} = 1$ and the model collapses to:

$$A_i = (\alpha_3 + \alpha_4) + \beta Y_i + \varepsilon_i \qquad \text{Equation 5.6}$$

where $\alpha_3 + \alpha_4 = \alpha_1$ from Equation 5.2. For female observations $X_{1i} = 0$ and thus Equation 5.5 becomes:

$$A_i = \alpha_3 + \beta Y_i + \varepsilon_i \qquad \text{Equation 5.7}$$

just as in Equation 5.3 but with $\alpha_3 = \alpha_2$.

That is, in order to estimate the parameters of the model as specified in Equations 5.2, 5.3 and 5.4 we simply regress $A$ on $X_1$ and $Y$. The coefficient on $Y_i$ will be the estimate of the common slope coefficient, $\beta$. The intercept term in Equation 5.2 is simply the sum of the constant term and the coefficient on $X_{1i}$ in Equation 5.5. The estimate of the intercept term in Equation 5.3 is given by the estimated intercept in Equation 5.5. (Note, that in combining Equations 5.2 to 5.4 into the single estimating equation in Equation 5.5 we have had to assume that the properties of the disturbance terms in Equations 5.2 and 5.3 are identical.)

The use of a dummy variable as described in Equation 5.5 is not the only way of producing an estimating equation to achieve the model specification in Equations 5.2 to 5.4. An identical specification can be achieved via the definition of two dummy variables. Thus we could define a second dummy variable, $X_2$, where:

$$X_2 = \begin{cases} 0 & \text{for male observations} \\ 1 & \text{for female observations} \end{cases}$$

The model could now be specified as:

$$A_i = \alpha_1 X_{1i} + \alpha_2 X_{2i} + \beta Y_i + \varepsilon_i \qquad \text{Equation 5.8}$$

Thus for males ($X_{1i} = 1$, $X_{2i} = 0$) Equation 5.8 collapses to Equation 5.2, and for females ($X_{1i} = 0$, $X_{2i} = 1$) Equation 5.8 collapses to Equation 5.3.

However, note that it would be inappropriate to include a constant term in Equation 5.8. Given the definitions of $X_1$ and $X_2$ above it must be the case that:

$$X_{1i} + X_{2i} = 1 \quad \text{for all } i$$

and consequently the inclusion of a constant term in Equation 5.8 would result in **perfect multicollinearity** – the constant term would be perfectly correlated with $X_1 + X_2$.

We could also use a dummy variable to allow for a difference in the slope coefficient between males and females. Thus a model which allows for differences in both the intercept and slope coefficients could be specified as:

$$A_i = \alpha_3 + \alpha_4 X_{1i} + \beta_1 Y_i + \beta_2 X_{1i} Y_i + \varepsilon_i \qquad \text{Equation 5.9}$$

where $X_1$ is defined as previously and $X_{1i} Y_i$ is a further variable which is simply the product of $X_1$ and $Y$. Thus for males ($X_{1i} = 1$) Equation 5.9 collapses to:

$$A_i = (\alpha_3 + \alpha_4) + (\beta_1 + \beta_2) Y_i + \varepsilon_i \qquad \text{Equation 5.10}$$

and for females ($X_{1i} = 0$) we have:

$$A_i = \alpha_3 + \beta_1 Y_i + \varepsilon_i \qquad \text{Equation 5.11}$$

A further and common application of dummy variables is for taking account of seasonality when modelling time-series data which contain seasonal variation. Thus let $Y$ be the dependent variable of interest. Assume that, say, quarterly observations are available on $Y$. Now, presumably $Y$ will vary from quarter to quarter according to the variation in a number of explanatory (or economic) variables, but some of the quarterly variation in $Y$ will also result from the influence of seasonal factors. Thus it might be argued that the purely seasonal variation in $Y$ is of no real interest (such variation can in a sense be 'explained' by the seasonality), and the investigator will wish to concentrate on explaining the more interesting non-seasonal variation (trend and cyclical movements). Thus we could define four dummy variables as follows:

$$X_1 = \begin{cases} 1 & \text{for 1st quarter observations} \\ 0 & \text{otherwise} \end{cases}$$

$$X_2 = \begin{cases} 1 & \text{for 2nd quarter observations} \\ 0 & \text{otherwise} \end{cases}$$

$$X_3 = \begin{cases} 1 & \text{for 3rd quarter observations} \\ 0 & \text{otherwise} \end{cases}$$

$$X_4 = \begin{cases} 1 & \text{for 4th quarter observations} \\ 0 & \text{otherwise} \end{cases}$$

The model could then be written as:

$$Y_t = \alpha_1 X_{1t} + \alpha_2 X_{2t} + \alpha_3 X_{3t} + \alpha_4 X_{4t}$$
$$+ \text{ other explanatory variables} + \varepsilon_t \qquad \text{Equation 5.12}$$

Note that the seasonality in Equation 5.12 is defined in terms of the variation in the constant term from quarter to quarter (it is $\alpha_1$ in the first quarter, $\alpha_2$ in the second, $\alpha_3$ in the third, and $\alpha_4$ in the fourth). In a two-dimensional context, seasonality is here defined as having the effect of simply shifting the regression line vertically from quarter to quarter, leaving the slope of the regression line unchanged. As such, this is the simplest assumption we could make about the nature of the seasonality in the data. (Note also, that for the reasons outlined above, it would be inappropriate to include a constant term in Equation 5.12. Alternatively, a constant term could be included and one of the dummy variables omitted.)

It may be the case that seasonally adjusted data are available on $Y$, in which case it would not be necessary to include seasonal dummy variables in the model. However, econometricians are often wary of modelling data that have already been 'tampered' with, and in general modelling data in their raw form is to be preferred. Indeed, it has been shown that some seasonal adjustment methods can actually introduce spurious variation into the data.

It will now be useful to consider an example of the use of a dummy variable.

Example 5.1

In this example we will consider the estimation of a production function for the UK coal mining industry. We will assume that a simple Cobb–Douglas production function is appropriate. That is, we will consider the estimation of the function:

$$Q = AK^{\alpha}L^{\beta}e^{\varepsilon} \qquad \text{Equation 5.13}$$

where

$Q$ = coal output
$K$ = capital inputs
$L$ = labour inputs
$\varepsilon$ = a disturbance term

$A$, $\alpha$, and $\beta$ are the parameters to be estimated. (Note, that the only justification we would offer here for the way in which the disturbance term enters Equation 5.13 is one of analytical convenience, so as to allow for the direct derivation of a linear estimating equation.)

Equation 5.13 is in a non-linear form and therefore we must first linearise the function. This can be achieved by taking logarithms of both sides. That is, the estimating equation becomes:

$$\ln(Q) = \ln(A) + \alpha \ln(K) + \beta \ln(L) + \varepsilon \qquad \text{Equation 5.14}$$

where ln denotes natural logarithm.

In order to estimate Equation 5.14 we will use a sample of time-series data over the period 1964 to 1980. These data are presented in Table 5.1. As is the case with the estimation of most production functions, it is the measurement of capital inputs that presents most difficulties. Here we have used gross capital stock in all mining and quarrying, as a series relating solely to the coal mining industry was not readily available. We would have to argue, then, that this series closely reflects the variation in the equivalent series for coal mining – that is, that this series is a good **proxy** for capital inputs in coal

**Table 5.1** Production and employment in coal mining gross capital stock in mining and quarrying, UK 1964 to 1980

| Year | Total coal production (million tonnes) | Total employment (coal mining) ('000) | Gross capital stock in mining and quarrying (1975 replacement cost) (£m) |
|------|------|------|------|
| 1964 | 196.7 | 597 | 4.1 |
| 1965 | 190.6 | 565 | 4.1 |
| 1966 | 177.4 | 518 | 4.3 |
| 1967 | 174.9 | 496 | 4.3 |
| 1968 | 166.7 | 446 | 4.3 |
| 1969 | 153.0 | 407 | 4.3 |
| 1970 | 144.6 | 382 | 4.3 |
| 1971 | 147.1 | 368 | 4.3 |
| 1972 | 119.5 | 330 | 4.3 |
| 1973 | 130.2 | 315 | 4.2 |
| 1974 | 109.3 | 300 | 4.2 |
| 1975 | 127.8 | 303 | 4.2 |
| 1976 | 122.2 | 297 | 4.3 |
| 1977 | 120.6 | 299 | 4.4 |
| 1978 | 121.7 | 295 | 4.6 |
| 1979 | 120.7 | 288 | 4.9 |
| 1980 | 128.2 | 286 | 5.2 |

*Source: Annual Abstract of Statistics, 1982, HMSO.*

mining. This is perhaps not an unreasonable assumption as the UK mining and quarrying industry is dominated by coal mining (approximately 80 per cent of the output of mining and quarrying is accounted for by coal).

However, a more fundamental difficulty concerns the appropriateness of gross capital stock as a measure of capital input. We will not concern ourselves with this particular problem, but rather we will concentrate on the statistical problems associated with estimating Equation 5.14, given the data in Table 5.1. We would stress, therefore, that our resulting estimated equation should not be interpreted as in any sense a definitive statement of the actual production function in coal mining – our approach here ignores many of the theoretical problems of production function specification and estimation, problems which are beyond the scope of this book.

The least squares estimate of Equation 5.14, using the data in Table 5.1, is as follows (absolute values of $t$-statistics in brackets):

$$\widehat{\ln}(Q_t) = -0.088 + 0.411\ln(K_t) + 0.750\ln(L_t) \qquad \text{Equation 5.15}$$
$$\quad\;\; (0.17) \quad (2.04) \qquad\quad (15.45)$$

$$R^2 = 0.954, \quad \bar{R}^2 = 0.947, \quad d = 3.28, \quad n = 17$$

Thus, superficially, the estimated equation appears to be highly satisfactory – both capital and labour are significant (although capital is just significant) and a very high proportion of the variation in output has been explained. However, we would also note that the Durbin–Watson statistic is significant (from Appendix IV, for a significance level of 2.5 per cent, 17 observations and two independent variables, we have $4 - d_U = 2.60$ and $4 - d_L = 3.10$). We must therefore attempt to identify the cause of this significant $d$ value – that is, does it result from the actual disturbance terms being autocorrelated, or is it caused by some misspecification in the model?

As a starting point, we present a graph of coal output against time in Figure 5.2.

A notable feature of Figure 5.2 is the relatively low levels of output in 1972 and 1974 (this can also be seen from Table 5.1). It so happens that in both of these years the UK coal mining industry suffered from exceptionally high levels of strike activity, and this would seem to be the most likely explanation of these low output levels. In order to confirm this, Table 5.2 shows the number of working days lost as a result of industrial stoppages in mining and quarrying over the sample period. Thus we can now consider a possible explanation as to why the estimated production function in Equation 5.15 should produce a significant Durbin–Watson statistic.

The model has attempted to explain the variation in coal output over time in terms of the variation in the levels of both capital and labour employed. However, we have now identified a further factor which might affect the level of coal output – strikes. Note that the variable we have used to measure labour inputs – total numbers employed – will not reflect the level of strike

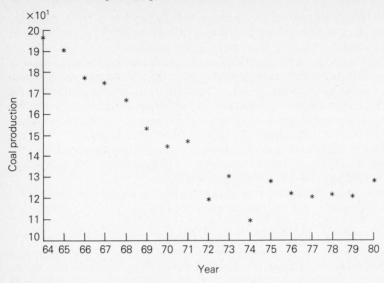

**Figure 5.2** Coal output against time.

activity, as this measure of labour inputs will remain unchanged during strikes – the numbers employed will simply not be working during these periods. Were a more detailed measure of labour inputs available – such as, say, the total number of hours actually worked by the labour force during each year – then such a variable should fully reflect the effects of strike activity (it might also be necessary to adjust the capital series to reflect actual capital utilisation, which would also be lower during strikes). Given such variables, then, it should not be necessary to take any further account of strikes in the model.

**Table 5.2** Working days lost due to industrial stoppages, mining and quarrying, 1964 to 1980 (millions)

| Year | Days lost | Year | Days lost | Year | Days lost |
|------|-----------|------|-----------|------|-----------|
| 1964 | 0.309 | 1970 | 1.092 | 1976 | 0.078 |
| 1965 | 0.413 | 1971 | 0.065 | 1977 | 0.097 |
| 1966 | 0.118 | 1972 | 10.800 | 1978 | 0.201 |
| 1967 | 0.108 | 1973 | 0.091 | 1979 | 0.128 |
| 1968 | 0.057 | 1974 | 5.628 | 1980 | 0.166 |
| 1969 | 1.041 | 1975 | 0.056 | | |

*Source: Annual Abstract of Statistics, 1982, HMSO.*

However, as the explanatory variables we have used here do not reflect the level of strike activity, then it could be argued that a 'strike' variable should be included in the model. Thus the reason, or possible reason, for Equation 5.15 producing a significant Durbin–Watson statistic is that the model has failed to account for this additional systematic factor. In particular, the model has been unable to explain the relatively low levels of output in both 1972 and 1974. The result is that the estimated disturbances will still reflect this systematic source of variation in the dependent variable and will not therefore be random – note that the level of the disturbance term will be particularly large in both 1972 and 1974, thus in a sense 'biasing' the calculated value of $d$ upwards.

The next problem, then, is to decide upon an appropriate means of accounting for this strike effect in the model. One approach would be to argue that as 1972 and 1974 were particularly atypical years with respect to strike activity then dummy variables accounting for these years might be a satisfactory solution. Thus we could define two dummy variables, one accounting for the 1972 strikes and the other accounting for the 1974 strikes. We will denote these dummy variables by D72 and D74, respectively. That is, D72 is simply a variable which takes on the value one in 1972 and zero in each of the other years in the sample period. Similarly, D74 takes on the value one in 1974, and zero elsewhere. Our model can now be specified as:

$$\ln(Q_t) = \beta_0 + \beta_1 \ln(K_t) + \beta_2 \ln(L_t) + \beta_3 \, D72_t + \beta_4 \, D74_t + \varepsilon_t$$

$$\text{Equation 5.16}$$

Note that we would expect both $\beta_3$ and $\beta_4$ to be negative – the effect of strikes is to suppress coal output, and in both 1972 and 1974 coal output will be lower than would be predicted by the levels of $K_t$ and $L_t$ in these years.

The least squares estimate of Equation 5.16 is as follows (absolute values of $t$-statistics in brackets):

$$\widehat{\ln}(Q_t) = 0.689 + 0.163 \ln(K_t) + 0.683 \ln(L_t)$$
$$\quad\quad (2.34) \quad (1.45) \quad\quad\quad (24.80)$$

$$\quad\quad -0.105 \, D72_t - 0.125 \, D74_t \quad\quad\quad\quad \text{Equation 5.17}$$
$$\quad\quad\quad (4.48) \quad\quad\quad (5.03)$$

$$R^2 = 0.989, \quad \bar{R}^2 = 0.986, \quad d = 1.81$$

From Equation 5.17 we note that both dummy variables are significant and with the expected sign. However, a cost of including these extra variables is that the coefficient on $\ln(K_t)$ is now insignificant. This presumably results from the added multicollinearity introduced by these two extra variables, which is also exacerbated by the relatively small sample which has been used here.

However, for our purposes, the main point to note from Equation 5.17 is that the associated Durbin–Watson statistic is now insignificant (the corresponding tabulated values are $d_L = 0.68$ and $d_U = 1.77$). Thus, the initial problem of a significant Durbin–Watson statistic would appear to have been caused by a misspecified model, rather than autocorrelation in the actual disturbance terms.

There are a number of other ways in which we could account for the strike effect in the above model. As a slight refinement to the model in Equation 5.16, we can note from the estimated equation in Equation 5.17 that the coefficients on D72 and D74 are very similar, thus suggesting the possibility of a single dummy variable being able to account for the strike effect.

We could formally test the hypothesis that $\beta_3$ and $\beta_4$ in Equation 5.16 are the same, via the following null hypothesis:

$$H_0: \beta_3 = \beta_4$$

or, equivalently

$$H_0: \beta_3 - \beta_4 = 0$$

Now, recall from Chapter 3, when discussing the general production function formulation in Equation 3.24, that we outlined the method for testing hypotheses concerning relationships between parameters in a model (see Equations 3.25 to 3.30). Thus we first require an estimate for $\beta_3 - \beta_4$. The best (and obvious) estimate for $\beta_3 - \beta_4$ is simply the difference between the estimated values of $\beta_3$ and $\beta_4$. Thus from Equation 5.17 we have:

$$\hat{\beta}_3 = -0.105 \quad \text{and} \quad \hat{\beta}_4 = -0.125$$

and therefore

$$\hat{\beta}_3 - \hat{\beta}_4 = 0.020$$

Next we require an estimate of the variance of $\hat{\beta}_3 - \hat{\beta}_4$, in order to calculate the $t$-statistic associated with the above null hypothesis. From Equation 3.27 (and note 2 of Chapter 3) we have:

$$\text{Var}(\hat{\beta}_3 - \hat{\beta}_4) = \text{Var}(\hat{\beta}_3) + \text{Var}(\hat{\beta}_4) - 2\,\text{Cov}(\hat{\beta}_3, \hat{\beta}_4) \qquad \text{Equation 5.18}$$

Thus the estimator of $\text{Var}(\hat{\beta}_3 - \hat{\beta}_4)$ can be written as:

$$S^2_{\hat{\beta}_3 - \beta_4} = S^2_{\hat{\beta}_3} + S^2_{\hat{\beta}_4} - 2\,\widehat{\text{Cov}}(\hat{\beta}_3, \hat{\beta}_4) \qquad \text{Equation 5.19}$$

$S^2_{\hat{\beta}_3}$ and $S^2_{\hat{\beta}_4}$ are simply the squares of the ratios of the coefficients and the $t$-statistics on D72 and D74, respectively, in Equation 5.17. The estimate of $\text{Cov}(\hat{\beta}_3, \hat{\beta}_4)$ can be obtained from the computer package used to derive Equation 5.17 (see the discussion of the variance–covariance matrix produced by the TSP regression package in Section 3.6 of Chapter 3). Therefore it can be shown that:

$$S^2_{\hat{\beta}_3 - \beta_4} = 0.001$$

Thus the *t*-statistic associated with the above null hypothesis is (see Equation 3.29):

$$t = \frac{\hat{\beta}_3 - \hat{\beta}_4 - (\beta_3 - \beta_4)}{S_{\beta_3 - \beta_4}}$$

which has a *t*-distribution with $n - (K + 1)$ degrees of freedom. Here, $\beta_3 - \beta_4$ is postulated to be zero, and thus the observed value of *t* is 0.63, which is clearly insignificant.

Thus we would conclude that the coefficients on D72 and D74 appear to be equal (or, strictly, there is no evidence to suggest that they are not equal), and therefore it does not seem unreasonable to use a single dummy variable to capture the influence of strikes in 1972 and 1974. Defining a third dummy variable, *D*, as a variable taking on the value one in 1972 and 1974, and zero in all other years, our estimated model becomes:

$$\widehat{\ln}(Q_t) = 0.661 + 0.173 \ln(K_t) + 0.685 \ln(L_t) - 0.114 D_t \qquad \text{Equation 5.20}$$
$$(2.33) \quad (1.59) \qquad (25.69) \qquad (6.42)$$

$$R^2 = 0.989, \quad \bar{R}^2 = 0.986, \quad d = 1.82$$

A comparison of Equations 5.17 and 5.20 reveals little to choose between them. They both have the same level of explanatory power, and for our purposes, the Durbin–Watson statistic remains insignificant in Equation 5.20. Thus as Equation 5.20 is the simpler formulation, and is in no respects inferior to Equation 5.17, it would be the preferred equation.

In the light of this example, we can now draw a number of conclusions concerning the use of dummy variables.

First, a dummy variable should be interpreted just like any other independent variable, in the sense that its inclusion in a model must be justified in theory. In practice, it will often be tempting to use dummy variables to account for extreme (or outlier) observations which have not been accounted for by the other variables in the model. However, only if there are clear and unambiguous reasons for the occurrence of such extreme observations would it be appropriate to include dummy variables. In the example we have used here a dummy variable was included to account for 'extreme strike activity'. In other words, the dummy variable could be theoretically justified, *a priori* (although in this case its relevance was not recognised initially).

Secondly, in the context of this example, it might be argued that the use of a dummy variable is not necessarily the appropriate way of capturing the strike effect. In particular, it might be argued that the obvious variable to include in the model is simply the variable shown in Table 5.2 – the actual number of days lost through strike activity in each of the years in the sample period. If we denote this variable by DAYS then the resulting estimated model is:

$$\widehat{\ln}(Q_t) = 0.453 + 0.235 \ln(K_t) + 0.705 \ln(L_t) - 0.012\,\text{DAYS}$$
$$\quad\quad (1.33) \quad (1.78) \quad\quad\quad (22.00) \quad\quad\quad (4.72)$$

Equation 5.21

$$R^2 = 0.983, \quad \bar{R}^2 = 0.979, \quad d = 2.14$$

Comparing Equations 5.21 and 5.20 we note that they are broadly similar. Whether DAYS or a dummy variable is used, the effect is negative and significant, and both equations produce insignificant Durbin–Watson statistics. However, the dummy variable in Equation 5.20 has a larger (and hence more significant) $t$-statistic than that associated with DAYS in Equation 5.21, resulting in the marginally greater explanatory power of Equation 5.20. Thus, on balance, Equation 5.20 would just be preferred to Equation 5.21. We might theoretically justify this choice by arguing that it will only be extreme strike activity which will have a significant effect on coal output. In years in which only a moderate level of strike activity occurs the resulting lost output can probably be made up via increased overtime working at those times during the year which are free of strike activity. However, in years of excessive strike activity overtime working will not be sufficient to make up all the lost output, resulting in a net fall in output over the year.

Thus, in short, the argument for using a dummy variable is that strike activity has a discrete effect on coal output rather than a continuous one. However, it must be emphasised that such an argument is far from clear-cut, and this example is useful both for illustrating the advantages of dummy variables and for highlighting some of the problems and ambiguities in their use.

So far we have only discussed dummy variables in the context of their use as independent variables. However, applications may occur in which it is appropriate to model a given dependent variable as a binary variable.

For example, consider the case of an investigator wishing to explain why certain firms in some given industry decide to adopt a particular form of new technology, and why other firms decide against its adoption. That is, the objective would be to isolate the various influences on the adoption decision and to attempt to measure the relative importance of these influences. Thus the dependent variable in such a model could simply be a variable which takes on the value one if a firm has adopted the technology and zero if it has not. The model could then be specified by identifying the various influences on the adoption decision (such as, for example, firm size, firm profitability, the specific nature of the firm's production processes and so on), and then deriving independent variables to measure these influences. Finally, a sample of firms could then be selected, data collected on the variables in the model and the model estimated.

Consider estimating such a model using ordinary least squares. The only difference here is that we now have a dependent variable which can take on only one of two possible values – zero or one – in contrast to other dependent variables we have considered which were all assumed to be continuous. Note also that the predicted or fitted values from the model will typically lie between zero and one, rather than being exactly equal to either zero or one (some or all of the independent variables will be continuous, and the parameter estimators will be continuous). Thus the predicted values from the model could be interpreted as probabilities – for some firm, given values of the independent variables, the model would predict the probability of that firm being an adopter of the technology. Given a predicted value in excess of 0.5 we would assume the firm is probably an adopter, and a value less than 0.5 would imply an assumption of non-adoption. Indeed the adequacy of the model could be judged on the basis of the proportion of the firms in the sample which are correctly categorised as adopters or non-adopters on the basis of the fitted values from the model.

However, in using ordinary least squares, two problems arise. First, given the estimated model, there is no guarantee that the predicted or fitted values of the dependent variable will all lie within the range zero to one. Thus predictions from the model (for given values of the independent variables) might produce negative values or values in excess of one, and therefore there will be difficulty in interpreting such predictions. One solution would be simply to assume that negative values indicate a zero value, and values in excess of one imply a predicted value of one. However, such a solution is somewhat *ad hoc* and therefore not particularly satisfactory. It would be much more satisfactory were the estimation method to ensure that predicted values of the dependent variable lie between zero and one.

The second problem in using ordinary least squares is that we can no longer assume that the disturbance term is normally distributed. Further, it can also be shown that the disturbance term must be heteroskedastic. For both of these reasons the ordinary least squares estimation of a model with a binary dependent variable will be sub-optimal. There are a number of alternatives which can be used, the most common of which is to respecify the model in a **probit** or **logit** form. This involves respecifying the model in a non-linear form and constrains the predicted values from the model to lie within the range zero to one. We will not discuss these models in any further detail, and the interested reader is referred to a more advanced econometrics text for a further discussion.[1]

## 5.3   Estimation of Models with Parameter Restrictions

So far, in specifying the various models we have estimated, we have implicitly assumed that these specifications have reflected all the available *a priori* theoretical information concerning the parameters in the model.

In general, we have been concerned with theoretical information which has been in the form of **inclusion** and **exclusion** restrictions. That is, at the very least, theory would indicate which variables should be included in the model and which variables should be excluded from it. Formally, we could consider a model such as the following:

$$Y_t = \beta_0 + \beta_1 X_{1t} + \beta_2 X_{2t} + \varepsilon_t \qquad \text{Equation 5.22}$$

Now, theory may indicate that $X_2$ is not in fact relevant in explaining $Y$. This *a priori* information could be expressed in the form of a **zero restriction** on the parameter $\beta_2$. That is:

$$\beta_2 = 0$$

and thus the model would now become:

$$Y_t = \beta_0 + \beta_1 X_{1t} + \varepsilon_t \qquad \text{Equation 5.23}$$

As a generalisation, then, theoretical analysis could be characterised, in part, as the process of determining all the valid zero restrictions which should be applied to a given model.

While this concept of a zero restriction may seem a somewhat over-formal way of describing the process of deciding which variables should or should not be included in a given model, there is an important point which should be emphasised. If a model fails to account for all the valid zero restrictions (that is, some irrelevant variables are left in the model) then the parameters in the model will be inefficiently estimated.

For example, the estimator of $\beta_1$ derived from the incorrect model in Equation 5.22 will tend to have a larger variance than the estimator which results from the use of Equation 5.23. This is because $X_2$ is theoretically unrelated to $Y$ and its inclusion in the model will not significantly explain any of the variation in $Y$. That is, the inclusion of $X_2$ will only marginally reduce the level of $\hat{\sigma}_\varepsilon^2$, and all that will be produced is an increased level of multicollinearity, and hence less reliable parameter estimators. Additionally, the inclusion of $X_2$ will use up an extra degree of freedom, thereby further reducing the efficiency of the estimation process.

Such an argument, then, can be interpreted as a more formal reason for ensuring that only theoretically relevant variables are included in any given model. Of course, the inclusion of largely irrelevant variables will have the effect of (marginally) increasing the value of $R^2$ (although not necessarily $\bar{R}^2$). However, given that the most important objective of estimating any model is to estimate the parameters of the model as accurately or efficiently as possible, then the maximisation of $R^2$ should be interpreted as very much a secondary consideration.

While the concept of a zero restriction might be useful for formalising the process of model building, of more practical importance is the consideration of **non-zero** restrictions. Thus *a priori* information may be available which allows the investigator to deduce the actual value of one or more of the parameters in the model. For example, previous studies may have produced very similar estimates for one of the parameters, thus resulting in a widely accepted value for this parameter and one which therefore excites no controversy. It would seem pointless, then, to re-estimate such an uncontroversial parameter, and more efficient estimates of the remaining parameters in the model can be derived by explicitly incorporating this parameter value into the model.

For example, assume that the model to be estimated is the following:

$$Y_t = \beta_0 + \beta_1 X_{1t} + \beta_2 X_{2t} + \beta_3 X_{3t} + \varepsilon_t \qquad \text{Equation 5.24}$$

Now, further assume that the generally accepted value of $\beta_2$ is $b$ (where $b$ is some known constant). Thus Equation 5.24 could be rewritten as:

$$Y_t - bX_{2t} = \beta_0 + \beta_1 X_{1t} + \beta_3 X_{3t} + \varepsilon_t \qquad \text{Equation 5.25}$$

That is, a new dependent variable, $Z_t$, say, would be generated, where $Z_t = Y_t - bX_{2t}$, and the remaining parameters can then be estimated by regressing $Z$ on $X_1$ and $X_3$. Note that $Z_t$ is simply the residual variation in $Y_t$ that is not explained by $X_{2t}$. Thus, in effect, in moving from Equation 5.24 to Equation 5.25 the number of independent variables has been reduced thereby increasing the degrees of freedom, reducing the level of multicollinearity and hence resulting in more efficient estimators.

Another, and more common, form of non-zero restriction is the specification of some form of relationship between some of the parameters in the model. For example, theory may imply that two parameters should be equal (or equal and opposite in sign), or that two parameters should sum to some known constant.

Again consider the model in Equation 5.24. Now assume that it is known that the coefficients on $X_1$ and $X_3$ are equal and opposite in sign. That is,

$$\beta_1 = -\beta_3 \qquad \text{Equation 5.26}$$

and we wish to incorporate this restriction into the model. Thus Equation 5.24 can now be written as:

$$Y_t = \beta_0 + -\beta_3 X_{1t} + \beta_2 X_{2t} + \beta_3 X_{3t} + \varepsilon_t \qquad \text{Equation 5.27}$$

or

$$Y_t = \beta_0 + \beta_3 W_t + \beta_2 X_{2t} + \varepsilon_t \qquad \text{Equation 5.28}$$

where $W_t$ is $X_{3t} - X_{1t}$. Thus again a model is produced in which the degrees of freedom have increased and multicollinearity has probably been reduced.[2]

Finally, we can consider parameter restrictions which imply that two or more of the parameters in the model add to some known constant.

Again consider Equation 5.24, but now assume that information is available which implies that the coefficients on $X_1$ and $X_2$ should sum to one, say. That is:

$$\beta_1 + \beta_2 = 1 \qquad \text{Equation 5.29}$$

or

$$\beta_2 = 1 - \beta_1 \qquad\qquad \text{Equation 5.30}$$

An example of such a parameter restriction would be a Cobb–Douglas production function with constant returns to scale – that is, we would require that the parameters $\alpha$ and $\beta$ in the model in Equation 5.13 (or 5.14) should sum to one.

Substituting Equation 5.30 into Equation 5.24, we can write:

$$Y_t = \beta_0 + \beta_1 X_{1t} + (1 - \beta_1) X_{2t} + \beta_3 X_{3t} + \varepsilon_t$$
$$\therefore Y_t - X_{2t} = \beta_0 + \beta_1 (X_{1t} - X_{2t}) + \beta_3 X_{3t} + \varepsilon_t$$

or

$$Z_t = \beta_0 + \beta_1 V_t + \beta_3 X_{3t} + \varepsilon_t \qquad\qquad \text{Equation 5.31}$$

where $Z_t = Y_t - X_{2t}$ and $V_t = X_{1t} - X_{2t}$. Estimates of $\beta_0$, $\beta_1$ and $\beta_3$ can therefore be obtained by regressing $Z$ on $V$ and $X_3$. An estimate of $\beta_2$ can then be derived by subtracting the estimated value of $\beta_1$ from one. Note, again, that the effect of incorporating such a parameter restriction into the model is to reduce the number of parameters that require estimation thereby increasing the efficiency with which the remaining parameters can be estimated.

We will now consider an example of estimating a model with parameter restrictions. We will continue with our example of estimating a production function for the coal industry, which we introduced in Example 5.1.

Example 5.2

Recall that the model that was finally accepted was given in Equation 5.20. That is:

$$\hat{q}_t = 0.661 + 0.173 k_t + 0.685\, l_t - 0.114 D_t \qquad\qquad \text{Equation 5.32}$$
$$\phantom{\hat{q}_t = }(2.33) \quad (1.59) \quad (25.69) \quad\;\; (6.42)$$

where, for convenience, we here use lower case letters to denote natural logarithms.

Now, a common hypothesis in the context of the estimation of production functions concerns the nature of the scale economies which exist in the firm, industry or economy which is being modelled. In particular, it will be of interest to examine whether it is reasonable to assume that constant returns to scale obtain.

Recall from our discussion of the production function in Equation 3.24 that constant returns are implied if the coefficients on the logs of capital and labour sum to one. Thus in terms of the specification of the model in Equation 5.16 (but assuming just a single dummy variable in the equation) the null hypothesis of constant returns to scale can be formally expressed as:

$$H_0: \beta_1 + \beta_2 = 1$$

which would be tested against the alternative hypothesis:

$$H_1: \beta_1 + \beta_2 \neq 1$$

The method of testing this hypothesis is exactly the same as the method we used above for testing whether the coefficients on the two dummy variables in Equation 5.16 were equal. Thus the associated $t$-statistic is:

$$t = \frac{\hat{\beta}_1 + \hat{\beta}_2 - 1}{S_{\beta_1 + \beta_2}}$$

where $\hat{\beta}_1 + \hat{\beta}_2$ here is 0.858, and the value of $S_{\beta_1 + \beta_2}$ can be shown to be 0.1136. Thus an insignificant $t$ value of $-1.25$ is produced, implying that $H_0$ must be accepted. That is, the statistical evidence is consistent with the coal industry operating under conditions of constant returns to scale (at least over the sample period). Thus, we could re-estimate the model by imposing the restriction that the parameter estimates on $k_t$ and $l_t$ sum to one, and thereby ensure that the estimated model explicitly exhibits constant returns to scale. Thus we wish to impose the restriction:

$$\beta_1 + \beta_2 = 1 \qquad\qquad \text{Equation 5.33}$$

From Equation 5.33 we can write:

$$\beta_2 = 1 - \beta_1 \qquad\qquad \text{Equation 5.34}$$

Ignoring the dummy variable and substituting Equation 5.34 into the logarithmic form of our production function specification, we have:

$$q_t = \beta_0 + \beta_1 k_t + (1 - \beta_1)l_t + \varepsilon_t \qquad\qquad \text{Equation 5.35}$$

Rearranging Equation 5.35 our estimating equation becomes:

$$z_t = \beta_0 + \beta_1 v_t + \varepsilon_t \qquad\qquad \text{Equation 5.36}$$

where $z_t = q_t - l_t$ and $v_t = k_t - l_t$.

The estimate of Equation 5.36 is shown in Equation 5.37, where we have also retained the dummy variable consistent with our previous specification.

$$\hat{z}_t = 0.357 + 0.293v_t - 0.107D_t \qquad\qquad \text{Equation 5.37}$$
$$\quad\ (4.22)\ \ (15.51)\ \ \ \ (6.41)$$

$$R^2 = 0.948, \quad \bar{R}^2 = 0.940, \quad d = 1.86$$

That is, $\hat{\beta}_1 = 0.293$ and therefore from Equation 5.34 we have:

$$\hat{\beta}_2 = 1 - 0.293$$
$$= 0.707$$

Note also that we can deduce the variance of $\hat{\beta}_2$ from Equation 5.34. That is

$$\hat{\beta}_2 = 1 - \hat{\beta}_1$$

$$\therefore \text{Var}(\hat{\beta}_2) = \text{Var}(1 - \hat{\beta}_1)$$

$$= \text{Var}(\hat{\beta}_1)$$

Therefore the estimated variance of $\hat{\beta}_2$ will equal the estimated variance of $\hat{\beta}_1$, and from Equation 5.37 we have:

$$\text{Var}(\hat{\beta}_1) = \text{Var}(\hat{\beta}_2) = \left(\frac{0.293}{15.51}\right)^2 = 0.00036$$

We will now go on to discuss a more generalised and widely used form of model specification – a distributed lag model – which also involves parameter restrictions, but restrictions which are non-linear.

## 5.4   Distributed Lag Models

A distributed lag model is a model specification which is relevant in the context of modelling time-series data.

In constructing models which attempt to explain the variation of some dependent variable over time, it will often be the case that lagged values of some of the independent variables will be relevant as explanatory influences. By a lagged value of a variable we mean the value of this variable in some previous time-period. Thus in explaining the level of the dependent variable in time-period $t$, say, we would generally expect that the value of an explanatory variable in period $t-1$ or $t-2$, or at some point in the past, will be of some relevance.

Indeed, time-series models containing lagged variables can be most usefully interpreted as the general form of time-series models in economics. That is, we would expect most economic behaviour to be influenced by what has occurred in the past, and in turn, we would expect current behaviour to influence future behaviour. As we shall see below, a distributed lag model represents a general statement of such models, and in this section we will be concerned with developing methods for estimating these models.

We have already discussed time-series models in which time-periods were assumed to be interdependent, and that was in our discussion of autocorrelation in Section 4.4 of Chapter 4. Distributed lag models, then, can be seen as a direct and generalised extension of the estimating models discussed in Section 4.4.

A typical context in which the role of lagged variables is important (and indeed the context in which distributed lag models were first developed) is in the analysis of investment decisions. Thus, at the level of the firm (or industry) current investment expenditure will probably be influenced to a large extent by the level of output or sales in previous time-periods. There are a number of reasons why this might be the case. First, if a firm (industry) is deciding whether to expand its productive capacity it will presumably require some indication of the likely level of demand for its output in the future. One source of information is the trend and level of its output in past time-periods. Second, given the gestation period involved in formulating investment plans, and the lags which occur between ordering and receiving investment goods, current investment expenditure is more likely to be a function of decisions made in the past. Finally, even in cases in which no reference is made to the past, actual investment expenditure is likely to be distributed over a number of time-periods, and particularly so in the case of relatively large investment programmes (such as investment in buildings and machinery).

Another, and related, context in which distributed lag models are considered to be relevant is in the analysis of a firm's or an industry's advertising expenditures. Thus it is generally argued that advertising expenditure has the characteristics of an investment in the sense that advertising can be interpreted as having the effect of building up a stock of goodwill for the firm's or the industry's product. In particular, the current level of sales will not only be influenced by current advertising expenditures but will also be influenced by past advertising, although presumably the influence of past advertising will die out over time.

In general, then, a distributed lag model could be expressed as follows:

$$Y_t = \alpha + \beta_0 X_t + \beta_1 X_{t-1} + \beta_2 X_{t-2} + \ldots + \beta_s X_{t-s} + \varepsilon_t \qquad \text{Equation 5.38}$$

where $Y_t$ is the level of the dependent variable in time-period $t$ and the general term, $X_{t-k}$, is the level of a relevant independent variable in period $t-k$, where $k$ can take on any integer value between zero and $s$ ($s > 0$). It would also be necessary to specify the appropriate time unit in Equation 5.38 – that is, whether the relevant time lags are weekly, monthly, quarterly, annual or whatever.

In terms of the above examples, $Y_t$ could denote the level of investment expenditure in period $t$ and $X_{t-k}$ would denote the level of output or sales $k$ periods in the past. For large investment expenditures the relevant time unit may be years or quarters. Or $Y_t$ could denote the level of a firm's sales in period $t$ and $X_{t-k}$ would denote advertising expenditure $k$ periods ago. As the influence of advertising expenditure dies out relatively quickly (particularly for non-durable consumer goods) then the relevant time unit would be much shorter – $t$ might refer to months or even weeks.

Note also that the values of the parameters $\beta_0, \beta_1, \ldots, \beta_s$ will reflect the relative importance of each of the lagged values of $X$. That is, the $\beta$s can be interpreted as the **weights** which can be attached to each of the current and previous levels of $X$.

In terms of the investment example, we might expect the current and most recent values of $X$ to have little influence on the current level of investment expenditure, and hence we might observe relatively small values for $\beta_0, \beta_1$ and possibly $\beta_2$, with the values of the $\beta$s perhaps peaking at $\beta_3$ or $\beta_4$ and declining thereafter. For the advertising example we would expect the current level of advertising expenditure to have the greatest influence on current sales with the past levels of advertising declining in influence. That is, we would expect a maximum value at $\beta_0$ with the $\beta$s declining as $k$ increases (or as the length of the lag increases).

Now, our objective here is to develop a method for estimating the parameters in Equation 5.38, and therefore for estimating the precise pattern of influence from current and past values of $X$ to the current value of $Y$. However, there are three problems which can occur in practice which will prevent the straightforward estimation of these parameters:

1   In general, theory will not be so specific as to enable the precise determination of the value of $s$ in Equation 5.38. That is, it will not be possible to determine, *a priori*, the length of the lag beyond which $X$ no longer significantly influences the current value of $Y$.
2   Even in those cases in which $s$ might be known, $s$ may be so large relative to the number of observations that are available to estimate the model that only few degrees of freedom remain. Note that not only must $s$ parameters be estimated, but $s$ observations will also be lost from the sample data. That is, the estimated model will have low effective explanatory power and the parameters will be estimated imprecisely. It may even be the case that $s$ exceeds the sample size and thus no estimates of the parameters can be derived.
3   There may be cases where $s$ is known but small relative to the sample size. However, it is very likely that the various lagged values of $X$ will be highly intercorrelated, thus producing a high degree of multicollinearity and therefore resulting in imprecise parameter estimators.

There are a number of estimation methods which are available for overcoming these problems, all of which involve making specific assumptions concerning the pattern of the $\beta$s over time. We will discuss two of these. The first method we will discuss is the **Koyck distributed lag scheme**,[3] which, primarily because of its simplicity, is the most commonly used solution. The second method we will discuss is the **Almon distributed lag scheme**,[4] which is more flexible than the Koyck solution but somewhat more complex.

### 5.4.1   *The Koyck Distributed Lag Scheme*

Again consider Equation 5.38, and for illustrative purposes assume that the model is attempting to explain a firm's current level of sales $(Y_t)$ in terms of its current and past levels of advertising expenditure $(X_{t-k}, k = 0, 1, \ldots, s)$. Assuming $s$ is unknown then the most general assumption that can be made is that $s$ is, in effect, infinite. That is, we begin by assuming that all past values of $X$ influence the current value of $Y$ (although upon estimation, presumably, it will be found that the influence of $X$ at longer lags is negligible). The approach here, then, is to allow the data to determine the value of $s$. Therefore we postulate the following model:

$$Y_t = \alpha + \beta_0 X_t + \beta_1 X_{t-1} + \beta_2 X_{t-2} + \dots + \varepsilon_t \qquad \text{Equation 5.39}$$

Now, given that the $\beta$s measure the relative influence (or importance) of each of the past levels of advertising expenditure, it would seem reasonable to assume here that the $\beta$s die out over time. That is, the further back in time any given level of advertising took place the weaker will be its influence on the current level of sales. If we also make the additional assumption that the $\beta$s decline geometrically over time we can then proceed to derive a method for estimating the parameters in Equation 5.39. That is, we assume that the $\beta$s are generated as follows:

$$\beta_k = \beta \lambda^k \qquad \text{Equation 5.40}$$

where $\beta$ and $\lambda$ are constants, and $\lambda$ is such that $0 < \lambda < 1$. Diagrammatically, the distribution of the $\beta$s over time could be interpreted as in Figure 5.3. The horizontal axis in Figure 5.3 represents the lag length (the value of $k$) and the vertical axis represents the corresponding value of $\beta$. That is, as $k$ increases (indicating time-periods further and further in the past) the corresponding $\beta$s decline.

Our objective, then, is to estimate the precise nature of the geometric decline in Figure 5.3 and hence to reach conclusions concerning the rate at which the $\beta$s die out over time. That is, we wish to determine how important past levels of advertising are in determining the current level of sales, and how rapidly (or slowly) the influence of past advertising dies out. In turn, this requires estimating $\beta$ and $\lambda$ in Equation 5.40.

Thus imposing Equation 5.40 on the model, Equation 5.39 can be written as:

$$Y_t = \alpha + \beta X_t + \beta \lambda X_{t-1} + \beta \lambda^2 X_{t-2} + \dots + \varepsilon_t \qquad \text{Equation 5.41}$$

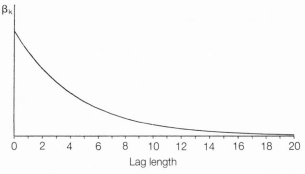

**Figure 5.3** Geometrically declining distributed lag coefficients.

Note that Equation 5.41 still contains an infinite lag (albeit of a restricted form) but the model now contains only three parameters – $\alpha$, $\beta$ and $\lambda$ – in contrast to the infinite number of parameters in Equation 5.39. However, Equation 5.41 is not yet in a form which will allow the estimation of these parameters, but this can be achieved via a simple algebraic manipulation.

First Equation 5.41 is lagged by one period and multiplied throughout by $\lambda$, producing the following equation:

$$\lambda Y_{t-1} = \alpha\lambda + \beta\lambda X_{t-1} + \beta\lambda^2 X_{t-2} + \dots + \lambda\varepsilon_{t-1} \qquad \text{Equation 5.42}$$

We now subtract Equation 5.42 from Equation 5.41, noting that all the terms in $\beta\lambda$ and above cancel out, and we obtain:

$$Y_t - \lambda Y_{t-1} = \alpha - \alpha\lambda + \beta X_t + \varepsilon_t - \lambda\varepsilon_{t-1} \qquad \text{Equation 5.43}$$

Rearranging Equation 5.43 produces the following estimating equation:

$$Y_t = \alpha(1-\lambda) + \lambda Y_{t-1} + \beta X_t + \varepsilon_t - \lambda\varepsilon_{t-1} \qquad \text{Equation 5.44}$$

Thus estimates of $\alpha$, $\beta$ and $\lambda$ can be derived by regressing $Y_t$ on $Y_{t-1}$ and $X_t$ (the estimate of $\alpha$ is obtained by dividing the estimated constant term in Equation 5.44 by one minus the estimated value of $\lambda$).

Finally, estimates of the original $\beta$s in Equation 5.39 can be obtained by substituting the estimated values of $\beta$ and $\lambda$ into Equation 5.40, for $k = 0, 1, 2, \dots$, and an estimated lag structure such as that in Figure 5.3 could be derived. Note that this method of estimating a distributed lag structure assumes that the decline in the $\beta$s begins from the current time-period (lag 0). This seemed a reasonable assumption in the context of our advertising example, but there may be cases in which this may be unrealistic.

Thus recall that in discussing the determinants of a firm's investment expenditure we argued that it might be more realistic to assume that output two or three periods ago exerts more of an influence on current expenditure than the current or immediately preceding output levels. This assumption can be easily incorporated into a Koyck model by imposing geometric decline on the $\beta$s beginning from, say, lag 3, and allowing the coefficients at lags 0, 1 and 2 to be determined freely. That is, the model could be written as:

$$Y_t = \alpha + \beta_0 X_t + \beta_1 X_{t-1} + \beta_2 X_{t-2} + \beta X_{t-3}$$
$$+ \beta\lambda X_{t-4} + \beta\lambda^2 X_{t-5} + \dots + \varepsilon_t \qquad \text{Equation 5.45}$$

The final estimating equation is then obtained in the same manner as described above (this is left as an exercise for the reader).

The Koyck distributed lag scheme is a relatively simple and an intuitively appealing method for estimating a distributed lag structure. However, the derived estimating equation (Equation 5.44) has not been achieved without cost. Three disadvantages of the method can be identified:

(1) Restrictive assumptions have had to be made concerning the functional

form which generates the $\beta$s. While an assumption of geometric decay in the $\beta$s may seem a reasonable one in the absence of any other information, it is essentially an arbitrary assumption, its use being conditioned by algebraic convenience.

(2) A second disadvantage of the Koyck solution is that it will result in an estimating equation which contains a complex disturbance term structure.

Thus note that the disturbance term in the final estimating equation (Equation 5.44) is $\varepsilon_t - \lambda\varepsilon_{t-1}$. That is, if the original disturbance term, $\varepsilon_t$, is independently distributed in each time-period then, by definition, the disturbance term in the estimating equation will no longer possess this property, and will therefore possess some structure. Note, however, that the nature of this structure is somewhat different from the first order autoregressive structure which we discussed in Section 4.4 of Chapter 4. There we defined a disturbance term, $\varepsilon_t$, as being autocorrelated if it was generated by the following relationship:

$$\varepsilon_t = \rho\varepsilon_{t-1} + u_t \qquad\qquad \text{Equation 5.46}$$

where $u_t \sim \text{NID}(0, \sigma_u^2)$. However if we denote the disturbance term in Equation 5.44 by $v_t$, then we have:

$$v_t = \varepsilon_t - \lambda\varepsilon_{t-1} \qquad\qquad \text{Equation 5.47}$$

where $\varepsilon_t \sim \text{NID}(0, \sigma_\varepsilon^2)$. In order to distinguish the disturbance term structure in Equation 5.47 from the autocorrelated structure in Equation 5.46, Equation 5.47 is referred to as a **moving average** structure of order one, or an MA(1).[5]

We can note, however, that if the disturbance term in the original model ($\varepsilon_t$ in Equation 5.41 or 5.45) is autocorrelated then there is the possibility that the Koyck transformation may in fact remove this autocorrelation. Thus assume that the original disturbance term is generated by Equation 5.46, which can be rewritten as:

$$u_t = \varepsilon_t - \rho\varepsilon_{t-1} \qquad\qquad \text{Equation 5.48}$$

But recall that the disturbance term in the final estimating equation of the Koyck transformation is given by $\varepsilon_t - \lambda\varepsilon_{t-1}$, and therefore if, by chance, $\rho = \lambda$ then a random disturbance term will be produced. In general, then, the closer $\rho$ is to $\lambda$ the more successful will the Koyck transformation be in removing the original autocorrelation.

(3) A third disadvantage of the Koyck transformation is that it produces an estimating equation which contains a lagged value of the dependent variable as an explanatory variable. This violates the assumption that all the explanatory variables in a regression model are non-stochastic (see the specification of the regression model in Equation 3.1) and hence we can no longer assume that each of the explanatory variables and the disturbance term is independent.

The implication for our ordinary least squares estimation procedures is that, at the very least, biased estimators will be produced. However, if we can assume that the disturbance terms in the final estimating equation are independently distributed (that is, if we can assume that $\rho = \lambda$) then the least squares estimators can be shown to be at least consistent. Indeed, under such conditions the least squares estimators can still be shown to be the best available estimators, despite their biasedness. We will discuss the estimation of models containing lagged values of the dependent variable as explanatory variables in greater detail in Section 5.5.

We will now discuss an example of estimating a distributed lag model using the Koyck transformation.

Example 5.3

We will continue with our example of estimating a consumption function which we introduced in Example 4.3.

Recall from Example 4.3 that a simple regression of consumption on income, using quarterly data, produced a statistically acceptable equation except that a significant Durbin–Watson statistic was produced (see Equation 4.94). However, recall from our discussion of the interpretation of the Durbin–Watson statistic that a significant value for $d$ can also be produced by a misspecified model.

Our approach here will be to consider the possibility of a misspecification. Thus, as we have already argued, it is somewhat simplistic to assume that the only determinant of consumption expenditure in time-period $t$ is income in period $t$. In particular, this ignores the role of habit persistence and would imply that consumers make no reference to past behaviour in reaching decisions concerning current consumption expenditure (indeed, it also assumes that current consumption patterns are unaffected by expectations consumers might hold concerning their future incomes).

Thus, as a starting point, it could be argued that it is not only current income but income in previous periods that influences current consumption decisions. The basic justification for such an argument is that previous income levels will have determined some pattern of consumption behaviour and this will be slow to change over time. In particular, this pattern will not respond immediately or fully to any short-run variation in income. A further justification may be in terms of arguing that current consumption is influenced, in part, by expected future income, and a predictor of future income trends is the pattern in the current and previous income levels.

A generalised statement of such a consumption function would be:

$$C_t = f(D_t, D_{t-1}, D_{t-2}, \ldots) \qquad\qquad \text{Equation 5.49}$$

Before going on to derive an estimating equation from Equation 5.49, we will make a slight modification to the consumption data which were used in Example 4.3.

Recall that in Example 4.3 consumption was measured by total consumers' expenditure. It is now generally accepted that in modelling consumption behaviour it is appropriate to distinguish between expenditure on durables and expenditure on non-durables. Consumers' expenditure on durable items, it is argued, should be interpreted more in terms of investment behaviour and consequently a somewhat different model used to explain this expenditure component. Therefore we will concern ourselves only with consumers' expenditure on non-durables. This series is shown in Appendix 5.2 and will be denoted by $CN_t$.

Using the data in Appendix 5.2 to estimate a simple consumption function produces the same estimation problems as in Equation 4.94 – that is, a significant Durbin–Watson statistic is still produced. Re-estimating this equation using the Cochrane–Orcutt procedure produces the following equation:

$$\widehat{CN}_t = 11{,}595.870 + 0.212D_t \qquad\qquad \text{Equation 5.50}$$
$$(10.77) \quad (4.38)$$

$$\bar{R}^2 = 0.989, \quad d = 2.71, \quad \hat{\rho} = 0.970, \quad n = 67$$

where $\hat{\rho}$ is the estimate of the parameter in the first-order autocorrelation structure.

There are two features we can note about Equation 5.50. First, the value of $d$ is still significant (the reader should confirm this by making reference to Durbin–Watson tables in Appendix IV). That is, it would appear that the adjustment procedure used in Equation 5.50 has, in effect, over-compensated for the original autocorrelation (this might indicate that the autocorrelation is more complex than a first-order structure). Second, the estimate of the marginal propensity to consume in Equation 5.50 (the coefficient on $D_t$) is considerably lower than would be predicted by theory.

In summary, then, the use of the Cochrane–Orcutt procedure has resulted in an equation which not only remains statistically unacceptable but is also theoretically unacceptable.

As we have already argued, the theoretical weaknesses of a simple consumption function formulation are alone sufficient to justify rejecting it from further consideration. However it is interesting to note the statistical problems which are still associated with Equation 5.50, and to consider the extent to which such problems are the result of theoretical shortcomings rather than the application of inappropriate statistical procedures. It could be argued that the resulting statistical problems are indeed a reflection of theoretical misspecification.

We will now go on to consider the estimation of the more generalised consumption function in Equation 5.49, and to determine whether this formulation resolves any of the problems associated with the estimation of the simple consumption function. Thus the linear version of Equation 5.49 could be written as:

$$CN_t = \alpha + \beta_0 D_t + \beta_1 D_{t-1} + \beta_2 D_{t-2} + \ldots + \varepsilon_t \qquad \text{Equation 5.51}$$

Assuming that the lag on $D$ is infinite, and that the $\beta$s decline geometrically, we can use the Koyck transformation to produce an estimating equation. The form of this estimating equation is (see Equation 5.44):

$$CN_t = \alpha + \lambda\, CN_{t-1} + \beta D_t + v_t \qquad \text{Equation 5.52}$$

The least squares estimate of Equation 5.52 is ($t$-statistics in brackets):

$$\widehat{CN}_t = 1206.614 + 0.666\, CN_{t-1} + 0.207 D_t \qquad \text{Equation 5.53}$$
$$\quad\;\; (4.17) \quad\; (8.93) \qquad\qquad (4.44)$$

$$\bar{R}^2 = 0.990, \quad d = 1.99, \quad n = 67$$

From an examination of Equation 5.53 and its associated summary statistics we would conclude that a very well determined equation has been produced. In particular, it would appear that the Koyck transformation has been remarkably successful. The transformation seems to have eliminated the problem of what initially appeared to be autocorrelation. (Although, as we shall see in Section 5.5, the use of the Durbin–Watson test is strictly invalid here due to the presence of $CN_{t-1}$ as an explanatory variable. But given that the sample is large and $d$ is so close to two acceptance of the conclusions of the Durbin–Watson test would seem reasonable in this case.)

The implication, then, is that the significant Durbin–Watson statistic associated with Equation 5.49 is a reflection of misspecification rather than an indication of autocorrelation in the actual disturbances.

Given the estimated model in Equation 5.53 we could also derive an estimate of the lag structure using Equation 5.40. That is, estimates of the original $\beta$s could be derived from:

$$\hat{\beta}_k = \hat{\beta}\hat{\lambda}^k \qquad \text{Equation 5.54}$$

where

$$\hat{\beta} = 0.207$$
$$\hat{\lambda} = 0.666$$

from Equation 5.53.

$$\therefore \hat{\beta}_0 = (0.207)(0.666)^0 = 0.207$$
$$\hat{\beta}_1 = (0.207)(0.666)^1 = 0.138$$
$$\hat{\beta}_2 = (0.207)(0.666)^2 = 0.092$$
$$\vdots \quad \vdots \quad\; \vdots \qquad \vdots$$

A graph of these estimated $\beta$s against $k$ (the lag length) is shown in Figure 5.4.

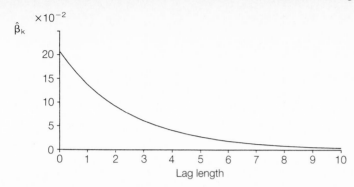

**Figure 5.4** Estimated lag structure from Equation 5.53.

### 5.4.2 The Almon Distributed Lag Scheme

Recall that one criticism which we made of the Koyck transformation was the rigidity it imposes on the functional form which generates the $\beta$s – in particular, it must be assumed that the $\beta$s decay geometrically. The Almon scheme, while still requiring that an assumption be made concerning the way in which the $\beta$s are generated, is much more flexible in the functional forms which can be imposed.

In contrast to the Koyck solution the Almon scheme requires the *a priori* specification of both the lag length and the functional form which generates the $\beta$s. However, as we shall see, the strength of the Almon approach is that it allows for considerable experimentation. Thus if the initial assumption concerning the lag length and functional form produces unsatisfactory statistical results then a shorter or longer lag can be tried and/or an alternative functional form imposed.

Thus, consider some dependent variable, $Y$, and an independent variable, $X$, and assume that an eight-period lag is considered appropriate. That is, the following model is postulated:

$$Y_t = \alpha + \beta_0 X_t + \beta_1 X_{t-1} + \ldots + \beta_8 X_{t-8} + \varepsilon_t \qquad \text{Equation 5.55}$$

We next require an assumption concerning the functional form that generates the $\beta$s. If we assume, for example, that the $\beta$s are generated by a quadratic function then we would specify:

$$\beta_k = a_0 + a_1 k + a_2 k^2 \qquad \text{Equation 5.56}$$

where $k$ is just an index, which can here take on any integer value between zero and eight, consistent with our assumption in Equation 5.55. However, in contrast to the Koyck solution, where only a geometrically declining lag structure can be accommodated, any one of the four lag structures shown in

Figure 5.5 can be generated by Equation 5.56. Thus the problem of estimating the coefficients in Equation 5.55 can be seen to be equivalent to estimating $a_0$, $a_1$ and $a_2$ in Equation 5.56. In turn, this will determine which of the four lag structures in Figure 5.5 is appropriate.

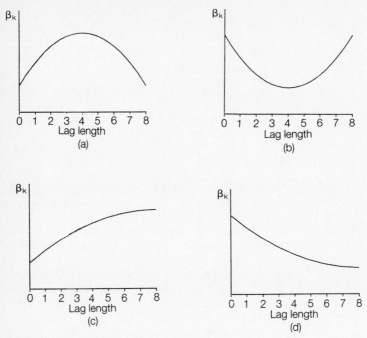

**Figure 5.5**  Lag structures generated by Equation 5.56.

Should it seem more realistic to assume that the $\beta$s are generated by a cubic, rather than a quadratic, then we need only add a term in $k^3$ to Equation 5.56 (requiring the estimation of a further parameter, $a_3$). If a quartic is appropriate then a term in $k^4$ would be added to Equation 5.56, and so on. In this way much more complex lag structures than simple geometric decay can be accommodated within this approach. We will now go on to discuss how the parameters of a given model can be estimated under an Almon approach.

Consider again the model specified in Equation 5.55, and assume that the $\beta$s are generated by Equation 5.56. We can now derive an equation which will allow the estimation of $a_0$, $a_1$ and $a_2$ and hence the estimation of the $\beta$s.

From Equation 5.56, successively substituting for $k = 0$ to 8, we have:

$$\beta_0 = a_0$$
$$\beta_1 = a_0 + a_1 + a_2$$

$$\beta_2 = a_0 + 2a_1 + 4a_2$$
$$\vdots \qquad \vdots \qquad \vdots \qquad \vdots$$
$$\beta_8 = a_0 + 8a_1 + 64a_2 \qquad\qquad\qquad \text{Equation 5.57}$$

Substituting for the $\beta$s in Equation 5.55 we can write:

$$Y_t = \alpha + a_0 X_t + (a_0 + a_1 + a_2) X_{t-1} + (a_0 + 2a_1 + 4a_2) X_{t-2} + \dots$$
$$+ (a_0 + 8a_1 + 64a_2) X_{t-8} + \varepsilon_t \qquad\qquad \text{Equation 5.58}$$

Rewriting Equation 5.58 by collecting all terms in $a_0$, $a_1$ and $a_2$ we have:

$$Y_t = \alpha + a_0(X_t + X_{t-1} + X_{t-2} + \dots + X_{t-8}) + a_1(X_{t-1} + 2X_{t-2} + \dots$$
$$+ 8X_{t-8}) + a_2(X_{t-1} + 4X_{t-2} + \dots + 64X_{t-8}) + \varepsilon_t \qquad \text{Equation 5.59}$$

Thus we can define three composite variables as follows:

$$V_{1t} = X_t + X_{t-1} + X_{t-2} + \dots + X_{t-8}$$
$$V_{2t} = \qquad X_{t-1} + 2X_{t-2} + \dots + 8X_{t-8}$$
$$V_{3t} = \qquad X_{t-1} + 4X_{t-2} + \dots + 64X_{t-8} \qquad\qquad \text{Equation 5.60}$$

and therefore the model in Equation 5.55, incorporating the assumption in Equation 5.56, can be written as:

$$Y_t = \alpha + a_0 V_{1t} + a_1 V_{2t} + a_2 V_{3t} + \varepsilon_t \qquad\qquad \text{Equation 5.61}$$

Thus estimates of $\alpha$, $a_0$, $a_1$ and $a_2$ are derived by regressing $Y_t$ on $V_{1t}$, $V_{2t}$ and $V_{3t}$.

Finally, estimates of the original $\beta$s can be obtained by substituting the resulting values of $\hat{a}_0$, $\hat{a}_1$ and $\hat{a}_2$ into Equation Set 5.57. That is:

$$\hat{\beta}_0 = \hat{a}_0$$
$$\hat{\beta}_1 = \hat{a}_0 + \hat{a}_1 + \hat{a}_2$$
$$\hat{\beta}_2 = \hat{a}_0 + 2\hat{a}_1 + 4\hat{a}_2$$
$$\vdots \qquad \vdots \qquad \vdots \qquad \vdots$$
$$\hat{\beta}_8 = \hat{a}_0 + 8\hat{a}_1 + 64\hat{a}_2 \qquad\qquad\qquad \text{Equation 5.62}$$

It is also straightforward (although tedious) to derive the variances of these estimators of the $\beta$s, and thus to test for their significance. Therefore as a direct extension of Equations 1.38 and 1.53, we can deduce that for two random variables, $R$ and $S$, and two constants, $c$ and $d$:

$$\text{Var}(cR + dS) = c^2 \text{Var}(R) + d^2 \text{Var}(S) + 2cd \text{Cov}(R, S) \qquad \text{Equation 5.63}$$

and this expression generalises to the case of three or more random variables. Thus from Equation Set 5.62 we have:

$$\mathrm{Var}(\hat{\beta}_0) = \mathrm{Var}(\hat{a}_0)$$

$$\mathrm{Var}(\hat{\beta}_1) = \mathrm{Var}(\hat{a}_0) + \mathrm{Var}(\hat{a}_1) + \mathrm{Var}(\hat{a}_0) + 2\,\mathrm{Cov}(\hat{a}_0, \hat{a}_1)$$
$$+ 2\,\mathrm{Cov}(\hat{a}_0, \hat{a}_2) + 2\,\mathrm{Cov}(\hat{a}_1, \hat{a}_2)$$

$$\mathrm{Var}(\hat{\beta}_2) = \mathrm{Var}(\hat{a}_0) + 4\,\mathrm{Var}(\hat{a}_1) + 16\,\mathrm{Var}(\hat{a}_2) + 4\,\mathrm{Cov}(\hat{a}_0, \hat{a}_1)$$
$$+ 8\,\mathrm{Cov}(\hat{a}_0, \hat{a}_2) + 16\,\mathrm{Cov}(\hat{a}_1, \hat{a}_2)$$

$$\vdots \qquad \vdots \qquad \vdots$$

$$\mathrm{Var}(\hat{\beta}_8) = \mathrm{Var}(\hat{a}_0) + 64\,\mathrm{Var}(\hat{a}_1) + 4096\,\mathrm{Var}(\hat{a}_2) + 16\,\mathrm{Cov}(\hat{a}_0, \hat{a}_1)$$
$$+ 128\,\mathrm{Cov}(\hat{a}_0, \hat{a}_2) + 1024\,\mathrm{Cov}(\hat{a}_1, \hat{a}_2) \qquad \text{Equation 5.64}$$

and the estimated variances and covariances of the $\hat{a}$s are obtained from the regression of $Y_t$ on $V_{1t}$, $V_{2t}$ and $V_{3t}$.

While the above estimation procedure may certainly appear tedious, many computer packages now contain a routine for estimating Almon lag structures, and therefore in practice the methodology is quite straightforward to use. All that is required on the part of the investigator is the specification of the required lag length and the degree of the polynomial which generates the $\beta$s. The computer package will then produce the regression of $Y_t$ on the $V_t$s, together with the derived estimates of the $\beta$s, their standard errors and $t$-statistics.

While the Almon approach is much more flexible that the Koyck solution, its disadvantage is that, in general, the appropriate lag length and degree of the polynomial which generates the $\beta$s will not be known in detail *a priori*. Typically a trial and error approach is thus adopted, with various lag lengths and polynomials tested and the optimum equation is selected on the basis of various statistical criteria – $R^2$, or corrected $R^2$, the significance of the resulting $\beta$s, the extent of autocorrelation amongst the residuals and so on. There may also be certain theoretical expectations which may aid in discriminating among the competing models. For example, theory may imply that all the $\beta$s should be positive, and hence any model producing negative $\beta$s would be rejected. Or by examining the shape of the resulting lag structure inconsistencies with theoretical expectations may be highlighted.

We will now illustrate the estimation of an Almon lag structure via an example.

## Example 5.4

In this example we will consider the estimation of a demand function for automobiles in the UK. In particular, we will consider the demand for new cars. In Appendix 5.3 we present quarterly data on new car registrations in the UK over the period first quarter, 1958 to fourth quarter, 1984.

Our approach here will be to consider only one of the influences on the demand for new cars, and that is the demand which derives from replacement purchases. In the UK this source of demand is particularly important, given that in 1970 91 per cent of new car purchasers already owned a car.[6] None the less, there will be many other potential influences on the decision to purchase a new car, such as price, income and consumer credit conditions, and therefore ignoring these factors (as, for simplicity, we propose to do here) necessarily means that any resulting model will be misspecified.[7] Thus the estimated models which we will present below should be treated with caution, and will be used only to demonstrate how an Almon lag structure might be estimated and interpreted.

Denote the number of new car registrations in quarter $t$ by $REG_t$. Now, arguing that an important influence on $REG_t$ is the demand which derives from replacement purchases implies that it is the pattern of past new car purchases that determines the level of demand in the current quarter. In turn, estimating the precise way in which past purchases influence current demand will provide information concerning the nature of replacement cycles. Thus a generalised model of replacement demand can be written as:

$$REG_t = \alpha + \beta_0\, REG_{t-1} + \beta_1\, REG_{t-2} + \beta_2\, REG_{t-3} + \ldots + \varepsilon_t$$

Equation 5.65

The values of the $\beta$s, then, are the weights which can be attached to past car purchases and thus reflect the proportion of car registrations in each of the previous quarters that is replaced in the current quarter. Therefore, theoretically, we would expect the $\beta$s to sum to marginally less than one.

We next require a method of estimating the $\beta$s. Equation 5.65 is a standard distributed lag model and thus we are faced with the usual estimation problems. However, the Koyck solution may not be particularly appropriate here as theory would not imply immediate geometric decay in the $\beta$s. In particular, we might expect an insignificant number of very new cars to be replaced – those, say, less than one quarter or so old. Thus a lag distribution something like that of Figure 5.5(a) may be more appropriate. However, as we shall see, there are a number of further features of the UK car market which also need to be considered and which will have some relevance for the shape of the resulting lag distribution.

Given the uncertainty concerning the expected shape of the lag distribution associated with Equation 5.65 the estimation of an Almon lag would appear preferable. Thus we first need to specify the length of the lag. We will begin with the (arbitrary) assumption that an insignificant level of replacement demand derives from cars which are seven years and older – that is, we will assume that all new cars are replaced within seven years and therefore we will estimate Equation 5.65 up to a lag of 27 quarters. Thus the model can be written as:

$$REG_t = \alpha + \beta_0\, REG_{t-1} + \beta_1\, REG_{t-2} + \ldots + \beta_{26}\, REG_{t-27} + \varepsilon_t$$

Equation 5.66

We next require the degree of the polynomial which generates the $\beta$s – that is, the maximum power of $k$ in Equation 5.56. For illustrative and comparative purposes we will consider a number of alternatives and, in particular, we will estimate lag structures generated by second, third, fourth and fifth degree polynomials. That is, we will consider lag structures generated by each of the following assumptions:

$$\beta_k = a_0 + a_1 k + a_2 k^2 \qquad\qquad \text{Equation 5.67}$$

$$\beta_k = a_0 + a_1 k + a_2 k^2 + a_3 k^3 \qquad\qquad \text{Equation 5.68}$$

$$\beta_k = a_0 + a_1 k + a_2 k^2 + a_3 k^3 + a_4 k^4 \qquad\qquad \text{Equation 5.69}$$

$$\beta_k = a_0 + a_1 k + a_2 k^2 + a_3 k^3 + a_4 k^4 + a_5 k^5 \qquad\qquad \text{Equation 5.70}$$

In turn, each of these assumptions will produce estimating equations of the form of Equation 5.61, but in the cases of the third, fourth and fifth degree polynomials additional composite variables will be required to allow of the estimation of $a_3$, $a_4$ and $a_5$ (that is, variables $V_{4t}$, $V_{5t}$ and $V_{6t}$ will have to be generated, consistent with the definitions in Equation Set 5.60).

In Table 5.3 we present summary statistics (corrected $R^2$s, Durbin–Watson

**Table 5.3** Summary statistics of Almon estimating equations produced by Equations 5.67 to 5.70

| Degree of polynomial generating the $\beta$s | $\bar{R}^2$ | Durbin–Watson | Sum of the estimated $\beta$s |
|---|---|---|---|
| 2nd | 0.299 | 2.14 | 0.878 |
| 3rd | 0.318 | 2.32 | 0.878 |
| 4th | 0.328 | 2.04 | 0.890 |
| 5th | 0.328 | 2.00 | 0.888 |

statistics and the sum of the estimated $\beta$s) produced by the estimating equations associated with each of the assumptions in Equations 5.67 to 5.70.

Thus on pure statistical criteria a fourth or fifth degree polynomial produces marginally superior estimation results. However we must also examine the resulting estimated lag structures with respect to their theoretical interpretation. In Figure 5.6(a)–(d), we present graphical interpretations of each of these four estimated lag structures.

We can immediately reject the second degree polynomial (a) as it does not make any theoretical sense – recall that, if anything, we might expect a lag structure with an inverted 'U' shape, such as that of Figure 5.5(a). Here we obtain the opposite structure. Similarly, the structure in (b) displays immediate geometric decline from lag 1, contrary to theoretical expectations. This leaves us only with (c) and (d), both of which exhibit two peaks, and thus

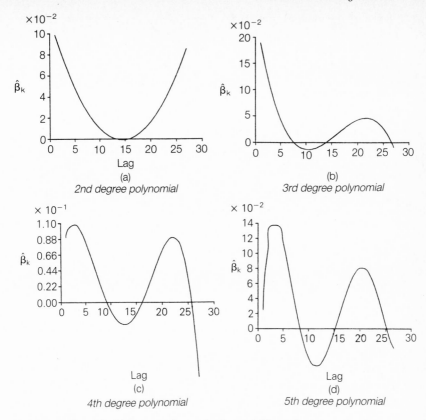

**Figure 5.6** Graphical interpretations of estimated Almon lags.

a theoretical rationalisation for these structures must be found before they can be considered any further.

An explanation for these shapes can be derived by considering the specific nature of the UK new car market. In particular, the market can be considered as consisting of two distinct segments – new cars which are purchased by companies for business purposes, including cars to be used as hire or rental vehicles, and new cars purchased by private individuals. In 1971 business demand for new cars accounted for more than 50 per cent of total demand[8] and this proportion has probably increased since then. Ideally, separate models for private and business demand should be constructed, as presumably the influences on both sectors are quite different. However, the available data on new car registrations do not distinguish between these sources of demand, and hence a joint model must be estimated.

The lag shapes in Figure 5.6(c) and (d), then, could be interpreted as reflecting the different nature of replacement behaviour in the company and private car markets. In the company sector we would expect much more frequent replacement as company cars are probably used more intensively than private cars, and are also used as a means of promoting company image. Typically, company cars are replaced within two years of purchase and thus the first peak in Figure 5.6(c) and (d) can be interpreted as reflecting business replacement behaviour. The second peak could then be argued to reflect replacement behaviour in the private car market, with an average replacement cycle of what appears to be about five to six years.

Note that in the cases of both of these lag structures theoretically unacceptable negative $\beta$s are produced at around lags 8 to 15 (recall that the $\beta$s can be interpreted as the proportion of cars purchased in each of the previous quarters which is replaced in the current quarter). However, the derived $t$-statistics associated with these negative $\beta$s are all insignificant, implying that an insignificant level of replacement demand occurs at these lag lengths. Hence the signs of these $\beta$s are in this sense irrelevant (although it would certainly have been neater if each of these $\beta$s were insignificant but positive).

Given this theoretical rationalisation for a bi-modal lag structure we would have to argue that the $\beta$s are in fact generated by a fourth degree polynomial, which would produce three turning points as required – a higher degree polynomial would produce an unnecessarily complex lag structure. Consequently, we would here argue for the selection of Figure 5.6(c), and this selection is reinforced by noting from Table 5.3 that none of the other polynomials produces superior statistical results.

In Table 5.4 we present the estimates of the derived $\beta$s and their associated $t$-statistics.

We must emphasise that we have used this example here purely for illustrative purposes – our only objective has been to demonstrate the

**Table 5.4** Estimated $\beta$s and $t$-statistics produced by a fourth degree Almon lag fitted to car registration data

| $k$ | $\hat{\beta}_k$ | $t$-statistic | $k$ | $\hat{\beta}_k$ | $t$-statistic | $k$ | $\hat{\beta}_k$ | $t$-statistic |
|---|---|---|---|---|---|---|---|---|
| 0 | 0.090 | 0.99 | 9 | −0.012 | −0.63 | 18 | 0.053 | 2.38 |
| 1 | 0.106 | 2.12 | 10 | −0.024 | −1.21 | 19 | 0.071 | 2.60 |
| 2 | 0.108 | 3.50 | 11 | −0.030 | −1.40 | 20 | 0.084 | 2.62 |
| 3 | 0.100 | 3.28 | 12 | −0.031 | −1.33 | 21 | 0.090 | 2.60 |
| 4 | 0.085 | 2.48 | 13 | −0.027 | −1.11 | 22 | 0.086 | 2.53 |
| 5 | 0.065 | 1.87 | 14 | −0.017 | −0.74 | 23 | 0.069 | 2.27 |
| 6 | 0.044 | 1.36 | 15 | −0.003 | −0.15 | 24 | 0.034 | 1.13 |
| 7 | 0.023 | 0.83 | 16 | 0.014 | 0.73 | 25 | −0.022 | −0.44 |
| 8 | 0.004 | 0.16 | 17 | 0.033 | 1.74 | 26 | −0.104 | −1.15 |

mechanics of estimating an Almon lag, and the importance of both theoretical and statistical analysis in the selection of a final lag structure. In terms of this particular example the following reservations must be made:

1   As we have already indicated the model we have estimated here, as specified in Equation 5.66, is misspecified, and any statistical results produced by such a model must be interpreted with care. In particular, our model has taken no account of price factors, relative price influences, income effects, credit restrictions and any other factors which might be relevant.
2   Our model has assumed very rigid replacement cycle behaviour on the part of car purchasers, in the sense that this behaviour is assumed fixed over the 27-year estimation period. It might be argued, however, that we would expect this behaviour itself to vary, and indeed it might vary in response to some of the factors omitted from the model and described in 1 above. For example, purchasers might respond to longer-term price and income changes via an adjustment in the frequency of vehicle replacement.
3   We have here only considered an arbitrarily selected lag length of 27 quarters. In fact, if this lag length is varied some very different lag shapes are produced, which casts doubt on the theoretical interpretation we have suggested here.

## 5.5   The Estimation of Dynamic Models

A distributed lag model could be interpreted as a particular form of dynamic model. In general, dynamic models are models which attempt to reflect the interconnections which exist between time-periods. Thus dynamic models will contain lagged variables, and attempt to model the way in which economic behaviour is influenced by the past (and the way it might also be influenced by expectations concerning the future).

Recall that the final estimating equation derived from the Koyck distributed lag scheme (Equation 5.44) contained as an explanatory variable a lagged value of the dependent variable. We indicated that this violates the assumption that all explanatory variables in the regression model are non-stochastic. The result is that it can be shown that the least squares estimators at the very least will be biased.[9] However not only distributed lag models can produce estimating equations containing lagged dependent variables.

Models containing lagged dependent variables could be justified by arguing that economic behaviour is often influenced by reference to the past – habit (or inertia) plays a central role in the decisions of many economic agents. That is, the level of some variable in a given time period will be partly influenced by its level in previous time periods. Recall that such an argument was used to justify the consumption function formulation which was derived from the Koyck transformation in Equation 5.52 above.

Another context in which estimating equations containing lagged dependent variables occur is in models in which expectations play a role. The **adaptive expectations model** is a typical example.

We begin by postulating that the level of some variable $Y$ in period $t$ will be influenced not by the actual value of some variable $X$ in period $t$ but by the value of $X$ that is expected to occur in $t$. Indeed there are many contexts in which decisions have to be taken on the basis of what agents expect will occur in the future, as generally information will not be available to indicate what will actually occur. A typical example is in modelling investment behaviour. Thus a firm's current investment decisions will be made on the basis of expectations concerning the strength of demand for the firm's output in the future. Hence when the actual investment expenditure is made it will be on the basis of the level of output that was expected to occur at that time.

Notationally, we can write:

$$Y_t = \alpha + \beta X_t^e + \varepsilon_t \qquad\qquad \text{Equation 5.71}$$

where $X_t^e$ denotes the level of $X$ that is expected to occur in period $t$, this expectation being held at the end of period $t-1$.

Now, the difficulty in estimating models such as Equation 5.71 is that in most applications expectations are not actually observable – we cannot, in general, collect a series of observations on $X_t^e$. Therefore in order to estimate $\alpha$ and $\beta$ we require some additional information and, in particular, information concerning the mechanism by which expectations are formed so that an estimating equation can be derived.

The adaptive expectations hypothesis argues that expectations will be altered (or updated) in response to the errors which are made in forecasting $X$. That is:

$$X_t^e - X_{t-1}^e = \delta(X_{t-1} - X_{t-1}^e) \qquad\qquad \text{Equation 5.72}$$

where $0 < \delta < 1$.

In words, the extent to which expectations are updated $(X_t^e - X_{t-1}^e)$ will be some fraction of the error which was made in forecasting $X$ in the previous time period $(X_{t-1} - X_{t-1}^e)$. The larger is $\delta$ then the stronger is the response of agents to their forecasting errors. Thus an additional parameter, $\delta$, has been introduced into the model. A simple algebraic manipulation can now produce an equation which contains only observable variables, thereby allowing the estimation of $\alpha$, $\beta$ and $\delta$.

Rewriting Equation 5.72 we have:

$$\delta X_{t-1} = X_t^e - (1-\delta) X_{t-1}^e \qquad\qquad \text{Equation 5.73}$$

Lagging Equation 5.71 by one period and multiplying throughout by $1-\delta$ produces:

$$(1-\delta) Y_{t-1} = (1-\delta)\alpha + \beta(1-\delta) X_{t-1}^e + (1-\delta)\varepsilon_{t-1} \qquad\qquad \text{Equation 5.74}$$

Subtracting Equation 5.74 from 5.71 and rearranging we have:

$$Y_t - (1-\delta)Y_{t-1} = \delta\alpha + \beta[X_t^e - (1-\delta)X_{t-1}^e] + \varepsilon_t - (1-\delta)\varepsilon_{t-1}$$

Equation 5.75

Noting that the term in square brackets in Equation 5.75 is equivalent to $\delta X_{t-1}$ in Equation 5.73 then the final estimating equation can be written as:

$$Y_t = \delta\alpha + (1-\delta)Y_{t-1} + \beta\delta X_{t-1} + \varepsilon_t - (1-\delta)\varepsilon_{t-1}$$

Equation 5.76

Thus, as in the Koyck solution, an estimating equation containing a lagged dependent variable on the right-hand side is produced. In fact, it can be shown that the adaptive expectations hypothesis can be interpreted in terms of a distributed lag model,[10] and thus the form of the estimating equation in Equation 5.76 is to be expected.

Another model which produces a Koyck-type estimating equation is the **partial adjustment model**. The partial adjustment model argues that in certain applications it might be realistic to assume that the change in the level of some variable from one period to the next is stimulated by the extent to which the variable deviates from some concept of an optimum or desired level. That is, if we consider a variable $Y$ and denote the optimum or desired level of $Y$ in period $t$ by $Y_t^*$, then the model could be written as:

$$Y_t - Y_{t-1} = \gamma(Y_t^* - Y_{t-1}) + \varepsilon_t$$

Equation 5.77

where $0 < \gamma < 1$.

Again, a typical application is in the analysis of investment behaviour. Thus if $Y_t$ denotes a firm's capital stock in period $t$ then Equation 5.77 implies that the change in the firm's capital stock from one period to the next (its net investment) is some fraction of the extent to which the level of its existing capital stock is sub-optimal. We would generally expect $\gamma$ to be less than one as there will be certain impediments to the firm fully and immediately responding to any sub-optimality. As in the case of expectations, $Y_t^*$ will be unobservable and therefore we require some additional information concerning the way in which $Y_t^*$ is determined. Assume for simplicity that $Y_t^*$ is determined by some other (observable) variable $X$, such that:

$$Y_t^* = \alpha + \beta X_t + \varepsilon_t$$

Equation 5.78

Then substituting Equation 5.78 into Equation 5.77 and rearranging again produces an estimating equation with a lagged value of the dependent variable on the right hand side.

In general, therefore, we are concerned with the problem of estimating dynamic models of the form:

$$Y_t = \alpha + \beta Y_{t-1} + \gamma X_t + \varepsilon_t$$

Equation 5.79

The method which is appropriate for estimating Equation 5.79 can be shown to depend on the nature of the disturbance term, $\varepsilon_t$. One of two assumptions can be made about $\varepsilon_t$:

1   $\varepsilon_t$ is randomly and independently distributed – that is, the assumption we made in the simplest specification of the regression model. If such an assumption can be made then it can be shown that although the least squares estimators are biased, they are still consistent.[11] Thus in practice these estimators would be used, as no superior estimator is available. Therefore the use of the least squares estimators could be theoretically justified in such situations, provided a relatively large sample was available.

2   $\varepsilon_t$ possesses some form of structure. At the simplest level, $\varepsilon_t$ could have either an AR(1) or an MA(1) structure. That is, $\varepsilon_t$ could be generated by:

$$\varepsilon_t = \rho \varepsilon_{t-1} + u_t \qquad\qquad \text{Equation 5.80}$$

or

$$\varepsilon_t = u_t - \lambda u_{t-1} \qquad\qquad \text{Equation 5.81}$$

where in both cases $u_t \sim \text{NID}(0, \sigma_u^2)$.

If $\varepsilon_t$ is generated by either Equation 5.80 or 5.81 it can be shown that the least squares estimators will not only be biased but they will also be inconsistent. The reason for this inconsistency is that as the disturbance terms are now related across time-periods then they must be correlated with the lagged dependent variable in Equation 5.79. Therefore the assumption of independence between the explanatory variables and the disturbance term will be violated.

Thus in the case of a structured disturbance term we require alternative methods for estimating dynamic models of the form of Equation 5.79. The appropriate estimation procedure in such cases is relatively complex and we will not attempt a full exposition here. Rather we will indicate some of the general approaches which are available.[12]

Now, the inconsistency in the estimators of the parameters in Equation 5.79 derives from the combination of the lagged dependent variable and the structured disturbance term. Thus the methods which are available for overcoming this inconsistency are directed at eliminating either one of these features. So, broadly, two approaches can be identified:

(1) Methods which explicitly incorporate the structure of the disturbance term into the estimation process. Essentially, such methods are variants of the Cochrane–Orcutt procedure which we discussed in Section 4.4 of Chapter 4. However, the precise estimation method which is used (or, in particular, the adjustments which are required to the simple least squares procedures) will be different depending on whether an autoregressive or moving average structure is assumed.

Thus the major disadvantage of these estimation methods is that they require the precise structure of the disturbance term to be known *a priori*. Further, even if the structure were known to be either moving average or autoregressive, an assumption of a simple first-order scheme is quite arbitrary, and essentially made in the interests of expediency. In the case of moving average structures, however, even if an assumption of a first-order scheme is realistic, the resulting estimation procedure becomes quite complex.

(2) A second approach to estimating models such as Equation 5.79 is to use some other variable to 'act' for the lagged dependent variable, with this other variable possessing the property that it is uncorrelated with the disturbance term. Such a variable is referred to as an **instrument** for the lagged dependent variable, and the estimation method is referred to as the method of **instrumental variables**.

The disadvantage of this approach is that it requires the derivation of an appropriate instrumental variable. Such a variable should possess two properties. First, as already indicated, this variable must be uncorrelated with the disturbance term. Second, this variable should be highly correlated with the variable for which it acts. This second property is not essential (any non-zero correlation is all that is theoretically required), but the higher this correlation is the more efficient will the resulting estimators be (as would seem intuitively plausible).

In terms of the model in Equation 5.79 an obvious instrument for $Y_{t-1}$ is $X_{t-1}$, and this would be the commonly used instrument for models of this form. That is, $X_{t-1}$ must be correlated with $Y_{t-1}$ as the initial specification of the model implied that $Y_t$, in part, is determined by $X_t$. In addition, as $X_{t-1}$ is assumed to be non-stochastic then it must be independent of the disturbance term.

However, while the use of $X_{t-1}$ will ensure that the resulting estimators are consistent the method cannot guarantee unbiasedness. In practice, finite sample properties are of far greater relevance. Further, it is difficult to draw conclusions concerning the efficiency of instrumental variable estimators in finite samples.

None the less, given that ordinary least squares estimation of models such as Equation 5.79 is known to produce biased and inconsistent estimators (given a structured disturbance term), an instrumental variable approach is to be preferred even though little is known about the performance of the resulting estimators in finite samples. We present a more detailed discussion of the mechanics of instrumental variable estimation in Appendix 5.1.

There remains a further difficulty in estimating models which contain lagged dependent variables. In the above discussion we concluded that the most serious estimation problems occur when the disturbance terms possess some structure, and in such cases alternative estimation methods are required. Therefore we first need to test for the independence of the disturbance terms. However it can be shown that our usual test – the Durbin–Watson test – is invalid when a lagged dependent variable is included in the model. The reason, in essence, is that as the inclusion of $Y_{t-1}$ results in biased, and possibly inconsistent, least squares estimators then the estimated residuals will themselves also be 'biased'. Hence these estimated residuals will provide a misleading basis for drawing inferences concerning the independence of the true disturbance terms.

A number of alternative tests have been proposed in the literature, but perhaps the most straightforward is the test proposed by Durbin himself.[13] The test is appropriate for large samples only and we proceed as follows:

The postulated model is estimated by ordinary least squares and from the estimated residuals $(e_t)$ we calculate a statistic, $r$, where:

$$r = \frac{\sum_{t=2}^{n} e_t e_{t-1}}{\sum_{t=1}^{n} e_t^2} \qquad \text{Equation 5.82}$$

and note that given the definition of the Durbin–Watson statistic, $d$ (see Equation 4.88 of Chapter 4), we have:

$$r \cong 1 - (1/2)d$$

and therefore $r$ can be calculated directly from the value of $d$.

We next define a statistic, $h$, where

$$h = r\sqrt{\frac{n}{1 - n\hat{V}(\hat{\beta}_1)}} \qquad \text{Equation 5.83}$$

and $\hat{V}(\hat{\beta}_1)$ is the estimated variance of the least squares estimator of the coefficient on $Y_{t-1}$.

Now, it can be shown that $h$ has an approximate standard normal distribution under a null hypothesis of an independently distributed disturbance term. We can therefore perform a test of significance on $h$ using our standard testing procedures. To carry out this test we only require $\hat{V}(\hat{\beta}_1)$, irrespective of how many other explanatory variables are included in the model, including further lagged values of $Y$ and $X$. Note, however, that the expression for $h$ in Equation 5.83 is only defined if the term, $1 - n\hat{V}(\hat{\beta}_1)$, is positive, and there is no guarantee that this will be the case in any given application. Thus the test cannot be performed in such cases.

However, even though the Durbin–Watson test is strictly invalid if $Y_{t-1}$ is included as an explanatory variable (or indeed any other lagged values of $Y$) experimental evidence seems to indicate that provided large samples are used (that is, in excess of about 30 observations) the Durbin–Watson test tends to lead to the correct conclusion in the majority of cases. This is more so the case the larger the number of $X$ variables (non-stochastic variables) that are included in the model. Therefore the Durbin–Watson test still tends to be used quite widely in empirical work despite its theoretical weaknesses.

We will now consider an example in order to illustrate some of these issues.

Example 5.5

We will continue with our example of estimating a consumption function, and further consider the estimated consumption function which was derived from the Koyck transformation in Example 5.3.

Recall from Equation 5.53 that a Koyck transformation appeared to produce a highly satisfactory consumption function. In particular, it was remarkably successful in eliminating what had initially appeared as a problem of autocorrelation (the reader should also confirm that the value of $h$ associated with Equation 5.53 is the insignificant value of 0.05). However, while Equation 5.53 certainly appears satisfactory in terms of all the diagnostic tests that we have so far used, these tests represent only the simplest of a range of possible tests of adequacy that could be performed on a given estimated model.

Thus, one important aspect of an estimated model which we would wish to examine is its forecasting performance. That is, up to this point we have been concerned with establishing how satisfactorily an estimated model performs with reference only to the sample data. However the real test of a model is its performance outside the sample period. By assumption, all the parameters in a specified model are constants, and the sample data are used simply to derive estimates of these constants. Therefore if the model being estimated is the true model then it should just as adequately explain the dependent variable outside the sample period as within it.

We will discuss forecasting in more detail in Chapter 6, and thus we will restrict ourselves here to an informal examination of how adequately the model specification in Equation 5.52 forecasts consumers' expenditure.

We will test the forecasting performance of Equation 5.52 by first re-estimating the model over the shorter sample period 1963, first quarter to 1974, fourth quarter. We will then use this re-estimated model to forecast $CN_t$ over the 'forecast period' 1975, first quarter to 1979, fourth quarter. Of course, actual $CN_t$ is known over this forecast period and so we can directly evaluate the forecasting performance of the model.

The estimate of Equation 5.52 over the shorter sample period is as follows:

$$\widehat{CN}_t = 1025.538 + 0.712\,CN_{t-1} + 0.180D_t \qquad \text{Equation 5.84}$$
$$\quad\ (3.08)\quad (8.24)\qquad\quad (3.28)$$

$$\bar{R}^2 = 0.987, \quad d = 2.12, \quad n = 47$$

Thus the broad features of the estimated model are little changed in moving from Equation 5.53 to 5.84.

There are two forecasting tests which can be set for Equation 5.84. The first and less stringent test is to forecast $CN_t$ using the actual value of $CN_{t-1}$ over the forecast period. This is generally referred to as a 'one-step ahead' forecast as, in effect, we forecast just one period at a time, at the point at which the actual value of $CN_{t-1}$ becomes known (although this is no problem here as

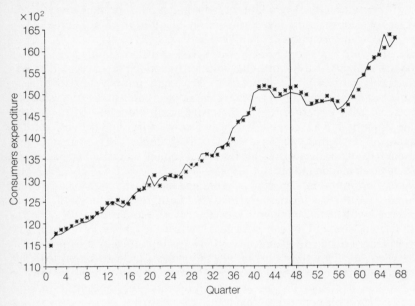

**Figure 5.7** One-step ahead forecasts from Equation 5.84.

we know $CN_{t-1}$ over the entire 'forecast' period). Thus the one-step ahead forecasts are derived by substituting into Equation 5.84 the actual values of $CN_{t-1}$ and $D_t$ over the forecast period (note that in a realistic forecasting situation $D_t$ would be unknown, and therefore forecasts of $D$ would have to be obtained from some source – but we will ignore this complication here).

The more stringent test for Equation 5.84 is to forecast $CN_t$ using as the value of $CN_{t-1}$ the forecast of $CN_t$ in the previous period – that is, we substitute $\widehat{CN}_{t-1}$ for $CN_{t-1}$ over the forecast period, in addition to the actual value of $D_t$. This is a more realistic test as in an actual forecasting situation we will not of course know the actual value of the lagged dependent variable over the forecast period (unless we were only forecasting one period at a time) and so we would have to use the lagged forecasts of the dependent variable. We will refer to these forecasts as the dynamic forecasts.

We will evaluate the forecasting performance of the model by graphical means only and leave to Chapter 6 a discussion of the more formal tests that

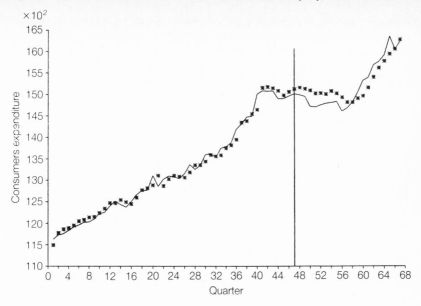

**Figure 5.8**  Dynamic forecasts from Equation 5.84.

could be performed. In Figure 5.7 we present the one-step ahead forecasts and in Figure 5.8 the dynamic forecasts. ($CN_t$ is shown as the unbroken line and the forecasts – $\widehat{CN}_t$ – are shown by the asterisks. Over the estimation period, 1963–74, the asterisks strictly represent the fitted values from the estimated model and thus provide an indication of the 'tracking' performance of the model.)

From a close inspection of Figure 5.7 it can be seen that there is a tendency to over-estimate $CN_t$ in the earlier part of the forecast period and a tendency for under-estimation in the latter part of the period. However, this tendency is much clearer in the dynamic forecasts in Figure 5.8. Further, if we examine the fitted values over the estimation period we note that $\widehat{CN}_t$ does not appear to fluctuate randomly around $CN_t$ – this is particularly apparent at both the beginning and end of the estimation period.

Hence, there is the suspicion that there remains a systematic component in $CN_t$ which has not been accounted for by the model, and this has resulted in the poor forecasting performance of Equation 5.84. We would expect therefore that this systematic component would result in some structure remaining in the estimated disturbance term. In effect, this implies that the structure in the original disturbance term ($\varepsilon_t$ in Equation 5.51) is more complex than a simple first-order scheme.[14]

In order to examine whether the model has captured all the systematic variation in the dependent variable (and in particular, whether there is any evidence of remaining structure in $\varepsilon_t$), we could examine the estimated residuals from the model in Equation 5.53 in more detail. Thus if we denote the estimated residual in time period $t$ by $e_t$, we could, for example, regress $e_t$ on a number of lagged values of itself, in addition to the independent variables already included in the model. That is, can a significant proportion of the unexplained variation in $CN_t$ $(e_t)$ still be explained by the explanatory factors in the model, but by now assuming a more complex disturbance term structure? The resulting estimated equation is as follows ($t$-statistics in brackets, and considering four lagged values of $e_t$):

$$\hat{e}_t = 117.7 + 0.005\,CN_{t-1} - 0.010D_t - 0.131e_{t-1} + 0.181e_{t-2}$$
$$\quad\;\;(0.37)(0.06) \qquad\quad (0.22) \qquad (0.96) \qquad\quad (1.36)$$

$$+\,0.350e_{t-3} + 0.185e_{t-4} \qquad\qquad\qquad\text{Equation 5.85}$$
$$\quad(2.52) \qquad\;\;(1.29)$$

$$R^2 = 0.169, \quad n = 63$$

Note from Equation 5.85 that the $t$-statistic associated with $e_{t-3}$ is significant, thus implying that some structure still remains in $e_t$. We could conclude therefore that the disturbance term in the model formulation in Equation 5.52 is autocorrelated (although no first-order autocorrelation would appear to be present). This neglected systematic factor may then explain the relatively poor forecasting performance of the model as highlighted by Figures 5.7 and 5.8. In turn, we would then have to establish whether this apparent structure in $e_t$ is a reflection of the actual disturbances having a relatively complex autocorrelated structure, or whether the model is still misspecified.

The approach which we have used in Equation 5.85 above for examining the possibility of a more complex disturbance term structure forms the basis of the **Lagrange Multiplier** test. However, we will not discuss the details of this procedure here.[15] We will consider the issue of more complex disturbance term structures in Chapter 7, where we will also further consider the modelling of consumers' expenditure.

### 5.6    Summary

In this chapter we have outlined a number of additional refinements which can be made to the basic regression model.

First, we discussed the use of dummy variables – that is, variables which are appropriate in those cases in which an explanatory factor exerts a discrete rather than a continuous influence on the dependent variable of interest. We also briefly indicated the way in which a dummy variable itself might be modelled as a dependent variable.

Next we discussed the way in which parameter restrictions can be incorporated into a model specification. In particular, we emphasised that the efficient estimation of any model depends not only on the use of appropriate estimation methods and satisfactory data, but also on the model specification reflecting all available *a priori* information.

We then introduced the concept of a distributed lag model and outlined some of the methods that are available for estimating these models. However, the estimation of such models is not necessarily straightforward, the complications involved deriving from the general problems associated with the estimation of dynamic models in economics. Thus the methods which we discussed could be characterised as uneasy compromises between strict theoretical considerations and empirical expediency. None the less the satisfactory estimation of time-series models is central to the theory and practice of econometrics. Our discussion here can therefore be most usefully viewed as an introduction to the issues involved, in that it has highlighted as many difficulties as it has provided solutions. We will return to a more detailed discussion of time-series modelling in Chapter 7.

## Notes

[1] For example, see R. J. Pindyck and D. L. Rubenfeld, *Econometric Models and Economic Forecasts*, 2nd edn (New York, McGraw-Hill, 1981), Ch. 10, or J. Kmenta, *Elements of Econometrics*, 2nd edn (New York, Macmillan, 1986), pp. 547–60 for an introductory discussion. A more advanced treatment can be found in G. S. Maddala, *Limited Dependent and Qualitative Variables in Econometrics* (Cambridge, Cambridge University Press, 1983).

[2] Note however that if $X_2$ and $X_3$ are highly collinear and that the form of this collinearity is such that:

$$X_{3t} = b + X_{2t}$$

where $b$ is some constant, then the difference $(W)$ between $X_3$ and $X_2$ would be approximately constant, and hence highly correlated with the constant term in Equation 5.28. That is, in moving from Equation 5.24 to 5.28 the level of multicollinearity might be only marginally reduced, and any gain in efficiency would result from the increased degrees of freedom in Equation 5.28.

[3] After L. M. Koyck, who first used such lag structures in his *Distributed Lags and Investment Analysis* (Amsterdam, North-Holland, 1954).

[4] See S. Almon, 'The distributed lag between capital appropriations and expenditures', *Econometrica*, 33 (1965), pp. 178–96.

[5] Just as in the case of autoregressive schemes we can generalise to higher order moving average schemes. Thus a *second order* moving average scheme (MA(2)) would be written as:

$$u_t = \varepsilon_t - \theta_1 \varepsilon_{t-1} - \theta_2 \varepsilon_{t-2}$$

and so on for higher order schemes. Models which incorporate more generalised disturbance term structures will be discussed in Chapter 7 below.

[6] The Motor Transactions Survey, 1971. *Economic Trends*, No. 242, HMSO, Dec. 1973.

[7] For a more detailed discussion of a fully specified demand function for new cars see A. G. Armstrong and J. C. Odling-Smee, 'The demand for new cars II – an empirical model for the UK', *Oxford Bulletin of Economics and Statistics*, Aug. 1979, pp. 193–214.

[8] The Motor Transactions Survey, 1971.

[9] See, for example, Kmenta, *Elements of Econometrics*, pp. 334–41.

[10] It is this feature of the adaptive expectations hypothesis – that agents only consider what has occurred in the past in forming their expectations (as opposed to what is occurring currently) – which has led, in part, to the development of the **rational expectations hypothesis**.

[11] Again, see Kmenta, *Elements of Econometrics*, pp. 334–41.

[12] Ibid., pp. 532–6, or any other more advanced econometrics text, for a fuller discussion.

[13] J. Durbin, 'Testing for serial correlation in least squares regression when some of the regressors are lagged dependent variables,' *Econometrica*, 38 (1970), pp. 410–21.

[14] Recall that the Koyck transformation could be expected to go some way towards eliminating first-order autocorrelation.

[15] See T. S. Breusch, 'Testing for autocorrelation in dynamic linear models', *Australian Economic Papers*, 17 (1978), pp. 334–55, and L. G. Godfrey, 'Testing against general autoregressive and moving average error models when the regressors include lagged dependent variables', *Econometrica*, 46 (1978), pp. 1293–302. See also Johnston, *Econometric Methods*, 3rd edn (New York, McGraw-Hill, 1984), pp. 319–21 for a summary of the procedure. It can be shown that under the null hypothesis of an unstructured disturbance term the statistic, $nR^2$, has a chi-square distribution with degrees of freedom equal to the number of lags on $e_t$ included in the estimating equation (Equation 5.85 here). We will briefly discuss the chi-square distribution in Chapter 6, and tables for the distribution are given in Appendix V. Thus from Equation 5.85 we would note that the value of $nR^2$ (10.65) is significant at the 5 per cent level.

## References and Further Reading

All of the texts listed in Chapters 2 and 3 cover the material we have presented here. Stewart offers the least technically/mathematically demanding exposition and Johnston is probably the most demanding in this respect (of the texts we have indicated), relying heavily on the use of matrix algebra. The remaining texts offer intermediate treatments of varying levels of complexity.

## Exercises

Exercises 1 and 2 cover Section 5.2 and Exercises 3–6 cover Sections 5.4 and 5.5.

*Section 5.2   Dummy Variables*

Exercise 1

Consider the specification of a model which seeks to explain the variation in the incomes of working women in the UK. In order to estimate such a model a sample of working women throughout the UK is selected. Describe the explanatory variables which you think should be included in this model. In particular, which explanatory factors might it be appropriate to specify as dummy variables?

Exercise 2

Consider a model in which the dependent variable is specified as a dummy variable. In particular, consider the following model:

$$Y_i = \alpha + \beta X_i + \varepsilon_i$$

where $Y_i$ can only take on the values zero or one. Explain why $\varepsilon_i$ cannot be assumed to be normally distributed, and also why it must be the case that the disturbance terms in this model are heteroskedastic. (Hint: determine the possible values that $\varepsilon_i$ can take on at each sample point.)

*Sections 5.4 and 5.5   Distributed Lag and Dynamic Models*

Exercise 3

Using the Koyck transformation, derive the estimating equation from the model specified in Equation 5.45. Can estimates of the original parameters as specified in Equation 5.45 be derived from the estimated parameters of the final estimating equation?

Exercise 4

Consider the following model:

$$Y_t = \alpha + \gamma Z_t + \beta_0 X_t + \beta_1 X_{t-1} + \beta_2 X_{t-2} + \ldots + \varepsilon_t$$

Using the Koyck transformation, derive an estimating equation from this model. Can unique estimates of the parameters in the above model be derived from this estimating equation?

Exercise 5

If you have access to an appropriate regression package, use the consumers' expenditure data in Appendix 5.2 and the income data in Table 4.3 to estimate consumption functions with the following lag structures:

(a)   An unrestricted eight-period lag on income.
(b)   An unrestricted four-period lag on income.
(c)   An eight-period Almon lag on income, with the $\beta$s generated by a quadratic (Equation 5.56).

(d)   A four-period Almon lag on income, with the $\beta$s generated by a quadratic.

Compare and contrast these various estimated models with respect to both their theoretical and statistical implications.

Exercise 6

Show that the adaptive expectations model specified in Equations 5.71 and 5.72 can be expressed as a distributed lag model.


**Appendix 5.1**   *The Estimation of Models Containing Lagged Values of the Dependent Variable and Autocorrelated Disturbance Terms by the Method of Instrumental Variables*

We require an appropriate estimation method for estimating models of the form:

$$Y_t = \alpha + \beta Y_{t-1} + \gamma X_t + \varepsilon_t \qquad \text{Equation A5.1.1}$$

In order to describe the method of instrumental variables, we will begin by describing instrumental variable estimation in general terms before considering the specific estimation of the model in Equation A5.1.1.
    Thus, consider the following simple model:

$$Y_t = \alpha + \beta X_t + \varepsilon_t \qquad \text{Equations A5.1.2}$$

where all the assumptions of the simple least squares model are satisfied and, in particular, $X_t$ is independent of $\varepsilon_t$. We will now derive a simple method for obtaining the least squares estimator of $\beta$.
    Re-expressing Equation A5.1.2 in terms of mean deviations (that is, simply subtract from Equation A5.1.2 the value of this equation averaged over the population values), we have:

$$y_t = \beta x_t + \varepsilon_t \qquad \text{Equation A5.1.3}$$

where $y_t = Y_t - E(Y)$ and $x_t = X_t - E(X)$. Multiplying Equation A5.1.3 throughout by $x_t$ and summing over the population, we obtain:

$$\sum_{t}^{N} y_t x_t = \beta \sum_{t}^{N} x_t^2 + \sum_{t}^{N} x_t \varepsilon_t \qquad \text{Equation A5.1.4}$$

Now, as $E(x_t \varepsilon_t) = 0$, by assumption, then we must have $\sum x_t \varepsilon_t = 0$, and thus solving for $\beta$ from Equation A5.1.4 produces:

$$\beta = \frac{\sum y_t x_t}{\sum x_t^2} \qquad \text{Equation A5.1.5}$$

Therefore a potential estimator for $\beta$ is simply Equation A5.1.5, but with summation occurring over the sample rather than the population values. That is,

$$\hat{\beta} = \frac{\sum_{t}^{n} y_t x_t}{\sum_{t}^{n} x_t^2}$$

Equation A5.1.6

But note that the estimator in Equation A5.1.6 is just the ordinary least squares estimator for $\beta$ which we presented in Chapter 2 (see Equations 2.20 and A2.1.10).

This 'short-cut' method for obtaining the least squares estimators in the simple regression model easily generalises to the case of a multiple regression. That is, if we consider the following model:

$$Y_t = \alpha + \beta_1 X_{1t} + \beta_2 X_{2t} + \varepsilon_t$$

Equation A5.1.7

where again all the assumptions of the least squares model are satisfied and, in particular:

$$E(X_{1t}\varepsilon_t) = E(X_{2t}\varepsilon_t) = 0$$

Equation A5.1.8

Rewriting Equation A5.1.8 in mean deviation form we have:

$$y_t = \beta_1 x_{1t} + \beta_2 x_{2t} + \varepsilon_t$$

Equation A5.1.9

Multiplying Equation A5.1.9 in turn by $x_{1t}$ and $x_{2t}$ and summing produces the following two equations:

$$\sum y_t x_{1t} = \beta_1 \sum x_{1t}^2 + \beta_2 \sum x_{2t} x_{1t} + \sum x_{1t}\varepsilon_t$$

Equation A5.1.10

$$\sum y_t x_{2t} = \beta_1 \sum x_{1t} x_{2t} + \beta_2 \sum x_{2t}^2 + \sum x_{2t}\varepsilon_t$$

Equation A5.1.11

Setting $\sum x_{1t}\varepsilon_t$ and $\sum x_{2t}\varepsilon_t$ equal to their population values of zero, solving simultaneously for $\beta_1$ and $\beta_2$ and then summing over the sample values will produce expressions for $\hat{\beta}_1$ and $\hat{\beta}_2$ which are equivalent to the ordinary least squares estimators for $\beta_1$ and $\beta_2$ (see Equation 3.6 for the case of $\beta_1$).

Thus, in general, for any multiple regression model with $K$ independent variables, we first express this model in mean deviation form, then multiply the resulting equation successively by each of the $K$ independent variables (in their mean deviation form), sum over each of these equations, set $\sum x_{kt}\varepsilon_t = 0$, for $k = 1, 2, \ldots, K$, and solve the resulting $K$ simultaneous equations for $\beta_1, \beta_2, \ldots, \beta_K$.

Now consider again the model in Equation A5.1.2. However, now assume that $X_t$ and $\varepsilon_t$ are not independent, and therefore we cannot set $\sum x_t\varepsilon_t$ to zero. Thus this short-cut method for deriving the least squares estimators breaks down. Recall that this is effectively what occurs in Equation A5.1.1 – in the notation used there, $Y_{t-1}$ and $\varepsilon_t$ are not independent, because $\varepsilon_t$ is autocorrelated, and this resulted in the least squares estimators being inconsistent. It is precisely because the sum of the product of the independent variable(s) and the disturbance term cannot be set to zero that the simple least squares estimators will be inconsistent.

Now consider an additional variable – $Z_t$, say – which has the property of being independent of $\varepsilon_t$ in Equation A5.1.2. That is:

$$E(Z_t \varepsilon_t) = 0 \qquad\qquad \text{Equation A5.1.12}$$

Multiplying Equation A5.1.3 by $z_t$ (where $z_t = Z_t - E(Z)$) and summing over the population produces:

$$\sum_{}^{N} y_t z_t = \beta \sum_{}^{N} x_t z_t + \sum_{}^{N} \varepsilon_t z_t \qquad\qquad \text{Equation A5.1.13}$$

Given the assumption in Equation A5.1.12 we can now validly set $\sum \varepsilon_t z_t$ to zero, and solving Equation A5.1.13 for $\beta$, but summing over the sample values, produces the following estimator for $\beta$:

$$\tilde{\beta} = \frac{\sum_{}^{n} y_t z_t}{\sum_{}^{n} x_t z_t} \qquad\qquad \text{Equation A5.1.14}$$

We next need to consider the properties of this estimator. First, we will establish whether or not $\tilde{\beta}$ is consistent. Substituting Equation A5.1.3 into Equation A5.1.14 we have:

$$\tilde{\beta} = \frac{\sum (\beta x_t + \varepsilon_t) z_t}{\sum x_t z_t}$$

$$= \frac{\beta \sum x_t z_t + \sum \varepsilon_t z_t}{\sum x_t z_t}$$

$$= \beta + \frac{\sum \varepsilon_t z_t}{\sum x_t z_t}$$

$$\therefore \operatorname{plim}(\tilde{\beta}) = \beta + \frac{\operatorname{plim}(1/n \sum \varepsilon_t z_t)}{\operatorname{plim}(1/n \sum x_t z_t)}$$

and as by assumption we have:

$$\operatorname{plim}(1/n \sum \varepsilon_t z_t) = 0$$

then we can conclude that:

$$\operatorname{plim}(\tilde{\beta}) = \beta$$

and thus that $\tilde{\beta}$ is a consistent estimator of $\beta$.

Next, we need to consider the efficiency of $\tilde{\beta}$ as an estimator of $\beta$. We state below, without proof, the expression for the estimated variance of $\hat{\beta}$. That is, it can be shown that:

$$S_{\hat{\beta}}^2 = \frac{\hat{\sigma}_\varepsilon^2 \sum z_t^2}{(\sum z_t x_t)^2}$$

Equation A5.1.15

Now, note from this expression that if $x_t$ and its instrument, $z_t$, are uncorrelated then $\sum z_t x_t = 0$ and $S_{\hat{\beta}}^2$ will therefore approach infinity. This is the reason, then, that we require that $z_t$ be correlated with $x_t$ – as long as there is some non-zero correlation between $x_t$ and $z_t$ then the resulting estimator will have a finite variance and some form of model evaluation can then be performed. Further, the higher the correlation between $x_t$ and $z_t$ then the smaller will $S_{\hat{\beta}}^2$ be. That is, the ideal instrument for $x_t$ is a variable which is uncorrelated with $\varepsilon_t$ (thus producing a consistent estimator) and a variable with which it is highly correlated (thus ensuring that the resulting estimator is relatively efficient).

Instrumental variable estimation generalises quite easily to the case of a multiple regression. Thus consider a regression model which contains $K$ independent variables. Assume that $G$ of these variables ($G \leqslant K$) are not independent of $\varepsilon_t$. We therefore require $G$ instrumental variables to act for these $G$ variables, and the remaining independent variables ($K - G$) can in effect act as their own instruments. Thus the mean deviation version of the model is successively multiplied through by the $G$ instrumental variables and the remaining $K - G$ original independent variables, and summed. The summations involving $\varepsilon_t$ are all set to zero and the instrumental variable estimators are obtained by solving the resulting set of simultaneous equations for the $\beta$s.

Algebraically, such a methodology is clearly tedious. However, computer packages are now widely available which simply require the investigator to indicate which of the variables in a regression model require instruments, and then of course to input into the package an appropriate set of instrumental variables. In practice, then, the problem is not so much one of actually deriving the instrumental variable estimators but, rather, obtaining a satisfactory set of instruments. Often no obvious candidates will be available and thus the methodology in such cases will have a somewhat arbitrary element, its justification then being derived from pure theoretical rather than practical considerations.

Returning finally to our starting point and the model in Equation A5.1.1, we are therefore faced with the problem of obtaining an appropriate instrument for $Y_{t-1}$. Two possibilities suggest themselves here:

1  $X_{t-1}$ could act as an instrument for $Y_{t-1}$. As $X_t$ (or $X_{t-1}$) is non-stochastic it will be independent of $\varepsilon_t$, and $X_{t-1}$ will certainly be correlated with $Y_{t-1}$ (the model itself implies that $X$ and $Y$ are contemporaneously correlated).
2  $Y_t$ could be regressed on lagged values of $X$ only and the fitted values for $Y_t$

from such a regression, lagged one period, could act as an instrument for $Y_{t-1}$. That is, we would have:

$$\hat{Y}_t = \hat{a}_0 + \hat{a}_1 X_{t-1} + \hat{a}_2 X_{t-2} + \ldots$$

and the appropriate instrument would be $\hat{Y}_{t-1}$. Note that as $\hat{Y}_t$ depends only on the $X$s then $\hat{Y}_t$ can be treated as being independent of $\varepsilon_t$.

The number of lagged values of $X$ to be included in the regression that produces the observations on $\hat{Y}_t$ (and hence $\hat{Y}_{t-1}$) could be determined either on the basis of the regression which produces the highest adjusted $R^2$, or alternatively, on the basis of some predetermined value of $R^2$ being achieved. Note that this second approach to obtaining an instrument for $Y_{t-1}$ gives some weight to ensuring that the resulting instrument is highly correlated with $Y_{t-1}$.

**Appendix 5.2** *Consumers' expenditure on non-durables, United Kingdom, quarterly – seasonally adjusted, 1963–1979, 1975 prices (£million)*

| Year | Quarter | Consumers' expenditure | Year | Quarter | Consumers' expenditure | Year | Quarter | Consumers' expenditure |
|------|---------|------|------|---------|------|------|---------|------|
| 1963 | 1 | 11,350 | 1969 | 1 | 13,079 | 1975 | 1 | 14,993 |
|      | 2 | 11,634 |      | 2 | 13,042 |      | 2 | 14,957 |
|      | 3 | 11,732 |      | 3 | 13,158 |      | 3 | 14,721 |
|      | 4 | 11,760 |      | 4 | 13,367 |      | 4 | 14,711 |
| 1964 | 1 | 11,837 | 1970 | 1 | 13,255 | 1976 | 1 | 14,760 |
|      | 2 | 11,918 |      | 2 | 13,350 |      | 2 | 14,799 |
|      | 3 | 11,961 |      | 3 | 13,600 |      | 3 | 14,817 |
|      | 4 | 12,024 |      | 4 | 13,622 |      | 4 | 13,842 |
| 1965 | 1 | 12,037 | 1971 | 1 | 13,540 | 1977 | 1 | 14,612 |
|      | 2 | 12,101 |      | 2 | 13,749 |      | 2 | 14,691 |
|      | 3 | 12,223 |      | 3 | 13,788 |      | 3 | 14,823 |
|      | 4 | 12,255 |      | 4 | 13,873 |      | 4 | 15,055 |
| 1966 | 1 | 12,403 | 1972 | 1 | 14,192 | 1978 | 1 | 15,330 |
|      | 2 | 12,518 |      | 2 | 14,312 |      | 2 | 15,396 |
|      | 3 | 12,437 |      | 3 | 14,478 |      | 3 | 15,689 |
|      | 4 | 12,374 |      | 4 | 14,491 |      | 4 | 15,763 |
| 1967 | 1 | 12,506 | 1973 | 1 | 15,013 | 1979 | 1 | 15,917 |
|      | 2 | 12,666 |      | 2 | 15,088 |      | 2 | 16,356 |
|      | 3 | 12,763 |      | 3 | 15,079 |      | 3 | 16,048 |
|      | 4 | 12,770 |      | 4 | 15,088 |      | 4 | 16,235 |
| 1968 | 1 | 13,111 | 1974 | 1 | 14,902 |      |   |        |
|      | 2 | 12,854 |      | 2 | 14,907 |      |   |        |
|      | 3 | 13,030 |      | 3 | 14,966 |      |   |        |
|      | 4 | 13,103 |      | 4 | 15,017 |      |   |        |

*Source: Economic Trends, Annual Abstract, 1981, HMSO.*

**Appendix 5.3** *Quarterly new registrations of cars, Great Britain 1956–1984, monthly averages – thousands*

| Year | Quarter | Regis-trations | Year | Quarter | Regis-trations | Year | Quarter | Regis-trations |
|------|---------|----------------|------|---------|----------------|------|---------|----------------|
| 1956 | 1 | 39.6 | 1966 | 1 | 116.1 | 1976 | 1 | 117.4 |
|      | 2 | 41.2 |      | 2 | 119.9 |      | 2 | 111.5 |
|      | 3 | 28.4 |      | 3 | 71.0 |      | 3 | 108.4 |
|      | 4 | 24.0 |      | 4 | 48.2 |      | 4 | 88.9 |
| 1957 | 1 | 26.9 | 1967 | 1 | 100.4 | 1977 | 1 | 118.9 |
|      | 2 | 41.5 |      | 2 | 102.3 |      | 2 | 108.3 |
|      | 3 | 38.3 |      | 3 | 87.7 |      | 3 | 123.4 |
|      | 4 | 35.1 |      | 4 | 81.9 |      | 4 | 87.2 |
| 1958 | 1 | 47.0 | 1968 | 1 | 129.7 | 1978 | 1 | 148.6 |
|      | 2 | 51.8 |      | 2 | 88.1 |      | 2 | 132.2 |
|      | 3 | 42.9 |      | 3 | 80.3 |      | 3 | 150.1 |
|      | 4 | 43.4 |      | 4 | 74.2 |      | 4 | 95.5 |
| 1959 | 1 | 48.9 | 1969 | 1 | 89.3 | 1979 | 1 | 154.6 |
|      | 2 | 61.1 |      | 2 | 94.4 |      | 2 | 182.2 |
|      | 3 | 46.5 |      | 3 | 83.3 |      | 3 | 126.4 |
|      | 4 | 58.6 |      | 4 | 62.1 |      | 4 | 105.1 |
| 1960 | 1 | 74.6 | 1970 | 1 | 95.9 | 1980 | 1 | 164.4 |
|      | 2 | 82.4 |      | 2 | 102.8 |      | 2 | 123.1 |
|      | 3 | 65.1 |      | 3 | 91.0 |      | 3 | 137.0 |
|      | 4 | 46.2 |      | 4 | 76.0 |      | 4 | 82.0 |
| 1961 | 1 | 68.9 | 1971 | 1 | 102.7 | 1981 | 1 | 138.8 |
|      | 2 | 80.0 |      | 2 | 105.1 |      | 2 | 124.3 |
|      | 3 | 57.6 |      | 3 | 117.9 |      | 3 | 138.2 |
|      | 4 | 41.1 |      | 4 | 108.1 |      | 4 | 96.9 |
| 1962 | 1 | 63.8 | 1972 | 1 | 133.7 | 1982 | 1 | 139.2 |
|      | 2 | 82.5 |      | 2 | 156.2 |      | 2 | 122.8 |
|      | 3 | 60.7 |      | 3 | 142.0 |      | 3 | 158.3 |
|      | 4 | 54.5 |      | 4 | 122.4 |      | 4 | 107.9 |
| 1963 | 1 | 77.8 | 1973 | 1 | 159.8 | 1983 | 1 | 165.6 |
|      | 2 | 107.7 |      | 2 | 142.2 |      | 2 | 141.5 |
|      | 3 | 80.2 |      | 3 | 145.9 |      | 3 | 183.2 |
|      | 4 | 70.5 |      | 4 | 100.6 |      | 4 | 111.8 |
| 1964 | 1 | 106.5 | 1974 | 1 | 109.1 | 1984 | 1 | 167.0 |
|      | 2 | 121.5 |      | 2 | 110.1 |      | 2 | 146.7 |
|      | 3 | 92.9 |      | 3 | 110.5 |      | 3 | 167.8 |
|      | 4 | 75.9 |      | 4 | 81.7 |      | 4 | 104.9 |
| 1965 | 1 | 120.2 | 1975 | 1 | 116.9 |      |   |      |
|      | 2 | 109.1 |      | 2 | 97.0 |      |   |      |
|      | 3 | 79.3 |      | 3 | 110.1 |      |   |      |
|      | 4 | 65.6 |      | 4 | 70.1 |      |   |      |

*Source: Economic Trends, Annual Abstract, 1986, HMSO*

# 6 An Introduction to Simultaneous Equation Models

## 6.1 Introduction

In this chapter we will present an introductory discussion of the role and nature of simultaneous equation modelling. We will begin by describing the structure and interpretation of simultaneous equation models, before going on to discuss the problems involved in estimating such models. Having discussed a number of estimation methods and associated methods of model evaluation, we will then describe the way in which a simultaneous equation model can be used for forecasting and policy evaluation. Finally, we will complete this chapter with a brief discussion of some of the compromises which have to be made between theory and practice in the application of simultaneous equation methods.

## 6.2 The Concept of a Simultaneous Equation Model

Up to this point, the various estimation methods which we have discussed have all been developed within the context of a single equation model. A single dependent variable was first identified as the focus of interest, and the variation in this variable was then explained in terms of the variation in a number of independent variables. That is, we have implicitly assumed that the variation in each of the independent variables requires no explanation – these variables are given or fixed (non-stochastic) and thus are of no further interest. However, it must be recognised that such an approach will generally represent a considerable abstraction from reality. In particular, it will often be

278

the case that some of the independent variables themselves will be of interest to the investigator and thus their variation will also require explanation.

We could relax the assumption of non-stochastic independent variables and assume that each independent variable is itself determined by some model (and therefore that each independent variable is stochastic). However, provided we can assume that the models that determine each of the independent variables have no bearing or influence on the dependent variable of interest, then, in effect, no estimation problems arise, and our usual estimation methods can be employed. That is, assuming that the independent variables are determined in some entirely unrelated context implies that they are independent of the disturbance term in the model, therefore allowing the valid application of ordinary least squares. However, in practice, it will often be more realistic to assume that the models that explain some (or all) of the independent variables are indeed related to the dependent variable. The most explicit form of such a relationship is the case of the dependent variable itself appearing as an explanatory variable in some of these models. That is, we must consider the possibility of **feedback** effects occurring between the dependent and some of the independent variables.

A simple example concerns the estimation of the consumption function, which we have considered at various points in this book (see Examples 2.1, 2.2, 4.3, and 5.3). For simplicity, we will only consider the naive formulation of the consumption function. That is:

$$C_t = \alpha + \beta D_t + \varepsilon_t \qquad\qquad \text{Equation 6.1}$$

where $C_t$ denotes consumption expenditure in year $t$ and $D_t$ is aggregate disposable income in year $t$.

Now, estimating Equation 6.1 by ordinary least squares (as we did in Example 2.1, for example) implicitly assumes that the level of $D_t$ is determined independently of the level of $C_t$. Note that we would certainly expect $D_t$ to be stochastic, and we would also expect that an explanation of the variation in the level of aggregate income over time will be of some importance to forecasters and policy-makers. But is the assumption of the independent determination of $D_t$ and $C_t$ a reasonable one? Clearly not, for the level of aggregate income in the economy must be determined, in part, by the level of consumers' expenditure. Thus an increase in consumption expenditure will lead to an increased level of economic activity which in turn will result in increased aggregate income. This increased income will then lead directly to a further increase in consumption expenditure via the consumption function, thus again increasing economic activity and hence income, and so on. Indeed, it is precisely this type of feedback effect that Keynes formalised via the multiplier mechanism.

Consequently, it will be much more realistic to assume that $C_t$ and $D_t$ are determined simultaneously, and a model must therefore be constructed to reflect this simultaneity. As we will show in Section 6.3, if this simultaneity is

ignored and Equation 6.1 estimated by ordinary least squares, then not only
will biased parameter estimators be produced but these estimators will also be
inconsistent. This will be the case irrespective of how complex a consumption
function formulation is used, provided that this formulation includes a term
in $D_t$. Note that the consumption function that we have so far specified and
estimated in our previous examples have all included a term in $D_t$ and thus it
could be argued that each of these functions has been inconsistently
estimated. Thus we require a methodology for modelling the simultaneous
determination of two (or more) variables.

Just as in the case of single equation models, the construction of
simultaneous equation models will be based upon considerations of economic
theory, and competing theories will produce different models. So any given
simultaneous equation model will be only as good as the theory used to
construct that model.

We will continue with our example of modelling the joint determination of
consumption and income. Consider the following simple three-equation
model:

$$C_t = \alpha_0 + \alpha_1(Y_t - T_t) + \varepsilon_{1t} \qquad\qquad \text{Equation 6.2}$$

$$I_t = \beta_1 Y_{t-1} + \beta_2 R_t + \varepsilon_{2t} \qquad\qquad \text{Equation 6.3}$$

$$Y_t = C_t + I_t + G_t \qquad\qquad \text{Equation 6.4}$$

where

$C_t$ = Consumers' expenditure in year $t$.
$I_t$ = Investment expenditure in year $t$.
$Y_t$ = National income in year $t$.
$T_t$ = Tax receipts in year $t$.
$R_t$ = Interest rate in year $t$.
$G_t$ = Government expenditure in year $t$.
$\varepsilon_{1t}, \varepsilon_{2t}$ = Disturbance terms.

Equation 6.2 is a simple consumption function in which tax receipts are
now explicitly included and thus $Y_t - T_t$ represents disposable income, as
previously. The final equation – Equation 6.4 – is an identity which is required
for the internal consistency of the model. It simply states that, by definition,
aggregate income must be equivalent to the sum of consumption, investment
and government expenditures. However, in defining aggregate income two
additional variables are introduced – investment and government
expenditure. Therefore we must decide whether these variables also require
explanation and hence whether additional equations are required.

We have assumed that investment is determined simultaneously with
consumption and income, and therefore Equation 6.3 is added, where it is
postulated that the level of investment is determined by lagged income and
the interest rate. Conversely, we have assumed that government expenditure

is determined outside the model: it might be argued that the government authorities reach their expenditure decisions independently of the levels of consumption, income and investment. (A similar argument might also be used in the case of $T_t$, and thus we do not require an equation for $T_t$.) Note also that in specifying the investment function in Equation 6.3 a further variable has been introduced, namely the interest rate. As in the case of government expenditure and taxes we have assumed that $R_t$ is determined outside the model and an equation for $R_t$ is not therefore required (the argument might be that the monetary authorities have full control over $R_t$ and set its level independently of the other variables in the model).

The above model, then, contains three simultaneously determined variables – $C_t$, $I_t$ and $Y_t$. These variables are referred to as **endogenous** variables, and the minimum requirement for the correct specification of any simultaneous equation model is that it contains as many equations as it does endogenous variables; each endogenous variable requires an equation explaining its variation. $R_t$, $T_t$ and $G_t$ are all held to be determined independently of the endogenous variables and are referred to as **exogenous** variables. By definition, all exogenous variables are independent of the disturbance terms in the model. The model also contains a lagged endogenous variable, $Y_{t-1}$, and this variable can also, in a sense, be treated as exogenous – its level is determined prior to the current time period. All strictly exogenous variables and lagged endogenous variables are referred to as **predetermined** variables.

Clearly this model is a highly simplified representation of the workings of the economy, and it is used here purely for illustrative purposes. However the process of constructing even so simple a model still serves the purpose of highlighting some of the basic difficulties and ambiguities of simultaneous equation model building.

We have argued that $R_t$, $T_t$ and $G_t$ are all strictly exogenous. However it might also be argued that each of these variables will be influenced, to some extent, by the other variables in the model. For example, government expenditure on unemployment benefits will depend directly on the level of unemployment, which in turn will depend on the level of economic activity in the economy ($Y_t$). That is, it could be argued that $G_t$ is partially endogenous. But once the unemployment rate is introduced into the model then an equation explaining the level of unemployment will be required, which will presumably introduce further variables, and in effect a sub-model explaining the workings of the labour market will be built up. Similarly, the level of $R_t$ will be influenced, in part, by the operation of the money market, and thus a model of the money market will be required.

That is, while it may be the case that the central authorities have some control over $R_t$, $T_t$ and $G_t$, there may be components of these variables which are beyond their control. Further, it might also be argued that even if these variables can be fully controlled by government, the decisions made concerning their levels will none the less be influenced by the state of the economy, and thus in this sense these variables can be interpreted as being determined by the model rather than outside it.

Indeed, it is difficult to conceive of any variable in the economy which could be defined as being strictly exogenous. However, as we shall see, in order to estimate a simultaneous equation model it is first necessary to categorise the variables in the model as either endogenous or exogenous. Therefore, in practice, a variable will be defined as exogenous if it can be assumed that its level is primarily determined outside the model – exogeneity can be more usefully considered as a relative rather than an absolute concept.

Thus in constructing a simultaneous equation model the categorisation of all relevant variables as endogenous or exogenous will determine the size and complexity of the model. The model in Equations 6.2 to 6.4 is also expressed in highly aggregated terms. Recall that in Example 5.3 we argued that it is appropriate to distinguish between consumption on durables and non-durables. Therefore, strictly, separate equations for these two consumption components are required, thus introducing additional variables, and hence further increasing the size of the model. Similarly, investment expenditure consists of a number of distinct components which should each be modelled separately, thus requiring the disaggregation of Equation 6.3. Our model also excludes a foreign sector which, for any trading nation, will presumably be of some importance in influencing the level of economic activity. That is, if we are to construct a realistic model of the economy such a model will contain many more equations and variables than is the case here. For example, the Treasury model of the UK economy contains over 500 equations and 750 variables (although it is a relatively large model compared to other operational models of the UK economy).

Returning to our highly simplified model in Equations 6.2 to 6.4, we will now examine the way in which this model can be re-expressed so as to highlight a number of underlying features of the economy which is being modelled.

The particular form of the model shown in equations 6.2 to 6.4 is referred to as the **structural** form of the model. It contains two **behavioural** equations (the consumption and investment functions) and an **identity**. The structural form directly reflects the theory used to construct the model – it reflects the theoretical relationships which are posited to exist amongst the variables.

However, the structural form is somewhat inconvenient for examining a number of issues. For example, consider the effect on an endogenous variable of a change in the level of one of the exogenous (or policy) variables – say, the effect of an increase in the level of government expenditure on the level of income (that is, the government expenditure multiplier). Let the increase in $G_t$ be denoted by $\delta$. From Equation 6.4 this increase in $G_t$ would directly result in an initial increase in $Y_t$ of $\delta$. This increased level of $Y_t$ would feed into the consumption function, increasing the level of consumption by $\alpha_1\delta$. A second-round increase in $Y_t$ would then occur via this increased level of $C_t$ in Equation 6.4, which again would feed back into the consumption function, further increasing consumption by $\alpha_1(\alpha_1\delta) = \alpha_1^2\delta$. Income would again be increased via Equation 6.4, and this process would continue until the initial increase of $\delta$ had died out. Thus the total increase in $Y_t$ as a result of the increase of $\delta$ in $G_t$ is:

$$\delta + \alpha_1\delta + \alpha_1^2\delta + \alpha_1^3\delta + \dots$$

$$= \delta(1 + \alpha_1 + \alpha_1^2 + \alpha_1^3 + \dots)$$

$$= \frac{1}{1-\alpha_1}\delta$$

using the expression for the sum of a geometric sequence where $\alpha_1$ (the marginal propensity to consume) is assumed to be less than one.

The coefficient on $\delta$ in the above expression is the familiar Keynesian multiplier, but it has been derived in a somewhat tedious manner. Similarly, we may also wish to determine the effects of a change in $G_t$ on $C_t$ and $I_t$, or the effects of changes in $R_t$ and $T_t$ on $C_t$, $I_t$ and $Y_t$. To determine these effects in the above way is clearly inconvenient, and so we define another form of the model – the **reduced form** – which allows the direct evaluation of all the various multipliers in the model.

The reduced form is derived by expressing each endogenous variable in terms only of **predetermined** variables. The process is a purely algebraic one. Thus we first note that the investment function is already in its reduced form. To obtain the reduced form equation for $C_t$ we substitute Equation 6.3 into Equation 6.4, substitute the resulting expression for $Y_t$ into Equation 6.2 and then solve for $C_t$. Finally, the reduced form equation for $Y_t$ is obtained by substituting Equations 6.2 and 6.3 into Equation 6.4 and then solving for $Y_t$. Thus the reduced form of the model can be written as follows:

$$C_t = \frac{\alpha_0}{1-\alpha_1} + \frac{\alpha_1\beta_1}{1-\alpha_1}Y_{t-1} + \frac{\alpha_1\beta_2}{1-\alpha_1}R_t + \frac{\alpha_1}{1-\alpha_1}(G_t - T_t)$$

$$+ \frac{\varepsilon_{1t} + \alpha_1\varepsilon_{2t}}{1-\alpha_1} \qquad\qquad \text{Equation 6.5}$$

$$I_t = \beta_1 Y_{t-1} + \beta_2 R_t + \varepsilon_{2t} \qquad\qquad \text{Equation 6.6}$$

$$Y_t = \frac{\alpha_0}{1-\alpha_1} + \frac{\beta_1}{1-\alpha_1}Y_{t-1} + \frac{\beta_2}{1-\alpha_1}R_t + \frac{1}{1-\alpha_1}G_t - \frac{\alpha_1}{1-\alpha_1}T_t$$

$$+ \frac{\varepsilon_{1t} + \varepsilon_{2t}}{1-\alpha_1} \qquad\qquad \text{Equation 6.7}$$

The coefficients on each of the exogenous variables in the reduced form are referred to as **impact multipliers** – they measure the total effect on each of the endogenous variables of changes in the exogenous variables (note the government expenditure multiplier as the coefficient on $G_t$ in equation 6.7).

As we shall see when we discuss the estimation of simultaneous equation models in Sections 6.3 and 6.4, a central issue concerns the estimation of the structural form versus the estimation of the reduced form. Both forms of the model provide different (although related) sets of information but, as we shall show, it is easier to derive an estimate of the reduced form. However, given an estimate of the reduced form, it will not necessarily be the case that we will be able to derive estimates of the structural parameters in Equations 6.2 to 6.4 (the problem of **identification**).

If the structural form contains lagged endogenous variables (and is therefore a dynamic simultaneous equation model), then it will also be of interest to examine the **time paths** of each of the endogenous variables. This can be achieved by deriving the **fundamental dynamic equation** for each endogenous variable – that is, expressing each endogenous variable in terms only of lagged values of itself and current and lagged values of the exogenous variables. Thus note that the reduced form equation for $Y_t$ (Equation 6.7) is also the fundamental dynamic equation for $Y_t$. The fundamental dynamic equations for $C_t$ and $I_t$ can be derived by algebraically manipulating the structural and reduced forms (this is left as an exercise for the reader).

From the fundamental dynamic equations each endogenous variable can finally be expressed in terms only of current and lagged values of the exogenous variables (plus the initial values of the endogenous variables). Thus from Equation 6.7 we can deduce that:

$$Y_t = \xi_t + \xi_0 Y_0 + \psi_t R_t + \psi_{t-1} R_{t-1} + \ldots + \psi_1 R_1$$
$$+ \eta_t G_t + \eta_{t-1} G_{t-1} + \ldots + \eta_1 G_1 + \zeta_t T_t + \zeta_{t-1} T_{t-1} + \ldots$$
$$+ \zeta_1 T_1 + u_t$$

where the coefficients in this equation are just functions of the original structural parameters, $u_t$ is a (complex) disturbance term and $Y_0$ is the initial (or given) value of $Y$. This equation is referred to as the **final form** equation for $Y_t$, and expressing each endogenous variable in this form produces the final form of the model. Thus note that from the final form we can deduce the way in which the current and past values of the exogenous variables affect the current levels of the endogenous variables. We can also examine the stability of the model (and hence the stability of the economy (industry, market) being modelled).

In summary, then, the structural form of the model directly reflects the economic theory which has been used to construct the model. The reduced form of the model allows the direct examination of the short-term properties of the model (that is, the effects on the current levels of the endogenous variables of current changes in the exogenous variables). The final form of the model allows the examination of the long-run properties of the model (the effect of past changes in the exogenous variables on the current levels of the endogenous variables, and the effect of current changes in the exogenous variables on future levels of the endogenous variables).

We will now go on to discuss the estimation of simultaneous equation models.

## 6.3 The Identification Problem

As we indicated above, the direct application of ordinary least squares to each structural form equation will generally produce biased and inconsistent estimators. However, estimation of the reduced form is generally more straightforward.

The identification problem, then, is concerned with the possibility of indirectly deriving estimates of the structural parameters (the coefficients in Equations 6.2 to 6.4) from the estimates of the reduced form parameters (the coefficients on the exogenous and the lagged endogenous variables in Equations 6.5 to 6.7). As Equations 6.5 to 6.7 explicitly show, the reduced form parameters are simply functions of the structural parameters. Hence it may be possible to solve for some or all of the structural parameters from the estimate of the reduced form, and thereby identify these parameters.

In order to simplify our discussion we will now consider an even simpler model than that in Equations 6.2 to 6.4. Thus consider the following model:

$$C_t = \alpha_0 + \alpha_1 Y_t + \varepsilon_{1t} \qquad\qquad \text{Equation 6.8}$$

$$I_t = \beta_0 + \beta_1 R_t + \varepsilon_{2t} \qquad\qquad \text{Equation 6.9}$$

$$Y_t = C_t + I_t \qquad\qquad \text{Equation 6.10}$$

where the notation is the same as previously. That is, we will ignore the role of government and use a simpler specification of the investment function.

From the model in Equations 6.8 to 6.10 we can now see why the ordinary least squares estimation of the consumption function will produce inconsistent estimators. Thus note from Equation 6.10 that $Y_t$ depends directly on $C_t$. In turn, $C_t$ depends on $\varepsilon_{1t}$ (from Equation 6.8) and thus $Y_t$ must also be a function of $\varepsilon_{1t}$. Therefore, as $Y_t$ and $\varepsilon_{1t}$ are related then one of the assumptions of the simple regression model is violated and the application of ordinary least squares will result in inconsistent parameter estimators.[1] Appendix 6.1 provides a more detailed discussion. However, note that the investment function in the above model depends only on a single exogenous variable ($R_t$) and hence no difficulties arise in the estimation of this equation – $R_t$ and $\varepsilon_{2t}$ are independent, by assumption.

Generally, however, some of the explanatory variables in each equation of a simultaneous equation model will appear as endogenous (or dependent) variables elsewhere in the model. This will result in correlation between such explanatory variables and the disturbance terms and hence render the application of ordinary least squares invalid. Alternative estimation methods are therefore required.

Now, as the reduced form of a model expresses each endogenous variable in terms only of predetermined variables, then ordinary least squares can be applied to each reduced form equation, thus producing consistent estimators of the reduced form parameters. That is, even if lagged endogenous variables appear in the reduced form equations least squares will still produce consistent (although generally biased) estimators provided the disturbance terms are random (recall the discussion of dynamic models in Section 5.5 of Chapter 5).

However, as the reduced form parameters are only functions of the structural parameters a potential method for deriving an estimate of the structural form suggests itself – that is, to express each structural parameter in terms of the consistent estimates of the reduced form parameters. This, then, is the essence of the identification problem – is it possible to solve for the structural parameters uniquely in terms of the reduced form parameters? As we shall now go on to see, this is a far from trivial question and the answer will depend on the precise structure of the model.

Consider again the simple three-equation model in Equations 6.8 to 6.10. Now, the concept of identification relates to each structural equation – can the parameters of each structural equation be identified from the reduced form? The problem, therefore, does not arise with identities, as identities do not contain unknown parameters. Consequently it is not necessary to examine Equation 6.10 with respect to its identification status.

In order to assess the identification status of each behavioural equation the easiest way of dealing with the identity is to substitute it into the two behavioural equations, thus effectively reducing the size of the model by one equation. Thus substituting Equation 6.10 into Equation 6.8 and re-arranging, the model can now be written as:

$$C_t = \frac{\alpha_0}{1-\alpha_1} + \frac{\alpha_1}{1-\alpha_1}I_t + \frac{\varepsilon_{1t}}{1-\alpha_1} \qquad\qquad \text{Equation 6.11}$$

$$I_t = \beta_0 + \beta_1 R_t + \varepsilon_{2t} \qquad\qquad \text{Equation 6.12}$$

As the model contains only one predetermined variable ($R_t$) the reduced form equations for $C_t$ and $I_t$ are:

$$C_t = a + bR_t + U_{1t} \qquad\qquad \text{Equation 6.13}$$

$$I_t = c + dR_t + U_{2t} \qquad\qquad \text{Equation 6.14}$$

where $a$, $b$, $c$ and $d$ are the reduced form parameters, which in turn are functions of the structural parameters $\alpha_0$, $\alpha_1$, $\beta_0$ and $\beta_1$. It is straightforward to show that, given the model in Equations 6.8 to 6.10 (or equivalently, Equations 6.11 and 6.12), then we must have:

$$a = \frac{\alpha_0 + \alpha_1 \beta_0}{1 - \alpha_1} \qquad b = \frac{\beta_1 \alpha_1}{1 - \alpha_1}$$

$$c = \beta_0 \qquad\qquad d = \beta_1$$

(this is left as an exercise for the reader). $U_{1t}$ and $U_{2t}$ are disturbance terms which are simply linear functions of the original disturbances, $\varepsilon_{1t}$ and $\varepsilon_{2t}$. That is:

$$U_{1t} = \frac{\alpha_1 \varepsilon_{2t} + \varepsilon_{1t}}{1 - \alpha_1} \qquad U_{2t} = \varepsilon_{2t}$$

We can apply ordinary least squares to Equations 6.13 and 6.14 and obtain consistent (and in this case, unbiased) estimators of $a$, $b$, $c$ and $d$. Thus, as we indicated previously, we can see immediately that no difficulties arise with the investment function – the reduced form equation for $I_t$ is equivalent to its structural equation and thus consistent estimators of $\beta_0$ and $\beta_1$ can be derived directly. This must be the case for any structural equation in which all explanatory variables are predetermined (although such equations should be interpreted as special cases).

Now consider the consumption function. We have two expressions for $C_t$ – the structural equation (Equation 6.11) and the reduced form equation (Equation 6.13). Equating these we can write:

$$a + bR_t + U_{1t} = \frac{\alpha_0}{1 - \alpha_1} + \frac{\alpha_1}{1 - \alpha_1} I_t + \frac{\varepsilon_{1t}}{1 - \alpha_1}$$

Substituting the reduced form equation for $I_t$ (Equation 6.14) and rearranging produces:

$$a + bR_t + U_{1t} = \frac{\alpha_0 + \alpha_1 c}{1 - \alpha_1} + \frac{\alpha_1 d}{1 - \alpha_1} R_t + \frac{\alpha_1 U_{2t} + \varepsilon_{1t}}{1 - \alpha_1} \qquad\qquad \text{Equation 6.15}$$

Noting that

$$U_{1t} = \frac{\alpha_1 \varepsilon_{2t} + \varepsilon_{1t}}{1 - \alpha_1} \quad \text{and} \quad U_{2t} = \varepsilon_{2t}$$

the two disturbance terms in Equation 6.15 must therefore cancel.

Equating the coefficients in Equation 6.15 we can now write:

$$a = \frac{\alpha_0 + \alpha_1 c}{1 - \alpha_1} \qquad\qquad \text{Equation 6.16}$$

$$b = \frac{\alpha_1 d}{1 - \alpha_1} \qquad\qquad \text{Equation 6.17}$$

Solving for $\alpha_0$ and $\alpha_1$ from Equations 6.16 and 6.17 we have:

$$\alpha_0 = \frac{ad-bc}{d+b}$$

Equation 6.18

and

$$\alpha_1 = \frac{b}{d+b}$$

Equation 6.19

Thus $\alpha_0$ and $\alpha_1$ can be expressed directly in terms of the reduced form parameters and we can conclude that the consumption function is identified. Note that in comparing the reduced form and structural equations for $C_t$, two equations were produced (Equations 6.16 and 6.17) which contained just two unknowns ($\alpha_0$ and $\alpha_1$). Consequently $\alpha_0$ and $\alpha_1$ could be expressed uniquely in terms of the reduced form parameters. The consumption function here, then, is referred to as being **exactly** identified. We can then go on to obtain estimates of $\alpha_0$ and $\alpha_1$ by first obtaining the least squares estimates of $a$, $b$, $c$ and $d$ – $\hat{a}$, $\hat{b}$, $\hat{c}$ and $\hat{d}$ – and substituting these estimates into Equations 6.18 and 6.19.

Thus, given the simultaneous equation model in Equations 6.8 to 6.10, we have established that each of the behavioural equations is exactly identified. This means that we can indirectly derive consistent estimators of the structural parameters by first obtaining the least squares estimate of the reduced form of the model. For this reason, this method of estimating the structural parameters is generally referred to as the method of **indirect least squares**. If the model does not contain any lagged endogenous variables then the estimators of the reduced form parameters must be unbiased, but it can be shown that this property does not carry over to the derived estimators of the structural parameters – these estimators will only be consistent.[2]

Now consider a slight modification to this model. In particular, we will introduce government expenditure – $G_t$ – as an exogenous variable but allow it to enter only via the identity. Thus the model becomes:

$$C_t = \alpha_0 + \alpha_1 Y_t + \varepsilon_{1t}$$

Equation 6.20

$$I_t = \beta_0 + \beta_1 R_t + \varepsilon_{2t}$$

Equation 6.21

$$Y_t = C_t + I_t + G_t$$

Equation 6.22

Again, substituting the identity into the remainder of the model, the investment function remains unchanged and the consumption function becomes:

$$C_t = \frac{\alpha_0}{1-\alpha_1} + \frac{\alpha_1}{1-\alpha_1} I_t + \frac{\alpha_1}{1-\alpha_1} G_t + \frac{\varepsilon_{1t}}{1-\alpha_1}$$

Equation 6.23

The reduced form of the model can be written as:

$$C_t = a' + b'R_t + c'G_t + U'_{1t}$$

Equation 6.24

$$I_t = d' + e'R_t + U'_{2t}$$

Equation 6.25

As previously, no difficulties arise in the estimation of the investment function – the structural form of the investment function is equivalent to its reduced form and therefore $\beta_0$ and $\beta_1$ can be estimated directly by ordinary least squares.

In order to examine the identification status of the consumption function we first equate the right-hand sides of Equations 6.23 and 6.24, and then substitute Equation 6.25 for $I_t$, producing:

$$a' + b'R_t + c'G_t + U'_{1t} = \frac{\alpha_0 + \alpha_1 d'}{1 - \alpha_1} + \frac{\alpha_1 e'}{1 - \alpha_1} R_t + \frac{\alpha_1}{1 - \alpha_1} G_t$$

$$+ \frac{\alpha_1 U'_{2t} + \varepsilon_{1t}}{1 - \alpha_1}$$

Equation 6.26

Again, the two disturbance terms cancel. Equating coefficients, we have:

$$a' = \frac{\alpha_0 + \alpha_1 d'}{1 - \alpha_1}$$

Equation 6.27

$$b' = \frac{\alpha_1 e'}{1 - \alpha_1}$$

Equation 6.28

$$c' = \frac{\alpha_1}{1 - \alpha_1}$$

Equation 6.29

Now, we can solve for $\alpha_1$ directly from Equation 6.28. That is:

$$\alpha_1 = \frac{b'}{e' + b'}$$

Equation 6.30

But note from Equation 6.29 that we can also write:

$$\alpha_1 = \frac{c'}{1 + c'}$$

Equation 6.31

Therefore, given the least squares estimates of $a'$, $b'$ and $e'$ two estimates of $\alpha_1$ will be available, one derived from Equation 6.30 and one derived from Equation 6.31, and, in general, these estimates will not be the same. Given two estimates of $\alpha_1$ then two estimates of $\alpha_0$ can also be derived from Equation 6.27.

The structural form equation for $C_t$ is therefore said to be **over**-identified. That is, in comparing the reduced form and structural form equations for $C_t$ three equations are produced (Equations 6.27, 6.28 and 6.29) in only two unknowns. In this sense, too much information is available to solve uniquely for the structural parameters. In practice this does not present any difficulties as estimation methods are available which, in effect, optimally combine this information to produce unique estimates of the structural parameters. These methods will be discussed in Section 6.4.

Finally, consider a third version of the model where $G_t$ is omitted, $R_t$ now appears as an explanatory variable in the consumption function (as $C_t$ represents total consumers' expenditure then it might be argued that $R_t$ influences expenditure on consumer durables), and investment expenditure is held to depend only on the level of aggregate income.[3] Thus the model becomes:

$$C_t = \alpha_0 + \alpha_1 Y_t + \alpha_2 R_t + \varepsilon_{1t} \qquad\qquad \text{Equation 6.32}$$

$$I_t = \beta_0 + \beta_1 Y_t + \varepsilon_{2t} \qquad\qquad\qquad \text{Equation 6.33}$$

$$Y_t = C_t + I_t \qquad\qquad\qquad\qquad \text{Equation 6.34}$$

Substituting Equation 6.34 into Equations 6.32 and 6.33 we have:

$$C_t = \frac{\alpha_0}{1-\alpha_1} + \frac{\alpha_1}{1-\alpha_1} I_t + \frac{\alpha_2}{1-\alpha_1} R_t + \frac{\varepsilon_{1t}}{1-\alpha_1} \qquad \text{Equation 6.35}$$

$$I_t = \frac{\beta_0}{1-\beta_1} + \frac{\beta_1}{1-\beta_1} C_t + \frac{\varepsilon_{2t}}{1-\beta_1} \qquad\qquad \text{Equation 6.36}$$

The reduced form equations for $C_t$ and $I_t$ can be written as:

$$C_t = a'' + b'' R_t + U_{1t}'' \qquad\qquad\qquad \text{Equation 6.37}$$

$$I_t = c'' + d'' R_t + U_{2t}'' \qquad\qquad\qquad \text{Equation 6.38}$$

First consider the consumption function. Equating the right-hand sides of Equations 6.35 and 6.37 and substituting Equation 6.38 for $I_t$ produces:

$$a'' + b'' R_t + U_{1t}'' = \frac{\alpha_0 + \alpha_1 c''}{1-\alpha_1} + \frac{\alpha_1 d'' + \alpha_2}{1-\alpha_1} R_t + \frac{\alpha_1 U_{2t}'' + \varepsilon_{2t}}{1-\alpha_1} \qquad \text{Equation 6.39}$$

The disturbance terms again cancel, and equating coefficients we have:

$$a'' = \frac{\alpha_0 + \alpha_1 c''}{1-\alpha_1} \qquad\qquad\qquad \text{Equation 6.40}$$

$$b'' = \frac{\alpha_1 d'' + \alpha_2}{1-\alpha_1} \qquad\qquad\qquad \text{Equation 6.41}$$

Note that we now only have two equations to solve for the three unknown structural parameters $\alpha_0$, $\alpha_1$, and $\alpha_2$. Thus we cannot obtain consistent estimators for the parameters of the consumption function, and the consumption function is therefore referred to as being **under**-identified – not enough information is available to allow the identification of $\alpha_0$, $\alpha_1$ and $\alpha_2$.

Now consider the investment function. Equating the right-hand sides of Equations 6.36 and 6.38 and substituting the reduced form equation for $C_t$

(Equation 6.37) produces:

$$c'' + d'' R_t + U_{2t}'' = \frac{\beta_0 + \beta_1 a''}{1 - \beta_1} + \frac{\beta_1 b''}{1 - \beta_1} R_t + \frac{\beta_1 U_{1t}'' + \varepsilon_{2t}}{1 - \beta_1} \qquad \text{Equation 6.42}$$

Equating coefficients (the disturbance terms cancel) we have:

$$c'' = \frac{\beta_0 + \beta_1 a''}{1 - \beta_1} \qquad \text{Equation 6.43}$$

$$d'' = \frac{\beta_1 b''}{1 - \beta_1} \qquad \text{Equation 6.44}$$

We now have two equations in two unknowns and we can solve uniquely for $\beta_0$ and $\beta_1$. That is:

$$\beta_0 = \frac{c'' b'' - a'' d''}{b'' + d''} \qquad \text{Equation 6.45}$$

and

$$\beta_1 = \frac{d''}{b'' + d''} \qquad \text{Equation 6.46}$$

Thus we can conclude that the investment function is **exactly** identified.

We will now consider an alternative interpretation of the identification problem in the context of this example. Thus consider once again the model as expessed in Equations 6.35 and 6.36, and for simplicity, ignore the disturbance terms. Note, that by assumption, this is the true model of the economy, and therefore any set of sample observations on $C_t$ and $I_t$ must have been generated by Equations 6.35 and 6.36 (or, equivalently, by Equations 6.32 and 6.33, together with the condition in Equation 6.34).

Consider adding together Equations 6.35 and 6.36. Ignoring the disturbance terms, and rearranging this composite equation so that $C_t$ is expressed in terms of $I_t$ and $R_t$ produces:

$$C_t = \frac{\alpha_0(1 - \beta_1) + \beta_0(1 - \alpha_1)}{(1 - 2\beta_1)(1 - \alpha_1)} - \frac{(2\alpha_1 - 1)(1 - \beta_1)}{(1 - 2\beta_1)(1 - \alpha_1)} I_t + \frac{\alpha_2(1 - \beta_1)}{(1 - 2\beta_1)(1 - \alpha_1)} R_t$$

$$\text{Equation 6.47}$$

Now, assume a set of sample observations is available on all the variables specified in the model. As Equation 6.47 is simply a linear combination of Equations 6.35 and 6.36, and as these two equations can be interpreted as having generated the data, then Equation 6.47 must also be perfectly consistent with the data. That is, given the values of the structural parameters, substituting the set of observations on $I_t$ and $R_t$ into Equation 6.35 will produce the actual series on $C_t$, and this will also be the case for Equation 6.47. However, note that although the data will exactly satisfy both Equations

**292**    *An Introduction to Simultaneous Equation Models*

6.35 and 6.47, the values of the constant term and the coefficients on $I_t$ and $R_t$ in these two equations must necessarily be different.

But of course the point here is that we do not know the true values of the structural parameters. Thus, consider the hypothetical situation of the values of the composite coefficients on $I_t$ and $R_t$ in both Equations 6.35 and 6.47 being made available to us (by some omniscient economic modeller, say). However, given this information, we are not told which equation is which – all we have is two equations 'explaining' $C_t$ in terms of $I_t$ and $R_t$, both of these equations being perfectly consistent with the data. Is it then possible to deduce the values of the original structural parameters? Clearly not, for how can we determine which of these two equations is the true consumption function in Equation 6.35? All that we can confirm is that both equations are consistent with the data and therefore that they have both been derived from the true model.

Further, any linear combination of Equations 6.35 and 6.36 will produce a data-consistent equation so there is potentially an infinite number of equations in which $C_t$ is a function of $I_t$ and $R_t$ and which are also data-consistent. All that we can do when presented with a candidate for consideration as an estimate of the consumption function is to confirm that it contains only $I_t$ and $R_t$ as independent variables, and to reject from further consideration any equation which does not satisfy the data. However we have no means of discriminating amongst the class of data-consistent consumption equations. Thus we conclude that the consumption function in this model is under-identified – the true consumption function cannot be distinguished from any linear combination of Equations 6.35 and 6.36, and therefore it is impossible to deduce the values of the structural parameters.

However, no such problem occurs with the investment function. By definition (Equation 6.36), $I_t$ is a function only of $C_t$ and thus it is only equations of this form that can be considered as potential investment functions. But there will only be one such equation which will also be consistent with the data – Equation 6.36 itself. That is, there is only one investment equation which is consistent with both the model and the data, and this is the linear combination of Equations 6.35 and 6.36 which attaches a weight of zero to Equation 6.35 and a weight of one to Equation 6.36. All other combinations attaching a non-zero weight to Equation 6.35 must produce an equation containing $R_t$ which, by definition, cannot be an investment function. Further, as there are two coefficients in Equation 6.36, which in turn are functions of just two structural parameters, then we can conclude that the investment function is exactly identified.

Note that a similar interpretation can be placed on the over-identified consumption function in Equation 6.23 of the model considered previously. Thus there is only one linear combination of Equations 6.21 and 6.23 that can produce a consumption function which is both model and data-consistent (that combination which attaches a weight of zero to Equation 6.21, given that the consumption function cannot contain $R_t$). Therefore we can conclude that the consumption function is identified. In addition, as Equation 6.23 contains three coefficients in two structural parameters, the consumption function is over-identified.

Therefore, the first step in deriving valid estimates of the structural parameters of a simultaneous equation model is to ensure that each structural equation is either exactly or over-identified. However, the method we have so far used for establishing the identification status of each structural equation is clearly tedious (and will be more so, the larger is the model), and we will now outline a simplified procedure.

Note first that our above discussion implies that a structural equation will tend to be under-identified the larger the number of variables in that equation – that is, the larger is the number of structural parameters which require estimation. Thus the basic problem in estimating Equation 6.32 (or equivalently Equation 6.35) is that the structural equation for $C_t$ contains three parameters ($\alpha_0$, $\alpha_1$ and $\alpha_2$), but its corresponding reduced form equation (Equation 6.37) contains only two parameters ($a''$ and $b''$). Hence only two equations could be derived to solve for the three unknown structural parameters.

Now, in general, each reduced form equation will contain all the predetermined variables which appear in the model. If we let $K$ denote the number of predetermined variables in the model then each reduced form equation will contain $K+1$ parameters (that is, the $K$ coefficients on each of the predetermined variables plus a constant term).

Consider a given endogenous variable. Assume that the structural equation for this variable contains $H$ explanatory variables (some of which may be endogenous and some of which may be predetermined). Therefore there will be $H+1$ structural parameters to be estimated (the $H$ coefficients on each of the explanatory variables plus a constant term). Now, the corresponding reduced form equation for this endogenous variable will contain $K+1$ parameters, and thus we can solve for the $H+1$ structural parameters in terms of these $K+1$ reduced form parameters provided that:

$$K+1 \geqslant H+1$$

or

$$K \geqslant H \qquad\qquad\qquad \text{Equation 6.48}$$

If $K = H$ then the structural equation is exactly identified. If $K > H$ the equation is over-identified, and if $K < H$ then the equation is under-identified. This condition for identification is referred to as the **order** condition. Thus this condition can be stated as follows:

A given structural equation will be identified if the number of explanatory variables appearing in that equation is less than or equal to the number of predetermined variables in the model.

The reader should confirm that the application of this order condition to the three models which we discussed above (Equations 6.8 to 6.10, Equations 6.20 to 6.22 and Equations 6.32 to 6.34) leads to the same conclusions as were derived from the detailed algebraic analyses of these models. Clearly, applying this order condition for identification is considerably more straightforward than attempting to solve explicitly for each of the structural parameters in terms of the reduced form parameters. This order condition can be expressed in a number of alternative forms, the applications of which are more convenient still. Thus two further forms of the order condition are as follows:

> In a model containing $G$ equations, a given equation will be identified if at least $G-1$ of the variables appearing in the model are omitted from this equation.

> A given equation will be identified if the number of predetermined variables excluded from that equation is greater than or equal to the number of endogenous variables appearing in the equation (including the dependent variable) minus one.

(The derivation of these alternative forms of the order condition is left as an exercise for the reader.)

Note that the application of the last of these conditions does not require knowledge of how many endogenous variables appear in the model (or how many equations the model contains), and thus is particularly convenient in the case of large models.

Now, while the order condition is certainly straightforward to apply, its disadvantage is that it is only a necessary condition for identification and not a sufficient condition. That is, models can be constructed in which the parameters of a given equation are identified by the order condition, and yet it will not be possible to solve for the structural parameters in terms of the reduced form parameters. This will occur in those cases in which the equations produced by a comparison of the structural form and reduced form equations for some given endogenous variable (such as Equations 6.16 and 6.17, for example) are not independent. That is, the order condition simply ensures that at least as many equations as there are structural parameters can be derived, but it cannot guarantee that the information contained in these equations is independent. An example will clarify this point.

Consider again the model specified in Equations 6.32 to 6.34. Now, recall that the consumption function was under-identified as it contained two explanatory variables whereas the model contained only one predetermined variable. Thus it would appear that this identification problem could be resolved if an additional predetermined variable was somehow incorporated into the model. However, as we shall see, the introduction of such a variable must be justified theoretically and thus the form in which it is introduced into the model will be of central importance.

For illustrative purposes consider adding a further equation to Equations 6.32 to 6.34. This equation must (necessarily) contain an additional endogenous variable, but to keep the argument straightforward we will ensure that this endogenous variable is a function only of an additional predetermined variable. For argument's sake, let the additional endogenous variable be the rate of inflation $(F_t)$ and assume that $F_t$ depends only on the money supply $(M_t)$, where $M_t$ is exogenous (that is, $M_t$ is assumed to be under the control of the central banking authorities). Thus, ignoring disturbance terms, the revised model becomes:

$$C_t = \alpha_0 + \alpha_1 Y_t + \alpha_2 R_t \qquad\qquad \text{Equation 6.49}$$

$$I_t = \beta_0 + \beta_1 Y_t \qquad\qquad \text{Equation 6.50}$$

$$F_t = \gamma_0 + \gamma_1 M_t \qquad\qquad \text{Equation 6.51}$$

$$Y_t = C_t + I_t \qquad\qquad \text{Equation 6.52}$$

The consumption function still contains two explanatory variables but the model now contains two predetermined variables $(R_t$ and $M_t)$. Thus according to the order condition the consumption function is exactly identified. Therefore, we should be able to go on to express $\alpha_0$, $\alpha_1$ and $\alpha_2$ in terms of the reduced parameters and thereby derive consistent estimators of these structural parameters. Proceeding as previously, the reduced form of the model in Equations 6.49 to 6.52 can be written as:

$$C_t = a + bR_t + cM_t \qquad\qquad \text{Equation 6.53}$$

$$I_t = d + eR_t + fM_t \qquad\qquad \text{Equation 6.54}$$

$$F_t = g + hR_t + kM_t \qquad\qquad \text{Equation 6.55}$$

Following the same algebraic procedures as previously, it is straightforward to show that the reduced form parameters of the consumption function can be expressed as:

$$a = \frac{\alpha_0 + \alpha_1 d}{1 - \alpha_1} \qquad\qquad \text{Equation 6.56}$$

$$b = \frac{\alpha_1 e + \alpha_2}{1 - \alpha_1} \qquad\qquad \text{Equation 6.57}$$

$$c = \frac{\alpha_1 f}{1 - \alpha_1} \qquad\qquad \text{Equation 6.58}$$

Thus, as expected, three equations are produced in the three unknown structural parameters.

However, consider explicitly deriving the reduced form equations for $C_t$ and $I_t$. Substituting Equation 6.52 into Equation 6.49 allows $C_t$ to be expressed as a function of $I_t$ and $R_t$. Substituting Equation 6.52 into Equation

6.50 allows $I_t$ to be expressed as a function of $C_t$. Thus we can deduce that the reduced form equation for $I_t$ will be a function only of $R_t$. But as $C_t$ can be expressed as a function of $I_t$ and $R_t$, then substitution of the reduced form equation for $I_t$ implies that the reduced form equation for $C_t$ will also be a function only of $R_t$. That is, in terms of the general statement of the reduced form in Equations 6.53 to 6.55 a closer examination of the structural form of the model allows us to conclude that:

$$c = f = 0$$

(similarly, it must also be the case that $h = 0$).

Given that $c = f = 0$ then Equation 6.58 is now meaningless with the result that only two equations are in fact available to solve for $\alpha_0$, $\alpha_1$ and $\alpha_2$. Therefore the consumption function still remains under-identified.

The problem that has occurred here is that the equation that was added to the original model (the 'inflation function' in Equation 6.51) is completely irrelevant in relation to the simultaneous determination of $C_t$, $I_t$ and $Y_t$. Neither $F_t$ nor $M_t$ appears in any other equation in the model and therefore there is no connection between Equation 6.51 and the remainder of the model. It is to be expected, then, that Equation 6.51 cannot provide any information that is relevant for the identification of the original structural equations.

Thus in constructing a simultaneous equation model not only must we ensure that each equation in the model makes theoretical sense (that is, that exactly the same principles are applied as in the specification of single equation models), but we must also ensure that each equation is theoretically relevant in relation to the remainder of the model. By definition, an endogenous variable is determined by the workings of the entire model and not just by the structural equation in which it appears as a dependent variable. This is precisely the confusion which occurred in the model in Equations 6.49 to 6.52. $F_t$ is not endogenous in terms of this model – it is exogenous in the sense that it is determined entirely independently of the model. As an exogenous variable it has no role to play in the model and its inclusion cannot therefore be justified.

It is possible to derive a condition for identification which is both necessary and sufficient. This condition is referred to as the **rank** condition for identification. However, this condition is complex to derive (and often complex to apply) and we will not provide a detailed discussion of its use here. In Appendix 6.2 we provide an informal description of the rank condition.

In general, the application of the rank condition, rather than simply establishing whether or not an equation is identified (as was the case in the model in Equations 6.49 to 6.52), will typically result in restrictions having to be placed on some of the parameters in the model. That is, the rank condition will imply that an equation is identified provided that some of parameters appearing elsewhere in the model do not take on certain pre-specified values. But of course as the investigator will not know the true parameter values such considerations are of theoretical rather than practical relevance. In practice, then, only the order condition is gradually examined, even though it is simply a sufficient condition for identification.

A further example will help to fix ideas.

## Example 6.1

A commonly used illustration of the under-identification problem concerns the estimation of supply and demand models. The simplest specification of such a model would be to assume that the level of demand for some commodity and the quantity supplied of this commodity are both functions only of the commodity's price. In particular, we would expect quantity demanded to be inversely related to price and quantity supplied to be positively related to price. Further, in the simplest form of such a model, we would assume that the market is always in equilibrium (the market continually clears) and hence that quantity demanded always equals quantity supplied. Thus, in a time series context, the model could be expressed as follows:

$$D_t = \alpha_0 + \alpha_1 P_t + \varepsilon_{1t} \qquad\qquad \text{Equation 6.59}$$

$$S_t = \beta_0 + \beta_1 P_t + \varepsilon_{2t} \qquad\qquad \text{Equation 6.60}$$

$$S_t = D_t = Q_t \qquad\qquad \text{Equation 6.61}$$

where:

$D_t$ = quantity demanded in time period $t$
$S_t$ = quantity supplied in time period $t$
$P_t$ = price in time period $t$
$Q_t$ = market clearing quantity

and $\varepsilon_{1t}$ and $\varepsilon_{2t}$ are disturbance terms.

*A priori* we would expect $\alpha_1 < 0$, and $\beta_1 > 0$.

The model can be reduced from three equations to two equations by substituting the market clearing assumption in Equation 6.61 into the remainder of the model. That is, an equivalent version of the model is:

Demand: $\quad Q_t = \alpha_0 + \alpha_1 P_t + \varepsilon_{1t} \qquad\qquad \text{Equation 6.62}$

Supply: $\quad Q_t = \beta_0 + \beta_1 P_t + \varepsilon_{2t} \qquad\qquad \text{Equation 6.63}$

We now have a two-equation model containing two endogenous variables, $Q_t$ and $P_t$. Thus we can see immediately that neither the demand nor the supply function is identified as the model does not contain any predetermined variables. (Note that, strictly, the original version of the model in Equations 6.59 to 6.61 is a four-equation model, with Equation 6.61 being a combination of the two equations $S_t = Q_t$ and $D_t = Q_t$. That is, the original version of the model contains four equations in four variables ($D_t$, $S_t$, $P_t$ and $Q_t$), and these variables are all endogenous, given that their levels are jointly determined within the model.)

We can derive the reduced form of the model in Equations 6.62 and 6.63 in order to examine the identification status of the structural equations. Thus the reduced form can be written as:

$$P_t = \frac{\alpha_0 - \beta_0}{\beta_1 - \alpha_1} + \frac{\varepsilon_{1t} - \varepsilon_{2t}}{\beta_1 - \alpha_1} \qquad \text{Equation 6.64}$$

$$Q_t = \frac{\alpha_0 \beta_1 - \alpha_1 \beta_0}{\beta_1 - \alpha_1} + \frac{\beta_1 - \alpha_1 \varepsilon_{2t}}{\beta_1 - \alpha_1} \qquad \text{Equation 6.65}$$

or

$$P_t = a + U_{1t} \qquad \text{Equation 6.66}$$

$$Q_t = b + U_{2t} \qquad \text{Equation 6.67}$$

That is, each reduced form equation consists only of a constant term and a disturbance term. We will therefore not be able to derive estimates of the four structural parameters ($\alpha_0$, $\alpha_1$, $\beta_0$ and $\beta_1$) from estimates of the two reduced form parameters ($a$ and $b$). The advantage of this simple example is that it allows for a direct interpretation of the reasons for the under-identification of the supply and demand functions.

To be concrete, consider the case of the market for some agricultural product – the market for oranges, say. Further assume that the model as specified in Equations 6.59 to 6.61 is considered to be an adequate description of the supply and demand forces governing this market.

Now consider the approach which might be used to estimate the parameters of the demand and supply functions in Equations 6.62 and 6.63. We first require a sample of data on price, quantity demanded and quantity supplied.

Assume that the investigator collects these data in a particular market by recording the average price of oranges during each of a sample of, say, 50 weeks, and also records the quantity of oranges sold in each of these weeks (which equals the quantity supplied as we assume that price always adjusts so as to clear the market). A series of observations on $P_t$ and $Q_t$ is thereby produced.

Now, the problem is that these price and quantity observations are observations on **equilibrium** price and quantity, and hence are neither exclusively generated by the supply function nor the demand function. What is being observed is the outcome of this equilibrating process, rather than the form that this process takes. Diagrammatically, a graph of these price and quantity observations would produce a scatter around the intersection of the supply and demand functions, such as in Figure 6.1. That is, it is clear from Figure 6.1 that it will not be possible to infer the form of the supply and

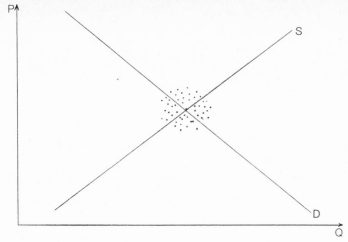

**Figure 6.1** A sample of observations on equilibrium price and quantity.

demand functions from the sample data, and hence we cannot identify the structural parameters.

We can of course validly estimate the reduced form parameters, $a$ and $b$, in Equations 6.66 and 6.67. Thus the least squares estimates of $a$ and $b$ will simply be the average of the price and quantity observations, respectively. That is:

$$\hat{a} = \bar{P} \qquad \text{Equation 6.68}$$

and

$$\hat{b} = \bar{Q} \qquad \text{Equation 6.69}$$

The estimate of the reduced form of this model, then, produces no more than estimates of equilibrium price and quantity, and no further inferences can be drawn concerning the nature of the supply and demand functions.

Note also the misleading conclusions which could be drawn if this problem of identification were not recognized. Thus assume that the investigator is unfamiliar with the concept of a simultaneous equation model, but collected data on price and quantity, as described above. The investigator then makes the further assumption that these data reflect the demand conditions in the market – the data measure the variation in the price of oranges over the 50-week period and the corresponding variation in the quantity of oranges demanded. The investigator then regresses $Q_t$ on $P_t$ in order to derive an estimate of the demand function. However, given the diagrammatic interpretation of the data in Figure 6.1, the likely outcome is that an insignificant relationship will be produced. The investigator may then be tempted to draw the erroneous conclusion that the demand for oranges appears to be insensitive to price and hence that the demand for oranges is perfectly inelastic.

Although the supply and demand model of the simple form shown in Equations 6.62 and 6.63 cannot be estimated by statistical means, it will be rare that such a simple formulation will be a reasonable description of reality. In turn, a more detailed theoretical specification will generally have the effect of improving the identification status of the model.

Consider again our example of a supply and demand model for oranges. Now, the demand function in Equation 6.62 is probably a reasonable description of the demand process – that is, it would seem reasonable to assume that current price is the sole determinant of the current demand for oranges. However, it might be argued that the supply function is somewhat unrealistic in that it assumes that the supply of oranges can respond immediately to any price changes. As is the case for any agricultural product, there will typically be some lag between changes in market price and the ability of farmers to respond to these price changes – the supply of oranges cannot be increased or decreased overnight. Consequently, a more realistic specification of the supply function would be to argue that the supply of oranges in time period $t$ is the result of planting decisions made in some previous time period, which in turn are a function of the market price prevailing at that time. Thus a more realistic model specification would be:

Demand:   $Q_t = \alpha_0 + \alpha_1 P_t + \varepsilon_{1t}$                Equation 6.70

Supply:   $Q_t = \beta_0 + \beta_1 P_{t-k} + \varepsilon_{2t}$               Equation 6.71

where $k$ denotes the length of time required by farmers to adjust supply. This amended model specification now contains a predetermined variable, $P_{t-k}$, and hence both equations are exactly identified by the order condition.

There are various other refinements that will generally be appropriate in the context of supply and demand models, and which will also improve the identification status of the model. For example, it is generally argued that the demand for some good will depend not only on price, but will also depend on the incomes of consumers. Thus a demand function would be specified which reflects both an income and a price effect. Formally, the following model could be postulated:

Demand:   $Q_t = \alpha_0 + \alpha_1 P_t + \alpha_2 Y_t + \varepsilon_{1t}$            Equation 6.72

Supply:   $Q_t = \beta_0 + \beta_1 P_t + \varepsilon_{2t}$               Equation 6.73

where $Y_t$ is assumed to be exogenous.[4]

Note that the supply function is now exactly identified but the demand function remains under-identified. In diagrammatic terms the inclusion of $Y_t$ in the model allows the supply curve to be 'traced out' and hence identified. That is, in a two-dimensional context, the demand curve will shift at each

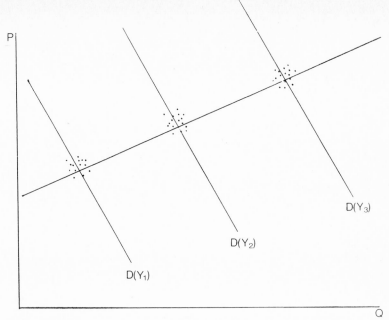

**Figure 6.2** Price and quantity observations at varying income levels.

income level (with its slope remaining constant) thus producing a scatter of observations on $Q$ and $P$ such as that in Figure 6.2.

An alternative way of interpreting the identification problem here is that which we used in the discussion associated with Equation 6.47. Given that the model in Equations 6.72 and 6.73 is the true model, then there will be just one equation in which $Q_t$ is a function only of $P_t$ and which will also satisfy the data. This equation must be the supply function – only one such equation can be both data and model-consistent. However, an infinite number of linear combinations of Equations 6.72 and 6.73 can be derived, all of which must satisfy the data and all of which will express $Q_t$ as functions of $P_t$ and $Y_t$. But presented with any one of these equations it will be impossible to ascertain whether this equation is the actual demand function in Equation 6.73. We can confirm that such an equation satisfies the data and we can confirm that the equation only contains $P_t$ and $Y_t$ as independent variables, but we have no further means of discrimination and therefore cannot identify the demand function.

Further refinements to this model (if considered theoretically appropriate) can have the effect of resulting in the identification of the demand function. Thus, as argued previously, it may be considered nore realistic to assume that supply is a function of lagged price and thus replacing Equation 6.73 with

Equation 6.71 will produce a model in which there are now two predetermined variables, resulting in the exact identification of the demand function and, strictly, the over-identification of the supply function (although such a supply function would also be a reduced form equation, hence permitting the direct estimation of the structural parameters).

Alternatively, it might be argued that the supply function should also include a variable reflecting, say, production costs. Thus denoting production costs by $W_t$ (and assuming $W_t$ to be exogenous) then the model could be specified as:

Demand:   $Q_t = \alpha_0 + \alpha_1 P_t + \alpha_2 Y_t + \varepsilon_{1t}$                      Equation 6.74

Supply:   $Q_t = \beta_0 + \beta_1 P_t + \beta_2 W_t + \varepsilon_{2t}$                      Equation 6.75

and thus both the supply and demand functions are now exactly identified.

In summary, provided a structural equation is either exactly or over-identified, no estimation problems arise. The central issue, then, is how to proceed in those cases in which a structural equation is found to be under-identified.

From our discussion of the supply and demand model in Example 6.1 there is the possibility that a more detailed theoretical analysis and specification of the model may resolve the problem. In addition to ensuring that each equation contains all relevant variables, it may also be considered appropriate to **disaggregate** some of the variables in the model. Recall, for example, that in modelling consumers' expenditure we argued that it was appropriate to disaggregate as between durable and non-durable expenditure and to specify separate models for these expenditure components (see Example 5.3). The general effect of such an approach is to increase the size of the model, introducing additional predetermined variables and hence tending to resolve any identification problems. However, the cost of such an approach is that larger and more complex models will be produced which will be more difficult to manipulate and interpret.

A further approach to overcoming under-identification is to ensure that all relevant information concerning the structural parameters has been incorporated into the model. Recall from our discussion of parameter restrictions in Section 5.3 that the effect of imposing such restrictions on the model is to reduce the number of parameters requiring estimation, which in turn will improve the identification status of the model.

There is one final point which should be emphasised. As we have already indicated, the identification problem is concerned with the consistent estimation of the structural parameters. However, no difficulty arises in the estimation of the reduced form parameters. Now, if the only objective of specifying and estimating some model is to generate forecasts of the endogenous variables, then we will only require an estimate of the reduced form of the model. For it is the reduced form that is the most convenient version of the model for forecasting purposes – each endogenous variable is expressed in terms only of predetermined variables, and hence given forecasts of the predetermined variables (from some source) corresponding forecasts of the endogenous variables can be generated directly from the reduced form. So for forecasting purposes we need not concern ourselves with the identification problem. However, if the model is to be used for testing theoretical postulates concerning the structural parameters (and hence for evaluating the economic theory upon which the model is based) then an estimate of the structural form will be required and any identification problems will need to be resolved.

## 6.4   Estimation Methods

Having checked for identification, the next step is to proceed to the estimation of the structural parameters. Broadly, two approaches to estimation are available: single equation methods, which involve estimating each equation in the model separately, and the more complex system methods, in which the approach is to estimate jointly all the equations in the model. We will discuss each of these methods in turn.

### 6.4.1   Single Equation Methods of Estimation

Assume that the following equation is the $g$th structural equation in a $G$-equation model:

$$Y_t = \beta_0 + \beta_1 Z_{1t} + \beta_2 Z_{2t} + \alpha_1 X_{1t} + \alpha_2 X_{2t} + \varepsilon_{gt} \qquad \text{Equation 6.76}$$

where $Y$, $Z_1$ and $Z_2$ are endogenous variables and $X_1$ and $X_2$ are predetermined. Now, our objective is to derive consistent estimators of the structural parameters $\beta_0$, $\beta_1$, $\beta_2$, $\alpha_1$, and $\alpha_2$. Recall that the application of ordinary least squares to Equation 6.76 will produce biased and inconsistent estimators as, in general, we would expect $\varepsilon_{gt}$ to be correlated with $Z_1$ and $Z_2$. Therefore we require an alternative method of estimating the structural parameters.

We have already briefly discussed one single equation method of estimation which is appropriate in the case of an exactly identified structural equation, and that is the method of indirect least squares. However, this method is tedious to employ as it requires the explicit derivation of the precise relationship between each structural parameter and the reduced form parameters. It is also awkward to derive the variances of these indirect least squares estimators, hence inhibiting hypothesis testing and interval estimation. In addition, it is not clear how this method could be extended to the much more common case of an over-identified structural equation. Consequently, a more generalised estimation procedure is required.

In Section 5.4.1, in our discussion of Koyck distributed lag models, we encountered a similar estimation problem to that associated with Equation 6.76. That is, models in which lagged values of the dependent variable appear as explanatory variables will generally result in correlation between such variables and the disturbance term, thus producing inconsistent least squares estimators. Now, one of the solutions to this problem, which we outlined in detail in Appendix 5.1, was the method of instrumental variables. Thus consistent estimators can be derived by, in effect, replacing the stochastic explanatory variables by proxy variables (or instruments). The properties we require of these instrumental variables are that they are uncorrelated with the disturbance term and, in order to ensure efficient estimation, highly correlated with the variables for which they act. Indeed, ordinary least squares could be interpreted in terms of instrumental variable estimation, with each independent variable, in a given equation, acting as its own instrument (recall the way in which instrumental variable estimation was justified in Equation A5.1.4 and A5.1.13).

Thus a potential method of estimating structural equations such as Equation 6.76 is to use instruments for the endogenous explanatory variables ($Z_1$ and $Z_2$ in Equation 6.76). The problem then is to obtain a set of instrumental variables.

In the case of simultaneous equation models a natural set of instruments is available, and that is the set of predetermined variables which do not appear in the structural equation being estimated. By definition all the predetermined variables are uncorrelated with the disturbance terms in the model (assuming that all the disturbance terms are random) and, by assumption, the predetermined variables are correlated with all of the endogenous variables (which can be seen explicitly in the reduced form of the model).

First consider the case of an exactly identified structural equation. Now, recall that the third version of the order condition which we presented above implied that a structural equation will be exactly identified if the number of predetermined variables excluded from the equation equals the number of endogenous variables that appear in the equation as explanatory variables.[5] Thus a unique set of instrumental variables is available – the set of excluded predetermined variables. It can be shown that in the case of exact identification, instrumental variable estimation, where the instruments are the excluded predetermined variables, is equivalent to the method of indirect least squares. However the method of instrumental variables is easier to employ (given that most regression computer packages have a routine for instrumental variable estimation), and it is easier to derive the variances of the resulting estimators.

We are then left with the case of an over-identified structural equation. By definition, an over-identified equation will contain fewer explanatory variables than there are predetermined variables in the model and hence such an equation will exclude more predetermined variables than there are explanatory endogenous variables. Therefore if instrumental variable estimation were to be used a number of potential sets of instruments would be available, each a sub-set of the excluded predetermined variables. However, different estimates of the structural parameters would be produced by each of these sets of instruments, and there is no reason for preferring one of these sets of estimates over any other. That is, in the case of over-identification, instrumental variable estimation will not produce unique estimators of the structural parameters.

The most commonly used solution in such cases is the method of **two-stage least squares** (2SLS). However, as we shall see, the method is perfectly general and can also be used for the estimation of exactly identified equations.

The basic approach of 2SLS is to derive unique instruments for each of the explanatory endogenous variables, these instruments being based on all the predetermined variables in the model. Thus consider the estimation of Equation 6.76. We first require instruments for $Z_1$ and $Z_2$. Consider regressing $Z_1$ and $Z_2$ on all the predetermined variables in the model. That is, we use ordinary least squares to estimate the following two equations:

$$Z_{1t} = \gamma_0 + \gamma_1 X_{1t} + \gamma_2 X_{2t} + \ldots + \gamma_K X_{Kt} + \varepsilon_{1t} \qquad \text{Equation 6.77}$$

$$Z_{2t} = \delta_0 + \delta_1 X_{1t} + \delta_2 X_{2t} + \ldots + \delta_K X_{Kt} + \varepsilon_{2t} \qquad \text{Equation 6.78}$$

assuming that there are $K$ predetermined variables in the model. Note that Equations 6.77 and 6.78 are simply the reduced form equations for $Z_1$ and $Z_2$.

From the estimates of Equations 6.77 and 6.78 we obtain the **fitted** values of $Z_{1t}$ and $Z_{2t}$. That is, we derive $\hat{Z}_{1t}$ and $\hat{Z}_{2t}$ where:

$$\hat{Z}_{1t} = \hat{\gamma}_0 + \hat{\gamma}_1 X_{1t} + \hat{\gamma}_2 X_{2t} + \ldots + \hat{\gamma}_K X_{Kt} \qquad \text{Equation 6.79}$$

$$\hat{Z}_{2t} = \hat{\delta}_0 + \hat{\delta}_1 X_{1t} + \hat{\delta}_2 X_{2t} + \ldots + \hat{\delta}_K X_{Kt} \qquad \text{Equation 6.80}$$

$\hat{Z}_{1t}$ and $\hat{Z}_{2t}$ can now be used as instruments for $Z_{1t}$ and $Z_{2t}$ and we can proceed to estimate Equation 6.76 by the method of instrumental variables. The basic justification for this approach is that as $\hat{Z}_{1t}$ and $\hat{Z}_{2t}$ are functions only of the predetermined variables then they can be interpreted as themselves being predetermined, and therefore uncorrelated with the disturbance terms in the model. It can be shown that this instrumental variable method is equivalent to simply substituting $\hat{Z}_{1t}$ and $\hat{Z}_{2t}$ for $Z_{1t}$ and $Z_{2t}$ in Equation 6.76 and then directly estimating the resulting equation by ordinary least squares.[6]

Therefore, for any given structural equation, the method of two-stage least squares would be implemented as follows:

1   The first stage is to regress each of the endogenous explanatory variables in the equation on all the predetermined variables in the model – that is, to estimate the reduced form equations for each of these endogenous variables. The fitted values of the endogenous variables are then obtained from these regressions.

2    The second stage is to substitute these fitted values for the original endogenous explanatory variables and then to apply ordinary least squares to this equation. That is, in terms of Equation 6.76, the following equation is estimated by ordinary least squares:

$$Y_t = \beta_0 + \beta_1 \hat{Z}_{1t} + \beta_2 \hat{Z}_{2t} + \alpha_1 X_{1t} + \alpha_2 X_{2t} + \varepsilon_{gt} \qquad \text{Equation 6.81}$$

If the given structural equation is exactly identified then it can be shown that the 2SLS estimators are equivalent to the indirect least squares estimators. Therefore, 2SLS provides a generalised method for estimating any identified structural equation. However, unlike indirect least squares, 2SLS directly produces unique estimates of the structural parameters (and estimates of the corresponding estimator variances). But just as in the case of any instrumental variable estimator, although the 2SLS estimators are consistent, they are biased in finite samples.

2SLS is an application of the principle of least squares to the estimation of simultaneous equation models. However, recall that in Chapter 2 we briefly discussed an estimation method which was derived from an alternative principle – the **maximum likelihood principle** (see Appendix 2.2) – and a simultaneous equation method based on this principle can also be derived. In the case of single equation estimation this method is referred to as **Limited Information Maximum Likelihood Estimation** ('Limited Information' because equations are estimated separately (as with 2SLS) thus ignoring linkages across equations). However we will not discuss this method here and the interested reader is referred to any more advanced econometrics text.[7]

### 6.4.2    System Methods of Estimation

2SLS, while being a consistent method of estimation, is not asymptotically efficient. That is, at least in the case of large samples, other estimation methods are available which produce estimators with smaller variances. Essentially, this is because 2SLS fails to take account of the covariance of the disturbance terms across equations, and hence does not fully utilise all available information.

The analogous system method of 2SLS is **three stage least squares** (3SLS). The application of 3SLS proceeds as follows:

1    Each equation in the model is first estimated by 2SLS, and the residuals from these equations are derived. Thus consider just two equations in the model – the $g$th and $k$th equations, say. The true disturbance terms in these equations would be denoted by $\varepsilon_{gt}$ and $\varepsilon_{kt}$, respectively. 2SLS estimation then allows the derivation of two sets of residuals (or estimated disturbances) – $e_{gt}$ and $e_{kt}$ – for $t = 1, \ldots, n$.

2    Now, it will generally be the case that some correlation will exist between $\varepsilon_{gt}$ and $\varepsilon_{kt}$ – after all, simultaneity implies that the equations in the model

are linked in some way and these links are likely to be reflected, in part, in correlation between $\varepsilon_{gt}$ and $\varepsilon_{kt}$ (and correlation amongst the other disturbance terms in the model). Thus, in general, the covariance between $\varepsilon_{gt}$ and $\varepsilon_{kt}$ will be non-zero. Hence the second stage of 3SLS is to estimate the covariance between $\varepsilon_{gt}$ and $\varepsilon_{kt}$ (and the other disturbance terms in the model), and the obvious estimator is the covariance between the estimated disturbance terms, $e_{gt}$ and $e_{kt}$.

Thus note the multi-dimensional nature of the disturbance terms in a simultaneous equation model. For a given equation, we must allow for the possibility of the disturbances being heteroskedastic and/or autocorrelated. However, over and above these problems (which we discussed in Chapter 4) we must now allow for the possibility of the disturbance terms being correlated across equations. In addition, even if the disturbance terms in each equation are homoskedastic there is no reason for the variances of the disturbance terms to be equal across equations – that is, it will generally be the case that:

$$\text{Var}(\varepsilon_{gt}) \neq \text{Var}(\varepsilon_{kt})$$

for $g, k = 1, \ldots, G, g \neq k$, where $G$ denotes the number of equations in the model.

3   Given estimates of the covariances of the disturbances across all equations, these estimates are then fed back into the estimation process, and the third stage of 3SLS is to re-estimate the structural parameters by applying the principle of least squares to the model as a whole (as opposed to estimating each equation separately).

A slight modification to this estimation procedure is to re-estimate the disturbance terms in the model, given these 3SLS estimates of the structural parameters, re-estimate the covariances between the disturbances and then to obtain a second-round 3SLS estimate of the model. This process continues until successive estimates of the structural parameters converge. This variant of 3SLS is referred to as **iterative** 3SLS.

If the disturbance terms are uncorrelated across equations then the 3SLS estimators can be shown to be equivalent to the 2SLS estimators. Thus the gains in efficiency of 3SLS over 2SLS will be greater the higher the cross-equation correlations between the disturbance terms.

Our exposition of 3SLS here has necessarily been intuitive in nature. Our objective has simply been to convey, in general terms, the rationale for the use of 3SLS and broadly what is involved in the implementation of the methodology. A more detailed exposition would require the use of matrix algebra which is beyond the scope of this book. The interested reader is referred to any more advanced econometrics text.[8]

In terms of maximum likelihood estimation the corresponding system method is referred to as **Full Information Maximum Likelihood** estimation. In essence the method involves the application of the maximum likelihood principle to the model as a whole. However, the method is a complex one, and consequently a method which is not widely used; we will not attempt an exposition here.[9]

## 6.5   The Evaluation of Estimated Simultaneous Equation Models

Having selected and applied a satisfactory estimation method to some simultaneous equation model, the next step, just as in the case of single equation models, is to evaluate the estimated model.

In general, we would begin by carrying out significance tests on all the estimated coefficients. Therefore, we first require expressions for the variances of each of the parameter estimators. However, in the case of simultaneous equation estimation the exact expressions for these variances are complex to derive. The derivation of the expressions for the asymptotic variances (that is, the expressions for the estimator variances assuming infinite sample sizes) is relatively straightforward, however, and it is these expressions which are generally used as approximations to the finite sample variances.

Thus using the expressions for the asymptotic variances of the estimators conventional $t$-tests can be performed using the parameter estimates (and/or confidence intervals derived). Although little analytical evidence exists to justify the use of the expressions for the asymptotic variances in a finite sample context, experimental evidence suggests that the use of these asymptotic estimators generally leads to correct inferences being drawn.

In practice, computer programs containing simultaneous equation estimation routines will produce these asymptotic estimates of the estimator variances and the associated $t$-statistics. So it is straightforward to identify insignificant coefficients (and of course also to confirm that all estimated coefficients in the model are of the expected sign). However, note that if a variable in some equation is found to be insignificant and the investigator then decides to omit this variable from the equation this can affect the estimated coefficients on the variables in the remainder of the model. This would certainly be the case if the omitted variable was an exogenous variable and only appeared in this one equation – that is, the omission of this variable from the equation would also result in the omission of the variable from the model, hence affecting all the parameter estimates. In the case of system methods of estimation, given that links between equations are explicitly incorporated into the estimation process, changes to the structure of any one equation will affect the estimation of the remaining equations.

Another criterion which might be useful in assessing an estimated model is some measure of the model's **goodness-of-fit** – that is, a simultaneous equation analogue of the single equation multiple correlation coefficient ($R^2$).

We could begin by simply obtaining a measure of $R^2$ for each equation in the model. Recall from equation 2.76 that $R^2$ could be expressed as:

$$R^2 = 1 - \frac{\sum e_t^2}{\sum (Y_t - \bar{Y})^2}$$  Equation 6.82

where $Y_t$ is the dependent variable, $\bar{Y}$ is the mean of the sample of observations on the dependent variable, and $e_t$ is the estimated disturbance term.

Therefore given any estimated equation in a simultaneous equation model we could certainly derive a value for $R^2$ from Equation 6.82 – given the estimated coefficients we can derive the estimated disturbance terms and then substitute these into Equation 6.82. However, the difficulty in interpreting the resulting value of $R^2$ is that if some consistent estimation method has been employed then no weight will have been given to achieving a high value of $R^2$ – it is only ordinary least squares that derives estimators which must necessarily minimise the dispersion of the estimated disturbance terms (or conversely, maximise $R^2$). Consequently, the use of some consistent estimation method must necessarily result in a lower $R^2$ than could be obtained via the use of (the invalid) ordinary least squares. Indeed, there is no reason why the value of $R^2$ in Equation 6.82 could not be negative, given a consistent estimation method, as in effect there are no bounds on the resulting value of $\sum e_t^2$.

In other words, it is meaningless to judge the success (or failure) of some consistent estimation method (2SLS or 3SLS) on the basis of a criterion $(R^2)$ to which these methods make no reference, and indeed a criterion which necessarily conflicts with the criterion of consistency. Consequently, a value for $R^2$ is not generally quoted if a consistent estimation method has been employed, and an initial evaluation of the model is simply carried out in terms of the significance of the $t$-statistics and theoretical expectations concerning the signs of the coefficients.

Further tests of the model's adequacy would concern the ability of the model to forecast satisfactorily, and the ability of the model to simulate the properties of the economy (market, industry, etc.) which is being modelled. These further aspects of model evaluation will be discussed in Section 6.6.

By way of an illustration of the foregoing discussion, we will now go on to discuss the estimation of a simple macroeconomic model.

Example 6.2
Consider the following simplified model of the economy:

$$C_t = \alpha_0 + \alpha_1 C_{t-1} + \alpha_2 Y_t + \varepsilon_{1t}$$  Equation 6.83

$$I_t = \beta_0 + \beta_1 Y_{t-1} + \beta_2 R_t + \varepsilon_{2t}$$  Equation 6.84

$$Y_t = C_t + I_t + G_t$$  Equation 6.85

where:

$C_t$   is consumers' expenditure in time period $t$
$Y_t$   is national income in time period $t$
$I_t$   is investment expenditure in time period $t$
$G_t$   is government expenditure in time period $t$
$R_t$   is the interest rate in time period $t$
$\varepsilon_{1t}$ and $\varepsilon_{2t}$ are disturbance terms.

Thus the model contains two behavioural equations (Equations 6.83 and 6.84) and an identity (Equation 6.85). We will here assume that $G_t$ and $R_t$ are exogenous and thus there are three endogenous variables ($C_t$, $I_t$ and $Y_t$) and four predetermined variables ($G_t$, $R_t$, $C_{t-1}$ and $Y_{t-1}$).

Before proceeding to estimate the parameters in this model we must first ensure that each equation is identified. As the model contains four predetermined variables and as each behavioural equation contains just two explanatory variables we can conclude that both equations are over-identified (although as all the explanatory variables in the investment equation are predetermined then this equation can be estimated directly). Therefore we can now proceed to estimate the model. For comparative purposes we will use three estimation methods – the inconsistent ordinary least squares (OLS), and the two consistent methods, 2SLS and 3SLS.

First we require data with which to estimate the model. We will use annual data for the UK economy over the period 1956 to 1981. For $C_t$ we will use a series on consumers' expenditure, for $I_t$ we will use a series on gross domestic fixed capital formation, $G_t$ will be measured by central government final consumption expenditure, and $R_t$ will be measured by the annual average of the minimum lending rate. In order for the identity in the model to be satisfied (Equation 6.85) we will use as a measure of $Y_t$ the sum of $C_t$, $I_t$ and $G_t$ as defined above. All data are in 1975 prices (except for the interest rate series). These data are shown in Appendix 6.3.

It must be emphasised that we are using this model here for illustrative purposes only. It is certainly not being presented as in any sense an accurate representation of the workings of the UK economy. The theory used to construct the model is far too simplistic and the data are in too aggregated a form. Among the obvious shortcomings are that we have ignored the role of taxation and we have only included that component of government expenditure which is accounted for by final consumption of goods and services. Current operational models of the UK economy typically contain hundreds of equations and variables, and are constructed on the basis of a much more rigorous theoretical analysis than has been employed here. None the less we will proceed on the (unrealistic) assumption that the structure of the model in Equations 6.83 to 6.85 is adequate and that the data used to measure each of the variables are satisfactory.

We present below the OLS, 2SLS and 3SLS estimates of the behavioural equations in the model. The numbers in brackets are the standard errors of the corresponding estimators.

*OLS*

$$\hat{C}_t = 1538.567 + 0.276 C_{t-1} + 0.428 Y_t \quad \bar{R}^2 = 0.993$$
$$\quad\quad (967.0655) \;\; (0.1209) \quad\quad (0.0724) \quad\quad d = 0.76$$

$$\hat{I}_t = -5342.233 + 0.286 Y_{t-1} - 460.607 R_t \quad \bar{R}^2 = 0.898$$
$$\quad\quad (1779.1211)\,(0.0304) \quad\quad (163.6192) \quad\quad d = 0.96$$

*2SLS*

$$\hat{C}_t = 1818.952 + 0.598 C_{t-1} + 0.233 Y_t$$
$$\quad\quad (1123.6549)\,(0.2097) \quad\quad (0.1262)$$

$$\hat{I}_t = -5342.233 + 0.286 Y_{t-1} - 460.607 R_t$$
$$\quad\quad (1779.1211)\,(0.0304) \quad\quad (163.6192)$$

*3SLS*

$$\hat{C}_t = 1820.032 + 0.578 C_{t-1} + 0.245 Y_t$$
$$\quad\quad (1123.6344)\,(0.2091) \quad\quad (0.1258)$$

$$\hat{I}_t = -5430.615 + 0.288 Y_{t-1} - 475.003 R_t$$
$$\quad\quad (1777.2135)\,(0.0303) \quad\quad (163.1393)$$

We first note that under each of the èstimation methods all the coefficients in the model are significant according to the conventional $t$-tests (except for the constant term in the consumption function which is marginally insignificant). All coefficients are also of the expected sign.

Second, there are quite marked changes in the estimated coefficients of the consumption function in moving from OLS to 2SLS. Notice also that the estimates of the investment function are identical under OLS and 2SLS. This simply reflects the fact that as the investment function does not contain any endogenous explanatory variables then it can be consistently estimated directly by OLS – the use of 2SLS here collapses to the direct application of OLS.

In moving from 2SLS to 3SLS the estimated coefficients change only marginally, and the standard errors of the 3SLS estimators are only slightly smaller than those of the 2SLS estimators. Thus, it might be inferred that there is only a slight gain in efficiency in employing 3SLS rather than 2SLS, perhaps indicating a relatively low level of cross-equation correlation of the disturbance terms.

Again, we would emphasise that these estimated models should not be taken too seriously. Our only objective has been to demonstrate that different estimation methods will, in general, produce different coefficient estimates. As we shall see in the following section, this will have certain implications when we come to use our model for policy evaluation and forecasting.

We can certainly conclude that 2SLS and 3SLS will produce 'better' estimates than OLS, provided that the model being estimated is the correct one. In practice, we will rarely (if ever) know the structure of the true model, and to argue that the 2SLS or 3SLS estimate of a given model is superior to the OLS estimate is conditional upon the model being correctly specified.

## 6.6    Forecasting and Policy Evaluation

Up to this point, the central focus of this book has been the development of a range of estimation techniques that can be used to estimate a variety of model specifications validly. However, once some given model has been satisfactorily estimated, we have not as yet discussed in any detail how this model might be used.

Apart from testing theoretical postulates concerning the model parameters, an estimated model can be used for two purposes – forecasting and policy evaluation. We will discuss each of these functions in turn.

### 6.6.1    *Forecasting with an Econometric Model*

Given an estimated single equation model it is straightforward to derive forecasts of the dependent variable, over some forecast period, conditional upon a set of forecasts for the independent variables. Recall that in Examples 2.2 and 5.5 we briefly discussed the forecasting of consumers' expenditure in this way, given an estimated consumption function.

Similarly, in a simultaneous equation context, we can also use an estimated model to derive a set of forecasts of the endogenous variables conditional upon a set of forecasts for the exogenous variables.

Using a model for forecasting purposes presupposes that the model is specified and estimated in time-series form. A cross-section model could be used for what we might term prediction, rather than forecasting. As a cross-section model is estimated at a single point in time it can strictly only be used to draw inferences concerning that point in time (although a set of cross-section models, each estimated at a different point in time, could conceivably be used to draw inferences about the future). For example, if we have a cross-section consumption function, estimated over a sample of households, this function could be used to predict household consumption for given levels of household income and given levels of any other relevant explanatory variables. In order to highlight the mechanics of forecasting with an econometric model we will begin by considering a simple single equation model, which contains just one explanatory variable. That is, consider the model:

$$Y_t = \alpha + \beta X_t + \varepsilon_t \hspace{4cm} \text{Equation 6.86}$$

This model is then estimated over the period $t = 1, \ldots, n$.

Assume that we require a forecast of $Y$ $k$ periods into the future. That is, we require a forecast of $Y$ at the time point $n+k$, or equivalently, a forecast of $Y_{n+k}$. The obvious method of deriving such a forecast is to substitute the estimates of $\alpha$ and $\beta$ into Equation 6.86, and to set the value of $\varepsilon_{n+k}$ equal to its expected value of 0. Thus the forecast of $Y$ at period $n+k$ ($\hat{Y}_{n+k}$) can be written as:

$$\hat{Y}_{n+k} = \hat{\alpha} + \hat{\beta}X_{n+k} \hspace{3cm} \text{Equation 6.87}$$

In order to derive a value for $\hat{Y}_{n+k}$ we first require a value for $X_{n+k}$. In general, $X_{n+k}$ will also be unknown and thus a forecast of $X_{n+k}$ must be obtained from some source. That is, the forecast for $Y_{n+k}$ derived from Equation 6.87 will be conditional upon the forecast of $X_{n+k}$. However, for our purposes, we will assume that a forecast for $X_{n+k}$ is available.

As an example of forecasting with a simple regression model, consider the simple gas consumption model which we estimated in Chapter 2. Thus recall from Equation 2.23 that the relationship between gas consumption and atmospheric temperature, estimated from the data in Table 2.1, was given by:

$$\hat{Y}_t = 577.910 - 25.354X_t \hspace{3cm} \text{Equation 6.88}$$

Now, assume that a forecast is required one period into the future – that is, a forecast is required of gas consumption for the month of January 1982 (and for argument's sake, assume that the current time-period is the end of December 1981). We first require a forecast of mean daily air temperature during January 1982. Assume that the weather forecasting authorities predict that daily air temperature during January 1982 will average 3.6 degrees. Thus, from Equation 6.88, the forecast of gas consumption (conditional on this weather forecast) is:

$$\hat{Y}_{n+1} = 577.910 - (25.354)(3.6)$$

$$= 486.6$$

Note that in deriving such a forecast we must assume that all other potential influences on gas consumption remain unchanged (as we also had to assume when estimating the model).

Returning to Equation 6.86, the error made in forecasting $Y_{n+k}$ can be written as:

$$Y_{n+k} - \hat{Y}_{n+k}$$

Thus we can write:

$$Y_{n+k} - \hat{Y}_{n+k} = \alpha + \beta X_{n+k} + \varepsilon_{n+k} - \hat{\alpha} - \hat{\beta}X_{n+k} \hspace{2cm} \text{Equation 6.89}$$

and therefore the expected value of the forecast error is:

$$E(Y_{n+k} - \hat{Y}_{n+k}) = \alpha + \beta X_{n+k} + E(\varepsilon_{n+k}) - E(\hat{\alpha}) - E(\hat{\beta})X_{n+k} \hspace{1cm} \text{Equation 6.90}$$

$$= \alpha + \beta X_{n+k} - \alpha - \beta X_{n+k}$$

$$= 0$$

Note from Equation 6.89 that the forecast error is linearly dependent on three random variables – $\varepsilon_{n+k}$, $\hat{\alpha}$ and $\hat{\beta}$. Given the simplest assumptions of the linear regression model each of these three variables will be normally distributed and thus $Y_{n+k} - \hat{Y}_{n+k}$ will also be normally distributed.

Given that the mean of the forecast error is zero then we can conclude that Equation 6.87 will produce unbiased forecasts of $Y_{n+k}$. That is, we can write:

$$E(\hat{Y}_{n+k}) = Y_{n+k} \qquad \text{Equation 6.91}$$

So finally, once we derive the variance of the forecast error, we will be able to place confidence limits around our forecasts. That is, we can write:

$$(Y_{n+k} - \hat{Y}_{n+k}) \sim N[0, \text{Var}(Y_{n+k} - \hat{Y}_{n+k})]$$

The derivation of the variance of the forecast error is somewhat tedious, and we will simply state it here without proof. Thus it can be shown that:[10]

$$\sigma_F^2 = \sigma_\varepsilon^2 \left[ 1 + \frac{1}{n} + \frac{(X_{n+k} - \bar{X})^2}{\sum (X_t - \bar{X})^2} \right] \qquad \text{Equation 6.92}$$

where $\sigma_F^2$ denotes the variance of the forecast error, $\sigma_\varepsilon^2$ is the variance of the disturbance term, $\bar{X}$ is the mean of the sample values of $X$, and $\sum (X_t - \bar{X})^2$ is also evaluated over the sample values. In practice $\sigma_\varepsilon^2$ will be unknown and the sample estimate, $\hat{\sigma}_\varepsilon^2$, will have to be used, and thus we can write:

$$S_F^2 = \hat{\sigma}_\varepsilon^2 \left[ 1 + \frac{1}{n} + \frac{(X_{n+k} - \bar{X})^2}{\sum (X_t - \bar{X})^2} \right] \qquad \text{Equation 6.93}$$

Therefore we can make the following statement:

$$\frac{Y_{n+k} - \hat{Y}_{n+k}}{\sigma_F} \sim N(0, 1)$$

Replacing $\sigma_F$ with $S_F$ we have:

$$\frac{Y_{n+k} - \hat{Y}_{n+k}}{S_F} \sim t_{n-2}$$

Thus we can write:

$$\Pr\left[ \hat{Y}_{n+k} - S_F t_{n-2, \gamma/2} < Y_{n+k} < \hat{Y}_{n+k} + S_F t_{n-2, \gamma/2} \right] = 1 - \gamma \qquad \text{Equation 6.94}$$

Equation 6.94 now allows us to place **confidence intervals** around the true value of $Y$ at time point $n+k$.

Note also from Equation 6.93 that the greater the difference between $X_{n+k}$ and the mean of the sample of $X$s used to estimate the model then the larger will be $S_F^2$. The larger is $S_F^2$ then the wider will be the confidence interval around the corresponding $Y_{n+k}$. This simply reflects the fact that the further we attempt to forecast outside the range of the sample the greater will be the uncertainty associated with the forecast. Thus, typically, a set of forecasts which are made into the future will have corresponding confidence intervals which 'fan out' over time.

As an example of deriving a forecast confidence interval consider once again our gas consumption model of Chapter 2. Further, consider the forecast of gas consumption which we derived from Equation 6.88 above, for a temperature of 3.6 degrees.

In order to derive the confidence interval for the actual value of $Y$ at time point $n+1$, we first require an estimate of $\sigma_F^2$. This estimate can be derived from Equation 6.93, where we also require the value of $\hat{\sigma}_\varepsilon^2$. From Equation 2.56 we obtained a value for $\hat{\sigma}_\varepsilon^2$ of 512.536, the value of $\Sigma(X_t - \bar{X})^2$ was 489.858, and $\bar{X}$ was 9.808. Therefore substitution into Equation 6.93 produces:

$$S_F^2 = 574.215$$

Thus the 95 per cent interval estimate for $Y_{n+1}$, derived from Equation 6.94 ($t_{22,0.025} = 2.07$), is:

$$436.997 < Y_{n+1} < 536.203$$

We have here discussed forecasting or prediction almost solely within the context of time-series models. However all the above results still apply in the case of cross-section models. Thus in a cross-section context we would be attempting to predict the value of the dependent variable for some given value of the independent variable. Confidence intervals such as Equation 6.94 can also be derived, where the expression for $S_F^2$ in Equation 6.93 would involve summations at a point in time, rather than over time.

Forecasting with a multiple regression model is a direct extension of the above results. Thus forecasts are made conditional upon forecasts for each of the independent variables. The variance of the forecast error, $\sigma_F^2$, can also be derived and hence confidence intervals placed around the value of the dependent variable at various forecast points. We will not here derive the expression for $\sigma_F^2$ for the case of a multiple regression model,[11] although it is a direct generalisation of the expression for $\sigma_F^2$ in the simple regression model.

Finally, we must consider how simultaneous equation models can be used for forecasting.

In Section 6.3 above we indicated that it is the reduced form of a simultaneous equation model which provides the most convenient means of deriving forecasts of the endogenous variables. Thus consider again the model which we estimated in Example 6.3. That is:

$$C_t = \alpha_0 + \alpha_1 C_{t-1} + \alpha_2 Y_t + \varepsilon_{1t} \qquad \text{Equation 6.95}$$

$$I_t = \beta_0 + \beta_1 Y_{t-1} + \beta_2 R_t + \varepsilon_{2t} \qquad \text{Equation 6.96}$$

$$Y_t = C_t + I_t + G_t \qquad \text{Equation 6.97}$$

The general statement of the reduced form of this model is as follows:

$$C_t = a_0 + a_1 C_{t-1} + a_2 Y_{t-1} + a_3 R_t + a_4 G_t + u_{1t} \qquad \text{Equation 6.98}$$

$$I_t = b_0 + b_1 C_{t-1} + b_2 Y_{t-1} + b_3 R_t + b_4 G_t + u_{2t} \qquad \text{Equation 6.99}$$

$$Y_t = c_0 + c_1 C_{t-1} + c_2 Y_{t-1} + c_3 R_t + c_4 G_t + u_{3t} \qquad \text{Equation 6.100}$$

As we have already indicated, each reduced form equation can be consistently estimated by the direct application of ordinary least squares. Thus to derive a set of forecasts for $C_t$, $I_t$ and $Y_t$ we simply substitute into these estimated reduced form equations a set of forecasts for $R_t$ and $G_t$. If we require forecasts just one period into the future then we can substitute the actual values of $C_{t-1}$ and $Y_{t-1}$ into Equations 6.98 to 6.100. However, if we require forecasts further into the future then we must use the forecasts of $C_{t-1}$ and $Y_{t-1}$ which are generated by the model.

In deriving the above reduced form equations it was not necessary to make any reference to the precise structure of the model in Equations 6.95 to 6.97. All that was required was knowledge of which variables are endogenous and which are predetermined. However, it will often be the case that the structural form will contain further information which is relevant for the structure of the reduced form. Thus note, for example, that the structural form equation for $I_t$ (Equation 6.96) is equivalent to its reduced form equation – Equation 6.96 does not contain any endogenous explanatory variables. Therefore in terms of the reduced form coefficients in Equation 6.99 we can deduce from Equation 6.96 that:

$$b_1 = b_4 = 0$$

and

$$b_0 = \beta_0$$
$$b_2 = \beta_1$$
$$b_3 = \beta_2$$

Indeed, by explicitly deriving the reduced form of the model the restriction that the structural form places on the reduced form can be seen directly. That is, algebraically manipulating the structural form produces the following explicit version of the reduced form:

$$C_t = \frac{\alpha_0 + \alpha_2 \beta_0}{1 - \alpha_2} + \frac{\alpha_1}{1 - \alpha_2} C_{t-1} + \frac{\alpha_2 \beta_1}{1 - \alpha_2} Y_{t-1} + \frac{\alpha_2 \beta_2}{1 - \alpha_2} R_t$$

$$+ \frac{\alpha_2}{1 - \alpha_2} G_t + u_{1t} \qquad \text{Equation 6.101}$$

$$I_t = \beta_0 + \beta_1 Y_{t-1} + \beta_2 R_t + u_{2t} \qquad \text{Equation 6.102}$$

$$Y_t = \frac{\alpha_0 + \beta_0}{1 - \alpha_2} + \frac{\alpha_1}{1 - \alpha_2} C_{t-1} + \frac{\beta_1}{1 - \alpha_2} Y_{t-1} + \frac{\beta_2}{1 - \alpha_2} R_t$$

$$+ \frac{1}{1 - \alpha_2} G_t + u_{3t} \qquad\qquad \text{Equation 6.103}$$

That is, from this explicit version of the reduced form we can now see that neither $C_{t-1}$ nor $G_t$ actually appears in the reduced form equation for $I_t$, in contrast to the general version of the reduced form in Equations 6.98 to 6.100.

Now, given the three sets of estimates of the structural parameters which we presented in Example 6.2 (that is, the OLS, 2SLS and 3SLS estimates), three different estimates of the reduced form can be derived by substituting these sets of parameter estimates into Equations 6.101 to 6.103. A further estimate of the reduced form can also be obtained by the direct estimation of Equations 6.98 to 6.100.

Thus, strictly, four sets of forecasts could be derived for $C_t$, $I_t$ and $Y_t$, each depending on the method used to estimate the reduced form.[12] Estimates of the reduced form which are obtained by first estimating the structural form and then substituting into the explicit version of the reduced form are referred to as the **restricted** estimates – they reflect all the restrictions concerning the reduced form that are contained in the structural form. The direct estimation of the reduced form – that is, applying OLS to each equation in the implicit version of the reduced form (Equations 6.98 to 6.100) – is referred to as **unrestricted** estimation. As may seem intuitively obvious, the use of a valid estimate of the restricted reduced form will produce more efficient forecasts than the use of the unrestricted reduced form. However, the computational costs associated with deriving a restricted estimate are clearly considerably higher than estimating the unrestricted reduced form, and this is particularly so the larger is the model. Thus, in practice, only the unrestricted estimate of the reduced form would be used for forecasting.

Just as in the case of single equation models, confidence limits can be derived from the estimation process and placed around the level of each endogenous variable at various forecast points. However, as we are forecasting a set of variables with a simultaneous equation model the issue is not as straightforward as simply placing confidence intervals around the individual values of each of the endogenous variables. Rather, we are concerned with deriving joint confidence limits and being able to make statements to the effect that, say, a 95 per cent confidence 'interval' can be attached to the joint forecasts of all the endogenous variables. This problem is a complex one and we will not concern ourselves with it any further. The interested reader is referred to a more advanced econometrics text.[13]

Forecasting with an econometric model also provides a further test of model adequacy. Recall that in Example 5.5 we carried out a forecasting test for our estimated consumption function (see Figures 5.7 and 5.8). Thus, in general, given a sample of data we could subdivide this sample into two data periods, estimate the model over the first period and then forecast into the second period. The advantage of this approach is that we will know the true values of the endogenous variable(s) over the 'forecast' period and thus we can directly evaluate the forecasting performance of the model (we will also know the true values of the predetermined variables and thus we will not require forecasts for these). Such a forecasting test can be performed with either a single equation or simultaneous equation model.

In terms of assessing the forecasting performance of a model, both formal and informal methods are available. In Example 5.5 our assessment was very much an informal one – the assessment was by graphical means only and hence was necessarily somewhat subjective. However a number of more formal assessment procedures can be developed.

An obvious starting point would be to consider the extent of the forecasting errors over the forecast period. Thus consider again the simple model in Equation 6.86 above. That is:

$$Y_t = \alpha + \beta X_t + \varepsilon_t$$
Equation 6.104

Assume that this model has been estimated over the period $1,\ldots,n$. It is then used to forecast over the $T$ periods $n+1,\ldots,n+T$. Also assume that the actual values of $Y$ are known over the forecast period (the forecasts are *ex post* rather than *ex ante*). Thus for each of the points over the forecast period the forecast error can be evaluated and is given by:

$$Y_{n+k} - \hat{Y}_{n+k} \quad \text{for} \quad k = 1,\ldots,T$$

We could begin by simply examining the average of these forecast errors. That is:

$$\text{Av. Error} = \frac{1}{T} \sum_{k=1}^{T} (Y_{n+k} - \hat{Y}_{n+k})$$
Equation 6.105

However, the obvious disadvantage of such a measure is that large positive forecast errors will offset large negative errors. Hence a small value for this average error will be consistent with either large or small fluctuations of the forecasts around the true value of $Y$. None the less, the average forecast error conveys some information, for if the forecasts are unbiased then we would expect this average error to be zero (just as the average value of the disturbance terms must be zero over the estimation period). Hence a non-zero value for the average forecast error gives some indication of the extent to which $Y$ is being over- or under-estimated.

As an example, again consider Example 5.5 where we derived quarterly forecasts of Consumers' Expenditure (CN) over the period 1975 to 1979, from a model which was estimated over the period 1963 to 1974. Consider only the one-step ahead forecasts which we presented in Figure 5.7. Now, the average forecast error over the 20 quarters of the forecast period can be shown to be

$-12.13$, and thus we can conclude that there is a very slight tendency for CN to be over-estimated (compared to the average value of CN over the forecast period of 15,297.75).

In order to derive a measure of forecast performance which reflects the overall magnitude of the forecast errors, we could proceed in one of two ways:

1  We could obtain the average of the absolute forecast errors, or
2  We could derive the average of the squared forecast errors, and then obtain the square root of this measure in order to return to the original units of measurement. Note, that this is simply a measure of the standard deviation of the forecasts around the actual value of $Y$ over the forecast period.

It is this latter measure which is the more commonly used, and is generally referred to as the **Root Mean Square Error** (RMSE). That is, we can write:

$$\text{RMSE} = \sqrt{\frac{1}{T}\sum_{k=1}^{T}(Y_{n+k}-\hat{Y}_{n+k})^2} \qquad \text{Equation 6.106}$$

Again, for the case of the one-step ahead forecasts of CN in Example 5.5, it can be shown that:

$$\text{RMSE} = 152.6$$

Therefore, relative to the magnitude of CN over the forecast period of between about 14,000 and 16,000, we could conclude that this value of RMSE is relatively small, and thus it would appear that the model forecasts reasonably well.

While the use of RMSE is certainly a more concise way of summarising the *ex post* forecasting performance of a model than a graphical examination of the forecasts (such as Figure 5.7), its interpretation is none the less still subjective – we do not have any absolute definition of what constitutes a 'large' or 'small' value for RMSE. In particular, we require some benchmark against which RMSE could be compared and hence conclusions drawn concerning the relative forecasting performance of the model.

One way of proceeding would be to compare RMSE with its equivalent over the estimation period – that is, the standard deviation of the disturbance terms. Thus if the true disturbance terms were known then the RMSE of the model over the estimation period would be given by:

$$\text{RMSE}^e = \sqrt{\frac{1}{n}\sum_{t=1}^{n}\varepsilon_t^2} \qquad \text{Equation 6.107}$$

$$= \sigma_\varepsilon$$

Now, if the model performs as well over the forecast period as it does over the estimation period – that is, it forecasts the data as well as it 'tracks' them –

then we would expect to observe:

$$\text{RMSE} \simeq \sigma_\varepsilon$$

Conversely, if RMSE substantially exceeds $\sigma_\varepsilon$ then this would indicate poor forecasting performance relative to the performance of the model over the estimation period. The model would therefore have to be rejected, given that it cannot replicate its estimation performance outside the estimation period. It cannot be the correct model. (Note that the converse does not necessarily follow – just because a model forecasts satisfactorily does not mean that the model must be the correct one. That is, satisfactory forecasting performance is only one of a range of properties we would require of any model purporting to be the true model.)

Formally, we could express the above discussion in terms of the following null hypothesis:

$H_0$: The forecasting performance of the model is equivalent to its estimation performance.

In order to test this hypothesis we could compare RMSE with $\sigma_\varepsilon$. Thus if $H_0$ were true, we would expect to observe:

$$\text{RMSE} = \sigma_\varepsilon$$

or

$$\frac{\text{RMSE}}{\sigma_\varepsilon} = 1 \qquad\qquad \text{Equation 6.108}$$

Squaring both sides of Equation 6.108 and multiplying throughout by $T$ finally produces:

$$\frac{\sum_{k=1}^{T} (Y_{n+k} - \hat{Y}_{n+k})^2}{\sigma_\varepsilon^2} = T \qquad\qquad \text{Equation 6.109}$$

Thus in order to test $H_0$ we use the sample data to calculate a value for the left-hand side of Equation 6.109, and if $H_0$ is true we would expect this value to be close to the value of $T$, the number of forecasts generated by the model. However, in order to test $H_0$ formally we first require the distribution of this test statistic. Thus consider the test statistic, $Z_1$, where:

$$Z_1 = \frac{\sum_{k=1}^{T} [Y_{n+k} - E(Y_{n+k})]^2}{\sigma_\varepsilon^2}$$

$$= \sum_{k=1}^{T} \left( \frac{Y_{n+k} - E(Y_{n+k})}{\sigma_\varepsilon} \right)^2.$$

Now, under the simplest assumptions of the regression model, $Y_{n+k}$ will be normally distributed with a mean of $E(Y_{n+k})$ and some variance. If $H_0$ is true then this implies that the properties of the model are the same over the estimation period as over the forecast period and, in particular, that the variance of the disturbance terms over the estimation period will equal the variance of the $Y$s over the forecast period. That is, under $H_0$ we have:

$$Y_{n+k} \sim N[E(Y_{n+k}), \sigma_\varepsilon^2] \quad \text{for} \quad k = 1, \ldots, T$$

Consequently,

$$\frac{Y_{n+k} - E(Y_{n+k})}{\sigma_\varepsilon} \sim N(0, 1)$$

Thus under $H_0$ $Z_1$ is simply the sum of the squares of $T$ standard normal variables. Now, it can be shown that the sum of the squares of $T$ standard normal variables has what is referred to as a $\chi^2$ **(chi-square) distribution** with $T$ degrees of freedom.[14] A $\chi^2$ distribution is just another statistical distribution (like the $F$, normal and $t$-distributions) and hence it can be used to calculate various probabilities. In particular, it can be shown that the mean of a $\chi^2$ distribution with $T$ degrees of freedom is just $T$. We present tables of the $\chi^2$ distribution in Appendix V.

Thus in terms of the above null hypothesis, given an observed value for $Z_1$, we make reference to the tables of the $\chi^2$ distribution, evaluate the probability that this value was in fact selected from a $\chi^2$ distribution with $T$ degrees of freedom, and then on the basis of this probability either accept or reject $H_0$.

However, in general, $\sigma_\varepsilon^2$ will be unknown and thus the sample estimate, $\hat{\sigma}_\varepsilon^2$ would have to be used. Therefore denoting the observed value of $Z_1$ by $z_1$ we have:

$$z_1 = \frac{\sum_{k=1}^{T} (Y_{n+k} - \hat{Y}_{n+k})^2}{\hat{\sigma}_\varepsilon^2} \qquad \text{Equation 6.110}$$

Thus as $\sigma_\varepsilon^2$ is unknown then $z_1$ in Equation 6.110 only has an approximate $\chi^2$ distribution. However, the larger is the sample used to estimate the parameters in the model the more satisfactory will $z_1$ be as an approximation of $Z_1$. That is, the use of $z_1$ rather than $Z_1$ is only asymptotically valid.[15]

Again consider the one-step ahead forecasts of Example 5.5. We have already indicated that RMSE is 152.6, and from the estimated model (see Equation 5.84) the value of $\hat{\sigma}_\varepsilon$ (the standard error of the regression) can be shown to be 122.502. Thus noting that we can write:

$$z_1 = \frac{T(\text{RMSE})^2}{\hat{\sigma}_\varepsilon} \qquad \text{Equation 6.111}$$

then the observed value of $z_1$ is:

$$z_1 = \frac{(20)(152.6)^2}{(122.502)^2}$$

$$= 31.04$$

This value exceeds the expected value of $Z_1$ (under $H_0$) of 20, and we next have to determine whether this difference is significant. From Appendix V, for a $\chi^2$ distribution with 20 degrees of freedom, there is only a 5 per cent chance of observing a value in excess of 31.4, and only a 10 per cent chance of observing a value in excess of 28.4. Therefore we can conclude that there is only between a 5 and 10 per cent chance of observing as extreme a value for $z_1$ as 31.04, if $H_0$ were true. Hence there is reasonable evidence for rejecting $H_0$, and concluding that the model's forecasts are unsatisfactory.

While the forecasting test described above certainly provides a reasonably rigorous basis for evaluating a model's forecasting performance, its disadvantage, as we have already indicated, is that it is strictly valid only in large samples.

However, a further criticism which could be made of the test is that it judges forecasting adequacy only with reference to the model's own performance over the estimation period. That is, no reference is made to any absolute criteria of forecasting adequacy – an estimated model could satisfy the above test if it performs equally poorly over the estimation and forecast periods.

Another commonly used measure of forecasting accuracy is **Theil's inequality coefficient** or **U-statistic**.[16] As we shall see, this measure does not involve any formal test of significance, with the justification for its use being more intuitive than rigorous.

Consider some estimated model and the *ex post* forecasts generated by this model over the forecast period $n+1,\ldots,n+T$. Given the $T$ forecasts of the dependent variable over the forecast period, $\hat{Y}_{n+1},\ldots,\hat{Y}_{n+T}$, we could derive the forecast relative (or percentage) change in $Y$ from one period to the next, for each of the time points in the forecast period. That is, denoting the forecast relative change in $Y$ from period $n+i$ to period $n+(i+1)$ by $\text{FRC}_i$, then we can write:

$$\text{FRC}_i = \frac{\hat{Y}_{n+(i+1)} - Y_{n+i}}{Y_{n+i}} \qquad \text{Equation 6.112}$$

Similarly the actual relative change in $Y$ from $n+i$ to $n+(i+1)$ ($\text{ARC}_i$) can be written as:

$$\text{ARC}_i = \frac{Y_{n+(i+1)} - Y_{n+i}}{Y_{n+i}} \qquad \text{Equation 6.113}$$

Theil's inequality coefficient is then defined as follows:

$$U = \sqrt{\frac{\sum\limits_{i=1}^{T-1} (\text{FRC}_i - \text{ARC}_i)^2}{\sum\limits_{i=1}^{T-1} (\text{ARC}_i)^2}}$$

Equation 6.114

The advantage of this measure is that it has a particularly straightforward interpretation. For consider the case of the model forecasting perfectly over the forecast period, so that $\text{FRC}_i = \text{ARC}_i$ for all $i$. The value of $U$ in Equation 6.113 would therefore be zero, and thus we can judge the forecasting performance of any model in terms of how small a value of $U$ it produces. Conversely, consider the case of $\text{FRC}_i = 0$. If $\text{FRC}_i = 0$ for all $i$ then this means that the model forecasts 'no change' from period to period, which is simply equivalent to the naive forecasting rule of using the current value of $Y$ as next period's forecast of $Y$. Now if $\text{FRC}_i = 0$ for all $i$ then note from Equation 6.114 that the value of $U$ will be one. Consequently, any forecasting model which produces a value of $U$ in excess of one is producing worse forecasts than a naive, no change forecasting rule (which of course does not require any model).

By way of an illustration of the use of $U$, again consider the one-step ahead forecasts of Example 5.5. Substituting the actual values of consumers' expenditure over the forecast period and the corresponding forecast values into Equation 6.114 produces a value of $U$ of 0.79. Thus the model produces better forecasts than the naive forecasts, but the value of $U$ is certainly closer to one than it is to zero and consequently we might conclude that the forecasts are not particularly impressive.

Although we have demonstrated the use of these various methods of evaluating forecast performance in terms of single equation models, the methods are perfectly general and can also be applied to the forecasts generated by simultaneous equation models. In Example 6.3 we will evaluate the forecasting performance of the simple simultaneous equation model which we estimated in Example 6.2 and thereby further demonstrate some of these methods.

### 6.6.2    Policy Evaluation with an Econometric Model

In addition to forecasting or prediction, an estimated model can also be used for **policy evaluation**. Thus given an estimated model the investigator (policy maker) may be able to control or influence the level of one or more of the exogenous variables. He can then use the model to infer what the effects on the endogenous variable(s) might be of given changes in these controllable exogenous variables (the policy variables).

For example, a manufacturer of some product may have obtained an estimate of the product's demand function, which can then be used to determine how demand will be affected (and consequently how profits will be affected) if the price of the product were to be altered. Or the Government, given an estimate of a model of the economy, can determine the effect of changes in its policy variables (the tax rate, its own expenditure, the interest rate, the exchange rate etc.) on important endogenous variables (the levels of unemployment, national income, investment, consumers' expenditure etc).

Certainly the issues involved in both forecasting and policy evaluation are closely related. However, the distinction which can be drawn between these two functions of an estimated model is that forecasting is typically carried out within the context of a given or unchanged policy regime, whereas the exercise of policy evaluation explicitly attempts to determine the effects of changes in the existing policy regime.

As in the case of forecasting, the reduced form of the model is the most convenient for policy evaluation purposes. In terms of short-term policy evaluation we are concerned with determining how the current levels of the endogenous variables are affected by changes in the current levels of the policy variables. These effects are measured directly by the reduced form coefficients (the impact multipliers).

Again consider the model which we specified in Example 6.2 (Equations 6.83 to 6.85). Recall that we presented the reduced form of this model in Equations 6.101 to 6.103.

Thus, for example, we can directly infer from Equation 6.103 that a one-unit change in the current level of government expenditure ($G_t$) will result in a $1/(1-\alpha_2)$ unit change in the current level of income ($Y_t$). Similarly, a one-unit change in the interest rate will result in a $\beta_2/(1-\alpha_2)$ unit change in income (and a $\beta_2$ unit change in investment (from Equation 6.102), and a $\alpha_2\beta_2/(1-\alpha_2)$ change in consumption expenditure (from Equation 6.101)). In general, then, the magnitude of the coefficients on the policy variables in the reduced form will reflect the responsiveness of the endogenous variables to changes in these policy variables (and, in turn, can be used to infer how effective various policies might be).

Strictly, it is the restricted reduced form which should be used for policy evaluation. In the case of the model in Equations 6.83 to 6.85, use of the unrestricted reduced form (Equations 6.98 to 6.100) would lead to the conclusion that $G_t$ exerts an influence on $I_t$. Thus in terms of policy evaluation it would be concluded that government expenditure policies will directly affect the level of investment expenditure. However, it can be seen from the restricted reduced form that no such influence from $G_t$ to $I_t$ exists. Thus, in this case, quite erroneous policy conclusions could be drawn through the use of the unrestricted reduced form. But the derivation of the restricted reduced form will generally be complex and costly, and an estimate of the unrestricted reduced form will be much more straightforward to obtain. Thus, in practice, the unrestricted reduced form would generally be used.

We will now go on to analyse the model which we estimated in Example 6.2 in terms of its forecasting performance and policy implications.

Example 6.3

Given the three sets of parameter estimates which we presented in Example 6.2 (OLS, 2SLS and 3SLS) there will be four sets of forecasts for $C_t$, $I_t$ and $Y_t$ which can be derived from the model in Equations 6.83 to 6.85. That is:

1  Forecasts derived from that estimate of the restricted reduced form which is obtained by substituting into Equations 6.101 to 6.103 the (inconsistent) OLS estimates of the structural parameters.
2  Forecasts derived from the restricted reduced form estimated using the 2SLS estimates of the structural parameters.
3  Forecasts derived from the restricted reduced form estimated with the 3SLS estimates of the structural parameters.
4  Forecasts derived from the OLS estimate of the unrestricted reduced form.

The forecasting test which we will perform is to re-estimate the model over the period 1956 to 1976, and then to forecast into the period 1977 to 1981. We will only derive the one-step ahead forecasts (that is, we will use the actual values of $C_{t-1}$ and $Y_{t-1}$ over the forecast period, in addition to the actual values of $R_t$ and $G_t$). We will also not concern ourselves with deriving confidence intervals for the levels of $C_t$, $I_t$ and $Y_t$ over the forecast period. Furthermore, we will only consider the forecasts generated under 3 and 4 above – that is, the forecasts generated by the 3SLS estimate of the restricted reduced form and forecasts generated by the unrestricted reduced form.

Equations 6.115 to 6.117 are the estimates of the reduced form equations obtained by substituting the 3SLS estimates of the structural parameters into Equations 6.101 to 6.103. The parameters were estimated over the period 1956 to 1976. No $t$-statistics or $R^2$ are presented as these would have to be derived indirectly (and tediously) from the estimate of the structural form.

$$C_t = -132.808 + 0.406C_{t-1} + 0.247Y_{t-1} - 370.745R_t + 0.758G_t$$
Equation 6.115

$$I_t = -8275.564 + 0.325Y_{t-1} - 489.253R_t \qquad \text{Equation 6.116}$$

$$Y_t = -8408.372 + 0.406C_{t-1} + 0.571Y_{t-1} - 859.998R_t + 1.758G_t$$
Equation 6.117

Equations 6.118 to 6.120 present the OLS estimates of the unrestricted reduced form equations (absolute values of $t$-statistics in brackets).

$$C_t = -2506.770 + 1.226C_{t-1} - 0.123Y_{t-1} - 604.274R_t + 0.366G_t$$
$$(0.86)\quad(3.22)\qquad(0.58)\qquad(3.13)\qquad(0.75)$$
$$\bar{R}^2 = 0.987 \qquad d = 1.81 \qquad \text{Equation 6.118}$$

$$I_t = -4855.461 - 0.337C_{t-1} + 0.566Y_{t-1} - 313.171R_t - 0.424G_t$$
$$\quad\quad\; (2.04)\quad (1.12)\quad\quad\;\; (3.25)\quad\quad\quad\; (1.99)\quad\quad (1.07)$$

$$\bar{R}^2 = 0.961 \quad\quad\quad d = 1.97 \quad\quad\quad \text{Equation 6.119}$$

$$Y_t = -7362.236 + 0.890C_{t-1} - 0.443Y_{t-1} - 917.445R_t + 0.942G_t$$
$$\quad\quad\; (1.68)\quad\;\; (1.60)\quad\quad\;\; (1.38)\quad\quad\quad\; (3.17)\quad\quad (1.29)$$

$$\bar{R}^2 = 0.991 \quad\quad\quad d = 2.04 \quad\quad\quad \text{Equation 6.120}$$

In terms of a comparison of these two estimates of the reduced form, note that there are considerable differences between some of the parameter estimates, with in some cases the signs of the estimates differing.

We will begin by graphically comparing the forecasts generated by these two estimated versions of the reduced form.

Figure 6.3 presents the forecasts of consumption expenditure derived from

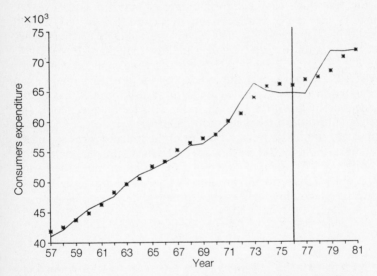

**Figure 6.3** Consumption forecasts – restricted reduced form (3SLS).

the (3SLS) restricted reduced form. The unbroken line is the actual value of consumption and the asterisks denote the forecasts (over the estimation period the asterisks strictly denote the fitted values of consumption). Figure 6.4 presents the forecasts of consumption derived from the unrestricted reduced form. Figures 6.5 and 6.6 present, respectively, the restricted and unrestricted reduced form forecasts of investment, and similarly, Figures 6.7 and 6.8 compare the income forecasts. An obvious feature of these two sets of forecasts is their broad similarity – although the parameter estimates of the

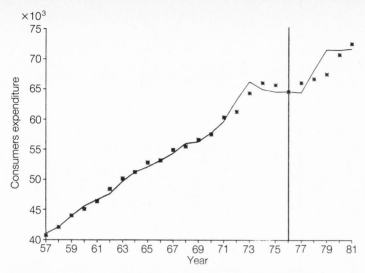

**Figure 6.4**  Consumption forecasts – unrestricted reduced form.

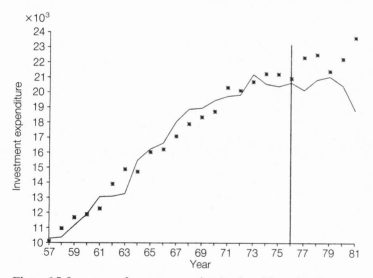

**Figure 6.5**  Investment forecasts – restricted reduced form (3SLS).

restricted and unrestricted reduced forms are in a number of cases very different, very similar forecasts are produced. Thus (at least in this particular application) it would seem that for forecasting purposes there is little to be gained from the tedious and costly derivation of the restricted reduced form.

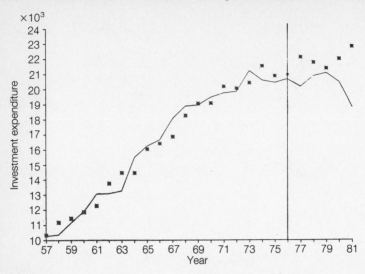

**Figure 6.6** Investment forecasts – unrestricted reduced form.

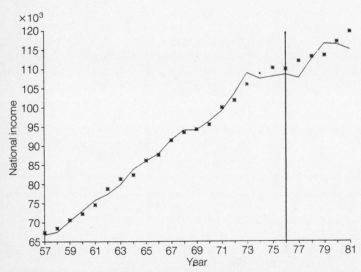

**Figure 6.7** Income forecasts – restricted reduced form (3SLS).

Note also that although reasonable (but certainly not outstanding) forecasts of consumption and income are produced, the investment forecasts are extremely poor. Indeed it is difficult to imagine how the investment forecasts could be any worse – when actual investment is increasing the model

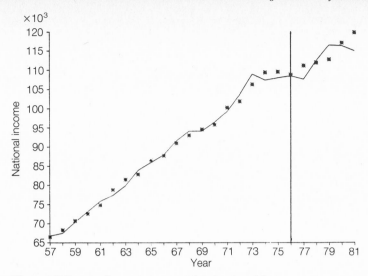

**Figure 6.8** Income forecasts – unrestricted reduced form.

forecasts declining investment, and when actual investment is falling the model forecasts an increase.

Although this simple graphical analysis of the model's forecasting performance has been sufficient to highlight the inadequacies of the model, it is also instructive to examine the forecasting assessment statistics which we described above – that is, the forecasting test statistic, $z_1$, and Theil's $U$-statistic.

In terms of the statistical test associated with $z_1$, we would first emphasise that as we have only used a relatively small sample here, the results of this test should be treated with caution. None the less, primarily for illustrative purposes, we will employ the test in the normal way. As the model has been used to generate five forecasts the appropriate distribution is a $\chi^2$ distribution with five degrees of freedom. From Appendix V, the critical value from the $\chi^2_5$ is 11.1 (at the 5 per cent level). That is, an observed value for $z_1$ in excess of 11.1 would indicate an inconsistency between the given equation's forecasting performance and its estimation performance, hence implying some model misspecification. A value for $z_1$ was obtained via the use of Equation 6.110, for each reduced form equation in each of the two estimated versions of the reduced form. A value for $\hat{\sigma}^2_\varepsilon$ in Equation 6.110 was derived by first using the estimated reduced form equations (Equations 6.115 to 6.120) to obtain the fitted values of each endogenous variable over the estimation period, and then deriving the sum of the squares of the deviations of these fitted values from the actual values. A value for $\hat{\sigma}^2_\varepsilon$ was then obtained by dividing this sum of squares by 20 (the sample size) minus the number of coefficients appearing in the corresponding reduced form equation (note that the restricted reduced form equation for investment only contains three coefficients).

A value for the $U$-statistic was obtained for each set of forecasts through the use of Equation 6.114.

In Table 6.1 we present the values of both $z_1$ and $U$ associated with each of the estimated reduced form equations. From Table 6.1 we can see that in all cases the $z_1$ statistic is significant, reinforcing our conclusions concerning the

**Table 6.1** Forecast summary statistics

| Endogenous variable: | METHOD USED TO ESTIMATE REDUCED FORM: | | | |
| | 3SLS estimates of structural parameters | | Unrestricted reduced form | |
| | $z_1$ | $U$ | $z_1$ | $U$ |
| --- | --- | --- | --- | --- |
| $C_t$ | 14.34 | 0.68 | 26.14 | 0.86 |
| $I_t$ | 57.74 | 2.82 | 40.75 | 2.28 |
| $Y_t$ | 23.36 | 0.83 | 26.34 | 0.91 |

inadequacies of the model derived from the graphical analysis. In terms of the $U$-statistic values of less than one are obtained for the consumption and income equations, and therefore we can conclude that these equations produce better forecasts than a no-change forecasting rule. However, these $U$ values are still quite large implying that the forecasts are not markedly superior to no-change forecasts. In terms of the investment equations, however, the values of both $z_1$ and $U$ emphasise their very poor forecasting performance. In particular, the values of $U$ indicate that the forecasts from the model are considerably worse than simple no-change forecasts.

Thus the assessment of this model on the basis of its forecasting performance has indicated that there is considerable room for improvement, particularly in terms of the investment function. As we argued earlier, the model used here is far too simplistic and its relatively poor forecasting performance is to be expected. The next step would be to go on to derive a more complex and disaggregated model which would presumably produce more satisfactory forecasts.

Finally, we can consider the model in terms of its implications for policy evaluation. Strictly, we should re-estimate the reduced form of the model over the entire sample period – 1956 to 1981 – in order to compare the various reduced forms with respect to their policy implications. However for our purposes we will simply consider the estimated reduced forms in Equations 6.115 to 6.120.

The policy variables are $R_t$ and $G_t$. An important impact multiplier is the government expenditure multiplier – the coefficient on $G_t$ in Equations 6.117 and 6.120. Certainly theory would predict that this multiplier will exceed one – it is simply the inverse of (one minus the marginal propensity to consume), and the marginal propensity to consume would certainly be expected to lie between zero and one. However, note that this multiplier in the unrestricted reduced form (Equation 6.120) is less than one, and in the restricted version of the reduced form, although greater than one, it is perhaps smaller than might be expected. Similarly the estimated impact of government expenditure on consumption differs considerably as between the unrestricted and restricted reduced forms.

Thus a further inadequacy of the model has been identified – some of its policy implications are contrary to theoretical expectations, and this is particularly so with the unrestricted reduced form. Hence further evidence is produced for the need to restructure or respecify the model.

## 6.7   The Estimation of Simultaneous Equation Models in Practice

So far we have discussed various simultaneous equation estimation methods without indicating how to discriminate between these methods for a given estimation problem – that is, for a given application, which method should be used?

We have indicated that theoretically the system methods (3SLS) are superior to the consistent single equation methods (2SLS), which in turn are superior to the inconsistent estimation of each structural equation by ordinary least squares. However, recall that this theoretical superiority was established on the basis of the asymptotic properties of the various estimation methods – that is, on the assumption that infinite sample sizes are available. In practice, only finite (and often small) samples are available, and we cannot draw any conclusions concerning the small sample properties of any estimation method on the basis of its asymptotic properties.

In general, 3SLS, 2SLS and OLS all produce biased estimators in finite samples, this bias only approaching zero as sample size increases for 3SLS and 2SLS. So the real question is – is OLS necessarily inferior to 3SLS and 2SLS in small or finite samples? This question cannot be (or as yet has not been) resolved analytically, but the experimental evidence that is available seems to indicate that the asymptotic advantages of the consistent estimation methods carry over to finite samples, although perhaps not to the same extent. Thus while 3SLS and 2SLS are probably superior to OLS in finite samples, this superiority may not be as marked as might be expected. It must also be emphasised that these conclusions follow only on the assumption that the theoretical model has been correctly specified.

For small models, such as the model used in Examples 6.3 and 6.4, use of, say, 3SLS rather than OLS did not involve a great deal of extra effort. However, in estimating larger models use of consistent estimation methods will be considerably more resource-intensive than the application of OLS to each structural equation. So with larger models there is a very clear trade-off between the inconsistent but far simpler OLS estimation and consistent estimation. Further, if the theoretical advantages of consistent estimation are perhaps not substantial then the advantage of the simplicity of OLS may dominate.

However, in practice, there is a much more serious problem in the application of 2SLS or 3SLS. Recall that the first step in using 2SLS or 3SLS is to regress each explanatory endogenous variable on all the predetermined variables in the model. Most macroeconomic models that are used today contain hundreds (sometimes thousands) of equations and variables. Thus, in general, it will not be possible to carry out the first step of 2SLS or 3SLS estimation – the number of predetermined variables in the model will generally exceed the number of sample observations. Note that this will also be the case in estimating even the unrestricted reduced form – each reduced form equation will contain more explanatory variables than there are observations.

Consequently, for large models – typically macroeconomic models – instrumental variable estimation, or even ordinary least squares, is commonly employed to estimate each structural equation directly (where the instruments would be some subset of the excluded predetermined variables). Therefore in assessing these models we return to the single equation techniques which we have discussed in Chapters 2 to 5. In certain cases it may be possible to define smaller sub-models within larger models which can be treated as more or less independent of the remainder of the model and thus estimated using a more sophisticated methodology.

Thus direct estimates of the reduced form cannot be obtained and forecasting with a large model is a complex exercise – given forecasts of the endogenous variables and estimates of the structural parameters the endogenous variables then have to be solved for in terms of these estimates in order to derive a set of forecasts.

The methodology which we have outlined in this chapter is therefore strictly appropriate only for small or medium sized models, and hence is more appropriate for microeconomic modelling.

## 6.8   Summary

In this chapter we have provided an introductory discussion of the specification, estimation and use of simultaneous equation models.

A simultaneous equation model, as opposed to a single equation model, should be interpreted as the general form of an econometric model. This is particularly so at the macroeconomic level, given the wide range of interrelationships which would be expected to exist amongst macroeconomic variables. However, while the specification of a simultaneous equation model might be argued to be a more satisfactory reflection of reality, the estimation and use of such models is not generally straightforward.

We have emphasised that the direct application of ordinary least squares to the structural equations in a simultaneous equation model is theoretically invalid, and consequently more complex (and hence costly) estimation techniques are required. We briefly discussed two such methods, 2SLS and 3SLS. However, for large simultaneous equation models, these estimation methods tend to become impractical, and we are therefore forced back to the use of less sophisticated methods. The general conclusion which might be drawn, then, is that simultaneous equation modelling is somewhat more advanced in theory than it is in practice.

The consequence is that in much applied econometric work single equation models and estimation methods are still widely used, despite their acknowledged shortcomings. Indeed, many of the recent advances in econometric theory and practice have been in terms of refining these single equation methods, rather than in terms of developing simultaneous equation methods. Thus, for the foreseeable future, it would appear that single equation estimation will still form the basis of most applied econometrics.

## Notes

[1] Recall that the same problem arose in estimating models containing lagged values of the dependent variable (see Section 5.5).

[2] For a proof of this result see, for example, A. Koutsoyiannis. *Theory of Econometrics*, 2nd edn (London, Macmillan, 1977), pp. 373–6.

[3] We are not here concerned with providing a rigorous theoretical justification for this version of the model. Rather, our objective is simply to demonstrate the consequences for identification of variations in the structure of the model.

[4] The assumption of $Y_t$ being exogenous is generally reasonable provided that the market being analysed is relatively small. That is, aggregate consumer income can be interpreted as being a function of all economic activity, and in particular, results from the operation of all submarkets in the economy. So $Y_t$ is influenced by each of the submarkets in the economy, and if it is included in the models of these submarkets then $Y_t$ should strictly be interpreted, in part, as endogenous to these submarket models. However, if the market is small it will have only a limited effect on $Y_t$ and thus $Y_t$ can be defined as being largely exogenous.

[5] Let $H$ denote the number of explanatory variables in an exactly identified structural equation. Assume that of these $H$ explanatory variables $P$ are predetermined and $E$ are endogenous, and further assume that there are a total of $K$ predetermined variables in the model. The equation must therefore exclude $K - P$ of

the predetermined variables appearing in the model. But if the equation is exactly identified then we must have:

$$H = P + E = K$$

and therefore:

$$E = K - P$$

That is, the number of endogenous explanatory variables must equal the number of excluded predetermined variables.

[6] For example, see J. Kmenta, *Elements of Econometrics*, 2nd edn (New York, Macmillan, 1986), pp. 681–5, for a proof of this equivalence.

[7] For example, see ibid., pp. 690–5.

[8] For example, see ibid., pp. 695–701.

[9] For example, see ibid., pp. 701–4.

[10] For example, see ibid., p. 250.

[11] For example, see ibid., pp. 426–30.

[12] Given that the structural form can also be estimated by maximum likelihood methods, more that four sets of forecasts could be derived.

[13] For example, see J. Johnston, *Econometric Methods*, 2nd edn (New York, McGraw-Hill, 1972), pp. 406–7.

[14] See any standard mathematical statistics text, such as R. V. Hogg and A. T. Craig, *Introduction to Mathematical Statistics*, 4th edn (Collier Macmillan, 1978), pp. 169–70. Also see Kmenta, *Elements of Econometrics*, pp. 139–41.

[15] For an illustration of the use of this forecasting test see J. E. H. Davidson *et al.*, 'Econometric modelling of the aggregate time-series relationship between consumers' expenditure and income in the United Kingdom', *Economic Journal*, Dec. 1978, pp. 661–92.

[16] See H. Theil, *Applied Economic Forecasting* (Amsterdam, North-Holland, 1966), pp. 26–36. Also see H. Theil, *Economic Forecasts and Policy* (Amsterdam, North-Holland, 1962), pp. 31–48.

### References and Further Reading

All of the texts indicated in Chapters 2 and 3 contain chapters covering simultaneous equation models. For a more detailed discussion of the structure and properties of the major macroeconomic models of the UK economy see: K. Holden, D. A. Peel and J. L. Thompson, *Modelling the UK Economy* (Martin Robertson, 1982), or K. F. Wallis *et al.*, *Models of the UK Economy* (2 vols, Oxford, Oxford University Press, 1984 and 1985).

For an introductory discussion of the mechanics of forecasting with simultaneous equation models see: L. R. Klein and R. M. Young, *An Introduction to Econometric Forecasting Models* (Lexington Books, 1980).

A concise discussion of some of the practicalities and compromises involved in forecasting with macro models is provided by M. J. C. Surrey and P. A. Ormerod, 'Formal and informal aspects of forecasting with an econometric model', *National Institute Economic Review*, August 1977.

## Exercises

### Exercise 1
Consider the model in Equations 6.2 to 6.4 (and its reduced form in Equations 6.5 to 6.7). Derive the fundamental dynamic equations for $C_t$ and $I_t$.

### Exercise 2
Confirm that the disturbance terms on the left- and right-hand sides of Equation 6.26 are equal.

### Exercise 3
Confirm the equivalence of the three versions of the order condition presented in Section 6.3.

### Exercise 4
Consider the following simple macroeconomic model:

$$C_t = \alpha_0 + \alpha_1 Y_t + \alpha_2 G_t$$
$$I_t = \beta_0 + \beta_1 Y_t + \beta_2 R_t$$
$$Y_t = C_t + I_t + G_t$$

where the notation is the same as previously, and $G_t$ and $R_t$ are exogenous (and, for simplicity, disturbance terms have been ignored).

Using the order condition, examine the identification status of each of the behavioural equations in this model.

Express each reduced form parameter explicitly in terms of the structural parameters. What would be the implications for the identification of the consumption function if $\beta_2 = 0$? How would the identification of the investment function be affected if $\alpha_2 = -1$?

### Exercise 5
Using Equation 6.88, forecast gas consumption for temperatures of $-5$ degrees, 10 degrees and 20 degrees. Place confidence intervals around your forecasts.

**Appendix 6.1** *Inconsistency and the Ordinary Least Squares Estimation of the Structural Form.*

Consider the least squares estimation of the consumption function in the model presented in Equations 6.8 to 6.10.

The least squares estimator of $\alpha_1$ in Equation 6.8 can be written as:

$$\hat{\alpha}_1 = \frac{\sum (C_t - \bar{C})(Y_t - \bar{Y})}{\sum (Y_t - \bar{Y})^2}$$ 

Equation A6.1.1

(See Equation 2.20)

For convenience, let lower case letters denote deviations from the mean. Then we can rewrite Equation A6.1.1 as:

$$\hat{\alpha}_1 = \frac{\sum c_t y_t}{\sum y_t^2}$$ 

Equation A6.1.2

where

$$c_t = C_t - \bar{C}$$
$$y_t = Y_t - \bar{Y}$$

Thus the consumption function in Equation 6.8 can be written as:

$$c_t = \alpha_1 y_t + \varepsilon_{1t}$$ 

Equation A6.1.3

Therefore, substituting Equation A6.1.3 into Equation A6.1.2 produces:

$$\hat{\alpha}_1 = \frac{\sum (\alpha_1 y_t + \varepsilon_{1t}) y_t}{\sum y_t^2}$$

$$= \frac{\alpha_1 \sum y_t^2 + \sum \varepsilon_{1t} y_t}{\sum y_t^2}$$

$$= \alpha_1 + \frac{\sum y_t \varepsilon_{1t}}{\sum y_t^2}$$

$$\therefore E(\hat{\alpha}_1) = \alpha_1 + E\left[\frac{\sum y_t \varepsilon_{1t}}{\sum y_t^2}\right]$$ 

Equation A6.1.4

Now if $y_t$ and $\varepsilon_{1t}$ were independent then we could write:

$$E\left[\frac{\sum y_t \varepsilon_{1t}}{\sum y_t^2}\right] = E\left[\frac{\sum y_t}{\sum y_t^2}\right] E(\varepsilon_{1t}) = 0$$

and thus $\hat{\alpha}_1$ would be both consistent and unbiased. However we have already informally indicated that $y_t$ (or $Y_t$) and $\varepsilon_{1t}$ are not independent. More formally, this can be seen by first deriving the reduced form equation for $Y_t$. That is:

$$Y_t = \frac{\alpha_0 + \beta_0}{1 - \alpha_1} + \frac{\beta_1}{1 - \alpha_1} R_t + \frac{\varepsilon_{1t} + \varepsilon_{2t}}{1 - \alpha_1}$$ 

Equation A6.1.5

Multiplying Equation A6.1.5 by $\varepsilon_{1t}$ we have:

$$Y_t \varepsilon_{1t} = \frac{\alpha_0 + \beta_0}{1 - \alpha_1} \varepsilon_{1t} + \frac{\beta_1}{1 - \alpha_1} R_t \varepsilon_{1t} + \frac{\varepsilon_{1t}^2 + \varepsilon_{2t} \varepsilon_{1t}}{1 - \alpha_1}$$

$$\therefore E(Y_t \varepsilon_{1t}) = \frac{1}{1 - \alpha_1} [E(\varepsilon_{1t}^2) + E(\varepsilon_{1t} \varepsilon_{2t})]$$

or

$$E(Y_t \varepsilon_{1t}) = \frac{1}{1 - \alpha_1} (\sigma_1^2 + \sigma_{12}) \qquad \text{Equation A6.1.6}$$

where $\sigma_1^2 = E(\varepsilon_{1t}^2)$, which is certainly non-zero and $\sigma_{12} = E(\varepsilon_{1t} \varepsilon_{2t})$, which will be non-zero if the disturbance terms are correlated across equations.

Also note that $E(R_t \varepsilon_{1t}) = 0$ as $R_t$ is exogenous.

From Equation A6.1.6 we can see that $Y_t$ and $\varepsilon_{1t}$ are not independent, and consequently that $\hat{\alpha}_1$ will be biased. Further, we have:

$$\text{plim} (\hat{\alpha})_1 = \alpha_1 + \frac{\text{plim} (1/n \sum y_t \varepsilon_{1t})}{\text{plim} (1/n \sum y_t^2)}$$

The dependence of $Y_t$ on $\varepsilon_{1t}$ implies that:

$$\text{plim} (1/n \sum y_t \varepsilon_{1t}) \neq 0$$

and thus $\hat{\alpha}_1$ will not only be biased but also inconsistent.

**Appendix 6.2** *The Rank Condition for the Identification of a Simultaneous Equation Model.*

Recall from our discussion of the model in Equations 6.49 to 6.52 that in order for an equation to be strictly identified then there must be some connection between the variables appearing in that equation and the variables appearing elsewhere in the model. That is, the rest of the model must contribute information which is relevant in terms of the equation under review.

Recall that one version of the order condition states that an equation is exactly identified if it excludes $G - 1$ of the variables appearing in the model, where $G$ is the number of endogenous variables (or equations). In terms of the consumption function (Equation 6.49) we note that this equation excludes three variables ($I_t$, $F_t$, and $M_t$), and as $G = 4$, the equation can be seen to be exactly identified by the order condition. The rank condition, then, requires that these excluded variables are connected in some way to the included variables. In other words, it must be possible to express the excluded variables ($I_t$, $F_t$, and $M_t$) in terms of the included variables ($C_t$, $Y_t$, and $R_t$).

The remainder of the model can be interpreted as three equations in the three excluded variables. Thus in order to determine whether the rank condition is satisfied we need to establish that these three equations can be solved for $I_t$, $F_t$ and $M_t$. Rewriting Equations 6.50 to 6.52, and explicitly including variables with zero restrictions, we have:

$$I_t + 0F_t + 0M_t = \beta_0 + 0C_t + \beta_1 Y_t + 0R_t \qquad \text{Equation A6.2.1}$$

$$0I_t + F_t - \gamma_1 M_t = \gamma_0 + 0C_t + 0Y_t + 0R_t \qquad \text{Equation A6.2.2}$$

$$I_t + 0F_t + 0M_t = 0 - C_t + Y_t + 0R_t \qquad \text{Equation A6.2.3}$$

However, note that Equations A6.2.1 and A6.2.3 have identical left-hand sides but differ on the right-hand side. Equations A6.2.1 and A6.2.3 are therefore not independent and it is not possible to solve for $I_t$, $F_t$ and $M_t$ in terms of $C_t$, $Y_t$ and $R_t$. Consequently, the consumption function remains under-identified.

Readers familiar with matrix algebra will recognise that the rank condition requires that the matrix of coefficients on the excluded variables in the remaining $G-1$ equations of the model be of rank $G-1$. In the case of an exactly identified equation the matrix of coefficients on the excluded variables will be of order $(G-1)$ by $(G-1)$. The rank condition then requires that this matrix have a non-zero determinant. Note that in Equations A6.2.1 to A6.2.3 the matrix of coefficients on $I_t$, $F_t$, and $M_t$ has a determinant of zero. In the case of an over-identified equation we need only establish that the matrix of coefficients on the excluded variables contains at least one $(G-1)$ by $(G-1)$ matrix with a non-zero determinant. Thus in order to examine the identification of the equations in any given model the following procedure can be adopted:

Each equation in the model is first re-expressed such that all zero restrictions are explicitly included, and each equation contains all variables on the left-hand side (in the same ordering). Then, for any given equation, the order condition can be directly checked by confirming that the equation contains at least as many zero coefficients as there are equations in the model minus 1 – that is, that the equation excludes at least $G-1$ variables.

To check the rank condition for any equation the matrix of coefficients on the excluded variables in the remaining equations in the model is formed. Thus the rank condition will be satisfied if this matrix contains at least one $(G-1)$ by $(G-1)$ sub-matrix with a non-zero determinant. In the case of exact identification, the matrix of excluded variable coefficients will be exactly $(G-1)$ by $(G-1)$, and thus the rank condition will be satisfied if this matrix has a non-zero determinant. Further, as the determinant of this matrix will be a function of the structural parameters, it will also be possible to deduce directly the values of the structural parameters for which this determinant will be zero. That is, it will be possible to deduce the values of the structural parameters which will result in the under-identification of the given equation.

Thus in terms of the model in Equations 6.49 to 6.52, this model can be re-expressed as follows:

$$C_t + 0I_t + 0F_t - \alpha_1 Y_t - \alpha_2 R_t + 0M_t - \alpha_0 = 0$$

$$0C_t + I_t + 0F_t - \beta_1 Y_t + 0R_t + 0M_t - \beta_0 = 0$$

$$0C_t + 0I_t + F_t + 0Y_t + 0R_t - \gamma_1 M_t - \gamma_0 = 0$$
$$-C_t - I_t + 0F_t + Y_t + 0R_t + 0M_t + 0 = 0$$

Rewriting the coefficients in tabular form produces:

| $C_t$ | $I_t$ | $F_t$ | $Y_t$ | $R_t$ | $M_t$ | 1 |
|---|---|---|---|---|---|---|
| 1 | 0 | 0 | $-\alpha_1$ | $-\alpha_2$ | 0 | $-\alpha_0$ |
| 0 | 1 | 0 | $-\beta_1$ | 0 | 0 | $-\beta_0$ |
| 0 | 0 | 1 | 0 | 0 | $-\gamma_1$ | $-\gamma_0$ |
| $-1$ | $-1$ | 0 | 1 | 0 | 0 | 0 |

Thus the row of coefficients corresponding to the consumption function contains three zeros, and is therefore exactly identified by the order condition. The matrix of coefficients on the excluded variables which appear in the remaining three equations is as follows:

$$\begin{matrix} 1 & 0 & 0 \\ 0 & 1 & -\gamma_1 \\ -1 & 0 & 0 \end{matrix}$$

The determinant of this matrix is zero, and therefore the consumption function is under-identified.

Consider the investment function. It contains four zero coefficients, and thus is over-identified by the order condition. The matrix of coefficients on the excluded variables is:

$$\begin{matrix} 1 & 0 & -\alpha_2 & 0 \\ 0 & 1 & 0 & -\gamma_1 \\ -1 & 0 & 0 & 0 \end{matrix}$$

In order to confirm that the investment function is identified by the rank condition we need to establish that at least one three by three matrix can be formed from this four by four matrix which has a zero determinant. This can be achieved *provided* that $\alpha_2 \neq 0$. Thus we would conclude that the investment function is identified on the condition that $\alpha_2 \neq 0$. In turn, this simply implies that the investment function will be identified provided $R_t$ appears in the model. Note that if $R_t$ did not appear in the model, then the investment function would still be identified by the order condition (due to the presence of the exogenous variable, $M_t$), but would then be under-identified by the rank condition (for the same reason as the consumption function was under-identified). The reader should confirm this.

**Appendix 6.3**   *Consumption, Investment, National Income, Government Expenditure and Interest Rates, United Kingdom 1956–1981 (1975 Prices).*

| Year | Consumers' expenditure (£m) | Gross domestic fixed capital formation (£m) | Government expenditure (£m) | National income (£m) | Minimum lending rate (%) |
|------|------|------|------|------|------|
| 1956 | 40,225 | 9747 | 15,685 | 65,657 | 5.50 |
| 1957 | 41,073 | 10,280 | 15,419 | 66,777 | 6.00 |
| 1958 | 42,145 | 10,366 | 15,006 | 67,517 | 5.00 |
| 1959 | 43,979 | 11,160 | 15,270 | 70,409 | 4.00 |
| 1960 | 45,623 | 11,905 | 15,576 | 73,104 | 5.50 |
| 1961 | 46,680 | 13,070 | 16,129 | 75,879 | 6.50 |
| 1962 | 47,653 | 13,096 | 16,621 | 77,370 | 5.00 |
| 1963 | 49,725 | 13,269 | 16,891 | 79,885 | 4.00 |
| 1964 | 51,274 | 15,494 | 17,161 | 83,929 | 6.00 |
| 1965 | 52,131 | 16,240 | 17,616 | 85,987 | 6.00 |
| 1966 | 53,184 | 16,643 | 18,083 | 87,910 | 7.00 |
| 1967 | 54,385 | 18,052 | 19,114 | 91,551 | 6.50 |
| 1968 | 56,026 | 18,878 | 19,186 | 94,090 | 7.25 |
| 1969 | 56,313 | 18,954 | 18,829 | 94,096 | 8.00 |
| 1970 | 57,814 | 19,460 | 19,103 | 96,377 | 7.25 |
| 1971 | 59,724 | 19,743 | 19,673 | 99,140 | 5.50 |
| 1972 | 63,270 | 19,823 | 20,484 | 103,577 | 7.75 |
| 1973 | 66,332 | 21,195 | 21;453 | 108,980 | 9.50 |
| 1974 | 65,049 | 20,562 | 21,774 | 107,385 | 12.00 |
| 1975 | 64,652 | 20,408 | 22,950 | 108,010 | 11.00 |
| 1976 | 64,707 | 20,640 | 23,178 | 108,525 | 12.00 |
| 1977 | 64,517 | 20,139 | 22,951 | 107,607 | 9.50 |
| 1978 | 68,227 | 20,845 | 23,438 | 112,510 | 8.50 |
| 1979 | 71,599 | 21,039 | 23,866 | 116,504 | 14.00 |
| 1980 | 71,550 | 20,443 | 24,311 | 116,304 | 15.00 |
| 1981 | 71,762 | 18,774 | 24,394 | 114,930 | 12.00 |

*Source: Economic Trends*, Annual Supplement, 1983, HMSO.

# 7 Some Further Aspects of Time-Series Modelling

## 7.1 Introduction

In this chapter we will present an introductory discussion of the Box–Jenkins approach to time-series modelling. The central objective of this approach is to estimate time-series models which can be used directly and exclusively for forecasting purposes (and particularly for short-term forecasting). In this sense, the objectives of Box–Jenkins modelling are considerably more modest than those of econometric modelling. Box–Jenkins models make no attempt to explain or isolate the economic forces which have generated the data series of interest. Rather, the approach is much more pragmatic, with the emphasis being placed on a rigorous analysis of the statistical properties of the data series. It is via such an analysis that an approximation of the statistical process which generated the data can be derived. Combined with the objective of keeping such models as simple as possible, the Box–Jenkins approach can provide a very powerful and efficient means of generating short-term forecasts.

However, in terms of economic modelling at least, there are limitations to the Box–Jenkins approach. The approach is not well suited to generating medium to longer-term forecasts, and the approach is of only limited use for policy evaluation purposes. Consequently, we will complete this chapter by once again returning to the consideration of modelling consumers' expenditure. We will demonstrate that by borrowing some of the ideas of the Box–Jenkins approach (particularly the emphasis which is placed on a detailed examination of the statistical properties of the data) it is possible to specify and estimate a consumption function which is both statistically rigorous and economically plausible.

## 7.2    An Introduction to the Box–Jenkins Approach to Time-Series Modelling

Throughout this book we have emphasised that the process of specifying and estimating econometric models involves satisfying the requirements of both economic and statistical theory. The role of economic theory could be characterised as providing the basis for selecting a model from among that class of competing statistical models that are all equally consistent with the available data. Often it may not be possible to derive a model which is both data and theory-consistent. The implication in such cases, then, is that the available economic theory may need to be refined and developed and/or that more reliable and relevant data should be obtained. Thus, via this iterative process of refining economic theory and examining the statistical properties of the available data it should be possible, ultimately, to derive an estimate of the true model.

However, in many respects, this approach to modelling economic data represents an ideal which can never be fully achieved in practice. Economic theory is continually evolving and is therefore not an infallible basis for discriminating between competing models, and 'perfect' data will never be available (at least in the social sciences). Thus it could be argued that this idealised approach to econometric modelling is over-optimistic, and if the economic modeller is to provide useful and immediate information for the economic policy maker then a more pragmatic approach must be made.

In essence, the Box–Jenkins approach to modelling time-series data (hereinafter referred to as B–J) could be characterised as just such a pragmatic approach. B–J gives no weight to satisfying the requirements of economic theory, its objective being solely to identify and estimate an appropriate statistical model, which can then be used for forecasting. This is achieved via a rigorous analysis of the statistical properties of the available sample data – the only criterion used for selecting an appropriate model is data consistency. In practice, it will often be possible to identify and estimate a *number* of competing models satisfactorily, all of which will be equally consistent with the data. The basis for discrimination in such cases is to select the simplest of these models – that is, that model with the smallest number of parameters (somewhat grandly referred to in the B–J literature as invoking the 'principle or parsimony').

The proponents of B–J do not necessarily argue that economic theory is irrelevant. Certainly it is accepted that any given economic data set will be the outcome of a variety of (generally complex) economic forces, but for forecasting purposes at least, it may not be necessary to isolate each of these economic influences – the data series itself may well contain all the information necessary (in some aggregated sense) to allow adequate forecasts of this series to be made. B–J has no pretensions to derive models which 'explain' how a given data series evolves over time, nor is any attempt made to identify the 'true' model. Rather, the approach is to derive as simple and concise a statistical description of the data as possible, thereby facilitating the forecasting process.

We will now go on to discuss B–J in more detail.

Let $Y$ denote the variable of interest. Assume that a time-series of $n$ observations is available on $Y$. Thus the sample observations can be denoted by:

$$Y_1, Y_2, \ldots, Y_n$$

Just as in the case of econometric modelling, $Y$ is assumed to be stochastic. That is, each $Y_t$ $(t = 1, \ldots, n)$ can be interpreted as having been selected from a distribution of possible values, the characteristics of this distribution being determined by the nature of a disturbance term, $\varepsilon_t$.

Before proceeding to apply B–J methodology we must first ensure that the sample data $(Y_1, \ldots, Y_n)$ are **stationary**. For practical purposes, by stationarity we mean that the sample data have a constant mean (that is, there is no trend in the data) and a constant variance (the disturbance terms are homoskedastic). The reason for requiring stationarity derives from the nature of B–J methodology. The objective of B–J is to identify and estimate a statistical model which can be interpreted as having generated the sample data. If this estimated model is then to be used for forecasting we must assume that the features of this model are constant through time, and particularly over future time periods. Thus the simple reason for requiring stationary data is that any model which is inferred from these data can itself be interpreted as stationary or stable, therefore providing a valid basis for forecasting.

In practice, most economic time-series will not be stationary – they will generally contain a trend of some form and will often reflect heteroskedasticity. As an example, consider the graph of quarterly consumers' expenditure in Figure 4.7. The data exhibit clear evidence of a trend and would also appear to be heteroskedastic. That is, in B–J terminology the data would be described as being non-stationary in both the mean and the variance. Thus before applying B–J methodology to such data they would first have to be transformed in some way in order to produce a stationary data series. A model would then be fitted to these stationary data and forecasts of the stationary series would be derived from this estimated model. These forecasts can then be 'untransformed' so as to produce forecasts of the original time-series.

For our present purposes, we will proceed on the assumption that the available sample data are stationary, and we will subsequently describe the data transformations which can be used to reduce a non-stationary series to a stationary one. For simplicity, we will also assume that the sample data have a zero mean (if the original data have a non-zero mean then we would simply express the data in mean deviation form and then proceed to analyse these mean deviations).

Given the variable, $Y$, the simplest assumption which could be made is that $Y_t$ is a function only of its own past values and a disturbance term. That is, forecasts of $Y$ can be generated via an analysis of the behaviour of $Y$ over previous time-periods. Formally, a model for $Y_t$ could be written as:

$$Y_t = \phi_1 Y_{t-1} + \phi_2 Y_{t-2} + \dots + \phi_p Y_{t-p} + \varepsilon_t + \theta_1 \varepsilon_{t-1} + \theta_2 \varepsilon_{t-2} + \dots + \theta_q \varepsilon_{t-q}$$

Equation 7.1

where $\varepsilon_t$ is a random disturbance term, the properties of which are identical to those specified in the simple regression model.

Equation 7.1 is not to be interpreted as a model which purports to explain the behaviour of $Y$ over time. Rather, it is an attempt to summarise the behaviour of $Y$ in terms only of its own past behaviour and that of a disturbance term. No doubt there is a set of variables or influences which can actually explain the behaviour of $Y$ (and which would be specified in the appropriate econometric model). However, the assumption implicit in Equation 7.1 is that all of these external influences are reflected in the past values of $Y$, and there is no need to identify each of these influences if our only objective is to forecast $Y$. The time-series observations on $Y$ could in this sense be interpreted as having a 'memory'.

Note also that the assumption concerning the structure of the disturbance term in Equation 7.1 is perfectly general, allowing for the possibility of much more complex structures than the simple first-order structures assumed in Chapter 4.

The model in Equation 7.1 describes the class of B–J **univariate** time-series models – that is, the attempt to model the variable of interest in terms only of its own past behaviour. This class of models represents the simplest form of B–J models and is the only class of models which we will discuss. However, more complex B–J models have been developed which attempt to incorporate the role which might be played by additional variables (these models are described as **transfer function** models). Thus the general approach of B–J would be first to estimate an appropriate univariate model. If this model then proved to be inadequate (that is, an unacceptable level of residual variation remained, hence producing unreliable forecasts) the estimation of an appropriate transfer function model would be attempted. However we will not offer a discussion of such models here.[1]

In order to estimate Equation 7.1, for some given data set, we must first specify the number of parameters that are to be included in the model (or the length of the lags which appear in Equation 7.1). That is, the first step in estimating a B–J model is to specify the values of $p$ and $q$ in Equation 7.1. This initial step is referred to as the **identification** stage, and the approach of B–J is to perform an initial statistical analysis of the data so as to determine tentative values for $p$ and $q$.

Given these initial values of $p$ and $q$, the next step is to estimate the parameters of the implied model. The estimation methods used are essentially those which we have already outlined in the previous chapters of this book – that is, least squares or maximum likelihood methods can be employed, although, in general, non-linear estimation methods will have to be used.

Having estimated the parameters of the model, the next step is to examine the adequacy of the estimated model. Again, the approach is similar to that employed by the econometrician. The $t$-statistics associated with each estimated parameter can be calculated, and any lagged variable with an insignificant $t$-statistic could be dropped from the model (recall that B–J is not concerned with any theoretical justification for retaining a variable in the model).

However, the major criterion employed is to check that the residuals from the estimated model are random. Note from Equation 7.1 that if the model is correctly specified (that is, the correct values of $p$ and $q$ have been selected) then, by definition, the disturbance term, $\varepsilon_t$, must be random. Thus given a correctly specified and estimated model we would expect the estimated disturbances – the $e_t$ terms – to reflect this property of randomness. If the estimated disturbances are found to be non-random then this would imply some model inadequacy, and therefore the need to respecify and re-estimate the model. That is, any structure remaining in the estimated residuals would directly imply the need for further lagged terms in Equation 7.1. Recall that the econometrician is also concerned with this aspect of model evaluation, and this was the role played by the Durbin–Watson test. However, in the case of B–J a much more generalised approach is taken, with consideration given to any form of structure in the disturbance term, not just the possibility of first-order autocorrelation.

The foregoing describes the basic approach to specifying and estimating B–J models. Thus an initial model is tentatively identified, this model is then estimated, and its adequacy then evaluated. If any model inadequacy is highlighted at the evaluation stage then this will imply the need to re-specify, re-estimate and re-evaluate the model. Indeed, it will often be the case that the form of model inadequacy that is highlighted at the evaluation stage will directly imply the specific nature of the model re-specification which is required. Thus the approach of B–J modelling is very much an iterative one. Once a model has been satisfactorily specified, estimated and evaluated (essentially, this will be that model which produces a random disturbance term using the smallest number of estimated parameters) then the model can be finally used for forecasting.

We will now go on to discuss each of these four iterative stages of B–J modelling – that is, identification, estimation, evaluation and forecasting.

### 7.2.1   *Identifying a Tentative Model*

The general form of the model specified in Equation 7.1 is referred to an **Autoregressive-Moving Average** model of order $p, q$, which is generally shortened to ARMA$(p, q)$. That is, the model contains $p$ autoregressive parameters ($p$ lagged values of $Y$) and $q$ moving average parameters ($q$ lagged values of the disturbance term).

For most applications values of $p$ and $q$ less than about two (or at the most three) will generally prove to be adequate. Thus, typically, we will not have to consider models more complex than an ARMA$(2, 2)$, which can be written as:

$$Y_t = \phi_1 Y_{t-1} + \phi_2 Y_{t-2} + \varepsilon_t + \theta_1 \varepsilon_{t-1} + \theta_2 \varepsilon_{t-2} \qquad \text{Equation 7.2}$$

Within the class of ARMA$(p, q)$ models we can also consider **pure** autoregressive models or **pure** moving average models. Thus a model containing only autoregressive parameters could be denoted by ARMA$(p, 0)$, or simply AR$(p)$. Similarly, a pure moving average model containing just $q$ moving average parameters would be denoted by MA$(q)$. Thus the expressions for AR$(1)$, AR$(2)$, MA$(1)$ and MA$(2)$ models would be as follows:

$$\text{AR}(1): Y_t = \phi_1 Y_{t-1} + \varepsilon_t \qquad \text{Equation 7.3}$$

$$\text{AR}(2): Y_t = \phi_1 Y_{t-1} + \phi_2 Y_{t-2} + \varepsilon_t \qquad \text{Equation 7.4}$$

$$\text{MA}(1): Y_t = \varepsilon_t + \theta_1 \varepsilon_{t-1} \qquad \text{Equation 7.5}$$

$$\text{MA}(2): Y_t = \varepsilon_t + \theta_1 \varepsilon_{t-1} + \theta_2 \varepsilon_{t-2} \qquad \text{Equation 7.6}$$

It is left to the reader to deduce the expressions for an ARMA$(1, 1)$ model, an ARMA$(1, 2)$ model and an ARMA$(2, 1)$ model. Note also that Equations 7.3 and 7.4 could be interpreted as dynamic econometric models.

Thus, given a time-series sample on $Y$, our objective is to derive a method for inferring which one of these various models is consistent with the data, and can therefore be used as a summary description of the statistical process which generated the data. We will begin by considering the case of pure autoregressive models.

### The Identification of Autoregressive Models

For illustrative purposes, consider again the data which we generated on a positively and a negatively autocorrelated disturbance term in Chapter 4 (see Equations 4.70 and 4.71). Thus recall from Equation 4.70 that we generated the positively autocorrelated disturbances via the equation:

$$P\varepsilon_t = 0.85 P\varepsilon_{t-1} + u_t \qquad \text{Equation 7.7}$$

where $u_t$ is a normally and independently distributed disturbance term, with a mean of zero and a variance of 10,000.

In terms of the notation we are using here let:

$$Y_t = P\varepsilon_t$$

and

$$\varepsilon_t = u_t$$

Therefore Equation 7.7 can be rewritten as:

$$Y_t = 0.85Y_{t-1} + \varepsilon_t \qquad\qquad \text{Equation 7.8}$$

That is, the observations on $P\varepsilon_t$ derived in Chapter 4 can be interpreted as having been generated by an AR(1) process with a value for $\phi_1$ of 0.85.

Our problem here is, given these sample observations (but without any knowledge of how they were generated), how can we infer that they were in fact generated by an AR(1)?

Consider being presented with the sample of observations on $P\varepsilon_t$ (which we will hereinafter denote by $Y_t$). As we have already indicated, before proceeding to apply B–J methods we must ensure that the data are stationary. A first step then would be simply to graph the sample observations against time. Recall that we did this in Figure 4.10(a), and we reproduce this graph in Figure 7.1.

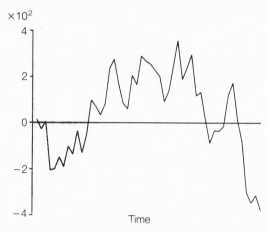

**Figure 7.1** Data generated by Equation 7.8.

Thus from Figure 7.1 there would appear to be no trend in the data, and there is no obvious evidence of any heteroskedasticity (we will describe more formal procedures which can be used for examining the stationarity of any given data set in Section 7.2.5). As a starting point, it would seem reasonable to assume that the data in Figure 7.1 are stationary. This is of course to be expected, given that we imposed stationarity on the process which generated the data – that is, from Equation 4.67 of Chapter 4, but using the notation we have adopted here, the AR(1) process:

$$Y_t = \phi_1 Y_{t-1} + \varepsilon_t \qquad\qquad \text{Equation 7.9}$$

has a constant mean and constant variance of:

$$E(Y_t) = 0 \quad \text{for all } t \qquad\qquad \text{Equation 7.10}$$

and

$$\text{Var}(Y_t) = \frac{\sigma_\varepsilon^2}{1 - \phi_1^2} \quad \text{for all } t \qquad \qquad \text{Equation 7.11}$$

where $\sigma_\varepsilon^2$ is the variance of the disturbance term $\varepsilon_t$.

In order to apply B–J methods to these data we must first introduce a number of additional statistical concepts.

Consider the correlation between $Y_t$ and $Y_{t-1}$. Now, we showed in Chapter 4 that if Equation 7.9 generated the data then the correlation between $Y_t$ and $Y_{t-1}$ is simply given by $\phi_1$ (see Equation 4.66, noting that we there used $\rho$ in place of $\phi_1$).

Now consider the correlation between $Y_t$ and $Y_{t-2}$. It is left as an exercise for the reader to show that, in the case of an AR(1), this correlation is simply $\phi_1^2$. Further, it can be shown that, in general, the correlation between $Y_t$ and $Y_{t-k}$ (if $Y_t$ is generated by an AR(1) process) is given by $\phi_1^k$ (again, this is left for the reader to confirm).

Define the correlation between $Y_t$ and $Y_{t-k}$ as the **autocorrelation of the process at lag k**. Denote this autocorrelation by $\rho_k$. The set of autocorrelations for $k = 1, \ldots, K$ is referred to as the **autocorrelation function** of the process (generally abbreviated to a.c.f.). That is, the a.c.f. of an AR(1) process is:

$$\rho_k = \phi_1^k, \quad k = 1, \ldots, K \qquad \qquad \text{Equation 7.12}$$

Finally, note that as $\phi_1$ can be interpreted as the correlation coefficient between $Y_t$ and $Y_{t-1}$ we must have $|\phi_1| < 1$ (note from Equation 7.11 that if $|\phi_1| > 1$ then $\text{Var}(Y_t)$ would be negative, and hence undefined).

Consequently, given that $|\phi_1| < 1$, we can deduce from Equation 7.12 that

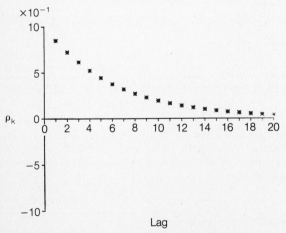

**Figure 7.2** The a.c.f. of an AR(1) with positive $\phi_1$.

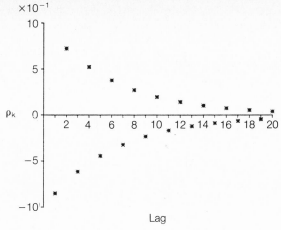

**Figure 7.3** The a.c.f. of an AR(1) with negative $\phi_1$.

the a.c.f. of a stationary AR(1) process will decay geometrically as the lag length, $k$, increases. In Figures 7.2 and 7.3 we present a diagrammatic interpretation of the theoretical a.c.f. of an AR(1), for positive and negative $\phi_1$, respectively. Therefore we now have a potential method for identifying the form of the statistical process which may have generated a given sample of data. That is, we could estimate the autocorrelations at the various lag lengths from the sample data, and if these autocorrelations approximate the behaviour of the theoretical a.c.f.s in either Figure 7.2 or Figure 7.3, then we could conclude that the data appear to have been generated by an AR(1). The next step would be to go on to estimate the parameter, $\phi_1$, of the implied AR(1) process. The problem, then, is how an estimate of the a.c.f. can be derived from the sample data.

Note first that, strictly, in order to estimate the autocorrelation at lag $k$ we require a sample of observations at time-period $t$ and a sample at period $t-k$. We could then calculate the correlation coefficient between these two sets of data. That is, the actual autocorrelation at lag $k$ can be written as:

$$\rho_k = \frac{\mathrm{Cov}(Y_t, Y_{t-k})}{\sqrt{\mathrm{Var}(Y_t)\,\mathrm{Var}(Y_{t-k})}} \qquad\qquad \text{Equation 7.13}$$

and as the process is assumed to be stationary then we have:

$$\mathrm{Var}(Y_t) = \mathrm{Var}(Y_{t-k})$$

and thus Equation 7.13 can be written as:

$$\rho_k = \frac{\mathrm{Cov}(Y_t, Y_{t-k})}{\mathrm{Var}(Y_t)} \qquad\qquad \text{Equation 7.14}$$

Therefore in order to estimate $\rho_k$ we require an estimate of the covariance between $Y_t$ and $Y_{t-k}$ and an estimate of the variance of $Y$ at period $t$.

However, given a sample of time-series observations, only one observation will be available at each time period, and therefore we will not be able to estimate the various autocorrelations in this way. This, then, is a further reason for requiring a stationary time series. For if the time series is stationary, then both the mean and variance of $Y_t$ will be constant at each time point, and this constant mean and variance can then be estimated by the mean and variance of the sample observations. That is:

$$\hat{\mu} = \frac{1}{n} \sum_{t=1}^{n} Y_t = \bar{Y}$$    Equation 7.15

(which we have assumed to be zero), and

$$\text{Var}(Y_t) = \text{Var}(Y_{t-1}) = \ldots = \text{Var}(Y_{t-k})$$

$$= \frac{1}{n} \sum_{t=1}^{n} (Y_t - \bar{Y})^2$$    Equation 7.16

Similarly, the covariance between $Y_t$ and $Y_{t-k}$ (referred to as the autocovariance at lag $k$) can be estimated by:

$$C_k = \frac{1}{n} \sum_{t=1}^{n-k} (Y_t - \bar{Y})(Y_{t+k} - \bar{Y})$$    Equation 7.17

since as the process is stationary then we must have:

$$C_k = \text{Cov}(Y_t, Y_{t-k}) = \text{Cov}(Y_t, Y_{t+k})$$

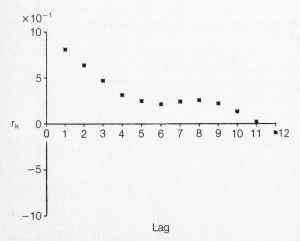

**Figure 7.4** Estimated a.c.f. from sample data on $Y_t$.

Denoting the estimate of Var $(Y_t)$ by $C_0$, to be consistent with the notation in Equation 7.17, the estimated a.c.f. associated with any data set can therefore be written as:

$$\hat{\rho}_k = r_k = \frac{C_k}{C_0} \quad \text{for } k = 1,\ldots,K \qquad \text{Equation 7.18}$$

In order to derive reliable estimates of $r_k$ a large sample should be used (in excess of about 40 or 50), and autocorrelations beyond lag $n/4$ should not be considered.

Thus we can now use the sample data generated by Equation 4.70 to estimate the a.c.f. of the underlying process. Using Equation 7.18, and considering only autocorrelations up to lag 12, it can be shown that:

$$r_1 = 0.809$$

$$r_2 = 0.636$$

$$r_3 = 0.470$$

$$= \ldots$$

$$r_{12} = -0.096$$

A graph of these autocorrelations is shown in Figure 7.4.

Although the estimated a.c.f. in Figure 7.4 does not perfectly mimic the behaviour of the corresponding theoretical a.c.f. in Figure 7.2 (it is only an estimate), evidence of geometric decay is certainly present (in the first six autocorrelations, at least). Therefore we would here tentatively accept that the data have been generated by an AR process.

However, while geometric decay in the a.c.f. certainly implies that AR parameters are involved in the underlying statistical process, it can be shown that all AR processes, irrespective of their order, will produce geometrically declining a.c.f.s. That is, we cannot deduce directly from Figure 7.4 that the underlying process is necessarily AR(1). Thus we require a method for identifying the order of the AR process which generated the data.

Consider the general expression for an AR($p$) process. That is:

$$Y_t = \phi_1 Y_{t-1} + \phi_2 Y_{t-2} + \ldots + \phi_p Y_{t-p} + \varepsilon_t \qquad \text{Equation 7.19}$$

Now, consider interpreting Equation 7.19 as a multiple regression equation, where $Y_t$ is regressed on $p$ lagged values of itself.

One possible method for determining the order of the underlying AR process is to use ordinary least squares to estimate varying versions of Equation 7.19, each with a successively increased value of $p$. That regression which produces an insignificant $t$-statistic for $\phi_p$ would therefore imply that the order of the AR process is $p-1$. That is, we could begin with $p = 2$, and thus estimate the equation:

$$Y_t = \phi_1 Y_{t-1} + \phi_2 Y_{t-2} + \varepsilon_t \qquad \text{Equation 7.20}$$

If the $t$-statistic associated with $\phi_2$ is insignificant then the implication is that the underlying process is AR(1). If the $t$-statistic is significant, then we would consider $p = 3$ and therefore estimate:

$$Y_t = \phi_1 Y_{t-1} + \phi_2 Y_{t-2} + \phi_3 Y_{t-3} + \varepsilon_t \qquad \text{Equation 7.21}$$

If the $t$-statistic associated with $\phi_3$ is insignificant then an AR(2) is implied. If the $t$-statistic is significant then $p = 4$ would be considered. This process could then be continued until an insignificant $t$-statistic on $\phi_p$ is produced. In effect, this is the approach which B–J adopts in identifying the appropriate order of an AR process. However, this procedure can be considerably shortened.

Consider an AR(1). We have already shown that for an AR(1) (see Equation 7.12):

$$\phi_1 = \rho_1 \qquad \text{Equation 7.22}$$

and therefore we could estimate $\phi_1$ with $r_1$ (see Equation 7.18, and note that $r_1$ is simply the least squares estimator of $\phi_1$).

If the process is AR(2), then it can be shown that:

$$\phi_2 = \frac{\rho_2 - \rho_1^2}{1 - \rho_1^2} \qquad \text{Equation 7.23}$$

and thus $\phi_2$ could be estimated by:

$$\hat{\phi}_2 = \frac{r_2 - r_1^2}{1 - r_1^2} \qquad \text{Equation 7.24}$$

(Again, note that the expression for $\hat{\phi}_2$ in Equation 7.24 is simply the expression for the least squares estimator of $\phi_2$ in Equation 7.19, for $p = 2$.)

Similarly, for an AR(3) it can be shown that:

$$\phi_3 = \frac{(\rho_3 - \rho_1\rho_2) - \rho_1(\rho_1\rho_3 - \rho_2^2) + \rho_1(\rho_1^2 - \rho_2)}{(1 - \rho_1^2) - \rho_1^2(1 - \rho_2) + \rho_2(\rho_1^2 - \rho_2)} \qquad \text{Equation 7.25}$$

and thus an estimate of $\phi_3$ can be derived by substituting $r_1$, $r_2$ and $r_3$ for $\rho_1$, $\rho_2$ and $\rho_3$ in Equation 7.25. (Again, it can be shown that the expression for $\hat{\phi}_3$ derived from Equation 7.25 is just the expression for the least squares estimator of $\phi_3$ in Equation 7.19, for $p = 3$.)

These expressions for $\phi_k$, $k = 1, 2, 3$, in Equations 7.22, 7.23 and 7.25 can be generalised, and thus a general expression derived for $\phi_k$, $k = 1, \ldots, K$. This general expression is referred to as the **partial autocorrelation function** (p.a.c.f.) of the process, and is denoted by $\phi_{kk}$ (a double subscript is used in order to distinguish these partial autocorrelations from the coefficients of the finally identified and estimated AR process).

Thus if the process is AR(1) then, from Equation 7.22, $\phi_{11} = \rho_1$. From Equation 7.12 we also have $\rho_k = \phi_1^k$, and therefore $\phi_{22}$ and $\phi_{33}$ in Equations

7.23 and 7.25 will both be zero (the reader can confirm that the numerator of both Equation 7.23 and Equation 7.25 will equal zero if $\rho_k = \phi_1^k$). It can be shown that for an AR(1) this result generalises to:

$$\phi_{11} = \rho_1$$

and

$$\phi_{kk} = 0 \quad \text{for all } k \geqslant 2$$

In terms of our multiple regression interpretation of an AR($p$) model in Equation 7.19, this result simply reflects the fact that, by definition, an AR(1) will have $\phi_1 \neq 0$, and $\phi_k = 0$ for all $k \geqslant 0$.

Similarly, it can be shown that for an AR(2), both $\phi_{11}$ and $\phi_{22}$ will be non-zero, and $\phi_{kk}$ will equal zero for all $k \geqslant 3$.

Therefore, it can be shown that we can generalise to the result that for an AR($p$) process the theoretical a.c.f. will exhibit some form of geometric decline, and that for the p.a.c.f.:

$$\phi_{kk} \neq 0 \quad \text{for } k = 1, \ldots, p$$

and

$$\phi_{kk} = 0 \quad \text{for } k \geqslant p+1$$

Thus the order of an AR($p$) process can be determined by the number of non-zero partial autocorrelations in the p.a.c.f. Diagrammatically, the theoretical a.c.f. and p.a.c.f. of an AR(1) would appear as in Figure 7.5 or Figure 7.6, depending on whether $\phi_1$ were positive or negative. Similarly, for an AR(2), four patterns are possible, as shown in Figures 7.7 to 7.10.

Of course, given a sample of data we can only estimate the a.c.f. and p.a.c.f. We have already indicated how the a.c.f. can be estimated (Equation 7.18). The estimate of the p.a.c.f. ($\hat{\phi}_{kk}$) is derived via the generalisation of Equation 7.25, with $r_k$ substituted for $\rho_k$.

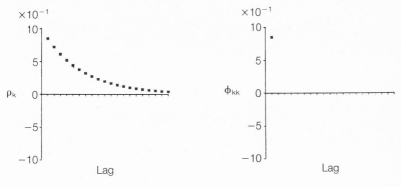

**Figure 7.5** Theoretical a.c.f. and p.a.c.f. for an AR(1) with $\phi_1 > 0$.

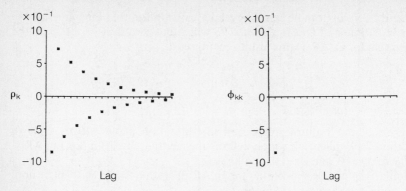

**Figure 7.6**  Theoretical a.c.f. and p.a.c.f. of an AR(1) with $\phi_1 < 0$.

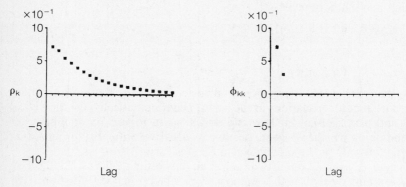

**Figure 7.7**  Theoretical a.c.f. and p.a.c.f. of an AR(2) with $\phi_1 > 0$ and $\phi_2 > 0$.

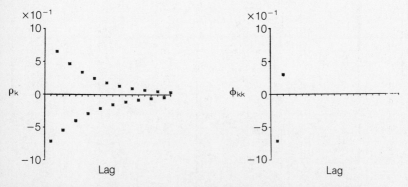

**Figure 7.8**  Theoretical a.c.f. and p.a.c.f. of an AR(2) with $\phi_1 < 0$ and $\phi_2 > 0$.

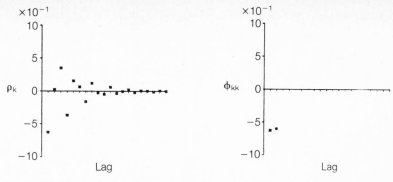

**Figure 7.9** Theoretical a.c.f. and p.a.c.f. of an AR(2) with $\phi_1 < 0$ and $\phi_2 < 0$.

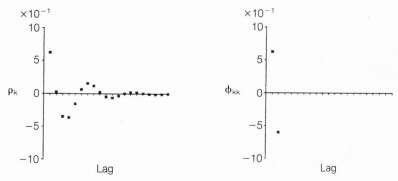

**Figure 7.10** Theoretical a.c.f. and p.a.c.f. of an AR(2) with $\phi_1 > 0$ and $\phi_2 < 0$.

However, as we can only estimate the partial autocorrelations we must allow for sampling error. That is, if the process is AR($p$) it is unlikely that exactly $p$ non-zero $\hat{\phi}_{kk}$s would be produced – rather, we must determine how many of the $\hat{\phi}_{kk}$s are significantly different from zero.

Now, it can be shown that if the process is AR($p$) then the variance of $\hat{\phi}_{kk}$ for $k \geqslant p+1$ is simply:

$$\text{Var}(\hat{\phi}_{kk}) = \frac{1}{n} \qquad\qquad \text{Equation 7.26}$$

For large $n$ it can also be shown that $\hat{\phi}_{kk}$ is normally distributed under the null hypothesis of $\phi_{kk} = 0$. Thus if the process is AR($p$) we would expect the absolute values of the first $p$ estimated partial autocorrelations to exceed about two standard errors (that is, to lie outside $\pm 2/\sqrt{n}$).

As an example, consider again the data which were generated by Equation 7.8 (or equivalently, by Equation 4.70) (which we have here denoted by $Y_t$).

From these data we indicated that we can derive estimates of $\rho_1, \rho_2$ and $\rho_3$ of:

$r_1 = 0.809$

$r_2 = 0.636$

$r_3 = 0.470$

Substituting these estimates of $\rho_1$, $\rho_2$ and $\rho_3$ into Equations 7.22, 7.23 and 7.25 the following estimates of the first three partial autocorrelations are produced:

$\hat{\phi}_{11} = 0.809$

$\hat{\phi}_{22} = -0.053$

$\hat{\phi}_{33} = -0.083$

Given a sample size of 50 then the standard error or $\hat{\phi}_{kk}$ is $1/\sqrt{50} = 0.141$. Thus as only $\hat{\phi}_{11}$ exceeds twice this standard error then the implication is that the data have been generated by an AR(1) (which of course we know to be the case). As in the case of the a.c.f. we can present the estimated p.a.c.f. diagrammatically. Thus in Figure 7.11 we present the a.c.f. (reproduced from Figure 7.4) and the p.a.c.f. of the sample data. The two standard error bands are also included for the p.a.c.f.

Thus from Figure 7.11 we can confirm that the theoretical behaviour of Figure 7.5 is approximated, therefore implying an AR(1) with positive $\phi_1$.

In order to illustrate this identification procedure for an AR(2) process, again consider simulating a set of sample observations from a known AR(2) model. In particular, consider the following AR(2) process:

$$Y_t = 0.85Y_{t-1} - 0.50Y_{t-2} + \varepsilon_t \qquad \text{Equation 7.27}$$

We will use the same sample of 50 observations for $\varepsilon_t$ as was used in Chapter 4

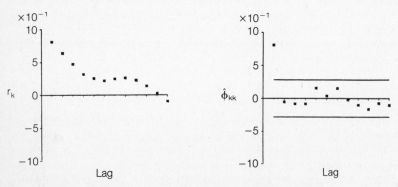

**Figure 7.11** Estimated a.c.f. and p.a.c.f. from the sample data on $Y_t$.

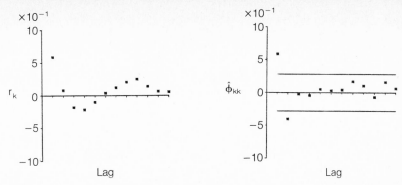

**Figure 7.12** Estimated a.c.f. and p.a.c.f. for the sample data generated by Equation 7.27.

(which we there denoted by $u_t$). In order to begin the simulation process we require values for $Y_{-1}$ and $Y_0$ (so as to generate values for $Y_1$ and $Y_2$). Arbitrary values of 36.010 and $-167.940$, respectively, were selected, and Equation 7.27 was then used recursively to build up a sample of 50 observations (in order to allow the process to 'settle down' 60 observations were in fact generated, and the first 10 were then discarded).

In Figure 7.12 we present the estimated a.c.f. and p.a.c.f. of these sample data. Note that Figure 7.12 approximates the theoretical behaviour of Figure 7.10, and therefore we would here conclude that the data appear to have been generated by an AR(2).

### The Identification of Moving Average Models

The general expression for an MA($q$) model can be written as follows:

$$Y_t = \varepsilon_t + \theta_1 \varepsilon_{t-1} + \theta_2 \varepsilon_{t-2} + \ldots + \theta_q \varepsilon_{t-q} \qquad \text{Equation 7.28}$$

As in the case of identifying AR models, we require a method for initially determining whether any given data set has been generated by an MA process, and if so, the order of the process which has generated the data (that is, the value of $q$ in Equation 7.28).

It can be shown that the theoretical behaviour of the a.c.f. and p.a.c.f. of an MA process is the exact opposite of that for an AR process. That is, an MA($q$) will exhibit some form of geometric decay in its p.a.c.f. and the first $q$ autocorrelations will be non-zero.

For illustrative purposes we will simulate a set of sample observations from a known MA process, and then derive the estimated a.c.f. and p.a.c.f. from these data. In particular, consider the following MA(1) and MA(2) models:

$$Y_t = \varepsilon_t + 0.85\varepsilon_{t-1} \qquad \text{Equation 7.29}$$

and

$$Y_t = \varepsilon_t - 0.85\varepsilon_{t-1} + 0.60\varepsilon_{t-2} \qquad \text{Equation 7.30}$$

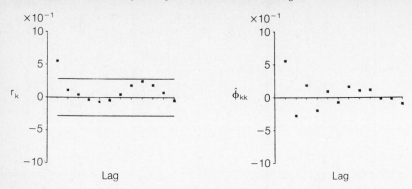

**Figure 7.13** Estimated a.c.f. and p.a.c.f. from data generated by Equation 7.29.

Again, using as a set of sample observations on $\varepsilon_t$ the observations on $u_t$ from Section 4.4.1, Equations 7.29 and 7.30 can then be used to build up a sample of observations from an MA(1) and MA(2) process, respectively. In Figures 7.13 and 7.14 we present the estimated a.c.f.s and p.a.c.f.s for these two data sets.

Thus, Figure 7.13 could be interpreted as exhibiting approximate geometric decay in the p.a.c.f., with a single significant autocorrelation at lag 1 in the a.c.f. An MA(1) is implied. Similarly, in Figure 7.14 two significant autocorrelations occur in the a.c.f. and the p.a.c.f. could be interpreted as exhibiting geometric decay. Thus, an MA(2) is implied.

We also include the two standard error bands in the estimated a.c.f.s of Figures 7.13 and 7.14, to test the null hypothesis that none of the autocorrelations is significant. Thus under the null hypothesis:

$$H_0 : \rho_k = 0 \quad \text{for } k > K$$

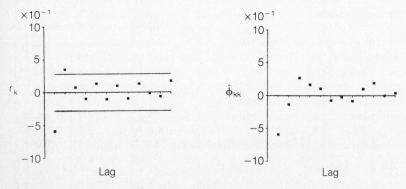

**Figure 7.14** Estimated a.c.f. and p.a.c.f. from data generated by Equation 7.30.

it can be shown that:

$$r_k \sim N(0, \mathrm{Var}\,(r_k)) \quad \text{for large } n$$

and an estimate of $\mathrm{Var}\,(r_k)$ is given by:

$$\widehat{\mathrm{Var}}\,(r_k) \simeq \frac{1}{n}\left(1 + 2\sum_{i=1}^{K} r_i^2\right) \qquad \text{Equation 7.31}$$

Thus, for example, to test the hypothesis:

$$H_0\colon \rho_k = 0 \quad \text{for } k \geqslant 2$$

(that is, that the process is MA(1)), then under $H_0$:

$$r_k \sim N(0, \widehat{\mathrm{Var}}\,(r_k)) \quad \text{for all } k \geqslant 2$$

where

$$\widehat{\mathrm{Var}}\,(r_k) \simeq \frac{1}{n}\left(1 + 2\sum_{i=1}^{1} r_i^2\right)$$

or

$$\widehat{\mathrm{Var}}\,(r_k) \simeq \frac{1}{n}(1 + 2r_1^2) \qquad \text{Equation 7.32}$$

Therefore we would accept $H_0$ if $r_1$ were relatively large, and all $r_k$ for $k \geqslant 2$ were within $\pm 2\sqrt{(1 + 2r_1^2)/n}$.

Note that if we were to test:

$$H_0\colon \rho_k = 0 \quad \text{for } k \geqslant 1$$

that is, that there are no significant autocorrelations, then under $H_0$:

$$r_k \sim N(0, \widehat{\mathrm{Var}}\,(r_k)) \quad \text{for all } k$$

and

$$\widehat{\mathrm{Var}}\,(r_k) \simeq \frac{1}{n}\left(1 + 2\sum_{i=1}^{0} r_1^2\right)$$

or, simply,

$$\widehat{\mathrm{Var}}\,(r_k) \simeq \frac{1}{n} \qquad \text{Equation 7.33}$$

That is, if all the estimated autocorrelations were within $\pm 2/\sqrt{n}$ (or if all the estimated partial autocorrelations were within $\pm 2/\sqrt{n}$) then we would conclude that there appears to be no structure in the data, and hence that the data have been randomly generated – the data generating process is 'white noise'. These are the standard error bands that we produce in the estimated a.c.f.s of Figures 7.13 and 7.14 (and in all the subsequent estimated a.c.f.s that we will present).

The Identification of Mixed ARMA Models

Finally, having discussed the identification of pure AR and MA models, we need to consider the theoretical behaviour of the a.c.f. and p.a.c.f. of models containing both AR and MA parameters. Recall that we presented the general form of such a model in Equation 7.1.

Identifying an appropriate $ARMA(p, q)$ model from the estimated a.c.f. and p.a.c.f. can often become difficult. Essentially, if the patterns in the estimated a.c.f. and p.a.c.f. do not neatly reflect the theoretical behaviour of either a pure AR or a pure MA process, then a mixed ARMA model is implied. That is, geometric decay in both the a.c.f. and the p.a.c.f. would imply an ARMA process. However, deducing the values of $p$ and $q$ will often not be straightforward, and typically a trial and error approach would have to be adopted.

As in the cases of illustrating the identification of AR and MA processes, we can consider simulating a set of sample observations from a known ARMA model. In particular, consider the following ARMA(1, 1) model:

$$Y_t = 0.9 Y_{t-1} + \varepsilon_t + 0.9 \varepsilon_{t-1} \qquad\qquad \text{Equation 7.34}$$

In the same manner as previously, Equation 7.34 can be used to generate 50 sample observations on $Y_t$. In Figure 7.15 we present the estimated a.c.f. and p.a.c.f. derived from these sample observations.

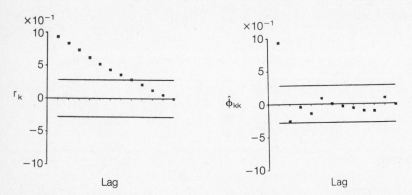

**Figure 7.15**   Estimated a.c.f. and p.a.c.f. from data generated by Equation 7.34.

Note from Figure 7.15 that the a.c.f. shows clear evidence of decay (although perhaps not strictly geometric), and hence AR parameters are implied. The p.a.c.f. could also be interpreted as exhibiting geometric decay, although this is far from clear-cut. Indeed, a much more obvious identification from Figure 7.15 would be decay in the a.c.f. and a single significant partial autocorrelation in the p.a.c.f., therefore implying an AR(1).

**Table 7.1** Theoretical behaviour of AR, MA, and ARMA processes

| Type of model | Behaviour of a.c.f. and p.a.c.f. |
|---|---|
| AR($p$) | Geometric decay in the a.c.f. and $p$ significant partial autocorrelations in the p.a.c.f. |
| MA($q$) | Geometric decay in the p.a.c.f. and $q$ significant autocorrelations in the a.c.f. |
| ARMA($p, q$) | Geometric decay in both the a.c.f. and p.a.c.f. |

However, as we shall see below, such an initial identification will be shown to be inadequate at the diagnostic checking phase of B–J.

In Table 7.1 we summarise the theoretical behaviour of the a.c.f.s and p.a.c.f.s of AR, MA, and ARMA processes.

### 7.2.2 Estimation of the Model Parameters

Having obtained a tentative identification of the statistical model which may have generated the sample data, the next step is to derive estimates of the model parameters – that is, estimates of the $\phi$s and the $\theta$s.

We will not discuss the details of estimating these models. The methods involved are the same as any econometrician would employ. That is, least squares and maximum likelihood estimators can be derived, although, in general, non-linear techniques will have to be used. This will be the case for any model which contains moving average parameters. For example, consider an MA(1) process. That is:

$$Y_t = \varepsilon_t + \theta_1 \varepsilon_{t-1} \qquad \text{Equation 7.35}$$

In order to derive the least squares estimator of $\theta_1$, $\varepsilon_t$ must be first expressed in terms of just $\theta_1$ and current and lagged values of $Y$. Thus rewriting Equation 7.35 we have:

$$\varepsilon_t = Y_t - \theta_1 \varepsilon_{t-1} \qquad \text{Equation 7.36}$$

From Equation 7.36 we can write:

$$\varepsilon_{t-1} = Y_{t-1} - \theta_1 \varepsilon_{t-2} \qquad \text{Equation 7.37}$$

Substituting Equation 7.37 into Equation 7.36 will produce an equation in which $\varepsilon_t$ is a function of $\theta_1$, $\theta_1^2$, $Y_t$, $Y_{t-1}$ and $\varepsilon_{t-2}$. Thus repeatedly substituting into Equation 7.36 in this way will eventually produce an equation in which $\varepsilon_t$ is a function only of current and lagged values of $Y$ and various powered terms in $\theta_1$. However note that the first derivative of $\Sigma \varepsilon_t^2$ with respect to $\theta_1$ will produce an equation which is non-linear in $\theta_1$, and hence a unique expression for $\theta_1$ cannot be derived. Consequently a non-linear estimation procedure is required, and while such a procedure is a tedious one, it is easily performed on a computer.

For illustrative purposes, we present below the estimated models using the various sets of simulated data which we derived above. That is, Equation 7.38 is the estimate of the AR(1) model using the data generated by Equation 7.8, and similarly, Equations 7.39 to 7.42 are the estimates of the AR(2), MA(1), MA(2) and ARMA(1, 1) models using the data derived from Equations 7.27, 7.29, 7.30, and 7.34, respectively (the computer package used to generate these estimates was SPSS).

$$Y_t = 0.904Y_{t-1} + e_t \qquad\qquad \text{Equation 7.38}$$

$$Y_t = 0.832Y_{t-1} - 0.412Y_{t-2} + e_t \qquad\qquad \text{Equation 7.39}$$

$$Y_t = e_t + 0.871e_{t-1} \qquad\qquad \text{Equation 7.40}$$

$$Y_t = e_t - 0.808e_{t-1} + 0.678e_{t-2} \qquad\qquad \text{Equation 7.41}$$

$$Y_t = 0.930Y_{t-1} + e_t + 0.978e_t \qquad\qquad \text{Equation 7.42}$$

### 7.2.3    Diagnostic Checking

Having estimated an initially identified model, the next step is to examine the adequacy of the model (just as would be the case for any estimated econometric model). Indeed, it will often be the case that the estimated a.c.f. and p.a.c.f. will not unambiguously imply a single model, and consequently the identification stage may well produce a number of competing models. Therefore, we require a means for discriminating between these models, and hence determining which model provides the most satisfactory description of the data.

For example, consider the estimated a.c.f. and p.a.c.f. derived from the ARMA(1, 1) model in Equation 7.34 and shown in Figure 7.15. Recall that in discussing Figure 7.15 we indicated that even though the data were known to have been generated by an ARMA(1, 1), and this could be interpreted as being reflected in the behaviour of the estimated a.c.f. and p.a.c.f., an AR(1) could also be inferred. Therefore, the procedure that would generally be adopted in such cases is to begin with the simplest model specification – the AR(1) in the case of Figure 7.15. This model would then be estimated and its adequacy assessed. If the model specification proved to be inadequate an alternative specification would be tried, and this procedure would continue until a satisfactory model had been obtained.

The first step in examining the adequacy of any estimated model is to test for the significance of the estimated parameters. The estimation process will also produce the estimated standard errors associated with each parameter and thus simple *t*-tests can be performed. If higher order parameters prove to be insignificant then the implication is that the process can be just as adequately described by a lower order process. Thus insignificant parameters would be dropped from the model, and the simpler specification then re-estimated. Note, that as the variables in a B–J model do not have a theoretical interpretation there is no need to be concerned with the theoretical relevance of retaining a variable in the model – only statistical criteria are relevant.

A second criterion is that the standard deviation of the estimated residuals be as small as possible. This is essentially a goodness-of-fit criterion. Thus that model with the smallest $\hat{\sigma}_e$, *ceteris paribus*, is to be preferred.

A third form of model evaluation is to examine the properties of the residuals from the estimated model. In particular, if the model is correctly specified then, by definition, the disturbance terms, the $\varepsilon_t$s, must be random. Therefore we would expect this property of randomness to be reflected in the estimated residuals, the $e_t$s.

One way of examining the randomness of $e_t$ is to derive the estimated residuals from the model and then to calculate the a.c.f. for these data. If $e_t$ is random then we would expect all the autocorrelations to be insignificant. Alternatively, if significant autocorrelations do occur and/or there is some pattern in the estimated a.c.f. for $e_t$ then the implication is that the model has not fully accounted for all the systematic behaviour in $Y_t$. Indeed, the nature of the estimated a.c.f. of $e_t$ will often directly indicate the form of model re-specification which is required – that is, whether additional AR or MA parameters should be included.

While an inspection of the a.c.f. of the estimated residuals will often be sufficient to indicate whether or not an assumption of randomness is justified, a simple test of significance can be derived. Thus rather than test for the significance of the individual autocorrelations, a test can be derived which examines the significance of the autocorrelations as a set – that is, we can test for the significance of the entire a.c.f.

The test statistic which is used is generally referred to as the **Box–Pierce Q-statistic**[2] (the corresponding test is also referred to as the 'portmanteau' test). Thus we could consider the first $K$ autocorrelations, and the null hypothesis would be that these autocorrelations are all insignificantly different from zero. That is:

$$H_0: \rho_1 = \rho_2 = \ldots = \rho_K = 0$$

Now, recall from Equation 7.33 and the discussion immediately preceding this equation that under the above null hypothesis each estimated autocorrelation, $r_k$, will be normally distributed with a mean of zero and a variance of $1/n$. Thus, under $H_0$, we can write:

$$\frac{r_k - 0}{1/\sqrt{n}} \sim N(0, 1) \quad \text{for } k = 1, \dots, K$$

Also recall from Chapter 6, and the discussion associated with Equation 6.110, that the sum of the squares of $n$ standard normal variables has a $\chi^2$ distribution with $n$ degrees of freedom. Thus considering the first $K$ autocorrelations we can write:

$$Q = \sum_{k=1}^{K} \left( \frac{r_k - 0}{1/\sqrt{n}} \right)^2 = n \sum_{k=1}^{K} r_k^2 \sim \chi_K^2 \qquad \text{Equation 7.43}$$

That is, $Q$ is just the sum of the squares of the first $K$ autocorrelations divided by their standard deviation and therefore, assuming $H_0$ to be true, should be distributed as a $\chi^2$ with $K$ degrees of freedom. However, as we are using the estimated residuals to calculate the $r_k$s, and as $p+q$ parameters were estimated in order to derive the $e_t$s, then the statistic, $Q$, in Equation 7.43 is only approximately distributed as a $\chi^2$, and with $K-p-q$ degrees of freedom, not $K$ degrees of freedom ($p+q$ degrees of freedom were 'lost' in estimating the $p+q$ parameters).

Thus having estimated a B–J model, the estimated residuals can be derived from this model and the value of $Q$ in Equation 7.43 calculated. The number of autocorrelations that are used to calculate $Q$ (the value of $K$ in Equation 7.43) will depend on the sample size. As it is only about the first $n/4$ estimated autocorrelations which are considered reliable then it would seem appropriate to set the value of $K$ to $n/4$. The resulting value of $Q$ can then be compared to the critical value of $Q$ from the corresponding tables for the $\chi^2$ distribution for $K-p-q$ degrees of freedom. If the observed value of $Q$ is unacceptably large (it exceeds the tabulated $\chi^2$ value) then we would conclude that $Q$ is significant, and hence that $H_0$ must be rejected. That is, the model is inadequate and requires respecification and re-estimation.

However, care must be taken in interpreting the value of $Q$ which is derived from an estimated model. For if the value of $K$ used to calculate $Q$ is relatively large, and should just one or two significant autocorrelations occur in the residual a.c.f., then these will tend to be 'washed out' by the much larger number of remaining insignificant autocorrelations. That is, the power of the $Q$-test to detect model inadequacies declines as $K$ increases. But if only a small value of $K$ is used then any significant autocorrelations at higher lags will be missed. In practice, we could select a number of different values of $K$ (say 6, 12, 18, 24) and then examine the significance of the corresponding $Q$ values. If all of the corresponding $Q$ values were insignificant then $H_0$ would be accepted. Otherwise the possibility of a model inadequacy could be further investigated.[3]

In order to illustrate these methods of model evaluation we can consider

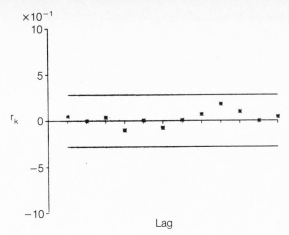

**Figure 7.16** Estimated a.c.f. of the residuals from Equation 7.38.

again the estimated models which we presented above in Equations 7.38 to 7.42.

Consider the AR(1) model in Equation 7.38. First, the $t$-statistic associated with the estimate of $\phi_1$ can be shown to be 12.70 and thus we would conclude that this estimate is highly significant. Second, the standard deviation of the estimated residuals is 89.108, which could be compared to the standard deviation of the original series ($Y_t$) of 180.230 (we could in fact calculate an $R^2$ statistic, if desired). Finally, in order to determine whether it is reasonable to infer that the disturbances in the model are random (and hence that the model has captured all the systematic variation in $Y_t$) we could examine the estimated a.c.f. of the residuals from Equation 7.38. In Figure 7.16 we present the estimated a.c.f. of the residual series from Equation 7.38.

Note from Figure 7.16 that none of the estimated autocorrelations lies outside the two-standard-error bands, and thus there is no evidence of any remaining systematic variation in $Y_t$. We could more conveniently test this hypothesis by calculating the $Q$-statistic associated with Equation 7.38. Thus for $K = 12$, and using Equation 7.43, we have:

$$Q = 4.48$$

In this case $Q$ will be distributed as a $\chi^2$ with $K - 1 = 11$ degrees of freedom. From the tables of the $\chi^2$ distribution in Appendix V, at a 5 per cent level of significance and for 11 degrees of freedom, the critical $\chi^2$ value is 19.7. Consequently, the observed value of $Q$ here is insignificant and we would conclude that the disturbance terms are random (for $K = 6$, the corresponding value of $Q$ is 1.21, which the reader should confirm is also insignificant).

Thus the estimated model in Equation 7.38 would appear to provide a satisfactory statistical description of the process that generated the data. We could now go on to use this model for forecasting purposes.

Similarly, via these same evaluation procedures, the remaining estimated models in Equations 7.39 to 7.42 can all be shown to provide adequate statistical descriptions of the corresponding data generating processes – that is, the estimated parameters in these models are all significant and in all cases insignificant $Q$-statistics are produced. This is of course hardly surprising as all these data series were derived from *known* models, and the models which we identified were all consistent with the known models. In practice, however, data will generally not be as 'well-behaved' as the simulated series which we have analysed here, and the identification process may not result in such unambiguous conclusions.

As an illustration of some of the ambiguities of identification, consider the data produced by the ARMA(1, 1) model in Equation 7.34. In particular, recall that the a.c.f. and p.a.c.f. of these data were consistent with the identification of an AR(1) model (see Figure 7.15), in addition to an ARMA(1, 1). Thus we could consider fitting an AR(1) model to these data. The resulting estimated AR(1) model is as follows (*t*-statistic in brackets):

$$Y_t = 0.975 Y_{t-1} + e_t \qquad\qquad \text{Equation 7.44}$$
$$(27.45)$$

Thus the *t*-statistic associated with the estimate of $\phi_1$ is highly significant. The next step is to examine the a.c.f. of the residuals from Equation 7.44. This a.c.f. is shown in Figure 7.17.

Note from Figure 7.17 that a significant autocorrelation occurs at lag 1.

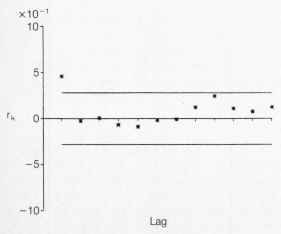

**Figure 7.17** Estimated a.c.f. of the residuals from Equation 7.44.

The $Q$-statistic associated with Figure 7.17 is 20.13, which, compared to the critical value of 19.7, is significant. Hence a model specification of AR(1) is inadequate – systematic variation still remains in $Y_t$, which is reflected in the a.c.f. of the residuals.

The next step then is to attempt to re-identify and re-estimate the model. However, we can deduce directly from Figure 7.17 the particular form of model inadequacy which is present. That is, given any estimated a.c.f., a single significant autocorrelation at lag 1 with no other obvious features in the a.c.f. would imply an MA(1). Thus Figure 7.17 could be interpreted as indicating that an MA(1) parameter has been omitted from the initial model specification. Thus re-identifying and re-estimating the model as ARMA(1, 1) produces the following equation ($t$-statistics in brackets):

$$Y_t = 0.930Y_{t-1} + e_t + 0.978e_{t-1} \qquad \text{Equation 7.45}$$
$$\;\;\;\;(18.01) \qquad\qquad (63.95)$$

The $Q$-statistic associated with the a.c.f. of the residuals of Equation 7.45 is 6.02, which can be compared to the critical value from the $\chi^2$ tables for ten degrees of freedom (Equation 7.45 contains two estimated parameters) of 18.3. The $Q$-statistic is therefore insignificant and Equation 7.45 would be accepted as an adequate description of the data generating process. In addition, in moving from Equation 7.44 to Equation 7.45 the standard deviation of the residuals is reduced from 124.180 to 94.476, further reinforcing the clear superiority of Equation 7.44 over Equation 7.45.

### 7.2.4   Forecasting with B–J models

Once a B–J model has been satisfactorily identified and estimated, it can then be used to generate forecasts of $Y_t$.

The use of estimated B–J models for forecasting is essentially a mechanical process. Consider the estimated ARMA(1, 1) model which we presented in Equation 7.45. Recall that this model was estimated using a sample of 50 observations. Thus for the last sample observation the model could be written as:

$$Y_{50} = 0.930Y_{49} + e_{50} + 0.978e_{49} \qquad \text{Equation 7.46}$$

Therefore the forecast of $Y$ one period into the future – $\hat{Y}_{51}$ – could be written as:

$$\hat{Y}_{51} = 0.930Y_{50} + e_{51} + 0.978e_{50} \qquad \text{Equation 7.47}$$

The value of $Y_{50}$ – the last sample observation – is of course known. $e_{50}$ is the estimated residual from the model at time period 50. The estimation procedure will produce a series of estimated residuals (which, recall, is used for diagnostic checking purposes), and hence a value for $e_{50}$ will also be available.[4] $e_{51}$ is the estimated residual one period into the future which is unknown. The obvious solution is to use as a value of $e_{51}$ the corresponding expected value of $\varepsilon_{51}$, which is just zero. Thus from the data used to estimate the model we have:

$$Y_{50} = -594.982$$

$$e_{50} = 38.277$$

and assuming that

$$e_{51} = 0$$

then $\hat{Y}_{51}$ is given by:

$$\hat{Y}_{51} = (0.930)(-594.982) + 0 + (0.978)(38.277)$$

$$= -515.898$$

Similarly, the forecast of $Y$ two periods into the future can be written as:

$$\hat{Y}_{52} = 0.930Y_{51} + e_{52} + 0.978e_{51} \qquad \text{Equation 7.48}$$

Setting both $e_{51}$ and $e_{52}$ to their corresponding expected values of zero, and using as a value of $Y_{51}$ the value of $\hat{Y}_{51}$ derived above we can write:

$$\hat{Y}_{52} = (0.930)(-515.898) + 0 + (0.978)(0)$$

$$= -479.785$$

Thus a series of forecasts of $Y$, for any desired number of periods into the future, can be derived in this way. The (computerised) estimation procedure will also produce confidence intervals which can be placed around the forecasts, and hence an evaluation of the precision of the forecasts can be carried out.

Note that the B–J forecasts derived in the above manner will approach zero (the mean of the series), and eventually settle down to zero. This is particularly the case with pure MA processes which depend only on $e_t$ terms. Thus the forecasts of an MA process will all be zero beyond $q$ periods into the future, where $q$ is the number of MA parameters in the model (or the number of lagged terms in the model). It is in this sense that B–J models are really only useful for short-term forecasting. The manner in which B–J models are used in practice is that as new data on $Y$ become available these are fed back into the estimation process, the model is then re-estimated and a constantly evolving series of short-term forecasts are produced.

### 7.2.5  *Stationarity*

So far we have assumed that the sample data have been generated by a stationary model. We have taken stationarity to mean that the underlying process has a constant mean and variance. In practice, most time-series, and particularly economic time-series, will be non-stationary. Typically a given time-series will contain a trend of some form, and it may also be the case that the data will be heteroskedastic with respect to time. Recall the example of quarterly consumers' expenditure which we graphed in Figure 4.7, which could be interpreted as being non-stationary in both mean and variance. Consequently before applying B–J methodology to a given sample of data the data must be first appropriately transformed so as to produce a stationary series.

The problem of a non-constant mean (a trend in the data) can be quite easily dealt with. For example, assume that the data contain a simple linear trend. Then letting $t$ denote time-period $t$, we can write the model for $Y_t$ as:

$$Y_t = a + bt + \text{stochastic terms} \qquad \text{Equation 7.49}$$

where the stochastic terms represent the ARMA component of the model. Ignoring these stochastic terms for the moment, then from Equation 7.49 we can write:

$$Y_{t-1} = a + b(t-1) = a + bt - b \qquad \text{Equation 7.50}$$

and therefore:

$$Y_t - Y_{t-1} = \Delta Y_t = b \qquad \text{Equation 7.51}$$

$\Delta Y_t$ is referred to as the **first difference** of $Y$ (that is, the difference between successive values of $Y$). Note from Equation 7.51 that if $Y$ contains a linear time trend, taking the first difference of $Y$ will eliminate this trend, leaving just a constant term (plus stochastic terms in some form). We would then proceed to fit an appropriate ARMA model to this first differenced series (a model which would also contain an estimate of the constant term, $b$).

If the trend in $Y$ is non-linear then further differencing would be required. For example, consider the case of a quadratic time-trend in $Y$. That is, the **deterministic** component of $Y$ could be written as:

$$Y_t = a + bt + ct^2 \qquad \text{Equation 7.52}$$

From Equation 7.52 we can write:

$$Y_{t-1} = a + b(t-1) + c(t-1)^2 \qquad \text{Equation 7.53}$$

$$\therefore \Delta Y_t = b - c + 2ct \qquad \text{Equation 7.54}$$

Thus the first difference in $Y$ now contains a linear trend and hence differencing $\Delta Y_t$ one further time will eliminate this trend. That is, it is straightforward to show that:

$$(Y_t - Y_{t-1}) - (Y_{t-1} - Y_{t-2}) = \Delta^2 Y_t = 2c \qquad \text{Equation 7.55}$$

A model can then be fitted to this twice differenced data.

In general, then, data which are non-stationary in the mean can be reduced to stationarity via an appropriate level of differencing. In particular, if the trend in the data follows a polynomial of order $d$ then differencing the data $d$ times will eliminate this trend. In practice, it would be unusual to have to difference the data more than twice.

In order to identify the appropriate level of differencing, given a sample of data, the simplest approach is to graph the data against time and informally evaluate the nature of any trend in the data. If the data follow an upward (or downward) trend then the variance of the data must be greater than if the data oscillate around a constant mean – trending data must necessarily contain larger deviations from the sample mean than non-trending data. Therefore, data should be differenced to the point at which the variance of the differenced data is at a minimum – over-differencing would be implied if the variance of the data begins to increase. A further indication of the need to difference data is if the a.c.f. of the data dies out only slowly or the auto-correlations die out linearly rather than geometrically. We will illustrate some of these features in Example 7.1.

We are then left with the problem of how to deal with heteroskedastic data. The approach, in effect, is the same as that outlined in Section 4.3, where we discussed the problem of heteroskedastic disturbance terms in the regression model. That is, an appropriate transformation of the data will result in homoskedasticity. Recall that in Chapter 4 heteroskedasticity was defined in terms of the variance of the disturbance term at each sample point being related in some way to the corresponding level of some exogenous variable (typically, one of the independent variables in the model). This exogenous variable could then be used to transform the data so as to render the transformed disturbance term homoskedastic. In the case of B–J models heteroskedasticity is simply defined as a change in the variance of the series over time. Therefore an appropriate mathematical transform of the data will have the effect of stabilising this variance.

For example, if it appears that the variance of the data is increasing over time, together with the mean of the data, (such as in Figure 4.7) then we would require a data transform that will attenuate the extreme observations, thereby stabilising the variance of the data. If we took the square root of the data, for example, then this would have the effect of reducing the larger observations proportionately more than the smaller observations thereby tending to reduce the rate of increase in the variance. This would be the case for any power transform of the data of the form:

$$Z_t = Y_t^\lambda \qquad\qquad \text{Equation 7.56}$$

where $0 < \lambda < 1$ (for a square root transformation $\lambda = 0.5$).

Taking the logarithms of the data would also have the effect of reducing the larger observations proportionately more than the smaller observations, again having the effect of reducing the rate of increase in the variance. As an example, we present in Figure 7.18 the natural logarithm of the consumers' expenditure data of Figure 4.7. We note from Figure 7.18 that the logarithmic transformation would appear to have had the effect of producing a constant variance. The next step would be to remove the trend from these data, and then to go on to fit an appropriate ARMA model to the resulting stationary data.

In practice, the problem is to determine the appropriate data transformation (the value of $\lambda$ in Equation 7.56, or whether a logarithmic, or any other form of transformation is appropriate). Our approach here has been simply to rely on an informal graphical analysis of the data, and then perhaps to experiment with a number of alternative transformations until an appropriate transformation is found. More formal procedures are available, but we will not concern ourselves with these here.[5]

The problem of data which are non-stationary in the variance is typically a problem associated with seasonal data (that is, seasonal data may contain a seasonal pattern which becomes more volatile over time, such as the consumers' expenditure data in Figure 4.7). We present a discussion of the B–J approach to modelling seasonal data in Appendix 7.1, where it can be seen that B–J can be quite easily extended to modelling seasonal data. Indeed, one of the more powerful features of B–J is its treatment of seasonality, particularly as compared to some of the more traditional econometric

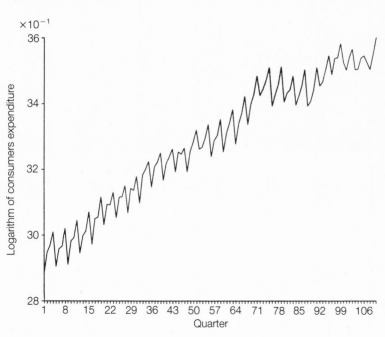

**Figure 7.18** Natural logarithm of consumers' expenditure 1955(1) to 1982(4).

approaches. That is, the econometrician might choose either to ignore seasonality by using deseasonalised data (thereby ignoring what might be a very important feature of the data), or to account for seasonality via the somewhat arbitrary use of dummy variables.

We will now illustrate B–J via an example.

Example 7.1

In Example 5.4 we discussed the estimation of an econometric model which purported to explain (partially) the demand for new cars in Great Britain. The data series which was used was the quarterly new registrations of cars over the period 1956 to 1984, and which we presented in Appendix 5.3.

We will now attempt to fit a Box–Jenkins model to the same data series. However, rather than using the raw seasonal data of Appendix 5.3, we will here use the corresponding deseasonalised data, as we have not developed B–J methods for modelling seasonal data (apart from our discussion in Appendix 7.1). This deseasonalised data series, available only from 1958 onwards, is shown in Appendix 7.2.

We must emphasise, however, that the use of deseasonalised data would be considered highly inappropriate according to strict B–J methodology. Given that the approach of B–J is to rely solely on the sample data to determine an

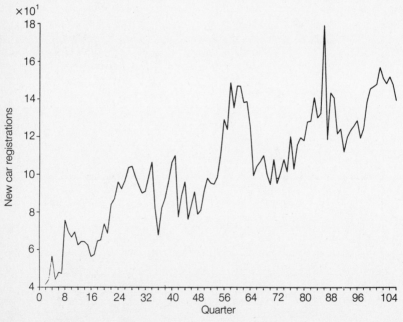

**Figure 7.19** Quarterly new car registrations – seasonally adjusted 1958(1) to 1984(4).

appropriate model, it is essential that the available data be in their raw and purest form. Many seasonal adjustment techniques presuppose a relatively rigid seasonal pattern, and the data are adjusted accordingly. The result is that the seasonally adjusted data may well contain spurious features which can be confusing and misleading in identifying and estimating a B–J model. Further, it is not at all clear to the B–J modeller why the seasonal features of any data set should be considered inherently less interesting or less important than any other features of the data, and therefore he can find no justification for the arbitrary removal of seasonality from the data. For our purposes we will ignore these (very valid) criticisms and we shall go on to use the data in Appendix 7.2 to illustrate B–J. However, for the interested reader, we present in Appendix 7.1 a discussion of fitting a seasonal B–J model to the raw car registration data of Appendix 5.3.

In Figure 7.19 we present a graph of the seasonally adjusted car registration data of Appendix 7.2. From the figure it can be seen that there is a clear upward trend in the data, and thus differencing of the data will be required. The data could also be interpreted as being heteroskedastic, the data appearing to exhibit increasing variation over time. Therefore a data transformation of some form is implied.

In terms of an appropriate data transformation we could begin by considering a logarithmic transformation. In Figure 7.20 we present a graph

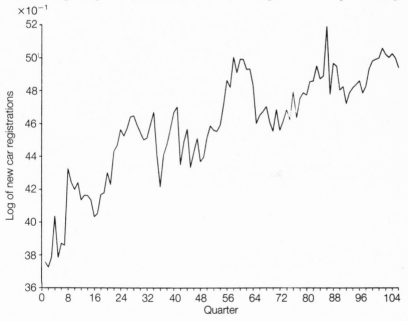

**Figure 7.20** Logarithms of quarterly new car registrations.

of the logarithms of the data against time. From the figure it would appear that the logarithmic transformation has produced an approximately homoskedastic series. However we would emphasise that our approach is very much an informal one here, and, strictly, a more rigorous analysis of the data should be performed in order to determine an appropriate transformation. For our purposes we will proceed on the assumption that this transformation is satisfactory, allowing the possibility of any inadequacies to be highlighted at the estimation and diagnostic checking stages.

Next we need to remove the trend from the data. From Figure 7.20 the

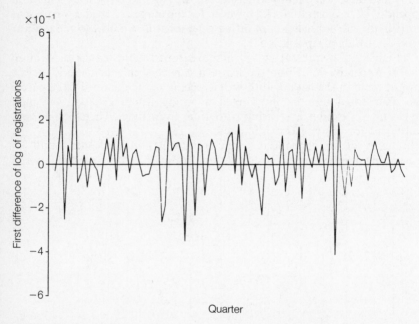

**Figure 7.21**  First differences of the logarithms of the car registration data.

trend would appear to be linear, and thus first differencing should be adequate. The first differences of the logarithms of the data are shown in Figure 7.21, from which it can be seen that an assumption of stationarity would seem reasonable. Recall from our discussion of stationarity in Section 7.2.5 that trending data should be differenced to the point at which the variance or standard deviation of the data is minimised. The standard deviation of the data in Figure 7.20 is 0.325, and the standard deviation of the first differences (Figure 7.21) is 0.122. Thus first differencing is certainly justified. The standard deviation of the twice differenced series is 0.200, and of the three times differenced series 0.357. Therefore first differencing would appear appropriate. We can now attempt to fit a B–J model to the data in Figure 7.21.

The first step, then, is to estimate the a.c.f. and p.a.c.f. from the stationary data in Figure 7.21. These are presented in Figure 7.22.

The main features of Figure 7.22 are the significant autocorrelation at lag 1 and the significant partial autocorrelations at lags 1 and 9. Given the difficulty of interpreting the relevance of a nine-period lag in a non-seasonal B–J model, we will begin by assuming that the significant partial auto-correlation at lag 9 is spurious (after all, at a significance level of 5 per cent we

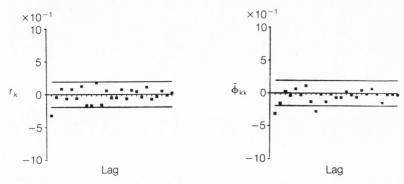

**Figure 7.22**   A.c.f. and p.a.c.f. of the data in Figure 7.21.

would expect an average of 1 in 20 spuriously significant autocorrelations and partial autocorrelations). Thus ignoring this significant partial autocor-relation for identification purposes, we are left with significance at lag 1 in both the a.c.f. and p.a.c.f. Thus either an AR(1), an MA(1), or possibly an ARMA(1, 1) is suggested.

Now, it might be argued that the p.a.c.f. shows (marginally) more evidence of geometric decay than is the case in the a.c.f., particularly amongst the first six or so lags. Such an interpretation would therefore imply an MA(1). Thus we could begin by estimating an MA(1) and then checking the adequacy of such an identification. If an MA(1) proves to be inadequate, then the adequacy of an AR(1) could be examined, and, if necessary, an ARMA(1, 1) could be finally tried.

The resulting estimated MA(1) model is as follows (*t*-statistics in brackets):

$$Y_t = 0.011 + e_t - 0.362e_{t-1} \qquad \text{Equation 7.57}$$
$$\phantom{Y_t = }(1.58) \qquad (4.10)$$

$$\hat{\sigma}_\varepsilon = 0.112$$

Given the insignificance of the constant term in Equation 7.57 it would seem reasonable to drop the constant from the model. Re-estimating the model without the constant produces the following results:

$$Y_t = e_t - 0.334 e_{t-1}$$
$$\quad\quad (3.75)$$

Equation 7.58

$$\hat{\sigma}_\varepsilon = 0.112$$

Thus the moving average parameter is significant.

Next, we need to examine the residuals from Equation 7.58 and hence to determine whether an hypothesis of random disturbance terms is supported. The a.c.f. of the residuals from the estimated model is presented in Figure 7.23.

From Figure 7.23 we note that there are significant autocorrelations at lags 8 and 9, and hence a possible model inadequacy is implied. The value of the $Q$ statistic derived from all 25 autocorrelations is 22.43. The corresponding critical value of the $\chi^2$ statistic from Appendix V, for 24 degrees of freedom and a significance level of 5 per cent, is 36.4. Thus we can conclude that the value of $Q$ here is insignificant and hence that an hypothesis of random disturbance terms is acceptable. In effect, we could argue that the significant autocorrelations at lags 8 and 9 are spurious, particularly as these lags have no obvious relevance within the context of the model (although an economic interpretation of these lags will be offered below).

However, as we indicated above in the discussion of the $Q$ statistic in Equation 7.43, care must be taken in interpreting an insignificant $Q$ statistic. Thus if we consider just the first 12 autocorrelations in Figure 7.23 then the resulting value of $Q$ is 17.09, which is still insignificant at the 5 per cent level, but only just insignificant at the 10 per cent level (the tabulated value at the 10 per cent level for 11 degrees of freedom is 17.3).

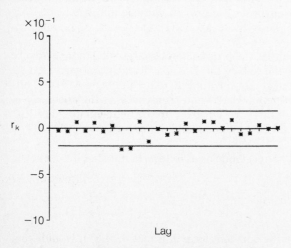

**Figure 7.23**   A.c.f. of residuals from Equation 7.58.

Equation 7.58 might therefore be accepted as an adequate (possibly just adequate) statistical summary of the process which generated the car registration data (or, strictly, the process which generated the first difference of the logs of these data). We could then go on to use Equation 7.58 for forecasting, although we may first wish to carry out a number of forecasting tests, such as those described in Chapter 6, before finally accepting Equation 7.58 as a satisfactory forecasting equation.

It is useful to also consider the alternative model specifications which were suggested by the a.c.f. and p.a.c.f. in Figure 7.22. That is, the possibility that the data were generated by an AR(1) or an ARMA(1, 1). The corresponding estimates of these models are as follows (omitting constant terms):

$$Y_t = -0.301 Y_{t-1} + e_t \qquad\qquad \text{Equation 7.59}$$
$$(3.33)$$

$$\hat{\sigma}_\varepsilon = 0.114, \quad Q_{12} = 17.96, \quad Q_{25} = 23.04$$

$$Y_t = -0.040 Y_t + e_t - 0.299 e_{t-1} \qquad\qquad \text{Equation 7.60}$$
$$(0.14) \qquad\quad (1.12)$$

$$\hat{\sigma}_\varepsilon = 0.113, \quad Q_{12} = 16.77, \quad Q_{25} = 22.00$$

where $Q_{12}$ and $Q_{25}$ are the Q statistics derived from the first 12 and 25 autocorrelations, respectively. In the cases of both of these models, the a.c.f. of the residuals again contain significant autocorrelations at lags 8 and 9. However, $Q_{12}$ is significant at the 10 per cent level in both cases (for 11 and 10 degrees of freedom, respectively), although $Q_{25}$ remains insignificant. Hence the marginal superiority of the MA(1) specification is implied. Given that both parameter estimates in the ARMA(1, 1) model are insignificant, and that the model does not appear to be superior to either the MA(1) or the AR(1) in any other respect, this model can be rejected from further consideration. We could conclude, therefore, that either an AR(1) or an MA(1) appears adequate, with the MA(1) being marginally superior. We could perhaps go on to compare the forecasting performance of these models, with a basis for discrimination possibly emerging from such a comparison.

## 7.3   A Comparison of the Box–Jenkins and Econometric Approaches to Time-Series Modelling

Given this brief exposition of B–J we can now contrast and compare econometric and B–J modelling. The statistical bases of the two approaches are clearly similar, and in the limit, identical. Both approaches are based on regression methods and the application of the standard theory of statistical inference and hypothesis testing. If anything, it might be argued that B–J is somewhat more rigorous and detailed in the application and interpretation of these methods, but this is no more than a difference in emphasis between the two approaches rather than any difference in substance. The major difference between the approaches is B–J's rejection of any role which might be played by economic theory in model specification and evaluation.

Under B–J it is the sample data that provide the sole basis for discriminating between competing models. Given that the data play such a crucial role, highly sensitive and rigorous statistical techniques are required, and the strength of B–J is that it provides an integrated body of such techniques. However, it is clearly essential that data which are subjected to such detailed analysis are highly reliable. If the data are unreliable, and by implication not amenable to sophisticated statistical analysis, then the result of a B–J analysis may well be that the 'wrong' model is very efficiently identified and estimated. It is for this reason that B–J techniques are most commonly applied to the analysis of what might be broadly termed natural phenomena, in which data are generated by laboratory-type 'experiments', and in which there is therefore some direct control over the reliability of the data. Thus typical applications are in the modelling and forecasting of daily energy demand, daily temperatures, airline passenger movements, and the outcomes of various industrial processes.[6] Note also the relatively simple (and often obvious) theoretical bases of these types of applications, hence possibly justifying the use of a simple B–J model, even in theory.

The econometrician would argue, however, that in the analysis of economic data, or social science data in general, theory can no longer be ignored. Economic data are typically generated by relatively complex theoretical processes, and while some simplified approximation to these processes will be required for practical purposes, there will be a limit to how far such simplification can occur. Thus, not only must any given econometric model be data-consistent (in the same sense as a B–J model), but the model must also satisfy the requirements of economic theory. Indeed, the requirement for an econometric model to be consistent with economic theory provides the modeller with a further means of discriminating between competing models. There may be any number of models which are consistent with the sample data, but only one of these will be consistent with accepted economic theory. This model, then, can be interpreted as the 'true' model. Note also that the application of economic theory to model specification can be interpreted in terms of placing restrictions on the parameters in the model, hence increasing the efficiency of the resulting parameter estimators (see the discussion in Section 5.3).

The only criterion available to B–J in discriminating between competing statistical models is the somewhat naive one of selecting the simplest of these models. An econometrician would argue that not only is such a criterion arbitrary, it is probably inappropriate, given the inherent complexity of most economic phenomena. Only models which reflect the complexities of economic behaviour can provide an effective and reliable basis for forecasting and policy formulation, particularly in the medium to longer term. In practice, the process of deriving a satisfactory econometric model will inevitably involve the need to abstract from reality – it is unlikely that all the complexities of economic behaviour can be fully captured by some manageable mathematical formulation. However, the econometrician would argue, model complexity should be treated as the norm rather than the exception. Thus central to effective model building is the need to develop a methodology which can accommodate relatively complex models. This contrasts with B–J's scepticism that such a methodology can be successfully developed, at least in a resource effective manner, which in turn results in the much more modest objectives of B–J modelling.

As a very simple illustration of how even the simplest of economic theory might assist in the formulation and interpretation of a B–J model, consider again Example 7.1. Recall that in modelling the car registration data we concluded that an MA(1) model provided a reasonably parsimonious description of the data. However the one reservation about the model was the significance of the autocorrelations at lags 8 and 9 in the residual a.c.f. As the data are non-seasonal some B–J modellers would tend to treat these autocorrelations as spurious and hence they would be ignored. But how would an econometrician interpret these autocorrelations? Recall that in Example 5.4 we fitted an Almon distributed lag to the car registration data. The main justification for doing so was the recognition that replacement cycles were involved, and might well be the main explanation for the quarterly variation in new car registrations. Upon estimation, replacement cycles of approximately two and six years duration were found to be present. In turn, these could be rationalised in terms of the differential purchasing behaviour of companies and private individuals. Consequently the significant auto-correlations at lags 8 and 9 in Figure 7.23, rather than being spurious, may well reflect this cyclical nature of the data (in particular, the two-year cycles), and the need for some adjustment to the initial MA(1) model is therefore implied.

The only point we would wish to make here is that in analysing any economic data set considerations of economic theory can provide a very effective input into the modelling process. We are certainly not suggesting that it is only such considerations that provide the potential for resolving possible model inadequacies of the type in Example 7.1. Given this particular application, it is perfectly conceivable that some other B–J analyst would not have rejected the significant autocorrelations in the residual a.c.f. as spurious, and would indeed have proceeded to amend the model in some way so as to account for these autocorrelations. However, the point we would make is that this process of model adjustment could be greatly facilitated if consideration were given to the possible economic explanations for the initial model inadequacy.

We will complete this chapter by going on to discuss one final application of econometric modelling. This application could be interpreted as being influenced by B–J in the sense that considerable weight is given to deriving a data-consistent model. However, the requirements of economic theory are also incorporated into the modelling process, with the result that a model which is both data- and theory-consistent is ultimately derived. As we shall see, this example is useful for illustrating the potential for deriving econometric models which fully satisfy both economic theory and the available data. This contrasts with perhaps more traditional econometric models which have often been criticised for representing a compromise between theory and data.

## 7.4   The Consumption Function Revisited

The application which we will be concerned with here is one which we have already discussed at various points in this book and that is the modelling of consumers' expenditure, or the consumption function.

This section will draw heavily upon an article by Davidson, Hendry, Srba and Yeo (hereinafter referred to as DHSY).[7] We will only provide a brief summary of the main conclusions of the article. However, the reader is strongly urged to read the article in full. It is also not our intention to provide a detailed discussion of the historical development of the theory and estimation of the consumption function, for which the interested reader is directed elsewhere.[8]

The approach taken by DHSY was to begin by considering a number of alternative formulations of the consumption function, and then to compare the statistical performance of these formulations using a common data set. In general terms, the consumption function was defined as being some form of relationship between consumption and income, with consumption being the dependent variable and income the independent variable. The central issue, then, is the specification of the precise form of this relationship.

The basic data set used was quarterly, seasonally unadjusted observations on non-durable consumption expenditure and personal disposable income, both in 1970 prices, over the period 1958 to 1975 (although 1957 data were used to generate some of the lagged variables). These data are presented in Appendix 7.3, together with a series on the consumers' expenditure deflator (the relevance of which will be seen presently).[9]

The data period was divided into two sub-periods – 1958(1) to 1970(4), and 1971(1) to 1975(4). The first period was used to estimate the parameters of the various competing consumption function formulations. The second period was used as a forecast period, over which the various consumption functions could be compared with respect to their forecasting performance. As some of the formulations which we will present involve five-period lags, the effective estimation period begins in 1958(2), and thus all equations will be estimated over the resulting 51 observations. In Figure 7.24 we present a graph of the

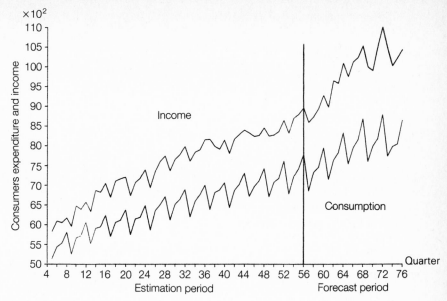

**Figure 7.24** Consumers' non-durable expenditure and personal disposable income, 1958 to 1975.

income and consumption data, in which the estimation and forecast periods are indicated.

An obvious feature of Figure 7.24 is the much more regular seasonal pattern in the consumption series as compared to the income series. Note the more variable behaviour of the income series over the forecast period relative to the estimation period, and similarly, the 'levelling out' of the consumption series over the estimation period. Also note the expanding seasonal pattern in the consumption series, a feature upon which we commented in Figure 4.7. In other words, the ability of any model, estimated only over the estimation period, to forecast the relatively atypical behaviour of consumption over the forecast period (given the volatility of the income series) provides a quite stringent forecasting test.

We begin with what could be termed the 'traditional' econometric approach to modelling consumption expenditure, which is essentially the approach which we took in Example 5.3. That is, assuming a simple Koyck lag structure then a formulation such as the following is produced:

$$C_t = \beta_0 + \beta_1 C_{t-1} + \beta_2 Y_t + \varepsilon_t \hspace{2cm} \text{Equation 7.61}$$

A number of theoretical justifications for such a formulation have been provided in the consumption function literature. However, they all essentially derive from an attempt to explain the much more regular pattern of consumption expenditure as compared to the irregular variation in income. Thus consumption expenditure is held to be primarily influenced by habit, and habits change only slowly over time. Short-term variations in income will not be fully reflected in changed consumption expenditure, but rather consumers will only adjust their behaviour in response to longer term (or permanent) movements in income. Hence some model which relates current consumption to current and past income is produced. A Koyck lag can then be imposed for estimation purposes.

As we have emphasised throughout this book, econometrics provides two forms of model evaluation. First, we can apply standard statistical criteria to examine the extent to which a given model specification is *data*-consistent. Second, we can also evaluate an estimated model in terms of *theory*-consistency.

In terms of the specification in Equation 7.61 there are a number of theoretical postulates concerning consumption behaviour which can be examined, relating both to short-run and long-run behaviour.

$\beta_2$ is the short-run marginal propensity to consume – that is, the proportion of an additional unit of current income which is devoted to current consumption. Clearly, $\beta_2$ must be positive and less than one, although theory might be a little unclear as to its order of magnitude. Therefore we would expect these properties to be reflected in any estimate of $\beta_2$. However, more interesting questions concern long-run behaviour, and here theory is somewhat more specific.

We could define the long-run as a point in time at which the economy reaches static equilibrium – that is, the economy will have settled down to a situation of no growth, and in particular, consumption and income will be constant from period to period. Thus in the long-run the average propensity to consume (APC) – the ratio of consumption to income $(C_t/Y_t)$ – must also be constant from period to period. Given that the marginal propensity to consume (MPC) is the proportion of an additional unit of income which goes on consumption then in the long-run the MPC must equal the APC. For if the marginal expenditure on consumption diverges from the average expenditure then the average expenditure will change over time and the economy will no longer be in static equilibrium.

Equality of the long-run APC and MPC implies a long-run elasticity of consumption to income of one. That is, we can express the elasticity of consumption with respect to income as:

$$\varepsilon_{cy} = \frac{dC_t}{dY_t} \times \frac{Y_t}{C_t}$$

$$= \text{MPC} \times (1/\text{APC})$$

and thus in the long-run we must have:

$$\varepsilon_{cy} = 1$$

In order to derive the long-run MPC from Equation 7.61 we simply set $C_t = C_{t-1}$, and then re-express the equation in terms of $C_t$. The long-run consumption function can then be written as:

$$C_t = \frac{\beta_0}{1-\beta_1} + \frac{\beta_2}{1-\beta_1} Y_t + \frac{\varepsilon_t}{1-\beta_1}$$  Equation 7.62

Therefore the long-run MPC is simply the coefficient on $Y_t$ in Equation 7.62, or

$$MPC_{LR} = \frac{\beta_2}{1-\beta_1}$$  Equation 7.63

Thus an estimate of the long-run MPC can be derived by estimating Equation 7.61 and dividing the estimate of $\beta_2$ by one minus the estimate of $\beta_1$. An estimate of the long-run APC could be obtained by simply dividing average quarterly consumption over the estimation period by average quarterly income. That is, from the sample data we have:

$$\bar{C} = 6490.152$$

$$\bar{Y} = 7563.333$$

and therefore

$$\widehat{APC} = 0.858$$

One difficulty relating to the estimation of Equation 7.61 is that the theory used to produce this model is not specific as to whether the relevant time-period is months, quarters, years, or whatever, or whether seasonally adjusted or unadjusted data should be used. The theory is perfectly general and presumably the form of the data used should make little difference to the resulting parameter estimates. As we have already indicated, the data used here are quarterly, seasonally unadjusted. Therefore we require a method for accounting for the seasonality in the data.

A common procedure is to use dummy variables. However, we have already noted that not only do the consumption data exhibit a regular seasonal pattern, but this pattern also appears to expand over time. Consequently, two sets of dummy variables are required, one to account for the constant seasonal pattern and the other to account for the expanding pattern. Thus we define the following dummy variables:

$D_{1t} = 1$  in Quarter 1, 0 otherwise

$D_{2t} = 1$  in Quarter 2, 0 otherwise

$D_{3t} = 1$  in Quarter 3, 0 otherwise

$T_t$  is a time trend variable, running from 1 to 51

$DT_{4t} = D_{1t} \times T_t$

$$DT_{5t} = D_{2t} \times T_t$$
$$DT_{6t} = D_{3t} \times T_t$$

Finally, there is one minor feature of the data which requires consideration. In the first quarter of 1968 advance warning was given of purchase tax increases which were to occur in the second quarter of 1968. This caused a considerable amount of switching of expenditure from the second quarter of 1968 to the first quarter. We can account for this expenditure-switching effect through the use of a dummy variable which takes on the value one in 1968(1), minus one in 1968(2) and zero at all other times. This dummy variable will be denoted by $D_t^0$ (a similar effect also occurred during the forecast period in the first two quarters of 1973, and for forecasting purposes $D_t^0$ was set to 1, $-1$ in 1973 (1)/(2)).

Thus the final estimating equation can be written as:

$$C_t = \beta_0 + \beta_1 C_{t-1} + \beta_2 Y_t + \beta_3 D_{1t} + \beta_4 D_{2t} + \beta_5 D_{3t} + \beta_6 T_t$$
$$+ \beta_7 DT_{4t} + \beta_8 DT_{5t} + \beta_9 DT_{6t} + \beta_{10} D_t^0 + \varepsilon_t \qquad \text{Equation 7.64}$$

Using the data in Appendix 7.3, and the above-defined dummy variables, the ordinary least squares estimate of Equation 7.64 is as follows (*t*-statistics in brackets):

$$\hat{C}_t = 2752.862 + 0.273 C_{t-1} + 0.225 Y_t - 486.539 D_{1t}$$
$$\quad (5.44) \quad (2.16) \qquad (4.57) \qquad (8.35)$$

$$- 118.573 D_{2t} - 190.338 D_{3t} + 17.012 T_t - 6.046 DT_{4t}$$
$$\quad (2.15) \qquad (5.18) \qquad (4.80) \qquad (5.32)$$

$$- 1.625 DT_{5t} - 0.286 DT_{6t} + 75.536 D_t^0 \qquad \text{Equation 7.65}$$
$$\quad (1.48) \qquad (0.27) \qquad (2.24)$$

$$R^2 = 0.997, \quad \hat{\sigma}_\varepsilon = 39.855, \quad d = 2.09, \quad n = 51$$

where $\hat{\sigma}_\varepsilon$ is the standard error of the regression (that is, the standard deviation of the residuals, adjusted for the degrees of freedom). Thus, superficially at least, a well determined equation is produced, with no obvious statistical shortcomings.

However, as indicated above, we can also assess Equation 7.65 with respect to its theoretical implications. Thus the estimate of the short-run MPC is 0.225, and perhaps might be argued to be somewhat on the low side. The long-run MPC is:

$$\text{MPC}_{LR} = \frac{0.225}{1 - 0.273} = 0.309$$

which is certainly lower than theory would predict, producing a long-run elasticity of only $0.309/0.858 = 0.360$. Thus we would conclude that although

Equation 7.65 appears statistically adequate, its theoretical implications are unacceptable.

Finally, we can examine Equation 7.65 with respect to its forecasting performance. Recall from Chapter 6 that we introduced a forecasting test involving a test statistic, $z_1$ (see Equation 6.110 and the associated discussion). Thus Equation 7.65 could be used to produce the one-step ahead forecasts over the 20-period forecast period, 1971(1) to 1975(4). The root mean square error (RMSE) can then be derived from these forecasts (recall that the actual value of $C_t$ is known over the 'forecast' period), and thus, given the value of $\hat{\sigma}_\varepsilon$ from Equation 7.65, a value for $z_1$ can be derived from Equation 6.111. As 20 forecasts are being produced, then the resulting value of $z_1$ can be compared to the corresponding tabulated value for the $\chi^2$ distribution with 20 degrees of freedom. At a significance level of 5 per cent the tabulated value from Appendix V is 31.4. Thus an observed value of $z_1$ in excess of 31.4 would imply an inconsistency between the equation's forecasting performance and its estimation performance, hence implying a model inadequacy.

The one-step ahead forecasts from Equation 7.65 produce a RMSE of 99.68. Therefore we have, from Equation 6.111:

$$z_1 = \frac{(20)(99.68)^2}{(39.855)^2} = 125.11$$

Equation 7.65 therefore fails the forecast performance test. This, together with the unacceptable theoretical implications of the estimated model, means we would have to reject it from further consideration. In the various estimated models which we will subsequently present we will also quote the associated value of $z_1$ amongst the summary statistics.

Recall that we previously argued that the apparent heteroskedasticity in the consumption data could be dealt with by an appropriate transformation (in particular, the logarithmic transformation – see Figure 7.18). This would certainly be the approach of a B–J modeller, who would argue, perhaps not unreasonably, that the use of the time-related dummy variables in Equation 7.64 is somewhat clumsy, and certainly wasteful of degrees of freedom. Consequently, Equation 7.64 could be re-estimated in logarithmic form, but omitting the time-related dummy variables. We present this estimated equation in Equation 7.66.

$$\ln \hat{C}_t = 0.476 + 0.765 \ln C_{t-1} + 0.182 \ln Y_t - 0.126 D_{1t}$$
$$\quad (2.93) \quad (9.27) \qquad\qquad (2.72) \qquad\quad (17.92)$$

$$+ 0.008 D_{2t} - 0.026 D_{3t} + 0.016 D_t^0 \qquad\qquad \text{Equation 7.66}$$
$$\quad (1.42) \qquad (8.41) \qquad (2.50)$$

$$R^2 = 0.994, \quad \hat{\sigma}_\varepsilon = 0.0079, \quad d = 2.08, \quad z_1 = 87.88$$

In comparing Equations 7.65 and 7.66 we note that the statistical performances of the two equations are virtually identical. That is, we could argue that the logarithmic transformation is a relatively efficient way of dealing with the heteroskedasticity in the data. Consequently all the remaining equations we will present will be in logarithmic form (although we will subsequently provide a theoretical, rather than a purely pragmatic, justification for the use of the logarithmic transformation).

We can also evaluate Equation 7.66 with respect to its theoretical implications. As the data are now in logarithmic form all the coefficients in Equation 7.66 can be interpreted as **elasticities**. In particular, the coefficient on ln $Y_t$ is the short-run elasticity of consumption with respect to income. In order to derive the short-run MPC we have:

$$\varepsilon_{cy} = \frac{dC_t}{dY_t} \times \frac{Y_t}{C_t}$$

$$\therefore \frac{dC_t}{dY_t} = \text{MPC} = \varepsilon_{cy} \times \frac{C_t}{Y_t}$$

Evaluating this MPC at the sample means produces:

$$\text{MPC}_{SR} = (0.182)(0.858) = 0.156$$

As in the case of Equation 7.65 it could be argued that this estimate is somewhat low.

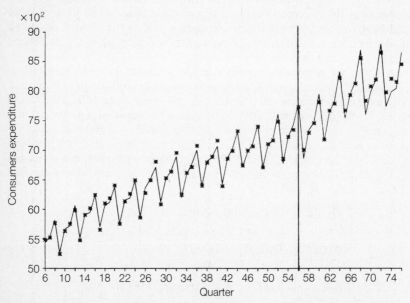

**Figure 7.25** Forecasts of consumption expenditure derived from Equation 7.66.

The long-run elasticity is straightforward to derive from Equation 7.66. Setting $C_t = C_{t-1}$, and solving for $\ln C_t$ the resulting coefficient on $\ln Y_t$ can be directly interpreted as the long-run elasticity. That is:

$$\varepsilon_{LR} = 0.182/(1 - 0.765) = 0.774$$

Again, a value less than one results, hence rendering the equation theoretically unacceptable.

Finally, Equation 7.66 still produces a significant value for $z_1$, providing a further justification for its rejection.

In order to allow a subjective evaluation of the forecasting performance of Equation 7.66 we present in Figure 7.25 the associated one-step ahead forecasts of $C_t$. The unbroken line denotes the actual value of $C_t$ and the asterisks denote the fitted values over the estimation period, and the one-step ahead forecasts over the forecast period. From the figure it could be argued that the forecasts are not unreasonable. However, the performance of the equation is somewhat poorer over the forecast period as compared to the estimation period, and particularly so towards the end of the forecast period. Again, this emphasises the role of the $z_1$ statistic. As we indicated in Chapter 6, $z_1$ is a measure of relative forecast accuracy and its value here reflects the poor forecasting performance of Equation 7.66 relative to its estimation performance. In turn, given that the equation cannot reproduce its estimation performance outside the estimation period, a model inadequacy is implied – the parameters of the model could be interpreted as being unstable.

Thus the general conclusion which could be drawn is that while the 'traditional' approach to modelling consumers' expenditure produces models which provide acceptable statistical descriptions of the available data, and could even be interpreted as generating reasonable forecasts (at least in some absolute sense), the models all have serious theoretical weaknesses. These models therefore provide an unreliable (or unstable) basis for forecasting and policy evaluation.

Finally, we could consider a B–J approach to modelling $C_t$. Rather than consider a univariate model, we will consider a **transfer function** model, in which $C_t$ is related to $Y_t$. We will not consider the details of this modelling approach, and we need only recognise that the resulting model is derived without reference to any economic theory, save that income is related to consumption in some way. As in the case of deriving a B–J univariate model, the objective is to estimate as concise a relationship between $C_t$ and $Y_t$ as possible, within the constraints only of statistical acceptability.

DHSY make reference to a particular B–J study of the consumption–income relationship,[10] and interpret the finally identified form of this relationship, in the context of their quarterly data, as follows:[11]

$$\Delta_4 \ln C_t = \beta_0 + \beta_1 \Delta_4 \ln Y_t + \beta_2 \Delta_1 \Delta_4 \ln Y_t + \beta_3 \Delta_4 D_t^0 + \varepsilon_t \qquad \text{Equation 7.67}$$

where $\Delta_1$ refers to the first difference of the data and $\Delta_4$ refers to the fourth difference. Equation 7.67 does not include any dummy variables to account for seasonality, as it is the fourth differences of the data that should perform this role (see Appendix 7.1 for a fuller exposition of the B–J approach to modelling seasonal data). We would also note that Equation 7.67 certainly provides a more concise summary of the consumption–income relationship that the econometric approach (although the theoretical implications of Equation 7.67 have yet to be examined).

The least squares estimate of Equation 7.67 is as follows:

$$\Delta_4 \ln \hat{C}_t = 0.010 + 0.450 \Delta_4 \ln Y_t - 0.157 \Delta_1 \Delta_4 \ln Y_t + 0.008 \Delta_4 D_t^0$$
$$\quad\quad (6.97)\ (11.21) \quad\quad\quad (3.51) \quad\quad\quad\quad (2.49)$$

Equation 7.68

$$R^2 = 0.751, \quad d = 1.67, \quad \hat{\sigma}_\varepsilon = 0.0063, \quad z_1 = 63.44$$

A graph of the forecasts of $C_t$ derived from Equation 7.68 is shown in Figure 7.26 (that is, by first deriving the forecasts of $\Delta_4 \ln C_t$ directly from Equation 7.68, and then 'undifferencing' and 'unlogging' the resulting forecasts to return to the original units of measurement).

One obvious feature of Figure 7.26 is that fourth differencing appears to have dealt quite adequately with the seasonality in the data. Consequently the Box–Jenkins approach would certainly appear to provide a more efficient means of accounting for seasonality than the somewhat arbitrary addition of dummy variables to the model. Indeed, it could be argued that the regular and

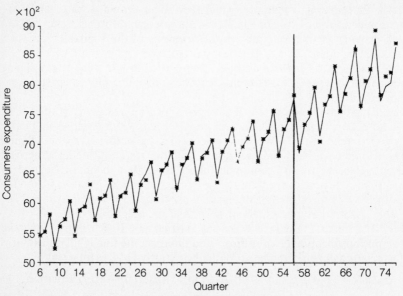

**Figure 7.26**  Forecasts of $C_t$ derived from Equation 7.68.

expanding seasonal pattern in consumption expenditure is one of the more interesting features of the data and therefore should be modelled with as much care as the non-seasonal components of the data. The use of dummy variables to account for seasonality is effectively an attempt to remove the seasonality from the data rather than to explain it. That is, it might be argued that even theoretically the B–J formulation in Equation 7.67 provides a more satisfactory means of modelling seasonal consumption data than the traditional econometric approach.

However, Equation 7.68 still produces a significant $z_1$ statistic, and consequently the basic forecasting problem of the earlier formulations remains unresolved. Further, while it might be argued that Equation 7.68 is a more satisfactory model of the seasonal components of the data, additional theoretical problems still remain. In particular, Equation 7.68 can provide no information concerning a situation of static equilibrium, for it has no static equilibrium solution. That is, if we assume a situation of no growth, then we must have:

$$\ln C_t = \ln C_{t-4}$$

and

$$\ln Y_t = \ln Y_{t-4}$$

However, Equation 7.68 cannot be solved for these conditions (the left-hand side will be zero and the right-hand side will simply equal the constant term). The only long-term solution that can be derived from Equation 7.68 is for the case of stable equilibrium, in which the economy is growing at some steady-state rate. Thus ignoring the dummy variable, $\Delta_4 D_t^0$, in stable equilibrium we must have:

$$\Delta_4 \ln Y_t = g$$

where $g$ is the constant steady-state growth rate, and consequently:

$$\Delta_1 \Delta_4 \ln Y_t = \Delta_1 g = 0$$

Therefore the estimate of the 'long-run' consumption function from Equation 7.68 becomes:

$$\Delta_4 \ln \hat{C}_t = 0.010 + 0.450 \Delta_4 \ln Y_t \qquad \text{Equation 7.69}$$

Thus an estimated long-run elasticity of only 0.45 is produced, again being inconsistent with the theoretically expected unit elasticity.

However, in a steady state the growth rate of consumption must equal that of income, and thus we must have:

$$\Delta_4 \ln C_t = \Delta_4 \ln Y_t = g$$

and solving Equation 7.69 for this constant growth rate produces:

$$g = 0.010/0.450 = 0.022$$

or a growth rate of 2.2 per cent per annum. That is, Equation 7.68 is consistent only with a fixed long-term growth rate. In other words, Equation 7.68 (and the formulation from which it is derived) is extremely restrictive with respect to any conclusions that can be drawn concerning the long-run behaviour of the economy. (A Box–Jenkins modeller would presumably reject such criticisms by arguing that B–J models only claim to be short-term models, and it is therefore unreasonable to evaluate them with respect to their long-term properties.)

While it is the case that the two econometric formulations (Equations 7.65 and 7.66) and the B–J formulation (Equation 7.68) have all been rejected for both inadequate theoretical and forecasting performances, it is still of some interest to determine which of these equations is statistically superior.

Certainly the B–J model is the most parsimonious description of the data, and does not appear to produce obviously inferior forecasts to the econometric models. In addition, it could be argued that this model provides a more satisfactory treatment of the seasonality in the data. Further, note that the formulation in Equation 7.67 can be interpreted as a set of parameter restrictions. For if we were to 'undifference' the variables in Equation 7.67 then the following model is produced:

$$\ln C_t = \beta_0 + \beta_1 \ln Y_t - \beta_1 \ln Y_{t-4} + \beta_2 \Delta_1 \ln Y_t - \beta_2 \Delta_1 \ln Y_{t-4}$$
$$+ \ln C_{t-4} + \beta_3 D_t^0 - \beta_3 D_{t-4}^0 + \varepsilon_t \qquad \text{Equation 7.70}$$

We could interpret Equation 7.70 as the unrestricted B–J model. Thus note that the B–J formulation in Equation 7.67 implies that the sets of coefficients on $\ln Y_t$ and $\ln Y_{t-4}$, $\Delta_1 \ln Y_t$ and $\Delta_1 \ln Y_{t-4}$, and $D_t^0$ and $D_{t-4}^0$ are each equal and opposite in sign, and the coefficient on $\ln C_{t-4}$ is one. Therefore if Equation 7.67 is an accurate summary of the statistical process which generated the sample data then we would expect the direct estimation of Equation 7.70 to be consistent with these implied parameter restrictions. Directly estimating Equation 7.70 produces the following results:

$$\ln \hat{C}_t = 0.130 + 0.437 \ln Y_t - 0.419 \ln Y_{t-4}$$
$$\quad (1.39) \quad (9.50) \qquad (8.73)$$

$$-0.131 \Delta_1 \ln Y_t + 0.165 \Delta_1 \ln Y_{t-4} + 0.968 \ln C_{t-4}$$
$$(2.61) \qquad\qquad (3.43) \qquad\qquad (24.78)$$

$$+ 0.009 D_t^0 - 0.008 D_{t-4}^0 \qquad\qquad\qquad \text{Equation 7.71}$$
$$(1.80) \qquad (1.78)$$

$$R^2 = 0.996, \quad \hat{\sigma}_\varepsilon = 0.0064, \quad d = 1.73, \quad z_1 = 51.49$$

Thus Equation 7.71 is remarkably consistent with the parameter restrictions implied by the strict B–J formulation in Equation 7.67.

The general conclusion which can be drawn, therefore, is that the B–J model would appear to provide the most satisfactory statistical description of the data. It is efficient in the use of parameters, it very adequately explains the seasonality in the data and it cannot be rejected in terms of its implied parameter restrictions.[12] However, in theoretical terms, the B–J formulation is probably the least satisfactory of the competing models in that it offers the potential for only short-term analysis.

Given that none of the models forecasts adequately and that they all have theoretical weaknesses, further model refinement is clearly required. As the B–J model produces the best statistical performance then it would seem reasonable to begin with this formulation, and to consider possible refinements, particularly in terms of introducing a long-term dimension to the model.

We require a model which produces a long-run elasticity of one. Thus consider a model which in the long run collapses to:

$$C_t = kY_t \qquad \text{Equation 7.72}$$

Note that, by definition, Equation 7.72 must produce a long-run elasticity of one, irrespective of the value of $k$. That is, from Equation 7.72 we have:

$$\frac{dC_t}{dY_t} = k = \text{MPC}_{\text{LR}}$$

and

$$\frac{C_t}{Y_t} = k = \text{APC}$$

Now, from Equation 7.72 we can write:

$$\ln C_t = \ln k + \ln Y_t \qquad \text{Equation 7.73}$$

$$\therefore \ln C_{t-1} = \ln k + \ln Y_{t-1} \qquad \text{Equation 7.74}$$

Subtracting Equation 7.74 from Equation 7.73 produces:

$$\ln C_t - \ln C_{t-1} = \ln Y_t - \ln Y_{t-1}$$

or

$$\Delta_1 \ln C_t = \Delta_1 \ln Y_t \qquad \text{Equation 7.75}$$

That is, in the long run the growth rate of consumption must equal that of income.

Consider a consumption function formulation such as the following:

$$\Delta_1 \ln C_t = k^* + \beta_1 \Delta_1 \ln Y_t + \gamma(\ln C_{t-1} - \ln Y_{t-1}) \qquad \text{Equation 7.76}$$

Now, in static equilibrium the growth rates of consumption and income must both be zero and thus we have:

$$\Delta_1 \ln C_t = \Delta_1 \ln Y_t = 0$$

and therefore Equation 7.76 collapses to:

$$\ln C_{t-1} = \frac{-k^*}{\gamma} + \ln Y_{t-1}$$

or

$$\ln C_t = \frac{-k^*}{\gamma} + \ln Y_t \qquad\qquad\text{Equation 7.77}$$

Note that Equation 7.77 is equivalent to Equation 7.73 (with $\ln k = -k^*/\gamma$), which in turn is equivalent to the long-run consumption function in Equation 7.72. That is, if the consumption function is given by Equation 7.76 then in static equilibrium it will collapse to a consumption function with unit elasticity, as required by theory (and irrespective of the values of the parameters in Equation 7.76).

Note also that Equation 7.76 could be solved for the case of stable equilibrium, where a common growth rate of $g$ can be assumed such that:

$$\Delta_1 \ln C_t = \Delta_1 \ln Y_t = g \qquad\qquad\text{Equation 7.78}$$

Substituting Equation 7.78 into Equation 7.76 again produces a long-run consumption function equivalent to Equation 7.72 (although with a different constant term), producing a long-run elasticity of one, as required by theory. Thus Equation 7.76 has both a stable and a static equilibrium solution, in both cases producing a long-run unit elasticity. This property results from the inclusion of the **disequilibrium** term, $\ln C_{t-1} - \ln Y_{t-1}$. Without this term the model would not have a static equilibrium solution, and would therefore only be a short-run model.

However, we have as yet provided no theoretical justification for Equation 7.76, nor have we evaluated its statistical performance.

A formulation such as Equation 7.76 could be justified by first arguing that the relevant dependent variable is the change in the level of consumption expenditure from one period to the next. That is, we require an explanation not so much for the level of consumption, but rather as to why it should change from period to period. In terms of explanatory variables, the obvious one is the change in the level of income, which is presumably the major explanation for the short-run movements in consumption expenditure. However, consumers might also be interpreted as responding to some longer-term 'target' consumption function – as reflected in the long-run consumption function of Equation 7.72. Thus the disequilibrium term reflects the extent to which this target is being achieved – the extent to which the levels of consumption and income are in equilibrium – and hence the adjustments which are required to current consumption expenditure in order to approach some concept of longer-run equilibrium.

Returning to the specifics of our quarterly consumption function, we first note that as seasonally unadjusted quarterly data are being used then the appropriate dependent variable is $\Delta_4 \ln C_t$. That is, we require an explanation for the change in consumption expenditure from the immediately preceding comparable quarter – the level of consumption expenditure four quarters previously. Thus the relevant dependent variable is that identified by the B–J analysis. Consequently, as the B–J model was considered the most satisfactory statistical model then it would seem appropriate to begin with this formulation, with the theoretical refinement of now adding a disequilibrium term. Again, as quarterly data are being used the appropriate disequilibrium term is:

$$\ln C_{t-4} - \ln Y_{t-4} = \ln\left(\frac{C_{t-4}}{Y_{t-4}}\right) = \ln(C/Y)_{t-4}$$

Thus the model can now be written as:

$$\Delta_4 \ln C_t = \beta_0 + \beta_1 \Delta_4 \ln Y_t + \beta_2 \Delta_1 \Delta_4 \ln Y_t$$
$$+ \beta_3 \ln(C/Y)_{t-4} + \beta_4 \Delta_4 D_t^0 + \varepsilon_t \qquad \text{Equation 7.79}$$

Note that we now have a further term which requires theoretical justification, $\Delta_1 \Delta_4 \ln Y_t$. Thus it could be argued that not only will $\Delta_4 \ln C_t$ repond to the corresponding change in income, but it might be expected to respond differently depending on whether income is increasing or decreasing. Note also that the logarithmic transformation of the variables in Equation 7.79 can be justified directly in terms of the theoretical specification of the model, beginning with the simple long-run model in Equation 7.72. That is, we can now provide a theoretical justification for the log transformation, rather than the pragmatic (and arbitrary) one of variance stabilisation.

There is one final practical point associated with the estimation of Equation 7.79. If, over the estimation period, $C_t$ and $Y_t$ are growing at a constant rate (as would appear approximately to be the case from Figure 7.24) then the term $\ln(C/Y)_{t-4}$ will be a constant. Consequently, it will be highly collinear with the constant term in Equation 7.79 leading to multicollinearity problems, and hence imprecise estimation. Thus either the constant term or the disequilibrium term could be dropped from the model with little effect on the model's goodness of fit. However, dropping the disequilibrium term would reduce the model to the simple B–J formulation, which we have already shown to be inadequate, and which would remove the long-run properties from the model. Dropping the constant term would leave the theoretical properties of the model unaltered.

The least squares estimate of Equation 7.79, omitting the constant, is as follows:

$$\Delta_4 \ln \hat{C}_t = 0.508 \Delta_4 \ln Y_t - 0.175 \Delta_1 \Delta_4 \ln Y_t$$
$$\phantom{\Delta_4 \ln \hat{C}_t =} (13.82) \qquad\qquad (3.75)$$

$$-0.056 \ln(C/Y)_{t-4} + 0.008 D_t^0 \qquad\qquad \text{Equation 7.80}$$
$$\phantom{-0.056} (6.25) \qquad\qquad (2.34)$$

$$R^2 = 0.729, \quad \hat{\sigma}_\varepsilon = 0.0066, \quad d = 1.58, \quad z_1 = 76.29$$

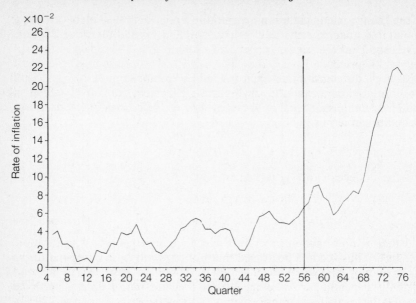

**Figure 7.27**  The annual rate of inflation the UK – 1958(1) to 1975(4).

However, the $z_1$ statistic associated with Equation 7.80 is still significant. Thus despite the superior theoretical specification of this model, it does not produce forecasts superior to those of the previously considered models. Therefore further theoretical refinement is required. This might also be justified by the inconclusive value of the Durbin–Watson statistic, implying the possibility of some misspecification.

Now, the forecast period of 1971(1) to 1975(4) was a period of exceptionally high inflation rates in the UK. In Figure 7.27 we present a graph of the annual rate of inflation over the entire sample period (defined in terms of the fourth difference of the log of the implied consumers' expenditure deflator shown in Appendix 7.3). From Figure 7.27 we can see the very different behaviour of prices over the forecast period as compared to the estimation period, hence providing a possible explanation for the poor forecasting performance of the model.

In terms of a theoretical justification for including an inflation effect in the model, it could be argued that unanticipated inflation (that is, inflation which is not immediately and fully reflected in changed income) will have the effect of a relative price change. Consumers will be purchasing a range of commodities and the relative prices of these commodities will be continually changing from time point to time point as the differential lags in inflationary price changes work their way through the system for each commodity. Over a longer time-period, assuming that the prices of all commodities are equally affected by inflation, no long-term changes in relative prices will occur. But at a point in time consumers will find it difficult to distinguish between a relative price change and a lag in inflationary effects being fully reflected in some commodity prices.

A fuller theoretical justification for such an argument can be found elsewhere.[13] For our purposes it is sufficient to recognise that a theoretical case for including inflation in the model can be made out, a case which is as plausible over the estimation period as it is over the forecast period. In any event, in estimating this inflation effect only the observations over the estimation period will be used. Therefore if the inclusion of inflation is to improve the forecasting performance of the model then it must be the case that the parameters which measure this effect are constant over both the estimation and forecast periods. That is, it must be argued that inflation has a constant or stable effect, but over the forecast period its presence is simply more marked than over the estimation period.

Let $P_t$ denote the implied consumers' expenditure deflator (derived by dividing consumers' expenditure in current prices by consumers' expenditure in 1970 prices, multiplied by 100). Then we could argue that $P_t$ should enter the model in the same way as $Y_t$ – that is, the relative change in consumption will be influenced by the corresponding change in prices, and whether inflation is increasing or decreasing. Thus two further variables are added to the model: $\Delta_4 \ln P_t$ and $\Delta_1 \Delta_4 \ln P_t$. Re-estimating the model with these two additional variables produces the following results:

$$\Delta_4 \ln \hat{C}_t = 0.495 \Delta_4 \ln Y_t - 0.208 \Delta_1 \Delta_4 \ln Y_t$$
$$\quad\quad (12.23) \quad\quad\quad\quad (4.10)$$

$$\quad - 0.086 \ln (C/Y)_{t-4} - 0.108 \Delta_4 \ln P_t$$
$$\quad\quad (3.73) \quad\quad\quad\quad\quad (1.49)$$

$$\quad - 0.171 \Delta_1 \Delta_4 \ln P_t + 0.008 D_t^0 \quad\quad\quad\quad \text{Equation 7.81}$$
$$\quad\quad (1.47) \quad\quad\quad\quad\quad (2.25)$$

$$R^2 = 0.770, \quad \hat{\sigma}_\varepsilon = 0.0062, \quad d = 1.80, \quad z_1 = 22.43$$

Thus from Equation 7.81 it can be seen that the associated $z_1$ statistic is now insignificant and therefore that the forecasting problem has been resolved. In Figure 7.28 we present the forecasts of $C_t$ derived from Equation 7.81, from which the impressive forecasting performance of the model can be confirmed. In particular, there does not appear to be any inconsistency between the model's estimation performance and its forecasting performance, thereby satisfying an important requirement of any model that purports to be the 'true' model.

In order to confirm that it is not just the consideration of inflation effects that resolves the forecasting problem, we could re-specify the model by dropping the disequilibrium term, adding a constant and leaving in the

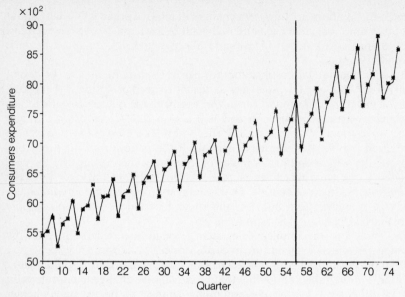

**Figure 7.28** Forecasts of $C_t$ derived from Equation 7.81.

inflation terms. That is, in effect we are returning to a B–J specification in which the effect of inflation is now included in the model. The resulting estimated model is as follows:

$$\Delta_4 \ln \hat{C}_t = 0.020 + 0.360 \Delta_4 \ln Y_t$$
$$\quad\quad\quad (5.49) \quad (7.11)$$

$$\quad -0.155 \Delta_1 \Delta_4 \ln Y_t - 0.206 \Delta_4 \ln P_t$$
$$\quad\quad (3.29) \quad\quad\quad\quad (3.03)$$

$$\quad -0.077 \Delta_1 \Delta_4 \ln P_t + 0.008 D_t^0 \quad\quad\quad\quad \text{Equation 7.82}$$
$$\quad\quad (0.73) \quad\quad\quad\quad (2.60)$$

$$R^2 = 0.816, \quad \hat{\sigma}_\varepsilon = 0.0055, \quad d = 1.93, \quad z_1 = 140.46$$

Thus Equation 7.82 produces a highly significant $z_1$ statistic. A graph of the forecasts from Equation 7.82 is shown in Figure 7.29, from which the equation's poor forecasting performance can be seen. The point we would wish to emphasise with this application is the very powerful role which can be played by economic theory in the modelling process. Theory does matter, and in this particular application it provided the means for producing a satisfactory (and indeed very impressive) forecasting model.

While B–J was very useful for highlighting the possibility of describing the statistical properties of the data in a considerably simplified form, it was only when considerations of economic theory were introduced that a satisfactory

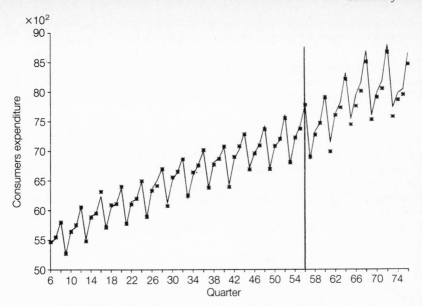

**Figure 7.29** Forecasts of $C_t$ derived from Equation 7.82.

model was finally derived. Central to the resolution of both the theoretical and forecasting problems of the various models initially considered was the identification of the disequilibrium term, $\ln(C/Y)_{t-4}$. B–J has no mechanism for identifying the importance of such a term. Indeed, over the estimation period, the statistical (as opposed to the theoretical) importance of this term was not particularly apparent, given the relative constancy of the growth rate over this period, and the stability of inflation. However, over the forecast period, where the income and inflation series in particular were more volatile, disequilibrium effects became much more important.

This application very forcibly emphasises the considerable benefits which can be derived from combining rigorous statistical analysis with appropriate theoretical analysis (although we have not here discussed a number of further statistical testing procedures adopted by DHSY). None the less, the approach outlined here should not be interpreted as representing any radical development of econometric methodology. Rather, it is an illustration of a rigorous and careful application of basic econometric methodology, and the advantages which can be derived from such an approach.

### 7.5 Summary

In this final chapter we have provided an introductory discussion of the Box–Jenkins approach to modelling time-series data. We emphasised that the objectives of the approach are modest, in the sense that it has been developed only for the purpose of producing short-term statistical forecasting models. None the less, judged against this objective, B–J provides a powerful and integrated set of statistical procedures for deriving such models.

However, to the econometrician, B–J is of only limited use, given its inability to incorporate the requirements of economic theory in a direct and effective manner. None the less, the B–J emphasis on the rigorous analysis of the statistical properties of a given data set can at least be interpreted as a valuable input into the econometric modelling process.

We completed this chapter with a relatively detailed discussion of a published study concerned with the econometric modelling of consumers' expenditure. In certain respects the study could be interpreted as being influenced by B–J methodology, in the sense that considerable weight was given to a rigorous analysis of the statistical properties of the data. However, the requirements of economic theory were still considered to be paramount, and via such an approach the possibility of deriving a satisfactory longer-term forecasting model was demonstrated.

## Notes

[1] For a full exposition of Box–Jenkins methodology the interested reader is referred to G. E. P. Box and G. M. Jenkins, *Time Series Analysis: Forecasting and Control* (San Francisco, Holden-Day, 1976). However, see the references to this chapter for alternative, and more accessible, sources.

[2] See G. E. P. Box and D. A. Pierce, 'Distribution of residual autocorrelations in autoregressive integrated moving average time-series models', *Journal of the American Statistical Association*, 65 (1970), Dec.

[3] A slight modification to the $Q$ statistic which has been proposed is to define $Q$ as:

$$Q = n(n+2) \sum_{k=1}^{K} r_k^2/(n-k)$$

rather than the expression in Equation 7.43. See G. M. Ljung and G. E. P. Box, 'On a measure of lack of fit in time series models', *Biometrika*, 65 (1978), pp. 297–303.

[4] In fact, the derivation of the residuals from an estimated B–J model is not an entirely straightforward procedure, particularly when moving average parameters are involved. In effect, the estimated residuals are simulated from the model, a process which is tedious but easily performed on a computer. For a fuller exposition, involving a numerical example, the interested reader is referred to Box and Jenkins, *Time-Series Analysis*, pp. 215–20.

[5] For a brief discussion of the approach recommended by Box and Jenkins see ibid., p. 328. The Goldfeld–Quandt test may also be useful – see R. J. Pindyck and D. L. Rubenfeld, *Econometric Models and Economic Forecasts*, 2nd edn (New York, McGraw-Hill, 1981), pp. 148–50, and Section 4.3.4.

[6] For example, see Box and Jenkins, *Time Series Analysis*, for a discussion of various examples of this nature.

⁷ J. E. H. Davidson, D. F. Hendry, F. Srba and S. Yeo, 'Econometric modelling of the aggregate time-series relationship between consumers' expenditure and income in the United Kingdom', *The Economic Journal*, Dec. 1978.

⁸ For example, see D. G. Mayes, *Applications of Econometrics* (Prentice-Hall International, 1981), ch. 2; K. F. Wallis, *Topics in Applied Econometrics*, 2nd edn (Oxford, Basil Blackwell, 1979), ch. 1; R. L. Thomas, *Introductory Econometrics* (London, Longman, 1985), ch. 7.

⁹ The data used here would appear to differ slightly from those used by DHSY, presumably because of the difficulty of generating a series on real non-durable consumption expenditure prior to 1962, for which no series is published in the source quoted by DHSY (*Economic Trends*, Annual Supplement, 1976, HMSO). The approach we took here was to use a later data source (*Economic Trends*, Annual Supplement, 1981), in which data in 1975 prices are published, and to derive the proportions of non-durable consumption prior to 1962. These proportions were then applied to real total consumers' expenditure in 1970 prices in order to derive a series on real non-durable consumption expenditure in 1970 prices. Consequently, the estimated equations which we will present differ slightly from those presented in DHSY.

¹⁰ K. D. Wall *et al.*, 'Estimates of a simple control model of the UK economy', in *Modelling the Economy*, ed. G. A. Renton (London, Heinemann Educational Books, 1975).

¹¹ In fact, DHSY use data in levels rather than logs, but we will retain logarithms here for consistency.

¹² DHSY perform a number of formal statistical tests to confirm the superiority of the B–J formulation. However we will only rely on an informal analysis.

¹³ See A. S. Deaton, 'Involuntary saving through unanticipated inflation', *American Economic Review* (1977), Dec., pp. 899–910.

## References and Further Reading

The seminal source for Box–Jenkins methodology is G. E. P. Box and G. M. Jenkins, *Time Series Analysis: Forecasting and Control* (San Francisco, Holden-Day, 1976). Briefer and more elementary treatments can be found in Pindyck and Rubenfeld, *Econometric Models*, chs. 16 to 20, and S. Makridakis, S. C. Wheelwright and V. E. McGee, *Forecasting: Methods and Applications*, 2nd edn (John Wiley and Sons, 1983), chs. 8 to 10 (both of which also include examples of modelling economic data series with B–J). Other useful references for economic applications are the *Journal of Forecasting* and *The International Journal of Forecasting*.

The main reference for Section 7.4 is J. E. H. Davidson, D. F. Hendry, F. Srba, and S. Yeo, 'Econometric modelling of the aggregate time-series relationship between consumers' expenditure and income in the United Kingdom', *Economic Journal* (1978), Dec. An additional useful reference, in which a broader perspective of the DHSY results is taken, and which also examines the robustness of the DHSY formulation, is D. F. Hendry, 'Econometric modelling: The consumption function in retrospect', *Scottish Journal of Political Economy* (1983), Nov., pp. 193–220.

**Exercises**

Exercise 1

Consider the AR(1) process:

$$Y_t = \phi_1 Y_{t-1} + \varepsilon_t$$

Derive the expression for the correlation coefficient between $Y_t$ and $Y_{t-2}$. What is the correlation coefficient between $Y_t$ and $Y_{t-3}$? Deduce the correlation coefficient between $Y_t$ and $Y_{t-k}$.

Exercise 2

Consider the AR(2) process:

$$Y_t = \phi_1 Y_{t-1} + \phi_2 Y_{t-2} + \varepsilon_t$$

First derive the expression for the autocovariance at lag $k$ (that is, simply multiply the above equation throughout by $Y_{t-k}$ and take expectations). Show that the a.c.f. of an AR(2) is given by:

$$\rho_k = \phi_1 \rho_{k-1} + \phi_2 \rho_{k-2}$$

Given this expression, derive the expressions for $\rho_1, \rho_2$ and $\rho_3$ in terms only of $\phi_1$ and $\phi_2$.

Exercise 3

Now consider the p.a.c.f. of any AR process. The first partial autocorrelation is defined as the expression for $\phi_1$, in terms of $\rho_1$, if the process were AR(1). The second partial autocorrelation is the expression for $\phi_2$, in terms of $\rho_1$ and $\rho_2$, if the process were AR(2). The third partial autocorrelation is the expression for $\phi_3$, in terms of $\rho_1, \rho_2$, and $\rho_3$, if the process were AR(3), and so on. Thus derive the expressions for the first three partial autocorrelations of an AR process.

From these expressions, confirm that if the actual underlying process is AR(1) then the first partial autocorrelation will be non-zero, and the second and third partials will be zero. If the underlying process is AR(2) confirm that the first and second partials are non-zero and the third is zero.

Exercise 4

Show that the expression for the second partial autocorrelation for an AR(2) process can be interpreted in terms of the least squares estimator of $\phi_2$. (Hint: Consider the expression for $\hat{\beta}_1$ in Equation 3.35 and deduce the expression for $\hat{\beta}_2$. Now amend the notation in Equation 3.35 to that used in the case of an AR(2) (noting that all means are zero).)

Exercise 5

Consider the MA(1) process:

$$Y_t = \varepsilon_t + \theta_1 \varepsilon_{t-1}$$

Derive expressions for the autocovariance at lags 0, 1 and 2, and generalise for the autocovariance at lag $k$. What are the expressions for the autocorrelations, in terms of $\theta_1$, at lags 0, 1, 2 and $k$?

Exercise 6

(Requires familiarity with the material in Appendix 7.1.) If you have access to a computer package with a facility for Box–Jenkins estimation, attempt to fit a Box–Jenkins model to the consumers' expenditure data in Appendix 7.3, using as the estimation period 1957(1) to 1970(4). Given your estimated model use the computer package to generate forecasts over the period 1971(1) to 1975(4), and compare these forecasts to those presented in Section 7.4 above. Comment.

Exercise 7

(Requires familiarity with the material in Appendix 7.1.) Fit Box–Jenkins models to the income and consumers' expenditure deflator series in Appendix 7.3. Discuss your identified and estimated models.

**Appendix 7.1**  *The Box–Jenkins Approach to Modelling Seasonal Data*

The B–J approach to modelling seasonal data is a direct and logical extension of the methodology developed for modelling non-seasonal data.

Essentially, a statistical model can be fitted to the seasonal observations, and then superimposed on the period-to-period model. For example, if the data are quarterly a B–J model can be fitted to the observations four periods apart (this will be the seasonal model – it will reflect the way in which observations at a given quarter are related to the observations at the corresponding quarter in previous years). Thus given a model of how the quarterly observations evolve we then impose this model on the model describing the way in which the non-seasonal observations evolve.

We will now describe this approach in more detail. Assume that we have a time-series of quarterly, seasonally unadjusted observations. Further assume that the model relating the observations four periods apart is ARMA(1, 1). This will be the seasonal model. That is, we have:

$$Y_t = \Phi Y_{t-4} + u_t + \Theta u_{t-4} \qquad \text{Equation A7.4.1}$$

(this can be generalised to any ARMA($P, Q$), where the $\Phi$s and the $\Theta$s are the seasonal parameters). However, Equation A7.4.1 explains only the seasonal features of the data – we still require a model which explains the non-seasonal features.

Now, $u_t$ in Equation A7.4.1 is the residual from the seasonal model, and can therefore be interpreted as that component of $Y_t$ which is not explained by the seasonality. Thus we can treat $u_t$ as we have previously treated $Y_t$, and we can therefore fit some ARMA$(p, q)$ model to $u_t$. Again assume that the appropriate model is ARMA$(1, 1)$. That is:

$$u_t = \phi u_{t-1} + \varepsilon_t + \theta \varepsilon_{t-1} \qquad \text{Equation A7.4.2}$$

(and this could be generalised to any ARMA$(p, q)$ model.)

Therefore Equation A7.4.1 can be interpreted as the seasonal model and Equation A7.4.2 is the non-seasonal model. These two models can now be combined into a single model via a simple algebraic manipulation. From Equation A7.4.2 we can write:

$$u_{t-4} = \phi u_{t-5} + \varepsilon_{t-4} + \theta \varepsilon_{t-5} \qquad \text{Equation A7.4.3}$$

and substituting Equations A7.4.2 and A7.4.3 into Equation A7.4.1 we have:

$$Y_t = \Phi Y_{t-4} + \phi u_{t-1} + \varepsilon_t + \theta \varepsilon_{t-1} + \Phi \phi u_{t-5} + \Theta \varepsilon_{t-4} + \Theta \theta \varepsilon_{t-5}$$

$$\text{Equation A7.4.4}$$

Consider the term

$$\phi u_{t-1} + \Theta \phi u_{t-5}$$

in Equation A7.4.4. From Equation A7.4.1 we can write:

$$Y_t - \Phi Y_{t-4} = u_t + \Theta u_{t-4} \qquad \text{Equation A7.4.5}$$

$$\therefore\ Y_{t-1} - \Phi Y_{t-5} = u_{t-1} + \Theta u_{t-5} \qquad \text{Equation A7.4.6}$$

Multiplying Equation A7.4.6 by $\phi$ we have:

$$\phi Y_{t-1} - \phi \Phi Y_{t-5} = \phi u_{t-1} + \phi \Theta u_{t-5} \qquad \text{Equation A7.4.7}$$

Therefore from Equation A7.4.7 we can substitute for $\phi u_{t-1} + \phi \Theta u_{t-5}$ in Equation A7.4.4 and thus obtain:

$$Y_t = \phi Y_{t-1} + \Phi Y_{t-4} - \phi \Phi Y_{t-5} + \varepsilon_t + \theta \varepsilon_{t-1} + \Theta \varepsilon_{t-4} + \Theta \theta \varepsilon_{t-5}$$

$$\text{Equation A7.4.8}$$

Thus in Equation A7.4.8 we have a model which purports to explain all the variation in $Y_t$, with its seasonal elements explained by an ARMA$(1, 1)$ and its non-seasonal elements also explained by an ARMA$(1, 1)$. This approach is perfectly general and easily generalises to the case of any seasonal ARMA$(P, Q)$ model and non-seasonal ARMA$(p, q)$ model, where the values of $P, Q, p$ and $q$ can be set at any appropriate value.

If instead of quarterly data we had monthly data, then a seasonal model would be required which explains how the observations 12 periods apart are generated. Thus Equation A7.4.8 would contain terms in $Y_{t-12}$, $Y_{t-13}$, $\varepsilon_{t-12}$, and $\varepsilon_{t-13}$, rather than lags of $t-4$ and $t-5$ (assuming that ARMA$(1, 1)$ models were appropriate).

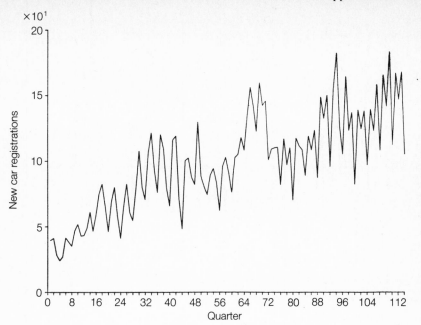

**Figure A7.4.1**  Seasonal quarterly new car registrations – 1956 to 1984.

We can now illustrate the fitting of B–J seasonal model by once again considering the quarterly car registration data in Appendix 5.3.

In Figure A7.4.1 we present a graph of the raw data against time. From the figure we can see that the data are non-stationary in the mean and would also appear to be heteroskedastic. As previously, we will assume that a logarithmic transformation adequately stabilises the variance. In terms of the trend in the data differencing is clearly required. However, as the data are quarterly and seasonal, we will have to difference both the seasonal and non-seasonal components of the data. That is, we will have to take first differences to remove the trend from the non-seasonal components, and fourth differences to remove the trend from the seasonal components. Thus if we denote the raw car registration data by $R_t$, then the following transformations would be performed:

$$W_t = \log(R_t)$$
$$X_t = W_t - W_{t-4}$$

and finally

$$Y_t = X_t - X_{t-1}$$

and thus we would expect the resulting series on $Y_t$ to be stationary. We would

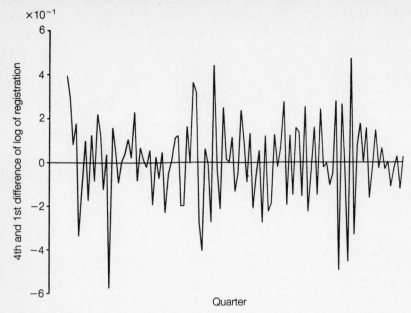

**Figure A7.4.2** First and fourth difference of the log of the car registration data.

then proceed to fit a model to $Y_t$. In Figure A7.4.2 we present a graph of the series on $Y_t$, from which we can see that an assumption of stationarity would seem reasonable.

In Figure A7.4.3 we present the estimated a.c.f. and p.a.c.f. derived from the data in Figure A7.4.2.

We can begin by attempting to identify a seasonal model. The procedure is exactly the same as in the identification of a non-seasonal model, except that

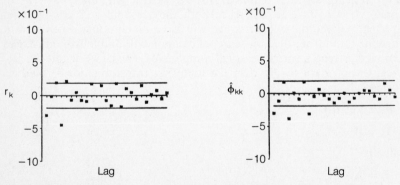

**Figure A7.4.3** Estimated a.c.f. and p.a.c.f. of data in Figure A7.4.2.

we only consider lags at the seasonal frequencies – that is, lags which are multiples of four. We then treat these lags as if they were adjacent and then look for the same patterns as in the identification of non-seasonal models.

Thus we note that there is a single significant autocorrelation at lag 4 (which we treat as lag '1'). A seasonal MA(1) is implied. To confirm such an identification we would expect to observe geometric decay in the p.a.c.f. at lags 4, 8, 12,.... From the p.a.c.f. the partial autocorrelations certainly decline at lags 4, 8, 12,..., although perhaps not geometrically. An alternative identification would be to treat the partial autocorrelations at lags 4 and 8 as significant, and then to argue that the a.c.f. decays at lags 4, 8, 12,.... A seasonal AR(2) model would be implied. Again, such an interpretation is not strictly consistent with the a.c.f. (the autocorrelations at lags 12, 16 and 20 remain relatively large). Thus we could begin with the simpler of these models (the MA(1)) and allow any model inadequacies to be highlighted at the diagnostic checking stage. It might also be argued that some form of mixed model is consistent with the estimated a.c.f. and p.a.c.f.

In terms of the non-seasonal model, we note the significant autocorrelation at lag 1 in the a.c.f. (plus the marginally significant autocorrelations at lags 3 and 5, which we will initially ignore). An MA(1) is implied. In terms of the p.a.c.f. geometric decay could be (liberally) inferred. (The large partials at lags 3 and 7 might be argued to reflect the seasonal components of the data, being adjacent to the seasonal frequencies at lags 4 and 8. That is, it can be shown that the estimated autocorrelations and partial autocorrelations are in fact intercorrelated, and therefore they can often be misleading reflections of the underlying process.)

Thus an initial (and by no means clear-cut) identification is an MA(1) for

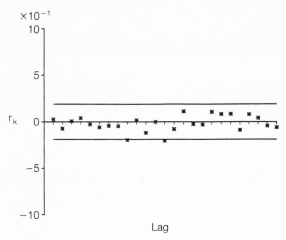

**Figure A7.4.4**  Estimated a.c.f. of residuals.

both the seasonal and non-seasonal components. We can now go on to estimate this model and evaluate its adequacy.

Using an appropriate computer package (SPSS was used here) the following parameter estimates and $t$-statistics are obtained:

|  | Parameter | Estimate | t-statistic |
|---|---|---|---|
| Non-seasonal MA | $\theta$ | 0.402 | 4.84 |
| Seasonal MA | $\Theta$ | 0.759 | 12.37 |

Thus we would note that both parameter estimates are significant. Next, we can examine the a.c.f. of the estimated residuals from this model. We present this estimated a.c.f. in Figure A7.4.4. From the figure we note that, except for the very marginally significant autocorrelations at lags 9 and 13, no structure would appear to remain. The Box–Pierce $Q$ statistic derived from all 25 estimated autocorrelations is 24.04, which at 23 degrees of freedom is insignificant. The corresponding values of $Q$ derived from the first 6, 12 and 18 autocorrelations are 1.51, 8.90 and 18.84, respectively, all of which are insignificant. We conclude therefore that a satisfactory model would appear to have been identified and estimated.

**Appendix 7.2** *Quarterly new registrations of cars, Great Britain (seasonally adjusted), 1958–1984, monthly averages – thousands*

| Year | Quarter | Registrations | Year | Quarter | Registrations | Year | Quarter | Registrations |
|------|---------|---------------|------|---------|---------------|------|---------|---------------|
| 1958 | 1 | 42.8 | 1967 | 1 | 82.3 | 1976 | 1 | 100.8 |
|      | 2 | 41.5 |      | 2 | 87.5 |      | 2 | 108.0 |
|      | 3 | 44.1 |      | 3 | 96.2 |      | 3 | 101.4 |
|      | 4 | 56.6 |      | 4 | 106.3 |      | 4 | 120.3 |
| 1959 | 1 | 44.0 | 1968 | 1 | 110.0 | 1977 | 1 | 102.7 |
|      | 2 | 48.0 |      | 2 | 77.4 |      | 2 | 115.7 |
|      | 3 | 47.4 |      | 3 | 88.8 |      | 3 | 119.7 |
|      | 4 | 75.7 |      | 4 | 96.1 |      | 4 | 117.9 |
| 1960 | 1 | 69.6 | 1969 | 1 | 76.1 | 1978 | 1 | 128.0 |
|      | 2 | 66.6 |      | 2 | 83.5 |      | 2 | 128.5 |
|      | 3 | 69.5 |      | 3 | 90.8 |      | 3 | 140.9 |
|      | 4 | 62.5 |      | 4 | 78.8 |      | 4 | 130.1 |
| 1961 | 1 | 64.4 | 1970 | 1 | 81.1 | 1979 | 1 | 132.5 |
|      | 2 | 64.3 |      | 2 | 91.1 |      | 2 | 179.1 |
|      | 3 | 62.5 |      | 3 | 98.1 |      | 3 | 118.4 |
|      | 4 | 56.4 |      | 4 | 95.4 |      | 4 | 143.3 |
| 1962 | 1 | 57.6 | 1971 | 1 | 94.8 | 1980 | 1 | 140.6 |
|      | 2 | 64.7 |      | 2 | 98.5 |      | 2 | 121.6 |
|      | 3 | 65.3 |      | 3 | 111.4 |      | 3 | 124.3 |
|      | 4 | 73.8 |      | 4 | 129.1 |      | 4 | 112.0 |
| 1963 | 1 | 68.6 | 1972 | 1 | 123.7 | 1981 | 1 | 120.0 |
|      | 2 | 84.1 |      | 2 | 148.6 |      | 2 | 123.5 |
|      | 3 | 87.2 |      | 3 | 135.1 |      | 3 | 125.9 |
|      | 4 | 96.0 |      | 4 | 146.9 |      | 4 | 128.7 |
| 1964 | 1 | 92.2 | 1973 | 1 | 146.7 | 1982 | 1 | 119.4 |
|      | 2 | 96.7 |      | 2 | 138.1 |      | 2 | 124.6 |
|      | 3 | 103.6 |      | 3 | 138.6 |      | 3 | 138.7 |
|      | 4 | 104.3 |      | 4 | 125.1 |      | 4 | 145.4 |
| 1965 | 1 | 98.7 | 1974 | 1 | 99.3 | 1983 | 1 | 146.6 |
|      | 2 | 94.2 |      | 2 | 104.3 |      | 2 | 147.8 |
|      | 3 | 90.1 |      | 3 | 106.8 |      | 3 | 156.8 |
|      | 4 | 91.2 |      | 4 | 110.1 |      | 4 | 150.9 |
| 1966 | 1 | 98.9 | 1975 | 1 | 100.1 | 1984 | 1 | 148.0 |
|      | 2 | 106.6 |      | 2 | 94.7 |      | 2 | 151.7 |
|      | 3 | 81.9 |      | 3 | 108.0 |      | 3 | 147.5 |
|      | 4 | 67.7 |      | 4 | 95.2 |      | 4 | 139.2 |

*Source: Economic Trends*, Annual Abstract, 1986, HMSO.

**Appendix 7.3**  *Consumers' non-durable expenditure, personal disposable income and the consumers' expenditure deflator, quarterly, 1957–1975, United Kingdom 1970 prices (£ million)*

| Year | Quarter | $C_t$ | $Y_t$ | $P_t$ | Year | Quarter | $C_t$ | $Y_t$ | $P_t$ |
|------|---------|-------|-------|-------|------|---------|-------|--------|-------|
| 1957 | 1 | 5011 | 5657 | 61.8 |      | 3 | 6882 | 7913 | 82.9 |
|      | 2 | 5368 | 6049 | 62.1 |      | 4 | 7068 | 8145 | 84.1 |
|      | 3 | 5424 | 5914 | 63.1 | 1967 | 1 | 6429 | 7802 | 84.5 |
|      | 4 | 5718 | 6115 | 62.2 |      | 2 | 6865 | 8169 | 84.9 |
| 1958 | 1 | 5147 | 5836 | 63.2 |      | 3 | 7029 | 8291 | 85.0 |
|      | 2 | 5439 | 6097 | 64.4 |      | 4 | 7310 | 8399 | 85.8 |
|      | 3 | 5537 | 6052 | 64.4 | 1968 | 1 | 6718 | 8323 | 86.8 |
|      | 4 | 5818 | 6175 | 65.1 |      | 2 | 6968 | 8236 | 88.8 |
| 1959 | 1 | 5253 | 5955 | 64.9 |      | 3 | 7115 | 8263 | 89.8 |
|      | 2 | 5669 | 6480 | 64.5 |      | 4 | 7430 | 8452 | 91.2 |
|      | 3 | 5722 | 6387 | 64.9 | 1969 | 1 | 6707 | 8248 | 93.0 |
|      | 4 | 6069 | 6578 | 65.5 |      | 2 | 7077 | 8273 | 94.0 |
| 1960 | 1 | 5510 | 6330 | 64.9 |      | 3 | 7181 | 8364 | 94.8 |
|      | 2 | 5913 | 6870 | 65.4 |      | 4 | 7617 | 8645 | 96.0 |
|      | 3 | 5951 | 6821 | 65.9 | 1970 | 1 | 6776 | 8313 | 98.0 |
|      | 4 | 6246 | 7051 | 66.7 |      | 2 | 7221 | 8698 | 99.1 |
| 1961 | 1 | 5702 | 6693 | 66.6 |      | 3 | 7426 | 8796 | 100.2 |
|      | 2 | 6062 | 7106 | 67.2 |      | 4 | 7786 | 8959 | 102.4 |
|      | 3 | 6122 | 7168 | 68.5 | 1971 | 1 | 6855 | 8589 | 104.9 |
|      | 4 | 6380 | 7205 | 69.2 |      | 2 | 7335 | 8733 | 107.9 |
| 1962 | 1 | 5749 | 6734 | 70.1 |      | 3 | 7467 | 8941 | 109.2 |
|      | 2 | 6154 | 7071 | 71.3 |      | 4 | 7952 | 9282 | 110.4 |
|      | 3 | 6194 | 7181 | 71.4 | 1972 | 1 | 7147 | 8972 | 112.9 |
|      | 4 | 6489 | 7398 | 71.8 |      | 2 | 7636 | 9655 | 114.5 |
| 1963 | 1 | 5866 | 6933 | 72.1 |      | 3 | 7829 | 9584 | 116.9 |
|      | 2 | 6367 | 7360 | 72.8 |      | 4 | 8332 | 10,100 | 118.9 |
|      | 3 | 6514 | 7605 | 72.4 | 1973 | 1 | 7539 | 9750 | 122.3 |
|      | 4 | 6718 | 7746 | 73.6 |      | 2 | 7948 | 10,125 | 125.1 |
| 1964 | 1 | 6123 | 7366 | 73.7 |      | 3 | 8157 | 10,241 | 127.6 |
|      | 2 | 6520 | 7656 | 75.2 |      | 4 | 8691 | 10,534 | 130.0 |
|      | 3 | 6651 | 7779 | 75.5 | 1974 | 1 | 7601 | 10,001 | 137.0 |
|      | 4 | 6895 | 7988 | 76.7 |      | 2 | 7985 | 9903 | 144.5 |
| 1965 | 1 | 6195 | 7607 | 77.6 |      | 3 | 8186 | 10,507 | 150.0 |
|      | 2 | 6592 | 7839 | 79.3 |      | 4 | 8798 | 11,016 | 154.4 |
|      | 3 | 6770 | 7902 | 79.6 | 1975 | 1 | 7735 | 10,473 | 165.0 |
|      | 4 | 7005 | 8158 | 80.4 |      | 2 | 7984 | 10,022 | 178.2 |
| 1966 | 1 | 6383 | 8167 | 81.0 |      | 3 | 8045 | 10,224 | 186.5 |
|      | 2 | 6816 | 7983 | 82.4 |      | 4 | 8646 | 10,434 | 191.1 |

*Source: Economic Trends,* Annual Supplements, 1976 and 1981, HMSO.

# Appendix I

*Tables of the Standard Normal Distribution*

Standard normal, cumulative probability in right-hand tail

| $z_0$ | 0 | 1 | 2 | 3 | 4 | 5 | 6 | 7 | 8 | 9 |
|-------|---|---|---|---|---|---|---|---|---|---|
| | | | | Next decimal place of $z_0$ | | | | | | |
| 0.0 | .500 | .496 | .492 | .488 | .484 | .480 | .476 | .472 | .468 | .464 |
| 0.1 | .460 | .456 | .452 | .448 | .444 | .440 | .436 | .433 | .429 | .425 |
| 0.2 | .421 | .417 | .413 | .409 | .405 | .401 | .397 | .394 | .390 | .386 |
| 0.3 | .382 | .378 | .374 | .371 | .367 | .363 | .359 | .356 | .352 | .348 |
| 0.4 | .345 | .341 | .337 | .334 | .330 | .326 | .323 | .319 | .316 | .312 |
| 0.5 | .309 | .305 | .302 | .298 | .295 | .291 | .288 | .284 | .281 | .278 |
| 0.6 | .274 | .271 | .268 | .264 | .261 | .258 | .255 | .251 | .248 | .245 |
| 0.7 | .242 | .239 | .236 | .233 | .230 | .227 | .224 | .221 | .218 | .215 |
| 0.8 | .212 | .209 | .206 | .203 | .200 | .198 | .195 | .192 | .189 | .187 |
| 0.9 | .184 | .181 | .179 | .176 | .174 | .171 | .169 | .166 | .164 | .161 |
| 1.0 | .159 | .156 | .154 | .152 | .149 | .147 | .145 | .142 | .140 | .138 |
| 1.1 | .136 | .133 | .131 | .129 | .127 | .125 | .123 | .121 | .119 | .117 |
| 1.2 | .115 | .113 | .111 | .109 | .107 | .106 | .104 | .102 | .100 | .099 |
| 1.3 | .097 | .095 | .093 | .092 | .090 | .089 | .087 | .085 | .084 | .082 |
| 1.4 | .081 | .079 | .078 | .076 | .075 | .074 | .072 | .071 | .069 | .068 |
| 1.5 | .067 | .066 | .064 | .063 | .062 | .061 | .059 | .058 | .057 | .056 |
| 1.6 | .055 | .054 | .053 | .052 | .051 | .049 | .048 | .047 | .046 | .046 |
| 1.7 | .045 | .044 | .043 | .042 | .041 | .040 | .039 | .038 | .038 | .037 |
| 1.8 | .036 | .035 | .034 | .034 | .033 | .032 | .031 | .031 | .030 | .029 |
| 1.9 | .029 | .028 | .027 | .027 | .026 | .026 | .025 | .024 | .024 | .023 |
| 2.0 | .023 | .022 | .022 | .021 | .021 | .020 | .020 | .019 | .019 | .018 |
| 2.1 | .018 | .017 | .017 | .017 | .016 | .016 | .015 | .015 | .015 | .014 |
| 2.2 | .014 | .014 | .013 | .013 | .013 | .012 | .012 | .012 | .011 | .011 |
| 2.3 | .011 | .010 | .010 | .010 | .010 | .009 | .009 | .009 | .009 | .008 |
| 2.4 | .008 | .008 | .008 | .008 | .007 | .007 | .007 | .007 | .007 | .006 |
| 2.5 | .006 | .006 | .006 | .006 | .006 | .005 | .005 | .005 | .005 | .005 |
| 2.6 | .005 | .005 | .004 | .004 | .004 | .004 | .004 | .004 | .004 | .004 |
| 2.7 | .003 | .003 | .003 | .003 | .003 | .003 | .003 | .003 | .003 | .003 |
| 2.8 | .003 | .002 | .002 | .002 | .002 | .002 | .002 | .002 | .002 | .002 |
| 2.9 | .002 | .002 | .002 | .002 | .002 | .002 | .002 | .001 | .001 | .001 |

# Appendix II

*Tables of the* t-*distribution*

t Critical points

| d.f. | $t_{.10}$ | $t_{.05}$ | $t_{.025}$ | $t_{.010}$ | $t_{.005}$ |
|---|---|---|---|---|---|
| 1 | 3.08 | 6.31 | 12.7 | 31.8 | 63.7 |
| 2 | 1.89 | 2.92 | 4.30 | 6.96 | 9.92 |
| 3 | 1.64 | 2.35 | 3.18 | 4.54 | 5.84 |
| 4 | 1.53 | 2.13 | 2.78 | 3.75 | 4.60 |
| 5 | 1.48 | 2.02 | 2.57 | 3.36 | 4.03 |
| 6 | 1.44 | 1.94 | 2.45 | 3.14 | 3.71 |
| 7 | 1.41 | 1.89 | 2.36 | 3.00 | 3.50 |
| 8 | 1.40 | 1.86 | 2.31 | 2.90 | 3.36 |
| 9 | 1.38 | 1.83 | 2.26 | 2.82 | 3.25 |
| 10 | 1.37 | 1.81 | 2.23 | 2.76 | 3.17 |
| 11 | 1.36 | 1.80 | 2.20 | 2.72 | 3.11 |
| 12 | 1.36 | 1.78 | 2.18 | 2.68 | 3.05 |
| 13 | 1.35 | 1.77 | 2.16 | 2.65 | 3.01 |
| 14 | 1.35 | 1.76 | 2.14 | 2.62 | 2.98 |
| 15 | 1.34 | 1.75 | 2.13 | 2.60 | 2.95 |
| 16 | 1.34 | 1.75 | 2.12 | 2.58 | 2.92 |
| 17 | 1.33 | 1.74 | 2.11 | 2.57 | 2.90 |
| 18 | 1.33 | 1.73 | 2.10 | 2.55 | 2.88 |
| 19 | 1.33 | 1.73 | 2.09 | 2.54 | 2.86 |
| 20 | 1.33 | 1.72 | 2.09 | 2.53 | 2.85 |
| 21 | 1.32 | 1.72 | 2.08 | 2.52 | 2.83 |
| 22 | 1.32 | 1.72 | 2.07 | 2.51 | 2.82 |
| 23 | 1.32 | 1.71 | 2.07 | 2.50 | 2.81 |
| 24 | 1.32 | 1.71 | 2.06 | 2.49 | 2.80 |
| 25 | 1.32 | 1.71 | 2.06 | 2.49 | 2.79 |
| 26 | 1.31 | 1.71 | 2.06 | 2.48 | 2.78 |
| 27 | 1.31 | 1.70 | 2.05 | 2.47 | 2.77 |
| 28 | 1.31 | 1.70 | 2.05 | 2.47 | 2.76 |
| 29 | 1.31 | 1.70 | 2.05 | 2.46 | 2.76 |
| 30 | 1.31 | 1.70 | 2.04 | 2.46 | 2.75 |
| 40 | 1.30 | 1.68 | 2.02 | 2.42 | 2.70 |
| 60 | 1.30 | 1.67 | 2.00 | 2.39 | 2.66 |
| 120 | 1.29 | 1.66 | 1.98 | 2.36 | 2.62 |
| $\infty$ | 1.28 | 1.64 | 1.96 | 2.33 | 2.58 |

# Appendix III

*Tables of the* F-*distribution*

F Critical points

| | | 1 | 2 | 3 | 4 | 5 | 6 | 8 | 10 | 20 | 40 | ∞ |
|---|---|---|---|---|---|---|---|---|---|---|---|---|
| | | | | | Degrees of freedom for numerator | | | | | | | |
| 1 | $F_{.10}$ | 39.9 | 49.5 | 53.6 | 55.8 | 57.2 | 58.2 | 59.4 | 60.2 | 61.7 | 62.5 | 63.3 |
| | $F_{.05}$ | 161 | 200 | 216 | 225 | 230 | 234 | 239 | 242 | 248 | 251 | 254 |
| 2 | $F_{.10}$ | 8.53 | 9.00 | 9.16 | 9.24 | 9.29 | 9.33 | 9.37 | 9.39 | 9.44 | 9.47 | 9.49 |
| | $F_{.05}$ | 18.5 | 19.0 | 19.2 | 19.2 | 19.3 | 19.3 | 19.4 | 19.4 | 19.4 | 19.5 | 19.5 |
| | $F_{.01}$ | 98.5 | 99.0 | 99.2 | 99.2 | 99.3 | 99.3 | 99.4 | 99.4 | 99.4 | 99.5 | 99.5 |
| 3 | $F_{.10}$ | 5.54 | 5.46 | 5.39 | 5.34 | 5.31 | 5.28 | 5.25 | 5.23 | 5.18 | 5.16 | 5.13 |
| | $F_{.05}$ | 10.1 | 9.55 | 9.28 | 9.12 | 9.10 | 8.94 | 8.85 | 8.79 | 8.66 | 8.59 | 8.53 |
| | $F_{.01}$ | 34.1 | 30.8 | 29.5 | 28.7 | 28.2 | 27.9 | 27.5 | 27.2 | 26.7 | 26.4 | 26.1 |
| 4 | $F_{.10}$ | 4.54 | 4.32 | 4.19 | 4.11 | 4.05 | 4.01 | 3.95 | 3.92 | 3.84 | 3.80 | 3.76 |
| | $F_{.05}$ | 7.71 | 6.94 | 6.59 | 6.39 | 6.26 | 6.16 | 6.04 | 5.96 | 5.80 | 5.72 | 5.63 |
| | $F_{.01}$ | 21.2 | 18.0 | 16.7 | 16.0 | 15.5 | 15.2 | 14.8 | 14.5 | 14.0 | 13.7 | 13.5 |
| 5 | $F_{.10}$ | 4.06 | 3.78 | 3.62 | 3.52 | 3.45 | 3.40 | 3.34 | 3.30 | 3.21 | 3.16 | 3.10 |
| | $F_{.05}$ | 6.61 | 5.79 | 5.41 | 5.19 | 5.05 | 4.95 | 4.82 | 4.74 | 4.56 | 4.46 | 4.36 |
| | $F_{.01}$ | 16.3 | 13.3 | 12.1 | 11.4 | 11.0 | 10.7 | 10.3 | 10.1 | 9.55 | 9.29 | 9.02 |
| 6 | $F_{.10}$ | 3.78 | 3.46 | 3.29 | 3.18 | 3.11 | 3.05 | 2.98 | 2.94 | 2.84 | 2.78 | 2.72 |
| | $F_{.05}$ | 5.99 | 5.14 | 4.76 | 4.53 | 4.39 | 4.28 | 4.15 | 4.06 | 3.87 | 3.77 | 3.67 |
| | $F_{.01}$ | 13.7 | 10.9 | 9.78 | 9.15 | 8.75 | 8.47 | 8.10 | 7.87 | 7.40 | 7.14 | 6.88 |
| 7 | $F_{.10}$ | 3.59 | 3.26 | 3.07 | 2.96 | 2.88 | 2.83 | 2.75 | 2.70 | 2.59 | 2.54 | 2.47 |
| | $F_{.05}$ | 5.59 | 4.74 | 4.35 | 4.12 | 3.97 | 3.87 | 3.73 | 3.64 | 3.44 | 3.34 | 3.23 |
| | $F_{.01}$ | 12.2 | 9.55 | 8.45 | 7.85 | 7.46 | 7.19 | 6.84 | 6.62 | 6.16 | 5.91 | 5.65 |
| 8 | $F_{.10}$ | 3.46 | 3.11 | 2.92 | 2.81 | 2.73 | 2.67 | 2.59 | 2.54 | 2.42 | 2.36 | 2.29 |
| | $F_{.05}$ | 5.32 | 4.46 | 4.07 | 3.84 | 3.69 | 3.58 | 3.44 | 3.35 | 3.15 | 3.04 | 2.93 |
| | $F_{.01}$ | 11.3 | 8.65 | 7.59 | 7.01 | 6.63 | 6.37 | 6.03 | 5.81 | 5.36 | 5.12 | 4.86 |
| 9 | $F_{.10}$ | 3.36 | 3.01 | 2.81 | 2.69 | 2.61 | 2.55 | 2.47 | 2.42 | 2.30 | 2.23 | 2.16 |
| | $F_{.05}$ | 5.12 | 4.26 | 3.86 | 3.63 | 3.48 | 3.37 | 3.23 | 3.14 | 2.94 | 2.83 | 2.71 |
| | $F_{.01}$ | 10.6 | 8.02 | 6.99 | 6.42 | 6.06 | 5.80 | 5.47 | 5.26 | 4.81 | 4.57 | 4.31 |

*Degrees of freedom for denominator* (left vertical label)

411

## Appendix III (continued)

|  | | Degrees of freedom for numerator | | | | | | | | | | |
|---|---|---|---|---|---|---|---|---|---|---|---|---|
| | | 1 | 2 | 3 | 4 | 5 | 6 | 8 | 10 | 20 | 40 | ∞ |
| 10 | $F_{.10}$ | 3.28 | 2.92 | 2.73 | 2.61 | 2.52 | 2.46 | 2.38 | 2.32 | 2.20 | 2.13 | 2.06 |
| | $F_{.05}$ | 4.96 | 4.10 | 3.71 | 3.48 | 3.33 | 3.22 | 3.07 | 2.98 | 2.77 | 2.66 | 2.54 |
| | $F_{.01}$ | 10.0 | 7.56 | 6.55 | 5.99 | 5.64 | 5.39 | 5.06 | 4.85 | 4.41 | 4.17 | 3.91 |
| 12 | $F_{.10}$ | 3.18 | 2.81 | 2.61 | 2.48 | 2.39 | 2.33 | 2.24 | 2.19 | 2.06 | 1.99 | 1.90 |
| | $F_{.05}$ | 4.75 | 3.89 | 3.49 | 3.26 | 3.11 | 3.00 | 2.85 | 2.75 | 2.54 | 2.43 | 2.30 |
| | $F_{.01}$ | 9.33 | 6.93 | 5.95 | 5.41 | 5.06 | 4.82 | 4.50 | 4.30 | 3.86 | 3.62 | 3.36 |
| 14 | $F_{.10}$ | 3.10 | 2.73 | 2.52 | 2.39 | 2.31 | 2.24 | 2.15 | 2.10 | 1.96 | 1.89 | 1.80 |
| | $F_{.05}$ | 4.60 | 3.74 | 3.34 | 3.11 | 2.96 | 2.85 | 2.70 | 2.60 | 2.39 | 2.27 | 2.13 |
| | $F_{.01}$ | 8.86 | 5.51 | 5.56 | 5.04 | 4.69 | 4.46 | 4.14 | 3.94 | 3.51 | 3.27 | 3.00 |
| 16 | $F_{.10}$ | 3.05 | 2.67 | 2.46 | 2.33 | 2.24 | 2.18 | 2.09 | 2.03 | 1.89 | 1.81 | 1.72 |
| | $F_{.05}$ | 4.49 | 3.63 | 3.24 | 3.01 | 2.85 | 2.74 | 2.59 | 2.49 | 2.28 | 2.15 | 2.01 |
| | $F_{.01}$ | 8.53 | 6.23 | 5.29 | 4.77 | 4.44 | 4.20 | 3.89 | 3.69 | 3.26 | 3.02 | 2.75 |
| 20 | $F_{.10}$ | 2.97 | 2.59 | 2.38 | 2.25 | 2.16 | 2.09 | 2.00 | 1.94 | 1.79 | 1.71 | 1.61 |
| | $F_{.05}$ | 4.35 | 3.49 | 3.10 | 2.87 | 2.71 | 2.60 | 2.45 | 2.35 | 2.12 | 1.99 | 1.84 |
| | $F_{.01}$ | 8.10 | 5.85 | 4.94 | 4.43 | 4.10 | 3.87 | 3.56 | 3.37 | 2.94 | 2.69 | 2.42 |
| 30 | $F_{.10}$ | 2.88 | 2.49 | 2.28 | 2.14 | 2.05 | 1.98 | 1.88 | 1.82 | 1.67 | 1.57 | 1.46 |
| | $F_{.05}$ | 4.17 | 3.32 | 2.92 | 2.69 | 2.53 | 2.42 | 2.27 | 2.16 | 1.93 | 1.79 | 1.62 |
| | $F_{.01}$ | 7.56 | 5.39 | 4.51 | 4.02 | 3.70 | 3.47 | 3.17 | 2.98 | 2.55 | 2.30 | 2.01 |
| 40 | $F_{.10}$ | 2.84 | 2.44 | 2.23 | 2.09 | 2.00 | 1.93 | 1.83 | 1.76 | 1.61 | 1.51 | 1.38 |
| | $F_{.05}$ | 4.08 | 3.23 | 2.84 | 2.61 | 2.45 | 2.34 | 2.18 | 2.08 | 1.84 | 1.69 | 1.51 |
| | $F_{.01}$ | 7.31 | 5.18 | 4.31 | 3.83 | 3.51 | 3.29 | 2.99 | 2.80 | 2.37 | 2.11 | 1.80 |
| 60 | $F_{.10}$ | 2.79 | 2.39 | 2.18 | 2.04 | 1.95 | 1.87 | 1.77 | 1.71 | 1.54 | 1.44 | 1.29 |
| | $F_{.05}$ | 4.00 | 3.15 | 2.76 | 2.53 | 2.37 | 2.25 | 2.10 | 1.99 | 1.75 | 1.59 | 1.39 |
| | $F_{.01}$ | 7.08 | 4.98 | 4.13 | 3.65 | 3.34 | 3.12 | 2.82 | 2.63 | 2.20 | 1.94 | 1.60 |
| 120 | $F_{.10}$ | 2.75 | 2.35 | 2.13 | 1.99 | 1.90 | 1.82 | 1.72 | 1.65 | 1.48 | 1.37 | 1.19 |
| | $F_{.05}$ | 3.92 | 3.07 | 2.68 | 2.45 | 2.29 | 2.17 | 2.02 | 1.91 | 1.66 | 1.50 | 1.25 |
| | $F_{.01}$ | 6.85 | 4.79 | 3.95 | 3.48 | 3.17 | 2.96 | 2.66 | 2.47 | 2.03 | 1.76 | 1.38 |
| ∞ | $F_{.10}$ | 2.71 | 2.30 | 2.08 | 1.94 | 1.85 | 1.77 | 1.67 | 1.60 | 1.42 | 1.30 | 1.00 |
| | $F_{.05}$ | 3.84 | 3.00 | 2.60 | 2.37 | 2.21 | 2.10 | 1.94 | 1.83 | 1.57 | 1.39 | 1.00 |
| | $F_{.01}$ | 6.63 | 4.61 | 3.78 | 3.32 | 3.02 | 2.80 | 2.51 | 2.32 | 1.88 | 1.59 | 1.00 |

Degrees of freedom for denominator

# Appendix IV

*Tables of the Durbin–Watson Statistic*

Significance points of $d_L$ and $d_U$: 5%

| n | K = 1 | | K = 2 | | K = 3 | | K = 4 | | K = 5 | |
|---|---|---|---|---|---|---|---|---|---|---|
| | $d_L$ | $d_U$ | $d_L$ | $d_U$ | $d_L$ | $d_U$ | $d_L$ | $d_U$ | $d_L$ | $d_U$ |
| 15 | 1.08 | 1.36 | 0.95 | 1.54 | 0.82 | 1.75 | 0.69 | 1.97 | 0.56 | 2.21 |
| 16 | 1.10 | 1.37 | 0.98 | 1.54 | 0.86 | 1.73 | 0.74 | 1.93 | 0.62 | 2.15 |
| 17 | 1.13 | 1.38 | 1.02 | 1.54 | 0.90 | 1.71 | 0.78 | 1.90 | 0.67 | 2.10 |
| 18 | 1.16 | 1.39 | 1.05 | 1.53 | 0.93 | 1.69 | 0.82 | 1.87 | 0.71 | 2.06 |
| 19 | 1.18 | 1.40 | 1.08 | 1.53 | 0.97 | 1.68 | 0.86 | 1.85 | 0.75 | 2.02 |
| 20 | 1.20 | 1.41 | 1.10 | 1.54 | 1.00 | 1.68 | 0.90 | 1.83 | 0.79 | 1.99 |
| 21 | 1.22 | 1.42 | 1.13 | 1.54 | 1.03 | 1.67 | 0.93 | 1.81 | 0.83 | 1.96 |
| 22 | 1.24 | 1.43 | 1.15 | 1.54 | 1.05 | 1.66 | 0.96 | 1.80 | 0.86 | 1.94 |
| 23 | 1.26 | 1.44 | 1.17 | 1.54 | 1.08 | 1.66 | 0.99 | 1.79 | 0.90 | 1.92 |
| 24 | 1.27 | 1.45 | 1.19 | 1.55 | 1.10 | 1.66 | 1.01 | 1.78 | 0.93 | 1.90 |
| 25 | 1.29 | 1.45 | 1.21 | 1.55 | 1.12 | 1.66 | 1.04 | 1.77 | 0.95 | 1.89 |
| 26 | 1.30 | 1.46 | 1.22 | 1.55 | 1.14 | 1.65 | 1.06 | 1.76 | 0.98 | 1.88 |
| 27 | 1.32 | 1.47 | 1.24 | 1.56 | 1.16 | 1.65 | 1.08 | 1.76 | 1.01 | 1.86 |
| 28 | 1.33 | 1.48 | 1.26 | 1.56 | 1.18 | 1.65 | 1.10 | 1.75 | 1.03 | 1.85 |
| 29 | 1.34 | 1.48 | 1.27 | 1.56 | 1.20 | 1.65 | 1.12 | 1.74 | 1.05 | 1.84 |
| 30 | 1.35 | 1.49 | 1.28 | 1.57 | 1.21 | 1.65 | 1.14 | 1.74 | 1.07 | 1.83 |
| 31 | 1.36 | 1.50 | 1.30 | 1.57 | 1.23 | 1.65 | 1.16 | 1.74 | 1.09 | 1.83 |
| 32 | 1.37 | 1.50 | 1.31 | 1.57 | 1.24 | 1.65 | 1.18 | 1.73 | 1.11 | 1.82 |
| 33 | 1.38 | 1.51 | 1.32 | 1.58 | 1.26 | 1.65 | 1.19 | 1.73 | 1.13 | 1.81 |
| 34 | 1.39 | 1.51 | 1.33 | 1.58 | 1.27 | 1.65 | 1.21 | 1.73 | 1.15 | 1.81 |
| 35 | 1.40 | 1.52 | 1.34 | 1.58 | 1.28 | 1.65 | 1.22 | 1.73 | 1.16 | 1.80 |
| 36 | 1.41 | 1.52 | 1.35 | 1.59 | 1.29 | 1.65 | 1.24 | 1.73 | 1.18 | 1.80 |
| 37 | 1.42 | 1.53 | 1.36 | 1.59 | 1.31 | 1.66 | 1.25 | 1.72 | 1.19 | 1.80 |
| 38 | 1.43 | 1.54 | 1.37 | 1.59 | 1.32 | 1.66 | 1.26 | 1.72 | 1.21 | 1.79 |
| 39 | 1.43 | 1.54 | 1.38 | 1.60 | 1.33 | 1.66 | 1.27 | 1.72 | 1.22 | 1.79 |
| 40 | 1.44 | 1.54 | 1.39 | 1.60 | 1.34 | 1.66 | 1.29 | 1.72 | 1.23 | 1.79 |
| 45 | 1.48 | 1.57 | 1.43 | 1.62 | 1.38 | 1.67 | 1.34 | 1.72 | 1.29 | 1.78 |
| 50 | 1.50 | 1.59 | 1.46 | 1.63 | 1.42 | 1.67 | 1.38 | 1.72 | 1.34 | 1.77 |
| 55 | 1.53 | 1.60 | 1.49 | 1.64 | 1.45 | 1.68 | 1.41 | 1.72 | 1.38 | 1.77 |
| 60 | 1.55 | 1.62 | 1.51 | 1.65 | 1.48 | 1.69 | 1.44 | 1.73 | 1.41 | 1.77 |
| 65 | 1.57 | 1.63 | 1.54 | 1.66 | 1.50 | 1.70 | 1.47 | 1.73 | 1.44 | 1.77 |
| 70 | 1.58 | 1.64 | 1.55 | 1.67 | 1.52 | 1.70 | 1.49 | 1.74 | 1.46 | 1.77 |
| 75 | 1.60 | 1.65 | 1.57 | 1.68 | 1.54 | 1.71 | 1.51 | 1.74 | 1.49 | 1.77 |
| 80 | 1.61 | 1.66 | 1.59 | 1.69 | 1.56 | 1.72 | 1.53 | 1.74 | 1.51 | 1.77 |
| 85 | 1.62 | 1.67 | 1.60 | 1.70 | 1.57 | 1.72 | 1.55 | 1.75 | 1.52 | 1.77 |
| 90 | 1.63 | 1.68 | 1.61 | 1.70 | 1.59 | 1.73 | 1.57 | 1.75 | 1.54 | 1.78 |
| 95 | 1.64 | 1.69 | 1.62 | 1.71 | 1.60 | 1.73 | 1.58 | 1.75 | 1.56 | 1.78 |
| 100 | 1.65 | 1.69 | 1.63 | 1.72 | 1.61 | 1.74 | 1.59 | 1.76 | 1.57 | 1.78 |

*Note:* $K$ = number of explanatory variables excluding the constant term.

Significance points of $d_L$ and $d_U$: 2.5%

| $n$ | $K = 1$ | | $K = 2$ | | $K = 3$ | | $K = 4$ | | $K = 5$ | |
|---|---|---|---|---|---|---|---|---|---|---|
| | $d_L$ | $d_U$ | $d_L$ | $d_U$ | $d_L$ | $d_U$ | $d_L$ | $d_U$ | $d_L$ | $d_U$ |
| 15 | 0.95 | 1.23 | 0.83 | 1.40 | 0.71 | 1.61 | 0.59 | 1.84 | 0.48 | 2.09 |
| 16 | 0.98 | 1.24 | 0.86 | 1.40 | 0.75 | 1.59 | 0.64 | 1.80 | 0.53 | 2.03 |
| 17 | 1.01 | 1.25 | 0.90 | 1.40 | 0.79 | 1.58 | 0.68 | 1.77 | 0.57 | 1.98 |
| 18 | 1.03 | 1.26 | 0.93 | 1.40 | 0.82 | 1.56 | 0.72 | 1.74 | 0.62 | 1.93 |
| 19 | 1.06 | 1.28 | 0.96 | 1.41 | 0.86 | 1.55 | 0.76 | 1.72 | 0.66 | 1.90 |
| 20 | 1.08 | 1.28 | 0.99 | 1.41 | 0.89 | 1.55 | 0.79 | 1.70 | 0.70 | 1.87 |
| 21 | 1.10 | 1.30 | 1.01 | 1.41 | 0.92 | 1.54 | 0.83 | 1.69 | 0.73 | 1.84 |
| 22 | 1.12 | 1.31 | 1.04 | 1.42 | 0.95 | 1.54 | 0.86 | 1.68 | 0.77 | 1.82 |
| 23 | 1.14 | 1.32 | 1.06 | 1.42 | 0.97 | 1.54 | 0.89 | 1.67 | 0.80 | 1.80 |
| 24 | 1.16 | 1.33 | 1.08 | 1.43 | 1.00 | 1.54 | 0.91 | 1.66 | 0.83 | 1.79 |
| 25 | 1.18 | 1.34 | 1.10 | 1.43 | 1.02 | 1.54 | 0.94 | 1.65 | 0.86 | 1.77 |
| 26 | 1.19 | 1.35 | 1.12 | 1.44 | 1.04 | 1.54 | 0.96 | 1.65 | 0.88 | 1.76 |
| 27 | 1.21 | 1.36 | 1.13 | 1.44 | 1.06 | 1.54 | 0.99 | 1.64 | 0.91 | 1.75 |
| 28 | 1.22 | 1.37 | 1.15 | 1.45 | 1.08 | 1.54 | 1.01 | 1.64 | 0.93 | 1.74 |
| 29 | 1.24 | 1.38 | 1.17 | 1.45 | 1.10 | 1.54 | 1.03 | 1.63 | 0.96 | 1.73 |
| 30 | 1.25 | 1.38 | 1.18 | 1.46 | 1.12 | 1.54 | 1.05 | 1.63 | 0.98 | 1.73 |
| 31 | 1.26 | 1.39 | 1.20 | 1.47 | 1.13 | 1.55 | 1.07 | 1.63 | 1.00 | 1.72 |
| 32 | 1.27 | 1.40 | 1.21 | 1.47 | 1.15 | 1.55 | 1.08 | 1.63 | 1.02 | 1.71 |
| 33 | 1.28 | 1.41 | 1.22 | 1.48 | 1.16 | 1.55 | 1.10 | 1.63 | 1.04 | 1.71 |
| 34 | 1.29 | 1.41 | 1.24 | 1.48 | 1.17 | 1.55 | 1.12 | 1.63 | 1.06 | 1.70 |
| 35 | 1.30 | 1.42 | 1.25 | 1.48 | 1.19 | 1.55 | 1.13 | 1.63 | 1.07 | 1.70 |
| 36 | 1.31 | 1.43 | 1.26 | 1.49 | 1.20 | 1.56 | 1.15 | 1.63 | 1.09 | 1.70 |
| 37 | 1.32 | 1.43 | 1.27 | 1.49 | 1.21 | 1.56 | 1.16 | 1.62 | 1.10 | 1.70 |
| 38 | 1.33 | 1.44 | 1.28 | 1.50 | 1.23 | 1.56 | 1.17 | 1.62 | 1.12 | 1.70 |
| 39 | 1.34 | 1.44 | 1.29 | 1.50 | 1.24 | 1.56 | 1.19 | 1.63 | 1.13 | 1.69 |
| 40 | 1.35 | 1.45 | 1.30 | 1.51 | 1.25 | 1.57 | 1.20 | 1.63 | 1.15 | 1.69 |
| 45 | 1.39 | 1.48 | 1.34 | 1.53 | 1.30 | 1.58 | 1.25 | 1.63 | 1.21 | 1.69 |
| 50 | 1.42 | 1.50 | 1.38 | 1.54 | 1.34 | 1.59 | 1.30 | 1.64 | 1.26 | 1.69 |
| 55 | 1.45 | 1.52 | 1.41 | 1.56 | 1.37 | 1.60 | 1.33 | 1.64 | 1.30 | 1.69 |
| 60 | 1.47 | 1.54 | 1.44 | 1.57 | 1.40 | 1.61 | 1.37 | 1.65 | 1.33 | 1.69 |
| 65 | 1.49 | 1.55 | 1.46 | 1.59 | 1.43 | 1.62 | 1.40 | 1.66 | 1.36 | 1.69 |
| 70 | 1.51 | 1.57 | 1.48 | 1.60 | 1.45 | 1.63 | 1.42 | 1.66 | 1.39 | 1.70 |
| 75 | 1.53 | 1.58 | 1.50 | 1.61 | 1.47 | 1.64 | 1.45 | 1.67 | 1.42 | 1.70 |
| 80 | 1.54 | 1.59 | 1.52 | 1.62 | 1.49 | 1.65 | 1.47 | 1.67 | 1.44 | 1.70 |
| 85 | 1.56 | 1.60 | 1.53 | 1.63 | 1.51 | 1.65 | 1.49 | 1.68 | 1.46 | 1.71 |
| 90 | 1.57 | 1.61 | 1.55 | 1.64 | 1.53 | 1.66 | 1.50 | 1.69 | 1.48 | 1.71 |
| 95 | 1.58 | 1.62 | 1.56 | 1.65 | 1.54 | 1.67 | 1.52 | 1.69 | 1.50 | 1.71 |
| 100 | 1.59 | 1.63 | 1.57 | 1.65 | 1.55 | 1.67 | 1.53 | 1.70 | 1.51 | 1.72 |

*Note:* $K$ = number of explanatory variables excluding the constant term.

# Appendix V

*Tables of the Chi-square Distribution*

$\chi^2$ Critical points

| d.f. | $\chi^2_{.10}$ | $\chi^2_{.05}$ | $\chi^2_{.025}$ | $\chi^2_{.010}$ | $\chi^2_{.005}$ |
|------|------|------|------|------|------|
| 1 | 2.71 | 3.84 | 5.02 | 6.63 | 7.88 |
| 2 | 4.61 | 5.99 | 7.38 | 9.21 | 10.6 |
| 3 | 6.25 | 7.81 | 9.35 | 11.3 | 12.8 |
| 4 | 7.78 | 9.49 | 11.1 | 13.3 | 14.9 |
| 5 | 9.24 | 11.1 | 12.8 | 15.1 | 16.7 |
| 6 | 10.6 | 12.6 | 14.4 | 16.8 | 18.5 |
| 7 | 12.0 | 14.1 | 16.0 | 18.5 | 20.3 |
| 8 | 13.4 | 15.5 | 17.5 | 20.1 | 22.0 |
| 9 | 14.7 | 16.9 | 19.0 | 21.7 | 23.6 |
| 10 | 16.0 | 18.3 | 20.5 | 23.2 | 25.2 |
| 11 | 17.3 | 19.7 | 21.9 | 24.7 | 26.8 |
| 12 | 18.5 | 21.0 | 23.3 | 26.2 | 28.3 |
| 13 | 19.8 | 22.4 | 24.7 | 27.7 | 29.8 |
| 14 | 21.1 | 23.7 | 26.1 | 29.1 | 31.3 |
| 15 | 22.3 | 25.0 | 27.5 | 30.6 | 32.8 |
| 16 | 23.5 | 26.3 | 28.8 | 32.0 | 34.3 |
| 17 | 24.8 | 27.6 | 30.2 | 33.4 | 35.7 |
| 18 | 26.0 | 28.9 | 31.5 | 34.8 | 37.2 |
| 19 | 27.2 | 30.1 | 32.9 | 36.2 | 38.6 |
| 20 | 28.4 | 31.4 | 34.2 | 37.6 | 40.0 |
| 21 | 29.6 | 32.7 | 35.5 | 38.9 | 41.4 |
| 22 | 30.8 | 33.9 | 36.8 | 40.3 | 42.8 |
| 23 | 32.0 | 35.2 | 38.1 | 41.6 | 44.2 |
| 24 | 33.2 | 36.4 | 39.4 | 32.0 | 45.6 |
| 25 | 34.4 | 37.7 | 40.6 | 44.3 | 46.9 |
| 26 | 35.6 | 38.9 | 41.9 | 45.6 | 48.3 |
| 27 | 36.7 | 40.1 | 43.2 | 47.0 | 49.6 |
| 28 | 37.9 | 41.3 | 44.5 | 48.3 | 51.0 |
| 29 | 39.1 | 42.6 | 45.7 | 49.6 | 52.3 |
| 30 | 40.3 | 43.8 | 47.0 | 50.9 | 53.7 |
| 40 | 51.8 | 55.8 | 59.3 | 63.7 | 66.8 |
| 50 | 63.2 | 67.5 | 71.4 | 76.2 | 79.5 |
| 60 | 74.4 | 79.1 | 83.3 | 88.4 | 92.0 |
| 70 | 85.5 | 90.5 | 95.0 | 100 | 104 |
| 80 | 96.6 | 102 | 107 | 112 | 116 |
| 90 | 108 | 113 | 118 | 124 | 128 |
| 100 | 118 | 124 | 130 | 136 | 140 |

# Solutions to Selected Exercises

**Chapter 1**

1  (b)  $\bar{X} = 91.144$

$V^2 = 896.158$

However, these summary measures do not reflect the movements of the data over time, and hence are only of limited value.

2                     March, 1982            March, 1971

$\bar{X} = 12.171$            $\bar{X} = 3.526$

$V^2 = 11.245$            $V^2 = 1.469$

4  (a)  $\sum_{i=1}^{5} P(X_i) = 1$

(b)  $E(X) = 11/3, \quad \mathrm{Var}(X) = 14/9$

(c)  (i) 3/5     (ii) 2/3     (iii) 1/5

5  (a)  $\int_{-2}^{4} f(X) = 1$

(b)  $E(X) = 2, \quad \mathrm{Var}(X) = 2$

(c)  (i) 8/9     (ii) 4/9     (iii) 1/36

6  (a) 0.309     (b) 0.227     (c) 0.341     (d) 0.136

7  (a) 0.044     (b) 0.099     (c) 0.546

9   21.86   to   30.84

10   March, 1971   3.104   to   3.948
     March, 1982  11.004   to  13.338

11   $H_0$: The accused is innocent
     $H_1$: The accused is guilty

   Type I error: Finding the accused guilty, when he/she is in fact innocent.
   Type II error: Finding the accused innocent, when he/she is in fact guilty.

   Under British law the cost of making a Type I error is considered more
   serious than making a Type II error, and hence emphasis is placed on
   minimising the probability of making a Type I error. However, the result
   is that the probability of making a Type II error is increased.

12   $H_0$: $\mu = 45$
     $H_1$: $\mu < 45$

   $\bar{X} = 43.5$, $S = 3.849$, $t_0 = -1.35$

   $H_0$ must be accepted at a 5 per cent significance level.

13   $\bar{Y} = 8.646$, $S = 2.826$, $t_0 = 18.10$. Reject $H_0$.

14   $r = 0.997$

15   $r = 0.911$. But relationship appears to be stronger for lower values than
     for higher values.

16   Relationship appears to be relatively weak, although a tendency towards
     a positive relationship is in evidence.

17   The relatively large and negative correlation between the exchange rate
     and the UK unemployment rate (and the relative UK unemployment
     rate) might be explained by arguing that an increase in UK unem-
     ployment (implying poor economic performance) adversely affects the
     valuation of sterling. The corresponding argument in terms of the
     exchange rate and the US unemployment rate would therefore imply a
     positive relationship. However a negative (although weaker) relationship
     is observed. Thus an alternative rationalisation must be sought for the
     sign of this correlation coefficient. The simplest explanation is that this
     observed correlation is spurious – the exchange rate has fallen over time
     due to the UK's poor economic performance, but movements in the US
     unemployment rate are related to other factors. Alternatively, additional
     forces may have caused a strengthening of the US dollar over time (and

hence a fall in the exchange rate) which may have had the effect of stimulating imports into the US and depressing the exporting industries, thereby causing an increase in US unemployment. However, the essential point is that these simple correlation coefficients are not capable of reflecting the complexity of many of the underlying explanatory factors, and hence can be very misleading as a basis for drawing any detailed inferences. A range of conflicting explanations can each be consistent with an observed correlation coefficient, but this correlation coefficient cannot be used to discriminate between these explanations.

**Chapter 2**

8    $\hat{R}_t = -43.886 + 2.180D_t$
     (3.36) (10.56)

$R^2 = 0.829, \hat{\sigma}_\varepsilon = 12.905$

(*t*-statistics in brackets)

From the above summary statistics the model appears adequate. However, the graph of the data in Exercise 15 of Chapter 1 implied a stronger association between $R$ and $D$ for lower values than for higher values, casting doubt on the above simple formulation. Even theoretically the model could be argued to be simplistic and naive (there will presumably be a range of factors which will influence new car registrations) and hence the relatively satisfactory statistical performance of the model should be interpreted with caution.

9   On purely statistical grounds Model (a) would be just preferred to Model (c) (and is clearly superior to Model (b)). From Model (b) we could deduce that while US is a significant determinant of $E$ it does not appear to be a particularly important one. Thus we could conclude that $E$ appears to be more directly related to UK (or RU) than it is to US. However, the determinants of exchange rate movements are clearly complex, and these simple formulations could each be argued to be theoretically inadequate.

**Chapter 3**

3  (a)  $\varepsilon_D = \dfrac{\partial D_t}{\partial P_t^C} \times \dfrac{P_t^C}{D_t} = (-3.07)(1.63/50) = -0.10$

Thus a 10 per cent increase in the price of coffee would result in a $(10)(0.10) = 1$ per cent fall in demand.
(b) Requires an estimate of the elasticity of demand for coffee with respect

to the price of tea. That is:

$$\varepsilon_D^T = \frac{\partial D_t}{\partial P_t^T} \times \frac{P_t^T}{D_t} = (2.63)(0.95/50) = 0.05$$

Given that $\varepsilon_D = 0.10$ then the price of coffee would have to be reduced by 7.5 per cent in order to offset a 15 per cent reduction in the price of tea.

(c) $\hat{D}_{88} = 49.19$

(d) $\bar{R}^2 = 0.790$ and $F = 18.84$ (see Equation 3.22) and therefore the equation appears relatively satisfactory in terms of explanatory power. The obvious feature of the summary statistics is the insignificance of the $t$-statistics on $P_t^T$ and $Y_t$. It is likely that the time-trend variable, $t$, is highly correlated with $Y_t$ and thus the insignificance of $Y_t$ may be a result of this multicollinearity. However, the insignificance of $P_t^T$ may reflect the theoretical irrelevance of this variable – that is, it might be argued that tea is not in fact a substitute for coffee (tea drinkers and coffee drinkers are quite separate and distinct consumer groups). If it is accepted that there is no theoretical justification for including $P_t^T$ in the model then the equation should be re-estimated and the estimates in (a) to (c) recalculated. In particular $\varepsilon_D^T$ would now be zero, and the forecast of coffee demand would not depend on the price of tea.

4  For Equation (i) we have $\bar{R}^2 = 0.58$, $F = 5.96$, for Equation (ii) $\bar{R}^2 = 0.62$, $F = 3.75$, and for Equation (iii) $\bar{R}^2 = 0.55$, $F = 2.00$. Thus in terms of pure explanatory power ($\bar{R}^2$) Equation (ii) is to be preferred. However, the $F$-statistics associated with Equations (ii) and (iii) are both insignificant (at the 5 per cent level) and therefore both of these equations must be rejected from further consideration. Therefore, by default, Equation (i) is the most satisfactory equation. The major problem with these regression equations is the very small sample which is used, thus precluding a rigorous regression analysis. The most obvious information which is required is just what each of the variables measures, so that each model can be theoretically evaluated.

5  Estimated equation is:

$$\hat{Y}_t = 686.7 - 25.638 X_{1t} - 1.746 X_{2t}, \quad R^2 = 0.967$$
$$(6.71)\ (24.33) \qquad\quad (1.07)$$

Given the insignificance of the coefficient on the price variable ($X_{2t}$) it would seem reasonable to conclude that price had an insignificant influence on $Y_t$ over the estimation period, and thus it could be omitted from the model. Further, the correlation between $X_1$ and $X_2$ is $-0.252$, and therefore the insignificance of $X_2$ cannot be attributed to multicollinearity. Thus the exclusion of $X_2$ from the model can now be justified statistically as well as theoretically.

## Chapter 4

1   The price elasticity of demand is defined as:

$$\frac{\partial D_t}{\partial P_t} \times \frac{P_t}{D_t}$$

Partially differentiating Equation 4.8 with respect to $P_t$ produces:

$$\frac{1}{D_t} \times \frac{\partial D_t}{\partial P_t} = \beta_1 \times \frac{1}{P_t}$$

or

$$\beta_1 = \frac{\partial D_t}{\partial P_t} \times \frac{P_t}{D_t}$$

Similarly,

$$\beta_2 = \frac{\partial D_t}{\partial Y_t} \times \frac{Y_t}{D_t}$$

which is the income elasticity of demand.

2   (a)   (i) $\ln Y_t = \beta \ln X_t$
     (ii) $\ln Y_t = \ln \beta X_t$
     (iii) $\ln Y_t = -\alpha - \beta X_t$
   (b) A disturbance term must enter each equation multiplicatively in the form $e^{\varepsilon_t}$. However, as $\varepsilon_t$ is a component of $Y_t$ it could be argued that $\varepsilon_t$ should simply enter each equation additively. That is, $Y_t$ consists of a systematic component of some form plus a disturbance term. But if $\varepsilon_t$ enters these equations additively then the above derived estimating equations cannot be justified.

3   $$Y_i/\sigma_i = \alpha(1/\sigma_i) + \beta(X_i/\sigma_i) + \varepsilon_i/\sigma_i \qquad \text{Equation 1}$$

Thus

$$\text{Var}(\varepsilon_i/\sigma_i) = (1/\sigma_i^2)\,\text{Var}(\varepsilon_i) = 1$$

Therefore the variance of the disturbance term in this transformed equation is now a constant (equal to one), thus justifying the direct application of ordinary least squares to this equation. That is, the BLUEs of $\alpha$ and $\beta$ are derived by regressing $Y_i/\sigma_i$ on $1/\sigma_i$ and $X_i/\sigma_i$ (without a constant term).

Consider the generalised multiple regression model, without a constant term:

$$Y_i = \beta_1 X_{1i} + \beta_2 X_{2i} + \varepsilon_i \qquad \text{Equation 2}$$

From Equation 3.6 we can deduce that the least squares estimator of $\beta_2$ is:

$$\beta_2 = \frac{\sum Y_i X_{2i} \sum X_{1i}^2 - \sum Y_i X_{1i} \sum X_{1i} X_{2i}}{\sum X_{1i}^2 \sum X_{2i}^2 - (\sum X_{1i} X_{2i})^2} \qquad \text{Equation 3}$$

(see the analogous expression for $\hat{\beta}$ for the simple regression model in Equation 4.13).

From Equation 1 above we have:

$$Y_i = Y_i/\sigma_i, \; X_{1i} = 1/\sigma_i \quad \text{and} \quad X_{2i} = X_i/\sigma_i$$

and substitution into Equation 3 and simplifying produces Equation 4.35.

4   We have:

$$C_i = \alpha + \beta D_i + \varepsilon_i$$
$$\hat{\beta} = \sum W_i C_i$$

where

$$W_i = \frac{(D_i - \bar{D})}{\sum (D_i - \bar{D})^2}$$

$$\hat{\alpha} = \bar{C} - \hat{\beta}\bar{D}$$
$$= \bar{C} - \bar{D}\sum W_i(\alpha + \beta D_i + \varepsilon_i)$$
$$= \alpha + (1/n)\sum \varepsilon_i - \bar{D}\sum W_i \varepsilon_i$$

$$\therefore E(\hat{\alpha}) = \alpha$$
$$\therefore \text{Var}(\hat{\alpha}) = E(\hat{\alpha} - \alpha)^2 = E[\sum (1/n - \bar{D}W_i)\varepsilon_i]^2$$
$$= \sum (1/n - \bar{D}W_i)\sigma_i^2$$

as $E(\varepsilon_i \varepsilon_j) = 0$ for all $i \neq j$.

5   The data are already in the appropriate order for application of the Goldfeld–Quandt test. Thus, omitting the middle five observations produces:

$$\hat{\sigma}_1^2 = 36.918 \quad \text{and} \quad \hat{\sigma}_2^2 = 254.084$$
$$\therefore F = 6.88$$

which is significant at the 5 per cent level. Thus we would conclude that the disturbance terms are heteroskedastic.

Consider the following three assumptions:

1   $\sigma_i^2 = b\sqrt{D_i}$

2   $\sigma_i^2 = bD_i$

3   $\sigma_i^2 = bD_i^2$

Respecifying the model consistent with each of these three assumptions, produces the following parameter estimates and standard errors:

|  | Parameter estimate | Standard error |
|---|---|---|
| Assumption 1 | $\hat{\alpha} = -46.90$ | 12.66 |
|  | $\hat{\beta} = 2.228$ | 0.204 |
| Assumption 2 | $\hat{\alpha} = -49.95$ | 12.31 |
|  | $\hat{\beta} = 2.278$ | 0.203 |
| Assumption 3 | $\hat{\alpha} = -56.16$ | 11.75 |
|  | $\hat{\beta} = 2.382$ | 0.202 |
| No Adjustment (See Exercise 8 of Chapter 2) | $\hat{\alpha} = -43.89$ | 13.04 |
|  | $\hat{\beta} = 2.180$ | 0.206 |

Thus under each assumption smaller standard errors are obtained, implying that failure to adjust for heteroskedasticity here gives the impression of unwarranted imprecision.

6 Using a significance level of 2.5 per cent, the tabulated $d$ values are:

(a) $4 - d_U = 2.67$, $4 - d_L = 2.84$, $d$ is insignificant
(b) $d_L = 1.18$, $d_U = 1.34$, $d$ is significant
(c) $d_L = 1.37$, $d_U = 1.54$, $d$ is significant
(d) $d_L = 0.90$, $d_U = 1.40$, $d$ is significant
    $d_L = 0.79$, $d_U = 1.58$, $d$ is inconclusive


## Chapter 5

1 In addition to various continuous explanatory variables, some of the dummy variables which might be examined are:

(a) Marital status. That is:
   1 – if married and living with husband
   0 – otherwise
(b) Nature of area of residence. For example:
   1 – if conurbation
   0 – otherwise
(c) Level of education. For example:
   1 – if university educated
   0 – otherwise
(d) Nature of financial commitments. For example:
   1 – if housing all paid for
   0 – otherwise

(e) Nature of employment. For example:
   1 – only works part-time
   0 – works full-time

2  If $Y_i = 1$, then $\varepsilon_i = 1 - \alpha - \beta X_i$, and if $Y_i = 0$, $\varepsilon_i = -\alpha - \beta X_i$. That is, given the value of $X_i$ at sample point $i$, $\varepsilon_i$ can only take on one of the two values $1 - \alpha - \beta X_i$ or $-\alpha - \beta X_i$. Thus $X_i$ is a discrete rather than a continuous variable and cannot possibly be normally distributed.

   Assume that the distribution of $\varepsilon_i$ at sample point $i$ is such that $\varepsilon_i$ can take on the value $1 - \alpha - \beta X_i$ with probability $p_i$ (and therefore can take on the value $-\alpha - \beta X_i$ with probability $1 - p_i$). Thus:

$$E(\varepsilon_i) = (1 - \alpha - \beta X_i) + (-\alpha - \beta X_i)(1 - p_i)$$

As $E(\varepsilon_i) = 0$, by assumption, then:

$$(1 - \alpha - \beta X_i)p_i + (-\alpha - \beta X_i)(1 - p_i) = 0$$

or

$$p_i = \alpha + \beta X_i$$

$$\therefore \text{Var}(\varepsilon_i) = E(\varepsilon_i^2)$$
$$= (1 - \alpha - \beta X_i)^2 p_i + (-\alpha - \beta X_i)^2(1 - p_i)$$
$$= (1 - \alpha - \beta X_i)(\alpha + \beta X_i)$$

Thus $\text{Var}(\varepsilon_i)$ is not a constant (it depends on the value of $X_i$), and therefore we can conclude that $\varepsilon_i$ is heteroskedastic.

3  $$Y_t = \alpha(1 - \lambda) + \lambda Y_{t-1} + \beta_0 X_t + (\beta_1 - \lambda \beta_0)X_{t-1}$$
$$+ (\beta_2 - \lambda \beta_1)X_{t-2} + (\beta - \beta_2 \lambda)X_{t-3} + \varepsilon_t - \lambda \varepsilon_{t-1}$$

An estimate of $\lambda$ is given by the estimated coefficient on $Y_{t-1}$, $\alpha$ is estimated by dividing the constant term by $1 - \hat{\lambda}$, and $\beta_0$ is estimated by the coefficient on $X_t$. Given $\hat{\lambda}$ and $\hat{\beta}_0$, $\hat{\beta}_1$ can be deduced from the estimated coefficient on $X_{t-1}$, and similarly $\hat{\beta}_2$ can be deduced from the coefficient on $X_{t-2}$, and $\hat{\beta}$ can be deduced from the coefficient on $X_{t-3}$.

4  Imposing a geometrically declining lag we have:

$$Y_t = \alpha + \gamma Z_t + \beta X_t + \beta \lambda X_{t-1} + \beta \lambda^2 X_{t-2} + \ldots + \varepsilon_t$$

and the Koyck solution therefore produces:

$$Y_t = \alpha(1 - \lambda) + \lambda Y_{t-1} + \gamma Z_t - \gamma \lambda Z_{t-1} + \beta X_t + \varepsilon_t - \lambda \varepsilon_{t-1}$$

$\lambda$ can be estimated by the estimated coefficient on $Y_{t-1}$. But a second estimate of $\lambda$ can be derived from the (negative) ratio of the estimated coefficients on $Z_{t-1}$ and $Z_t$, respectively. Given two estimates of $\lambda$, two estimates of $\alpha$ can be derived, and thus we cannot derive unique estimates of all the parameters ($\lambda$ and $\alpha$ are said to be over-identified).

5   Using the Cochrane–Orcutt procedure to adjust for autocorrelation in each case, the estimation results are as follows:

(a)  Unrestricted eight-period lag on income

| Variable | Coefficient | $t$-statistic |
|---|---|---|
| Constant | 4585.619 | 5.98 |
| $D_t$ | 0.235 | 4.71 |
| $D_{t-1}$ | 0.178 | 3.30 |
| $D_{t-2}$ | 0.000 | 0.00 |
| $D_{t-3}$ | 0.147 | 2.75 |
| $D_{t-4}$ | $-0.020$ | 0.36 |
| $D_{t-5}$ | $-0.046$ | 0.86 |
| $D_{t-6}$ | 0.118 | 2.08 |
| $D_{t-7}$ | $-0.037$ | 0.67 |
| $D_{t-8}$ | $-0.016$ | 0.29 |

$\bar{R}^2 = 0.987$, $d = 2.51$, $n = 59$, $\hat{\rho} = 0.799$

(b)  Unrestricted four-period lag on income

| Variable | Coefficient | $t$-statistic |
|---|---|---|
| Constant | 4243.006 | 6.73 |
| $D_t$ | 0.268 | 5.62 |
| $D_{t-1}$ | 0.164 | 3.32 |
| $D_{t-2}$ | 0.028 | 0.55 |
| $D_{t-3}$ | 0.134 | 2.69 |
| $D_{t-4}$ | $-0.014$ | 0.27 |

$\bar{R}^2 = 0.989$, $d = 2.48$, $n = 63$, $\hat{\rho} = 0.791$

(c)  Eight-period Almon lag on income

| Variable | Coefficient | $t$-statistic |
|---|---|---|
| Constant | 4384.083 | 6.76 |
| $D_t$ | 0.229 | 6.19 |
| $D_{t-1}$ | 0.161 | 8.39 |
| $D_{t-2}$ | 0.104 | 7.07 |
| $D_{t-3}$ | 0.058 | 3.11 |
| $D_{t-4}$ | 0.025 | 1.19 |
| $D_{t-5}$ | 0.003 | 0.15 |
| $D_{t-6}$ | $-0.007$ | 0.47 |
| $D_{t-7}$ | $-0.006$ | 0.28 |
| $D_{t-8}$ | 0.007 | 0.19 |

$\bar{R}^2 = 0.987$, $d = 2.43$, $n = 59$, $\hat{\rho} = 0.752$

(d) Four-period Almon lag on income

| Variable | Coefficient | $t$-statistic |
|----------|-------------|---------------|
| Constant | 4217.318 | 6.91 |
| $D_t$ | 0.247 | 5.90 |
| $D_{t-1}$ | 0.164 | 7.46 |
| $D_{t-2}$ | 0.099 | 3.46 |
| $D_{t-3}$ | 0.051 | 2.25 |
| $D_{t-4}$ | 0.020 | 0.47 |

$\bar{R}^2 = 0.989$, $d = 2.47$, $n = 63$, $\hat{\rho} = 0.779$

Except for (d) theoretically unacceptable negative coefficients are produced (although they are in all cases insignificantly different from zero). In
the cases of (a) and (b) the resulting lag structures are very erratic, making
little, if any, theoretical sense (this presumably results from the high level
of multicollinearity amongst the lagged values of $X$ thus resulting in
imprecise estimation). In all cases $d$ falls in the inconclusive region, casting
further doubt on the model specifications.

6   Equation 5.72 can be re-expressed as:

$$X_t^e = \delta X_{t-1} + (1-\delta)X_{t-1}^e$$
$$= \delta X_{t-1} + (1-\delta)[\delta X_{t-2} + (1-\delta)X_{t-2}^e]$$
$$= \ldots$$
$$= \delta X_{t-1} + (1-\delta)\delta X_{t-2} + (1-\delta)^2 \delta X_{t-3} + \ldots$$

and substitution into Equation 5.71 produces a distributed lag model.

# Chapter 6

1
$$C_t = \frac{\alpha_0(1-\beta_1)}{1-\alpha_1} + \frac{\beta_1}{1-\alpha_1} C_{t-1} - \frac{\alpha_1}{1-\alpha_1} T_t + \frac{\alpha_1 \beta_1}{1-\alpha_1} T_{t-1}$$
$$+ \frac{\alpha_1 \beta_2}{1-\alpha_1} R_t + \frac{\alpha_1}{1-\alpha_1} G_t + \frac{\varepsilon_{1t} - \beta_1 \varepsilon_{1t-1} + \alpha_1 \varepsilon_{2t}}{1-\alpha_1}$$

$$I_t = \frac{\alpha_1 \beta_1}{1-\alpha_1} + \frac{\beta_1}{1-\alpha_1} I_{t-1} + \frac{\beta_1}{1-\alpha_1} G_{t-1} - \frac{\beta_1 \alpha_1}{1-\alpha_1} T_{t-1} + \beta_2 R_t$$
$$+ \frac{\beta_1 \varepsilon_{1t-1} + (1-\alpha_1)\varepsilon_{2t}}{1-\alpha_1}$$

3   Let $H$ denote the number of explanatory variables appearing in a given structural equation, of which $P$ are predetermined and $E$ are endogenous. Thus the equation contains $E+1$ endogenous variables (including the dependent variable). Assume that the model contains a total of $K$ predetermined variables and $G$ endogenous variables (that is, the model contains $G$ equations).

From Equation 6.48 an equation will be identified if:

$$K \geqslant H$$

and this is the form in which the first form of the order condition was presented.

The number of variables in the model which are excluded from a given equation is:

$$G-(E+1)+K-P = G-1+K-(E+P) \qquad \text{Equation 1}$$

However, as $H = E+P$, and as the equation is identified if:

$$K \geqslant E+P \qquad \text{Equation 2}$$

or

$$K-(E+P) \geqslant 0$$

then from the right-hand side of Equation 1 we can deduce that an equation will be identified if it excludes at least $G-1$ variables. Thus we have confirmed the second version of the order condition.

The number of predetermined variables excluded from an equation is $K-P$. Thus from Equation 2 above an equation will be identified if:

$$K-P \geqslant E$$

or

$$K-P \geqslant (E+1)-1$$

thus confirming the third version of the order condition.

4   Both behavioural equations are exactly identified by the order condition. The reduced form equations for $C_t$ and $I_t$ can be written as:

$$C_t = a+bG_t+cR_t$$
$$I_t = d+eG_t+fR_t$$

where

$$a = \frac{\alpha_0(1-\beta_1)+\alpha_1\beta_0}{1-\alpha_1-\beta_1} \qquad \text{Equation 1}$$

$$b = \frac{\alpha_1+\alpha_2(1-\beta_1)}{1-\alpha_1-\beta_1} \qquad \text{Equation 2}$$

$$c = \frac{\alpha_1 \beta_1}{1 - \alpha_1 - \beta_1} \qquad \text{Equation 3}$$

$$d = \frac{\beta_0(1 - \alpha_1) + \beta_1 \alpha_0}{1 - \alpha_1 - \beta_1} \qquad \text{Equation 4}$$

$$e = \frac{\beta_1(1 + \alpha_2)}{1 - \alpha_1 - \beta_1} \qquad \text{Equation 5}$$

$$f = \frac{\beta_2(1 - \alpha_1)}{1 - \alpha_1 - \beta_1} \qquad \text{Equation 6}$$

If $\beta_2 = 0$ then $R_t$ would not appear in the model, and the model would therefore contain just one predetermined variable. The consumption function would still contain two explanatory variables and therefore would be underidentified (the investment function would remain exactly identified as it would now only contain one explanatory variable).

Now consider the investment function. Substituting the identity into the investment function, and then substituting the reduced form equation for $C_t$ produces:

$$I_t = \frac{\beta_0 + a\beta_1}{1 - \beta_1} + \frac{\beta_1(1 + b)}{1 - \beta_1} G_t + \frac{c\beta_1 + \beta_2}{1 - \beta_1} R_t$$

Thus we can deduce from the reduced form that:

$$d = \frac{\beta_0 + a\beta_1}{1 - \beta_1} \qquad \text{Equation 7}$$

$$e = \frac{\beta_1(1 + b)}{1 - \beta_1} \qquad \text{Equation 8}$$

$$f = \frac{c\beta_1 + \beta_2}{1 - \beta_1} \qquad \text{Equation 9}$$

Now, if $\alpha_2 = -1$, then $b = -1$ and $e = 0$ (see Equations 2 and 5 above). Thus Equation 8 becomes meaningless and we now only have two equations to solve for $\beta_0$, $\beta_1$ and $\beta_2$. That is, if $\alpha_2 = -1$, the investment function would be underidentified.

Thus we would conclude that the consumption function is identified provided that $\beta_2 \neq 0$ (which is a trivial requirement as it simply requires that $R_t$ appears in the model). And the investment function is identified provided that $\alpha_2 \neq -1$. These conditions constitute the rank conditions for the identification of the consumption and investment functions, respectively (in Appendix 6.2 we present a more direct method for establishing the rank condition).

5   For $X_{n+k} = -5$, we have from Equation 6.88:

$$\hat{Y}_{n+k} = 704.68$$

Using Equation 6.93, and the data derived in Chapter 2 we have for $X_{n+k} = -5$:

$$S_F^2 = 763.320$$

and therefore the 95 per cent interval estimate for $Y_{n+k}$ is:

647.490   to   761.870

For $X_{n+k} = 10$, $\hat{Y}_{n+k} = 324.37$, and the 95 per cent interval estimate for $Y_{n+k}$ is:

276.539   to   372.013

For $X_{n+k} = 20$, $\hat{Y}_{n+k} = 70.83$, and the 95 per cent interval estimate for $Y_{n+k}$ is:

18.357   to   123.303

## Chapter 7

1   From Equation 7.9:

$$E(Y_t Y_{t-1}) = \gamma_1 = \phi_1 E(Y_{t-1}^2) + E(\varepsilon_t Y_{t-2}) = \phi_1 \gamma_0$$

$$\therefore \rho_1 = \frac{\gamma_1}{\gamma_0} = \phi_1$$

Similarly,

$$\gamma_2 = \phi_1 \gamma_1 = \phi_1^2 \gamma_0$$

$$\therefore \rho_2 = \phi_1^2$$

and

$$\rho_3 = \phi_1^3$$

and in general

$$\rho_k = \phi_1^k$$

2   $$\rho_1 = \frac{\phi_1}{1 - \phi_2}$$

$$\rho_2 = \frac{\phi_1^2 + \phi_2 - \phi_2^2}{1 - \phi_2}$$

$$\rho_3 = \frac{\phi_1^3 + 2\phi_1 \phi_2 - \phi_1 \phi_2^2}{1 - \phi_2}$$

3  If the process is AR(1), then:

$$\rho_1 = \phi_1$$

or

$$\phi_{11} = \rho_1$$

If the process is AR(2), then from Exercise 2 above:

$$\rho_k = \phi_1\rho_{k-1} + \phi_2\rho_{k-2}$$
$$\therefore \rho_1 = \phi_1 + \phi_2\rho_1$$

and

$$\rho_2 = \phi_1\rho_1 + \phi_2$$

Solving for $\phi_2$ in terms of $\rho_1$ and $\rho_2$ from these two equations produces:

$$\phi_{22} = \frac{\rho_2 - \rho_1^2}{1 - \rho_1^2}$$

In the case of an AR(3) it is straightforward to establish that:

$$\rho_k = \phi_1\rho_{k-1} + \phi_2\rho_{k-2} + \phi_3\rho_{k-3}$$

and therefore:

$$\rho_1 = \phi_1 + \phi_2\rho_1 + \phi_3\rho_2$$
$$\rho_2 = \phi_1\rho_1 + \phi_2 + \phi_3\rho_1$$
$$\rho_3 = \phi_1\rho_2 + \phi_2\rho_1 + \phi_3$$

Solving for $\phi_3$ in terms of $\rho_1$, $\rho_2$ and $\rho_3$ from these three equations produces:

$$\phi_{33} = \frac{(\rho_3 - \rho_1\rho_2) - \rho_1(\rho_1\rho_3 - \rho_2^2) + \rho_1(\rho_1^2 - \rho_2)}{(1 - \rho_1^2) - \rho_1^2(1 - \rho_2) + \rho_2(\rho_1^2 - \rho_2)}$$

5  
$$\gamma_0 = \sigma_\varepsilon^2(1 + \theta_1^2)$$
$$\gamma_1 = \theta_1\sigma_\varepsilon^2$$
$$\gamma_2 = 0$$
$$\gamma_k = 0 \quad \text{for all } k \geqslant 2$$
$$\rho_0 = 1$$
$$\rho_1 = \frac{\gamma_1}{\gamma_0} = \frac{\theta_1}{1 + \theta_1^2}$$
$$\rho_2 = 0$$
$$\rho_k = 0 \quad \text{for all } k \geqslant 2$$

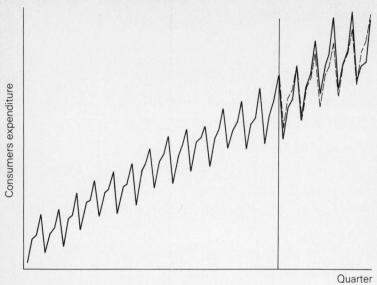

**Figure EA.1** Box–Jenkins forecasts of consumers' expenditure.

6    Stationarity is achieved by logging and first and fourth differencing the data. The simplest model specification which appears to provide an adequate description of the data generating process is an MA(1) fitted to both the seasonal and non-seasonal observations. The estimation results for the first 56 observations are:

|  | Parameter | Estimate | $t$-statistic |
|---|---|---|---|
| Non-seasonal MA | $\theta$ | $-0.405$ | 3.48 |
| Seasonal MA | $\Theta$ | $-0.862$ | 16.98 |

$\hat{\sigma}_\varepsilon = 0.008$, $Q_6 = 4.74$, $Q_{12} = 7.07$

The forecasts generated by this model over the period 1971(1) to 1975(4) are shown diagrammatically in Figure EA.1 (actual consumers' expenditure is the unbroken line, and the forecasts are shown as the broken line).

# Index